MW01202083

THE ANNOTATED LUTHER

Volume 4
Pastoral Writings

Additional Praise for *Pastoral Writings*

"Martin Luther profoundly shaped Protestant worship, preaching, and prayer practices. This volume presents Luther's most sensitive and influential pastoral writings, including essential sermons, catechisms, hymns, and letters of consolation. Modern readers will appreciate the fresh translations of original German and Latin texts, generous notes, and illustrations."

—**Michael J. Halvorson** | Pacific Lutheran University

THE ANNOTATED LUTHER

Volume 4
Pastoral Writings

VOLUME EDITOR
Mary Jane Haemig

GENERAL EDITORS
Hans J. Hillerbrand
Kirsi I. Stjerna
Timothy J. Wengert

Fortress Press
Minneapolis

THE ANNOTATED LUTHER, Volume 4
Pastoral Writings

Fortress Press Publication Staff: Scott Tunseth, Project Editor; Alicia Ehlers, Production Manager; Laurie Ingram, Cover Design; Michael Moore, Permissions.

Copyeditor: David Lott
Series Designer and Typesetter: Ann Delgehausen, Trio Bookworks
Proofreader: Paul Kobelski, The HK Scriptorium

Library of Congress Cataloging-in-Publication Data is available.

ISBN: 978-1-4514-6272-2
eISBN: 978-1-4514-6510-5

Contents

PASTORAL CARE AND CONSOLATION

REFLECTIONS ON REFORM

Series Introduction

Engaging the Essential Luther

Even after five hundred years Martin Luther continues to engage and challenge each new generation of scholars and believers alike. With 2017 marking the five-hundredth anniversary of Luther's *95 Theses*, Luther's theology and legacy are being explored around the world with new questions and methods and by diverse voices. His thought invites ongoing examination, his writings are a staple in classrooms and pulpits, and he speaks to an expanding assortment of conversation partners who use different languages and hale from different geographical and social contexts.

The six volumes of The Annotated Luther edition offer a flexible tool for the global reader of Luther, making many of his most important writings available in the *lingua franca* of our times as one way of facilitating interest in the Wittenberg reformer. They feature new introductions, annotations, revised translations, and textual notes, as well as visual enhancements (illustrations, art, photos, maps, and timelines). The Annotated Luther edition embodies Luther's own cherished principles of communication. Theological writing, like preaching, needs to reflect human beings' lived experience, benefits from up-to-date scholarship, and should be easily accessible to all. These volumes are designed to help teachers and students, pastors and laypersons, and other professionals in ministry understand the context in which the documents were written, recognize how the documents have shaped Protestant and Lutheran thinking, and interpret the meaning of these documents for faith and life today.

The Rationale for This Edition

For any reader of Luther, the sheer number of his works presents a challenge. Well over one hundred volumes comprise the scholarly edition of Luther's works, the so-called Weimar Ausgabe (WA), a publishing enterprise begun in 1883 and only completed in the twenty-first century. From 1955 to 1986, fifty-five volumes came to make up *Luther's Works* (American Edition) (LW), to which Concordia Publishing House, St. Louis, is adding still more. This English-language contribution to Luther studies, matched by similar translation projects for Erasmus of Rotterdam and John Calvin, provides a theological and historical gold mine for those interested in studying Luther's thought. But even these volumes are not always easy to use and are hardly portable. Electronic forms have increased availability, but preserving Luther in book form and providing readers with manageable selections are also important goals.

Moreover, since the publication of the WA and the first fifty-five volumes of the LW, research on the Reformation in general and on Martin Luther in particular has broken new ground and evolved, as has knowledge regarding the languages in which Luther wrote. Up-to-date information from a variety of sources is brought together in The Annotated Luther, building on the work done by previous generations of scholars. The language and phrasing of the translations have also been updated to reflect modern English usage. While the WA and, in a derivative way, LW remain the central source for Luther scholarship, the present critical and annotated English translation facilitates research internationally and invites a new generation of readers for whom Latin and German might prove an unsurpassable obstacle to accessing Luther. The WA provides the basic Luther texts (with some exceptions); the LW provides the basis for almost all translations.

Defining the "Essential Luther"

Deciding which works to include in this collection was not easy. Criteria included giving attention to Luther's initial key works; considering which publications had the most impact in his day and later; and taking account of Luther's own favorites, texts addressing specific issues of continued importance for today, and Luther's exegetical works. Taken as a whole, these works present the many sides of Luther, as reformer, pastor, biblical interpreter, and theologian. To serve today's readers and by using categories similar to those found in volumes 31–47 of Luther's works (published by Fortress Press), the volumes offer in the main a thematic rather than strictly chronological approach to Luther's writings. The volumes in the series include:

Volume 1: *The Roots of Reform* (Timothy J. Wengert, editor)
Volume 2: *Word and Faith* (Kirsi I. Stjerna, editor)
Volume 3: *Church and Sacraments* (Paul W. Robinson, editor)
Volume 4: *Pastoral Writings* (Mary Jane Haemig, editor)
Volume 5: *Christian Life in the World* (Hans J. Hillerbrand, editor)
Volume 6: *The Interpretation of Scripture* (Euan K. Cameron, editor)

The History of the Project

In 2011 Fortress Press convened an advisory board to explore the promise and parameters of a new English edition of Luther's essential works. Board members Denis Janz, Robert Kolb, Peter Matheson, Christine Helmer, and Kirsi Stjerna deliberated with

Fortress Press publisher Will Bergkamp to develop a concept and identify contributors. After a review with scholars in the field, college and seminary professors, and pastors, it was concluded that a single-language edition was more desirable than dual-language volumes.

In August 2012, Hans Hillerbrand, Kirsi Stjerna, and Timothy Wengert were appointed as general editors of the series with Scott Tunseth from Fortress Press as the project editor. The general editors were tasked with determining the contents of the volumes and developing the working principles of the series. They also helped with the identification and recruitment of additional volume editors, who in turn worked with the general editors to identify volume contributors. Mastery of the languages and unique knowledge of the subject matter were key factors in identifying contributors. Most contributors are North American scholars and native English speakers, but The Annotated Luther includes among its contributors a circle of international scholars. Likewise, the series is offered for a global network of teachers and students in seminary, university, and college classes, as well as pastors, lay teachers, and adult students in congregations seeking background and depth in Lutheran theology, biblical interpretation, and Reformation history.

Editorial Principles

The volume editors and contributors have, with few exceptions, used the translations of LW as the basis of their work, retranslating from the WA for the sake of clarity and contemporary usage. Where the LW translations have been substantively altered, explanatory notes have often been provided. More importantly, contributors have provided marginal notes to help readers understand theological and historical references. Introductions have been expanded and sharpened to reflect the very latest historical and theological research. In citing the Bible, care has been taken to reflect the German and Latin texts commonly used in the sixteenth century rather than modern editions, which often employ textual sources that were unavailable to Luther and his contemporaries.

Finally, all pieces in The Annotated Luther have been revised in the light of modern principles of inclusive language. This is not always an easy task with a historical author, but an intentional effort has been made to revise language throughout, with creativity and editorial liberties, to allow Luther's theology to speak free from unnecessary and unintended gender-exclusive language. This important principle provides an opportunity to translate accurately certain gender-neutral German and Latin expressions that Luther employed—for example, the Latin word *homo* and the German *Mensch* mean "human being," not simply "males." Using the words *man* and *men* to translate such terms would create an ambiguity not present in the original texts. The focus is on linguistic accuracy and Luther's intent. Regarding creedal formulations and trinitarian language, Luther's own expressions have been preserved, without entering the complex and important contemporary debates over language for God and the Trinity.

The 2017 anniversary of the publication of the *95 Theses* is providing an opportunity to assess the substance of Luther's role and influence in the Protestant Reformation. Revisiting Luther's essential writings not only allows reassessment of Luther's rationale and goals but also provides a new look at what Martin Luther was about and why new generations would still wish to engage him. We hope these six volumes offer a compelling invitation.

Hans J. Hillerbrand
Kirsi I. Stjerna
Timothy J. Wengert
General Editors

Abbreviations

AWA	Archiv für die Weimarer Ausgabe
BC	*The Book of Concord*, ed. Robert Kolb and Timothy J. Wengert (Minneapolis: Fortress Press, 2000)
Brecht	Martin Brecht, *Martin Luther*, trans. James L. Schaaf, 3 vols. (Philadelphia and Minneapolis: Fortress Press, 1985–1993)
CA	Augsburg Confession
CSEL	*Corpus scriptorum ecclesiasticorum latinorum*
LC	*The Large Catechism*
LW	*Luther's Works* [American edition], ed. Helmut Lehmann and Jaroslav Pelikan, 55 vols. (Philadelphia: Fortress Press; St. Louis: Concordia, 1955–86)
MLStA	*Martin Luther: Studienausgabe*, ed. Hans-Ulrich Delius, 6 vols. (Berlin and Leipzig: Evangelische Verlagsanstalt, 1979–99)
MPG	*Patrologiae cursus completus, series Graeca*, ed. Jacques-Paul Migne, 166 vols. (Paris, 1857–1866)
MPL	*Patrologiae cursus completus, series Latina*, ed. Jacques-Paul Migne, 217 vols. (Paris, 1844–1864)
ODCC	*The Oxford Dictionary of the Christian Church*, ed. F. L. Cross, 3rd ed. rev., ed. E. A. Livingstone (Oxford: Oxford University Press, 2005)
OER	*Oxford Encyclopedia of the Reformation*, ed. Hans J. Hillerbrand, 4 vols. (New York and Oxford: Oxford University Press, 1996)
SA	*The Smalcald Articles*
SC	*The Small Catechism*
SD	*Solid Declaration*
TAL	The Annotated Luther
VD	*Verzeichnis der im deutschen Sprachbereich erschienenen Drucke des Jahrhunderts* (Munich: Bayerische Staatsbibliothek; Herzog August Bibliothek in Wolfenbüttel, Stuttgart: Hiersemann [1983–])
WA	*Luthers Werke: Kritische Gesamtausgabe* [*Schriften*], 73 vols. (Weimar: H. Böhlau, 1883–2009)
WA Bi	*Luthers Werke: Kritische Gesamtausgabe: Bibel*, 12 vols. (Weimar: H. Böhlau, 1906–61), 7:206
WA Br	*Luthers Werke: Kritische Gesamtausgabe: Briefwechsel*, 18 vols. (Weimar: H. Böhlau, 1930–1985)
WA DB	*Luthers Werke: Kritische Gesamtausgabe: Deutsche Bibel*, 12 vols. (Weimar: H. Böhlau, 1906–61)
WA TR	*Luthers Werke: Kritische Gesamtausgabe: Tischreden*, 6 vols. (Weimar: H. Böhlau, 1912–21)

REFORMATION EUROPE
in the 16th century

- – - Holy Roman Empire boundary
---- Provincial boundary

ATLANTIC OCEAN

NORWAY

SCOTLAND
Edinburgh

SWEDEN
Stockholm

ESTONIA
LIVONIA
KURLAND

IRELAND

North Sea

DENMARK

Baltic Sea

York

ENGLAND

Copenhagen

Königsberg

PRUSSIA

London

Hamburg

POMERANIA

BRANDENBURG

POLAND

Ghent

ARTOIS

NETHERLANDS

FLANDERS

HESSE

COLOGNE

LUXEMBOURG

SAXONY

SILESIA

Paris

Mainz

UPPER PALITANATE

BOHEMIA

Nantes

LOWER PALITANATE

MORAVIA

Orleans

BAVARIA

FRANCE

FRENCH COMTE

Augsburg

AUSTRIA

Vienna

IMPERIAL HUNGARY

SWISS CONFEDERATION

TYROL

CARINTHIA

Budapest

BOURBON LANDS

SAVOY

Milan

Trent

CARNIOLA

HUNGARY

Valladolid

Toulouse

Avignon

Pavia

Venice

Mohacs

NAVARRE

Genoa

VENETIAN REPUBLIC

PORTUGAL

SPAIN

Barcelona

Florence

PAPAL STATES

OTTOMAN EMPIRE

Lisbon

Madrid

CASTILE

Toledo

ARAGON

CORSICA (TO GENOA)

ITALY

Rome

Seville

BALERIC ISLANDS

Granada

GRANADA

SARDINIA (TO SPAIN)

Naples

NAPLES

Tangier

Mediterranean Sea

SICILY (TO SPAIN)

Algiers

Bizerte

0   300 Miles

Tunis

Lucidity Information Design, LLC

LUTHER'S GERMANY

- - - Major political subdivisions

N

DENMARK

Baltic Sea

Wolgast

Hamburg

POMERANIA

Bremen

Stettin

Amsterdam

Elbe

NETHERLANDS

Magdeburg

Wittenberg

POLAND

Brussels

Cologne

Eisenach

Eisleben

Torgau

Marburg

Erfurt

Leipzig

Breslau

Oder

Schmalkalden

LUXEMBURG

Mansfeld

Prague

Worms

Nuremberg

Metz

Strasbourg

Rhine

Regansburg

Danube

Augsburg

AUSTRIA

FRANCE

Zürich

Salzburg

Vienna

SWISS CONFEDERATION

HUNGARY

Milan

Venice

VENETIAN DOMINION

0   200 Miles

Florence

Adriatic Sea

Introduction to Volume 4

MARY JANE HAEMIG

The reader may well ask why the writings included in this volume—and not other writings—are subsumed under the heading "Pastoral Writings." In some sense, all of Luther's works were pastoral, driven by a deep concern not for "correct" theology but to provide consolation and hope to people suffering in body, mind, and spirit. Certainly his early questions about indulgences derived as much from a deep pastoral concern for people as from a theoretical questioning of the entire indulgence system.

Luther the pastor is often overlooked.[a] Succeeding generations have thought of him as the great prophet, steadfast reforming figure, mover and shaker of his time, best-selling writer, brilliant theologian—even the national or denominational hero. But Luther was also a pastor who explained the basics of the Christian faith, taught people how to pray, visited and comforted the sick and dying, encouraged the doubtful, advised the prominent and the obscure, counseled the faithful, doubting, and

---

a   For a broad and recent treatment of pastoral care in this era see Ronald Rittgers, *The Reformation of Suffering: Pastoral Theology and Lay Piety in Late Medieval and Early Modern Germany* (New York: Oxford University Press, 2012). See also Gerhard Ebeling, *Luthers Seelsorge an seinen Briefen dargestellt* (Tübingen: Mohr Siebeck, 1997); and Timothy J. Wengert, ed., *The Pastoral Luther: Essays on Martin Luther's Practical Theology* (Grand Rapids: Eerdmans, 2009).

1. Fred W. Meuser notes, "Luther's preaching ministry was remarkable, his productivity prodigious—almost miraculous . . . in 1528 he preached nearly two hundred times in spite of severe headaches and dizzy spells . . . most years he preached over a hundred times. . . . Of the approximately 4,000 sermons he preached in his lifetime, about 2,300 have been preserved in some form." See Meuser, "Luther as Preacher of the Word of God," in Donald K. McKim, ed., *The Cambridge Companion to Martin Luther* (Cambridge: Cambridge University Press, 2003), 136–48, at 136.

suffering, and offered concrete help in a number of situations. Luther's actual pastoral work was broad ranging. It is estimated that he preached approximately four thousand sermons in his lifetime.[1] His skills as a poet still inform the ordinary Christian through his radiant hymnody. He shaped new Evangelical worship, catechetical, and prayer practices. He never considered himself above the usual activities of a pastor. Luther never wrote a manual for pastors, a genre used by medieval priests and later by Lutheran pastors.[b] Nevertheless, his works provided guidance as to how his pastoral work was done.

A quick glance at the other volumes in The Annotated Luther series assures one that any number of other pieces could also have been considered "pastoral" and included in this volume. See for example, the *Sermon on Indulgences and Grace* (1518) in volume 1, which provides an explanation of the theological problems of indulgences at the lay level, or *Whether Soldiers too Can Be Saved* (1526) in volume 5. Surely Luther's reform of worship, including the *German Mass* (1526) in volume 3, could also be considered "pastoral." Any number of pastoral works are not included in The Annotated Luther series at all; see for example, *Fourteen Consolations* (1520)[c] or his numerous letters.

The pieces in this volume are arranged thematically rather than chronologically. It was the editors' opinion that this would aid the reader in considering Luther's thought on particular issues of pastoral ministry. Of course, no piece fits solely into one category.

The volume begins with the theme "Sermon and Song." Luther was an incredibly active and productive preacher. While some works published under the title of "sermons" were probably never preached, the *Invocavit Sermons* (1522), also known as *Eight Sermons at Wittenberg*, illustrate Luther preaching into a

b See, for example, Scott Hendrix, trans. and ed., *Preaching the Reformation: The Homiletical Handbook of Urbanus Rhegius* (Milwaukee: Marquette University Press, 2003). See also Amy Nelson Burnett, "The Evolution of the Lutheran Pastors' Manual in the Sixteenth Century," *Church History* 73 (September 2004): 536–65. A later rector at the Latin school in Eisleben, however, did assemble a variety of passages from Luther's writings in his *Pastorale Lutheri* (Eisleben, 1582). See Robert Kolb, "Luther the Master Pastor: Conrad Porta's *Pastorale Lutheri*, Handbook for Generations," *Concordia Journal* 9 (1983): 179–87.

c LW 42:121–66. Jane Strohl, "Luther's Fourteen Consolations," *Lutheran Quarterly* ns 3 (1989): 169–82.

particular situation of crisis. Returning from the Wartburg in 1522, Luther had to take in hand a reforming movement that, in his view, had gotten out of hand by claiming to carry reform to its logical ends yet returning to a legalism that Luther's reform opposed.

The *Selected Sermons* illustrate Luther's preaching on a number of topics and texts. Although Luther wrote down few of his actual sermons, the notes taken by listeners allow us to appreciate his forthright, energetic, and clear manner of expressing key Reformation insights in ways that all would understand. A sermon from one of his postils is also included. In the sixteenth century, a pastor's library typically included several *postils*, collections of sermons on Gospel and/or Epistle lectionary texts arranged according to the church year. Luther sought through his postils to provide preaching aids to other pastors and thus influenced the course of evangelical preaching. They provide a glimpse of how Luther wanted his insights preached and taught. Only recently have scholars started recognizing the importance of postils in the spread of Reformation preaching and teaching.[d]

Luther was well aware of the power of hymnody to preach and teach the faith as well as provide opportunity for the laity to confess the faith. The first Evangelical hymnals were published in 1524, five years before Luther's catechisms. Luther continued to compose hymns throughout his life; some of these are sung to this day by Christians around the world. The hymns provided in this volume give insight into Luther's poetic genius for conveying the gospel in this form.

"Teaching and Prayer" contains several pieces specifically intended to teach prayer: *A Sermon on Prayer and Procession during Rogation Days* (1519), the *Little Prayer Book* (1522), Luther's *Small*

A 1548 printing of Luther's *Hausspostil*, with a historiated border that depicts images of God's instructions to Adam and Eve, the Fall and expulsion from Eden, Adam and Eve working the ground, John the Baptist pointing the way, the crucifixion, infant baptism, and the Eucharist.

---

d   See, for example, John Frymire, *The Primacy of the Postils: Catholics, Protestants, and the Dissemination of Ideas in Early Modern Germany* (Leiden: Brill, 2010).

Catechism (1529), and *A Simple Way to Pray* (1535). Often ignored, Luther's reformation of prayer theology and practice has gained more attention in recent decades. The works here illustrate how Luther used different genres—sermon, prayer book, letter, and catechism—to teach prayer. The *Little Prayer Book* is sometimes seen as a forerunner to *The Small Catechism*, as it contains many catechetical elements. Like the *Little Prayer Book, The Small Catechism* went beyond teaching prayer and illustrates Luther's efforts to concentrate his theology in an easily understandable (and learnable) form focused on the most important elements of the Christian faith. *The Small Catechism* is probably the most influential of all his works, shaping generations of Lutherans across several continents, who memorized and reflected upon its contents.

The pieces in "Pastoral Care and Consolation" show Luther dealing with a diverse set of pastoral challenges. In *A Sermon on Preparing to Die* (1519) he consciously moved away from the advice given in the medieval *Ars Moriendi* literature while retaining some of the form of that literature. Departing from medieval Roman Catholic beliefs and practices surrounding death, Luther stressed that the dying could be certain of God's forgiveness because God had promised to forgive. Luther's instructions for dying removed the threat that one's disposition on the deathbed might put one's salvation in peril. Rather than focusing on death, sin, and hell, the Christian is to be consoled by God's sure promise.

Luther knew well that high regard for and devotion to the Virgin Mary were prominent in medieval piety and key to how laity understood and practiced their faith. While Luther firmly rejected any notion that Mary was a mediator between God and humans, he did not eliminate all mention of her but, rather, sought to teach a proper understanding and appreciation of Mary. He began his commentary on Mary's song in Luke 1 (*The Magnificat*) before he left for the Diet of Worms in 1521[2] but he did not complete it until he was at the Wartburg. Luther saw Mary's "humility" not as a virtue but, rather, as a description of her status as a lowly, poor, and even despised person. Rather than ascribing virtue to Mary, Luther praised her for her great faith and willingness to be the mother of God. Written for those who, like Mary, were "humble" and "simple," this piece served also as a gift for the young prince John Frederick. Castigating

2. An imperial diet was an assembly of the political representatives of the Holy Roman Empire called by the Holy Roman Emperor. Luther was under the threat of excommunication by Pope Leo X (r. 1513–1521), which by tradition meant that Emperor Charles V (1500–1558) should declare Luther an outlaw. Even so, Charles did allow Luther to appear at the Diet of Worms to get a hearing where he was expected to retract his writings against papal teachings. Luther did not retract, and supporters secretly stole him away to safety and exile at the Wartburg, the castle of Elector Frederick III (1463–1525) in May 1521.

many of the vices and failures that plague leaders, including their pride and presumption, it taught what a good and pious prince should be careful to avoid. A right understanding of Mary's song, with its teaching about God and how God regards the proud and the humble, can teach rulers how to conduct themselves.

Whether One May Flee from a Deadly Plague (1527) responded to a concrete challenge and offers opportunity to reflect on what Christian vocation means in the midst of threat and death. Plague—with its attendant threat of sudden death—was a regular event in Luther's era. While much of today's Western world may have lost the sense that one could be swept away quickly by epidemic disease, this threat was common up into the modern era and still exists in many parts of the world today.

That Christians Should Bear Their Cross with Patience (1530) illustrates Luther's use and extension of his theology of the cross. These were probably notes for his

The plague known as Black Death is depicted in this image called "Dance of Death," published in the German printed edition of Hartman Schedel's *Chronicle of the World* (Nuremberg, 1493). The artist is thought to be Michael Wolgemut (1434–1519).

sermon to the Wittenberg entourage headed for the Diet of Augsburg (1530).[3] Facing a potentially negative outcome of the Diet, and the resulting suffering and pain, Luther sought to give comfort and confidence to his fellow reformers. Readers may want to read these notes in connection with the sermon included under "Selected Sermons."

Consolation for Women Whose Pregnancies Have Not Gone Well (1542) addressed an all-too-common issue. It demonstrates not only Luther's pastoral care for women but also his response to the concern of all parents for the salvation of unbaptized children.

Luther carried on an extensive correspondence with a very diverse set of individuals, including rulers, church leaders, former students, relatives, friends, and strangers. The sampling of letters in this volume show Luther using this genre to extend pastoral care to those far away from him.

3. Emperor Charles called this diet and summoned Elector John Frederick (1486–1532) with the hope of ending religious division in his empire. Elector John asked Luther, Philip Melanchthon (1497–1560), and others to write and present a clear statement of their faith and teachings. Melanchthon submitted the *Augsburg Confession* to the emperor, but Luther did not attend in person for reasons of safety.

The volume concludes with "Reflections on Reform," containing Luther's *Preface to the German Works* (1539) and *Preface to the Latin Works* (1545). Luther was reluctant to let his works be assembled and published but realized that this would probably happen regardless of his wishes. He knew that a significant part of the audience for these would be pastors. He chose to use the prefaces to those editions to reflect on what was most important to him—namely his approach to Scripture and his Reformation breakthrough.

Luther's Reformation breakthrough—the realization that God considers humans righteous for the sake of Christ, not on the basis of any human merit or worthiness, and that faith (trust) in this promise, a faith itself given by the Holy Spirit, is all that is needed for salvation—shaped his pastoral work and that of his followers in ways very different from their medieval predecessors. Both pastoral practice and lay piety changed significantly as a result of Luther's insights into the heart of the Christian faith.

The Invocavit Sermons

1522[a]

MARTIN J. LOHRMANN

INTRODUCTION

Following an almost year-long exile at Wartburg Castle, Martin Luther returned to Wittenberg in early March 1522 and resumed his ministry there by preaching these eight sermons over eight days. He preached the first of them on *Invocavit* Sunday, the first Sunday in Lent. Although delivered for a unique set of local circumstances, these sermons provide excellent witness to Luther's knowledge and use of Scripture, his ability to share the gospel message of justification by faith, and his skill in applying that saving faith to the challenges of daily life.

Historical Background

Luther came back to Wittenberg at a critical time.[b] In the months since Luther had been summoned to the Diet of Worms in April 1521, reforms in Wittenberg continued under the leadership of colleagues such as Justus Jonas (1493–1555), Nicholas von Amsdorf (1483–1565), Andreas Bodenstein von Karlstadt

This 1522 illustration by Lucas Cranach the Elder (1472–1553) depicts Luther as Junker Jörg.

---

a   The first published title of these sermons was *Eight Sermons Preached by Dr. Martin Luther in Wittenberg during Lent, in Which the Mass, Images,*

An etching of Andreas Bodenstein von Karlstadt, sixteenth century. Karlstadt received his doctorate in Wittenberg in 1510 and also studied canon law and civil law in Erfurt, Cologne, and Rome. Highly interested in social and church reform, he held many official positions at the university and its church, including theology department chair, archdeacon, and dean.

(1486–1541), and Philip Melanchthon (1497–1560); Gabriel Zwilling (1487–1558) led reform efforts at the town's Augustinian monastery. Outside the school and churches, Luther's teachings also inspired townspeople to embrace the need for religious and social reforms—for instance, how to care for the poor and improve church oversight on the local level.

While away from Wittenberg, Luther corresponded with Melanchthon, Amsdorf, and the court advisor Georg Spalatin (1484–1545) and stayed informed of Wittenberg events. In those months, some priests had begun to marry, in opposition to centuries of mandatory clerical celibacy.[1] In September, Melanchthon led a small group in privately receiving both the wine and the bread of Holy Communion.[2] At the Augustinian monastery and at the All Saints Church (the Castle Church) priests refused to hold the customary private Masses. Luther supported these reforms, though a tract against rioting written in December 1521 after a discreet visit to Wittenberg suggests that he knew greater social upheaval was possible.[c]

That Christmas, Karlstadt took reforms a step further, as he presided at communion without wearing his vestments, used a modified liturgy, and served communion in both kinds, even to people who had not made confession.[d] The following day he announced that he, too, was going to marry. These events did not provoke any criticism from Luther. That relative harmony began to change in January 1522 with the appearance of a new Wittenberg Ordinance to reform city and church practices, put forth by Karlstadt and the city council with the approval of the

1. Clerical celibacy became a general requirement in the Western church under Pope Gregory VII (d. 1085) and his successors in the eleventh and twelfth centuries. It was included in the decrees of the First and Second Lateran Councils, held in the years 1123 and 1139, respectively.

2. This "reception in both kinds" went against the dominant practice that only priests received the wine of communion. It was an early focus in Luther's call for sacramental reform,

Both Kinds of the Sacrament, Foods and Private Confession Are Briefly Treated (Speyer: Jakob Schmidt, 1523).

b Many primary sources for the history of this period appear in Nikolaus Müller, ed., *Die Wittenberger Bewegung, 1521 und 1522* (Leipzig: Nachfolger, 1909) [hereafter NM]. Several detailed studies of the Wittenberg Movement exist in English: Mark U. Edwards Jr., *Luther and the False Brethren* (Stanford: Stanford University Press, 1975); James S. Preus, *Carlstadt's* Ordinaciones *and Luther's Liberty* (Cambridge: Harvard University Press, 1974); Ronald J. Sider, ed., *Karlstadt's Battle with Luther* (Philadelphia: Fortress Press, 1978); and Amy Nelson Burnett, *The Eucharistic Pamphlets of Andreas Bodenstein von Karlstadt* (Kirksville, MO: Truman State University Press, 2011).

c *A Sincere Admonition by Martin Luther to All Christians to Guard against Insurrection and Rebellion* (WA 8:676–87; LW 45:57–73).

d Preus, *Carlstadt's* Ordinaciones, 28.

university.[e] Interpretations of these events favorable to Karlstadt view this as a bold step forward to reform church and society; in that light, Luther's later critique of this ordinance signifies his inability to accept his own conclusions and reveals his subservience to the nobility. On the other hand, interpretations more sympathic to Luther's view identify the Wittenberg Ordinance as the moment when Karlstadt reached too far and revealed himself to be a radical reformer.[3] Careful engagement with primary documents continues to leave many questions unanswered, so that a variety of interpretations are possible. The dramatic events of these months have led some to describe this period as the "Wittenberg Unrest."

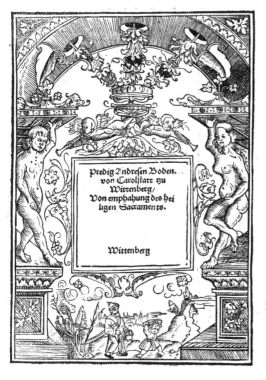

This is a title page to a 1522 publication of Karlstadt's sermon on the reception of Holy Communion. Karlstadt was himself a prolific writer and an important voice in launching church reforms. The illustration refers to Abraham's near sacrifice of Isaac (Gen. 22).

included in his 1519 *The Blessed Sacrament of the Holy and True Body of Christ, and the Brotherhoods* (LW 35:50; TAL 1:225–56) and in the 1520 work *The Babylonian Captivity of the Church* (LW 36:13–17; TAL 3:15–21). A century before Luther, Jan Hus of Prague (1369–1415) had called for similar reforms, which remained practiced by some in Bohemia despite Hus's condemnation and execution for heresy at the 1415 Council of Constance. An 8 October, 1521, letter by Sebastian Heinemann, who was a student in Wittenberg at the time, includes the report, "Philip Melanchthon, with all his students, communed in both kinds on St. Michael's Day [September 29] in the parish"; NM nr. 4 (trans.).

3. Although he had not yet expressed such beliefs, in the following years Karlstadt went on to advocate many of the same ideas later held and practiced by members of the so-called Radical Reformation, including believers' baptism, the rejection of Christ's physical presence in Holy Communion, anticlericalism, and an emphasis on personal piety and sanctification.

---

e   The text of the Wittenberg Ordinance appears in Emil Sehling, ed., *Die evangelischen Kirchenordnungen des XVI. Jahrhunderts.* Vol. 1/1, 696–98 (Leipzig: Reisland, 1902); Hans Lietzman, ed., *Die Wittenberger und*

4. See Edwards, *Luther and the False Brethren*, 14: "The Reichsregiment had recently forbade innovations and commanded that preachers admonish the populace to remain within the old faith."

5. Melanchthon has often been criticized in literature about this period, since disruptions in the city and the confusion surrounding the Wittenberg Ordinance are supposed to show that he was too weak a leader in Luther's absence. Heinz Scheible has disproved these critiques in recent decades. For instance, although he contributed where he could, the young professor (then twenty-four years old) had almost no official civic, ecclesial, or academic authority to assert. Luther had asked that Melanchthon might take his place as preacher in the City Church, but officials denied that request because Melanchthon was not ordained. Within days after the Wittenberg Ordinance appeared, Melanchthon composed a set of propositions to conclude that the new document may be rightly revoked for these reasons (NM, nr. 85). His invocation of Christian freedom on these points was reminiscent of Luther's 1520 tract *The Freedom of a Christian* (LW 31:327–77; TAL 1:466–538) and foreshadowed the argument that Luther made a month later in the *Invocavit Sermons*. See Heinz Scheible, "Luther and Melanchthon," *Lutheran Quarterly* 4 (Autumn 1990): 321–28; and idem, "Fifty Years of Melanchthon Research," *Lutheran Quarterly* 26 (Summer 2012): 169.

One complicating factor is that an imperial law forbidding religious changes had just been enacted on January 20, making it politically untenable for Saxon elector Frederick the Wise (1463–1525) to support or even consider local reform efforts like the January 22 Wittenberg Ordinance.[4] Though the Wittenberg Ordinance required the gradual removal of church images and altars, the situation deteriorated when impatient mobs started to destroy many religious images on their own. This made it appear as if reformers such as Karlstadt and Zwilling, who most favored removing the images, had incited an uproar despite their own concern for order.[f]

It is hard to know how much support the ordinance enjoyed. Although town mayor Christian Beyer (1482–1535) wrote the following day to the elector's representative that the ordinance had the support of the university and the council, he also said that he had spoken in favor of keeping crucifixes but that others overruled him by citing the biblical prohibitions against images (Exod. 20:4; Deut. 5:8; and Baruch 6). The fact that court painter Lucas Cranach the Elder (1472–1553) was a member of the city council beginning in 1519 also raises a question about how much agreement there could have been regarding the removal of images and altars.[g] Finally, within days of its passage, Melanchthon wrote a set of theses against the ordinance's conclusions about images and communion.[5] The Wittenberg Ordinance had quickly become a main point of contention in the town's religious, social, and political life.

Leisniger Kastenordnung 1522–1523 (Berlin: de Gruyter, 1935), 4–6; and Hans-Ulrich Delius, ed., Martin Luther: *Studienausgabe*, vol. 2 (Berlin: Evangelische Verlagsanstalt, 1982) [hereafter MLStA], 525–29. See also NM, nr. 75.

f   Preus, *Carlstadt's* Ordinaciones, 41.

g   Steven Ozment, *The Serpent and the Lamb: Cranach, Luther, and the Making of the Reformation* (New Haven: Yale University Press, 2011), 102–3 and 136–39.

Andreas Bodenstein von Karlstadt and the destruction of images.
This copper engraving from the seventeenth century shows that
even though he had not advocated rash iconoclasm, Karlstadt has
often been linked with the actions of an unruly mob ever since.

6. Luther wrote pointed letters to Frederick about his return on February 22 and March 5, 1522 (WA Br 2:448–49; LW 48:386–87 and WA Br 2:454–57; LW 48:388–93), including the following from the March 5 letter: "I have written this so Your Electoral Grace might know that I am going to Wittenberg under a far higher protection than the Elector's. I have no intention of asking Your Electoral Grace for protection. Indeed I think I shall protect Your Electoral Grace more than you are able to protect me. And if I thought that Your Electoral Grace could and would protect me, I should not go. The sword ought not and cannot help a matter of this kind. God alone must do it—and without the solicitude and co-operation of men. Consequently he who believes the most can protect the most" (LW 48:391).

7. The tonsure results from shaving part of the head as a sign of religious humility and was one of the marks of a monk in the Middle Ages.

The *Invocavit Sermons*: Content and Effects

Having decided, against the elector's wishes, that it was time to leave Wartburg Castle, Luther arrived back in Wittenberg on March 6, 1522.[6] He shaved off Junker Jörg's beard and received again a monk's tonsure.[7] On March 9, the first Sunday in Lent, he re-entered his pulpit in the City Church and spoke these gripping words: "The summons of death comes to us all, and no one can die for another."

One firsthand report says that Luther preached on the appointed text from Matthew for the day and then "left the text" to discuss the issues at hand.[h] While that may be so, Luther's message in these sermons matched the appointed Bible readings

---

h WA 10/3:lii. Although given by a witness, the report itself was not written until about 1533.

Painting of Luther preaching on the altarpiece
at the City Church (St. Mary's Church) in Wittenberg.
By Lucas Cranach the Younger, 1547.

8. Luther was perhaps thinking back to events in Wittenberg in 1522 when in his 1525 Lenten Postils he commented on the words "By the power of God" (2 Cor. 6:7): "False spirits go ahead and act with their own power, rage against images, make regulations in the churches, but do not ask if God's power does that or not; nothing good comes of this" (WA 17/2:185; LW 76:362–63).

very well. For instance, the first Sunday in Lent was long known as *Invocavit* Sunday, because the opening Introit for the day's worship began with Ps. 91:15, a fitting introduction for the sermons that followed: *Invocabit me et exaudiam eum* ("When they call to me, I will answer them"). The appointed epistle was 2 Cor. 6:1-10, which begins, "As we work together with him [Christ], we urge you not to accept the grace of God in vain." Repeatedly in the *Invocavit Sermons*, Luther accused his fellow Wittenbergers as having used their evangelical faith and freedom in vain.[8] The Gospel for *Invocavit* Sunday was Matt. 4:1-11, the temptation of Jesus by the devil. Indeed, Luther's primary opponent in the pulpit that week in Wittenberg was not flesh and blood but the clever arguments and damning accusations of the devil. However intentionally Luther followed the appointed biblical texts, these sermons are powerful and contextual reflections on the Lenten call to contend against evil, repent, pray, practice self-discipline, and serve others through works of love.

Luther's sermons were met immediately with positive acclaim and effect.[i] Many in the congregation wrote glowing accounts of

what they had heard. Before the week was even finished, Zwilling admitted to having acted immoder-
ately.[j] By the end of the month, Melanchthon viewed
the sermons as having helped bring calm to Wittenberg, saying, "Everything here has been well restored
by Doctor Martinus."[k]

What about Karlstadt? It seems that a little room
had been left open for a constructive relationship
between Luther and Karlstadt, though this would
have involved at least a little loss of face and status
for Karlstadt.[9] Indeed, Karlstadt soon showed his
continuing sympathy with more radical elements of
the Reformation. If events surrounding the *Invocavit
Sermons* are viewed as a battle of wills or methods,
then Luther's vision for reform carried the day and
set a lasting tone for the Wittenberg Reformation.[10]

The *Invocavit Sermons* remain rich sources for learning from
and about Martin Luther. They demonstrate his ability to
reason scripturally and to share the gospel through effective
preaching.[l] These sermons also stand as a fitting companion to
and case study for *The Freedom of a Christian*,[m] which had been
published before Luther left for the Diet of Worms.[n] As in that
work, the *Invocavit Sermons* emphasize the primacy of faith alone
in Christ alone, the power of God's Word to change the world,
and the new opportunity that liberated believers have in Christ
and the Holy Spirit to love and serve their neighbors. Histori-
cally, these sermons also provide a powerful conclusion to the
"Wittenberg Unrest." Karlstadt's influence had peaked, and an
important Lutheran precedent for responding to religious and
social change had appeared: Christians look first to Christ, who
frees them and in turn sends them back to care for others.

Scenes of Satan tempting Jesus
in the wilderness from Luther's
*Interpretation of the Epistles and Gospels
from Advent to Easter*, 1540 printing.

9. On this point, historian Ronald Sider
writes, "At this point Karlstadt could
have apologized for his excessive zeal
and worked behind the scenes as one
of Luther's important lieutenants to
foster as much change as possible"
(*Andreas Bodenstein von Karlstadt* [Leiden:
Brill, 1974], 173); and idem, *Karlstadt's
Battle with Luther*, 174. Offering a less
positive view of the relationship, Preus
concludes, "Luther's attack upon the
Ordnung is *ipso facto* an assault upon
Carlstadt" (*Carlstadt's* Ordinaciones,
65).

10. Though he objected to the
Wittenberg Ordinance in his *Invocavit
Sermons*, Luther was not against
"institutionalizing" reforms. In 1523
he supported the town of Leisnig's
reforming ordinance (WA 12:11–30;
LW 45:169–94) and established
liturgical changes in his 1523 *Order
of Mass and Communion for the Church
at Wittenberg* (WA 12:205–20;
LW 53:19–40).

i   WA 10/3:li–lv; and Martin Brecht, *Martin Luther: Shaping and Defining the
      Reformation, 1521–1532*, trans. James L. Schaaf (Minneapolis: Fortress
      Press, 1990), 61 (hereafter Brecht 2).

j   Edwards, *Luther and the False Brethren*, 26.

k   Brecht 2:61.

l   On Luther's use of rhetoric in the *Invocavit Sermons*, see Neil Leroux,
      Luther's Rhetoric: Strategies and Style from the Invocavit Sermons (St. Louis:
      Concordia Academic, 2002).

m   See TAL 1:467–538.

n   See n. 37, p. 22.

About This Edition

Though the text presented here is not an entirely new translation of the *Invocavit Sermons*, it is a significant revision of "Eight Sermons at Wittenberg, 1522" included in volume 51 of *Luther's Works*, American Edition. That version, edited by Dr. John Doberstein and published in 1959, was a revision of the translation by Rev. Augustus Steimle included in the 1915 Philadelphia Edition of *Luther's Works*, volume 2.[11]

Three reasons for the significant revisions commend themselves. First, the English language has changed enough since Steimle's translation that new word choices and revised sentence structures are warranted. Second, in relatively few cases, significant alterations have been made to better represent the original German text. Third, The Annotated Luther series has aimed to use gender-inclusive language where possible. Since Luther often addressed himself explicitly to "brothers and sisters," "friends," and "neighbors" in these sermons, the more expansive language of this edition fits Luther's original meaning. In all cases, faithfulness to the letter and spirit of the sermons has remained central. The original sources consulted in this translation were *Martin Luther: Studienausgabe* 2:530–58 and *Luthers Werke*, Weimar Ausgabe 10/3:1–64.

THE INVOCAVIT SERMONS[12]

The First Sermon, 9 March 1522, *Invocavit* Sunday

THE SUMMONS OF DEATH comes to us all, and no one can die for another. All must fight their own battle with death by themselves, alone. We can shout into one another's ears but everyone must individu-

11. LW 51:67–100; and *Works of Martin Luther*, vol. 2 (Philadelphia: n.p., 1915), 390–425.

12. In LW 51, titled *Eight Sermons at Wittenberg*.

ally be prepared for the time of death, for I will not be with you then nor you with me. Therefore each person must personally know and be armed with the chief things that concern a Christian. And these are what you, my beloved, heard from me many times in the past.

In the first place, we must know that we are the children of wrath and all our works, intentions, and thoughts are nothing at all. Here we need a clear, strong text to bear out this point. Such is the saying of St. Paul in Eph. 2[:3]. Note this well; and though there are many such in the Bible, I do not wish to overwhelm you with many texts. "We are all the children of wrath." And please do not start to say: I have built an altar, given a foundation for Masses, etc.

Second, God has sent us the only-begotten Son that we may believe in him so that whoever trusts in him shall be free from sin and a child of God, as John declares in his first chapter, "To all who believed in his name, he gave power to become children of God" [John 1:12]. Here we should all be well versed in the Bible and ready to confront the devil with many passages.[13] With respect to these two points I do not feel that there has been anything wrong or lacking. They have been rightly preached to you, and I should be sorry if it were otherwise. Indeed, I am well aware and dare say that you are more learned than I, and that there are not only one, two, three, or four, but perhaps ten or more who have this awareness.

Third, we must also have love and through love we must do to one another as God has done to us through faith. For without love faith is nothing, as St. Paul says (1 Cor. 2[13:1]): "If I had the tongues of angels and could speak of the highest things in faith, and have not love, I am nothing." And here, dear friends, have you not grievously failed? I see no signs of love among you and I observe very well that you have not been grateful to God for his rich gifts and treasures.[14]

Here let us beware lest Wittenberg become Capernaum [cf. Matt. 11:23].[15] I notice that you have a great deal to say of the doctrine of faith and love which is preached to you, and this is

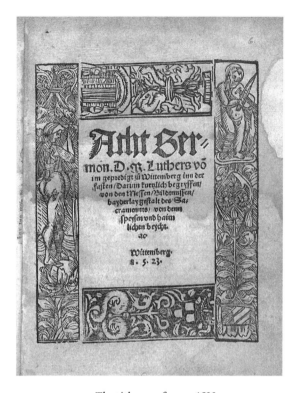

The title page from a 1523 printing of the *Eight Sermons* (*Acht Sermon D. M. Luthers*)

13. This resonates with the appointed Gospel for the day, Matt. 4:1-11.

14. This recalls the epistle for the day, 2 Cor. 6:1-10.

15. In Matt. 11:23, Jesus lamented the unbelief of towns where he had preached and healed.

This title page image is from a section of Lutheran hymnist Joseph Clauder's (1586–1653) hymn collection that is dedicated to the themes of the believer's crucifixion with Jesus and the suffering of persecution. This woodcut print features a man giving praise to God, having laid down his harp and crown to do so, a gesture of exultation in renunciation for the sake of the Kingdom of God.

no wonder; an ass can almost intone the lessons, and why should you not be able to repeat the doctrines and formulas? Dear friends, the kingdom of God—and we are that kingdom—does not consist in talk or words but in activity, in deeds, in works and exercises [1 Cor. 4:20; 1 John 3:18]. God does not want hearers and repeaters of words but followers and doers, and this occurs in faith through love [Jas. 1:22; Gal. 5:2]. For a faith without love is not enough—rather it is not faith at all, but a counterfeit of faith, just as a face seen in a mirror is not a real face, but merely the reflection of a face [1 Cor. 13:12].[16]

Fourth, we also need patience. For whoever has faith trusts in God and shows love to their neighbor, practicing it day by day, will undoubtedly suffer persecution. For the devil never sleeps, but constantly gives believers plenty of trouble. But patience works and produces hope [Rom. 5:4], which freely yields itself to God and realizes itself in God. Thus faith, by much affliction and persecution, ever increases, and is strengthened day by day. A heart thus blessed with virtues can never rest or restrain itself, but rather pours itself out again for the benefit and service of the brethren, just as God has done to it.

And here, dear friends, believers must not insist upon their own rights, but must see what may be useful and helpful to their brothers and sisters, as Paul says, *Omnia mihi licent, sed non omnia expediunt*, "'All things are lawful for me,' but not all things are helpful" [1 Cor. 6:12]. For we are not all equally strong in faith and some of you have even stronger faith than I. Therefore we must not look upon ourselves, or our strength, or our prestige, but upon our neighbor, for God has said through Moses: I have borne and reared you, as a mother does her child [Deut. 1:31].

What does a mother do to her child? First she gives it milk, then gruel, then eggs and soft food, whereas if she turned about and gave it solid food, the child would never thrive [cf. 1 Cor. 3:2; Heb. 5:12-13]. So we should also deal with our brothers and sisters, have patience with them for a time, have patience with their weakness and help them bear it [Gal. 6:2]; we should also give them milk-food, too [1 Pet. 2:2; cf. Rom. 14:1-3], as was done with us, until they, too, grow strong. In this way, we do not travel heavenward alone but bring those brothers and sisters who are not yet our friends with us. If all mothers were to abandon their children, where would we have been? Dear friend, if you have suckled long enough, do not at once cut off the breast, but let your neighbor be suckled as you were. If I had been here, I would not have gone so far as you have. The cause is good but there has been too much haste. For there are still brothers and sisters on the other side who belong to us and must still be won.

Let me illustrate. The sun has two properties, light and heat.[17] No king has power enough to bend or guide the light of the sun; it remains fixed in its place. But the heat may be turned and guided, even as it always still comes from the sun. Thus faith must always remain pure and immovable in our hearts, never wavering; but love bends and turns so that our neighbor may grasp and follow it. There are some who can run, others must walk, still others can hardly creep [cf. 1 Cor. 8:7-13]. Therefore we must not look upon our own abilities, but upon our neighbor's powers, so that those who are weak in faith and attempt to follow the strong may not be snatched up by the devil. Therefore, dear friends, follow me; I have never been a destroyer. I was also the first whom God set to this task. I cannot run away but will remain as long as God allows. I was also the first one to whom God revealed that his word should be preached to you. I am also sure that you have the clear word of God.[18]

Let us, therefore, act with fear and humility, casting ourselves at one another's feet, reaching out our hands to one another, and helping each other. I will do my part, which is no more than my duty, to love you even as I love my own soul.[19] For here we battle not against popes, bishops, or anyone else, but against the devil, and do you imagine he is asleep [cf. Eph. 6:12; 1 Pet. 5:8]? He sleeps not, but sees the true light rising, and to keep it from shining into his eyes he would like to make a flank attack—and he will succeed, if we are not on our guard. I know him well, and I hope, too, that with the help of God, I am his master.[20] But if we yield him but an inch, we must soon look to it how we may be rid of him. Therefore all those have erred who have helped and consented to abolish the Mass; not that it was not a good thing, but that it was not done in an orderly way. You say it was

16. Though Luther is known to have called James "an epistle of straw" (LW 35:362), he could also cite it approvingly, as he did here and in the *Large Catechism*'s words about prayer (BC 456.123). The reference to straw was likely an allusion to 1 Cor. 3:11-12, which names straw as a poor building material. Luther's critique of James, then, was that on its own it can be poor material upon which to build faith.

17. Luther was fond of using illustrations from the natural world in his sermons and writings.

18. Luther made a very strong appeal to his own call to preach, identifying himself as the first to have preached this message to the congregation in Wittenberg. Some have interpreted Luther's appeal here and elsewhere to his own heavenly call, his proper congregational call, and his experience in debates with Rome to indicate that he wanted to reassert personal control of reforms in Wittenberg over against other leaders like Karlstadt and Zwilling. Whether or not that personal challenge is exactly what Luther meant, the appeal to his own experience and authority

is a powerful rhetorical tool employed to gain support from his audience.

19. Here is a reference both to Luther's personal call to love the people through his call as a local preacher and to Jesus' summary of the greatest commandment, to "love your neighbor as yourself" (Matt. 22:39).

20. The devil appears again as the great adversary to faith, a theme of the Gospel for the day and of the *Invocavit Sermons* in general. For more on Luther's understanding of the devil, see Heiko Oberman, *Luther: Man between God and the Devil*, trans. Eileen

Walliser-Schwarzbart (New Haven: Yale University Press, 2006), 154–56.

21. Note the use of "order" or "orderly" in this place. Luther was likely contrasting the relationship between real "orderliness" and the "ordinances" that had recently caused so much "disorder" and controversy in Wittenberg.

22. Once again, Luther focused on the devil's ability to undermine faith, especially during intense moments like a deathbed scene. This section recalls the teaching and counsel that Luther gave in his 1519 *Sermon on Preparing to Die* (LW 42:101; in this volume, p. 283).

23. While somewhat similar to the previous appeal to his own authority, Luther here refers to the external call of the council as a source of comfort from the attacks and accusations of the devil. That is, no matter what doubts or weaknesses he might have had about himself as a leader and preacher, Luther could rely on the outside word of assurance that the church and its leaders had appointed him to this exact work of preaching and teaching the gospel. While the precise details surrounding Luther's call from the city council remain unclear, he had been serving as a properly called preacher at the City Church since 1514; Martin Brecht, *Martin Luther: His Road to Reformation, 1483–1521*, trans. James L. Schaaf (Philadelphia: Fortress Press, 1985), 150–51 (hereafter Brecht 1).

right according to the Scriptures. I agree, but what becomes of order? For it was done in wantonness, with no regard for proper order and with offense to your neighbor.[21] If, beforehand, you had called upon God in earnest prayer and had obtained the aid of the authorities, one could be certain that it had come from God. I, too, would have taken steps toward the same end if it had been a good thing to do; and if the Mass were not so evil a thing, I would introduce it again. For I cannot defend your action, as I have just said. To the papists and blockheads I could defend it, for I could say: How do you know whether it was done with good or bad intention, since the work in itself was really a good work? But I would not know what to assert before the devil.[22] For if on their deathbeds the devil reminds those who began this affair of texts like these, "Every plant which my Father has not planted will be rooted up" [Matt. 15:13], or "I have not sent them, yet they ran" [Jer. 23:21], how will they be able to withstand? He will cast them into hell. But I shall poke the one spear into his face, so that even the world will become too small for him, for I know that in spite of my reluctance I was called by the council to preach.[23] Therefore I was willing to accept you as you were

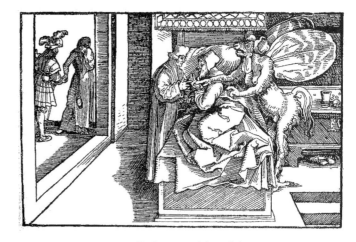

An evangelical pastor visits a dying man
who has turned his back on the devil.

willing to accept me, and, besides, you could have consulted me about the matter.

I was not so far away that you could not reach me with a letter, whereas not the slightest communication was sent to me.[24] If you were going to begin something and make me responsible for it, that would have been too much for me. I will not do it [i.e., assume the responsibility]. Here one can see that you do not have the Spirit, even though you do have a deep knowledge of the Scriptures. Take note of these two things, "must" and "free."[25] The "must" is that which necessity requires, and which must ever be unyielding; as, for instance, the faith, which I shall never permit anyone to take away from me, but must always keep in my heart and freely confess before everyone. But "free" is that in which I have choice, and may use or not, yet in such a way that it profit my neighbor and not me. Now do not make a "must" out of what is "free," as you have done, so that you may not be called to account for those who were led astray by your loveless exercise of liberty. For if you entice people to eat meat on Fridays and they become troubled by it on their deathbed, thinking, "Woe is me, for I have eaten meat and I am lost!" until they can no longer stand it, then God will call you to account for that soul. I, too, would like to begin many things, in which but few would follow me, but what is the use? For I know that when the conflicts come those who have begun such things would not be able to persevere and would be the first to retreat. How would it be, if I brought the crowds to the point of attack and then if I—who had been the first to exhort others—would then flee death rather than steadfastly face it? How the poor people would be deceived![26]

Let us, therefore, feed others also with the milk which we received, until they too become strong in faith. For there are many who are otherwise in accord with us and who would also gladly accept this thing, but they do not yet fully understand it—these we drive away. Therefore, let us show love to our neighbors; if we do not do this, our work will not endure. We must have patience with them for a long time yet and not cast out those who are still weak in faith; how much to do or not to do depends on what love requires and what does no harm to our faith. If we do not earnestly pray to God and act rightly in this matter, it looks to me as if all the complaints that we have heaped upon the papists will fall upon us. Therefore I could no longer remain away, but was compelled to come and say these things to you.

24. Though Luther had been in regular contact with colleagues, it appears that he is correct in saying that he had not known about the Wittenberg Ordinance as it was being written or instituted.

25. Here begins Luther's crucial distinction between matters that are essential for salvation ("musts") and matters that do not affect salvation and are therefore "free." Faith in the mercy of God given freely through Christ is the "must" of Christian life. Compared to faith, even the great works of love that follow such saving faith are nothing when it comes to salvation. Rather, faith that trusts Christ alone sees that there are no personal interests to defend or prop up when it comes to righteousness before God. Because it is entirely externally oriented, this justifying faith in Christ similarly leads to free and selfless service to one's neighbors. This paradoxical relationship between faith and love was the subject of Luther's 1520 tract *The Freedom of a Christian* (see n. 5, p. 10 above). It remains a uniquely fruitful, albeit challenging, interpretation of Christian life. Later Lutherans would discuss this relationship between necessity and freedom as the doctrine of adiaphora, as in the *Formula of Concord*, article 10 (BC 635.1–640.31).

26. This set of comments indicates that Luther was well aware of the real possibility for demagoguery and mob mentality arising from his or other reforming efforts. Such worries were well founded, as smaller mob actions in Wittenberg and elsewhere were followed by a mass uprising across German lands, the Peasants' War of 1524–25, which took tens of thousands of lives.

27. Because this sermon did not explicitly discuss the Mass or Holy Communion, this conclusion might seem surprising. Nevertheless, this comment shows that Luther's words about faith and love were spoken with the practical effects of liturgical reform in mind.

28. The phrase "private Masses" refers to those services of Holy Communion that priests said apart from corporate worship. These private Masses were paid for by donors who in return would receive forgiveness of sins and reduced time in purgatory for themselves or their loved ones.

29. As in *To the Christian Nobility of the German Nation concerning the Reform of the Christian Estate* (LW 44:123–217; TAL 1:369–465) and *The Babylonian Captivity of the Church* (LW 36:11–126; TAL 3:8–129).

This is enough about the Mass; tomorrow we shall speak about images.[27]

The Second Sermon, 10 March 1522, Monday after *Invocavit*

Dear friends, you heard yesterday the chief characteristics of Christians, that their whole lives and beings are grounded in faith and love. Faith is directed toward God, while love is directed toward people and consists in sharing with neighbors the love and service that we have received from God without our having worked for it or deserved it. Thus, there are two things: the one, which is the most needful and must happen before all else; the other, which is free and not of necessity, which may be kept or not without endangering faith or incurring hell. In both, love must deal with our neighbor in the same manner as God has dealt with us; it must walk the straight road, straying neither to the left nor to the right [cf. Matt. 7:13-14]. In the things that are "musts" and are matters of necessity, such as believing in Christ, love still never uses force or undue pressure. Thus the Mass is an evil thing, and God is displeased with it, because it is performed as if it were a sacrifice and work of merit. Therefore it must be abolished. Here, there can be no question or doubt, any more than you should ask whether you should worship God. Here we are entirely agreed: the private Masses must be abolished.[28] As I have said in my writings,[29] I wish they would be abolished everywhere and only the common evangelical Mass be retained. Nevertheless, Christian love should not employ harshness here nor force the matter. However, it should be preached and taught with tongue and pen that to hold Mass in such a manner is sinful, even though no one should be dragged away from it by the hair; for it should be left to God, whose word should be allowed to work alone, without our work or interference. Why? Because it is not in my power or hand to mold human hearts as the potter molds the clay and fashion them at my pleasure [Ecclus. 33:13]. I can get no further than their ears; their hearts I cannot reach. And since I cannot pour faith into their hearts, I cannot, nor should I, force anyone to have faith. That is God's work alone, who causes faith to live in the heart. Therefore we should give free course to the word and not add our works to it. We have the *jus verbi* [right to speak] but not the *executio* [power to accomplish]. We should preach the word but the results must be left solely to God's good pleasure.

Now if I should rush in and abolish it by force, there are many who would be compelled to consent to it without knowing where they stand, whether it is right or wrong, saying, "I do not know if it is right or wrong, I do not know where I stand, I was compelled by force to submit to the majority."[30] And this forcing and commanding results in a mere mockery, an external show, a fool's play, human ordinances, sham-saints, and hypocrites. For where the heart is not good, I care nothing at all for the work. We must first win the hearts of the people. But that is done when I teach only the word of God, preach the gospel, and say: "Dear lords or pastors, abandon the Mass. It is not right and you are sinning when you do it; I cannot refrain from telling you this." But I would not make it an ordinance for them, nor urge a general law.[31] Whoever would want to follow me could do so and whoever did not want to would remain outside. In the latter case the word would sink into the heart and do its work, so that such people would become convinced, acknowledge the error, and fall away from the Mass; tomorrow another would do the same. Thus God would accomplish more with the word than if you and I were to pile all our power into one heap. So when you have won the heart, you have won the person such that the thing itself must finally fall of its own weight and come to an end. And if the hearts and minds of all are agreed and united, abolish it. But if all are not heart and soul for its abolition, then leave it in God's hands, I beseech you, or else the result will not be good. Not that I would again set up the Mass; I let it lie in God's name. Faith must not be chained and imprisoned, nor bound by an ordinance to any work. This is the principle by which you must be governed. For I am sure you will not be able to carry out your plans. And if you should carry them out with such general laws, then I will recant everything that I have written and preached and I will not support you.[32] This I am telling you now. What harm can it do you? You still have your faith in God, pure and strong so that this thing cannot hurt you.

Love, therefore, demands that you have compassion on the weak, as all the apostles had. Once, when Paul came to the mighty city of Athens (Acts 17[:16-32]) he found in the temple

30. Luther often included hypothetical conversations in his sermons, as here when he anticipated questions or objections. A few sentences later (beginning, "Dear lords or pastors . . .") he put words in his own mouth. Even more dramatically in these and other sermons, Luther could put words in the mouth of God, Christ, or the devil to express what was at stake, using the logic and flow of a conversation or direct speech to get a point across.

31. As in the first sermon, in this section Luther rejected the idea that reforms are best effected by means of ordinances, laws, or general laws (*gemeyne ordnung*).

32. This is the first of several instances in which Luther threatened to either remove his support of the Wittenberg Reformation or even leave town if things continued as they were, adding a direct and personal entreaty to his preaching.

33. Luther refers to his personal experiences of conflict with the church authorities to show that reform can happen in many ways.

34. A reference to Luther's own early Reformation writings, beginning with the *95 Theses* of 1517 (WA 1:233–38; LW 31:25–33; TAL 1:13–46).

35. Luther's colleagues, Philip Melanchthon and Nicholas von Amsdorf.

36. This is an excellent example of Luther's belief that God's word creates real change in the world.

37. Luther was summoned to appear at the imperial assembly, the Diet of Worms, in the spring of 1521. He did not recant his criticisms of the pope and Roman church, but also did not try to incite crowds to protest.

Acts 17:16–32. Paul preaches on Mars Hill about Jesus beginning with the statue to the unknown god depicted in the background. Illustration by Pierre Eskrich (c. 1550–c. 1590).

many ancient altars, and he went from one to the other and looked at them all, but he did not kick down a single one of them with his foot. Rather he stood up in the middle of the marketplace and said they were nothing but idolatrous things and begged the people to forsake them; yet he did not destroy one of them by force. When the word took hold of their hearts, the people forsook them of their own accord and thus the thing fell of itself. Likewise, if I had seen people holding Mass, I would have preached to them and admonished them. Had they heeded my admonition, I would have won them; if not, I would nevertheless not have torn them from it by the hair or by using any force but would have let the word act and kept praying for them. For the Word created heaven and earth and all things [Ps. 33:6], so that the Word must do this thing and not we poor sinners.

In short, I will preach it, tell it, write it, but I will constrain no one by force, for faith must come freely without compulsion. Take an example from me.[33] I opposed indulgences and all the papists, but never with force.[34] I taught, preached, and wrote God's word alone; otherwise I did nothing. And while I slept [cf. Mark 4:26-29], or drank Wittenberg beer with my friends Philip and Amsdorf,[35] the word did so much that the papacy weakened in such a way that no prince or emperor ever inflicted such damage upon it. I did nothing; the word did everything.[36] Had I desired to proceed with violence, I could have brought great bloodshed upon Germany; indeed, even at Worms[37] I could have started such trouble that even the emperor would not have been safe. But what would it have been? Mere fool's play. I did nothing; I let the Word do its work. What do you suppose the devil thinks when one tries to establish something by making a big noise? He sits back in hell and thinks, "Oh, what a fine game the fools are up to now!" But it does him harm when we spread the word alone and let it alone do the work, for it is almighty and captures hearts. And when hearts are captured the work will fall of itself. Here's a simple example: In former times there were sects, too, of Jewish and Gentile Christians, differing on the law of Moses with respect to circumcision. The former wanted to keep it; the latter did not. Then Paul came preaching that it might be kept or not, for there was no power in it. He also said that they should not make a "must" of it but leave it as a matter of freedom; there was no danger in either keeping it or not [1 Cor. 7:18-24; Gal. 5:1]. So it was up to the time of Jerome, who came and wanted to make a "must" out of it, desiring to make an ordinance and a law that it be prohibited. Then came St. Augustine and he was of the same opinion as St. Paul that it might be kept or not, as one wished. St. Jerome was a hundred miles away from St. Paul's opinion. The two doctors bumped heads rather hard, but when St. Augustine died, St. Jerome was successful in having it prohibited.[38] After that came the popes, who also wanted to add something and they, too, made laws, such that from one law grew a thousand laws, until they have completely buried us under laws. And so it would happen here, too: one law will soon become two, two become three, and so forth.

Let this be enough at this time concerning the things that are necessary,[39] and let us beware lest we lead astray those of weak conscience [1 Cor. 8:12].

The Third Sermon, 11 March 1522, Tuesday after *Invocavit*

We have heard the things that are "musts," which are necessary and must be done, things which must be so and not otherwise: the private Masses must be abolished. For all works and things that are either commanded or forbidden by God and thus have been ordered by the supreme Majesty are "musts." Nevertheless, no one should be dragged to them or away from them by the hair, for—to say it plain enough—I cannot push anyone into heaven nor beat them into it with a club.[40] I believe you have understood what I said.

Now come the things which are not necessary but have been left open by God and which we may keep or not, such as whether a person should marry or not, or whether monks and nuns should leave the cloisters. These things are matters of freedom and must not be forbidden by anyone. If they are forbidden, the

38. Augustine (354–430) and Jerome (c. 347–420) debated the role of circumcision in the life of Christians in their correspondence. For bibliographic information about this controversy, see MLStA 2:538 nn.116–18, which also mentions discussion of this subject by Luther's contemporaries Faber Stapulensis (c. 1455–1536) and Erasmus of Rotterdam (1466–1536).

39. With this conclusion, Luther summarized his second sermon as expressing the difference between what is essential (faith in God) and what is not essential for salvation (human acts of love and rules of the church).

40. Luther uses physical words—dragging, pushing, and beating—to describe reforms that may be experienced as coercive. The image of "pulling by the hair" appears elsewhere in these sermons.

41. In this case, "God's ordinance" is to declare freedom.

42. Again, Luther's concern was that believers be able to withstand the condemnations of sin, death, and the devil in their time of greatest need, especially in the hour of death.

43. The dean (*Probst*) of the Castle Church at the time was Justus Jonas, who remained a longtime colleague and leader in the Reformation. Dr. Karlstadt was Andreas Bodenstein von Karlstadt, a leader in the effort to produce the Wittenberg Ordinance (a document discussed in the introduction). This is the only place in the *Invocavit Sermons* in which Karlstadt is singled out by name. Gabriel refers to Gabriel Zwilling, the leader of the local Augustinian monastery who had led reforms there. Additionally, the use of only his first name and the succeeding naming of Michael suggests that Luther was also intentionally then referring to the archangels Gabriel and Michael, which then calls to mind Gal. 1:8: "But even if we or an angel from heaven should proclaim to you a gospel contrary to what we proclaimed to you, let that one be accursed!" Such a rhetorical move would not necessarily represent a complete condemnation of Jonas, Karlstadt, or Zwilling. Instead, as the sentence continues and as Luther said in the beginning of the first sermon, it would emphasize that all need to know and claim the gospel for themselves.

44. The German here is *Spruch Ston*, which is reminiscent of Melanchthon's *loci communes* (commonplaces or touchstones) method of interpreting Scripture. Adapting the method of Erasmus of Rotterdam, Melanchthon read texts looking for the little steps

forbidding is wrong, since it is contrary to God's ordinance.[41] In the things that are free, such as marrying or not marrying, you should take this attitude: if you can keep to it without burden, then keep it; it must not be made a general law, rather everyone must be free. So if there is a priest, monk, or nun who cannot abstain, let him take a wife and she a husband,[o] in order that your conscience may be relieved; and see to it that you can stand before God and the world when you are assailed, especially when the devil attacks you in the hour of death.[42] It is not enough to say: this man or that man did it, I followed the crowd, according to the preaching of the dean, Dr. Karlstadt, or Gabriel, or Michael.[43] Not so [*neyn*]; all must stand on their own feet and be prepared to give battle to the devil. You must rest upon a strong and clear text of Scripture if you want to remain standing. If you do not have that, you will never be able to stand, for the devil will pluck you like a parched leaf. Therefore the priests who have taken wives and the nuns who have taken husbands in order to save their consciences must stand squarely upon a clear text of Scripture,[44] such as this one by St. Paul, although there are many more: "In later times some will depart from the faith by giving heed to deceitful spirits and doctrines of the devil" (I think St. Paul is plain enough here!) "and will forbid marriage and the foods which God created" [1 Tim. 4:1-3]. With this text, the devil will not be able to overthrow or devour you; it will overthrow and devour him instead. Therefore any monks or nuns who find themselves too weak to remain abstinent should conscientiously examine themselves; if their hearts and consciences are thus strengthened, let him take a wife and she a husband. Would to God all monks and nuns could hear this sermon and properly understand this matter and would all forsake the cloisters, and thus all the cloisters in the world would cease to exist; this is what I would wish. But now they have no understanding of the matter, for no one preaches it to them. They hear about others who are leaving the cloisters in other places, who, however, are well pre-

o   LW 51:79 n.10 was mistaken. The German here is *"dere neme ein weyb / vnnd sy ein man."* The same formulation appears a little further below, too. LW has translated: "let him take a wife and be a husband," reading the *sy* as a form of *sein*. However, in many other places in these sermons, *sy* clearly refers to the relative pronoun *sie* and not to *sein*, so that Luther really is speaking to both men and women, retaining the parallelism of his address to monks and nuns.

pared for such a step, and then they want to follow their example, but have not yet fortified their consciences and do not know that it is a matter of freedom. This is bad, and yet it is better that the evil should be outside rather than inside. Therefore I say, what God has made free shall remain free. If anybody forbids it to you (as the pope, the Antichrist,[45] has done), you should not obey. Whoever can do so without harm and for love of his neighbor

of logic, rhetoric, and theology that the biblical writers used to persuade their audiences of the gospel message. Melanchthon's 1521 edition of the *Loci communes theologici* applied exactly this method to Paul's epistle to the Romans. Luther commended the use of such firm words of Scripture as sources of comfort and assurance from the attacks of the devil.

45. Because the papacy of Luther's day rejected the evangelical teaching about justification by faith alone, Luther began to identify the papacy as the biblical Antichrist in early 1520; see Oberman, *Luther*, 42; and Scott Hendrix, *Luther and the Papacy: Stages in a Reformation Conflict* (Philadelphia: Fortress Press, 1981). The term *antichrist* appears in 1 and 2 John. Second Thessalonians 2 identifies a man of sin or lawlessness who "takes his seat in the temple of God" and deceives people about God's truth. The reformers especially connected this ungodliness within the church with the papacy on the basis of 1 Timothy 4, which says that signs of the "teaching of demons" will be the forbidding of marriage and forced fasting, both of which the reformers were working against, including in these sermons.

The whore of Babylon (Revelation 17) rides the beast with cup in hand, while being worshiped by the kings of the earth. The triple tiara is on her head, identifying her as the pope. Woodcut designed by Lucas Cranach the Elder (1472–1553), a close friend of Martin Luther.

46. This is perhaps ironic, as Luther himself was "tonsured and garbed once again as an Augustinian" as he gave these sermons; Edwards, *Luther and the False Brethren*, 26.

47. The following section is a strong example of Luther's refutation (*refutatio*) of possible counterarguments; see Leroux, *Luther's Rhetoric*, 78.

may wear a cowl or a tonsure,[46] since it will not injure your faith. The cowl will not strangle you, if you are already wearing one.

Thus, dear friends, I have said it clearly enough, and I believe you ought to understand it and not make liberty a law, saying: "This priest has taken a wife, therefore all priests must take wives."[47] Not at all. Or, "this monk or that nun has left the cloister, therefore they must all come out." Again, no. Or, "this man has broken the images and burnt them, therefore all images must be burned." Not at all, dear friend! Or, "this priest has no wife, therefore no priest may marry." Not at all! For they who cannot abstain should take wives, and for others who can abstain, it is good that they maintain their restraint, as people who live in the Spirit and not in the flesh [Rom. 8:4; 1 Cor. 7:1-9]. Neither should they be troubled about the vows they have made, such as the monks' vows of obedience, chastity, and poverty, even though these are quite superfluous. For we cannot vow anything that is contrary to God's commands. God has made it a matter of freedom to marry or not to marry. Yet like a fool you think this freedom allows you to create a vow contrary to the ordinance of God! Therefore you must let freedom remain and not make it a requirement, for your vow goes against God's freedom. For example, if I vowed to strike my father on the mouth, or to steal someone's property, do you believe God would be pleased with such a vow? Therefore, little as I ought to keep a vow to strike my father on the mouth, so little ought I to abstain from marriage because I am bound by a vow of chastity, for in both cases God has ordered it otherwise. God has ordained that I should be free to eat fish or flesh, so that there should be no commandment concerning them. Therefore all the Carthusians[48] and all monks and nuns are departing from God's ordinance and freedom when they believe that if they eat meat they are defiled.

48. As he did frequently, Luther here named the strictest of the monastic orders. The Carthusian order, founded in France in 1084, was known for its strict vows of renunciation and silence.

Concerning Images

But now we must come to the images. Concerning them also it is true that they are unnecessary, and we are free to have them or not, although it would be much better if we did not have them at all. I am not partial to them. A great controversy arose on the subject of images between the Roman emperor and the pope; the emperor held that he had the authority to banish the images, while the pope insisted that they should remain, and both were wrong. Much blood was shed, but the pope emerged as victor and the emperor lost.[49] What was it all about? They wished to make a "must" out of that which is free. God cannot tolerate this. Do you presume to do things differently from the way the supreme Majesty has decreed? Surely not; let it alone. You read in the Law (Exod. 20[:4]), "you shall not make yourself a graven image, or any likeness of anything that is in heaven above, or that is in the earth beneath, or that is in the water under the earth."[50] There you take your stand; that is your ground. Now let us see what happens when our adversaries say: "The meaning of the first commandment is that we should worship only one God and not any image, even as it is said immediately following, 'You shall not bow down to them or serve them'" [Exod. 20:5].[51] When they say

Le peuple d'Israël ayant offensé Dieu, est puny par la morsure des serpens ardens, & depuis guary.

L E peuple Israëlite continuant son voyage, vint de la montagne de Hor par la voye qui meine à la mer Rouge, pour circuir la terre d'Edom, & se fascha du labeur du chemin, & parloit contre le Seigneur, & Moyse luy disant : Pourquoy nous as-tu tirez d'Egypte pour mourir au desert, où n'y a pain ny eau : nostre ame a vn degoust de ce pain tant leger. Parquoy le Seigneur enuoya sur le peuple murmurans des serpens pleins de feu : pour la blessure desquels, & la mort de plusieurs, le peuple vint à Moyse, disant ; Nous auons peché, parce que nous auons parlé contre le Seigneur, & contre toy : Prie-le qu'il fasse retirer de nous les serpens Et Moyse pria pour le peuple. Et le Seigneur luy dist, Fais vn serpent d'airain ; & le mets pour signe ; quiconque sera mors & le verra, il viura. Moyse donc fit esleuer vn serpent d'airain, & le mit pour signe. Et quand ceux qui estoient frappez des serpens le regardoient, ils estoient guaris. Et les Israëlites partirent, & poserent leur camp en Oboth : de là passant outre, trauerserent plusieurs deserts, & prierent le Roy des Amorrhéens de passer seulement par le chemin public, ce qu'il ne voulut accorder. Enfin ayant esté vaincu par les Israëlites, ils occuperent ses villes & villages, comme ils firent aussi celles d'Og, Roy de Basan.

Nombres 21. Chap.

Moses fashions a snake of bronze that heals
whoever looks upon it (Num. 21:1–9).

49. A reference to the iconoclastic controversy, initiated by Emperor Leo III (680–741), who prohibited the veneration of images in 718, contested by Pope Gregory II (r. 715–731), and finally settled in 843. *Invocavit* Sunday is the "Feast of Orthodoxy" in commemoration of the Seventh Ecumenical Council of 783, which dealt with this question.

50. What follows is an argument from the books of Moses against absolutizing the Mosaic prohibition of images.

51. What follows is more *refutatio*, that is, anticipating the counterarguments of one's opponents. In this case, Luther used the *refutatio* to show that since arguments against images are not foolproof, it is appropriate to show tolerance for images.

that it is the worship of images which is forbidden and not the making of them, they are shaking our foundation and making it uncertain. And if you reply, "The text says, 'You shall not make any images,'" then they will say: "It also says, 'You shall not worship them.'" In the face of such uncertainty who would be so bold as to destroy the images? Not I. But let us go further. They say: "Did not Noah, Abraham, and Jacob build altars?" [Gen. 8:20; 12:7; 13:4; 13:18; 33:20]. And who will deny that? We must admit it. Again, "Did not Moses erect a bronze serpent, as we read in his fourth book? (Num. 22 [21:9]). Moses forbade the making of images, yet he himself made one? It seems to me that such a serpent is an image, too." How shall we answer that? Again, "Do we not read also that two cherubim were erected on the mercy seat [Exod. 37:7], the very place where God willed that he should be worshiped?" Here we must admit that we may have images and make images, but we must not worship them. If they are worshiped, they should be put away and destroyed, just as King Hezekiah broke in pieces the bronze serpent erected by Moses [2 Kgs. 18:4]. And who will be so bold as to say, when he is challenged to give an answer: "They worship the images"? They will say, "Are you the man who dares to accuse us of worshiping them?" Do not believe that they will acknowledge it. To be sure, it is true, but we cannot make them admit it. Just look how they acted when I condemned works without faith.[52] They said: "Do you believe that we have no faith, or that our works are performed without faith?" At that point, I cannot press them any further, but must put my flute back in my pocket;[53] for if they gain a hair's breadth, they make a hundred miles out of it.

Therefore it should have been preached that images were nothing and that no service is done to God by erecting them; then they would have fallen of themselves. That is what I did; that is what Paul did in Athens, when he went into their churches and saw all their idols. He did not punch anyone in the mouth, but stood in the marketplace and said, "You men of Athens, you are all idolatrous" [Acts 17:16, 22]. He preached against their idols, but he overthrew none by force. And you want to rush about, create an uproar, smash the altars, and cast out the images! Do you really believe you can abolish the images in this way? No, you will only set them up more firmly. Even if you overthrew the images in this place, do you think you have overthrown those in Nürnberg and the rest of the world? Not

52. Here Luther moved from biblical examples to reflections based on his own experience.

53. That is, he would have to change his tune and give up his argument.

at all. St. Paul, as we read in the book of Acts [28:11], sat in a ship on whose prow were painted or carved the Twin Brothers [i.e., Castor and Pollux]. He went on board and did not bother about them at all, neither did he break them off. Why must Luke describe the Twins at this point? Without doubt he wanted to show that outward things could do no harm to faith as long as the heart does not attach itself to them or put its trust in them. This is what we must preach and talk about, and let the word alone do the work, as I said before. The word must first capture peoples' hearts and enlighten them; we will not be the ones who will do it. For this reason, the apostles boasted in their service, *ministeri* [Rom. 11:13], and not in its effect, *executio*. Let this be enough for today.[54]

The Fourth Sermon, 12 March 1522, Wednesday after *Invocavit*

Dear friends, we have now heard about the things which are "musts," such as that the Mass is not to be observed as a sacrifice. Then we considered the things that are not necessary but free, such as marriage, the monastic life, and the abolishing of images. We have treated these four subjects, and have said that in all these matters love is the captain. On the subject of images, in particular, we saw that they ought to be abolished when they are worshiped; otherwise not—although because of the abuses they give rise to, I wish they were everywhere abolished. This cannot be denied. For people who place an image in a church imagine they have performed a service to God and done a good work, which is downright idolatry.[55] But this, the greatest, foremost, and highest reason for abolishing images, you have passed by, and fastened on the least important reason of all. For I suppose there is nobody—or certainly very few—who does not understand that yonder crucifix is not my God, for my God is in heaven, but that this is simply a sign. But the world is full of that other abuse; for who would place a silver or wooden image in a church unless he thought that by so doing he was rendering God a service? Do you think that Duke Frederick, the bishop of Halle, and the others would have dragged so many silver images into the churches, if they thought it counted for nothing before God?[56]

54. The conclusion to this sermon re-emphasizes the place of freedom in Christian life. If God has ordained freedom, then Christians can preach and share this freedom without coercion.

55. Luther referred to the common medieval practice of endowing private Masses and works of art in order to receive spiritual benefits, a so-called economy of salvation; Carter Lindberg, *Beyond Charity: Reformation Initiatives for the Poor* (Minneapolis: Fortress Press, 1993), 92.

56. Duke Frederick is Elector Frederick the Wise of Ernestine Saxony (1463–1525). It is significant that Luther would challenge his prince by name in this sermon. Frederick possessed a large collection of religious relics. In 1510, this collection received an indulgence from Rome, so that those who visited the collection would receive remission of the penalty of their sin in purgatory; Ozment, *Serpent and the Lamb*, 81. The "bishop of Halle" is Cardinal Albrecht of Hohenzollern, archbishop of Mainz and of Magdeburg (1490–1545), who also had a residence in Halle. In 1521 Albrecht increased the relic collection in Halle's cathedral, which Luther protested from Wartburg Castle in a tract entitled *Against the "Idol" in Halle*; ibid., 139–40. Though Luther's tract was never published (and was eventually lost), letters and information concerning this 1521 exchange between Luther and Albrecht appear in LW 48:315–17, 339–50.

57. An echo of number 43 of Luther's *95 Theses* (1517): "Christians are to be taught that he who gives to the poor or lends to the needy does a better deed than he who buys indulgences" (LW 31:29; TAL 1:40).

58. Here Luther makes a number of increasingly dramatic *ad absurdum* arguments to show the weakness of iconoclastic arguments.

59. *Kirchmess*: service for consecration or commemoration of the consecration of a church, an occasion for placing images or embellishments in the church.

No, they would not bother to do it. But this is not sufficient reason to abolish, destroy, and burn all images. Why? Because we must admit that there are still some people who hold no such wrong opinion of them, but to whom they may well be useful, although they are few. Nevertheless, we cannot and ought not condemn a thing that may be in any way useful to a person. You should rather have preached that images are nothing and that God cares nothing for them, being neither served nor pleased when we make an image, but that we would do better to give a poor person a goldpiece than God a golden image; for God has forbidden the latter, but not the former.[57] If they had heard this teaching that images count for nothing, they would have ceased of their own accord, and the images would have fallen without any uproar or tumult, as they are already beginning to do.

We must, therefore, be on our guard, for the devil, through his apostles, is after us with all his craft and cunning. Now, although it is true and no one can deny that the images are evil because they are abused, nevertheless we must not on that account reject them, nor condemn anything because it is abused. This would result in utter confusion. God has commanded us in Deut. 4[:19] not to lift up our eyes to the sun [and the moon and the stars], etc., that we may not worship them, for they are created to serve all nations. But there are many people who worship the sun and the stars. Therefore we propose to rush in and pull the sun and stars from the skies.[58] No, we had better let it be. Again, wine and women bring many a man to misery and make a fool of him [Ecclus. 19:2; 31:30]; so we kill all the women and pour out all the wine. Again, gold and silver cause much evil, so we condemn them. Indeed, if we want to drive away our worst enemy, the one who does us the most harm, we shall have to kill ourselves, for we have no greater enemy than our own heart, as the prophet, Jer. 17[:9], says, "The heart of man is crooked," or, as I take the meaning, "always twisting to one side." And so on—but what would we really achieve?

Whoever wants to smear the devil must have good charcoal, for he, too, wears fine clothes and is invited to the annual parish festival.[59] But I can catch him by asking him: "Do you not place the images in the churches because you think it a special service to God?" And when he says "Yes" (as he must), it becomes clear that what was meant as a service to God he has turned into idolatry by abusing the images and practicing what God has not commanded. For he has neglected God's command, which is that he should be helpful to his neighbor. But I have not yet caught him, though actually he is caught and will not admit it; he escapes me by saying: "Yes, I help the poor, too. Cannot I give to my neighbor and at the same time donate images?" This is not so, however, for who would not rather give his neighbor a gold-piece than God a golden image? No, he would not trouble himself about placing images in churches if he did not believe, as he actually does, that he was doing God a service. Therefore I must admit that images are neither here nor there, neither evil nor good, we may have them or not, as we please. This trouble has been caused by you;[60] the devil would not have accomplished it with me, for I cannot deny that it is possible to find someone to whom images are useful. And if I were asked about it, I would confess that none of these things gives offense to one, and if just one man were found on earth who used the images aright, the devil would

Portrait of Cardinal Albrecht painted by Lucas Cranach the Elder in 1526

soon draw the conclusion against me: "Why, then, do you condemn what may be used properly?" Then he is in the right and I would have to admit it. He would not have got nearly so far if I had been here. Proudly he ravaged us, though it has done no harm to the word of God. You wanted to smear the devil but you forgot the charcoal and used chalk. If you want to fight the devil you must know the Scriptures well and, besides, use them at the right time.[61]

Concerning Meats

Let us proceed and speak of the eating of meats and what our attitude should be in this matter. It is true that we are free to eat any kind of food, meats, fish, eggs, or butter. This no one can deny. God has given us this liberty; this is true.[62] Nevertheless, we must know how to use our liberty, and in this matter treat

60. This "devil's advocate" conversation has shown first that the devil is a powerful and even tyrannical logician and second demonstrated how Luther would have acted differently in the same situation, another appeal to his own authority as a gospel preacher.

61. Recalling the Gospel for *Invocavit* Sunday (Matt. 4:1-11), Luther reminded his hearers that the devil also knows and can use Scripture. Therefore, right use of the word is not a matter of mere recitation but also of discerning the Spirit.

62. The English words *freedom* and *liberty* both translate the same German word, *Freiheit*. In this case, "liberty"

better expresses the state of being that Luther referred to as a gift of God. Biblical supports frequently cited by the Lutheran reformers for freedom regarding foods include 1 Corinthians 8; Col. 2:16; and 2 Tim. 4:3.

63. Rather than a "one-size-fits-all" approach to conflict resolution or community life, Luther suggested that Christians rightly respond to conflicts differently depending on the situation and the people involved. It is instructive, too, that "weak" and "stiff-necked" are biblical categories (see Rom. 14:1 and Acts 7:51, respectively).

64. While this section nearly commands disobedience when confronted with an injustice, it is immediately tempered by the following paragraph, which emphasizes awareness of how using one's freedom might negatively affect others.

65. The phrase "free will" (*freyen willen*) appears here, emphasizing the extent to which Luther viewed freedom/liberty to be a gift of God in respect to matters not affecting salvation.

66. The "weak in faith" were those who resisted gospel-centered reforms due to caution or out of deference to existing traditions. Luther was convinced that clear and patient teaching would lead such people to embrace Evangelical reforms.

the weak among us quite differently from the stiff-necked.[63] Observe, then, how you ought to use this liberty.

First, if you cannot abstain from meat without harm to yourself, or if you are sick, you may eat whatever you like, and if any take offense, let them be offended. Even if the whole world took offense, you are not committing a sin, for God can approve it in view of the freedom so graciously bestowed upon you and of the necessities of your health, which would be endangered by your abstinence.

Second, if you should be pressed to eat fish instead of meat on Friday,[p] and to eat fish and abstain from eggs and butter during Lent, etc., as the pope has done with his foolish and burdensome laws, then you must in no way allow yourself to be drawn away from the liberty in which God has placed you but do just the contrary to spite him, and say: "Because you forbid me to eat meat and presume to turn my liberty into law, I will eat meat in spite of you."[64] And thus you must do in all other things that are matters of liberty. To give you an example: if the pope or anyone else were to force me to wear a cowl, just as he prescribes it, I would take off the cowl just to spite him. But since it is left to my own free will, I wear it or take it off, according to my pleasure.[65]

Third, there are some who are still weak in faith, who ought to be instructed and who would gladly believe as we do.[66] But their ignorance prevents them, and if this were preached to them, as it was to us, they would be one with us. Toward such well-meaning people we must assume an entirely different attitude from that which we assume toward the stiff-necked. We must bear patiently with these people and not use our liberty; since it brings no peril or harm to body or soul; in fact, it is rather beneficial, and we are doing our brothers and sisters a great service besides. But if we use our liberty unnecessarily and deliberately cause offense to our neighbor, we drive away the very one who in time would come to our faith. Thus St. Paul circumcised Timothy [Acts 16:3] because simple-minded Jews had taken offense; he thought: "What harm can it do, since they are offended because of their ignorance?" But when, in Antioch, they insisted that he ought and must circumcise Titus [Gal. 2:3], Paul withstood them all

p   This portion of canon law can be found in *Corpus iuris canonici,* editio Lipsiensis secunda post AE Richteri . . . instruxit AE Friedberg (Leipzig, 1879) [hereafter, Friedberg], 1:267–71, dist. 76, can. 1-12.

and to spite them refused to have Titus circumcised [Gal. 2:11]. And he stood his ground. He did the same when St. Peter by the exercise of his liberty caused a wrong conception in the minds of the unlearned. It happened in this way: when Peter was with the Gentiles, he ate pork and sausages with them, but when the Jews came in, he abstained from this food and did not eat as he did before. Then the Gentiles who had become Christians thought: "Oh no! We, too, must be like the Jews, eat no pork, and live according to the law of Moses." But when Paul learned that they were acting to the injury of evangelical freedom,[q] he reproved Peter publicly and read him an apostolic lecture, saying: "If you, though a Jew, live like a Gentile, how can you compel the Gentiles to live like Jews?" [Gal. 2:14]. Thus we, too, should live, using our liberty at the right and pleasing time, so that Christian liberty may suffer no injury and no offense be given to our weak brothers and sisters who are still without the knowledge of this liberty.[67]

67. This conclusion shows that the sermon was not about deciding which things are free or bound in themselves but about how Christians can deal with matters of freedom and order with flexibility and a sense of right.

The Fifth Sermon, 13 March 1522, Thursday after *Invocavit*[r]

We have heard of the things that are necessary, such as that the Mass is not to be performed as a sacrifice, and of the unnecessary things, such as monks leaving the monasteries, the marriage of priests, and images. We have seen how we must treat these matters, that no compulsion or ordinance must be made of them, and that no one shall be dragged from them or to them by the hair, but that we must let the word of God alone do the work. Let us now consider how we should keep the blessed sacrament.

You have heard how I preached against the foolish law of the pope and opposed his precept,[s] that no woman shall wash the altar linen on which the body of Christ has lain, even if it be a pure nun, except it first be washed by a pure priest.[t] Likewise,

---

q   For more on "evangelical freedom," see Luther's *The Freedom of a Christian* (LW 31:329–77; TAL 1:466–538).

r   This sermon also bears the title "A Sermon on the Sacrament."

s   Reference to *The Misuse of the Mass* (1521), WA 8:477–563, especially pp. 508 and 540; LW 36:133–230.

t   Friedberg 1:86, dist. 23, can. 25.

when anyone has touched the body of Christ, the priests come running and scrape his fingers, and much more of the same sort. But when a maid has slept with a naked priest, the pope winks at it and lets it go. If she becomes pregnant and bears a child, he lets that pass, too. But to touch the altar linen and the sacrament [i.e., the host], this he will not allow. But when a priest grabs it, both top and bottom, this is all right.

We have preached against such foolish laws, making such things public in order that it might be made known that no sin is involved in these foolish laws and commandments of the pope, and that the laity do not commit sin if they touch the cup or the body of Christ with their hands. You should give thanks to God that you have come to such clear knowledge, which many great men have lacked. But now you go ahead and become as foolish as the pope, in that you think that people must touch the sacrament with their hands. You want to prove that you are good Christians by touching the sacrament with your hands, and thus you have dealt with the sacrament, which is our highest treasure, in such a way that it is a wonder you were not struck to the ground by thunder and lightning. All the other things God might have suffered, but this the Lord cannot allow, because you have made a compulsion of it.[68] And if you do not stop this, neither the emperor nor anyone else need drive me from you, because I will go without urging. I dare say that none of my enemies, though they have caused me much sorrow, have wounded me as you have.

If you want to show that you are good Christians by handling the sacrament and boast of it before the world, then Herod and Pilate are the chief and best Christians, since it seems to me that they really handled the body of Christ when they had him nailed to the cross and put to death.[69] No, my dear friends, the kingdom of God does not consist in outward things, which can be touched or perceived, but in faith [Luke 17:20; Rom. 14:17; 1 Cor. 4:20].

But you may say: "We live and are supposed to live according to the Scriptures, and God has so instituted the sacrament that we must take it with our hands, for he said, 'Take, eat, this is my body'" [Matt. 26:26]. The answer is this: though I am convinced beyond a doubt that the disciples of the Lord took it with their hands, and though I admit that you may do the same without committing sin, nevertheless I can neither make it compulsory nor defend it. For the devil, when he really pushes us to the wall,

68. Luther's attack is inaccurate or an overstatement, since the Wittenberg Ordinance said that communicants "may" (not "must") take the bread and cup in their hands; MLStA 2:528.

69. Using heavy irony, Luther has taken the logic of "touching" the body of Christ to an absurd conclusion. Further "devil's advocate" arguments follow in order to lead people to trust in Christ and the promises of God rather than external actions, even with respect to the sacraments.

will argue: "Where have you read in the Scriptures that 'take' means 'grasping with the hands'?" How, then, am I going to prove or defend it? Indeed, how will I answer him when he cites from the Scriptures the very opposite and proves that "take" does not mean to receive with the hands only but also to convey to ourselves in other ways? "Listen to this, my good fellow," he will say, "is not the word 'take' used by three evangelists when they described the Lord's taking of gall and vinegar? [Matt. 27:34; Mark 15:23; Luke 23:36]. You must admit that the Lord did not touch or grab it with his hands, for his hands were nailed to the cross." This verse is a strong argument against me. Again, he cites the passage: *Et accepit omnes timor*, "Fear seized them all" [Luke 7:16], where again we must admit that fear has no hands. Thus I am driven into a corner and must concede, even against my will, that "take" means not only to receive with the hands but to receive for myself in whichever way it might be done. Therefore, dear friends, we must be on firm ground if we are to withstand the devil's attack [Eph. 6:11]. Although I must acknowledge that you committed no sin when you touched the sacrament with your hands, nevertheless I must tell you that it was not a good work, because it caused offense throughout the world. For the universal custom is to receive the blessed sacrament from the hands of the priest. Why will you not in this respect also serve those who are weak in faith and abstain from your liberty, particularly since it does not help you if you do it, nor harm you if you do not do it?

Therefore no new practices should be introduced. Instead, the gospel should be preached and understood through and through, as it has been among you. On this account, dear friends, let us deal soberly and wisely in the things that pertain to God, for God will not be mocked [Gal. 6:7]. The saints may endure mockery, but with God it is vastly different. Therefore, I beseech you, give up this practice.

Concerning Both Kinds in the Sacrament

Now let us speak of the two kinds. Although I hold that it is necessary that the sacrament should be received in both kinds

In this drawing by Lucas Cranach (1472–1553) Luther and Jan Hus are depicted serving the communion elements in both kinds to Saxon nobility.

according to the institution of the Lord, nevertheless it must not be forced or turned into a general law. We must rather promote, practice, and preach the word, and then afterward let the word drive it home and take root, leaving everyone free in this matter. Where this is not done, the sacrament becomes for me an outward work and a hypocrisy, which is just what the devil wants. But when the word is given free course and is not bound to any external observance, it takes hold[70] of one today and sinks into his heart, tomorrow it touches another, and so on. Thus quietly and soberly it does its work, and no one will know how it all came about.

I was glad to know when someone wrote me, that some people here had begun to receive the sacrament in both kinds.[71] You should have allowed it to remain thus and not forced it into an ordinance. But now you go at it pell mell, and headlong force everyone to it. Dear friends, you will come to ruin that way. For if you desire to be seen as better Christians than others just because you take the sacrament into your hands and also receive it in both kinds, then you are bad Christians as far as I am concerned. In this way even a sow could be a Christian, for she has a big enough snout to receive the sacrament outwardly. We must deal soberly with such high things. Dear friends, this dare be no mockery, and if you are going to follow me, stop it. If you are not going to follow me, however, then no one need drive me away from you—I will leave you unasked, and I shall regret that I ever preached so much as one sermon in this place. The other things could be passed by, but this cannot be overlooked; for you have acted so coarsely that people are saying: "In Wittenberg there are very good Christians, for they take the sacrament in their hands and grasp the cup, and then they go to their brandy and swill themselves full."[u] So the weak and well-meaning people, who would come to us if they had received as much instruction as we have, are driven away.

But if there are any who are so ignorant that they must touch the sacrament with their hands, let them have it brought home to his house where they may handle it to their hearts' content. But in public such people should abstain, since that will bring them no harm and the offense will be avoided which is caused to our brothers, sisters, and neighbors, who are now so angry with

70. A dramatic reversal: instead of people taking hold of the host, the word takes hold of the heart!

71. This first occurred among Melanchthon and a group of his students in the City Church (29 September 1521) and then among Zwilling and the Augustinian monks in October; NM, nrs. 4 and 10.

---

u   Such critiques from the period can be found; MLStA 2:551 n. 291.

us that they are ready to kill us. I may say that of all my enemies who have opposed me up to this time none have brought me so much grief as you.

This is enough for today; tomorrow we shall say more.

The Sixth Sermon, 14 March 1522, Friday after *Invocavit*

In our discussion we have moved from the primary matters [of faith] to the reception of the sacrament, which we have not yet finished. Today we shall see how we must conduct ourselves here as well as who is worthy to receive the sacrament and who belongs there.

It is very necessary here that your hearts and consciences be well instructed and that you make a big distinction between outward reception and inward spiritual reception. Bodily and outward reception is that in which we receive with our mouths the body of Christ and his blood. Such reception can very well take place in anyone, without faith and love. But this does not make a person a Christian, for if it did, even a mouse would be a Christian, for it, too, can eat the bread and perchance even drink out of the cup. It is such a simple thing to do. But the true, inward, spiritual reception is a very different thing, for it consists in the right use of the sacrament and its fruits.

First, we should say that this reception occurs in faith and is inward. We Christians have no external sign by which we may be distinguished from others except this sacrament and baptism; nevertheless, without faith outward reception is nothing. Faith must be present to make the reception worthy and acceptable before God, or else it is nothing but a sham and a mere external show, which is not Christianity at all. Christianity consists solely in faith and no outward work must be attached to it.

But the true faith that we all must have if we wish to go to the sacrament worthily is that we firmly believe that Christ, the Son of God, stands in our place, has taken all our sins upon his shoulders, and is the eternal satisfaction for our sin who reconciles us with God the Father. Whoever has this faith rightfully belongs at this sacrament, and neither devil nor hell nor sin can harm them.[72] Why? Because God is their protector and has their

72. Here and immediately below, Luther names the real adversaries of faith: sin, death, hell, and the devil.

73. This law goes back to the Fourth Ecumenical Lateran Synod, 1215, under Pope Innocent III; Friedberg 2:887, *Decretum Gratiani* IX, lib. 5, tit. 38, de poenitentiis et remissionibus, cap. 12.

74. Luther's concept of freedom included the conviction that only God can know another person's heart or faith; therefore faith cannot be judged or forced from outside. Luther was even able to invoke canon law on this point, as in his tract in *Temporal Authority: To What Extent It Should Be Obeyed* (early 1523; LW 45:107 and n. 61), *"De occultis non iudicat ecclesia"* ("the church does not judge hidden matters"); this is a gloss to the canon *Erubescant impii*, dist. XXXII, C. XI, in the *Decreti magistri Gratiani prima pars*, where the glossed phrase reads, *"De manifestis quidem loquimur, secretorum autem cognitor et iudex est Deus"* ("We indeed speak of open things, but God is the witness and judge of secret things"). *Corpus iuris canonici*, I, col. 120. The marginal gloss is found in *Decretum Gratiani emendatum et notationibus illustratum una cure glossis* (Paris, 1612), col. 175.

backs. When I have this faith, then I know for sure that God is fighting for me despite the devil, death, hell, and sin and all the harm they do to me. This is the great, inestimable treasure given to us in Christ, which no one can describe or grasp in words. Faith alone grasps this in the heart. Because not everyone has such faith [2 Thess. 3:2], this sacrament must not be made an ordinance, as the most holy father, the pope, has done with his foolish law: "All Christians must go to the sacrament at the holy Eastertide, and whoever does not go shall not be buried in consecrated ground."[73] Is not this a foolish law that the pope has set up? Why? Since we are not all alike, we do not all have equal faith; the faith of one is stronger than that of another. It is therefore impossible that the sacrament can be made a general ordinance. Instead, the greatest sins are committed at Easter solely on account of this un-Christian command, whose purpose is to drive and force the people to the sacrament. For if robbery, usury, unchastity, and all sins were piled into one big heap, this sin would exceed all others, at the very time when they [who come to the sacrament] want to be most holy. Why? Because the pope cannot look into people's hearts to see if they have faith or not.[74]

But if you believe that the Lord stands in your place and stakes all he has and sheds his blood for you, as if he were saying: "Step boldly and briskly behind me and let us see what can harm you. Should the devil, death, sin, and hell, and anything in creation come against you, then I shall stand in for you to be your rear guard and your vanguard [Isa. 52:12]. Trust me and boldly rely upon me. Whoever believes cannot be harmed by the devil, hell, sin, or death, for if God fights for such people, what harm can be done to them?"[v]

Those who have such faith take their rightful place here and receive the sacrament as an assurance, seal, or proof that assures them that God's promise and grace are most certainly for them. But, of course, we do not all have such faith; would God one tenth of the Christians had it! See how such rich, inestimable treasures [Eph. 2:7] God showers upon us by grace cannot belong to everyone equally, but only to those who suffer physical or spiritual tribulation: physically through human persecution, spiritually through the accusation of the conscience that comes either from outside or inside when the devil causes your heart to

v   A paraphrase of Rom. 8:31, "If God is for us, who is against us?"

be weak, timid, and discouraged, so that you do not know how you stand with God when he casts your sins into your face. In such terrified and trembling hearts alone God desires to dwell, as the prophet Isaiah says in the sixth chapter [Isa. 66:2].[75] For who would seek a shelter or someone to watch their back and go before them, if they feel no tribulation within themselves, making them distressed and daily tormented on account of their sins? Such people would not yet be ready for this food. This food wants a hungering and longing person, for it delights to enter a hungry soul that is constantly battling with its sins and eager to be rid of them.[76]

Those who are not thus prepared should abstain for a while from this sacrament, for this food will not enter a sated and full heart. If it does come to such a heart, it is harmful.[77] Therefore, if we meditate upon and discover within us such distress of conscience and the fear of an accused heart, we shall come with all humbleness and reverence, without running to it brashly and hastily, without due fear and humility. So we do not always find that we are worthy; today I have the grace and am worthy for it, but maybe not tomorrow. Indeed, it may be that for six months I may have no desire or worthiness for it.

Therefore the ones who are most worthy are those who are constantly being assailed by death and the devil. They are the ones to whom it is most confidently given, in order that they may remember and firmly believe that nothing can harm them, since they now have with them the one who can never be taken away. Death, devil, or sin cannot harm them, come as they may.

This is what Christ did when he was about to institute the blessed sacrament. First he terrified his disciples and shook their hearts by saying that he was going to leave them [Matt. 26:2], which was exceedingly worrisome to them. Then he went on to say, "One of you will betray me" [Matt. 26:21]. Do you think that that did not cut them to the heart? Of course they received that saying with all fear, sitting there as

75. Isaiah 66:2 reads: "All these things my hand has made, and so all these things are mine, says the LORD. But this is the one to whom I will look, to the humble and contrite in spirit, who trembles at my word."

76. The reference to "hungering and longing" comes from Augustine, *Preaching on Psalm 21 (Ennaratio in psalmos XXI)*. Compare this section about who is worthy to receive the sacrament (namely, the downcast, troubled, and humble) with similar statements in the *Large Catechism*, for instance, "it is the highest art to realize that this sacrament does not depend upon our worthiness" (BC 473.59).

77. The primary New Testament text for discussing who is worthy to receive the Sacrament of Holy Communion is 1 Cor. 11:17-29.

In this illustration by monogramist H.A., the last supper and crucifixion are pictured in the upper background and a scene of receiving the Sacrament of Communion is pictured in the foreground.

though they had all been traitors to God. And after he had made them all tremble with fear and sorrow, only then did he institute the blessed sacrament as a comfort and consoled them again. For this bread is consolation for the sorrowing, medicine for the sick, life for the dying, food for all who hunger, and a rich treasure for all the poor and needy.

Let this be enough for this time concerning the use of this sacrament and how you should use it. I commend you to God.[78]

The Seventh Sermon, 15 March 1522, Saturday before *Reminiscere*[w]

Yesterday you heard about the use of this holy and blessed sacrament and that those who are worthy to receive it are those in whom there is the fear of death, who have frightened and accused consciences and who are afraid of hell. These rightly come to partake of this food to strengthen their weak faith and to comfort their conscience. This is the true use and practice of this sacrament. Those who do not find themselves in this state, let them refrain from coming until God eventually touches and moves them through the word.

We shall now speak of the fruit of this sacrament, which is love; that is, that we should treat our neighbor as God has treated us.[x] We have received nothing but love and favor from God, for Christ has established and given us his righteousness and everything he has.[79] He has poured out upon us all his treasures, which no one can measure and no angel can grasp or fathom, for God is a glowing furnace of love, reaching even from the earth to the heavens.

Love, I say, is a fruit of this sacrament.[80] But this I do not yet sense among you here in Wittenberg, even though you have had much preaching and ought to have practiced anyway. This is the chief thing and the only business of a Christian. But nobody wants to actually concern themselves with this, wanting instead

78. Although there would be later controversies and discussions about Christ's presence in the sacrament (as in Luther's *Confession concerning Christ's Supper*, 1528), this sermon has focused on the immediate pastoral issue at hand: the use of the sacrament. This focus will lead into the next sermon on the fruits or effects of the sacrament. This move from what a thing is (*quid sit*) to what a thing does (*quid effectus*) is a hallmark of Lutheran theology; see Timothy Wengert, *Human Righteousness, Christian Freedom* (New York: Oxford University Press, 1998), 53; and Martin Lohrmann, *Bugenhagen's Jonah: Biblical Interpretation as Public Theology* (Minneapolis: Lutheran University Press, 2012), 95.

79. Luther discusses this "happy exchange" in which Christ gives his righteousness to believers and takes their sins upon himself in *The Freedom of a Christian* (LW 31:351–53; TAL 1:499–503).

80. See the note at the end of the previous sermon about the typical Lutheran move from what a thing is (*quid sit*) to what a thing does (*quid effectus*). Here, love between Christians is an effect or benefit of what God gives in the sacrament.

---

w   On *Reminiscere*, see the introduction to the next sermon.

x   A paraphrase of John 13:34 and 1 John 4:11.

to practice unnecessary and useless things. If you do not want to prove yourselves Christians by your love [John 13:35], then let the other things remain undone, too, for St. Paul says in 1 Cor. 11 [1 Cor. 13:1], "If I speak in the tongues of men and of angels, but have not love, I am a noisy gong or a clanging cymbal." This is a terrifying saying of Paul. "And if I have prophetic powers, and understand all mysteries and all knowledge, and if I have all faith, so as to remove mountains, but have not love, I am nothing. If I give away all I have, and if I deliver my body to be burned, but have not love, I gain nothing" [1 Cor. 13:2-3]. You have not yet come so far as this, even though you have received great and rich gifts from God, the highest of which is a knowledge of the Scriptures. It is true, you have the true gospel and the pure word of God but no one as yet has given his goods to the poor,*y* no one has yet been burned,[81] and even these things would be nothing without love. You are willing to take all of God's goods in the sacrament but are not willing to pour them out again in love. Nobody extends a helping hand to another, nobody seriously considers the other person, but all look out for themselves and their own gain, insisting upon their own way and looking after their own interests. If anybody is helped, well and good; but nobody looks after the poor to see how you might be able to help them.[82] This is a pity. You have heard many sermons about it and all my books are full of it and have this one purpose, to urge you to faith and love.

And if you will not love one another, God will allow a great plague to come upon you; let this be a warning to you. For God will not have the word revealed and preached in vain.[83] You are tempting God too hard, my friends; for if in times past someone had preached the word to our forefathers, they would perhaps have acted differently. Or if it were preached even now to many poor children in the cloisters,[84] they would receive it more joyfully than you. You are not heeding it at all and you are playing around with all kinds of useless tomfoolery.[85]

I commend you to God.

81. The first to be burned at the stake for their evangelical faith were the Antwerp Augustinian monks Jahn van den Esschen and Henry Vos, executed together on July 1, 1523, in Brussels; Brecht 2:102.

82. This is a vague and possibly unjust critique, since many points within the Wittenberg Ordinance focused on poor relief and the establishment of a common chest (*gemeine Kasten*) MLStA 2:525–29.

83. A reference to the Second Commandment, especially as later discussed in the *Large Catechism* (BC 393:53–55; TAL 2:305).

84. The "poor children" might refer to actual children sent to monasteries or convents at an early age or more generally to those in the cloisters, many of whom would not have chosen that path for themselves if they had the opportunity or the knowledge to do otherwise.

85. This conclusion is nearly as sharp as Luther's conclusion to the fifth sermon. Here Luther has contrasted the kind of self-giving love that he believes defines communion with the reforming efforts of the Wittenbergers, dismissing the latter as "useless tomfoolery" (*gaückelwerk* [*Gaukelei*]).

y   Karlstadt would experiment with that in the future; Carter Lindberg, *The European Reformations* (Malden, MA: Blackwell, 1996), 135–36.

The Eighth Sermon, 16 March 1522, *Reminiscere* Sunday[86]

A Short Summary of the Sermon of D[r.] M[artin] L[uther] Preached on *Reminiscere* Sunday on Private Confession

86. The second Sunday in Lent was often called *Reminiscere* Sunday, after the appointed Introit: *Reminiscere miserationum tuarum, Domine, et misericordiarum tuarum, quae a saeculo sunt* ("Remember, O Lᴏʀᴅ, thy tender mercies and thy lovingkindnesses; for they have been ever of old" [Ps. 25:6, KJV]). The epistle for the day was 1 Thess. 4:1-7 and the Gospel was Matt. 15:21-28. Because this sermon is called a "short summary" and because of the firsthand report cited in WA 10/3:lii, which said that Luther began the first of the sermons by preaching on the text and then addressing the contemporary issues at hand, it is likely that Luther preached more on the biblical text before taking up the practical reform of private confession as he did here. Luther's 1525 *Lenten Postil*s on this text show that Luther did connect the Gospel text with confessing one's sins (WA 17/2:203–4; LW 76:381).

87. That is, such a practice had no longer become the standard confessional practice of the church.

Now we have heard all the things that ought to be considered here, except confession. Of this we shall speak now.

In the first place, there is a confession that is founded on the Scriptures, and it is this: when people committed a public sin or one that became known, they were accused in front of the congregation. If they turned away from their sin, the congregation prayed to God for them. But if they would not listen to the entire group, they were cast out and excluded from the assembly, so that no one would have anything to do with them. This confession was commanded by God in Matt. 18[:15], "If your brother sins against you (so that you and others are offended), go and tell him his fault, between you and him alone." We no longer have any trace of this kind of confession anymore, so that on this point the gospel is in abeyance.[87] Anybody who was able to re-establish it would be doing a good work. Here is where you should have exerted yourselves to re-establish this kind of confession, letting the other things go; for no one would have been offended by this and everything would have gone smoothly and quietly. It should be done in this way: When you see a usurer, adulterer, thief, or drunkard, you should go to him in secret, and admonish him to give up his sin. If he will not listen, you should take two others with you and admonish him once more, in a brotherly way, to give up his sin. But if he scorns that, you should tell the pastor in front of the whole congregation (bringing your witnesses with you) and accuse him before the pastor in the presence of the people, saying: "Dear pastor, this man has done this and that and would not take our brotherly admonition to give up his sin. Therefore I accuse him, together with my witnesses, who have heard this." Then, if he will not give up and willingly acknowledge his guilt, the pastor should exclude him and put him under the ban before the whole assembly, for the sake of the congregation until he comes to his senses and is received back again. This would be Christian. But I would honestly not try to establish this single-handedly.[88]

Second, we need a kind of confession when we go into a corner by ourselves and confess to God directly, pour out all our faults to the Lord. This kind of confession is also commanded. From this comes the familiar word of Scripture: *Facite judicium et justitiara. Judicium facere est nos ipsos accusare et detonate; justitiam autem facere est fidere misericordiae Dei.*[89] As it is written, "Blessed are they who observe justice, who do righteousness at all times" [Ps. 106:3]. Judgment is nothing else than when people know, judge, and condemn themselves, for this is true humility and self-abasement. Righteousness is nothing else than when people know themselves and pray to God for the mercy and help through which God will raise them up again. This is what David means when he says, "I have sinned; I will confess my transgressions to the LORD and thou didst forgive the guilt of my sin; for this all thy saints shall pray to thee" [Ps. 32:5-6].

Third, there is also the kind of confession in which you take another aside to talk about something that troubles you, so that you may hear from the other a word of comfort; this confession is commanded by the pope. It is this urging and compulsion that I condemned when I wrote concerning confession.[z] I refuse to confess simply because the pope has commanded it and insists upon it. For I wish him to keep his hands off of my confession

88. As in other cases, Luther argued that just because a certain practice might be an improvement does not mean that it ought to be instituted immediately, if at all. Being put "under the ban" is a reference to excommunication, especially as described in Matt. 18:17.

89. "To do judgment is to accuse and condemn ourselves; but to do righteousness is to trust in the mercy of God." It is a saying Luther often used and a possible blending of Gen. 18:19 and Prov. 18:17.

A scene depicting private confession

---

z   *Von der Beicht, ob die der Papst macht habe zu gebieten* (1521), WA 8:138–204.

90. The Wittenberg Ordinance did not specifically forbid making private confession.

91. Luther made the point that whether one is accused by the devil or by God, in either case confession and absolution have been given by God to comfort and free people from sin.

92. In the first example, absolution comes from the word itself. The later examples of absolution in baptism, confession, and the Lord's Supper reveal the actions and effectiveness of those central pillars of faith (word, prayer, and sacraments) that Luther later treated in his catechisms.

and not make of it a compulsion or command, which he has not the power to do.[90] Nevertheless, I will not allow anyone to take private confession away from me, and I would not give it up for all the treasures in the world, since I know what comfort and strength it has given me. No one knows what it can do except one who has struggled with the devil. Yes, the devil would have slain me long ago, if confession had not sustained me. For there are many doubtful matters that we cannot resolve or find the answer to by ourselves, and so we take a friend aside and tell them our trouble. What harm is there if we humble ourselves a little before a neighbor, put ourselves to shame, look for a word of comfort, accept it and believe it, as if hearing it directly from God, as we read in Matt. 18[:19], "If two of you agree about anything they ask, it will be done for them."

Moreover, we must have many absolutions, so that we may strengthen our timid consciences and accused hearts against the devil and against God.[91] Therefore, no one should forbid confession nor keep or draw anyone away from it. For if any are wrestling with their sins, want to be rid of them, and desire a sure word on the matter, let them go and confess to another in secret, accepting what is said as if spoken directly from God through the mouth of this person. However, those who have a strong, firm faith that their sins are forgiven may let this confession go and confess to God alone. But how many have such a strong faith? Therefore, as I have said, I will not let this private confession be taken from me. But I will not have anybody forced to it, but left to each one's own desire.

For our God, the God we have, is not so stingy to have left us with only one comfort or strength for our conscience, or only one absolution, but we have many absolutions in the gospel and are richly showered with many absolutions.[92] For instance, we have this in the gospel: "If you forgive others their trespasses, your heavenly Father will also forgive you" [Matt. 6:14]. Another comfort we have in the Lord's Prayer: "Forgive us our trespasses," etc. [Matt. 6:12]. A third is our baptism, when I reason thus: "See, my Lord, I have indeed been baptized in your name so that I may be assured of your grace and mercy." Then we have private confession, when I go and receive a sure absolution as if God directly spoke it to me, so that I may be assured that my sins are forgiven. Finally, I take to myself the blessed sacrament, when I eat his body and drink his blood as a sign that I am rid of my sins and

God has freed me from all my faults. So that God may make me sure of this, he gives me his body to eat and his blood to drink, so that I truly shall not and cannot doubt that I have a gracious God.[93]

Thus you see that confession must not be despised but that it is a comforting thing. And since we need many absolutions and assurances as we fight against the devil, death, hell, and sin, we must not allow any of our weapons to be taken away but keep intact the whole armor and weaponry which God has given us to use against our enemies [cf. Eph. 6:11]. For you do not yet know what labor it costs to fight with the devil and overcome him. But I know it well, for I have eaten a bit of salt or two with him. I know him well, and he knows me well, too.[94] If you had known him, you would not have taken confession away from me in this way.[95]

I commend you to God. Amen.

93. As early as the *Explanations of the 95 Theses* (1518), Luther emphasized that believers can have total certainty in the word of absolution (WA 1:540–41; LW 31:100).

94. Before closing, Luther returned to the fight against sin, death, and especially the devil, with which he began these sermons. He also made another vivid appeal to his own experience fighting the devil with the word of God.

95. The "from me" was not included in the American Edition of *Luther's Works*, even though it clearly stands in the best edition of the text. It adds a personal appeal to this conclusion; namely, Luther's own need for and benefit from the many forms of confession available, including private confession. As an ending, it asks listeners to attend to the needs of their neighbors and reminds leaders to be mindful of others in their reforms of the church.

A preacher addresses a congregation from the pulpit,
a scene that illustrates the petition
in the Lord's Prayer, "Hallowed be your name."

Selected Sermons

MARY JANE HAEMIG

INTRODUCTION

When the preacher speaks, God speaks![a] Luther believed that God uses the preacher as an agent to convey God's word. For Luther, the sermon is not merely human words; rather, the preached word is a means of grace. In that preached word, the Holy Spirit is active to create both repentance and faith, to kill the old sinner and to make alive the new person. For Luther, the preached word is essential to any worship service. "When God's Word is not preached, one had better neither sing nor read, or even come together," he wrote.[b]

Preaching had become increasingly important in the late Middle Ages. Some larger towns established preacherships at their large churches; preachers strove to enlighten an increasingly sophisticated audience that demanded good preaching. But preaching, though generally in the vernacular, was not the center of worship in the late medieval Roman Catholic Church. Rather, the celebration of the Lord's Supper was central, with preaching seen as a helpful commentary or preparation for that

---

a   For general discussion of Luther on preaching, see Fred Meuser, *Luther the Preacher* (Minneapolis: Augsburg, 1983).

b   Martin Luther, *Concerning the Order of Public Worship*, LW 53:11.

event. Preaching was based on a biblical text. Sometimes the preacher discussed that text, its meanings, and exegetical issues, but on occasion the text was merely a launching pad to discuss other matters. Often sermons centered on moral admonition. Late medieval preachers produced a number of postils, collections of lectionary sermons designed to help ordinary priests with the task of preaching.

Luther's understanding of preaching differed from the late medieval understanding.[c] For him, the living word, Jesus Christ, both addresses and gives himself to us in human words. The Holy Spirit uses the preached word to create repentance and trust in God. Preaching is intended to let both God's law and God's promise speak, as Luther said:

> For we must preach not only one word of God but both, "bringing forth new and old from the treasure"—both the voice of the law and the word of grace. The voice of the law ought to be "brought forth" so that people may be terrified and led to a knowledge of their sins and thereby directed toward repentance and a better basis for life. But the word must not stop here. For this would be only "to wound" and not "to bind up"; "to strike down" and not "to heal"; "to kill" and not "to make alive"; "to lead into hell" and not "to lead out"; "to humble" but not "to exalt." Therefore, the word of grace and promised forgiveness ought also to be preached in order to instruct and awaken faith. . . . A person, who has been humbled by the threats and fear of the divine law and led to self-knowledge, is consoled and raised up through faith in the divine promise.[1]

Faith comes from hearing this word. Preaching is not primarily the conveyance of information, the discussion of a theological

1. *The Freedom of a Christian* (1520), in TAL 1:518–19; see also LW 31:364.

---

c   Fred Meuser, "Luther as Preacher of the Word of God," in Donald K. McKim, ed., *The Cambridge Companion to Martin Luther* (Cambridge: Cambridge University Press, 2003), 136–48; Mary Jane Haemig, "The Influence of the Genres of Exegetical Instruction, Preaching, and Catechesis on Luther," in Robert Kolb, et al., eds., *The Oxford Handbook of Martin Luther's Theology* (New York: Oxford University Press, 2014), 449–61; and Jeffrey G. Silcock, "Luther on the Holy Spirit and His Use of God's Word," in ibid., 294–309.

topic, or moral admonition. Preaching is not merely preparatory to the Lord's Supper but is itself sacramental—that is, it contains the gift of Christ and his benefits in, with, and under the human words. Preaching is where the Holy Spirit engages in battle with the forces of evil, a battle intended to conquer those forces and free the human for service to God and neighbor.

Luther's sermons were rooted in biblical texts but were not primarily or merely learned commentary on those texts. His focus was not on explaining or commenting on the text but, rather, on preaching God's word, both law and promise, as embodied in the text. His preaching proclaimed God's work as both law and gospel (threats and promises) and distinguished carefully between law and gospel. Luther's early sermons often reflect a verse-by-verse expository style common in the late Middle Ages. As time went on, he moved to focus his sermons on what he saw as the central message of a text, often embodied in one or two verses.

Luther was a prolific preacher; most years he preached on over one hundred occasions. He preached many Sundays and many weekdays. Sundays he followed the one-year lectionary cycle, containing both Gospel and Epistle texts for each Sunday and feast day, used by the late-medieval church. Luther did not revise this lectionary, an indication that his Reformation was not a matter of selecting different biblical texts but, rather, of preaching and hearing Reformation insights, both law and gospel, from the same texts. Sunday afternoons and weekdays he preached seriatim through biblical books or on the catechism.[2] He also preached at special occasions such as baptisms, weddings, and funerals.[d]

Luther's preaching activity in varied settings meant that he had to learn to formulate his message in ways that a nonlearned audience could understand. For him, conveying the message was more important than impressing listeners with his rhetorical style or learnedness. Luther commented that he preached for "Hans and Greta," that is, ordinary people. He used a simple and understandable style, including easily recognizable illustrations, earthy metaphors, and words that ordinary people would understand. He did not use lengthy introductions, preferring to state and begin to elucidate the main point of the text in the

A historiated title page border surrounds a central woodcut that illustrates a moneylender at work. This engraving adorns the title page of a sermon by Luther against usury published in 1520. Woodcut by Hans Schäufelein (c. 1480–c. 1539).

2. Luther described Wittenberg preaching in his *German Mass* (1526), WA 19:79,9–80, 24; LW 53:68–69; TAL 3:131–61.

---

d   On Luther's preaching activity, see Brecht, vol. 2, 284–92.

first few sentences of the sermon. Luther seldom wrote out a full manuscript of a sermon. The sermons we have from him are usually from notes written by hearers and may reflect to some extent the perspectives of those transcribers.[e]

Luther grasped early the practical importance of preaching for his reforming work. A number of his early sermons, published individually as pamphlets, aided the spread of his ideas.[f] Luther never wrote a preaching manual, as did some other reformers.[g] He did, however, recognize early the importance of providing evangelical preachers with materials that would help them in preaching. Luther criticized the popular late-medieval postils[3] that pastors often used to aid lectionary sermon preparation. He saw clearly that thoroughgoing reform of preaching would involve providing new postils. Already in his stay as an exile at the Wartburg (1521/22) he worked on the model sermons for the Advent and Christmas seasons. Luther continued to publish postils to counteract late-medieval postils and to help evangelical pastors preach truly evangelical sermons. One such postil sermon is included here. Luther's postils were the first of a flood of Evangelical postil literature, as the reformers sought to strengthen Evangelical preaching.[h]

3. A postil was a collection of model sermons. These commonly included sermons on the lectionary texts (Gospel and Epistle) for Sundays and feast days.

e   The complicated history of the transcription, transmission, and printing of Luther's sermons is too lengthy to describe in detail here. See, for example, Christopher Boyd Brown, "Introduction to Volume 58," in *Luther's Works*, vol. 58, ed. Christopher Boyd Brown (St. Louis: Concordia, 2010), xxiii–xxviii. The complicated history of the postils is covered in Benjamin T. G. Mayes, "Introduction to the Luther–Cruciger *Church Postil* (1540–1544)," in *Luther's Works*, vol. 75, ed. Benjamin T. G. Mayes and James L. Langebartels (St. Louis: Concordia, 2013), xiii–xxxi.

f   Mark U. Edwards Jr., *Printing, Propaganda, and Martin Luther* (Berkeley: University of California Press, 1994), 41–56.

g   See, for example, the handbook published by Lutheran reformer Urbanus Rhegius (1489–1541), in Scott Hendrix, ed., *Preaching the Reformation: The Homiletical Handbook of Urbanus Rhegius* (Milwaukee: Marquette University Press, 2003). For a more general discussion of pastoral manuals, see Amy Nelson Burnett, "The Evolution of the Lutheran Pastors' Manual in the Sixteenth Century," *Church History* 73 (2004): 536–65. This article includes a discussion of Conrad Porta's *Pastorale Lutheri*, a collection of citations from Luther dealing with various aspects of the pastoral office, including preaching.

h   See John Frymire, *The Primacy of the Postils: Catholics, Protestants, and the Dissemination of Ideas in Early Modern Germany* (Leiden: Brill, 2010).

Luther's sermons appear at several points in The Annotated Luther series, though not every "sermon" (*sermo*) was actually preached.[i]

SELECTED SERMONS[4]

Sermon Preached at Erfurt on the Journey to Worms, John 20:19-20, 7 April 1521[j]

The title of this sermon in its original printed form reads: "A Sermon by Dr. Martin Luther on his way to His Imperial Majesty[5] *at Worms, preached at Erfurt at the request of eminent and very learned men without previous preparation or special study, owing to the shortness of time. . . ." The Gospel for the day,* Quasimodo Geniti *(the first Sunday after Easter Sunday), was John 20:19-31, but Luther focused his sermon on the first few verses.*

On his way to the Diet at Worms,[6] *Luther was received with great enthusiasm in Erfurt; the church of the Augustinians where he preached was full to overflowing.*[7] *The sermon emphasizes the core of Christianity: faith in Christ on the foundation of the word of God, and contains sharp criticism of Rome, philosophy, and pulpit "fables." The transcriber of the sermon is unknown. The sermon was printed eight times in 1521, in Augsburg, Erfurt, Leipzig, and Wittenberg.*[k]

4. The translations of sermons here, except for the postil sermon, were originally made by John Doberstein. The translation of the postil sermon was originally made by John G. Kunstmann. Translations have been reviewed and updated by Mary Jane Haemig.

5. Holy Roman Emperor Charles V (1550–1558) summoned Luther to appear before an imperial diet, or assembly of the political representatives of the Holy Roman Empire, in Worms. See also the introduction to this volume, p. 4.

6. For the location of Erfurt and Worms, see the map of Luther's Germany at the front of this volume.

7. "The balcony threatened to collapse, so some of the participants broke the windows in order to jump to safety. Luther, however, calmed the congregation over this trick of the devil and then no accident occurred." Martin Brecht, *Martin Luther: His Road to Reformation 1483–1521*, trans. James L. Schaaf (Philadelphia: Fortress Press, 1985), 449. See also WA 7:803.

---

i   See TAL 1:57–65, 167–255; TAL 2:9–24; TAL 7–45, 147–57, 283–305.

j   WA 7:808–13; LW 51:60–66.

k   VD 16 L6138–45. See also the publishing information in WA 7:803–5.

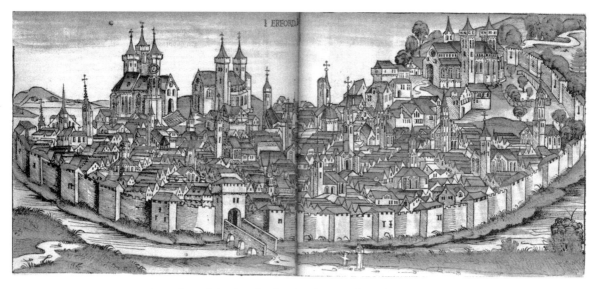

A woodcut of the city of Erfurt in *The Nuremberg Chronicle* (1493)

8. The Gospel for this Sunday was John 20:19-31, the story now popularly known as "doubting Thomas."

DEAR FRIENDS, I shall pass over the story of St. Thomas[8] this time and leave it for another occasion, and instead consider the brief words uttered by Christ: "Peace be with you" [John 20:19]¹ and "Behold my hands and my side" [John 20:27], and "as the Father has sent me, even so I send you" [John 20:21]. Now, it is clear and manifest that every person likes to think that he will be saved and attain eternal salvation. This is what I want to discuss now.

You also know that all philosophers, doctors, and writers have studiously endeavored to teach and write what attitude each person should take to piety. They have gone to great trouble, but, as is evident, have accomplished little. Now genuine and true piety consists of two kinds of works: alien works, which are the right kind, and those done for ourselves, which are unimportant.

1   Items in brackets (often scriptural citations) were not in WA. They are placed here for the reader's convenience.

In order to build a basis for this, one person builds churches; another goes on a pilgrimage to St. James's or St. Peter's; a third fasts or prays, wears a cowl,[9] goes barefoot, or does something else of the kind.[10] Such works are nothing whatever and must be completely destroyed. Mark these words: none of our works has any power whatsoever. For God has chosen a man, the Lord Christ Jesus, to crush death, destroy sin, and shatter hell, since there was no one before he came who did not inevitably belong to the devil. The devil therefore thought he would also get a hold upon the Lord, when he hung between two thieves and was suffering the most contemptible and disgraceful of deaths, which was cursed both by God and by humans [cf. Deut. 21:23; Gal. 3:13]. But the Godhead was so strong that death, sin, and even hell were destroyed. Therefore you should note well the words that Paul writes to the Romans [Rom. 5:12-21]. Our sins have their source in Adam, and because Adam ate the apple, we have inherited sin from him. But Christ has shattered death for our sake, in order that we might be saved by his works, which are alien to us, and not by our works.

But the papal dominion treats us altogether differently. It makes rules about fasting, praying, and butter-eating, so that whoever keeps the commandments of the pope will be saved and whoever does not keep them belongs to the devil. It thus seduces the people with the delusion that piety and salvation lie in their own works. But I say that none of the saints, no matter how holy they were, attained salvation by their works. Even the holy mother of God did not become pious, was not saved, by her virginity or her motherhood, but rather by the will of faith and the works of God, and not by her purity, or her own works.[11] Therefore, mark me well: this is the reason why salvation does not lie in our own works, no matter what they are; it cannot and will not be brought about without faith.

Now, someone may say: Look, my friend, you are saying a lot about faith, and claiming that our salvation depends solely upon it; now, I ask you, how does one come to faith? I will tell you. Our Lord Christ said, "Peace be with you. Behold my hands, etc."[m] [John 20:26-27]. [In other words, he is saying:] Look, I alone am the one who has taken away your sins and redeemed you, etc.; now be at peace. Just as you inherited sin from Adam—not that

9. The hooded robe worn by monks.

10. Luther lists some of the good works believed to be meritorious toward salvation: giving a financial contribution to help build a church, going on a pilgrimage to St. James of Compostella (a popular goal for pilgrimages, in Spain) or St. Peter's (in Rome), or becoming a monk (fasting, praying, wearing a cowl, going barefoot).

11. As a counter to late-medieval piety, Luther often discussed Mary's faith. See also, in these years, his comments on the Rosary in his *Little Prayer Book* (p. 194 of this volume), and his lengthy commentary on the Magnificat (pp. 307–83 of this volume).

m In the original these words are in Latin.

12. Cf. Rom. 4:5.

13. The sixteenth century was a time of intense eschatological expectation. Luther was not alone in seeing God's judgment and the end of the world as imminent. See Robin Barnes, *Prophecy and Gnosis: Apocalypticism in the Wake of the Lutheran Reformation* (Stanford: Stanford University Press, 1988).

you committed it, for I did not eat the apple, any more than you did, and yet this is how we came to be in sin—so we have not suffered [as Christ did], and therefore we were made free from death and sin by God's work, not by our works. Therefore God says: Behold, I am your redemption [cf. Isa. 43:3]; just as Paul said to the Corinthians: *Christus est iustificatio, redemptio, etc."* [1 Cor. 1:30]. Christ is our justification and redemption, as Paul says in this passage. And here our [Roman] masters say: Yes, *Redemptor*, Redeemer; this is true, but it is not enough.

Therefore, I say again: Alien works, these make us good! The Lord Christ says: I am your justification. I have destroyed the sins you have upon you. Therefore believe only in me; believe that I am he who has done this; then you will be justified. For it is written, *Justicia est fides*,[12] righteousness is faith and comes through faith. Therefore, if we want to have faith, we should believe the gospel, Paul, etc., and not the papal breves, or the decretals, but rather guard ourselves against them as against fire. For everything that comes from the pope cries out: Give, give; and if you refuse, you are of the devil. It would be a small matter if they were only exploiting the people. But, unfortunately, it is the greatest evil in the world to lead the people to believe that outward works can save or make a man good.

At this time the world is so full of wickedness that it is overflowing, and is therefore now under a terrible judgment and punishment,[13] which God has inflicted, so that the people are perverting and deceiving themselves in their own minds. For to build churches, and to fast and pray and so on has the appearance of good works, but in our heads we are deluding ourselves. We should not give way to greed, desire for temporal honor, and other vices but rather be helpful to our poor neighbor. Then God will arise in us and we in him; this means a new birth. What does it matter if we commit a fresh sin? If we do not immediately despair, but rather remember? "O God, you still live! Christ my Lord is the destroyer of sin," then at once the sin is gone. And also the wise man says: "*Septies in die cadit iustus et resurgit*," "A righteous man falls seven times in a day, and rises again" [Prov. 24:16].

The reason why the world is so utterly perverted and in error is that for a long time there have been no genuine preachers.

---

n   The Latin is in the original.

There are perhaps three thousand priests,[14] among whom one cannot find four good ones—God have mercy on us in this crying shame! And when you do get a good preacher, he runs through the Gospel superficially and then follows it up with a fable about the old ass° or a story about Dietrich of Berne,[15] or he mixes in something of the pagan teachers, Aristotle, Plato, Socrates, and others, who are all quite contrary to the gospel, and also contrary to God, for they did not have the knowledge of the light which we possess. Indeed, if you come to me and say: The Philosopher says: Do many good works, then you will acquire the habit, and

14. Luther wants preachers who will proclaim God's word, not priests who will merely perform rituals. The distinction reflects medieval practice that saw priests and preachers as distinct positions. The main role of the priest was to preside over sacramental rituals and convey the grace necessary for salvation. On the other hand, preachers were appointed to preach.

15. A heroic figure of German legend whose legend was associated with the Ostrogoth king Theodoric the Great (r. 493–526), though they are not likely one and the same. Berne is the German name for Verona in Italy, which was in the empire of Theodoric. Dietrich appears in the epic German poem *Nibelungenlied* associated with Attila. Cf. C. M. Gayley, ed., *The Classic Myths in English Literature and in Art* (Boston: Ginn & Co., 1911), 409, 537. Cf. WA 9:620.

Dietrich is depicted capturing the dwarf Alfrich in this xylograph by Johannes Gehrts (1883).

---

o   *Von dem alten Esel.* A variant text reads, *von dem alten Ezel (Etzel),* "about the ancient Attila," which was probably what Luther originally said. Cf. WA 7:810 n.1.

16. "Junkers" was a term used in German-speaking and Dutch-speaking areas of Europe for nobles or a class of nobles.

finally you will become good;*p* then I say to you: Do not perform good works in order to become good; but if you are already good, then do good works, though without affectation and with faith. There you see how contrary these two points of view are.

In former times the devil made great attacks upon the people and from these attacks they took refuge in faith and clung to the Head, which is Christ; and so he was unable to accomplish anything. So now the devil has invented another device; he whispers into the ears of our Junkers[16] what they should lay upon people and gives them laws. This way it looks well on the outside, but inside it is full of poison. So the young children grow up in a delusion; they go to church thinking that salvation consists in praying, fasting, and attending Mass. For so it is the preacher's fault. But there would be no need [for this], if only we had right preachers.

The Lord said three times to St. Peter: "*Petre, amas me? etc.; pasce oves meas*" [John 21:15-17]. "Peter, feed, feed, feed my sheep." What is the meaning of *pascere*? It means to feed. How should one feed the sheep? In no other way than by preaching the word of God, that is faith. Then our Junkers come along and say: *Pascere* means *leges dare*, to enact laws, but with deception. Yes, they are well fed! They feed the sheep as the butchers do on Easter eve. Whereas one should speak the word of God plainly to guide the poor and weak in faith, they mix in their beloved Aristotle, who is contrary to God, despite the fact that Paul says in Col. [2:8]: Beware of laws and philosophy. What does "philosophy" mean? If we knew Greek, Latin, and German, we would see clearly what the Apostle is saying.

Is not this the truth? I know very well that you don't like to hear this and that I am annoying many of you; nevertheless, I shall say it. I will also advise you, no matter who you are: If you have preaching in mind or are able to help it along, then do not become a priest or a monk, for there is a passage in the thirty-third and thirty-fourth chapters of the prophet Ezekiel, unfortunately a terrifying passage, which reads: If you forsake your neighbor, see him going astray, and do not help him, do not preach to him, I will call you to account for his soul [Ezek. 33:8; 34:10]. This is a passage that is not often read. But I say, you

p   Cf. Aristotle, *Nichomachean Ethics*, Book II, chap. I (London: Dent/Everyman's Library, 1934), 26–27.

become a priest or a monk in order to pray your seven canonical hours and say Mass, and you think you want to be godly. Alas, you're a fine fellow! It [i.e., being a priest or monk] will fail you.[17] You say the Psalter, you pray the rosary, you pray all kinds of other prayers, and say a lot of words; you say Mass, you kneel before the altar, you read confession, you go on mumbling and murmuring; and all the while you think you are free from sin and yet in your heart you have such great envy. If you could choke your neighbor and use a creditable pretext, you would do it. Then you would say Mass, and it would be no wonder if a thunderbolt struck you to the ground. But if you have eaten three grains of sugar or some other seasoning, no one could drag you to the altar with red-hot tongs.[18] You have scruples! And that means to go to heaven with the devil. I know very well that you don't like to hear this. Nevertheless, I will tell the truth, I must tell the truth, even though it cost me my neck twenty times over, that the verdict[19] may not be pronounced against me. Yes, you say, there were learned people a hundred or fifty years ago too.[20] That is true; but I am not concerned with the length of time or the number of persons. For even though they knew something of it then, the devil has always been a mixer, who preferred the pagan writers to the holy gospel. I will tell the truth and must tell the truth; that's why I'm standing here,[21] and not taking any money for it either. Therefore, we should not build upon human law or works, but rather have true faith in the One who is the destroyer of sin; then we shall find ourselves growing in him. Then everything that was previously bitter for us is sweet.[22] Then our hearts will recognize God. And when that happens we shall be despised, and we shall pay no regard to human law, and then the pope will come and excommunicate us. But then we shall be so united with God that we shall pay no heed whatsoever to any hardship, ban, or law.

Then someone may go on and ask: Should we not keep the human laws at all? Or, can we not continue to pray, fast, and so on, as long as the right way is present? I answer and say: if there is present a right Christian love and faith, then everything a human does is meritorious; and each may do what he wills [cf. Rom. 14:22], so long as he has no regard for works, since they cannot save him.

In conclusion, then, every person should reflect and remember that we cannot help ourselves, but only God [can help us]. Also that our works are utterly worthless. So we have the peace

17. Luther was preaching in the church of the Augustinians and undoubtedly had at least some monks in his audience.

18. Because of the rule that the priest must say Mass while fasting.

19. Possibly referring to the last judgment.

20. Luther in this paragraph may be anticipating and responding to the Roman Catholic criticism which said that the weight of church doctrine and practice over hundreds of years was certainly more true and proper than Luther's thinking.

21. These words echo Luther's words spoken eleven days later at the Diet of Worms, "Here I stand."

22. Luther frequently made use of oppositions in his sermons—here *bitter* and *sweet*.

of God and every person should so perform his work that it benefits not only himself, but also another, his neighbor. If he is rich, his wealth should benefit the poor. If he is poor, his service should benefit the rich. When persons are servants or maidservants, their work should benefit their masters. Thus no one's work should benefit him alone; for when you note that you are serving only your own advantage, then your service is false. I am not troubled; I know very well what man-made laws are. Let the pope issue as many laws as he likes; I will keep them all so far as I please.

Therefore, dear friends, remember that God has risen up[23] for our sakes. Therefore let us also arise to be helpful to the weak in faith, and so direct our work that God may be pleased with it. So shall we receive the peace he has given to us today. May God grant us this every day. Amen.

The Second Sermon on Matt. 22:37-39, the Afternoon of 19 October 1522[q]

In October 1522 Luther journeyed to Weimar and Erfurt, having been invited to preach in Weimar by Duke John of Saxony (1468–1532) and his son John Frederick (1503–1554), through the court preacher, Wolfgang Stein. There he preached six sermons, two on 19 October, one on the 24th, another on the 25th, and two on the 26th. 19 October was the eighteenth Sunday after Trinity. (On 21 and 22 October he visited Erfurt, where he preached three times.) He was accompanied on the journey by Philip Melanchthon (1497–1560), Johann Agricola (1494–1566), and Jacob Propst (1486–1562).[24] It appears these Weimar sermons were not published until the nineteenth century.[r]

23. A possible allusion to the bull *Exsurge Domine* ("Arise, O Lord"), which threatened Luther's excommunication.

24. Melanchthon came to Wittenberg to teach alongside Luther in 1518. Agricola was a student of Luther at Wittenberg and accompanied him as a kind of traveling secretary at times. Later, especially in 1536 when Agricola returned to Wittenberg to teach, he and Luther engaged in heated debate over the meaning of the Mosaic law for Christians. Luther accused Agricola of taking an Antinomian position. Probst was an Augustinian monk who was imprisoned twice in the Netherlands in 1522, accused of preaching Luther's heretical teachings. He escaped prison and came to Wittenberg in 1522. In 1523 he became the leader of the Reformation in Bremen.

q   WA 10/3:347–52; LW 51:111–17.
r   WA 10/3:clxi–clxii.

IOANNES AGRICOLA ISLEBIVS THEOLOGVS.

Oannes in Saxonia natus, & in omni genere lite rarum optimè educatus fuit. Is cum prima artiũ fundamenta feliciter iecisset, sese ad Vuitebergen sem Academiam contulit, & Theologiæ magna di ligentia incubuit. Hinc factum ut sacrarum literarũ usum sibi familiarem reddiderit, & ob multifariam eruditionem postea doctissimis Theologis cõnu meratus fuerit. Id cum Ioannes elector Saxonię in tellexisset, eum plurimùm dilexit, & aliquotties se cum ad Imperij comitia perduxit, ut aduersarijs se opponeret, & doctrinam Euangelij ex uerbo Dei cõfirmaret. quod etiam Ioannes gnauiter præstitit.
præsertim 1526 Spiræ, & 1530 Augustæ Vindelicorũ, ubi cum Melanchtone et Brentio idem sentiens in magna existimatione fuit. Postea uerò simultate quadam cum Luthero orta Vuiteberga discessit, & tan dem ad illustris. principem Ioachimum electorem Brandeburgicum peruenit, atq aliquandiu latuit. Cum autem postea Carolus bello Smalkaldico ui ctor esset, Islebius cum suo principe 1548 Augustam uenit, & sese pontificio rum Theologis coniunxit. Ibi quoq (ut ferebatur) unà cum Iulio Pflugio, & Michaële Sidonio nouam religionis formam composuit. quam interim dum Concilium celebraretur, omnes obseruare deberent. Vnde etiam à Cæsare & Ferdinando liberale donum tulit. Postea quoq cum in Saxonia de Adiapho ris cõtentio esset, Islebius Ioachimi principis iussu Theologorum colloquijs interfuit, & suam sententiã copiosè proposuit. Hoc modo factum, ut non mo dò apud Germanos, sed etiam apud exteras nationes magnum sibi nomen compararit. Ioan. Sleid.

Johann Agricola

The Second Sermon Preached by Martin [*sic*] at Weimar
in the Parish [Church] on the Afternoon
of the Above-named Sunday

This morning you heard the Gospel.[25] Nevertheless we shall deal with its main point.

Now you know that we have all been baptized and are called Christians. Accordingly, we should endeavor to know what it means to be a Christian person and have the name of Christian, and also what one must do to be one. Similarly, when a shoe-maker, a tailor, or some other craftsman wants to pursue a trade, he must know his trade, in order that he may fairly be called a tailor. If he could not demonstrate his name it would be a dis-grace. Likewise, if a person called himself a Carthusian, a Ber-nardine [i.e., a Cistercian], or a Benedictine[26] and did not know the rule of the order, he would be a laughingstock. Accordingly,

25. This was the eighteenth Sunday after Trinity. The lectionary Gospel for this Sunday was Matt. 22:34-46. The morning sermon was on Matt. 22:37-39, "You shall love . . ."

26. The Carthusian, Cistercian, and Benedictine orders were monastic orders established in the Middle Ages.

A view of Weimar in a 1650 publication

we, too, must establish our name and demonstrate that we are rightly called Christians.

Therefore a person must first guard against human teachings and human commandments, in order that they may not take root in him. He should first open his mouth wide to rejoice in the teaching of Christ and also cultivate it in his heart; which teaching is the gospel, which Paul [Rom. 1:16], Peter [1 Pet. 1:12], and especially Christ in all the Gospels call the Word of God, because God through him gave it and sent it from heaven. Neither I nor anyone else can ever preach the Word adequately; the Holy Spirit alone must utter and preach it. It is not being preached these days, not by a long shot, God have mercy on us. Where it is not being preached, there you have tomfoolery, corruption, and the devil himself. Therefore, the first thing to learn is the teaching of Christ and not that of men. For these latter teachings should be thrown out, which is highly necessary at the present time, for through them many people are being led astray. Now we shall preach only the gospel, which came from God and was proclaimed and revealed from heaven.

Moreover, the gospel proclaims nothing else but salvation by grace, given to humans without any works and merits whatsoever. The gospel cannot abide, hear, or see nature.[27] Nor does it (the gospel) enter into the hypocrites, for it casts out their works, declaring that they are nothing and not pleasing to God. Therefore nature is constantly fighting against the gospel; it will not tolerate it. It keeps saying: Ah, should we not do good works? After all, were there not devout people in earlier times who did good works? My father and mother believed this, and where they have gone I want to go, too.[28] These people preach against God and do wrong.

Using such words, the teaching of Christ pleases them not at all, and finally makes them furious. Now this is surely a sign that one is preaching the gospel and that it is beginning to be heard. Where the preaching or the preacher is not persecuted or spoken against it is not the gospel at all and the preacher is not preaching it. The gospel is always persecuted, and the hypocrites murmur against it, but their works are nothing. Direct yourself by that!

Thus you must prove your name as a Christian by faith and nothing else, so that you believe that Christ's righteousness is yours, that his life, death, and everything that Christ is, is yours, given to you, as Paul says in Gal. 1 [2:20], "It is no longer I who live, but Christ who lives in me." It is as if Paul were saying: Christ gives me life, he lives in me; what I do I am not doing; what I say and preach is not my word; Christ is in me. Therefore, he who does not conduct and exercise himself in the Spirit and in the work of Christ is condemned. Thus Paul says in Rom. 8[:9], "Any one who does not have the Spirit of God does not belong to Christ." Even though a person did everything, if the Spirit of God is not at work and in the person, it is all nothing. Therefore, let all cast away all their works, for without faith they [the works] are all condemned.

This the world and nature cannot tolerate, for they are constantly grumbling about our taking their good works away

27. The reference here is not to "nature" as the natural created world but, rather, to nature, and specifically humanity, as corrupted by sin.

28. Luther here repeats Roman Catholic arguments commonly made against his insights.

from them and saying: If our works are nothing, how can we get there? It is no good. In fact, you do not know what you are talking about. Do you think that you can perform the work? It is not your works. If that were the case, you would have to despair of your works altogether. It pains you and yet we must not keep silent about the gospel on account of them. God will send a Spirit of truth (John 16[:7-9]); he will punish us for our unbelief. Therefore we shall preach Christ and his faith even though it be a pain to everybody, as Paul says: We preach the crucified Christ, a stumbling block to the Jews, to the Gentiles foolishness or stupidity, and to believers salvation and consolation [1 Cor. 1:23-24].

Therefore works are nothing. For our monks who think they will be saved by their works, Christ is foolishness. So it must be that in the world the gospel should be called folly.[29] If we can so preach that the gospel is rejected, then things will be going as they should. So if you see that today some are saying that the gospel is right and praise it, too; others blaspheming and saying that it is wrong; some calling it a curse, and so on, then you see that things are going well. So whomever the gospel hits, it hits, and whomever it helps, it helps; and we must act according to it and nothing else. It follows from this that a Christian name is an utterly unfathomable thing; and that one is a Christian who believes in God and acknowledges and loves him above all things. The Christian knows all things, even what the devil has in mind.

So, does the Augustinian order[30] make me a Christian, or is any other monk made a Christian by his order? No, we are all Christians through faith and baptism. Now Christ is called the Anointed, and through his name I, too, can be called an anointed one. It follows that that person is a Christian who has received Christ and believes in God with his whole heart.[31] Take, for example, a faster, who fasts every day on water and bread. He should rather be called a faster than a Christian; his fasting does not make him a Christian, not at all. One who constantly prays much should rather be called a pray-er than a Christian. Likewise with a pilgrim, a flagellant,[s] a virgin, a founder of churches

29. Luther picks up Paul's theme of the gospel as folly or foolishness, a theme he had discussed in the *Heidelberg Disputation* (1518); see TAL 1:99.

30. Luther was a member of the Augustinian order.

31. "Heart" for Luther and his contemporaries meant what was most central to or characteristic of a person.

---

s   *Trescher*; cf. Jacob and Wilhelm Grimm's *Deutsches Wörterbuch*, 16 vols. (Leipzig: S. Hirsel, 1854–1954), 2:1403, where a derivative meaning of *dreschen* or *treschen* is that of inflicting pain.

and altars—this does not make them Christians. What makes one a Christian is to have God and everything that is God's, that is, to have the unsurpassable treasure, Christ, who is called rich in grace. As we call a rich man rich because he has many guldens and goods, so Christ is called the richest of the rich.

How, then, do we have Christ? After all, he is sitting at the right hand of the Father; he will not come down to us in our house. No, this he will not do. But how do I gain and have him? Ah, you cannot have him except in the gospel in which he is promised to you, that gospel which is folly to the Pharisees and salvation and consolation to believers, as Paul declared [1 Cor. 1:18]. And so Christ comes through the gospel into our heart, and he must also be grasped by the heart.[32] As I now believe that he is in the gospel, so I receive him and have him already. So Paul says: I carry Christ in my heart, for he is mine, etc. [cf. Eph. 3:17]. Thus Christ is given to us through the gospel in the same way as a person is given a letter in which he is promised a city or a kingdom, and now the letter is sealed as a sign that this promise should and will be kept. So we, too, through faith in Christ become rich in all his goods and riches.

There are some who say that faith is such a trifling thing[33] always to be preaching about it. Yes, it is such a trifling thing that it can never be sufficiently spread abroad and understood! Would God that it had been well preached! But now we are going to begin and preach it. Christ, too, must be abbot[34] for once, and not man-made laws. Christ gives to humans a letter, which is the gospel, and this God seals with his baptism and faith. He says to humans: Look, I tell you and assure you that Christ Jesus, my Son, is yours, and I have given you baptism and the sacrament as a true sign and seal, in order that you may believe me when I say that Christ is yours. His grace and mercy are given to you without any merit of yours; only believe me, you will find eternal life in him. If you believe this, even though you have not seen the place that he has deeded to you, you nevertheless have the letter and the seal as a true sign. Then you will say: If I have Christ, the great treasure and Lord over death, sin, devil, and hell, I shall not despair, and I know that I, too, shall be lord over these things, and I, too, have eternal life. Then blind nature opens up and recognizes Christ, and it is also glad that it is lord over death.

What could bring a person greater joy than to be told that he need not die? That's why this assurance of Christ is unfathom-

32. "Heart" for Luther includes both reason and emotion, that is, he does not share the modern tendency to let "heart" refer merely to the emotions. "For Luther, thought is intimately connected to emotion. The mutual connection between thought and emotion is a major presupposition of Luther's anthropology. . . . This classic conception of the human heart has a very wide range of meaning from thinking to feeling. Today, the metaphorical sense of 'heart' is restricted to mere 'feeling.'" Birgit Stolt, "Luther's Faith of 'the Heart,'" in Christine Helmer, ed., *The Global Luther: A Theologian for Modern Times* (Minneapolis: Fortress Press, 2009), 135. See also Birgit Stolt, *"Lasst uns fröhlich springen!" Gefühlswelt und Gefühlsnavigierung in Luthers Reformationsarbeit* (Berlin: Weidler, 2012), esp. 252–54.

33. Late-medieval theologians saw faith as a knowledge of facts about God and as insufficient for salvation. They believed that faith had to be completed or "formed" by doing good works in order to attain salvation.

34. An abbot was the head of a monastery. Monks were obligated to be obedient to him.

able. A human, after all, is too fainthearted, our hearts are too small, and we hear a lot of preaching, but still no faith is there. This is the reason why we get other ideas and beliefs. When we hear the gospel we walk away and say: Yes, I believe in God and his gospel. No, that is not sufficient Christian faith. Listen to God; this is what he said through David, "O Israel, open your mouth wide, and I will fill it with good" [Ps. 81:8, 10]. It is as if Christ were saying: Oh yes, it is true that your heart is small and faint, but open it up and believe in me, I will give you all things. And Christ did say this: You fainthearted, you poor little flock, you need not fear, for it has pleased God to give you the kingdom of heaven [Luke 12:32]. Therefore, for us humans it is an altogether great thing for Christ to give us a kingdom, but for him it is a small thing.

So you can see that nature[35] is always hostile to the gospel, for it is ambitious and wants to become good through good works. Wearing a black or a white or a blue cap, a long cloak, or a big tonsure[36] doesn't make a Christian name. No, my monastic order is nothing; before Christ it must fall to the ground. But rejection of their works is something that will not go into the hearts of the Jews and monks. In short, through faith all things are subject to the human, as Paul shows [Rom. 8:2].

Therefore, faith, eternal life, grace, mercy, and all good is to be sought in the eternal God. And this he wants to give to each person. Each one should freely count upon this and make bold to assume that all the things of Christ are his through pure grace without his works. For if we had to be saved through our works, then Christ would be nothing at all. So you see that works contribute nothing to salvation or to establishing the name of Christian. No Carthusian, no Franciscan, no preaching monk [Dominican] gives me salvation, as we have so long wanted it to be. No, they cannot do it; for they are subject to death, as Paul says: Death became my master [Rom. 7:10]. Therefore, I say very bluntly that all monks and nuns are the devil's (there is no other conclusion you can draw), because they all set their salvation on cowls, tonsures, or good works and expect to be saved through them, which is something that will never happen and does not help, for their works are nothing in the sight of God. Do you think the kingdom of heaven will be given to you because you sit home by the stove and say a couple of psalms? No; nor will it be given to you if you go running around.[37]

---

35. Again, "nature" here refers to corrupted human nature rather than to the natural created world.

36. Different monastic orders wore different colors of caps; similarly, robes and tonsures (shaven heads) were characteristic of monks.

37. In the last sentence, Luther is referring to the mendicant ord In the last sentence, ers. The mendicant orders were not tied to a self-supporting monastery but, rather, begged for their income. They were also known for their preaching.

Therefore, let us give attention to having Christ, that we receive him and may say: O you eternal heavenly Father, you have given your Son to me in order that I in him might be saved and in him possess all good. Now I make bold to believe that he is mine and has been given to me. And for a seal upon it I also have your true body, flesh and blood, your sacrament and baptism; to these I firmly cling. Then all the desires of the flesh must be taken away in order that it may be kept submissive. That is why Christ bids men to take young women and the young women to take men. That is why the monks and nuns enter the monastery, to preserve their chastity; they can hardly bear it there, however. They should take spouses.

When we have Christ by true faith, then he causes us to live in such a way that we are strengthened in faith, in such a way that I do these works which I do for the benefit and the good of my neighbor. For my Christian name would not be sufficient, despite my baptism and my faith, if I did not help my neighbor and draw him to faith through my works in order that he may follow me. Then a person, after he has given all glory to Christ, always remembers to do to his neighbor as Christ has done to him, in order that he may help him and everyone else. Thus Christ lives in him and he lives for the betterment of his neighbor, giving to everyone a good example of doing all things in love. So princes and officials should also carry out their offices in love. If he rules well, he should not boast that he is gracious and good to his people. God will not forget to reward him. No, he should commit the matter of reward to God. So the monk should direct his whole life to his neighbor in love. He should not say: Oh, I have made the vow to my God in order to be saved. If he does this, he is denying Christ, for this is not helping his neighbor. And even if he brought with him to Christ a whole cloakful of rosaries, it would not help him at all. Even if he took with him all the fish he ate when he was fasting, and the bones too, they would not help him at all.

Without faith you will not be saved. That's why Peter says we should desire the gospel and faith as a child longs for milk [1 Pet. 2:2]. The child drinks milk in order to become strong. It does not drink it in order to become a human being; it is a human before it drinks. Thus, if I have faith, I am already saved, without any works or merit. It follows that it is faith alone that does it and not works. For God's work, the love that he teaches today in the gospel, goes on. And so, if somebody accuses you of forbidding good works, you say to them: We do not forbid them; we are only pointing out the abuse of them and showing that they should be done for the inspiration and good of our neighbor and that we should not put our trust in them. So, when I help my neighbor, I prove my name as a Christian. God does not want our work. Guide yourself strictly by that.

It follows from this that to us believers Christ is salvation and consolation, but to the monks he is foolishness, for the gospel does not bring anything into their kitchens, cellars, or closets, as their laws did before. That's why they are persecuting us now. But patiently take the cross of Christ upon you in order to be able to suffer this patiently, if you want to be Christians. Take your faith and your Christian name to heart, for it is highly necessary for you and for me. In the whole gospel nothing is more clearly emphasized than faith and love, as I said this morning. This sinks very slowly into the heads of the lazy monks and sleepers; therefore you should pray to God for them constantly.

Let us call upon God. Amen.

Sermon at Coburg on Cross and Suffering[t]
1530

This sermon was preached on 16 April 1530, the Saturday before Easter, on the day after Luther arrived at Feste Coburg.[u] He stayed at the Coburg during the Diet of Augsburg, at which the Augsburg Confession was presented. Among the congregation in the chapel of the castle were the elector John, Count Albrecht of Mansfeld (1480–1560), Philip Melanchthon, Justus Jonas (1493–1555), Veit Dietrich (1506–1549), Johann Agricola, and some thirty retainers of the elector. Notes of the sermon were taken down by Veit Dietrich, who prepared the printed version of 1530.[38] The sermon was published at least four times in the sixteenth century, once in Nuremberg in 1530 and three times in Wittenberg in 1531.[v] It was also included in collections of Luther's works.[w]

38. The notes that Luther likely drafted in preparation for this sermon are found in this volume, *That Christians Should Bear Their Cross with Patience* (pp. 411–17).

---

t   The text of the sermon is found in LW 51:195–208; WA 32:28–39.

u   See also Brecht 2:372.

Coburg Castle

A Harmony of Matthew 27, Luke 25, and John 19

Dear friends, you know that it is customary in this season to preach on the Passion, so I have no doubt that you have heard many times what kind of passion and suffering it was. You have also heard why it was that God the Father ordained it, namely, that through it he wanted to help, not the passion of Christ, for Christ had no need at all for this suffering; but we and the whole human race needed this suffering. Thus it was a gift that was given and presented to us out of pure grace and mercy. But we shall not deal with this point now, for I have often spoken of it on other occasions.

But since there are many false fanatics around and about, who only distort the gospel and accuse us and say that we have nothing else to teach and preach except faith alone, that we leave out the doctrine of good works and the holy cross and suffering; and they also say that they have the true Spirit, who moves them to teach as they do, we shall at this time speak only of the

Veit Dietrich

v VD 16 L6257–60.

w WA 32:28–39.

example which this Passion gives to us, what kind of cross we bear and suffer, and also how we should bear and suffer it.

Therefore we must note in the first place that Christ by his suffering not only saved us from the devil, death, and sin, but also that his suffering is an example, which we are to follow in our suffering. Though our suffering and cross should never be so exalted that we think we can be saved by it or earn the least merit through it, nevertheless we should suffer in the manner of Christ, that we may be conformed to him. For God has appointed that we should not only believe in the crucified Christ, but also be crucified with him, as he clearly shows in many places in the Gospels: "He who does not take his cross," he says, "and follow me is not worthy of me" [Matt. 10:38]. And again: "If they have called the master of the house Beelzebul, how much more will they malign those of his household" [Matt. 10:25].

Therefore each one must bear a part of the holy cross; nor can it be otherwise. St. Paul too says, "In my flesh I complete what is lacking in Christ's afflictions" [Col. 1:24]. It is as if he were saying: His whole Christendom is not fully completed; we too must follow after, in order that none of the suffering of Christ may be lacking or lost, but all brought together into one. Therefore every Christian must be aware that the cross[39] will not fail to come.

It should be, however, and must be the kind of suffering that is worthy of the name and honestly grips and hurts, such as some great danger of property and honor, body and life. Such suffering we really feel and it weighs us down; otherwise, if it did not hurt us badly, it would not be suffering.

Beyond this, it should be the kind of suffering that we have not chosen ourselves, as the fanatics choose their own suffering. It should be the kind of suffering which, if it were possible, we would gladly be rid of, suffering visited upon us by the devil or the world. Then what is needed is to hold fast and submit oneself to it, as I have said, namely, that one knows that we must suffer, in order that we may thus be conformed to Christ, and that it cannot be otherwise, that everyone must have his cross and suffering. When one knows this it is the more easy and bearable, and one can comfort oneself by saying: Very well, if I want to be a Christian, I must also wear the colors of the court; the dear Christ issues no other garment in his court; suffering there must be. This the fanatics, who select their own cross, cannot do; they resist it and fight against it with their fists. What a fine and

39. Luther often uses "the cross" to denote suffering.

admirable suffering that is! And yet they can reproach us, as if we did not teach aright concerning suffering and they alone can do it. But our teaching is this, that none should dictate or choose his own cross and suffering, but rather, when it comes, patiently bear and suffer it.

But they are wrong, not only with respect to their choosing their own cross, but also in that they flaunt their suffering and make a great merit of it and thus blaspheme God, because it is not a true suffering but a stinking, self-chosen suffering. But we say that we earn nothing by our suffering and therefore do not frame it in such beautiful monstrances[40] as they do. It is enough that we know that it pleases God that we suffer in order that we may be conformed to Christ, as I have said. So we see that the very ones who boast and teach so much about cross and suffering know the least of the cross and of Christ, because they make their own suffering meritorious. Dear friends, it isn't that kind of thing at all; nor is anybody forced or compelled to it. If you don't want to do it for nothing and without any merit, then you can let it lie and so deny Christ. The way is at hand, but you must know that if you refuse to suffer you will also not become Christ's courtier. So you may do either one of these two, either suffer or deny Christ.

If you are willing to suffer, very well, then the treasure and consolation that is promised and given to you is so great that you ought to suffer willingly and joyfully because Christ and his suffering is being bestowed upon you and made your own. And if you can believe this, then in time of great fear and trouble you will be able to say: Even though I suffer long, very well then, what is that compared with that great treasure which my God has given to me, that I shall live eternally with him? Look what happens then: the suffering would be sweet and easy and no longer an eternal suffering, but only a modicum[41] which lasts only a short time and soon passes away, as St. Paul [2 Cor. 4:17], and St. Peter [1 Pet. 1:6], and also Christ himself says in the Gospels [John 16:16-22]. For they look to that great, immeasurable gift, which is that Christ with his suffering and merit has become altogether ours. Thus the suffering of Christ has become so mighty and strong that it fills heaven and earth and breaks the power and might of the devil and of hell, of death and sin. And then if you compare this treasure with your affliction and suffering, you will consider it but a small loss, compared to

A monstrance illustrating one of Luther's published sermons (1519)

40. In Roman Catholic practice a monstrance is a vessel, often placed on the altar, in which the consecrated bread of the Lord's Supper is displayed for purposes of veneration.

41. Small portion.

such treasure, to lose a little property, honor, health, wife, child, and even your own body and life. But if you refuse to regard this great treasure and to suffer for it, so be it; go on and let it lie. He who does not believe will also receive none of these unspeakable goods and gifts.

Furthermore, every Christian should so submit himself to this suffering that he is sure that it will work for his good and that Christ, for his word's sake, will not only help us to bear this suffering but also turn and transform it to our advantage. And again what makes this cross more agreeable and bearable for us is the fact that our dear God is ready to pour so many refreshing aromatics and cordials into our hearts that we are able to bear all our afflictions and tribulations, just as St. Paul says in 1 Cor. 10[:13], "God is faithful, and will not let us be tempted beyond our strength, but with the temptation will also provide the way of escape, that we may be able to endure it." This is true. When the suffering and affliction is at its worst, it bears and presses down so grievously that one thinks he can endure no more and must surely perish. But then if you can think of Christ, the faithful God will come and will help you, as he has always helped his own from the beginning of the world; for it is the same God as always has been.

Moreover, the cause of our suffering is the same as that for which all the saints[42] have suffered from the beginning. Of course the whole world must bear witness that we are not suffering because of public scandal or vice, such as adultery, fornication, murder, etc. Rather we suffer because we hold to the word of God, preach it, hear it, learn it, and practice it. And since this is the cause of our suffering, so let it always be; we have the same promise and the same cause for suffering which all the saints have always had. So we too can comfort ourselves with the same promise and cling to it in our suffering and tribulation, as is highly necessary.

So in our suffering we should so act that we give our greatest attention to the promises, in order that our cross and affliction may be turned to the best, to something which we could never have asked or thought. And this is precisely the thing that makes a difference between the Christian's suffering and afflictions and those of all other people. For other people also have their afflictions, cross, and misfortune, just as they also have their times when they can sit in the rose garden and employ their

42. For Luther, all believers were saints. The saints were not those whom the Roman Church regarded as particularly meritorious and therefore worthy of "sainthood" and veneration. See Robert Kolb, *For All the Saints: Changing Perceptions of Martyrdom and Sainthood in the Lutheran Reformation* (Macon, GA: Mercer University Press, 1987).

good fortune and their goods as they please. But when they run into affliction and suffering, they have nothing to comfort them, for they do not have the mighty promises and the confidence in God that Christians have. Therefore they cannot comfort themselves with the assurance that God will help them to bear the affliction, much less can they count on it that their affliction and suffering will be turned to good.

So it is, as we see, that they cannot endure even the small afflictions. But when the big, strong afflictions occur, they despair altogether, destroy themselves, or they want to jump out of their skin because the whole world has become too cramped for them. Likewise they cannot observe moderation either in fortune or misfortune. When things go well, they are the most wanton, defiant, and arrogant people you can find. When things go wrong, they are utterly shattered and despondent, more than any woman; as we see those who are now bridling, bragging, and boasting were so timid and nervous during the peasant uprising[43] that they hardly knew where to go. So it must be when one does not have the promises and God's word. But Christians have their consolation even in the worst of suffering and misfortune.

But in order that you may better understand this, I will give you a fine example in which the Christian's suffering is sketched and depicted. All of you are doubtless familiar with the way in which St. Christopher[44] has at times been portrayed. But you should not think that there ever was a man who was called by that name or who actually did what is said about St. Christopher. Rather the person who devised this legend or fable was without a doubt a fine, intelligent man, who wanted to paint this picture for the simple people so that they would have an example and image of a Christian life and how it should be lived. And actually he did hit it off very well; for a Christian is like a great giant, with great strong legs and arms, as Christopher is painted, for he bears a burden which the whole world, which no emperor, king, nor prince could carry. Therefore every Christian is a Christopher, that is, a Christ-bearer,[45] because he embraces the faith.

How goes it then with such a person? This way: when a person receives the faith, that one does not think of it as something burdensome. It appears as a little child, which is beautiful and well formed and easy to carry, as Christopher found. For at first

43. The Peasant's War took place during 1524–25. Peasants in southern Germany inspired by Luther's Reformation attacks on authority began to demand agrarian rights and freedom from a feudal system in which they were oppressed by nobles and landlords. Luther eventually condemned the uprising, likely contributing to its downfall.

44. St. Christopher, made popular by the *Golden Legend* (thirteenth century) of Jacobus de Voragine (c. 1230–1298), was one of the most venerated saints of the Middle Ages. In Western Christianity, Christopher was a giant who lived near a river and performed the charitable work of carrying travelers across the river. One day a child asked to be taken across the river. Christopher took him on his shoulder but halfway across staggered under what seemed to be a crushing weight and had trouble reaching the opposite bank. Christopher complained to the child that if he had carried the whole world on his back, it could not have been heavier. The child responded that he had carried both the world and the one who created it. See s.v. "Christopher," in André Vauchez, ed., *Oxford Encyclopedia of the Middle Ages* (New York: Oxford University Press, 2002).

45. Christopher is derived from the Greek contraction of the name of Christ (*Christos*) and the verb *pherein* ("to bear").

St. Christiopher
carrying the Christ child
by Albrecht Durer, 1511

the gospel looks like a fine, pleasant, friendly, and childlike teaching; as we saw at the beginning, when it started everybody grabbed it and wanted to be an Evangelical. There was such a yearning and thirst for it that no oven is as hot as the people were then. But what happened? The same thing that happened with Christopher. He did not find out how heavy the child was until he got into the deepest water.

So it was with the gospel; when it began to take hold the waves rolled out and pope, bishops, princes, and the crazy rabble set themselves against it. Then one first begins to feel how heavy the child is to carry. For it came so close to the good Christopher that he came very near to drowning. As you see, the same thing is happening now; on the other side, which is against the word, there are so many tricks and stratagems, so much deceit and cunning, everything aimed at one purpose, to drown us in the water. There is such threatening and terror that we would be frightened to death if we did not have another consolation to oppose to it.

All right then, anybody who has taken upon himself the burden of the Christ, the beloved child, must either carry him all the way across the water or drown; there is no middle way. It's no good to drown; therefore we'll go through the water with Christ, even though it looks again as though we would have to stay in it. After all, we have the promise that he who has Christ and relies and believes on him can boldly say with David in Ps. 27[:3], "Though a host encamp against me, my heart shall not fear; though war arise against me, yet will I be confident." Let them paw and stamp their feet, let them threaten and frighten as they please, were the water never so deep we shall nevertheless go through it with Christ.

So it is with all other things; when it gets going it becomes too heavy, whether it be sin, devil, death, or hell, or even our own conscience. But how are we going to do it? Where shall we go and hide ourselves? For us it looks as if the whole thing would fail. But on the other side they are confident and proud; they think they already have won the day. I, too, see the good Christopher sinking; nevertheless he gets through, for he has a tree that he holds on to. This tree is the promise that Christ will do something remarkable with our suffering. "In the world," he says, "you shall have afflictions and tribulations, but in me you shall have peace" [cf. John 16:33]. And St. Paul says, "We have a faithful God who helps us out of affliction, so that we can bear it" [cf. 1 Cor. 10:13]. These sayings are staves, yea, trees, which we can hold on to and let the waters roar and foam as they will.

So in Christopher we have an example and a picture that can strengthen us in our suffering and teach us that fear and trembling is not as great as the comfort and the promise, and that we should therefore know that in this life we shall have no rest if we are bearing Christ, but rather that in affliction we should turn our eyes away from the present suffering to the consolation and promise. Then we will learn that what Christ says is true: "In me you shall have peace" [John 16:33]. For this is the Christian art, which we must all learn, the art of looking to the word and looking away from all the trouble and suffering that lie upon us and weigh us down. But the flesh is utterly incapable of this art, it sees no further than the present suffering. For this also is the way of the devil; he removes the word far from one's eyes, so that one sees nothing but the present difficulty, just as he is doing with us now. What he wants is that we should deny and forget the word altogether and gaze only at the danger which threatens us from the pope and the Turks.[46] Then if he wins the game, he drowns us in the difficulty, so that we see nothing but its rush and roar. But this should not be. For this is what happens: when a person wants to be a Christian and wants to act according to his feelings, he soon loses Christ. Drive the suffering and cross from your heart and mind as quickly as you can; otherwise if you think about it for long the evil grows worse. If you are in affliction and suffering, say: I have myself not chosen and prepared this cross; it is because of the word of God that I am suffering and that I have and teach Christ. So let it ever be in God's name. I will let him take care of it and fight it out who long ago foretold that I should have this suffering and promised me his divine and gracious help.

If you give yourself to Scripture, you will feel comfort and all your concerns will be better, which otherwise you cannot control by any act, means, or methods of your own. After all, a merchant can bring himself, for the sake of gaining money and wealth, to leave house and home, wife and child, and risk body and life for the sake of disgraceful profit, and still have no sure promise or assurance that he will return home in health to wife and child; and yet he is foolhardy and rash enough to venture boldly into such danger without any promise whatsoever. Now,

46. With the Diet of Augsburg approaching, many of Luther's followers feared for the future of the Evangelical movement. Not only was the Evangelical movement threatened by the Roman Catholics, but the Muslims (identified with the Turks) posed an ongoing military and political challenge.

if a merchant can do that for money and riches, fie upon you, that we should not want to bear a little cross and yet want to be Christians, even though besides we have in our hands the tree to which we cling against the waves, namely, the word and the fine strong promises that we shall not be drowned by the waves.

So the knight does, too. He surrenders himself to battle, where innumerable spears, halberds, and firearms are directed against him. He too has no promise with which to console himself except his own mad spirit; and yet he goes on, even though his whole life is nothing but hard living and hard suffering. And so it is with the papists too. They begrudge no effort or labor to re-establish their abomination and idolatry. How often, just since the time when the gospel has been proclaimed anew, have they taken counsel together, even to this day, one deliberation after another, all of which have failed and fallen to ashes. And yet they want to imagine and are even sure they can sing this thing away and suppress the word of God, so in sheer foolhardiness they go into it.

Now if merchants, knights, papists, and such riffraff can muster up such courage to take upon themselves and suffer such peril, effort, and labor, we should simply be ashamed that we rebel against suffering and the cross, even though we know, in the first place, that God has appointed that we should suffer and that it cannot be otherwise. In the second place, we also know our promise and assurance, that, even though we are not such good Christians as we ought to be and are timid and weak both in life and faith, God will nevertheless defend his word simply because it is his word. Therefore we know that we can quite rightly bid defiance and say: Even though there were ten popes or Turkish emperors, I would like to see whether all of them together are a match for the Man who is called Christ. They may very well start a game that will grow too big for them to handle, but they will not demolish the word. And this will happen even though we are weak in faith.

This then is the true art, that in suffering and cross we should look to the word and the comforting assurance, and trust them, even as he said, "In me you shall have peace, but in the world, tribulation" [cf. John 16:33]. It is as if he were saying: Danger and terror will surely hit you if you claim my word; but let it come, this will happen to you because of me. So be of good cheer; I will not forsake you, I will be with you and will help you. No matter how great the affliction may be, it will be small and light for you, if you are able to draw such thoughts from the word of God.

Therefore in affliction all Christians should so arm themselves[47] that they may defend and guard themselves with the fine, comforting assurances which Christ, our dear Lord, has left us when we suffer for his Word's sake. But if we do not do this, if we let the comforting sayings go, then when the cross comes the same thing that happened to Eve in paradise will happen to us. She had God's commandment and with it she should have beaten down the devil's suggestions and instigations. But what did she do? She let the word go and kept thinking what a fine apple it was and that after all such a little thing was of no great importance. So she went her way. And when one lets the word go, there can be no other result. But when we stay with the word and hold on to it, we shall certainly have the experience of conquering and coming out of it fine. You see that we teach these two things when we preach on suffering and cross. And anybody who accuses us of teaching nothing about the cross is doing us an injustice. But this we do not do; we do not make our suffering meritorious before God. No, far from it. Christ alone did that and nobody else, and to him alone belongs the glory.

In the third place we want also to consider why it is that our Lord God sends us such suffering. And the reason is that in this way he wants to make us conformed to the image of his dear Son, Christ, so that we may become like him here in suffering and there in that life to come in honor and glory [cf. Rom. 8:29; 8:17; 2 Tim. 2:11-12], as he says, "Was it not necessary that the Christ should suffer and enter into glory?" [cf. Luke 24:26]. But God cannot accomplish this in us except through suffering and affliction, which he sends to us through the devil or other wicked people.[48]

The second reason is this, that even though God does not want to assault and torment us, the devil does, and he cannot abide the word. He is by nature so malicious and venomous that he cannot endure anything that is good. It irks him that an apple should be growing on a tree; it pains and vexes him that you have a sound finger, and if he were able he would tear everything apart and put it out of joint. But there is nothing to which he is so hostile as the beloved word. And the reason is that he can conceal himself beneath every created thing; only the word exposes him, so that he cannot hide himself, and shows everybody how

47. The pronouns in the original are masculine singular.

48. Luther here echoes the themes he took up in the *Heidelberg Disputation* (see TAL 1:67–120).

black he is. Then he fights back and resists and draws together the princes and the bishops, thinking thus to conceal himself again. But it is of no avail; the word nevertheless drags him out into the light. Therefore he, too, does not rest, and because the gospel cannot stand him, so he cannot stand the gospel, and that makes it equal. And if our dear God were not guarding us through his angels and we were able to see the devil's cunning, attacks, and lying, we should die of the sight of it alone, so many are the cannon and guns he has ranged against us. But God prevents them from striking us.

So the two heroes meet, each doing as much as possible. The devil brews one calamity after another; for he is a mighty, malicious, and turbulent spirit. So it is time that our dear God be concerned about his honor; for the word which we wield is a weak and miserable word, and we who have and wield it are also weak and miserable people, bearing the treasure as Paul says [2 Cor. 4:7], in earthen vessels, which can easily be shattered and broken. Therefore the evil spirit spares no effort and confidently lashes out to see if he can smash the little vessel; for there it is under his nose and he cannot stand it. So the battle really begins in earnest, with water and fire to dampen and quench the little spark. Then our Lord God looks on for a while and puts us in a tight place, so that we may learn from our own experience that the small, weak, miserable word is stronger than the devil and the gates of hell. They shall storm the castle, the devil and his cohorts. But let them storm; they will find something there that will make them sweat, and still they will not gain it; for it is a rock, as Christ calls it, which cannot be conquered. So let us suffer what comes upon us and so we shall learn that God will stand by us to guard and shield us against this enemy and all his adherents.

Thirdly, it is also highly necessary that we suffer not only that God may prove his honor, power, and strength against the devil, but also in order that, when we are not in trouble and suffering, this excellent treasure which we have may not merely make us sleepy and secure. We see so many people, unfortunately it is all too common, so misusing the gospel that it is a sin and a shame, as if now of course they have been so liberated by the gospel that there is no further need to do anything, give anything, or suffer anything. This kind of wickedness our God cannot check except through the cross. Hence God must keep disciplining and driving us, that our faith may increase and grow stronger and thus bring the Savior more deeply into us. For just as we cannot get along without eating and drinking so we cannot get along without affliction and suffering. Therefore we must necessarily be afflicted by the devil through persecution or else by a secret thorn that thrusts into the heart, as also St. Paul laments [cf. 2 Cor. 12:7]. Therefore, since it is better to have a cross than to be without a cross, nobody should dread or be afraid of it. After all, you have a good strong promise with which to comfort yourself. So the gospel cannot come to the fore except through and in suffering and cross.

Lastly, Christian suffering is nobler and more precious above all other human suffering because, since Christ himself suffered, he also made holy the suffering of all Christians. Are we not then poor, foolish people? We have run to Rome, Trier, and other places to visit the shrines;[49] why do we not also cherish cross and suffering, which was much nearer to Christ and touched him more closely than any garment did his body. This touched not only his body but his heart. Through the suffering of Christ, the suffering of all his saints has become utterly holy, for it has been touched with Christ's suffering. Therefore we should accept all suffering not otherwise than as a holy thing, for it is truly a holy thing.

Since we know then that it is God's good pleasure that we should suffer, and that God's glory is manifested in our suffering, better than in any other way, and since we are the kind of people who cannot hold on to the word and our faith without suffering, and moreover since we have the noble, costly promise that the cross which God sends to us is not a bad thing, but rather an utterly precious and noble holy thing, why should we refuse to suffer? As for those who will not suffer, let them go and be cavaliers; we preach this only to the devout who want to be Christians, the others wouldn't carry it out anyhow. After all, we have so many assurances and promises that he will not allow us to remain in our suffering but will help us out of it, even though all people should doubt it. Therefore, even though it hurts, so be it, you have to go through some suffering anyhow; things cannot always go smoothly. It is just as well, nay, a thousand times better, to have suffered for the sake of Christ, who promised us comfort and help in suffering, than to suffer and despair and perish without comfort and help for the sake of the devil.

49. A reference to the medieval practice of making pilgrimages to shrines containing the relics of saints, in the hope of gaining merit. Luther not only opposed the theology undergirding relics, he thought that pilgrimages took people away from their proper Christian vocations and opposed true holiness.

This, you see, is the way we teach concerning the cross, and you should also accustom yourself to distinguish carefully between the suffering of Christ and all other suffering and know that his is a heavenly suffering and ours is worldly, that his suffering accomplishes everything, while ours does nothing except that we become conformed to Christ, and that therefore the suffering of Christ is the suffering of a lord, whereas ours is the suffering of a servant. And those who teach otherwise know neither what Christ's suffering is nor what our suffering is. Why? Because reason cannot do otherwise; it likes to put on a display with its suffering, as with all other works, so that it may gain some merit. That's why we must learn to distinguish. We have said enough for this time concerning the example of the Passion and concerning our suffering. God grant that we may understand and learn it aright. Amen.

Sermon on the Twelfth Sunday after Trinity
1531

Preached in the parish church in Wittenberg, this sermon on the bold and confident certainty of the true preacher is a bright picture of Luther himself as a preacher. It is even more noteworthy when one considers that Luther had quit preaching in Wittenberg at the beginning of 1530. He had become totally discouraged and, though he preached some on his trip to Coburg, the Wittenberg congregation did not hear him again until fall 1530.[x] By 1531 he had resumed his intense preaching activity, with over 180 sermons in that year.

Sermon on the Epistle for the Twelfth Sunday after Trinity, 2 Cor. 3:4-6, Preached on the Afternoon of 27 August 1531[y]

This is the Epistle for today and it is our custom to preach on it, but I do not like to preach on this Epistle because it is not for the

---

x   For a full description of this see Fred Meuser, *Luther the Preacher* (Minneapolis: Augsburg, 1983), 28–34.

y   Text in macaronic Latin; WA 34/2:156–65; LW 51:219–27.

people who cannot follow it. However, in order not to disturb the order, I shall deal with it briefly.

This was the situation at the time after Paul had preached at Corinth: When he turned his back, other preachers had come in his place, and everything he had planted they rooted out and did much better. But there were also some sincere hearts there, who remained in the doctrine which Paul had given them, though many defected. And yet they were few and therefore the sectarians entered in force, as we read in the First Epistle. This is what happened to Paul, and in the very church where he himself had preached and installed preachers. It grieved him and it was a rotten business, for he did not know what to do. If he kept silent, this would not be good; if he said nothing concerning his office, it would be regrettable; if he were to praise himself, it would not sound well. Meanwhile the godless went on extolling themselves. This is the general meaning of what he outlines in this chapter: he lauds himself but yet does not laud himself and then lashes out and gives the false apostles a slap. In short, the office of preaching is an arduous office, especially when it is like what Paul encountered here. I have often said that, if I could come down with good conscience, I would rather be stretched upon a wheel[50] or carry stones than preach one sermon. For anyone who is in this office will always be plagued; and therefore I have often said that the damned devil and not a good man should be a preacher. But we're stuck with it now. Our Lord God was a better man than we are. And so it was with Jeremiah [Jer. 20:14-18]. If I had known I would not have let myself be drawn into it with twenty-four horses. Ingratitude is our reward; and after that we still have to bother ourselves with the sectarians and give an account to God on the last day. And for this we have let the peasants and the noblemen starve us until we feel like turning in our key and saying, "Go, preach yourselves, in the name of all the devils!"

So Paul here hardly knows what to do. "Do we need, as some do, letters of recommendation to you, or from you? You yourselves are our letter of recommendation" [2 Cor. 3:1-2]. His words are kindly for the sake of the devout, who have the gospel in their hearts and have not been defected, not for those who are evangelical in name but are devils nevertheless. But he says, "Such is the confidence that we have through Christ toward God" [2 Cor. 3:4]. And that we can set down and let stand. If I

50. A reference to a method of torture or execution.

can't convert the whole crowd, then I'll gain one or two. This is our confidence: when we have preached, it will not have been in vain. If the townsmen, peasants, and the big fellows don't want it, let them leave it; let them go; they will see for themselves that they will regret it. And then there are some who always know better, like the sectarians and our young noblemen, who can handle it better than we can. But when it comes to a showdown, they turn out to be scamps and traitors. The townsmen, the fellows who, when they have read one book are full of the Holy Spirit, are the worst. If I were to follow my own impulse I would say, "Let the damned devil be your preacher!" So I have often thought, but I cannot bring myself to do it. But then confidence returns and we say, let happen what may, we still have our confidence through Christ.

"Not that we are sufficient of ourselves" [2 Cor. 3:5]. We have something else in which we put our confidence and that's the end of it. I cannot boast of anything higher except that I am preaching by God's command and will; it is his will and I know that it is not fruitless. Nevertheless, it is disgusting for me to have to look at the pope, the sectarians, and our own people chewing up the gospel. But we must shut our eyes and look to him and remember that I did not invent this word of God and this office. It is God's word, God's work, God's office. There we two [i.e., God and I] are at one in the cause. It didn't grow in my garden. If he that is above is pleased, what can the world do to me? And I lump them all together: the wise, the powerful, and the hypocrites. It is our confidence, no matter how much the world may boast, that God has qualified us to be ministers, and, secondly, that it is not only pleasing to the heart of God but also that we shall not preach in vain and that this ministry will lift to heaven some few who receive the word. So Paul comforted himself, since he was having the same trouble that we are. All of Asia[51] defected from Paul to the false apostles, as most of Germany now. What should he do? Should he fall into desperation and disputation as to whether God had really sent him? No, he says, "Fall away who will, be wise who will, we have confidence through Christ toward God." But quickly he turns and says, "Not that we are sufficient of ourselves." Before he says, "Such confidence have we," he says, "It has pleased God to call me to the ministry. I have taught the Corinthians rightly and God sent me and qualified me. But they do not consider me qualified. Therefore we have

51. Asia refers to the Roman province of Asia, located in present-day west central Turkey.

confidence that God has qualified us. If he does so, that's all that matters. If the world does not consider us qualified, so be it!" So Paul says about him. "Not that we are sufficient of ourselves." As if he were saying: This is what the others, the noblemen, are doing; they qualify themselves, just like my little squires, the dunces who do not even have one little spark of faith and haven't even begun with works. We can't do things right for them; they can do much better, these fellows who know nothing and yet dispute our preaching. And it is true, when they come to make a speech they can talk a lot, but when you examine it by daylight it's nothing but chaff. So they are sufficient of themselves. And Paul says: These godless people, whom God did not send and who are not qualified by God and do not have the Holy Spirit, are self-qualified and what they preach, they think is right. So he gives them a slap. The truth is that no matter how learned a man may be, if he has no sure call and does not rightly teach the Scriptures, he may talk as he will but there is nothing behind it. And the same is true of those who want to judge others; if they understand a single word, then the devil take me!

So there you have two kinds of preachers. First those who qualify themselves and preach whatever they please. But Paul says: Such we do not want to be. We are not sufficient of ourselves, but God has made us sufficient, so that we know what the whole world does not know. So poor Paul is obliged to praise himself and rebuke others, even though it is courteously spoken. They speak as they please. That is politely said but nevertheless it is a rough slap. And this is high praise to say, God has qualified me; nor can I be censured by those who say God does not praise me and has not qualified me. Therefore anybody who wants to be a preacher, and especially one who is going to fight the battle, must learn this. We shall have these two kinds, Mr. Smartass and the good preachers, if not here, then outside. If they dared to do it, they would stop my mouth and that of all the learned men here. So it's a rotten office to have to deal with these people, not to speak of having to suffer such physical misery and give an accounting on the last day, that a man would rather be a swineherd. But this is our consolation, I can boast to them: if it pleases God, good enough; if it does not please him, let it fall. I wouldn't risk a hair of my head to uphold my office. But if it pleases God, God will preserve it; I'd like to see the fellow who would knock it down.

"Our sufficiency is from God" [2 Cor. 3:5]. What Paul means is that whatever good we do in preaching is done by God; when we preach it is God's work if it has power and accomplishes something among humans. Therefore if I am a good preacher who does some good, it isn't necessary for me to boast. It's not my mind, my wisdom, my ability. Otherwise at this hour all of you would be converted and the godless would be damned and all the smartasses, anti-sacramentalists, sectarians, and Anabaptists who say, "The gospel in Wittenberg is nothing, because it does not make people holy," would be held in check. Let Paul give the answer here! "If I were the one who could make people holy, I would begin with myself and make everybody else holy. I do not ascribe this to myself but to God. If my ministry is profitable, I ascribe it to God. If it produces fruit, I do not glory in myself; this is not my work, but the mercy of God, who has used me to do this. This the false scholars, smartasses, and fanatics cannot do." These are real blows, thunder and lightning hurled against the false apostles, who also were boasting that they would make the people holy and who today are saying, "A good beginning has been made but we're going to do better." But the answer to that is that what we have done was done by God. If anybody can do it better, then by God's grace I have the humility to say: If somebody else can do better, we will follow him. There are many who want to do it, but how many are able? I would help to pay him myself, if there were such a person. I know what preaching is.

"Who has qualified us to be ministers of a new covenant, not in a written code but in the Spirit; for the written code kills, but the Spirit gives life" [2 Cor. 3:6]. These are all words of attack and they are all aimed at vile preaching. We know nothing; you know everything, as he says in 1 Cor. 4[:10], "We are fools for Christ's sake, but you are wise in Christ." If I say, I am more learned than you, I am a proud dunce. If I humble myself, then nobody will want to learn from me. Therefore I say, I am utterly nothing, God knows it. But when I accomplish anything through God, I do not for the sake of the crowd but to commend our office, that is, good luck to you,[52] but we still preach better than you; we preach the New Testament. Here he sets up a mark for them. Emulate me in this! You are preachers and learned men. We know the New Testament and preach it; you preach the Old Testament.[53]

"Not in a written code but in the Spirit." These are Pauline words. You have heard that Paul exalted his office over against

52. Irony.

53. Luther speaks about two distinct messages, law and gospel, and uses Old Testament and New Testament to designate these messages, rather than as designations for parts of the Bible. In other writings he makes clear that the Old Testament in the Bible does contain gospel as well as law.

those who have put themselves forward and gloried in its fruits over against the sectarians. Now he also glories in the doctrine. And this is the controversy: We preach the Spirit and the New Testament, you the letter and the Old Testament. None of you preaches the Spirit and no smartass teaches the New Testament; you all preach the letter and the Old Testament, that is, the law. Nobody preaches the New Testament except those whom God has qualified. In all the apostles who taught at that time you can see how they fought against the false apostles who taught the Old Testament. And look at the Anabaptists today. When they rise up they say, "We must follow Christ's example, leave wife and child." That has a fine shine on it, but if you examine it you see that this is only preaching about what I should do. Likewise the anti-sacramental fanatics will not admit that there is forgiveness of sins in the sacrament and insist that it is only a work. The pope, too, says the Mass is a good work. One who makes himself wise can never preach the New Testament, no matter how he preaches. In short, it is impossible for a sectarian to preach the New Testament. Therefore we can boast that we have not only the ministry and the fruits that proceed from it but also the doctrine; for I know that nobody except us proclaims this doctrine. They do not know what the New Testament is. Even though they talk about it they still deviate into juridical legalism. They preach what magistrates and kings should be preaching. But Paul calls all this the "letter" which kills. All doctrine that does not preach the New Testament, the Spirit, he calls the "letter." Ah, dear Paul, you are a vexing preacher when you shoot back at these fellows and say that when they preach long sermons it still is nothing but words in a man's mouth and letters in a book. All their blabbering is like a letter in a book; it produces nothing. He who lacks the New Testament does not love God, does not believe, hear and teach God's word, and there is nothing there but what is written in a book. It is letter and remains letter, it produces nothing, and a man remains an angry, envious man, a thief, rascal, backbiter, adulterer. That's what it means to preach the letter, which teaches nothing more than what I should do. Then I and the preacher have nothing but letters and a book has just as many of them as we do. It lies like a dead letter in the heart, but I do not make it my own, it is a dead letter in a book. Therefore where the only preaching is, "Do this," it remains only a letter. So Paul is against the false apostles who disparaged and reviled him. He could not please anybody. In short, they preach the letter, but they themselves neither hear nor do what they preach, they remain without God and with the Spirit. Hence there is no fear, no faith, no obedience to God, no chaste heart, no humility.

Therefore we preach something better: the Spirit and the New Testament, which is that Jesus Christ has come for your sake and taken your sins upon himself. There you hear, not what you should do, but what God gives on account of Christ, which means, of course, faith and the Holy Spirit. This is what it means to preach the New Testament and the Holy Spirit. But nobody who wants to make people good through laws is practicing this preaching. That's Moses' and the hangman's business. Otherwise all people would long since have been good; for I preach daily that you should be good and not steal, but the more you hear it the worse you become; you remain the same rascals you were before. Therefore it remains merely letter. When the hangman comes he can chop off a finger, but the heart remains a rogue. I don't want to talk in subtleties about the law and how it frightens people, but only crassly. We have the confidence to say that we preach rightly, that we are sufficient and the fruit follows, that our doctrine is true, and that our ministry is pleasing to God. If we have these three things, then I who preach and you who hear have enough. If the vulgar crowd departs, what is that to me? I might well be angry on account of ingratitude and the fanatics, but I must let it be, as Paul did. If it does not please the world, it is enough that it pleases God. If it does not produce fruit in all, it is enough that it produces fruit in some. If the doctrine be true, let those who preach falsely go. There I can defend myself against spite and vexation. But that I should wish to stop their mouths and persuade the people not to despise me and to be grateful, this confidence we must not have. God is my Lord, the world is my enemy. The fruit will come and the third[z] will come, too. So in the fourth chapter also, Paul comforts himself and his followers, admonishing them not to be offended when it appears that our doctrine is lost, if only it please the One who is above.

---

z   I.e., that my ministry shall please God.

Sermon in Castle Pleissenburg, Leipzig
1539

This sermon has historical importance because of the occasion on which it was preached. It was delivered on Saturday afternoon before Pentecost, 1539, the day before the formal introduction of the Reformation in the city where twenty years before Luther had debated[54] so fervently and effectively and which was the seat of the university that opposed Wittenberg. Luther was ill but nevertheless preached to a crowded chapel in the presence of Duke Henry of Saxony (1473–1541), who had recently become ruler upon the death of Duke George (1471–1539), the champion of Rome and most bitter opponent of the Reformation. He preached again the next afternoon in St. Thomas' Church, but only the first sermon has been preserved.[a] Luther was accompanied to Leipzig by Philip Melanchthon, Justus Jonas, and Caspar Cruciger (1504–1548),[55] and the conjecture is that it was the latter who prepared the transcript. The sermon was not published until 1618.

54. Luther debated Johann Eck (1486–1543) at the Pleissenburg in Leipzig in the summer of 1519. See the image below.

55. Caspar Cruciger, the Elder, edited the Wittenberg edition of Luther's works and helped draft the Leipzig Interim.

Luther and Eck debating in 1519 at the Pleissenburg in Leipzig. Painting by Rudolf Julius Huebner, nineteenth century.

a   For further detail see Brecht, vol. 3, 287–88.

Reformation theologian
Caspar Cruciger

---

56. Luther here identifies the desire for an earthly kingdom with the Jews.

Sermon Preached in Castle Pleissenburg on the Occasion of the Inauguration of the Reformation in Leipzig, John 14:23-31, 24 May 1539[b]

Because I cannot depend upon my head, owing to physical infirmity, to venture upon expounding the teaching in its entirety, I shall adhere by God's grace to the text of the Gospel customarily dealt with in the churches tomorrow.

These words of the Lord Christ, "Those who love me will keep my word, etc." [John 14:23], were prompted by the fact that shortly before this the Lord Christ had expressed himself in almost the same way: "They who have my commandments and keep them are those who love me; . . . and I will love them and reveal myself to them" [John 14:21].[c] For this reason the good Judas (not Iscariot) asked, "Lord, how is it that you will reveal yourself to us, and not to the whole world?" [John 14:22]. It is to this question that the Lord Christ is replying here. And here one sees the fleshly and Jewish[56] notions that the apostles held; they were hoping for a worldly kingdom of the Lord Christ and they wanted to be the chief ones in that kingdom. Already they had disputed about who should be the greatest in that kingdom [Mark 9:34] and had divided it up into provinces. To this day the Jews have this same attitude and hope for an earthly messiah.

Thus since the Lord Christ said here, "those who have my commandments and keep them, they will I love and reveal myself to them" [John 14:21],[d] Judas says: Are we to be the only ones? Is it to be such a meager revelation and manifestation? Will it not be manifest to the whole world, including both Jews and the Gentiles? *Was sol das seyn*? [What is it going to be?] Are we to be the only ones to inherit you, and the Gentiles shall know nothing? This false Jewish delusion was in the apostles; that is why this Gospel here describes the kingdom of the Lord Christ and paints a far different picture of it for the disciples. It is as if he were saying: No, the world has a different kingdom, my dear Judas; that's why I say: If a man loves me, he will keep my word, and I will be with him along with my Father and the Holy Spirit and

---

b   WA 47:772–79; LW 51:301–12.

c   The text of John 14:21, 23 taken from NRSV.

d   Based on NRSV.

make our home with him. This home is God's dwelling, as Jerusalem was called the dwelling of God, which he himself chose as his own: Here is my hearth, house, and dwelling [Isa. 31:9]; just as today the churches are called God's dwellings on account of the word and sacraments. Here I think that Christ is pronouncing a severe judgment, here he is prophesying and forgetting the dwelling of Jerusalem, of which all the prophets said: Here will I dwell forever. This dwelling the Lord Christ pulls down and erects and builds a new dwelling, a new Jerusalem, not made of stones and wood, but rather: "If anyone loves me and keeps my word," there shall be my castle, my chamber, my dwelling.

In saying this Christ gave the answer to the argument concerning the true church; to this day you still hear our papists boasting and saying: the church, the church![57,e] It is true that Christ wants to have his home where the Father and the Holy Spirit want to be and to dwell. The entire Trinity dwells in the true church; what the true church does and directs is done and directed by God. Now the new church is a different dwelling from that of Jerusalem; he tears down all the prophecies concerning Jerusalem, as if Jerusalem were nothing in his eyes, and he builds another dwelling, the Christian church. Here we agree with the papists that there is one Christian church; but Christ wants to be everywhere in the land.

These are fine, heart-warming words—that God wants to come down to us, God wants to come to us and we may not climb up to him, he wants to be with us to the end of the world: Here dwells the Holy Spirit, effecting and creating everything in the Christian church.

But what is the dissension between the papists and us? The answer is: about the true Christian church. Should one then not be obedient to the Christian church? Yes, certainly, all believers owe this obedience; for St. Peter commands in the fourth chapter of his First Epistle: "Whoever speaks should speak as one who utters God's word" [1 Pet. 4:11]. If anybody wants to preach, let him suppress his own words and let them prevail in worldly and domestic affairs; here in the church he should speak nothing but the word of this rich Householder; otherwise it is not the

57. In the 1530s Luther often responded to the Roman Catholic accusation that the Evangelicals were not the true church. See Mark U. Edwards Jr., *Luther's Last Battles: Politics and Polemics* (Minneapolis: Fortress Press, 1983; rev. ed., 2004).

e   Luther discussed what defines the true church in other places in the 1530s. See, e.g., the *Smalcald Articles* (1537) [TAL 2:463; BC, 324–25]; and *On the Councils and the Church* (1539) [TAL 3:317–443; LW 41:3–178].

58. Latin: *administratio*, "stewardship"; cf. 1 Cor. 4:1.

59. I.e., in danger that Christ may say that his dwelling is not among them.

60. In this and the following paragraphs, Luther discusses what defines the true church: the speaking and hearing of God's word, baptism, Lord's Supper, and absolution. These means of grace create the faith that prays.

true church. This is why it must be said: God is speaking. After all, this is the way it must be in this world; if a prince wants to rule, his voice must be heard in his country and his house. And if this happens in this miserable life, so much the more must we let God's word resound in the church and in eternal life. All subjects and governments must be obedient to the Word of their Lord. This is called administration.[58] Therefore a preacher conducts the household of God by virtue and on the strength of his commission and office, and he dare not say anything different from what God says and commands. And even though there may be a lot of talk that is not the Word of God, the church is not in all this talk, even though they begin to yell like crazy. All they do is to shriek: church, church! One should listen to the pope and the bishops!

But when they are asked: What is the Christian church? What does it say and do? they reply: The church looks up to the pope, cardinals, and bishops. This is not true! Therefore we must look to Christ and listen to him as he describes the true Christian church in contrast to their phony shrieking. For one should and one must rather believe Christ and the apostles, that one speaks God's word, and do as St. Peter and here the Lord Christ says: He who keeps my word, there is my dwelling, there is the Builder, my word must remain in it; otherwise it shall not be my house. Our papists want to improve on this, and therefore they may be in peril.[59] Christ says: "We want to make our home with him"; there the Holy Spirit is at work. There must be a people that loves me and keeps my commandments. Quite bluntly, this is what he wants.

Here Christ is not speaking of how the church is built, as he spoke above concerning the dwelling. But when it has been built, then the word must certainly be there, and a Christian should listen to nothing but God's word.[60] Elsewhere, in worldly affairs, he hears other things, how the wicked should be punished and the good protected, and about the economy. But here in the Christian church it should be a house in which only the word of God resounds. Therefore let them shriek themselves crazy, with their cry: church, church! Without the word of God it is nothing. My dear Christians are steadfast confessors in word, in life, and in death. They do not want to forsake this dwelling, so dearly do they love this Prince. Whether in favor or not, for this they will leave country and people, body and life. Thus we read of a Roman centurion, a martyr,[61] who, when he was stripped of everything, said, "This I know; they cannot take away from me my Lord Christ." Therefore a Christian says: This Christ I must have, though it cost me everything else, that I cannot take with me. This remains: Christ alone is enough for me. Therefore all Christians should stand strong and steadfast upon the word alone, as St. Peter says, "by the strength which God supplies" [1 Pet. 4:11].

Behold, how it all happens in weakness. Look at baptism, it is water; where does the sanctifying and the power come from? From the pope? No, it comes from God, who says, "He who believes and is baptized" [Mark 16:16]. For the pope puts trust in the consecrated water.[62] Why, pope? Who gave you the power? The *ecclesia*, the church? Yes, indeed, where is it written? Nowhere![f] Therefore the consecrated water is Satan's bath, which cripples, blinds, and consecrates the people without the word. But in the church one should teach and preach nothing besides or apart from the word of God. For the pastor who does the baptizing says: It is not I who baptize you; I am only the instrument of the Father, Son, and Holy Spirit; this is not my work.

Likewise, the blessed sacrament is not administered by humans, but rather by God's command; we only lend our hands to it. Do you think this is an insignificant meal, with which one feeds not only the soul but also the mortal body of a poor, condemned sinner for the forgiveness of sins in order that the body too may live? This is God's power, this Householder's power, not human power.

So also in the absolution, when a distressed sinner is pardoned. By what authority and command? Not by human command, but by God's command. Behold, here by God's power I deliver you from the kingdom of the devil and transfer you to the kingdom of God [Col. 1:13]. So it is too with our prayer, which gains all things from God, not through its own power, or because it is able to do this, but because it trusts in God's promise. In the world you see how hard it is to approach the Roman emperor and gain help; but a devout Christian can always come to God with a humble, believing prayer and be heard.

In short, the word and the Holy Spirit, who prepares us for prayer, are in God's power. It is the word that we believe—this is

61. The reference is to Martin, Roman citizen and martyr. Cf. Ernst Schäfer, *Luther als Kirchenhistoriker* (Gütersloh: Bertelsmann, 1897), 235-36.

62. In discussing baptism and the Lord's Supper, Luther always emphasized that the word makes the sacrament. For example, in his *Small Catechism*, he states, "Baptism is not simply plain water. Instead it is water enclosed in God's command and connected with God's Word" (BC, 359; this volume, p. 231).

f   Luther's phrase is more crude: *im Rauchloch*, i.e., "in the anus."

63. Luther refers here to his Evangelical understanding of prayer. The one praying relies on God's promise to hear rather than upon her own worthiness to gain a hearing.

what makes our hearts so bold that we dare to call ourselves the children of the Father. Where does this come from? The answer is: From God, who teaches us to pray in the Lord's Prayer and puts into our hands the book of Psalms. For if we prayed without faith, this would be to curse twice over, as we learned in our nasty papistical holiness. But where there is a believing heart and that heart has before it the promise of God it quite simply and artlessly prays its "Our Father" and is heard.[63] Outside of this church of God you may present your prayers and supplications to great lords and potentates to the best of your ability, but here you have no ability to pray except in Christ Jesus, in order that we may not boast that we are holy as they do in the papacy, who protest, of course, and say: Oh, it would be a presumption for anybody to call himself holy and fit; and yet they teach that man of himself has a "certain preparation"[g] for prayer.

They also teach prayer according to this doctrine in their chants and say: I have prayed in doubt[h] as a poor sinner. Oh, stop that kind of praying! It would be better to drop such praying altogether if you doubt. For doubt ruins everything and if you go to baptism, prayer, and the sacrament without faith, in doubt, you are actually mocking God. What you should quickly say, however, is this: I am certain that my dear God has so commanded and that he has promised me the forgiveness of sins; therefore I will baptize, absolve, and pray. And immediately you will receive this treasure in your heart. It does not depend on our worthiness or unworthiness, for both of these can only make us despair. Therefore do not allow yourself by any means to be driven to despair. For it is a mockery of God when we do not believe the words "Go and baptize" [Matt. 28:19], that is, baptize those who repent and are sorry for their sins. Here you hear that this is not human work, but the work of God the Father; he is the Householder who wills to dwell here. But if we doubt, then we should stay away from the sacrament and from prayer, and first learn to say: All right, it makes no difference that I am unworthy, God is truthful nevertheless, and he has most certainly promised and assured us; I'll stake my life on this. And this we did

g　Latin: *praeparationem quandam.*

h　*Mit Zweifel*, literally "with doubt," which also includes despair, fear, and anxiety. In this paragraph *Zweifel* is sometimes translated "doubt" and sometimes "despair."

not know under the papacy. Indeed, I, Martin Luther, for a long time could not find my way out of this papistical dream, because they were constantly blathering to me about my worthiness and unworthiness. Therefore, you young people, learn to recognize the church rightly.

Concerning penitence or penance we teach that it consists in the acknowledgment of sins and genuine trust in God, who forgives us all of them for Christ's sake. The pope, on the contrary, does nothing but scold and devise intolerable burdens; and besides he knows nothing of grace and faith, much less does he teach what the Christian church really is.

But don't you forget the main point here, namely, that God wants to make his dwelling here. Therefore, when the hand is laid upon your head and the forgiveness of sins is proclaimed to you in the words "I absolve you in the name of Christ from all your sins," you should take hold of this word with a sure faith and be strengthened out of the mouth of the preacher. And this is what Christ and St. Peter are saying: He, the Lord, wants to dwell in this church; the word alone shall resound in it.

In short, the church is a dwelling, in order that God may be loved and heard. Not wood or stones, not dumb animals, it should be people, who know, love, and praise God. And that you may be able to trust God with certainty in all things, including cross and suffering, you should know that it is the true church, even though it be made up of scarcely two believing persons. That's why Christ says: "He who loves me keeps my word"; there I want to dwell, there you have my church.

So now you must guard yourselves against the pope's church, bedaubed and adorned with gold and pearls; for here Christ teaches the opposite. To love God and keep his Word is not the pope's long robe and crown, nor even his decretals. There is a great difference between what God commands and what humans command. Look how the pope brazenly announces—we should invoke the saints and conduct ourselves according to his human precepts. Does God's word command this too? I still do not see it. But this I know very well, that God's word says: I, Christ, go to the Father, and whoever believes in me will be saved. For I, I have suffered for that one and I also give that one the Holy Spirit from on high.

So the Lord Christ and the pope each has his own church, but with this mighty difference, which Christ himself, the best

64. This awkward word is a better translation of the sense of *rechtgleubtge* than "orthodox."

65. *Zeitliche Partecke*: "our poor, beggarly possessions, temporal bread, and well-being." See the phrase "bit of bread" in the next paragraph.

66. *Es ist der liebe Wilpret (der Friede) im Himmelreich gar seltsam*. This is a double-edged use of a proverbial saying applied to princes (Luther is addressing princes in this sermon), who were obsessed with hunting: "There is no game in heaven, what would a prince do with himself there?"

67. Note the echo of the last verse of Luther's famous hymn "A Mighty Fortress Is Our God": "If they should take my life, goods, honor, child, spouse, though life be wrenched away, they cannot win the day, the kingdom's ours forever" (see this volume, p. 134).

68. "Bread" here is an expression for all things related to temporal well-being.

69. *Vollkommenen*, "perfect," includes the sense of "complete." Luther may be referring, among other things, to the fact that the introduction of the Reformation meant that laypeople could receive the wine of the Lord's Supper.

dialectitian,[i] here describes, telling us what it is and where it is, namely, where his word is purely preached. So where you hear this, there you may know that this is the true church. For where the word of God is not present, there also are no true-believing[64] confessors and martyrs. And if the word of God were lacking, then we would have been deceived by Christ; then he really would have betrayed us!

Oh, if we could only stake it all on Christ and mock and laugh at the pope, since Christ clearly says here, not "he who has my word," but "he who keeps it loves me" and is also my disciple. There are many of you who have the word, true enough, but do not keep it, and in time of trouble and trial fall away altogether and deny Christ.

It would, of course, be desirable if we could always have both: the word and our temporal crumbs,[65] but the good venison, peace, is very scarce in the kingdom of heaven.[66] It is therefore something that must be recognized as a great blessing of God when there is peace among temporal lords and mutual understanding. But if not, then let them all go—goods, fame, wife, and child—if only this treasure remain with us.[67]

I fear, however, that unfortunately there will be among us many weathercocks, false brethren, and similar weeds; and yet I am not going to be a prophet, because I must prophesy nothing but evil, and who would presume to be able to fathom it all? It will turn out all right; now we have it, let us see to it that we hold on to it. But let us be valiant against Satan, who intends to sift us like wheat [cf. Luke 22:31]. For it may well be that you will have your bit of bread[68] under a good government and then the devil will soon set a snare for you in your security and presumption, so that you will no longer trust and give place to the word of God as much as you did before. That's why Christ says: My sheep not only hear me, they also obey and follow me [John 10:3-5]; they increase in faith daily through hearing the word of God and the right and perfect[69] use of the blessed sacraments. There is strength and consolation in this church. And it is also the true church, not cowls, tonsures, and long robes, of which the word of God knows nothing, but rather wherever two or three are gathered together [Matt. 18:20], no matter whether it be on the ocean or in the depths of the earth, if only they have before them the

i   Der beste Dialecticus.

word of God and believe and trust in the same, there is most certainly the real, ancient, true, apostolic church.

But we were so blinded in the papacy that, even though St. Peter tells us that "we have a sure prophetic word" and that you "do well to pay attention to this as to a lamp shining in a dark place" [2 Pet. 1:19], we still cannot see what a bright light we have in the gospel. Therefore we must note here once again the description of the Christian church that Christ gives us, namely, that it is a group[70] of people who not only have his Word but also love and keep it and forsake everything for the sake of love.

From this then you can answer the screamers and spitters who have nothing in their snouts but "church! church!": Tell me, dear pope, what is the church? Answer: the pope and his cardinals. Oh, listen to that; you anointed idols,[71] where is it written in God's word that Father Pope and Brother Cardinal are the true church? Was it because that was what the fine parrot bird said to the black jackdaw?[72]

But Christ tells you and me something far different, namely, my church is where my word is preached and kept pure and unadulterated. Therefore St. Paul warns that we should flee and avoid those who would lead us away from God's word. For whoever defiles God's temple, which we are, God will destroy that person [1 Cor. 3:17]. And St. Peter also says: Take heed, if you are going to preach, then you should preach nothing but God's word [1 Pet. 4:11], otherwise you will defile God's church.

Accordingly, it is once again to be diligently noted how Christ described his church for us; for this description is a strong thunderbolt against the miserable pope and his decretals by which he has made of the church of God a filthy privy.[73]

If anybody wants to teach human precepts, let him do so in secular and domestic affairs and leave the church alone. After all, the papists are really empty spewers and chatterers since Christ himself here says: He who hears my word and keeps it, to him I and my Father want to come and make our home with him. This is the end of Jerusalem and Moses; here there is to be a little band of Christ [*Heufflein Christi*], who hear God's word and keep the same and rely upon it in every misfortune. This is my church. In this Lord we shall trust, even though the pope bristles with anger over it.

But in these words Christ also wanted to answer the apostle Judas, who also allowed himself to imagine that Christ would

70. *Hauffe*, literally a "heap" or "mass" of people.

71. *Oelgoetze*, "anointed idols," refers to Roman Catholic priests, bishops, and popes.

72. A jackdaw is a member of the crow family.

73. The original repeats this in Latin: *contra Papam, qui fecit ex Ecclesia cloacam*, and also includes an untranslatable play on words: *Decret* ("decree") and *Secret* ("privy").

become a great secular emperor and that they, the apostles, would become great lords in the nations when he would manifest himself. But how wrong he was! Here Christ tells them straight out that his kingdom is not of this world, but that they and all believers should be that kingdom of heaven in which God the Father, Son, and Holy Spirit themselves dwell. He does not place angels, emperors, kings, princes, and lords into that church. He himself wants to be the Householder and be the only one to speak and act; there I will dwell, he says, and with me all believers from everlasting to everlasting.

But Judas, the good man, still cannot understand this and therefore the Holy Spirit must come and teach it to him. Of this future and this ministry, dear Christians, you will hear tomorrow, God willing. If I cannot do it, then it will be done by others who can do it better than I, though they will not admit it.[74] Let this today serve as an introduction or the early sermon. May the Lord help us, I cannot go on further now.

The Gospel for the Early Christmas[j] Service, Luke 2[:15-20]

Luther wrote his Church Postil (Kirchenpostille) or Wartburg Postil during his time at the Wartburg in 1521–1522. This sermon was not actually preached by Luther but was intended by him to be a guide or model for those preparing their own sermons on this text. The Christmas portion of this postil was published at least eight times between 1522 and 1536.[75]

This Gospel can be understood quite easily from the interpretation of the preceding one;[76] for it contains an example and carrying out of the teaching which is contained in the previous lesson in that the shepherds did and found what the angels had told them. So the present lesson deals with the consequences and fruits of the word of God and the signs by which we recognize whether the word of God is in us and has been effective.

74. The next day Paul Lindenau (c. 1489–1541), Justus Jonas, and Frederick Myconius (1490–1546) preached in Leipzig churches in the morning. Luther preached in St. Thomas' Church in the afternoon (LW 51:312 n.11).

75. Frymire, *The Primacy of the Postils*, 454.

76. The Gospel for Christmas Eve was Luke 2:1-14; the Gospel for the main Christmas service was John 1:1-14.

j   WA 10/1/1:128–41; LW 52:32–40; LW 75:248–55.

The first and chief item is faith. If these shepherds had not believed the angel, they would not have gone to Bethlehem nor would they have done any of the things told about them in the Gospel. But if anybody should say: Of course, I, too, surely would believe if the message were brought to me by an angel from heaven, then such a person deceives himself. For whoever does not accept the word on its own account is never inclined to accept it on account of any preacher, even if all the angels were preaching to him. And whoever accepts it on account of a preacher believes neither the word, nor in God through the word, but believes the preacher and in the preacher.[77] For this reason his faith does not last long. But whoever believes the word pays no attention to the one who proclaims it. He does not honor the word because of the person who preaches it, but, on the contrary, he honors the person who preaches because of the word; he never elevates the person[78] above the word, and even if the person should perish or, as a renegade, preach a different message, he gives up the person preaching rather than the word. He abides with what he has heard—no matter who the person preaching might be, no matter whether that person be coming or going, and no matter what happens.

This is also the real difference between godly faith and human faith: human faith clings to a person; it believes, trusts, and honors the word on account of the one who speaks it. But godly faith clings to the word, which is God himself; it believes, trusts, and honors the word not on account of the one who has spoken it, but feels that here is such a certainty of truth that nobody can ever tear it away, even if the very same preacher should try to do so. The Samaritans prove this, John 4[:42]: initially they heard of Christ from the pagan woman, and left town and came to Christ on her word. Having heard him with their own ears, they said to the woman: "We do not believe any longer on account of what you have said; for now we recognize that this is the Savior of the world." Again, all those who believed Christ on account of his person and his miracles deserted him when he was crucified. That is the way it is now and has always been. The word itself, without any regard for the person, must satisfy the heart, must embrace and capture the person so that he, like one who is imprisoned in it, feels how true and right it is, even if all the world, all angels, all the princes of hell said something else, indeed, even if God had a different message. For God at times

77. In this paragraph Luther discusses the issues of authority that were key in the Reformation. The Roman Catholic Church located authority in the pope, his bishops, and his priests; their words were to be believed because they occupied these positions. Luther locates authority in God's word and places this above any person or any office that may convey that word.

78. That is, the preacher.

tests his chosen ones and pretends to want something other than he previously indicated, as happened to Abraham when he was ordered to sacrifice his son Isaac and to Jacob, when he struggled with the angel, and to David when he was driven away by Absalom, his son, etc.

This faith persists, in both life and death, even as in hell and heaven, and nothing can overthrow it; for it rests on the word alone, without regard to any person. These shepherds also had such a faith; for they agree and they adhere to the word so much that they forget the angels who told it to them. They do not say: "Let us go and see the story which the angels have told us," but "which the Lord has made known to us." The angels are quickly forgotten, and only the word of God remains. Likewise Luke says that Mary kept and pondered the words in her heart and that, without a doubt, she was not troubled by the lowly estate of the shepherds, but considered everything the word of God. She was not the only one who did this; all the others who heard the account from the shepherds and were filled with wonder also did the same, as the text says. All clung only to the word. Although it is a peculiarity of the Hebrew language that, when talking about an action it expresses it by referring to the word as Luke does here (because the action is comprehended in words and thus made known), yet God also arranged that there be described the faith which clings to the word and acquiesces in the word which expresses the action. For if Christ's life and suffering were not comprehended in the word to which faith might cling, they would have availed nothing, for all those who were eyewitnesses received no benefit from their experience, or only very little.

The second item is the single-mindedness of the spirit. It is the nature of the Christian faith to make the hearts one, so that they are of one mind and of one will, as Ps. 68[:6] says in this regard: "God the Lord, Christ, our God makes harmonious inhabitants in the house," and Ps. 133[:1] states: "Ah, how beautiful and joyful it is that brothers dwell with one another in unity." St. Paul speaks of the unity of the spirit in many places: Rom. 12[:16], 1 Cor. 12[:4-31], and Eph. 5[4:3], and he says: Be ever diligent to be of one mind, of one will. Such unity is not possible outside of faith. As the saying goes, "Each one likes his own ways best, and so the land is full of fools." Experience teaches us how the religious orders, the estates, and the sects are divided among themselves. Each believes that his order, his estate, his ways, his works, his undertaking is best and the right road to heaven, and looks down upon the others, taking no interest in them. We observe this nowadays among the priests, monks, bishops, and the entire clergy. But those who have a right faith know that the one important thing is faith; on this they all are in accord. Thus there is no disunity among them and no division because of some external estate, action, or work. Externals make no difference to them, no matter how varied they may be. Thus in this story the shepherds are of one mind, of one will; they voice one opinion among themselves, they speak one and the same words when they say, "Let us go," etc.

The third item is humility, that they [the shepherds] acknowledge themselves as human beings. For this reason the evangelist adds the words: "the men, the shepherds," etc. For faith teaches immediately that whatever is human is nothing in the sight of God. For this reason they despise themselves and consider themselves to be nothing, and this is true and real humility and self-knowledge. Humility means that they are not interested in all those things which are high and mighty in the world and that they associate with lowly, poor, despised people. As St. Paul teaches and says in Rom. 12[:16]: "Do not be haughty, but associate with those who are lowly." And as Ps. 15[:4] also says: "The just one despises the despiser and honors those who fear God." From all of this, then, comes peace; for whoever considers all

A depiction of the angels telling the shepherds of the birth of Jesus. From a 1540 publication of Martin Luther's *Interpretation of the Epistle and Gospel Texts from Advent to Easter.*

external and big things to be nothing gives them up easily and does not fight with anybody about them. He feels within himself, in the faith of his heart, something that is better. No doubt one also finds concord, peace, and humility among murderers and public sinners, as also among those who put on a show of virtue. However, this is a unity of the flesh, not of the spirit, as when Pilate and Herod became united with one another and practiced peace and humility with one another [Luke 23:13]. The Jews did the same thing as Ps. 2[:2] says. "The kings and princes of this earth have become united among themselves against the Christ." In the same manner, too, the pope, monks, and priests are united, whenever they direct their activities against God, whereas at other times they are split into factions. For this reason this is called concord, humility, and peace of the spirit, because it is related to and deals with spiritual things, that is to say, with Christ.

The fourth item is love of one's neighbor and renunciation of self. The shepherds demonstrate this by leaving their sheep and by proceeding, not to the high and mighty lords in Jerusalem, not to the town councilors at Bethlehem, but to the lowly people[k] in the stable. They present themselves to the lowly and are ready and willing to serve and to do what was expected of them. Had they not had faith, they would not have left their sheep, as they did, and they would not have left their property lying around, especially as the angels had not commanded them to do so. For they did this out of their own free will and following their own counsel, as the text says: They talked about it among themselves and they came in haste, even though the angel did not command, admonish, or advise them to do so. All he did was to indicate what they would find; he left it up to their free will whether they wanted to go and to look. Love operates in exactly the same manner. Love needs no command; it does everything of its own accord, does not tarry, but hurries, and considers it sufficient that the direction is pointed out. Love does not need—and will not tolerate—someone to goad it along. Oh, much could be said on this topic. Thus a Christian life should move freely in love, should forget himself and that which is his, and should think only of and hasten to help the neighbor, as St. Paul says in Ephesians 5 [Phil. 2:4]:[l] "Let no one consider what is his, but what is the other's"; and Galatians 5 [6:2]:[m] "Let each one bear the other's burden and thus you will fulfill the law of Christ." But these days the pope with his bishops and priests has filled the world with laws and restraints, and there is nothing in all the world but sheer compulsion and intimidation; voluntary orders

---

k   *Heufflein,* a diminutive, literally, "little pile" or "little group."

l   Phil. 2:4 corrects the Ephesians 5 reference.

m   Gal. 6:2 corrects the Galatians 5 reference.

or estates no longer exist, in accordance with the prophecy that love would be extinguished and the world corrupted with the doctrines of men.

The fifth item is joy which expresses itself in words that we like to talk and hear about, that faith has received in the heart. Thus the shepherds chatter with one another happily and amicably concerning what they had heard and believed. They use many words as if they were chattering aimlessly. It is not enough for them to say, "Let us go to Bethlehem and see what has happened there." No, they add to this and say: "which God has done and has made known to us." Is it not superfluous talk when they say: "that has happened there, which God has done"? They could have said it briefly in this fashion: Therefore let us see the word*n* that God has done there. But the joy of the spirit flows over, as it were, with happy words, and yet there is not too much said, indeed, all too little; they are unable to say it as much as they really would like to, as Ps. 45[:1] reads: "My heart gulps forth a good word," as if the psalmist wanted to say: I should like to say it right out, but I cannot. It is greater than I can express, so that my word is scarcely more than a gulp. This accounts for the expression found in Ps. 50 [35:28]*o* and in several other places: "My tongue shall gulp forth your righteousness," i.e., it will talk, sing, and speak while I jump for joy. And Ps. 119[:171] says: "My lips will gush forth your praise," just as a boiling pot seethes and gushes.

The sixth item is that they follow through with action; for, as St. Paul says in 1 Corinthians 3 [4:20]:*p* "God's kingdom does not consist in words but in deeds." Accordingly the shepherds here do not merely say: "Let us go and see," but they actually go. Indeed, they do more than what they say; for the text speaks: "They came with haste." This is a great deal more than ordinary walking, as they had agreed to do. Thus faith and love always do more than they say and their works are in every respect alive, industrious, active, and overflowing. Thus a Christian should produce few words but many deeds, as he certainly will, if he is a true Christian. If he does not act in this manner, then he is as yet not a true Christian.

n   *Das Wort*, that is, a word that is a deed.
o   Ps. 35:28 corrects the Psalm 50 reference.
p   1 Cor. 4:20 corrects the 1 Corinthians 3 reference.

The seventh item is that they freely confess and publicly proclaim the word that was told them concerning the child. This is the greatest work in the Christian life, and for it one must be willing to risk life and limb and goods and reputation. For the evil spirit does not attack someone very vigorously if he has the right faith and lives rightly but privately and only for himself. But if someone is willing to go out and to spread the word, to confess, preach, and praise for the benefit of others, that he does not tolerate.[79] Therefore Luke reports that they not only came and saw, but that they also proclaimed—not only to Mary and Joseph but also to everyone—the news they had heard in the field concerning the child. Do you not think that there were many people who considered them fools and out of their minds because they dared, as uncouth and unschooled laypeople, to speak of the angels' song and message? How would they be received today, should they tell the pope, the bishops, and scholars such a tale? Or even a less important one? But the shepherds, filled with faith and joy, were happy for the sake of God to be considered foolish in the sight of humans. A Christian does the same; for God's word must be considered foolishness and error in this world.

The eighth item is Christian liberty that is not tied to any work. On the contrary, all works are the same to a Christian, no matter what they are. For these shepherds do not run away into the desert, they do not don monk's garb, they do not shave their heads, neither do they change their clothing, schedule, food, drink, nor any external work. They return to their place in the fields to serve God there! For being a Christian does not consist in external conduct, neither does it change anyone according to the external position; rather it changes him according to the inner disposition, that is to say, it provides a different heart, a different disposition, will, and mind which do the works which another person does without such a disposition and will.[80] For a Christian knows that it all depends upon faith; for this reason he walks, stands, eats, drinks, dresses, works, and lives as any ordinary person in his calling, so that one does not become aware of his Christianity, as Christ says in Luke 17[:20-21]: "The kingdom of God does not come in an external manner and one cannot say, 'Lo, here and there,' but the kingdom of God is within you." Against this liberty the pope and the spiritual estate fight with their laws and their choice of clothing, food, prayers, places, and persons. They catch themselves and every-

79. Luther reflected on this theme in other places. In *On the Councils and the Church* he noted that one of the seven signs of the true church was that it must endure misfortune, persecution, and all kinds of trials and evils (LW 41:164–65; TAL 3:317–443).

80. This paragraph echoes themes found in, for example, *The Freedom of a Christian* (TAL 1:466–537).

body else with such soul snares, with which they have filled the world, just as St. Anthony saw in a vision.[q] For they are of the opinion that salvation depends on their person and work. They call other people worldly, whereas they themselves in all likelihood are seven times more worldly, inasmuch as their doings are entirely human works concerning which God has commanded nothing.

The ninth and last item is to praise and thank God. For we are unable to give to God anything, in return for his goodness and grace, except praise and thanksgiving, which, moreover, proceed from the heart and have no great need of organ music, bells, and mumblings. Faith teaches such praise and thanksgiving; as is written here concerning the shepherds that they returned to their flocks with praise and thanksgiving and were well satisfied, even though they did not become wealthier, were not awarded higher honors, did not eat and drink better, and were not obliged to carry on a better trade. See, in this Gospel you have a picture of true Christian life, especially as pertains to its external aspects: on the outside, it shines forth not at all or at most a little bit in the sight of the people so that, indeed, most people see it as error and foolishness; but on the inside it is sheer light, joy, and blessedness. Thus we see what the apostle has in mind when he enumerates the fruits of the spirit in Galatians 5[:22]: "The fruits of the spirit (that is, the works of faith) are love, joy, peace, kindness, friendliness, patience, confidence, mercy, chastity." No person, time, food, garment, location, or any self-selected human work of this kind, as we see them swarming about in the lives of the papists, is enumerated.

But what it means to find Christ in such poverty and what his baby diapers and the manger signify have been stated in the previous Gospel. We saw that his poverty teaches how we are to find him in our neighbor, in the lowliest and the neediest. And that his diapers are Holy Scripture.[81] Thus in our active life we are to stick with the needy, while in our studies and in our contemplative life we are to stick to Scripture, so that Christ alone is head of both lives and in all respects before us. The books of Aristotle and those of the pope and of any other human should be avoided or they should be read in such a way that we do not seek the edification of the soul, but we should use them to improve

81. Luther referred to the Scriptures as "the swaddling clothes and the manger in which Christ lies" in his *Preface to the Old Testament* (LW 35:236; TAL, vol. 6, forthcoming).

q   Cf. *On the Lives of the Fathers* (*De vitis patrum*), III (MPL 73, 785).

our temporal life, to learn a trade or civil law. It was not without intention that Luke writes mentioning Mary before Joseph and both of them before the infant: "They found Mary and Joseph and the babe in the manger." As we said above, Mary is the Christian church and Joseph the servant of the church, and this is exactly what the bishops and priests should be when they preach the gospel. Now the church comes before the prelates of the church, as Christ, too, says in Luke 21 [22:26]: "He who wishes to be the greatest among you, must be the least." Nowadays this has been reversed, and one need not be astonished about it because they have rejected the gospel and exalted human babblings. The Christian church, on the contrary, keeps all the words of God in her heart and ponders them, compares one with the other and with Holy Scripture. Therefore those who want to find Christ must first find the church. How would one know Christ and faith in him if one did not know where they are who believe in him? Those who would know something concerning Christ must neither trust in themselves nor build bridges into heaven by means of their own reason, but should go to the church, attend it, and ask questions there.

The church is not wood and stone but the assembly[r] of people who believe in Christ. To this church one must cling and see how the people believe, live, and teach. They certainly have Christ in their midst, for outside the Christian church there is no truth, no Christ, no salvation. It follows that the pope or a bishop erroneously claims that he alone should be believed, posing as master; for all of them err and may be in error. Their teaching should rather be subject to the assembly of believers. What they teach should be subject to the judgment and verdict of the congregation; to this judgment one should defer, so that Mary may be found ahead of Joseph and the church preferred to the preachers.[82] For it is not Joseph but Mary who keeps these words in her heart, who ponders them and keeps them or compares them. The apostle taught the same thing in 1 Cor. 14[:29-30] when he says: "One or two are to interpret Scripture, the others shall sit in judgment, and whenever a revelation comes to one who sits, then the former must be silent." But nowadays the pope and his followers have become tyrants; they have reversed this Christian, divine, apostolic order and have introduced an altogether

82. Luther struck some of the same themes in *To the Christian Nobility* (1520). There he emphasized the right of every Christian to interpret Scripture; holding a particular office did not give one greater right or authority in regard to scriptural interpretation. See TAL 1:369–466.

r   *Hauff*, "mass" or "pile."

heathenish and Pythagorean order, so that they are able to talk, babble, and act foolishly according to their own whims. Nobody is permitted to judge or interrupt them, or to command them to be silent. In this manner, too, they have quenched the spirit, so that one finds among them neither Mary, nor Joseph, nor Christ, but only the rats, mice, adders, and serpents of their poisonous teachings and hypocrisy.

This is not really a Gospel of strife,[83] for, although it teaches Christian conduct and works, it does not state the articles of faith in plain language, even though there might be enough in its allegories, as has been shown; but allegorical passages must not be used in polemics. We need plain utterances that clearly set forth the articles of faith.

83. *Eyn Streytt Euangelium,* "a debatable or contentious gospel." Luther thinks that the contents of this Gospel text should not cause strife, for it talks about morals and works, something all agree on.

Selected Hymns

DOROTHEA WENDEBOURG

INTRODUCTION

"Grace and peace! I am planning, according to the examples of the prophets and the ancient Fathers, to create vernacular psalms, that is hymns, for the common folk, so that the Word of God remain with the people also through singing. Therefore we are looking everywhere for poets."[a] These lines, written by Martin Luther in December 1523 to Georg Spalatin,[1] mark the origin of one of the most typical and most successful fruits and means of the Reformation, the Protestant hymn. They do so not only for the Wittenberg Reformation but also for the one stamped by Geneva, although there the impulse that Luther set was taken up in a particular way.[2] This is not meant to say that there had not been hymns in the vernacular before. Such hymns had existed in the Middle Ages, when they were sung at different occasions such as processions or pilgrimages, and sometimes, although not officially, and repeatedly forbidden, even at Mass. Luther himself had composed his first hymn in German a few months before the letter to Spalatin when the shock about the news of the first martyrdoms of the Reformation[3] found release in the creation

1. Georg Spalatin (1484–1545), secretary, father confessor, and preacher at the Wittenberg court.

2. Namely, in the form of the *Genevan Psalter*, restricted to the Psalms and other biblical hymns and to be performed only by human voice without the use of musical instruments.

3. Two young Augustinian friars from Antwerp had been burned at the marketplace of Brussels.

a   WA Br 3, nr. 698.

of the hymn "A New Song Here Shall Be Begun."[b] Thus the Wittenberg professor whose linguistic mastery had already expressed itself in different genres of prose at the age of forty discovered his poetic vein. Three other hymns followed soon, among them "Dear Christians, Let Us Now Rejoice"[c] and "From Trouble Deep I Cry to Thee."[d] What was new, however, in the letter to Spalatin was that now Luther started a project of planned production of hymns in the vernacular. The reason for this unprecedented step was the stage of the liturgical development reached at Wittenberg by December 1523.

Although in the multicolored early Reformation liturgical pieces and orders in the vernacular had already appeared at some places,[4] Luther's first liturgy, the *Formula missae et communionis*,[e] published in December 1523, which was in many respects still a transitional formulation, was in Latin. Nevertheless, precisely this formulary contained a remark that, nearly in passing, set in motion a truly revolutionary development: the elevation of the vernacular hymn to an integral part of the Sunday Mass. Luther wrote that the Latin parts of the Mass sung by the choir could be followed or regularly replaced and should in the end be wholly supplanted by German hymns sung by the congregation. But, of course, such a vision required a large and diverse stock of vernacular hymns. That is why Luther in the same month wrote his letter asking for new German hymns. He named a few medieval examples and enclosed his "From Trouble Deep" as a model. This hymn was composed on the basis of a psalm, and indeed, the first hymns Luther required were such "psalm hymns" (*Psalmlieder*), and thus a new poetic genre was born. He added a few principles on how the hoped-for poets should proceed. They should not stick to the biblical wording. The biblical message must come through clearly and faithfully, but the poets should feel free to render it in their own German ways, with words that were common, but not vulgar; easy, but also to the point.

Luther's letter was sent not only to Spalatin, but at the same time to several colleagues, for, in order to fulfill the pressing need, he said that "we are looking everywhere for poets." Since

4. The most important was the *Deutsch Kirchenamt* by Thomas Müntzer (1489–1525), from 1523.

---

b See below, hymn 1, pp. 109 and 122.

c See below, hymn 2, pp. 110 and 126.

d See below, hymn 4, pp. 113 and 131.

e WA 12:205–20; LW 53:19–40.

he was not successful with his call, he had to do the work himself and did so immediately. In the following year, 1524, two-thirds of all his hymns were composed. These hymns, together with a few more written by others, were enough to allow the publication of the *Deutsche Messe* (German Mass)[f] in 1525/26, whose *ordinarium* is completely in the vernacular and which requires that all hymns including—as soon as possible—those to be sung *de tempore* were in German as well. Thus, full and active participation of the congregation in the service— hearing, understanding, praying, singing—was possible, the liturgical realization of the priesthood of all believers.

The year 1524 was thus the birth year of the Protestant hymn. In the same year appeared, besides a host of broadsheets with individual hymns, the first Lutheran hymnals, among them one for choirs with four voices set by Luther's musical advisor, Johann Walter.[5] Six hymnals,[g] growing in size from year to year, were published under Luther's personal supervision. He sought to control the content and the form of his own hymns in an age that knew no copyright laws. Many more hymnals were published across and beyond the Holy Roman Empire without his participation, altogether about a hundred Lutheran hymnals before his death.[6] This number mirrors the enormous popularity of the hymns written by Luther and his followers. As sources of the time show, they were widely sung inside and outside of churches, in services, in families, in open places, and at work. Thus, they came to be one of the most effective means of propagating the message of the Reformation and, practically from the beginning, one of the distinguishing marks of those congregations that followed the Wittenberg Reformation.[h]

In many cases Luther used existing hymns, ancient and medieval, in German and in Latin, which he reshaped, enlarged,

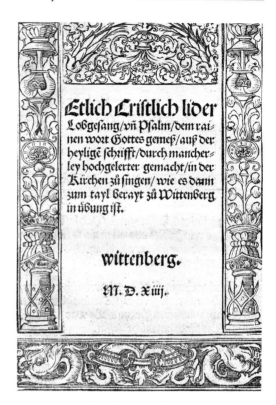

The title page of the *Achtliederbuch*, the first German hymnal, published in 1524. It contained only eight hymns, four of which were written by Luther. The title in German is *Etlich Cristlich lider Lobgesang un Psalm dem rainen wort Gottes . . . zü Wittenberg in übung ist.*

5. Johann Walter (1496–1570), court musician in Wittenberg and Dresden, founder of the first congregational choir and thus the father of this new institution, which was to become one of the trademarks of the Lutheran church.

6. The enormity of this number is made plain in the introduction to Ulrich S. Leupold's Luther's hymns in LW

---

f *German Mass*, WA 19:72–113; LW 53:61–90; TAL 3:131–61.

g Cf. LW 53:191–94 (WA 35:317–33).

h See, for example, Christopher Boyd Brown, *Singing the Gospel: Lutheran Hymns and the Success of the Reformation* (Cambridge: Harvard University Press, 2005).

53:194 n.25: "In comparison, the English Reformation produced thirteen hymnals up to the end of the sixteenth century (Scottish hymnals included)."

and, in the latter case, translated. In other cases, as mentioned above, he made biblical texts into German hymns—in the first place, the Psalms. A few times he created hymns out of catechetical material, and not rarely he composed a hymn without a preexisting textual base. In every case his hymns were songs of the Christian faith, which expressed itself in them. They displayed the Christian's joys and hopes before God and humans, not in a modern way oriented at subjective emotions, but as echoes of the gospel message that they wanted to convey. Since the hymns were meant for the people in the pews, Luther chose—among the different options present in the poetic usage of a time before literary standardization of vernacular poetry—a simple style with short sentences, containing mainly nouns and verbs with few adjectives and adverbs, devoid of abstract words and rich in images. He used rhymes, but in the rather loose way common at the time, and he applied alliteration.

For many hymns Luther used music that was already available. He reshaped tunes, especially in order to adapt their rhythms and melodic lines to the texts he had composed. He tended to choose rather strong, at times even complicated, rhythmical structures. The melodic lines followed the traditional church modes, although some already pointed to the new major and minor scales that were being advanced in his time. In all this, not only his musical talent, but also the solid musical education, both practical and theoretical, he had received at school and university bore fruit. Luther, who loved to sing in his spare time with friends and family, considered music to be God's second best gift after theology. Moreover, he attributed to music itself a theological role. Not only did he consider singing hymns a vital realization of the priesthood of all believers, he also underlined that music, especially sung music, possesses a particular affinity with the gospel: the gospel is not a written, bookish thing; neither is it something merely inward and spiritual, but it is a "living voice," vocal and audible, in need of advancement through speaking and singing. It is "a good message, good news, a good report, a good shout, which one sings and tells with gladness."[i] Therefore,

---

i   LW 35:358. In the German "*gute botschafft, gute meher, gutte newzeytung, gutt geschrey, davon man singet, saget und frolich ist*" (WA DB 6:2,24). See how the good news of Christ's birth is to be spoken and sung, as the first stanza of "From Heaven on High I Come to You" states.

Luther criticized "spiritualists" who rejected church music: they despised the word of God in its external, audible mode, as sound, just as they despised it in its tasteable and visible mode, as sacraments, in favor of a purely spiritual understanding. Yet, in fact, the word by definition has an external, sensual nature, and for its audible mode this becomes apparent in the strongest and most beautiful way when it is sung.[j]

The Hymn Texts

1. A New Song Here Shall Be Begun (1523)[k]

With "A New Song" Luther's activity as a hymnwriter began, both in terms of text and melody, and the hymnological history of the Reformation began.[l] Obviously, an emotion as deep as the one triggered by the news of the martyrdom of two young friars from his own order[7] in the Netherlands was needed to make him express himself for the first time in poetic form. After all, the excommunication and the Edict of Worms that had been pronounced upon him and all his followers in 1521 stipulated the same fate for him. The protection of his prince, Frederick the Wise,[8] spared Luther a similar death. Yet in the Netherlands, under the immediate rule of the Habsburgs, who suppressed the Reformation with all their might, there was no way out for adherents of the Reformation, as the two young Augustinian hermits and a third one to follow later[9] had to experience.

For his song Luther chose the genre of folk ballad. This was the poetic form for telling stories of heroes and villains, of battles and victories, of love and death. Ballads were dramatic and gripping: their language was simple, but colorful; their melodies, to be accompanied by the lute or another string instrument, were easy. Such ballads were sung by wandering bards in marketplaces and in taverns; they were printed and sold on broadsheets and quickly disseminated. Thus, the story they told

7. That is, the Augustinian Order. Friars Jahn van den Esschen and Henry Vos refused to renounce Lutheran teachings and were executed in Brussels on July 1, 1523.

8. Frederick the Wise (1483–1525), elector of Saxony.

9. Lambert Thorn, who was imprisoned and executed only later in 1528.

---

j   See Dorothea Wendebourg, "Luther und das Kirchenlied im lutherischen Protestantismus," *Berliner Theologische Zeitschrift* 28. Jahrgang (2011), Heft 2: 44–59.

k   LW 53:211–16.

l   See above pp. 105–6.

made its way across the country. Indeed, Luther wanted the story of the two Augustinian friars to be known everywhere. It was a story of faithfulness in extremity, of simplicity in the midst of cunning, of victory over cruelty and death. Whoever listened to it or sang it could not but take sides with the two martyred "boys." Indeed, that was, besides honoring the two, the scope of the song. For taking sides with them implied taking sides with the cause for which they had died, the gospel itself as it was proclaimed anew by the Reformation. At the dramatic climax of the ballad, immediately before the "two huge great fires" are kindled for the young friars, the message of the Reformation for which they are going to be burnt is explicitly cited (stanza 7): they have to read "a paper small" on which their "fault" is written, namely, that they trusted "solely in God"—the bell is rung for the Reformation catchword "alone." In fact, their "ashes" will spread this message, as the blood of the martyrs has from the beginning of Christianity been the seed of the church. Moreover, the "reappearance" of the word of God testified to by the two faithful "boys" points further, toward the ultimate goal (stanza 12): it announces the "summer" that will finally end the long winter of spiritual cold, the longed-for second coming of Christ (cf. Matt. 24:32). Thus, the ballad closes with an expression of eschatological hope and joy.

2. Dear Christians, Let Us Now Rejoice (1523)[m]

"Dear Christians," which followed soon after "A New Song," is also a kind of ballad that pictures a dramatic story of life and death and final victory. But this time the story is not a historical event in Luther's time but the divine history behind the scenes that makes victories like the martyrdoms in Brussels possible: the struggle between God and the devil over sinful humans, or, from the human perspective, the rescue from the devil's dominion and from death to the joyful life of the justified Christian. The narrative is retrospective, told from the point of the happy result that the poet and singer shares with all those "dear Christians" who are invited to sing with him (stanza 1). Yet the poet tells it and invites everybody to tell it in the first person singular, for the divine story becomes existential reality in faith for

m LW 53:217–20.

every Christian individually. The nine stanzas (2–10), which contain the struggle-and-rescue story, present the basic insights of Luther's theology: the first act looks back at the singer's being lost under devil, death, and sin, his lack of good works and the bondage of his will, his anguish and despair. The second act presents God's decision, rooted alone in the mercy of his "father-heart," to rescue the captive, and his request that his own son, his "heart's most precious crown," "go down," kill death, and let the captive live with him. The third act deals with the Son's obedient fulfillment of his Father's command. It alludes to the incarnation, the Christmas event ("a maiden mother"), and indicates that its purpose was to "catch the devil."

One would expect the narrative to continue in the same way—with the cross, resurrection, and so forth. But it does not; it stops here, at the point of the Son's having come "down to me"—in other words, the narrative stops at Christmas. Instead of continuing to report on the Son's story, the hymn now lets the Son himself talk: the whole rest of the hymn (stanzas 7–10) is one long speech of the Son incarnate to the captive, to the "me" for whom he just "came down." He tells the captive to "hold by" him, because he is now going to fight his battle. "For I am thine and thou art mine, and my place also shall be thine" (stanza 7)—the ancient nuptial formula, which reminds the reader of the image of the "Happy Exchange" (*fröhlicher Wechsel und Tausch*), about which Luther wrote in his famous treatise *The Freedom of a Christian*." As the Son has taken on the captive's existence in the incarnation, now the captive is encouraged to make the Son's existence his own. Because of this exchange the Son will die the captive's bloody death, and the captive in turn will profit from the victorious Son's eternal life with God, to be experienced on earth through the gift of the Holy Spirit. All these consequences of the *fröhlicher Wechsel* appear as part of the Son's speech and therefore in the future tense (stanzas 8 and 9). With this linguistic trick Luther does not want to give the impression that Christ's death, resurrection, and the rest had not yet happened. Rather, he underlines that what once has happened aims at becoming the basis and sense of the Christian's life today: such uniting of Christ and the Christian and thereby also of Christ's fate and the Christian's life takes place when the gospel becomes audible as Christ's own

n LW 31:333–77; TAL 1:467–538.

word spoken to a hearer and when the hearer "cleaves" to this word and thus "holds by" him who spoke it. It is this intricate relationship between Christ and the human, between Christ's story and human presence that is not simply the content of the hymn "Dear Christians," but which is acted out poetically in it.

"Dear Christians" is Luther's most theologically and hermeneutically refined hymn. One could say it is *the* hymn of the Reformation. No wonder that in the final stanza Christ strongly exhorts the singer to act and teach accordingly and to beware of corruptions of the gospel. Possibly because of its programmatic significance, "Dear Christians," included in Lutheran hymnals from the beginning, was circulated with three different tunes, one by Luther himself and two older ones that might have been proposed because they are easier to sing. Luther's own tune is bold in its intervals and melodic line, thus a congenial musical translation of his words.

3. From Heaven on High I Come to You (1535)°

Like "A New Song" and "Dear Christians," this hymn is also one of Luther's free compositions, both in regard to text and tune, with no earlier textual or melodic base. Yet it does not come from the early, groundbreaking years of the Reformation, but from a later period of Luther's life when he did not often write hymns. In the first editions it carries the title "A Childrens' Song"—and that is indeed what it is. Some interpreters claim that Luther, who by now was a father of several children, wrote this Christmas hymn for them. Originally, it came with a melody already in use, before Luther composed his own that begins, as he loved, with a high note and is particularly fitting for the movement of the angel who descends "from heaven on high" to proclaim the birth of Christ.

The setting of the hymn is the biblical story of the angels' appearance before the shepherds (Luke 2:9-16). The stanzas obviously reflect the reenactment of this scene in popular Nativity plays: the message of the angel, the conversation of the shepherds, their walk to the manger in which the congregation joins. Yet the hymn deviates from this pattern in a peculiar way. Mary and Joseph do not appear, only the child, for the hymn concen-

---

o LW 53:289–91.

trates completely on the relationship of the person who sings it and the Christ child. In fact, the second half of the hymn (stanzas 8–14) consists only in one long prayer addressed to the child. It is a prayer of welcome to the newborn Christ, who comes into a miserable environment not fitting to the "Lord, the maker of us all," as Luther specifies in a series of traditional rhetorical contrasts (stanzas 8, 9, 11). The scope of this welcome, however, is not the child's lying down in the manger. The bed in which he is asked to take his place is the praying person's heart. As in "Dear Christians," the Christ story must become the Christian's own story. Luther indicates how that will happen: contrary to what is normal, this child is asked to "make" himself "a soft, white little bed" (stanza 13). In other words, the initiative is Christ's; he makes the believer's heart his cradle—he awakens the believer's faith in him. In the imagery of the Christmas story, such faith is the rocking of the child in the cradle-heart that cannot but be accompanied by the song of "lullaby" (stanza 14).

4. From Trouble Deep I Cry to Thee (1523)[p]

"From Trouble Deep" was one of Luther's earliest hymns.[q] Yet, contrary to the three hymns presented so far, it is not a free composition but a poetic reshaping of a much older poem, Psalm 130. With it started a new genre and the long series of psalm hymns in the Lutheran, the Reformed, and other Protestant traditions. From early on "From Trouble Deep" was published with different melodies, some taken from other hymns. Two of them belong specifically to this hymn, one in C major and one in the Phrygian mode, the latter by Luther himself.

If one wanted to create vernacular hymns, it was obvious that one would have recourse to the hymn-book of the Bible itself, the psalter. This hymnal had provided daily sustenance for the former monk Luther. Of all the parts of the Bible, none other was treated by the Wittenberg professor more often

A setting of "Aus tiefer Not schrei ich zu dir" ("From Deep Trouble I Cry to Thee") printed in the Erfurt *Enchiridion* (1524)

---

p   LW 53:221–24.

q   See above, p. 106.

than the psalter and to no other did he turn more frequently for personal consolation. It was understood that he, like the tradition before him and his Christian contemporaries, read, interpreted, and sang the psalter as a Christian book that spoke of Christ and wanted to strengthen and gladden Christian believers. This was so much a matter of fact that in the Christian use of the Psalms the name Christ did not even have to be spelled out. Such is the case in "From Trouble Deep." In the form of an urgent prayer it expresses the central insight of the Reformation that is enclosed in the formulas "alone through grace" and "alone by faith." As the negative background the hymn depicts the "trouble deep" of sin and unrighteousness, the impossibility to produce "good works" and rely on "my deserts."[10] The only way out is the gracious word of God on which the sinner can rely. This decisive message is strategically placed in the third stanza, that is, in the center of the hymn. And it is presented in a way that implies a specific understanding. Whereas the psalmist simply says that he hopes for God's word, the hymn characterizes this word as the one in which God "promises" divine grace—"promise" being a key word for the gospel of Jesus Christ. Consequently, those whom the singer calls to put their trust upon this divine word are the "Israel . . . born of [the] Holy Ghost" (stanza 4). The God who will finally redeem them is the Good Shepherd (stanza 5). With this image before him, the Christian singer could not but think of the Good Shepherd from John 10, Jesus Christ.

5. A Mighty Fortress Is Our God (1528/29)[r]

This hymn is the most famous of Luther's seven psalm hymns, if not of all his hymns; its original title was simply "The 46th Psalm," *Deus noster refugium et virtus*[s]—the first words of Psalm 46. We do not know when it was written, but it was published in 1529. The melody, which in its flow and rhythm corresponds perfectly to the poetic text, can safely be considered also to be from Luther's hand.

As much as this hymn is based on Psalm 46, Luther uses the biblical text with great liberty. Only a few words are taken from

10. "Deserts" here means "what I deserve."

---

r   LW 53:283–85.

s   "God is our refuge and strength" (RSV).

the psalm; the imagery of his hymn is different, as is the existential situation in which it is set. However, the theme of both psalm and hymn is identical: both praise God as the singer's only refuge and strength, and for both God proves to be this by destroying the singer's powerful enemies. Yet, whereas the psalmist thinks of pagan peoples attacking the city of Jerusalem, whose military might is countered by God, Luther's hymn speaks of the last battle that "the world's prince," the devil, wages against the faithful before the end of the world. In this final assault of the *"alt böse feind"* (the old evil foe) the faithful have but God as their "fortress" in which to take refuge (stanza 1). What they can do themselves is "all in vain"; the only one—once again the motif of "grace alone"—who can sucessfully "fight for" them is God, the "Lord of hosts" (Lord Zebaoth). The latter conviction is already expressed by the psalm. What is new in Luther's hymn is the identification of this "Lord of hosts": he is Jesus Christ, at the same time human ("the right man") and divine ("God but him is none"), and thus sure "to win the battle" (stanza 2). To this "Lord of hosts," who is obviously not a man of military might, corresponds a specific weapon: the "word," the gospel (stanza 3). Through the "word" alone—the German original reads "one little word" in order to underline the contrast between the apparent powerlessness and the actual power of this means—Jesus Christ overturns "the world's prince" and brings about his "kingdom." Through the same word he fortifies the faithful with his Spirit and protects them (stanza 4). The last stanza hints at the specific context in which the hymn expresses its confidence: the menace coming from the enemies of the Reformation who do not want to "allow the word to stand," and possibly the threat of martyrdom. Those who have Christ as their fortress will not lose the kingdom of God even when they lose everything else.

6. Our Father Who in Heaven Art (1539)[t]

Psalms are not the only biblical pieces Luther made into hymns. He also did so with other texts, for instance, the Song of Simeon (Luke 2:29-32) (*Nunc dimittis*), the vision of Isaiah (Isa. 6:1-4), the Ten Commandments, and the Lord's Prayer ("Our Father"). The latter two were at the same time part of his versification of

t   LW 53:295-98.

the *Small Catechism*, whose "Main Parts" (*Hauptstücke*)—Ten Commandments, Apostles' Creed, Lord's Prayer, Baptism, and Lord's Supper*—were all presented in the form of hymns. Thus, they not only could be meditated upon in the textual form of the *Small Catechism*, but also be committed to memory and understanding through singing. The hymn "Our Father" is one of the few for which Luther's handwritten draft, both of text and music, is extant. The text was, however, printed with another melody, taken from the hymnal of the Bohemian Brethren and adapted to the text. Since this happened under Luther's eyes it might be that he was not satisfied with his own music and even did the adaptation of the Bohemian melody himself. The hymn has always been used with this latter melody.

The structure of the hymn closely follows that of the Lord's Prayer. Each of the seven petitions has its own stanza that always opens with the biblical words and continues with an interpretation of the petition. What is requested is in each case given a broader perspective than the literal meaning would suggest. These interpretations obviously mirror the respective passages of Luther's catechisms. The petition stanzas are framed by one that meditates on the first line of the prayer, its address "Our Father," which makes all those who pray and sing this prayer equally his children, and one that is dedicated to the final "Amen." The implicit topic of this last stanza is the notion through "the word alone—by faith alone," for it is stressed that the basis for genuine praying and genuinely saying "Amen!" is faith that trusts solely in the word of God.

7. All Praise to Thee, O Jesus Christ (1523/4)ᵛ

The first stanza of this Christmas hymn is a medieval song that dates at the latest from the fourteenth century. The "*Kyrioleis*" at the end marks it as a "*Leise*," that is, a stanza that developed from a vernacular acclamation to a Latin sequence.[11] "*Kyrioeleis*" ("Lord, have mercy!") was the closing word of such a *Leise*. The melody, at least in its general line, most probably was also medieval.

11. A sequence is an elaborate liturgical piece sung in the Mass on special feast days by the choir before the reading of the Gospel.

---

u   See below, hymn 10, pp. 120 and 144.

v   LW 53:240–41.

Luther took over this *Leise*, as he did in several other cases,[w] and added six new stanzas of his own. In the first stanza itself he made only one significant change: whereas the medieval version praised Christ because he is born "today," Luther's version praises him because he is born "man," thus shifting the accent from the liturgical remembrance of the Bethlehem event to its theological depth: the incarnation. What is immediately striking, however, is the change in the rhetorical direction between the first and the new stanzas: the first stanza is a prayer of praise directed to Jesus Christ who was "born as a human." The following six stanzas proclaim this event and therefore speak about him in the third person. Why this proclamation follows—and why Luther added his stanzas to the medieval one—as well as how it takes place is expressed in the finale (stanza 7): the fact of the incarnation that is celebrated in the first stanza as such has to be communicated and appropriated as a deed of "great love" performed by the Son of God "for us." Only if the event of Bethlehem is seen in this relational perspective[12] does "Christendom" have a reason for its Christmas joy and praise. Stanzas 2 and 3 describe the Son's deed of love by depicting the contrast between his divine majesty and the lowliness of the human existence he took upon himself—the same rhetorical strategy as in the Christmas hymn "From Heaven on High." Stanzas 4 through 6 point out what this step of loving condescension—described in three different images as the coming of light into darkness, of a noble guest into a miserable world, and of a rich one into poverty—means "for us": to become children of light, royal heirs, and rich inhabitants of heaven like the angels, a dense web of biblical allusions drawing on verses like John 1:4-9; 12:36; Rom. 8:17; 1 Thess. 5:5; Titus 3:7; 2 Cor. 8:9; and Heb. 12:22.

12. Cf. "From Heaven on High" (hymn 3 above, pp. 112–13), where this same scope of putting the Christmas event in a relational perspective is reached in another way: not in the form of proclamation of Christ's love, but through prayer to the child for faith in his love.

8. Death Held Our Lord in Prison (1524)[x]

The history of this hymn is complicated, as its original title, "The Song of Praise 'Christ Is Arisen,' amended," indicates. "Christ Is Arisen" is a medieval Easter *Leise*, one of the oldest German vernacular hymns. Luther loved it dearly and included it in 1529 among the hymns to be sung in the congregations

w   See below, hymn 8, pp. 117 and 139.
x   LW 53:255–57.

of the Reformation.*y* "Amended" therefore does not imply that this hymn in his eyes needed correction of faults. Luther, rather, thought the medieval hymn needed theological deepening. More precisely, as in his Christmas hymns he wanted to expose what the underlying Gospel story, in this case the event that "Christ was arisen," means for the believers who sing about it. To this end he presented the *Leise* in a new form (stanza 1) and added six stanzas of his own, for one of which, the central stanza 4, he made use of another medieval piece, the Latin sequence "Praise to the Paschal Victim" (*Victimae paschali laudes*), which had once given occasion for the birth of "Christ Is Arisen" as its acclamation. For the melody of his hymn Luther also took this sequence as its base, in addition to the music of "Christ Is Arisen," which had itself already been dependent on the melody of the sequence.

The first stanza introduces the theme "Christ Is Arisen" in the wake of the *Leise*. Yet several significant changes foreshadow what follows. Luther not only drops the *Kyrioleis*, but he also underlines the purpose of what happened to Christ "for us," the bestowal of forgiveness and life. In accordance with this two-dimensional aim, Christ's resurrection itself has a reverse side, his death, which needs to be addressed. In fact, the hymn "Death Held Our Lord" could just as well be taken for a Good Friday hymn; not accidentally, Luther wrote no hymn on Christ's passion and crucifixion. On the basis of Rom. 4:25, stanza 1 first speaks about Christ's death for the sake of "our sins" before it refers to his resurrection for the sake of our "life." The following six stanzas unfold this short Pauline formula as a dramatic story. The Good Friday/Easter event is told in a ballad of liberation. Thus, there is close affinity between "Death Held Our Lord" and "Dear Christians, Let Us Now Rejoice."*z* The latter hymn tells the liberation drama in the perspective of the individual believer's justification, whereas the Easter hymn presents it as a revolution that happened once and for all (stanzas 2–4) and then speaks about the believer's involvement in a second unit (stanzas 5–7). The drama evolves in four acts: the life of the sons of men under the captivity of death (stanza 2), the victorious interference of Christ (stanza 3), the duel between death and life (stanza 4), and the banquet of the liberated (stanzas 5–7). The

---

y   Namely in the *Klugsche Gesangbuch*, from 1529.

z   See above, hymn 2, p. 110.

center is stanza 4 which, on the basis of Hos. 13:14, depicts the Easter event as one death "eating" the other. Even more drastic is the image presented in stanza 5: Christ as the paschal lamb which on the cross was "roasted" in the passion of God's love—a blending of Exod. 12:3-8 and Luther's image of God being an "oven of love."[a] This image opens up to the dimension of personal appropriation of God's love: appropriation through communion in the Lord's Supper, which is hinted at indirectly by way of the clue "lamb," and appropriation through faith, which is addressed directly by saying that faith "holds" Christ's blood "before Death's eyes" (cf. Exod. 12:7), that is, it holds the forgiveness achieved by Christ against the debt brought on by sin (cf. stanza 3). Thus, the word comes into play that is the goal of the last stanza and thus of the whole hymn, faith. The joy of Easter (stanza 6) springs from the faith that is fed by the crucified and risen Christ alone (stanza 7).

9. Come, Holy Ghost Lord and God (1524)[b]

All three of Luther's hymns for Pentecost were based on medieval hymns, one of them Latin and two in the vernacular. The first stanza of "Come, Holy Ghost" was likely a fifteenth-century German translation of an eleventh- or twelfth-century Latin antiphon. Luther held it in the highest esteem; indeed, he said about it: "'Come, Holy Ghost Lord and God etc.' is a hymn composed by the Holy Ghost about himself, both words and music."[c] Nevertheless, since 1529 his hymn bore the title "'Come, Holy Ghost . . .' amended by Martin Luther." Again, "amended" is not to be understood in the sense of correction, but of theological deepening. For this purpose Luther added two stanzas of his own that interpret the medieval piece in a specific way. The melody was also taken over from the medieval stanza, though slightly simplified.

After the first stanza has prayed to the Holy Spirit to fill the hearts of the believers whom the Spirit's light has united in one faith with God's grace and kindle their love, the second stanza makes this desire specific by introducing the notions of word and

---

a   See WA 36:425, 1/13.

b   LW 53:265–67.

c   WA TR 4, nr. 4478.

Ertödt vns durch deyn gute/erweck vns durch
deyn gnadt. Den alten menschen krencke/das der
new leben mag. Wol hie auff dyser erden/den syn
vnd all begerden/vnd dancken han zu dir.

Das Lied S. Johannes hus gebessert.

Jhesus Christus vnser heylandt/der von vns den
zorn Gottis wand/durch das bitter leyden seyn/
halff er aus der helle peyn.
Das wir nymmer des vergessen/gab er vns seyn
leib zu essen/verborgen ym brott so klein/vnnd zu
trincken seyn blut ym weyn.
Wer sych zum tisch wil machen/der hab woll

This version of "Jesus Christ, Our God and Savior" appeared with the title "The Hymn of St. John Hus" in 1524.

---

13. Jan Hus (1369–1415), a Czech theologian who was burned at the Council of Konstanz, was considered to be such a "forerunner" because of parallels with the Reformation in his demands for reform of the church.

faith. Asking for the Spirit's light means asking for illumination through the divine word, the gospel, which enables the believer to recognize God in the right way, as loving Father instead of demanding judge, and to trust in Christ alone with true faith. The third stanza proceeds from faith to life in faith that is a life in the service of God. Such service in a world of troubles resembles the service of a knight for which the Spirit is asked to send comfort, joy, and strength.

10. Jesus Christ, Our God and Savior (1524)[d]

This hymn on the Lord's Supper again presents itself as an "amendment": it bears the title "The Hymn of St. John Hus, amended." In fact, it was only attributed to the Bohemian "forerunner" of the Reformation who had been martyred for his criticism of the church and is therefore here called a saint.[13] Luther used material from this Latin hymn and revised it as he did other medieval hymns. Here, however, his revision went considerably further than in the previous cases. Luther undertook not only a theological deepening, but a complete theological revision of the medieval hymn, which can only in parts, mainly in stanza 1, still be recognized. The music is also medieval, but did not originally belong to this hymn.

The "Hymn of St. John Hus" praised the wondrous real presence of Christ's body and blood in the sacrament. In his revision, Luther also speaks about this real presence (stanza 2). But in his perspective, Christ's sacramental presence is not a static reality but part of a movement of self-giving: what makes the presence of Christ's body and blood remarkable is that they are given to eat and to drink. Thus, the sacrament is an element in the overarching movement of grace that the Christ story is in itself (stanza 1) and which is "unforgettably" remembered by receiving the sacrament (stanza 2). After the first two stanzas have delineated this movement of grace from the cross to the distribution of the sacrament and have characterized it as a movement for all of "us," the following eight stanzas

d   LW 53:249–51.

look at the other pole of the movement, the communicant. Or, more precisely, they speak to him and do so in the second person singular. In stanzas 4 and 5 it is even Christ himself who speaks to the communicants and tells them what he is giving them here and now at the sacramental table. The hymn thus becomes a personal proclamation of the gospel. On the part of the communicant who hears and eats there is only one attitude that corresponds to this divine communication: faith—faith which is aware of one's own destitution (stanza 6) and inability to change the situation (stanza 8), and which expects everything from Christ (stanzas 7 and 9). Who comes to the table with such faith is well "prepareth" and "worthy" to receive the body of Christ (stanza 3; cf. 1 Cor. 11:27-29). The hymn closes with a reminder that faith is not idle. The love of God received by the communicant cannot but bring forth fruit, that is, works of love for one's neighbor (stanza 10).

14. The hymn texts in this volume are based primarily on the translation in LW 53 by George MacDonald, revised by Ulrich S. Leupold. According to the introduction of that volume, "faithfulness to the original wording, style, and meter seemed more important than a completely idiomatic English rendition" (LW 53:199). Further, Leupold states the LW edition "would like to represent Luther's hymns in an English form that is as close as possible to the original German text and at the same time singable to the original melodies" (LW 53:201). Some changes to the hymn texts have been made in this current edition, but they are not specifically noted.

SELECTED HYMNS [14]

Hymn 1: "A New Song Here Shall Be Begun"

15. Walter's Wittenberg hymnal of 1524 and most later hymnals have the final cadence lead to the dominant instead of the tonic.

so rich-ly hath a-dorn-ed.

e   See n. 3, p. 105 and n. 7, p. 109.

2. The first right fitly John[16] was named,
So rich he in God's favor;
His brother, Henry[17]—one unblamed,
Whose salt lost not its savor.
From this world they are gone away,
The diadem they've gained;
Honest, like God's good children, they
For his word life disdained,
And have become his martyrs.

3. The old arch-fiend[18] did them immure[19]
With terrors did enwrap them.
He bade them God's dear Word abjure,
With cunning he would trap them:
From Louvain many sophists came,[20]
In their curst nets to take them,
By him are gathered to the game:
The Spirit fools doth make them—
They could get nothing by it.

4. Oh! they sang sweet, and they sang sour;
Oh! they tried every double;
The boys they stood firm as a tower,
And mocked the sophists' trouble.
The ancient foe it filled with hate
That he was thus defeated
By two such youngsters—he, so great!
His wrath grew sevenfold heated,
He laid his plans to burn them.

5. Their cloister-garments[21] off they tore,
Took off their consecrations;
All this the boys were ready for,
They said Amen with patience.
To God their Father they gave thanks
That they would soon be rescued
From Satan's scoffs and mumming pranks,
With which, in falsehood masked,
The world he so befooleth.

16. Jahn van den Esschen (see n. 7, p. 109, above).

17. Henry Vos (see n. 7, p. 109, above).

18. I.e., Satan (the devil).

19. I.e., imprison.

20. The Catholic University of Louvain was founded in 1425 in Louvain (Leuven), Belgium. The "sophists" refer to Scholastic scholars at the university who demanded that the Augustinian brothers recant their public support of Reformation teachings.

21. The tunics worn by the friars were torn from them to show that they were no longer part of the order.

6. Then gracious God did grant to them
To pass true priesthood's border,
And offer up themselves to him,
And enter Christ's own order,
Unto the world to die outright,
With falsehood made a schism,
And come to heaven all pure and white,
To monkery be the besom,*f*
And leave men's toys behind them.

7. They wrote for them a paper small,
And made them read it over;
The parts they showed them therein all
Which their belief did cover.
Their greatest fault was saying this:
"In God we should trust solely;
For man is always full of lies,
We should distrust him wholly":
So they must burn to ashes.

Augustinian friars Jahn
van den Esschen and Henry Vos
being burned at the stake

8. Two huge great fires they kindled then,
The boys they carried to them;
Great wonder seized on every man,
For with contempt they view them.
To all with joy they yielded quite,
With singing and God-praising;
The sophs had little appetite
For these new things so dazing.
Where God was thus apparent.

9. They now repent the deed of blame,*g*
Would gladly gloss it over;
They dare not glory in their shame,
The facts almost they cover.
In their hearts gnaweth infamy—

f   I.e., broom.
g   WA 35:414–15 prints this verse and the next one at the
end of the poem.

They to their friends deplore it;
The Spirit cannot silent be:
Good Abel's blood out-poured
Must still besmear Cain's forehead.[h]

10. Leave off their ashes never will;
Into all lands they scatter;
Stream, hole, ditch, grave—nought keeps them still
With shame the foe they spatter.
Those whom in life with bloody hand
He drove to silence double,
When dead, he them in every land,
In tongues of every people,
Must hear go gladly singing.

11. But yet their lies they will not leave,
To trim and dress the murther;[22]
The fable false which out they gave,
Shows conscience grinds them further.
God's holy ones, e'en after death,
They still go on belying;
They say that with their latest breath,
The boys, in act of dying,
Repented and recanted.[23]

12. Let them lie on for evermore—
No refuge so is reared;
For us, we thank our God therefore,
His word has reappeared.
Sure at the door is summer nigh,
The winter now is ended,
The tender flowers come out and spy;
His hand when once extended
Withdraws not till he's finished.

22. I.e., murder.

23. Their Louvain accusers falsely claim the boys recanted their support of Protestant teachings as they died.

[h] A reference to Cain's murder of Abel in Gen. 4:1-16.

Hymn 2: "Dear Christians, Let Us Now Rejoice"

Nürnberg 1523

1 {Dear Chris - tians, let us now re - joice,
  {That of good cheer and with one voice,

and dance in joy - ous meas - ure:
we sing in love and pleas - ure.

Of what to us our God hath shown,

and the sweet won - der he hath done;

full dear - ly hath he wrought it.

24. Some of the later hymnals substitute D for the F here to avoid the high note.

2. Forlorn and lost in death I lay,
A captive to the devil,
My sin lay heavy, night and day,
For I was born in evil.[25]
I fell but deeper for my strife,
There was no good in all my life,
For sin had all possessed me.[26]

25. Ps. 51:7.

26. Rom. 7:17.

3. My good works they were worthless quite,
A mock was all my merit;
My will did hate God's judging light,
To all good dead and buried.
E'en to despair my anguish bore,
That nought but death[27] lay me before;
To hell I fast was sinking.

27. Rom 7:24.

4. Then God felt sorry on his throne
To see such torment rend me;
His tender mercy he thought on,
His good help he would send me.
He turned to me his father-heart;
Ah! then was his no easy part,
For of his best it cost him.

5. To his dear Son he said: "Go down;
'Tis time to take compassion.
Go down, my heart's most precious crown,
Be the poor man's salvation.
Lift him from out sin's scorn and scath,[28]
And strangle for him cruel Death,
That he with thee live ever."

6. The Son he heard obediently,
And by a maiden mother,
Pure, tender—down he came to me,
For he would be my brother.
Secret he bore his strength enorm,
He went about in my poor form,
For he would catch the devil.

7. He said to me: "Hold thou by me,
Thy matters I will settle;
I give myself all up for thee,
And I will fight thy battle.
For I am thine, and thou art mine,
And my place also shall be thine;
The enemy shall not part us.

8. "He will as water shed my blood,
My life he from me reave[29] will;
All this I suffer for thy good—
To that with firm faith cleave well.
My life from death the day shall win,
My innocence shall bear thy sin,
So were you blest forever.

28. I.e., injury.

29. I.e., deprive of; seize, carry away.

9. "To heaven unto my Father high,
From this life I am going;
But there thy Master still am I,
My spirit on thee bestowing,
Whose comfort shall thy trouble quell,
Who thee shall teach to know me well,
And in the truth shall guide thee.

10. "What I have done, and what I've said,
Shall be thy doing, teaching,
So that God's kingdom may be spread—
All to his glory reaching.
Beware all doctrines man will do,
For that corrupts the treasure true;
With this last word I leave thee."

Hymn 3: "From Heaven on High
I Come to You"

Nürnberg 1523

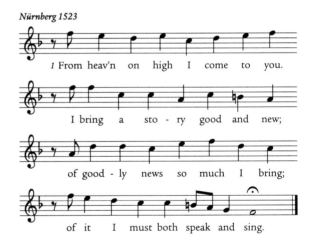

2. To you a child is come this morn,
A child of holy maiden born,
A little babe so sweet and mild—
Your joy and bliss shall be that child.

3. It is the Lord Christ, our own God.
He will ease you of all your load;
He will himself your Savior be,
And from all sinning set you free.

4. He brings you all the news so glad
Which God the Father ready had—
That you shall in his heavenly house
Live now and evermore with us.

5. Take heed then to the token sure,
The crib, the swaddling clothes so poor;
The infant you shall find laid there,
Who all the world doth hold and bear.

6. Hence let us all be gladsome then,
And with the shepherd folk go in
To see what God to us hath given,
With his dear Son endowed from heaven.

7. Take note, my heart; see there! look low:
What lies then in the manger so?
Whose is the lovely little child?
It is the darling Jesus-child.

8. Welcome thou art, thou noble guest,
With sinners who dost lie and rest,
And com'st into my misery!
How thankful I must ever be!

9. Ah Lord! the maker of us all!
How hast thou grown so poor and small,
That there thou liest on withered grass,
The supper of the ox and ass?

"The Nativity at Night," painted
by Geertgen tot Sint Jans, c. 1490

10. Were this world wider many fold,
And decked with gems and cloth of gold,
'Twere far too mean and narrow all,
To make for thee a cradle small.

11. The silk and velvet that are thine,
Are rough hay, linen not too fine,
Yet, as they were thy kingdom great,
Thou li'st[30] in them in royal state.

30. I.e., liest.

12. And this hath therefore pleased thee
That thou this truth mightst make me see—
How all earth's power, show, good, combined,
Helps none, nor comforts thy meek mind.

13. Dear little Jesus! in my shed,
Make thee a soft, white little bed,
And rest thee in my heart's low shrine,
That so my heart forget not thine.

14. And so I ever gladsome be,
Ready to dance and sing to thee
The lullaby thou lovest best,
With heart exulting in its guest.

15. Glory to God in highest heaven,
Who his own Son to us hath given!
For this the angel troop sings in
Such a new year with gladsome din.

Hymn 4: "From Trouble Deep I Cry to Thee"[31]

31. The first melody shown is F major. The second melody is Phrygian.

Strassburg 1525

32. *Ordnung des Herren Nachtmahl* (Strassburg, 1525) and later sources substitute E for F.

Erfurt 1524

2. With thee counts nothing but thy grace
To cover all our failing.
The best life cannot win the race,
Good works are unavailing.
Before thee no one glory can,
And so must tremble every man,
And live by thy grace only.

3. Hope therefore in my God will I,
On my deserts[33] not founding;
Upon him shall my heart rely,
All on his goodness grounding.
What his true Word doth promise me,
My comfort shall and refuge be;
That will I always wait for.

4. And though it last into the night,
And up until the morrow,
Yet shall my heart hope in God's might,
Nor doubt or take to worry.
Thus Israel must keep his post,
For he was born of [the] Holy Ghost,
And for his God must tarry.

5. Although our sin be great, God's grace
Is greater to relieve us;
His hand in helping nothing stays,
The hurt however grievous.
The Shepherd good alone is he,
Who will at last set Israel free,
From all and every trespass.

33. I.e., deserved rewards or punishments.

Hymn 5: "A Mighty Fortress Is Our God"

Klug 1533

1 { A might - y for - tress is our God,
{ he sets us free from ev - 'ry wrong

a good mail - coat and weap - on;
that wick - ed - ness would bring on.

The old knav - ish foe,[35] he

means ear - nest now; force and cun -

ning sly his hor - rid pol - i - cy,

on earth there's noth - ing like him.

34. In the first edition of Walter's hymnal that contains "Our God He Is a Castle Strong," the edition of 1544, Walter changed this figure.

35. I.e., Satan (the devil).

2. 'Tis all in vain, do what we can,
Our strength is soon dejected.
But he fights for us, the right man,
By God himself elected.
Ask'st thou who is this?
Jesus Christ it is,
Lord of Hosts alone,
And God but him is none,
So he must win the battle.

3. And did the world with devils swarm,
All gaping to devour us,
We will not fear the smallest harm,
Success is yet before us.
This world's prince accurst,
Let him rage his worst,
No hurt brings about;
His doom it is gone out,
One word can overturn him.

4. The word they must allow to stand,
Nor any thanks have for it;[i]
He is with us, at our right hand,
With all gifts of his spirit.
If they take our life,
Wealth, name, child, and wife—
Let everything go:
They have no profit so;
The kingdom ours remaineth.

Hymn 6: "Our Father Who in Heaven Art"

2. Hallowed be thy name, O Lord;
Help us keep pure thy holy word,
That we too may live holily,
And keep in thy name worthily.
Defend us, Lord, from lying lore;
Thy poor misguided folk restore.

3. Thy kingdom come now here below,
And after, up there, evermo'.
The Holy Ghost his temple hold
In us with graces manifold.
The devil's wrath and greatness strong,
Crush, that he do thy church no wrong.

---

i   Or: Nor any choice have in it.

Luther Ms.

1 Our Fa - ther who in hea - ven art,

who tell - est all of us, in heart

broth-ers to be and on thee call,

and wilt have prayer from us all,

grant that the mouth not on - ly pray,

[sic]

from deep - est heart, O help its way.

Schumann 1539

1 Our Fa - ther who in hea - ven art,

who tell - est all of us, in heart

broth - ers to be and on thee call,

and wilt have prayer from us all,

grant that the mouth not on - ly pray,

from deep - est heart, O help its way.

4. Thy will be done the same, Lord God,
On earth as in thy high abode;
In pain give patience for relief,
Obedience in love and grief;
All flesh and blood keep off and check
That 'gainst thy will makes a stiff neck.

5. Give us this day our daily bread,
And all that doth the body stead;
From strife and war, Lord, keep us free,
From sickness and from scarcity;
That we in happy peace may rest,
By care and greed all undistressed.

6. Forgive, Lord, all our trespasses,
That they no more may us distress,
As of our debtors we will let
Pass all the trespasses and debt.
To serve make us all ready be
In honest love and unity.

7. Into temptation lead us not.
E'en though the foe makes battle hot
Upon the right and the left hand,
Help us with vigor to withstand,
Firm in the faith, armed 'gainst a host
Through comfort of the Holy Ghost.

8. From all that's evil free thy sons—
The time, the days are wicked ones.
Deliver us from endless death;
Comfort us in our latest breath;
Grant us also a blessed end,
Our spirit take into thy hand.

9. Amen! that is, let this come true!
Strengthen our faith ever anew,
That we may never be in doubt
Of that we here have prayed about.
In thy name, trusting in thy word,
We blithely say Amen, O Lord.

Hymn 7: "All Praise to Thee, O Jesus Christ"

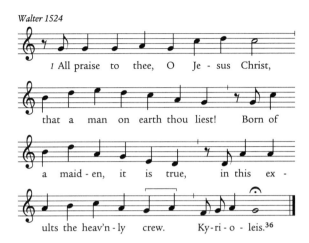

Walter 1524

1 All praise to thee, O Je - sus Christ,

that a man on earth thou liest! Born of

a maid - en, it is true, in this ex -

ults the heav'n - ly crew. Ky - ri - o - leis.[36]

36. *Kyrie eleison*, a common contraction in medieval sacred folk song.

2. The Father's only son begot
In the manger has his cot,
In our needy flesh and blood
Doth mask itself the endless good.
Kyrioleis.

3. Whom all the world could not enwrap,
Lieth he in Mary's lap;
A little child he now is grown,
Who everything upholds alone.
Kyrioleis.

4. Here the eternal light breaks through,
Gives the world a glory new;
It brightly shines amid the night,
And makes us children of the light.
Kyrioleis.

5. The Father's Son, God is his name,
In the world a guest became
He leads us from the vale of tears,
And in his palace makes us heirs.
Kyrioleis.

❡ Eyn deutſch hymnus oder Lobſang.

❡Gelobet ſeyſtu Jeſu Chriſt/ dz du menſch geboren biſt/von eyner jungfraw das iſt war/ des frewet ſych der engel ſchar/ Kyrioleys.

Des ewigen vaters eynig kind / ytz man ynn der krippen fynd/ Ijnｮonſer armes fleiſch vñ blut verkleydet ſych das ewig gut/ Kyrioleys.

Den aller welt kreyſſ nye beſchloſ der ligt ynn Maria ſchoſs Er iſt eyn kindlin worden klein/ der alle ding erhelt alleyn Kyrioleys.

Das ewig liecht gehet da herein/gibt der welt ein newen ſcheyn Es leucht wol mitten ynn der nacht/ vnd vns des liechtes kinder macht/ Kyrioleys.

Der ſon des vatters Gott von ard/ eyn gaſt ynn der welt ward. Vnnd furt vns aus dem yamer tal/er macht vns erben ynn ſeym ſaal/ Kyrioleys.

Er yſt auff erden kommẽ arm/ das er vnſer ſych erbarm. Vnd ynn dem hymel machet reych/ vnd ſeynen lieben Engeln gleich. Kyrioleys.

Das hat er alles vns gethan/ſeyn groſz lieb zu zeygen an . Des frew ſych all Chriſtenheyt/ vñ danck yhm des ynn ewigkeit/ Kyrioleys.

Martin Luther's *Weihnachtslied* (Christmas song)
"Gelobet seist du, Jesu Christ" as it appeared
in *Erfurter Enchiridion* (1524)

6. Poor to the earth he cometh thus,
Pity so to take on us,
And make us rich in heaven above,
And like the angels of his love.
Kyrioleis.

7. All this for us the Son did do,
his great love for us to show.
Let Christendom rejoice therefore,
And give him thanks for evermore.
Kyrioleis.

Hymn 8: "Death Held Our Lord in Prison"[37]

37. Two melodies are provided for this text.

Walter 1524

1 { Death held our Lord in pris - on   for sin
{ but   he hath up a - ris - en,   and brought

Erfurt 1524

1 { Death held our Lord in pris - on   for sin
{ but   he hath up a - ris - en,   and brought

that did un - do us;
our life back to us.   There-fore we must

that did un - do us;
our life back to us.   There-fore we must

glad-some be,   Ex-alt God and   thank - ful   be

glad-some be,   Ex - alt God and thank - ful be

and sing a - loud: Al - le - lu - ia! Al-le - lu - ia!

and sing a - loud: Al - le - lu - ia!

2. Death no one yet overcame—
All sons of men were helpless;
Sin for this was all to blame,
For no one yet was guiltless.
So Death came that early hour,
O'er us he took up his power,
And held us all in his kingdom. Alleluia!

3. Jesus Christ, God's only Son,
Into our place descending,
Away with all our sins hath done,
And therewith from Death rending
Right and might, made him a jape,[38]
Left him nothing but Death's shape:
His ancient sting—he has lost it. Alleluia!

4. That was a right wondrous strife
When Death in Life's grip wallowed:
Off victorious came Life,
Death he has quite upswallowed.
The Scripture has published that—
How one Death the other ate.
Thus Death is become a laughter. Alleluia!

5. Here is the true Paschal Lamb
On which we shall have feasted.
That was on the tree of shame
In flaming passion roasted
His blood on our doorpost lies;
Faith holds that before Death's eyes;
The smiting angel can do nought. Alleluia!

6. So we keep high feast of grace,
Hearty the joy and glee is
That shines on us from his face:
The sun himself, ah! he is,
Who, by his brightness divine,
His light in our hearts makes shine:
The night of our sins is over. Alleluia!

38. Something designed to arouse laughter.

The Resurrection by Lucas Cranach the Younger, 1558

7. We eat—and so we well fare—
Right Easter cakes sans leaven;
The old leaven shall not share
In the new word from heaven.
Christ himself will be the food,
Alone fill the soul with good:
Faith will live on nothing other. Alleluia!

Hymn 9: "Come, Holy Ghost Lord and God"

Erfurt 1524

1 Come, Ho - ly - Ghost Lord and God;

fill full with thine own gra - cious good

the faith - ful ones' heart, mind, de - sire;

in them light of thy love the fire.

O Lord, through thy light's flash - es fast,

In - to the faith thou gath - ered hast

the folk from ev - 'ry land and tongue.

This to thy praise, O our God, be sung.

Al - le - lu - ia, al - le - lu - ia.

2. Thou holy light, sure resort,
Shine on us your life-giving word.
Teach us to know our God aright
And call him Father with delight.
O Lord, protect us from strange lore,
That we may seek no masters more,

But Jesus with true faith solely,
And him with all our might trust wholly.
Alleluia, Alleluia.

3. Thou holy fire, comfort sweet,
Now help us, glad with cheer complete,
That in thy service nought shake us,
From thee let trouble ne'er take us.
Lord, by thy power us prepare,
And make the weak flesh strong to bear,
That as good knights we here with force
Through life and death to thee steer our course.
Alleluia, Alleluia.

A printing of Luther's
"Come, Holy Ghost Lord
and God" (Erfurt, 1524)

Hymn 10: "Jesus Christ, Our God and Savior"

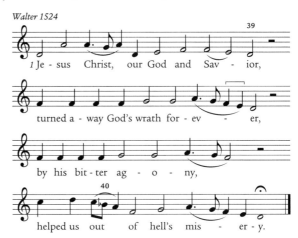

39. Most other hymnals have two quarter notes, F and E, in this place.

40. This slur appears in many different forms. For example, here are two variations:

Wittenberg 1524

Zwickau 1524, Klug 1533

2. That we never should forget it
Gave he us his flesh to eat it,
Hidden in this bit of bread,
And to drink gave he us his blood.

3. Whoso to this board repaireth,
Take good heed how he prepareth.
Who unworthy thither goes,
He not life then, just death he knows.

4. God the Father praise thou duly,
That he thee would feed so truly,
And for ill deeds by thee done
Unto death has he giv'n his Son.

5. Have this faith, and do not waver,
It is food for every craver
Who, his heart with sin opprest,
Can no more for its anguish rest.

6. Such a love and grace to get,
Seeks a heart with agony great.
Is it well with thee? take care,
Lest at last thou shouldst evil fare.

7. Lo, he saith himself, "Ye weary
Come to me and I will cheer ye;
Needless were the doctor's skill
To the souls that be strong and well.

8. "Hadst thou any claim to proffer,
Why for thee then should I suffer?
This table is not for thee,
If thou wilt set thine own self free."

9. If such faith thy heart possesses,
And the same thy mouth confesses,
Fit guest then thou art indeed,
And this food thine own soul will feed.

10. Fruit of faith therein be showing
That thou art to others loving;
To thy neighbor thou wilt do
As in love God hath done to you.

Ain Sermon
von dem gebeet vñ proces-
sion/in der Creützwochen
Mit ainer kurtzen außle-
gung des Vatter vnsers/
fürsich vnnd hindersich/
Doctor Martini Lu-
thers Augustiner
zů Wittemberg.

Historiated woodcut title page of 1519 printing
of Luther's *Sermon on Prayer and Procession
during Cross Week (Rogation Days)*

A Sermon on Prayer and Procession during Rogation Days

1519[1]

MARY JANE HAEMIG

INTRODUCTION

Martin Luther followed common late medieval practice in preaching on prayer during Rogation days.[a] Rogation days were the three days of prayer and procession between the fifth Sunday after Easter (Rogate) and Ascension; in 1519 these days were May 30 through June 1. The Gospel text for Rogate was John 16:23-30; this was usually used as an opportunity to preach on prayer. The emphasis continued in the following days, with the texts for Rogation being James 5:16-18 and Luke 11:5-13. Often sermons centered on "Ask, and it will be given you . . ." (Luke 11:9). In the late medieval era, it was also common to preach on the Lord's Prayer during Rogation days.[b]

The observance of Rogation days before Ascension has been traced to fifth-century Vienne, France.[c] Bishop Mamertus (d. c. 475) mandated a three-day fast and intercessory processions

1. The German title is *Ein Sermon von dem Gebet und Prozession in der Kreuzwoche*. *Kreuzwoche*—literally "cross week"—was the term used for the week of the "cross days," the three days before Ascension. Crosses were carried in the processions of these days, hence the name.

a See Paul Robinson, "Sermons on the Lord's Prayer and the Rogation Days in the Later Middle Ages," in Roy Hammerling, ed., *A History of Prayer: The First to the Fifteenth Century* (Leiden: Brill, 2008), 441–62.

b Ibid., 453: "Evidence from sermon collections suggests that by the late Middle Ages a sermon on the Lord's Prayer was a common, if not indispensable, part of the observance of the Rogation days."

before Ascension to ask God's blessings and deliverance from calamities afflicting the city. The Synod of Orleans prescribed this observance for all of Gaul in 511. It was not a part of Roman use until the early ninth century. Rome had developed its own festival of prayer, a Major Litany associated with the festival of St. Mark on April 25. The days before Ascension were often called the Minor Litany to distinguish them from the April 25 observance. These days before Ascension became an occasion in medieval Europe not only for asking for protection from adversity but also to pray for the crops, asking God to grant a good harvest. Elaborate processions around fields and parishes often accompanied Rogation observances.[d] After the introduction of the Reformation, many Lutheran areas continued to observe these days, particularly as an occasion for prayer for crops and general well-being.[e]

Not long after the Rogation days of 1519, Luther participated in the Leipzig Debate in July 1519. While the focus there was on some of the great theological issues of the day, debated in a manner worthy of university professors, the focus in this sermon is quite different. This work was part of Luther's concerted effort in the early years of the Reformation movement to shape a new evangelical piety for all people, particularly in regard to prayer. This piety was based on Luther's Reformation breakthrough,

c   See ibid., 441–42. Also see Adolf Adam, *The Liturgical Year: Its History and Its Meaning after the Reform of the Liturgy*, trans. Matthew J. O'Connell (New York: Pueblo, 1981), 190–92.

d   See Emil Joseph Lengeling, "Die Bittprozessionen des Domkapitels und der Pfarreien der Stadt Münster vor dem Fest Christi Himmelfahrt," in *Monasterium. Festschrift zum 700-jährigen Weihegedächtnis des Paulus-Domes zu Münster* (Münster: Regensberg, 1966), 151–220. See also Robert Scribner's description of the Rogation processions as a "boundary circuit" "which marked out boundaries as a form of sacred space, thus banishing evil spirits and protecting against natural disaster for the coming year." Scribner, *Religion and Culture in Germany (1400–1800)*, ed. Lyndal Roper (Leiden: Brill, 2001), 307.

e   Ernst Walter Zeeden, *Faith and Act: The Survival of Medieval Ceremonies in the Lutheran Reformation* (St. Louis: Concordia, 2012), 57–58, 65. Robert Scribner notes the "inability of Protestant authorities to prohibit Rogation day processions which sought divine protection for ripening crops against pests and damaging storms led to a distinctively evangelical form of the *Hagelfeier*, a procession around the fields with hymns and prayers . . ." Scribner, *Religion and Culture*, 280, 327.

This detail from a thirteenth-century codex
by Alfonso X of Castile, the Wise, depicts prayers
and procession during Rogation festival days.

an understanding of how God relates to humans that definitively reshaped and recast prayer as human response to God's word in command and promise.[f] In this sermon Luther made no mention of prayer to the saints, a standard element of medieval Rogation processions. Rather, Luther emphasized themes that he repeats in later writings on prayer:[g] prayer depends on God's promise to hear us, not on any purported human worthiness. Faith (trust) in God's promise to hear is the only thing a human need bring to prayer; such faith is produced not by the human but by the promise itself. Luther's views on prayer differed from standard medieval views, which tended to stress that the correct human disposition (often, humility) or mindset was essential to prayer;[2] some even stressed the importance of physical postures for the efficacy of prayer.[h] For medieval Christians, pious acts, human effort, and the proper attitude were key to the logic of prayer. Medieval theologians saw prayer as a pious and worthy act, through which Christians sought to cultivate a reciprocal relationship with God. As a reward for this, they hoped to receive help in this life and salvation in the future life.[i] In contrast, Luther, on the one hand, decisively rejected the notion that prayer could earn anything from God; on the other hand, he was firmly convinced that God did hear prayers and could change the divine will in response to human request.

Not until fairly late in this sermon did Luther criticize the processions that accompanied the Rogation days. He firmly rejected abuses and misuse of this practice and even suggested that bishops and temporal authorities may want to abolish

---

2. A late medieval pastoral manual illustrates this point: Guido of Monte Rochen, *Handbook for Curates: A Late Medieval Manual on Pastoral Ministry*, trans. Anne T. Thayer, with an introduction by Anne T. Thayer and Katharine J. Lualdi (Washington, DC: Catholic University of America Press, 2011). In the discussion of the Lord's Prayer, Guido alludes to the matter of worthiness: "it is necessary that it [prayer] be done with devotion of soul. Just as it is necessary for there to be fire for smoke to ascend from a censer, so in order for prayer to ascend to God it is necessary that it ascend from the fire of charity," 287.

---

f   A description of the historical circumstances surrounding the publication of Luther's writings on prayer from 1517 to 1519 is found in Brecht 1: 351–53.

g   For Luther's writings on prayer, see also in this volume, *A Simple Way to Pray* (253–81), *Little Prayer Book* (159–99), and *The Small Catechism* (201–51); also *The Large Catechism*, 1529 (TAL 2:366-87).

h   See, for example, the drawings of prayer postures and the descriptions in the prayer book of Peter the Chanter (d. 1197). Richard C. Trexler, *The Christian at Prayer: An Illustrated Prayer Manual Attributed to Peter the Chanter (d. 1197)* (Binghamton, NY: Center for Medieval and Early Renaissance Studies, 1987).

i   See Virginia Reinburg, "Prayers," in Miri Rubin, ed., *Medieval Christianity in Practice* (Princeton: Princeton University Press, 2009), 162–63.

them. In keeping with his own views that practices not expressly forbidden by the Bible may be reformed and used in an evangelical manner, Luther suggested the ways in which Rogation processions should be reformed.

Eight editions of this work appeared in 1519, and fourteen total between 1519 and 1525. In those six years it was printed in a broad range of cities in German-speaking lands: Augsburg, Leipzig, Nuremberg, Strassburg, Wittenberg, Zurich, and Lippe.[j] Several of the early editions included an explanation of the Lord's Prayer. This sermon was also included in some collections; parts were included in some editions of the *Betbüchlein* (*Little Prayer Book*; see pp. 159–99 in this volume).

A SERMON ON PRAYER AND PROCESSION DURING ROGATION DAYS[3]

Dr. Martin Luther, Augustinian Monk in Wittenberg

3. The translation here is based on *Ein Sermon von dem Gebet und Prozession in der Kreuzwoche* in WA 2:(172) 175–79, and updates the translation by Martin H. Bertram found in LW 42:87–93.

TO BEGIN WITH, two things are necessary so that a prayer is good and so that it is heard.[k] First, we must have a promise or a pledge from God. We must reflect on this promise and remind God of it, and in that way be emboldened to pray with confidence. If God had not commanded us to pray and if God had not promised fulfillment,[l] no

---

j   VD16 L6325–6338.

k   The German *erhöret* has the double meaning of "heard" and "fulfilled" or "brought to fruition."

l   The German *Erhörung* is here translated "fulfillment."

4. Notice that, for Luther, prayer starts with God! In all his writings on prayer he stresses God's command to pray and God's promise to hear our prayers. Implicitly, he rejects prayer to the saints, a common element of Rogation observances.

5. Luther's teaching on prayer reflects the central theme of Luther's theology. God is a merciful God, justifying sinners while they are yet sinners, not waiting for them to achieve righteousness. This means that merciful God hears and responds to the prayers of sinners without regard to their worthiness.

6. This was part of the lectionary text for Rogation days. It comes immediately after verses 2-4, the Lukan version of the Lord's Prayer.

7. In Luther's German, this paragraph and the next use the singular masculine pronoun but undoubtedly mean all people.

creature would be able to obtain so much as a kernel of grain despite all his petitions.[4]

It follows from this that not one of us obtains anything from God by our own virtue or the worthiness of our prayer, but solely by reason of the boundless mercy of God,[5] who, by anticipating all our prayers and desires, induces us through a gracious promise and assurance to petition and to ask so that we might learn how much more God provides for us and how God is more willing to give than we to take or to seek. God wants to encourage us to pray with confidence, since God offers us more than we are able to ask for.

Second, it is necessary that we never doubt the promise of the truthful and faithful God. For this very purpose God promises us a hearing, yes, the reason God commands us to pray is so we will be filled with a sure and firm faith that we will be heard. Thus God declares in Matt. 21[:22] and in Mark 11[:24], "Therefore I tell you, whatever you ask in prayer, believe that you receive it, and you certainly will." And in Luke 11[:9-13][6] he says, "Ask, and it will be given you; seek, and you will find; knock, and it will be opened to you. Where among you is a son who asks his father for bread, only to have him give him a stone? Or if he asks him for a fish, his father gives him a snake? Or if he asks for an egg, who gives him a scorpion? If you then, who are not good, are yet able to give good gifts to your children, how much more will the heavenly Father give the good Spirit to those who ask him?" We should cheerfully rely on these and similar promises and commands and pray with true confidence.

Third, if people pray while doubting God's fulfillment, if they[7] pray without certainty in whether or not their prayer is fulfilled, they make two mistakes. First, they destroy their own prayer and labor in vain. Thus we read in St. James 1[:6-8], "He who would ask of God, let him so ask that there is no doubt in his faith, for he who doubts is like a wave of the sea that is driven back and forth by the wind. That person must not suppose that he will receive anything from God." James means that God cannot give anything to such a person because that person's heart is unstable. Faith, however, keeps the heart firm and makes it receptive to all God's gifts.

The other mistake is that such people regard their very faithful and truthful God as a liar and as fickle and unreliable, neither able nor willing to keep promises. Thus through their doubts they rob God of his honor and of his reputation for faithfulness and truth.[8] This sin is so grave that it changes people from Christians into heathens, into people who deny and lose their own God. If they persist in this, they will be eternally and hopelessly damned. And if something for which they prayed is granted them, this does not redound to their salvation, but to their temporal and eternal harm. It is not the result of their prayer, but of the wrath of God, who thus rewards the good words which were spoken in sin, unbelief, and divine dishonor.

Fourth, some say, "I would indeed have confidence that my prayer would be answered if I were worthy and possessed merit." I reply: If you refuse to pray until you know or feel yourself worthy and fit you need never pray any more. For as was said before, our prayer must not be based upon or depend upon our worthiness or that of our prayer, but on the unwavering truth of the divine promise. Whenever our prayer is founded on itself or something else, it is false and deceptive, even though it wrings your heart with its intense devotion or weeps sheer drops of blood.[9]

We pray after all because we are unworthy to pray. The very fact that we are unworthy and that we dare to pray confidently, trusting only in the faithfulness of God, makes us worthy to pray and to have our prayer answered. Be as unworthy as you may, but know most seriously that it is a thousand times more important, yes, that everything depends on your honoring God's truthfulness and your never giving God's promise the lie by your doubts. Your worthiness does not help you; and your unworthiness does not hinder you. Mistrust condemns you, but confidence makes you worthy and sustains you.

All your life you must, therefore, guard against deeming yourself worthy or fit to pray or to receive, unless it be that you proceed with bold courage, trusting in the truthful and certain promises of your gracious God, who thereby wants to reveal divine mercy to you. Thus, just as God, unasked, promised out of sheer grace to hear you, an unworthy and undeserving person, God will, in sheer mercy, also give heed to you, an unworthy petitioner. And for all this you have not your own worthiness to thank, but divine truth, whereby God has fulfilled the divine promise, and God's mercy, which prompted the promise. This is supported in the statement found in Ps. 25[:10], "All the works of God are mercy and truth," mercy as manifested in the promise, truth in the keeping and fulfillment of the promise. We also find

8. This presages remarks that Luther makes in 1520 in *The Freedom of a Christian*. There Luther remarks that one of the powers of faith is that "It honors the one in whom it trusts with the most reverent and highest regard possible for this reason: Faith holds the one in whom it trusts to be truthful and deserving." And he asks, "what greater rebellion against God, godlessness, and contempt of God is there than not to believe the One who promises? What is this but either to make God out a liar or to doubt that God is truthful?" (TAL 1:497–98).

9. Luther emphasizes again that prayer is not dependent on human effort, attitude, or worthiness. This contrasts sharply to medieval Roman Catholic views.

it in the words of Ps. 85[:10], "Mercy and truth have kissed," that is, they are joined in every work and gift for which we pray, etc.

Fifth, your trust must not set a goal for God, not set a time and place, not specify the way or the means of fulfillment, but it must entrust all of that to God's will, wisdom, and omnipotence. Just wait cheerfully and undauntedly for the fulfillment without wanting to know how and where, how soon, how late, or by what means. God's divine wisdom will find an immeasurably better way and method, time and place, than we can imagine. In fact, even miracles will take place, as in the Old Testament. When the children of Israel trusted in God to redeem them, even though no conceivable possibility was in sight, the Red Sea opened up and afforded them free passage and also drowned all their enemies at once [Exod. 14:21-29]. Likewise also in Judith 8[:9-14]:[10] When the holy woman heard that the citizens of Bethulia intended to surrender the city in five days if God would not come to their assistance in the meantime, she rebuked them and said, "Who are you to put God to the test? By doing that, one wins not mercy, but more anger. Do you want to set the time when God will show mercy to you, and determine a day according to your own will?" etc. Therefore God helped Judith miraculously so that she beheaded the mighty Holofernes and the enemy was driven away. St. Paul also declares that God is able to do abundantly more and better than we ask or understand [Eph. 3:20]. Hence we must acknowledge that we are too paltry to be able to mention, specify, or suggest time, place, mode, measure, or any other circumstances regarding our requests of God. All this we must leave entirely to the discretion of God and most firmly believe that God will hear us.

Sixth, we must now learn to conduct ourselves properly in Rogation Week[11] and in all processions[12] and litanies. All should see to it that their litany and prayer are in accord with God's name and should petition God with a true and sincere faith, reminding God of the divine and merciful promise. Anyone who is not willing to do that is to remain at home and away from the procession, lest God be more angered by that one than appeased by others.

Unfortunately, the processions[13] have become scandalously misused. People want only to see and to be seen in them. They indulge in inane babble and hilarity, to say nothing of even worse conduct and sin. The village processions have become espe-

10. Luther appreciated and used the books of the Apocrypha, such as Judith, in his preaching. The book of Judith tells the story of Judith, a beautiful widow who tricked and beheaded the Assyrian general Holofernes, whose troops were besieging her town, and thereby preserved her town.

11. Here and elsewhere Luther does not reject the liturgical calendar of his time but, rather, seeks to use it for the proclamation of the gospel.

12. In medieval Europe processions were supposed to demonstrate the humility of those participating and obtain other spiritual benefits for them. Philip M. Soergel, "Ritual and Faith Formation in Early Modern Catholic Europe," in John Van Engen, ed., *Educating People of Faith* (Grand Rapids: Eerdmans, 2004), 324–29. Notice in what follows how Luther shifts the focus from what we do to what we pray that God will do.

13. William Durandus (c. 1230/35–1296), writing in *Rationale divinorum officiorum* in the thirteenth century, describes Rogation processions as featuring the cross and relics "so that with the standard of the cross and the prayers of the saints the demons might be expelled." The banners represent "the victory of the resurrection and ascension of Christ." See Robinson, "Sermons," 444–46. Jacobus de Voragine (c. 1230–1298), a contemporary of Durandus, wrote that "we carry the cross . . . to make the devils flee in terror." Ibid., 447.

cially disgraceful. These people give themselves to drinking and carousing in the taverns. They handle the processional crosses and banners in such a manner that it would not be surprising if God would let us all perish in one year.[14] Things have come to such a point that today there is more valid reason for entirely abolishing all processions and also the holy days than there ever was for instituting them.[15]

The bishops and also the temporal government should make it their business to remove the abuses or to do away entirely with the processions. It would be far better to gather in the churches for prayer and song than to mock God and his sacred symbols with such impudent behavior. The authorities, both temporal and spiritual, will have to give a grave account for tolerating these abuses or, in the event that they cannot overcome the abuses, for not putting an end to the processions completely. No procession at all is preferable to these.[m]

Seventh, we must pray for two things during the procession and Rogation Week. First, that God may graciously protect the crops in the fields and cleanse the air—not only that God may send blessed rain and good weather to ripen the fruit, but rather that the fruit may not be poisoned, and we, together with the animals, eat and drink thereof and become infected with pestilence, syphilis, fever, and other illnesses. St. Paul declares that "the creatures are blessed and sanctified by the word of God and prayer" [1 Tim. 4:4-5]. For where do pestilence and other plagues come from other than from the evil spirits who poison the air and then also the fruit, wine, and grain?[16] And so we, through the acquiescence of God, eat and drink death and sickness from our own goods. The Gospels are therefore read publicly in the fields[17] and in the open so that through the power of the holy

14. Notice that Luther does not criticize the practice of using crosses and banners in these processions but rather the misuse and abuse of the practice. He does not mention the common practice of carrying the relics of the saints in rogation processions.

15. Luther commented in his sermon for Rogate Sunday, May 21, 1525, that in this week it was customary to pray and process with crosses. He noted that those who instituted this perhaps meant well but that it had developed badly so that in the processions "many unchristian things happened and that so little or absolutely no prayer occurred, so that these were abolished and ignored." He then went on to note that he had often admonished them to prayer but "because the mouth flapping prayer and murmuring [*plapper gebet* and *murmeln*] is no longer done, we no longer pray. In this one can recognize that even though we previously prayed much, we were not really praying" (WA 17/1:248–49).

16. In the late medieval era, poisoned air was believed to cause plague. See Ronald K. Rittgers, "Protestants and Plague: The Case of the 1562/63 *Pest* in Nuremberg," in Franco Mormando and Thomas Worcester, eds., *Piety and Plague: From Byzantium to the Baroque* (Kirksville, MO: Truman State University Press, 2007), 134.

17. Durandus indicates that in some (not all) places "the litany is made through the fields"; Robinson, "Sermons," 446.

---

m For an analysis of one example of evangelical polemic in both text and picture against Roman Catholic processions, see Robert Scribner, *For the Sake of Simple Folk: Popular Propaganda for the German Reformation* (Cambridge: Cambridge University Press, 1981), 95–99. Scribner notes, "For evangelical belief, [processions on feast days and at times of distress] epitomized Catholicism in its most superstitious form, the notion that God's intervention was at the disposal of man's behest. It was the more offensive because processions involved the display of the Sacrament, the chanting of litanies invoking the saints and display of the Church hierarchy" (96).

word of God the devils may be weakened and the air kept pure and, subsequently, that the fruit may grow vigorously and be a blessing to us. Therefore, we should view the processions and especially the Word of God seriously, devoutly, and with honor and hear it with true faith, that the Word of God will exert its power on the fruit and on the air against all the princes of the air, that is, the devils, who inhabit the air, as St. Paul says [Eph. 6:12].

Eighth, we should ask God much more to bless the creation for us, not merely in the interest of our bodies, as was just said, but even more for the benefit of our souls, lest the poor soul also be stricken with pestilence and other plagues. This is what I mean: the pestilence and plague of the soul is sin. Whenever God grants us abundant crops in the field, we see how these gifts affect us. We drink ourselves into a stupor every day and lead idle lives. Then unchastity, adultery, cursing, swearing, murder, quarrels, and every other evil follow, so that it would have been far better if the fields had not been so productive. We then discover that what we asked for in the processions, God gives us abundantly and blesses everything for the welfare of the body, but for the soul all this is a fatal poison and results in the increase of abominable and horrible sin. For to be sated and idle is the greatest plague on earth, the source of all other plagues. No one heeds this pestilence, but we flee from the physical pestilence, pray, and try all kinds of remedies. We willingly enter into this spiritual pestilence, desiring only to have enough earthly goods and to be free of physical pestilence so that we may feast even more on this pestilence and plague. And God, who now sees and recognizes the thoughts of our hearts and our scorn for this plague, closes God's eyes and lets matters take their course, gives plentifully to us, blinds us, and immerses us so deeply in our sins that sin thus becomes a habit and a custom, and we no longer regard it as sin.

In our day there is truly a need for daily processions accompanied by scourging of the body and directed against the visibly rising deluge of all kinds of sin, especially in this country of so much gluttony, tippling, idleness, and what stems from these, in the hope that God might give us grace to use God's gifts for our souls' salvation and the betterment of our life, and thus the fruits become the means for maintaining and increasing the health of our body and soul. However, God blinds us so that we do not heed this, but rather use God's gifts for the passions of the body and for the soul's eternal damnation. In addition, God gives us a perverted mind[18] so that instead of improving matters we aggravate them and ruin the processions and the day of prayer with our sin. Thus God is angry, and no one can resist this divine anger, while prayer and procession, which should disarm this wrath, serve only to increase it.

May God help us all to come to our senses and to pray in true faith so that God may avert his anger. Amen.

18. Here and in the previous sentence Luther seems to refer to God's hidden work, a work of wrath. See the *Heidelberg Disputation* (LW 31:39–58; TAL 1:81–85, 88–105).

Ein bet-
büchlin / mit
eym Calender vnd
Passional / hübsch
zu gericht.

Marti.   Luther.

Wittemberg.

M. D. xxix.

The cover of a 1529 version
of Luther's *Little Prayer Book*

Little Prayer Book

1522

MARY JANE HAEMIG

INTRODUCTION

Luther's *Betbüchlein* (*Little Prayer Book*) was first published at the end of May 1522.[a] Luther had returned to Wittenberg from the Wartburg in early March 1522. The Reformation had advanced rapidly in Wittenberg, and not always in ways that Luther found helpful and evangelical. He clearly saw the need to reform worship and devotional practices but rejected enforced measures (such as the destruction of images or compelling people to receive both kinds), and instead desired a reformation embodying evangelical freedom based on the proclaimed word and faith. His *Invocavit Sermons*[b] expressed his vision of such reform.

The events of the first half of 1522 illustrate key theological insights. Luther believed that God deals with humans first outwardly, then inwardly. The external word—the speaking of the gospel, baptism, and the Lord's Supper—precedes and causes the inward experience of the Holy Spirit and faith. God gives the inward only through the outward. Faith then produces outward

---

a   Martin Brecht, *Martin Luther: Shaping and Defining the Reformation 1521–1532*, trans. James L. Schaaf (Minneapolis: Fortress Press, 1990), 119 (hereafter Brecht 2).

b   See above, pp. 7–45.

expressions. Decisions on outward matters of Christian practice, matters neither commanded nor forbidden by God, follow in evangelical freedom from faith. Luther complained that Andreas Bodenstein von Karlstadt (1486–1541) and his followers had, in both cases, reversed the direction.[1] Luther's *Betbüchlein* can be seen as a continuation of his message in the *Invocavit Sermons* and elsewhere; it provided both another proclamation of God's word and the resources for the life of faith and its outward expressions in practice that follow from that proclamation of the word. It did not mandate certain prayers and practices but provided resources for Christians to use in exercising their faith in freedom.

Luther's efforts in these months aimed at reorienting the reforming movement to its central message. In late April and early May 1522, Luther undertook a preaching tour to other cities in Electoral Saxony.[c] He was also revising his translation of the New Testament for its publication in September. It was this flurry of activity that may have prompted his comment that he "did not have the time" for a basic and thorough reformation of prayer books. Nevertheless, this work continued Luther's efforts to reform prayer practice. Already published were his sermons on the Lord's Prayer and on Rogation prayer.[d] The *Betbüchlein* reveals how profoundly Luther's Reformation insights affected the most ordinary aspects of Christian practice.

Medieval monastic prayer practices, patterns, and materials often set the pattern or ideal for lay prayer. The daily routine of monks and nuns included set times for prayer. Prayer was systematically taught even in mendicant orders.[e] The Franciscans, for example, developed a rich literature to instruct novices and friars in proper prayer practice. While they considered vocal prayer, and particularly the Lord's Prayer, as important, they also sought to reach beyond vocal prayer to mental or spiritual prayer, viewed as more advanced because it involved the human soul rising to God and attaining insights into divine secrets. Prayer was also shaped by confessional practices. It was part of

---

1. Luther later went into great detail on his differences with Karlstadt. See *Against the Heavenly Prophets in the Matter of Images and Sacraments* (1525) (LW 40:79–223; TAL 2:39–125). For more on Karlstadt in this volume, see the introduction to the *Invocavit Sermons*, pp. 7–14.

---

c Brecht 2:67.

d See above, pp. 147–57.

e See, e.g., Bert Roest, "The Discipline of the Heart: Pedagogies of Prayer in Medieval Franciscan Works of Religious Instruction," in Timothy J. Johnson, ed., *Franciscans at Prayer* (Leiden/Boston: Brill, 2007), 413–48.

the "satisfaction" stage in penance, in that saying prayers after proper contrition and confession to a priest helped satisfy the penitent's remaining temporal penalty for sin. Pastoral and devotional materials made clear that prayer was an activity that gained merit for the one praying, but that such merit depended on the fulfillment of the proper conditions.[2]

In the late Middle Ages, Books of Hours also became popular,[f] many being designed for and used by laity. Some are known to us today as finely bound and richly illuminated books used by nobility. With the invention of printing in the mid-fifteenth century, such books were available to a broader audience. These books centered on a cycle of prayers to the Virgin Mary (the Hours of the Virgin), designed for recitation throughout the day. The books offered materials and patterns that paralleled monastic practices but were aimed at a lay audience. Commonly, such books included calendars with feast days and commemorations of saints, Gospel lessons touching on major events in the life of Christ and often supplemented by John's account of Christ's passion, the Hours of the Virgin (eight separate hours including psalms, hymns, prayers, and lessons), the Hours of the Cross, the Hours of the Holy Spirit, specialized prayers to the Virgin, the seven penitential psalms (6, 32, 38, 51, 102, 130, and 143), the office of the dead, and prayers to the saints. The books

2. As Guido of Monte Rochen wrote in a popular pastoral manual in his discussion of the Sacrament of Penance: "For prayer to be entirely meritorious and effective as satisfaction, it is required to have thirteen conditions, namely, that it be faithful, untroubled,

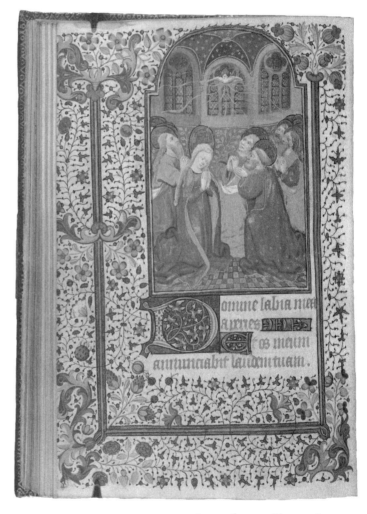

A scene from an illustrated Book of Hours printed in the fifteenth century depicts prayer and the Holy Spirit as dove.

f   Roger S. Wieck, "Prayer for the People: The Book of Hours," in Roy Hammerling, ed., *A History of Prayer: The First to the Fifteenth Century* (Leiden: Brill, 2008), 388–416.

humble, discrete, shameful, devout, secret, pure, tearful, attentive, fervent, painstaking, and constant." Guido of Monte Rochen, *Handbook for Curates: A Late Medieval Manual on Pastoral Ministry*, trans. Anne T. Thayer, with an introduction by Anne T. Thayer and Katharine J. Lualdi (Washington, DC: Catholic University of America Press, 2011), 247.

The *Stabat Mater*. Mary, the mother of Jesus, stands by Christ's cross along with the apostle John. Painting by Roger van der Weyden (1399/1400–1464).

also exhibited a wide variation in other content. Some contained Masses, that is, the prayers said by the priest or sung by the choir; some contained a variety of other prayers, including the *Stabat Mater* and prayers to one's guardian angel. Some prayers were accompanied by indulgences that provided the user with extra merit.

In Germany, beginning at the end of the fifteenth century, the most popular and widely disseminated prayer books were known as the *Hortulus animae* ("Garden of the Soul" or "Garden of the Spirit"). While including the typical contents of the Books of Hours, these shifted the focus of prayer away from the monastic routine and toward the personal and devotional use of prayer. They included prayers for arising and going to bed, prayers for leaving the house and for entering the church, prayers (often from the church fathers) to gain indulgences, prayers while receiving the sacraments of penance and the Lord's Supper, and prayers while attending Mass.[g]

Other extant works offer insight into the practice of prayer in the late medieval period. One prayer book for laity, probably dating from the late fifteenth or early sixteenth century, contained a hymn of praise to Mary, three prayers to one's personal angel, two prayers to an apostle chosen to be one's patron saint, and three prayers to Saint Erasmus.[h]

The lines between catechism, prayer book, and breviary were not strictly drawn in the Middle Ages, nor were lines between materials meant for communal worship and those meant for private devotion. The Ten Commandments, Apostles' Creed, Lord's Prayer, and Hail Mary (*Ave Maria*) were common elements of medieval catechisms. Typically, these catechisms also con-

g   Traugott Koch discusses the *Hortulus animae* in *Johann Habermanns "Betbüchlein" im Zusammenhang seiner Theologie* (Tübingen: Mohr Siebeck, 2001), 12–13. For more on these prayer books, see Austra Reinis, *Reforming the Art of Dying: The* Ars Moriendi *in the German Reformation (1519–1528)* (Burlington, VT: Ashgate, 2007), 40–45.

h   Peter Matheson, "Angels, Depression, and 'The Stone': A Late Medieval Prayer Book," *Journal of Theological Studies* (NS) 48, no. 2 (October 1997): 517–30.

tained other materials designed to guide conduct, educate the Christian in the faith, and teach prayer.[i] As most people were illiterate, they would have learned their prayers by hearing them spoken and repeating them.

Luther sought to reform both the theology and practice of prayer. He realized that unless his insights were conveyed on a popular, understandable level, they would not succeed in changing longstanding, strongly rooted ideas and practice. Medieval prayer books and practices had left people with many ideas that undermined God's mercy received in faith. Luther sought to encourage simple direct prayer to God, who had promised to hear the one praying, rather than to the Virgin Mary and the saints. Luther stressed that God hears prayers, despite unworthiness, because God has promised to listen to prayer. Prayer is not a good work and does not earn indulgences[3] or anything else from God; it is honest communication with God. Mindless repetition of prayer is not helpful; instead, Christians should contemplate the meaning of each petition and boldly, honestly, and persistently present their needs to God.

This illustration from a *Hortulus animae* published in 1550 depicts the branch springing from the stump of Jesse (Isaiah 11). As Jesse, the father of David, lies on the ground a tree grows from his side at whose center is the Madonna and child.

The *Betbüchlein* gave laypeople an evangelical counterpart to the problematic prayer books that Luther saw in use. In its effort to shape lay piety by focusing on the Ten Commandments, Apostles' Creed, and Lord's Prayer, the work is decidedly catechetical and reflects what would later become the structure of his catechisms.[4] Luther thought that the best way to teach prayer was to introduce people to the faith and thereby to incite them

3. Indulgences purported to remit a certain number of years that the Christian had to serve in purgatory.

4. See Luther's reflections in the *Prayer Book*'s introduction (below). See also his comment in the preface to the *Deutsche Messe* (German Mass), 1525 (LW 53:64–66; TAL 3:142–46), where he emphasizes the need for a catechism and suggests using the *Betbüchlein* as a basis for evangelical catechisms.

---

i   See for example, Dietrich Kolde's "Mirror for Christians" (1480), in Denis Janz, *Three Reformation Catechisms: Catholic, Anabaptist, Lutheran* (Lewiston, NY: Edwin Mellen Press, 1982), 29–130 (hereafter Kolde).

5. Commenting on Strassburg, Miriam Usher Chrisman writes, "The most popular prayerbook, of which five editions were printed between 1560 and 1591, was Luther's own *Betbüchlein.*" Miriam Usher Chrisman, *Lay Culture, Learned Culture: Books and Social Change in Strasbourg, 1580–1599* (New Haven: Yale University Press, 1982), 88.

6. See Luther's preface to Casper Cruciger's *Summer Postil* (1544) (LW 77:9; WA 21:201): "So also the shameful, false, slanderous prayer books, of which the world was full, have been cleared out, and in place of them pure prayers and good Christian hymns have been published, especially the Psalter, the finest and most precious prayer book and hymnal of them all, concerning which no theologian of our time could boast that he had understood a single psalm as well and as thoroughly as the laypeople, men and women, understand them now."

7. The title *"Betbüchlein"* literally means "Little Prayer Book." The *"-lein"* is a diminutive in German. This translation is based on the German text in WA 10/2:375–501 and the translation by Martin H. Bertram in LW 43:11–45.

to prayer. Here, as in other places, he focused his discussion of prayers on the Lord's Prayer. As he did frequently in later works, he also advocated the use of biblical texts, here the Psalms, as prayer for Christians. Luther and his followers saw clearly that in order to shape faith and practice, accessible materials had to make his insights available and usable at the popular level.

It is striking that this work is not a collection of prayers. For this reason, one scholar has called it an "anti-prayer book."[j] It actually is not a "prayer book" as that literary genre had been understood, for it contains no written prayers (such as the morning, evening, and table prayers that his *Small Catechism* later included) but, rather, direction and advice concerning prayer. Luther encouraged the use of biblical texts—particularly the Lord's Prayer and the Psalms—as something the Christian could use to pray meditatively and in so doing bring his or her own situation before God.[k] Luther's prayer book exhibits both Luther's reforming insights and his pastoral insights into how to convey them. He used familiar elements, common in medieval prayer books but now understood in an evangelical way, to convey Reformation content. The absence of other elements indicated that they did not fit his theology.

The work has a complicated publication history, as Luther himself—and those after him—modified its contents. Ironically, the same thing happened to it that happened to many medieval prayer books: while the basic core (Ten Commandments, Creed, Lord's Prayer, and Hail Mary) remained intact, various elements were added to and subtracted from it. Luther sometimes included translations of various books of the New Testament, psalms, and relevant sermons. Subsequent editors of the work also added various elements—for example, forms for use in confessing sin, instruction for the dying, short explanations of the Lord's Prayer, and the like. One of the more thorough revisions, probably done under Luther's supervision, took place in 1529, when the printer added a set of fifty woodcuts depicting the basic story of salvation from the creation, through the fall,

j Johannes Wallmann, "Zwischen Herzensgebet und Gebetbuch. Zur protestantischen deutschen Gebetsliteratur im 17. Jahrhundert," in *Gebetsliteratur der frühen Neuzeit als Hausfrömmigkeit* (Wiesbaden: Harrassowitz, 2001), 19.

k See the discussion in ibid., 18–21.

the incarnation, death, resurrection, and ascension of Christ, to the second coming, ending with the spreading of the gospel throughout the world.

Luther's *Betbüchlein* became popular immediately. It was printed at least seventeen times between 1522 and 1525 (in Augsburg, Erfurt, Grimma, Wittenberg, Jena, and Strassburg) and at least forty-four times by the end of the century.[1] In some areas, it was the most popular prayer book.[5] Writing in 1544, Luther claimed success for all evangelical efforts, including his own, to reform prayer practice.[6]

LITTLE PRAYER BOOK[7]

TO ALL MY DEAR MASTERS and brothers[8] in Christ, grace and peace.

Among the many harmful books and doctrines by which Christians are misled and deceived and countless false beliefs have arisen, I regard the little prayer books as by no means the least objectionable. They drub into the minds of simple people such a wretched counting up of sins[9] and going to confession, such un-Christian foolishness about prayers to God and the saints! Moreover, these books are puffed up with promises of indulgences[10] and come out with decorations in red ink and pretty titles; one is called *Hortulus animae*, another *Paradisus animae*,[11] and so on. These books need a basic and thorough reformation if not total extermination. And I would make the same judgment about those passionals[12] or books of legends into which the devil has tossed his own additions. But I just don't have the time and it is too much for me to undertake such a reformation alone. So until God gives me more time and grace, I

8. Luther prefaced his new prayer book with a letter of explanation addressed to "*herrn*" and "*brudern*." *Herrn* ("sirs") could refer to *Pfarrherrn* (parish pastors) or to *Ratsherrn* (civil officials) while *brudern* could refer to monks or others in ecclesiastical positions. Their opinions about Luther's bold supplanting of the old traditional prayer books would be solicited by many people. The support of these authorities for the new book and their recommendation would help greatly Luther's effort at reforming the forms of personal piety among the laity.

9. Numbering types of sins was common in late medieval Europe. So, for example, the seven deadly sins, the nine alien sins, the six sins against the Holy Spirit, and the five commandments of the church were all discussed in Kolde's catechism and other devotional works.

10. In medieval Roman Catholicism, certain prayers were thought to earn indulgences, that is, remission or reduction of the time one was obligated to spend in purgatory because of one's sins.

11. *Hortulus animae* ("Garden of the Soul" or "Garden of the Spirit") and *Paradisus animae* ("Paradise of the Soul") were titles for popular late medieval prayer books.

12. Passionals were histories of Christ's passion, often an amalgam of the scriptural accounts. Often other things were added to these works as well, for example, other Bible stories, stories concerning Mary, and stories concerning saints. Medieval prayer books sometimes contained one or more of these.

1 VD16, L4081–L4125.

13. The "mirror" was a literary genre. Many different types of "mirrors" were written in the late medieval to early modern era. Typically, a mirror declared what was acceptable and unacceptable conduct in a particular profession or situation. As the word *mirror* indicates, they were meant for self-examination and improvement.

14. The Lord's Prayer was commonly included in medieval catechisms and prayer books. Luther sees it as the preeminent prayer, not simply one among many.

15. Luther here implicitly rejects the imposition of monastic prayer practices on the laity. Such attempts manifested themselves, for example, in attempts to encourage laypeople to pray in accordance with the canonical hours. See Kolde's catechism, 88–90, where laypersons are given a prayer for each canonical hour.

16. St. Bridget (1303–1373) was a Swedish saint and mystic who was canonized in 1391. Her literary works include four prayers, but in the flowering of legends around her captivating personality, a set of fifteen prayers was ascribed to her and used frequently in the spiritual exercises of the devout. Personal prayer books promised that the Bridget prayers would gain for the user the salvation of forty souls of the same sex as the person offering the prayers, the conversion of forty sinners, and the strengthening of forty-six righteous persons.

will limit myself to the exhortation in this book. To begin with, I offer this simple Christian form of prayer and mirror[13] for recognizing sin, based on the Lord's Prayer and the Ten Commandments. And I am convinced that when Christians[m] rightly pray the Lord's Prayer[14] at any time or use any portion of it as they may desire, their praying is more than adequate.[15] What is important for a good prayer is not many words, as Christ says in Matthew 6[:7], but rather a turning to God frequently and with heartfelt longing, and doing so without ceasing [1 Thess. 5:17].

Birgitta (St. Bridget) of Sweden on an altarpiece in Salem church, Södermanland, Sweden

And herewith I urge everyone to break away from using the Bridget prayers[16] and any others that are ornamented with indulgences or rewards and urge all to get accustomed to praying this plain, ordinary Christian prayer. The longer one devotes one's self to this kind of praying, the more sweet and joyous it becomes. To that end may this prayer's Master, our dear Lord Jesus Christ, help us, to whom be blessings in all eternity. Amen.

m This term and corresponding pronouns are masculine singular in the German.

Foreword

It was not unintended in God's particular ordering of things that a lowly Christian person who might be unable to read the Bible[17] should nevertheless be obligated to learn and know the Ten Commandments, the Creed, and the Lord's Prayer.[18] Indeed, the total content of Scripture and preaching and everything a Christian needs to know is quite fully and richly comprehended in these three items. They summarize everything with such brevity and clarity[19] that no one can complain or make any excuse that the things necessary for salvation are too complicated or difficult to remember.

Three things people must know in order to be saved.[20] First, they*n* must know what to do and what to leave undone. Second, when they realize that, by their own strength, they cannot measure up to what they should do or leave undone, they need to know where to seek, find, and take the strength they require. Third, they must know how to seek and obtain that strength. It is just like sick people who first have to determine the nature of their sickness, and what to do or to leave undone. After that they have to know where to get the medicine which will help them do or leave undone what is right for a healthy person. Third, they have to desire to search for this medicine and to obtain it or have it brought to them.

Thus the commandments teach humans to recognize their sickness, enabling them to see and perceive what to do or refrain from doing, consent to or refuse, and so recognize themselves to be sinful and wicked persons.[21] The Creed will teach and show them where to find the medicine—grace—which will help them to become devout and keep the commandments. The Creed points them to God and God's mercy, given and made plain in Christ. Third, the Lord's Prayer teaches how they may seek, get, and bring to themselves all this, namely, by proper, humble, consolatory prayer. So it will be given to them, and through the fulfillment of God's commandments they will be blessed. In these three are the essentials of the entire Bible.

17. Literacy rates were low, estimated at 3 to 4 percent of Germany's population, about 400,000 people. Steven Ozment, *The Age of Reform 1250-1550: An Intellectual and Religious History of Late Medieval and Reformation Europe* (New Haven: Yale University Press, 1980), 201. Also, although vernacular Bibles were available, some had no access to them.

18. In the Middle Ages, people were expected to memorize the Hail Mary, the Ten Commandments, the Apostles' Creed, and the Lord's Prayer. Luther views only the last three as necessary but does not neglect the Hail Mary.

19. Luther implicitly contrasts the simplicity of these three elements to the many elements found in medieval prayer books and catechisms.

20. In medieval catechisms, the Apostles' Creed was often placed before the Lord's Prayer and the Ten Commandments. See, for example, Kolde. Luther here explains why he has a different order of parts.

21. The Ten Commandments were used as a confessional aid in the late medieval era. The priest could, by going through the commandments, lead the penitent to recognize and confess sin. The commandments were also used as instruments and guidelines for use in forming one's faith (intellectual knowledge of Christianity) into a life pleasing to God.

n   Here and following the plural pronoun replaces the singular male pronoun in the original.

For this reason, we begin with the commandments,[o] to teach and perceive our sin and wickedness, that is, our spiritual sickness that prevents us from doing or leaving undone as we ought.[22]

22. Luther emphasized human inability to fulfill the commandments, rather than human ability to please God through them.

Image of Moses receiving the Ten Commandments, from a seventeenth century reprint of Luther's Bible

The First Tablet

Properly, the first or right-hand tablet[23] of the commandments includes the first three, in which a person is instructed concerning his duty toward God—what he should do or leave undone, that is, how he should conduct himself in relation to God.

The First Commandment teaches a person the right attitude in his[24] own heart toward God, that is, what he should always keep in mind and consider important. In particular a person should expect all good things from God as from a father or good friend in all trust, faith, and love, with fear at all times, so he should not offend God, just as a child avoids offending his father. For Nature teaches us that there is a God who grants every good thing and who helps in all difficulties, as even the

23. Luther often used the distinction between the first and second tables (or tablets) of the law, between the obligations humans owe to God and those humans owe to other humans.

24. Though the masculine pronoun is used here and in the following paragraphs, Luther intended that this apply to all people.

---

o   Luther went into greater detail as to what each commandment requires in his *Treatise on Good Works* (1520) (LW 44:21–114; TAL 1:257–368).

false gods of the heathen declare. So the First Commandment says: "You shall have no other gods."

The Second Commandment[25] teaches how a person should govern himself in relation to God both in his outward speech to others and also in his inward, personal attitude. That is, he should honor God's name. For no one can express God's divine nature, either to himself or to others, except by using God's name. Thus this commandment says: "You shall not take the name of your God in vain."

The Third Commandment teaches how a person should govern his actions toward God, that is, in service to God.[26] It says: "You shall sanctify the Sabbath."[27] In this way these three commandments teach a person how to govern himself toward God in thought, word, and deed, that is, in all of life.

The Second Tablet

The second or left-hand tablet of the commandments includes the following seven commandments, in which a person is taught his obligation toward his fellow humans and neighbors, what he should do and leave undone.

The first teaches how to conduct one's self toward everyone in authority—those who act in God's place [Rom. 13:1-6; Eph. 6:5-8]. Hence this commandment comes immediately after the first three that relate to God's person, and it deals with those who are like God—father and mother, master and mistress. It says: "You shall honor your father and your mother."

The next commandment teaches how to deal with the person of our neighbor and fellow humans, that we are not to harm these, but help and assist them wherever they need it. It says: "You shall not kill."

The third teaches a person how to act in relation to what, next to his person, is the neighbor's most valuable possession—his wife, or child, or friend. We must not bring them into disgrace but preserve their reputation as much as we can. The commandment says: "You shall not commit adultery."

The fourth teaches a person how to act with regard to his neighbor's worldly property. One should not steal it or hinder it, but help him prosper. It says: "You shall not steal."

The fifth teaches a person how to act toward his neighbor's worldly reputation and honor. One should not weaken it but

25. Luther continues in the medieval tradition in that he does not consider the commandment against "graven images" to be the Second Commandment. See Albrecht Peters, *Commentary on Luther's Catechisms: Ten Commandments*, trans. Holger Sonntag (St. Louis: Concordia, 2009), pp. 141–46, "Appendix: The Prohibition of Images."

26. The German is *gottis diensten*, which is sometimes translated "worshiping" or "worship service," but means literally "God's service" or "service to God."

27. The German is *Feiertag heiligen*. *Fiertag* does not mean "day of celebration" but, rather, a day on which one rests from one's labors.

support, protect, and preserve it. It says: "You shall not give false testimony against your neighbor."

What is thus forbidden is harming one's neighbor in anything he owns; rather one should help him prosper. When we look at natural law, we see how right and universal all these commandments are. They require nothing toward God or our neighbor but that which anyone would want to see done, either from a divine or from a human point of view.

The last two commandments teach how evil our nature is and how unstained we should keep ourselves from all desires of the flesh and from greed—for us a lifelong task and struggle. These commandments read: "You shall not covet your neighbor's house. You shall not covet his wife, his servants or maids, his livestock, or anything that is his."

Christ himself summarizes the Ten Commandments briefly, saying, "Whatever you want others to do to you, do the same to them; this is the whole Law and the Prophets" [Matt. 7:12]. No one wants to see his kindness repaid by ingratitude or have someone defame his name. No one wants to be treated arrogantly, no one wants to be disobeyed, or treated with anger, or to have an unchaste wife, or to be robbed of his possessions, or endure falsehood against himself, or be betrayed, or be slandered. On the contrary, everyone wants a neighbor to show love and friendship, gratitude and helpfulness, truthfulness and loyalty—all required by these Ten Commandments.

What It Means
to Break[28] the Commandments[29]

Breaking the First

Whoever tries to do away with trouble by witchcraft, by the black arts, or by an alliance with the devil.

Whoever uses [magic] writings, signs, herbs, words, spells, and the like.[p]

---

28. Luther uses the term *Ubertrettung*, which means "crossing a boundary."

29. Here, as later in the *Small Catechism* (1529), Luther considers first how one breaks the commandments, and second, how one fulfills them.

---

p   For a discussion of popular magic and its manifestations during this era, see Robert Scribner, "The Reformation, Popular Magic, and the 'Disenchantment of the World,'" in Lyndal Roper and Rober Scribner, eds., *Religion and Culture in Germany (1400–1800)* (Leiden: Brill, 2001), 346–65.

Whoever uses divining rods, uses incantations to find treasure, resorts to crystal-gazing, travels by a magic cloak, or steals milk.

Whoever governs his[30] life and work according to certain days, celestial signs, and the advice of fortune-tellers [Lev. 20:6].

Whoever uses certain incantations as blessings and charms to protect himself, his cattle, his children, and any kind of property against danger from wolves, sword, fire, or water.

Whoever ascribes any bad luck or unpleasantness to the devil or to evil persons and does not, with love and praise, accept both evil and good as coming from God alone [Phil. 4:11], responding to God with gratitude and willing submission.

Whoever tempts God and exposes himself to unnecessary danger to body [Luke 4:12] and soul.

Whoever shows arrogance because of his piety, knowledge, or other spiritual gifts.

Whoever honors God and the saints only to gain some temporal advantage, forgetting the needs of his soul.

Whoever does not trust God at all times and rely upon God's mercy in everything he does.

Whoever doubts the Creed or God's grace.

Whoever does not defend others against unbelief and doubt and does not do all in his power to help them believe and trust in God's grace.

Here belongs every kind of unbelief, despair, and false belief.

Breaking the Second Commandment

Whoever swears needlessly or habitually.

Whoever swears a false oath or breaks his vow.

Whoever vows or swears to do evil.

Whoever curses using God's name.

Whoever tells silly stories about God and whoever carelessly misconstrues the words of Scripture.

Whoever does not call upon God's name in adversity and does not praise him in joy and sorrow, in fortune and misfortune [2 Cor. 6:8].

Whoever uses piety and wisdom to seek praise, honor, or reputation.

Whoever calls upon God's name falsely, as do heretics and all arrogant saints.

30. Though Luther uses the male pronoun here and in other places in this list of what it means to break the commandments, he means all persons.

Whoever does not praise God's name, no matter what may happen to him.

Whoever does not restrain others from dishonoring God's name, from using it wrongly or for evil purposes.

Hence self-conceit, boasting, and spiritual pride belong here.

Breaking the Third Commandment

Whoever does not listen to God's word or try to understand it.

Whoever does not pray and serve God spiritually.

Whoever does not regard all he does as God's work.

Whoever, in all he does and endures, does not quietly allow God to do with him as God pleases.

Whoever does not help the other person do all this and does not restrain him from doing otherwise.

Breaking the Fourth Commandment

Whoever is ashamed that his parents are poor, have faults, or are not highly regarded.

Whoever does not provide clothing and food for his parents in their need.

Especially whoever curses or strikes his parents, slanders them, and is hateful and disobedient toward them.

Whoever does not in all sincerity regard them highly simply because God has so commanded.

Whoever does not hold his parents in honor even though they might do wrong and use force.

Whoever does not honor those in authority over him, remain loyal and obedient to them, no matter whether they are good or bad.

Whoever does not help others to obey this commandment and resist those who break it.

Here belongs every kind of arrogance and disobedience.

Breaking the Fifth Commandment

Whoever is angry with his neighbor.

Whoever says to him, "Raca" [Matt. 5:22]—which represents any expression of anger and hatred.

Whoever says to him, you nitwit,[31] you fool [Matt. 5:22], that is, uses all sorts of insults, profanity, slander, backbiting, condemnation, scorn against his neighbor.

Whoever makes his neighbor's sin or shortcomings public and does not cover and excuse [these].

Whoever does not forgive his enemies, does not pray for them, is not friendly, and does them no kindness.

Breaking this commandment includes all sins of anger and hatred, such as murder, war, robbery, arson, quarreling and feuding, begrudging a neighbor's good fortune, and rejoicing over his misfortune [1 Cor. 13:6].

Whoever fails to practice merciful deeds even toward his enemies [Matt. 5:44; Rom. 12:20].

Whoever sets persons against one another and incites them to strife [Prov. 16:28].

Whoever causes disunity between persons.

Whoever does not reconcile those who are at odds with one another [Matt. 5:9].

Whoever does not prevent or forestall anger and discord wherever he can.

Breaking the Sixth Commandment

Whoever violates virgins, commits adultery, incest, and similar kinds of sexual sins.

Whoever commits sexual perversions (called the silent sins) [Rom. 1:26-27; Lev. 18:22-23; 20:10-16].

Whoever uses lewd words, ditties, stories, pictures to incite sexual lust or displays evil lust.

Whoever stirs up sexual desires in himself and contaminates himself by ogling, touching, and sexual fantasies.

Whoever does not avoid provocation to sexual sins—heavy drinking and eating, laziness and idleness, sleeping too much, and associating with persons of the opposite sex.

Whoever incites others to unchastity by excessive personal adornment, suggestive gestures, and other means.

Whoever allows his house, room, time, or assistance to be used for such sexual sins.

Whoever does not do and say what he can to help another person to be chaste.

31. Luther uses an old Latin term of scorn, *fatue*, from which the word *fatuous* is derived. Evidently the ancient epithet was still used in his time.

Breaking the Seventh Commandment

Whoever steals, robs, and practices usury.

Whoever uses short weights and measures [Deut. 25:15], or who passes off poor merchandise as good.

Whoever gets an inheritance or income by fraud.

Whoever withholds earned wages [Deut. 24:15] and whoever refuses to acknowledge his debts.

Whoever refuses to vouch for or lend money without interest to a needy neighbor.

All who are avaricious and want to get rich quickly.

Whoever in any way keeps what belongs to another or keeps for himself what is only entrusted to him for a time.

Whoever does not try to prevent loss to another person.

Whoever does not forewarn his neighbor against possible loss.

Whoever hinders what is advantageous to his neighbor.

Whoever is vexed by his neighbor's increase in wealth.

Breaking the Eighth Commandment

Whoever conceals and supresses the truth in court.

Whoever does harm by untruth and deceit.

Whoever uses flattery to do harm, or spreads gossip, or uses double-talk.

Whoever brings his neighbor's conduct, speech, life, or wealth into question or disrepute.

Whoever allows others to speak evil about his neighbor, helps them, and does nothing to oppose them.

Whoever does not speak up in defense of his neighbor's good repute.

Whoever does not take a backbiter to task.

Whoever does not speak well about all his neighbors and does not keep silent about what is bad about them.

Whoever conceals the truth or does not defend it.

Breaking the Last Two Commandments

The last two commandments set a goal or target which we should attain. Daily and penitently we must strive toward this goal with God's help and grace because our evil desires will not die completely until our flesh is reduced to dust and then created anew.

32. Luther in this paragraph refers to devices or lists that were commonly included in medieval prayer books and catechisms. He implicitly makes the point that these are unnecessary because everything important is included in the Ten Commandments. Luther rejects all these other lists and returns the Christian to the Ten Commandments.

33. Kolde (106) discusses seven works of physical mercy and seven works of spiritual mercy. The works of physical mercy are feeding the hungry, giving drink to the thirsty, freeing prisoners, visiting the sick, clothing the naked, sheltering pilgrims and other suffering people, and burying the dead. The works of spiritual mercy are: "Counseling naïve and simple people. Teaching the ignorant. Punishing the sinful. Comforting the grieving. Forgiving those who have offended you. Enduring and tolerating for God's sake, those who are burdensome and annoying. Interceding for all faithful souls, hearing mass for them, giving alms, fasting, and praying for them."

The five senses are comprehended in the Fifth and Sixth Commandments;[32] the six works of mercy[33] in the Fifth and Seventh; the seven mortal sins[34]—pride in the First and Second, lust in the Sixth, wrath and hatred in the Fifth, gluttony in the Sixth, sloth in the Third, and, for that matter, in all of them. The alien sins[35] are covered by all the commandments, for it is possible to break all the commandments just by talking, advising, or helping someone. The crying and silent sins[36] are committed against the Fifth, Sixth, and Seventh Commandments. In all of these deeds we can see the same thing: love of self which seeks its own advantage, robs both God and one's neighbor of their due, and concedes neither to God nor man anything of what they have, or are, or could do or become. Augustine expressed this succinctly when he said, "Self-love is the beginning of every sin."

The conclusion of all this is that the commandments demand or forbid nothing other than love. Only love fulfills and only love breaks the commandments. Therefore St. Paul declares that "love is the fulfilling of the law" [Rom. 13:8-10], just as an evil love breaks all the commandments.

34. Arrogance (pride), greed, unchastity (lust), anger, gluttony, envy, idleness.

35. Kolde (68) discusses nine "alien" sins, that is, sins that involve the sin of others. These include such things as requiring others to sin, providing aid to the commission of sin, consenting to sin, praising sin, harboring and protecting thieves, murderers, etc., eating and drinking from ill-gotten wealth, and failing to prevent sin when one could do so.

36. Along with "openly discussed sins," Kolde includes a discussion (69–70) of "the mute sins against nature that are seldom or never discussed." Kolde comments that it "occurs in myriad ways, such as with thoughts, with touching, with women, with men, or in various self-indulgent and forsaken ways."

This seven-paneled painting (polyptych)
by Master of Alkmaar (1504)
depicts the seven works of charity.
Located in Museum Boijmans Van Beunigen,
on loan from the Rijksmuseum Amsterdam.

Fulfilling the Commandments

The First

Fear and love God in true faith,[37] at all times, firmly trusting him in all that he does, accepting in simple, quiet confidence everything whether good or bad. What all of Scripture records about faith and hope and the love of God [1 Cor. 13:13] belongs here and is briefly comprehended in this commandment.

The Second

Praise, honor, glorify, and call upon God's name, and rather sink into utter nothingness so that God alone be exalted, who is in all things and works in everything [Rom. 8:28; 11:36; Eph. 4:6]. Here belongs all that Scripture teaches about giving praise, honor, and thanksgiving to God and rejoicing in God's name.

The Third

Yield to God so that all we do is done by him alone through us. This commandment requires us to be poor in spirit [Matt. 5:3], to sacrifice our nothingness to God so that God is our only God and that in us God's deeds may be glorified [2 Cor. 9:13] as the first two commandments require. Here belongs everything required of us: serving God,[38] listening to what is preached, doing good deeds, subjecting the body to the spirit [1 Cor. 9:27], so that all our works are God's and not our own.

The Fourth[39]

Show a willing obedience, humility, submissiveness to all authority as pleasing to God, as the Apostle St. Peter says [1 Pet. 2:13], without protesting, complaining, and murmuring. Here belongs all that is written regarding obedience, humility, submissiveness, and giving honor.

The Fifth

Patience, meekness, kindness, peacefulness, mercy, and in every circumstance a tender and friendly heart, devoid of all hatred,

---

37. This presages how Luther explains the First Commandment in the *Small Catechism* (1529), namely, that we should "fear, love, and trust God above all things."

38. The German is *gottis diensten* (see p. 169, n. 26 above).

39. In other places, Luther's explanation of the Fourth Commandment also includes a discussion of the duties and obligations of those in authority. See, for example, the *Large Catechism*, in BC, 409–10 ; TAL 2:314–27..

anger, and bitterness toward any person, even our enemies. Here belong all precepts concerning patience, meekness, peace, and harmonious relationships with others.

The Sixth

Chastity, decency, modesty in deeds, speech, attitude, and thought. Also moderation in eating, drinking, sleeping, and doing whatever encourages chastity. Here belong all precepts concerning chastity, fasting, sobriety, temperance, praying, being vigilant, working hard, and whatever else furthers chastity.

The Seventh

To be poor in spirit [Matt. 5:3], generous, willing to lend or give of our possessions, and to live free of avarice and covetousness. Here belongs all teaching about avarice, fraudulent gain, exploitative interest, deceit, craftiness, and allowing harm to happen to or hindering our neighbor's worldly goods.

The Eighth

A peaceful and beneficial manner of speech which harms no one and benefits everyone, reconciles the discordant, excuses and defends the maligned, that is, a manner of speech which is truthful and sincere. Here belong all precepts concerning when to keep silent and when to speak in matters affecting our neighbor's reputation, rights, concerns, and happiness.

The Last Two

They mean: perfect chastity and thorough disregard for all temporal pleasures and possessions—something not attainable until we reach the life beyond this one.

In all such actions we see nothing but an alien, comprehensive love toward God and our neighbor that never seeks its own advantage but only what serves God and our neighbor [1 Cor. 13:5]. And devotes itself freely to belonging to one's neighbor and serving him and his concerns.

Now you see that the Ten Commandments contain in a brief and orderly manner all precepts needful for a person's life.[40]

40. Luther emphasizes again that the Ten Commandments suffice—one does not need the various lists (of works of mercy, of various types of sin, etc.) common in medieval devotional works.

Anyone wishing to keep them all will find enough good deeds to do to fill every hour of the day; he need not hunt for other things to do, running here and there to do things which are not commanded.

We have clearly emphasized that these commandments prescribe nothing that a person is to do or leave undone for his own advantage, or expect of others for himself, but rather what a person is to do or leave undone toward others, toward God, and toward neighbor. Therefore we must comprehend the fulfillment of the commandments always as meaning love for others and not for ourselves. For a person is more than enough inclined to occupy himself with whatever benefits himself as things are. He needs no precepts for doing this, but needs rather to be restrained. The person who lives the best life does not live for himself; he who lives for himself lives the most dastardly kind of life. This is what the Ten Commandments teach, and they show us how few persons really live a good life, yes, that not one person is able to live this good life. Now that we recognize this, we must find out where to get the [medicinal] herbs to enable us to live a good life and fulfill the commandments.

Jesus

The Creed[41]

The Creed is divided into three main parts, each telling about one of the three persons of the holy divine Trinity.[42] The first— the Father; the second—the Son; and the third—the Holy Spirit. For this is the most important article in our faith, on which all the others are based.

Notice here that faith is exercised in two ways. First, a faith about God, meaning that I believe that what is said about God is true, just as I might say I believe that what people say about the Turks,[43] the devil, and hell is true. This kind of believing is more an item of knowledge or an observation than a creed. The second kind of faith means believing in God—not just that I believe that what is said about God is true, but that I put my trust in him, that I make the venture and take the risk to deal with him, believing beyond doubt that what God will be toward me or do with me will be just as they[q] say. I do not believe in this manner

41. The Apostles' Creed, the most common creed taught in western Europe in the medieval era.

42. Luther breaks with medieval tradition and discusses the Creed in terms of three parts, linking each to a member of the Trinity. Medieval works commonly discussed the Creed in twelve parts, linking each part to a particular apostle. By dropping from twelve to three, Luther not only simplifies the discussion but also puts the focus on the work of each member of the Trinity.

43. "Turks" may refer to people from the Ottoman Empire or to Muslims, the main religious group of the Ottoman Empire.

regarding any Turk or human being, no matter how highly he be praised. It is easy for me to believe that a certain man is outstandingly religious, but that is no reason for me to build [my life] upon him. Only a faith that ventures everything in life and in death on what is said of God makes a person a Christian and obtains all he desires from God.[44] No corrupt or hypocritical heart can have such a faith; this is a living faith as the First Commandment demands: I am your God; you shall have no other gods.

So that little word *in* is well chosen and should be noted carefully; we do not say, I believe God the Father, or I believe about the Father, but rather, I believe *in* God the Father, *in* Jesus Christ, in the Holy Spirit. And one should give this faith to no one except God alone and through it we confess the deity of Christ and of the Holy Spirit, thus believing in them just as we do in the Father. And just as there is one faith in all three Persons so the three Persons are one God.

The top portion of this 1511 painting by Albrecht Dürer (1471–1528) depicts God as Trinity. God the Father holds Christ the crucified Son, as the Holy Spirit as a dove flies above.

The First Part of the Creed

I believe in God, the Father almighty, maker of heaven and the earth. This means: I renounce the evil spirit, all idolatry, all sorcery, and all false belief.

I put my trust in no person on earth, not in myself, my power, my skill, my possessions, my piety, nor in anything else I may have.

I place my trust in no creature, whether in heaven or on earth.

I take the risk of placing my confidence only in the one, invisible, inscrutable, and only God, who created heaven and earth

44. Luther here discusses saving faith, contrasting it to mere intellectual knowledge.

q   A reference to the Scriptures.

and who alone is superior to all creation. Again, I am not terrified by all the wickedness of the devil and his cohorts because God is superior to them all.

I would believe in God not a bit less if I were to be forsaken and persecuted by all people.

I would believe in God no less if I were poor, unintelligent, uneducated, despised, or lacking in everything.

I believe no less though I am a sinner. For this manner of faith will of necessity rise over all that does or does not exist, over sin and virtue and all else, thus depending purely and completely upon God as the First Commandment enjoins me to do.

I do not ask for any sign from God to put God to the test.

I trust in God steadfastly, no matter how long God may delay, and prescribe neither a goal, nor a time, nor a measure, nor a way [for God to respond to me], but leave all to God's divine will in a free, honest, and genuine faith.

If God is almighty, what could I lack that God could not give or do for me?

If God is the Creator of heaven and earth and Lord over every thing, who, then, could deprive me of anything, or do me harm [Rom. 8:31]? Yes, how can it be otherwise than that all things work for good for me [Rom. 8:28] if the God whom all creation obeys and serves is well intentioned toward me?

If God is God, God can and knows how to do what is best with me. Since God is Father, God will do all this and do it gladly.

And since I do not doubt this but place my trust in God, I am assuredly God's child, servant, and eternal heir, and it will be with me as I believe.

The Second Part

And in Jesus Christ, his only Son, our Lord: who was conceived by the Holy Spirit, born of the virgin Mary, suffered under Pontius Pilate, was crucified, dead, and buried: he descended into hell, the third day he rose from the dead, he ascended into heaven, and is seated at the right hand of God, the Father almighty, whence he shall come to judge the living and the dead.

I do not only believe that Jesus Christ is the one true Son of God, begotten of him in eternity with one eternal divine nature and essence—but I also believe that the Father has made all things subject to him, that according to his human nature he has been made one Lord over me and all things which he created together with the Father in his divinity.

I believe that no one can believe in the Father and that no one can come to him by any ability, deeds, understanding, or anything that may be named in heaven or on earth [Eph. 3:15] but only in and through Jesus Christ, his only Son, that is, through faith in his name and lordship.

I firmly believe that for my welfare Christ was conceived by the Holy Spirit, by no human or carnal act and without any physical father or seed of man, so that he gives me and all who believe in him a pure, spiritual being, cleansing me of my sinful, carnal, impure, damnable conception [Ps. 51:5]—all this through his and the Almighty Father's gracious will.

I believe that for my sake he was born of the immaculate Virgin Mary,[45] without changing her physical and spiritual virginity, so that according to his fatherly mercy he might render my sinful and damnable birth blessed, innocent, and pure, as he does for all his believers.

I believe that for my sin and the sin of all believers Christ bore his suffering and cross and thereby transformed all suffering and every cross into a blessing—doing [the believer] no harm and even being salutary and most beneficial.

I believe that Christ died and was buried to put my sin to death [2 Tim. 1:10] and bury it and do the same for all believers and, moreover, that he slew human death [1 Cor. 15:26], transforming it into something that does no harm and is beneficial [Phil. 1:10] and salutary.

I believe that for me and all his believers Christ descended into hell to subdue the devil [1 Pet. 3:18-20] and take him captive along with all his power, cunning, and malice so that the devil can no longer harm me, and that he redeemed me from the pains of hell, transforming them into something nondestructive and beneficial.

I believe that he was resurrected from the dead on the third day to give a new life to me and all believers, thus awakening us with him by his grace and spirit henceforth to sin no more [Rom. 6:4; Gal. 2:20] but to serve him only with every grace and virtue, thus fulfilling God's commandments.

I believe that he ascended into heaven and received power and honor over all angels and creatures [Phil. 2:9-10] and now sits at God's right hand [Eph. 1:20-22]. This means that he is King

45. Luther shared the medieval belief that Mary remained a virgin even after the birth of Jesus.

and Lord over all that is God's in heaven, earth, and hell. Hence he can help me and all believers against all troubles and against every adversary and foe [Rom. 8:38-39].

I believe that Christ will return from heaven on the Last Day to judge those who are alive at that time and those who have died before that day [1 Thess. 4:16-17], that all humankind, angels, and devils will have to appear before his judgment [Matt. 18:35; Rom. 14:10; 1 Pet. 1:17] throne to see him visually. Then he will redeem me and all who believe in him from bodily death and every infirmity and will eternally punish his enemies and adversaries and deliver us from their power forever [Rev. 20:11-14].

The Third Part

I believe in the Holy Spirit, one holy Christian church,[46] one communion of saints, one forgiveness of sins, resurrection of the body, and life everlasting. Amen.

I believe not only what this means—that the Holy Spirit is truly God together with the Father and the Son—but also that except through the Holy Spirit's work no one can come in and to the Father through Christ and his life, his suffering and death, and all that is said of him, nor can anyone appropriate any of this to himself. Working through the Spirit, Father and Son stir, awaken, call, and beget new life in me and in all who are his. Thus the Spirit in and through Christ quickens, sanctifies, and awakens the spirit in us and brings us to the Father, so that the Father through Christ and in Christ is active and life-giving everywhere.

I believe that throughout the whole wide world there is only one holy, universal, Christian church, which is nothing other than the gathering or congregation of saints—pious believers on earth. This church is gathered, preserved, and governed by the same Holy Spirit and is given daily increase by means of the sacraments and the word of God.

I believe that no one can be saved who is not in this gathering or community, harmoniously sharing with it in one faith, word, sacraments, hope, and love. And that no Jew, heretic, pagan, or sinner can be saved along with this community unless he becomes reconciled with it and unites with it in full agreement in all things.

I believe that in this community or Christendom all things

46. Luther continues the late medieval German tradition of translating the Latin *Catholicam* as "Christian" rather than "catholic" or "universal." See Albrecht Peters, *Commentary on Luther's Catechisms: Creed*, trans. Thomas H. Trapp (St. Louis: Concordia, 2011), 267–72.

This illustration depicts the church gathered around the word preached and the sacraments of Baptism and Eucharist.

are held in common; what each one possesses belongs also to others and no one has complete ownership of anything. Hence, all the prayers and good deeds of all the Christian community benefit, aid, and strengthen me and every other believer at all times, both in life and in death, and that each one bears the other's burden, as St. Paul teaches [Gal. 6:2].

I believe that there is forgiveness of sin nowhere else than in this community and that beyond it nothing can help to gain it—no good deeds, no matter how many or how great they might be; and that within this community nothing can invalidate this forgiveness of sin—no matter how gravely and often one may sin; and that such forgiveness continues as long as this one community exists. To this [community] Christ gave the power of the keys,[47] saying in Matthew 18[:18], "Whatever you bind on earth shall be bound in heaven." He said the same to Peter as an individual, representing and taking the place of the one and only one church, "Whatever you bind on earth," etc., Matthew 16[:18-19].

I believe that there will be a resurrection from the dead in the future in which all flesh will be raised from the dead through the Holy Spirit, that is, all humankind, good and evil, will be raised bodily to return alive in the same flesh in which they died, were buried, and decayed or perished in various ways.

I believe that after the resurrection the saints will have eternal life and the sinners eternal dying. And I do not doubt all this, that the Father through his Son Jesus Christ our Lord and with the Holy Spirit will let all this happen to me. Amen, that is, this is a sure and trustworthy truth.

The Lord's Prayer

Preface and Preparation
for Praying the Seven Divine Petitions

Our Father who art in heaven
    What this means:
    O Almighty God, in your unmerited[48] goodness to us and through the merit and mediation of your only beloved Son, our Lord Jesus Christ, you have not only permitted but also commanded and taught us to regard you and call upon you as one Father of

47. Luther's assertion that the keys are given to the community directly contradicts the Roman view that Christ gave the keys to the disciple Peter and through him to his successors, the popes.

48. The German *grundlossz* has the double meaning of "unmerited" and "bottomless" or "unfathomable."

Jesus teaches his disciples
about prayer (Luke 11:1–13).

us all. You have done so although instead you could rightly and properly be a severe judge over us sinners since we have acted so often and gravely against your divine and good will and have aroused your wrath. Now through this same mercy implant in our hearts a comforting trust in your fatherly love, and let us experience the most sweet and pleasant savor of a childlike certainty that we may joyfully call you Father, knowing and loving you and calling on you in every trouble.[49] Watch over us that we may remain your children and never become guilty of making you, dearest Father, our fearful judge, and making ourselves, your children, into your foes.

You do not wish us just to call you Father but that we all, together, should call on you, Our Father, and so harmoniously pray for all. Therefore grant us a harmonious love so that we may all regard and accept each other as true brothers and sisters and turn to you as the dear Father of us all, praying for all persons as one child might entreat his father for someone else. Let us not seek only our own advantage in prayer before you, forgetting the other person, but let us strip ourselves of all hatred, envy, and discord, and love each other as true pious children of God, and thus all repeat together not *my* Father, but *our* Father.

Moreover, since you are not a physical father here on earth but a spiritual Father in heaven, not like an earthly, mortal father who dies and is not always dependable and may not be able to help himself, show us what an immeasurably better Father you are and teach us to regard earthly fatherhood, fatherland, friends, possessions, body and blood as far less in value than you. Grant us, O Father, that we may be your heavenly children, and teach us to value only our spiritual and heavenly inheritance, lest an earthly father, fatherland, or earthly goods delude, catch, and hinder us and make us into merely children of this world. And grant that we might say with true conviction: O our heavenly Father, we are truly your heavenly children.

The First Petition

Hallowed be your name
What this means:
O Almighty God, dear heavenly Father, in this wretched vale of tears your holy name is sadly profaned, blasphemed, and reviled in so many ways. In so many instances it is regarded with-

49. Luther's description of the child calling on the father here contrasts sharply with other medieval descriptions of prayer. Kolde (87) tells his readers they should ask in three ways: "First, you should ask as a criminal who asks the judge not to sentence him to death. Second, you should ask as a poor man asking a rich lord for gifts and possessions. Third, you should ask as a dear child fondly asks his dear father."

out honor to you and is often misused in many matters and in sinning, so that to live a disgraceful life might well be regarded as the same as disgracing and dishonoring your holy name.

Therefore grant us your divine grace that we might guard against all that does not serve to the honor and glory of your holy name. Help to do away with all sorcery and magic incantations. Help put an end to conjuring by the devil or other creatures by your name. Help root out all false belief and superstition. Help bring to naught all heresies and false doctrines that are spread under the guise of your name. Help that no one be deceived by the many kinds of falsehood that go under the pretense of truth, piety, and holiness. Help that no one may use your name to swear, lie, or deceive. Protect us from all false and imaginary consolation that might be given in your name. Protect us against all spiritual arrogance and false pride based on temporal fame or reputation. Help us to call upon your holy name in all our troubles and infirmities. Help us not to forget your name when we lie on our deathbed and our conscience is troubled. Help that we may use all our possessions, speech, and deeds to glorify and honor you alone and that we do not seek to claim or seek a reputation in doing this, but that all we do be done for you to whom alone everything belongs. Protect us from the shameful vice of ingratitude.

Help that our good deeds and conduct may incite others to praise not us, but you in us and to honor your name. Help so that our evil actions and shortcomings may not offend anyone, leading them to dishonor your name or to neglect your praise. Protect us from asking you for anything temporal or eternal which would not serve the glory and honor of your name. Should we petition you in such a way, do not listen to our folly. Help us conduct all our life in such a way that we may be found to be true children of God, so that your fatherly name is not named among us falsely or in vain. Amen.

And in this prayer belong all psalms and prayers in which one praises, honors, sings, and thanks God and every alleluia.

The Second Petition

May your kingdom come near[50]
>What this means:
>This wretched life is a realm[51] of every sin and malice, whose

50. Luther's German reads *zukomme dein Reich. Zukommen* means "to approach," "to come near," or "to send forward."

51. The German here is *Reich,* or "kingdom."

one lord is the evil spirit, the initiator and villainous instigator of all sin and wickedness. Yours is a realm, however, of every virtue and grace, whose one Lord is Jesus Christ, your dear Son, the Author and Beginner of every grace and truth. For this, dear Father, give us help and grace. Above all else grant us a true and constant faith in Christ, a fearless hope in your mercy overcoming all the stupidity of our sinful conscience, and a kindly love toward you and all people.

Protect us from unbelief, despair, and from boundless envy. Deliver us from the filthy lust of unchastity and grant us a love of every kind of virginity and chastity. Deliver us from discord, war, and dissension, and let the virtue, peace, harmony, and tranquility of your kingdom draw near. Help us that anger or other bitterness may not reign over us, but that by your grace, genuine kindness, loyalty, and every kind of friendliness, generosity, and gentleness may reign in us. Grant that inordinate sadness and depression may not prevail in us, but let joy and delight in your grace and mercy come over us. And finally may all sins be averted from us and, being filled with your grace and with all virtues and good deeds, may we become your kingdom so that in heart,[52] feeling, and thought we may serve you with all our strength inwardly and outwardly, obediently serving your commandments and will, being governed by you alone and not following self-love, the flesh, the world, or the devil.

Help that your kingdom, begun in us, may daily increase and improve, lest cunning malice and apathy for doing good overcome us so that we slip back. Rather grant us both an earnest resolve and an ability not only to begin to live a pious life but also to make vigorous progress in it and reach its goal. As the prophet says, "Lighten my eyes, lest I sleep the sleep of death or become slothful in the good life I have begun, and my enemy again have power over me."[r]

Help, that we may thus remain steadfast and that your future kingdom may be the end and consummation of the kingdom you have begun. Help us get free from this sinful and perilous life. Help us to yearn for that future life and be an enemy of this

---

52. "Heart" for Luther includes both reason and emotion, that is, he does not share the modern tendency to let "heart" refer merely to the emotions. "For Luther, thought is intimately connected to emotion. The mutual connection between thought and emotion is a major presupposition of Luther's anthropology. . . . This classic conception of the human heart has a very wide range of meaning from thinking to feeling. Today, the metaphorical sense of 'heart' is restricted to mere 'feeling.'" Birgit Stolt, "Luther's Faith of 'the Heart,'" in Christine Helmer, ed., *The Global Luther: A Theologian for Modern Times* (Minneapolis: Fortress Press, 2009), 135. See also Birgit Stolt, *"Lasst uns fröhlich springen!" Gefühlswelt und Gefühlsnavigierung in Luthers Reformationsarbeit* (Berlin: Weidler, 2012), esp. 252–54.

r   Psalm 13:3b-4. To this passage, Luther added "become slothful in the good life I have begun."

present life. Help us not to fear death but to desire it. Turn us from love and attachment to this life so that in everything your kingdom may be accomplished in us.

And in this petition belong all psalms, verses, and prayers that implore God for grace and virtue.

The Third Petition

Your will be done on earth as it is in heaven

What this means:

Compared with your will, our will is never good but always evil. Your will is at all times the best, to be cherished and desired above everything else. Therefore have mercy upon us, O dear Father, and let nothing happen just because it is our own will. Grant and teach us a deep patience in times when our will is prevented from happening or comes to nothing. Help when others contradict our will by what they say or do not say, do or leave undone, that we not become angry or vexed, not curse, complain, protest, condemn, disparage, or contradict. Help us to yield humbly to our adversaries and those who obstruct our will, surrendering our own will so that we praise, bless, and do good to these adversaries as persons who are carrying out your best and godly purposes in contradiction to our own.

Grant us grace to bear willingly all sorts of sickness, poverty, disgrace, suffering, and adversity and to recognize that in this your divine will is crucifying our will. Help us also to endure injustice gladly and preserve us from taking revenge. Let us not repay evil with evil [Matt. 5:39; Rom. 12:19, 21] nor meet violence with violence, but rather let us rejoice that these things happen to us according to your will and so let us praise and give thanks to you [Matt. 5:11]. Let us not ascribe to the devil or to evil persons anything that happens contrary to our will, but solely ascribe this to your divine will which orders everything that may hinder our will in order to increase the blessedness of your kingdom. Help us to die willingly and gladly and readily accept death as your will so that we do not become disobedient to you through impatience or discouragement.

Grant that we do not give our bodily members—eyes, tongue, heart, hands, and feet—free rein for what they desire or purpose, but make them captive to your will, bring them to a stop, and subdue them. Protect us from any kind of evil will—rebellious, stubborn, stiff-necked, obstinate, or capricious. Grant us true obedience, a perfect, calm, single-minded composure in all things—spiritual, earthly, temporal, and eternal. Protect us from the horrible vice of character assassination, from slander, back-biting, frivolously judging, condemning others, and misrepresenting what others have said. O hold far from us the plague and tragedy that such speech can cause; rather, whenever we see or hear anything in others that seems wrong or displeasing to us, teach us to keep quiet, not to publicize it, and to pour out our complaints to you alone and to commit all to your will. And so let us sincerely forgive all who wrong us and be sympathetic toward them.

Teach us to recognize that none can harm us without first harming themselves a thousand times more in your eyes, so that we might thus be moved more to pity rather than to anger toward such persons, to commiserate with them rather than to count up their wrongs. Help us to refrain from rejoicing whenever those who did not do our will or did us harm in their conduct are struck with adversity or other misfortune in their lives. Also help us not to be saddened by their good fortune.

To this petition belongs every psalm, verse, or prayer which petitions for help against sin and our foes.

The Fourth Petition

Give us this day our daily bread

What this means:

This bread is our Lord Jesus Christ who feeds and comforts the soul [John 6:51].[53] Therefore, O heavenly Father, grant grace that the life, words, deeds, and suffering of Christ be preached, made known, and preserved for us and all the world. Help that we may find in his words and deeds a powerful example and mirror of all virtues for all of life. Help that we may be strengthened and comforted in suffering and adversity in and through his suffering and cross. Help that we through his death overcome our own death with a firm faith and thus boldly follow our beloved Guide into the life beyond this one.

Graciously grant that all pastors preach your word and Christ throughout the world in a way effective for salvation. Help that all who hear the preaching of your word may learn to know Christ and thus sincerely lead better lives. May you also

53. This explanation of the fourth petition does not relate "daily bread" to bodily needs as does the explanation in the *Small Catechism*. Medieval interpretations often gave "bread" a spiritual meaning, including an understanding of "bread" as the bread of the Lord's Supper. Luther appropriated and changed this tradition. In his early works he understood "bread" as the Word of God, or Christ. See Paul W. Robinson, "Luther's Explanation of Daily Bread in Light of Medieval Preaching," *Lutheran Quarterly* (NS) 13 no. 4 (Winter 1999), 435–47.

graciously drive out of the holy church all foreign doctrine and preaching that do not teach Christ.

Be merciful to all bishops, priests, other clergy, and to all in authority that illumined by your grace they may teach and lead us correctly through speech and good example.

Protect all who are weak in faith that they may not be offended by the bad example set by those in authority.

Protect us against heretical and apostate teachers[54] so that we may remain united in one daily bread—the daily teaching and word of Christ. Teach us by your grace to contemplate Christ's suffering in a proper manner, to take it to heart and rejoice to copy it in our lives. Let us not be deprived of the holy and true body of Christ at our final end. Help all priests to administer and use the sacred sacrament worthily and blessedly for the betterment of all Christendom. Help that we and all Christians blessedly receive the holy sacrament with grace at the proper time.

And in summary, give us our daily bread so that Christ may remain in us eternally and we in him [John 15:5], and that we may worthily bear the name of Christian as derived from Christ.[55]

In this petition belong all prayers or psalms offered for those in authority and especially those directed against false teachers, those for the Jews, heretics, and all persons who err, those also for the grief-stricken and those who suffer without hope.

The Fifth Petition

And do not hold us accountable for our sins, as we do not hold accountable those who sin against us

What this means:

This petition has one supplement and condition: we must first forgive those who sin against us. When we have done that, then we may say, "Forgive us our sins." That is what we prayed for earlier in the Third Petition—that God's will be done, the will that one should endure everything with patience and not repay evil with evil, not seek revenge, but give good for evil as our Father in heaven does, who lets his sun rise on the pious and the evil and sends rain to those who thank him and to those who do not [Matt. 5:45]. Therefore we implore you, O Father, comfort us in the present and in the hour of our death[56] when

54. Luther probably had in mind here not only his Roman Catholic opponents but also those who claimed to follow him but, to his way of thinking, had taken his thinking in directions he did not intend.

55. Albrecht Peters traces the change in Luther's understanding of "bread" in the fourth petition. Prior to 1523, Luther understood "bread" as Christ, the bread of life, the food for the soul; beginning in 1523 he gives physical bread a broader place and by 1528 actual bread, the meeting of physical needs, is paramount. See Albrecht Peters, *Commentary on Luther's Catechisms: Lord's Prayer*, trans. Daniel Thies (St. Louis: Concordia, 2011), 124–30. See also Rudolf Dellsperger, "Unser tägliches Brot . . . Die Brotbitte bei Erasmus von Rotterdam, Martin Luther, Wolfgang Musculus und Petrus Canisius SJ," in Emidio Campi, Leif Grane, and Adolf Martin Ritter, eds., *Oratio: Das Gebet in patristischer und reformatorischer Sicht* (Göttingen: Vandenhoeck & Ruprecht, 1999), 211–26.

56. Here Luther understands the petition to be asking God to console us when we die. Much medieval devotional literature was intended to console the dying and help them take proper actions to prepare for death.

our conscience is and will be frightened terribly by our sins and by your judgment.

Grant your peace in our hearts that we may anticipate your judgment with joy. Let us not feel the harshness of your judgment, for no one could then be found righteous before you [Ps. 143:2]. Teach us, dear Father, not to rely on or find consolation in our good deeds or in merit, but simply to venture all upon your boundless mercy, committing ourselves with utter firmness to it alone. Likewise, let not our guilty and sinful life bring us into despair, but rather let us regard your mercy as higher, broader, and stronger than anything in our lives.

Help all who in peril of death and times of temptation are frightened by despair, particularly those whom we name. Have mercy upon all poor souls in purgatory, especially those we name [in our prayer]. Forgive them and all of us our sins, comfort them, and take them under your mercy.

Repay our wickedness with your goodness, as you have commanded us to do [to others]. Silence that evil spirit—the cruel backbiter, accuser, and magnifier of our sin—now and in our last hour, and in every torment of conscience, just as we, on our part, hold back from backbiting and magnifying the sins of others. Do not judge us according to the accusations of the devil or our wretched conscience, and pay no heed to the voice of our enemies who accuse us day and night before you, just as in turn we will pay no heed to the backbiters and accusers of others.

Relieve us of every heavy burden of sin and conscience so that we may live and die, suffer and conduct ourselves with a light and happy heart in complete confidence of your mercy.

In this petition belong all psalms and prayers which invoke God's mercy for our sin.

The Sixth Petition

And lead us not into temptation

What this means:

Three temptations or trials confront us: the flesh, the world, and the devil. Hence we pray: Dear Father, grant us grace that we may overcome fleshly lusts. Help that we may withstand excesses in eating and drinking, sleeping too much, idleness, and laziness. Help us through fasting, moderation in food, dress, and sleep, waking and working, to become serviceable and skilled in good works. Help us, with Christ, to crucify and put to death the evil inclination to unchastity and all of its desires and entice-ments [Rom. 6:6] that we may not yield to any temptations of the flesh or follow them. Help that when we look at a beautiful person or picture or any other creature, that this may not bring us into temptation but rather be an occasion for cherishing chas-tity and praising you in your creatures. Help that when we hear something pleasant or feel something pleasurable that we do not seek to indulge our lust in this but rather seek to praise and glo-rify you for it.

Protect us from the great vice of avarice and covetousness with regard to the riches of this world. Protect us from seeking honor and power in this world, or from even being inclined in this direction. Protect us that the deceit, delusion, and entice-ment of this world may not stir us to follow them. Keep us that we be not drawn into impatience, vindictiveness, anger, or other vices by the world's evil and unpleasantness.

Help us to renounce and forsake the world's deceit and delu-sion, promises and fickleness—all its good or evil—as we vowed to do in baptism. Help that we may remain steadfast and grow daily in [the promise of our baptism].

Protect us from the devil's whisperings so that we do not give in to pride, our own pleasure, and a contempt for others in order to gain wealth, high rank, power, skill, beauty, or any other good gift of yours. Protect us that we may not fall into hatred or envy for any reason whatsoever. Protect us that we may not fall victim to temptation of faith and despair, now and at our last hour.

Heavenly Father, may all who work and struggle against these great and manifold temptations be committed to your care. Strengthen those who are unbowed, raise up those who have fallen and are defeated. And give us all your grace, that we in the wretched insecurities of this life, being surrounded con-stantly by so many foes, may do battle with a firm and valiant faith, and may obtain an eternal crown.

The Seventh Petition

But deliver us from evil

What this means:

This petition bids for deliverance from every evil of pain and punishment, as the holy church does in the litanies. Deliver us,

O Father, from your eternal wrath and from the pangs of hell. Deliver us, O Father, in death and on Judgment Day, from your severe condemnation. Deliver us from sudden death. Protect us from fire and flood, from lightning and hail. Protect us from hunger and inflation. Protect us from war and bloodshed. Protect us from your plagues, pestilence, venereal disease, and other grave sickness. Protect us from every bodily evil and woe, to the end, that your name may be honored, your kingdom increased, and your divine will accomplished. Amen.

Amen

God grant that we may obtain all these petitions with certainty. Let us not doubt that you have heard us in the past and will do so in the future, answering us with a Yes and not a No or a Maybe. So we cheerfully say Amen—this is true and certain. Amen.

The Hail Mary[57]

Take note of this: no one should put his trust or confidence in the Mother of God or in her merits, for such confidence is worthy of God alone and is the lofty service due only to him.[58] Rather praise and thank God through Mary and the grace given her. Laud and love her simply as the one who, without merit, obtained such blessings from God, sheerly out of his mercy, as she herself testifies in the Magnificat [Luke 1:46-55].

It is very much the same when I, viewing the heavens, the sun, and all creation, am moved to praise the creator of all these and say: O God, Author of such a beautiful and perfect creation, grant to me. . . . Similarly, our prayer should include the Mother of God and say: O God, what a noble person you have created in her! May she be blessed! And so on. And you who honored her so highly, grant also to me . . . etc.

Let not our hearts cling to her in faith, but through her penetrate to Christ and to God himself. Thus what the Hail Mary says is that all glory should be given to God, using these words: "Hail, Mary, full of grace. The Lord is with you [Luke 1:28]; blessed are you among women and blessed is the fruit of thy body, Jesus Christ. Amen."

You see that these words are not concerned with prayer but purely with giving praise and honor, just as in the first words of

57. Luther includes one of the most common elements of medieval piety, the Hail Mary. Mary was seen as a patron of childbirth. But her appeal was broader. By the late Middle Ages, regional church synods were mandating that the Hail Mary be taught and recited, along with the Lord's Prayer and the Creed. It was considered one of the basic prayers of the church for both clergy and lay. See, for example, Anne L. Clark, "The Cult of the Virgin Mary and Technologies of Christian Formation," in John Van Engen, ed., *Educating People of Faith* (Grand Rapids: Eerdmans, 2004), 227–39.

58. Luther immediately makes a statement about how Mary is to be regarded. Rejecting medieval views that encourage prayer to Mary and even see her as a mediator between God and humans, he encourages an evangelical view of Mary. Luther's inclusion of the Hail Mary in his prayer book is another example of Luther taking a common element of medieval piety and, rather than rejecting it outright, giving it an evangelical interpretation.

the Lord's Prayer there is also no prayer but rather praise and glory to God, that he is our Father and is in heaven. Therefore we should make the Hail Mary neither a prayer nor an invocation because it is improper for us to interpret the words beyond what they mean in themselves and beyond the meaning given them by the Holy Spirit.

But there are two things we can do. First, we can use the Hail Mary as a meditation in which we recite what grace God has given her. Second, we can add a wish that everyone may know and respect her [as one blessed by God].

In the first place, she is full of grace, so that she is known as entirely without sin—something exceedingly great. For God's grace fills her with everything good and makes her devoid of all evil.

In the second place, God is with her, meaning that all she does or leaves undone is divine and the action of God in her. Moreover, God guards and protects her from all that might be hurtful to her.

Madonna under the Fir Tree by Lucas Cranach the Elder (1510)

In the third place, she is blessed above all other women, not only because she gave birth without labor, pain, and injury to herself, not as Eve and all other women, but because by the Holy Spirit and without sin, she became fertile, conceived, and gave birth in a way granted to no other woman.

In the fourth place, her [bodily] fruit is blessed in that it is spared the curse upon all children of Eve who are conceived in sin [Ps. 51:5] and born to deserve death and damnation. But only the fruit of her body is blessed, and through the same we are all blessed.

Furthermore, a prayer or wish is to be added, so that one prays for all who speak evil against this Fruit and the Mother. But who is it that speaks evil of this Fruit and the Mother? All who persecute and speak evil against his word, the gospel, and the faith, as Jews and papists are now doing.

From the above it follows that in the present no one speaks evil of this Mother and her Fruit as much as those who bless her

59. Luther was very familiar with medieval Marian piety. We know that he read a devotional work (*Marienpsalter*) containing the rosary. His marginal notes indicate his doubts about claims made about the rosary's antiquity as well as his complaint that, instead of being pointed to Christ, humans are left to rely on their own works. See D. G. Kawerau, "Luthers Randglossen zum Marienpsalter 1515," *Theologische Studien und Kritiken* 80 (1917): 81–87.

with many rosaries and constantly mouth the Hail Mary. These, more than any others, speak evil against Christ's word and faith in the worst way.[59]

Therefore, notice that this Mother and her Fruit are blessed in a twofold way—bodily and spiritually. [Those who bless her] bodily with lips and the words of the Hail Mary blaspheme and speak evil of her most dangerously. And [those who bless her] spiritually in their hearts praise and bless her child, Christ in all his words, deeds, and sufferings. No one does this except the one who has the true Christian faith because without such faith no heart is good but is naturally stuffed full of evil speech and blasphemy against God and all the saints. For that reason the one who has no faith is advised to refrain from saying the Hail Mary and all other prayers. For it is written of such people: *Oratio eius fiat ynn peccatum*: Let his prayer be sin [Ps. 109:7].

60. Luther appended the German texts of eight psalms at this point in his prayer book. Only the psalm numbers and Luther's captions are given in our translation. There seems to be no readily apparent reason for choosing these eight psalms. It may be that Luther chose these in place of the penitential psalms in some prayer books and as psalms which stated the most needed emphases of Christian prayer, as the captions Luther wrote seem to indicate.

61. Just a few years later, Luther used Psalms 12 and 67 as the bases for two of his early hymns: "Ach Gott vom Himmel sieh darein . . ." (Psalm 12; LW 53:225–28) and "Es wollt uns Gott gnädig sein . . ." (Psalm 67; LW 53:232–34; WA 10/2:339).

Psalm 12[60]
To be prayed for the exaltation of the holy gospel

Psalm 67[61]
To be prayed for the increase of faith

Psalm 51
Concerning the whole matter, that is, the essential [matter] and original sin together with its fruits

Psalm 103
For thanking God for all his goodness

Psalm 20
For good government and for earthly authorities

Psalm 79
Against the enemies of the Christian church and the gospel

Psalm 25
A general prayer to submit to God in all things

Psalm 10
To be prayed against the Antichrist and his kingdom

The Epistle of St. Paul to Titus[62]

To give instruction for living a Christian life

Preface to St. Paul's Epistle to Titus[5]

This letter is a brief but finely formed model for Christian instruction, in which a number of things are masterfully discussed, that a Christian needs to know and to live. In the first chapter he [St. Paul] teaches what kind of person a bishop or pastor should be—namely, pious and educated for preaching the gospel and for refuting the false teaching of [salvation by] works and human precepts which continually do battle against faith and lead a person's conscience away from Christian liberty into the prison of their human works, which, after all, are vain.

In the second chapter he [St. Paul] instructs persons in all situations of life—the old and the young, women and men, masters and servants—how to conduct themselves as those whom Christ has won through his death to be his own.

In the third chapter he [St. Paul] teaches [us] to honor and obey governmental authorities in this world and calls attention again to the grace which Christ has gained for us, lest anyone think that obedience to the government suffices because before God all our righteousness amounts to nothing. And he commands us to shun those who are stubborn and heretics.

[Here Luther appended his German text of the Epistle to Titus.]

62. Luther included a translation of Titus in the earliest editions. The text (not translated here) shows some variations from the version that appeared later that year in his translation of the New Testament (the *September Testament*), indicating that he polished the text after he translated it for his prayer book. Later editions of the prayer book included that revised text.

---

5   The preface for Titus was added in the fifth printing of 1522. It was the same preface Luther wrote for use in his *September Testament* (1522).

63. Luther's Passional did not appear in the 1522 edition on which our prayer book translation is based. It was first printed in the Wittenberg edition of 1529. His substitute for the traditional passion history of the old prayer books with their legends about the Virgin Mary and the saints was a collection of fifty full-page woodcuts to illustrate stories from the Bible ranging from the creation to the last judgment. Under each woodcut Luther placed a title and a brief biblical text (indicated by the Bible references given). The selection of subject matter is significant because it indicates what Luther thought was important for a layperson to know about the Bible and to use for personal edification. In editions after 1529 woodcuts from Dürer's *Short Passion History* were substituted.

64. Luther's focus on teaching the biblical story here stands in contrast to medieval uses of the passion story. The popular late medieval prayer book *Hortulus animae* ("Garden of the Soul") contained many prayers focusing on the passion of Christ: "A description of the contents of the 1530 edition . . . [includes] the hours of the passion of Christ attributed to Bonaventure, a prayer entitled the 'golden passional,' a prayer attributed to Ambrose about each of the 'articles' of the passion of Christ, an abbreviated version of the said prayer, a prayer attributed to the Venerable Bede based on the seven last words of Christ and a prayer hailing the five wounds of Christ. This section of prayers concludes with the text of the passion according to John, which in turn is followed by the seven penitential psalms and the litany to the saints." See Reinis, *Reforming the Art of Dying*, 40.

65. Christ's passion was one of the key devotional themes of the late Middle

Passional[63]

Martin Luther[64]

I thought it expedient to add to the *Little Prayer Book* the old "Passional"[65] especially for the sake of children and simple people who are more apt to retain the divine stories when taught by picture and parable than merely by words or instruction. As St. Mark testifies,*t* Christ also preached in ordinary parables for the sake of simple folk.*u*

I have added some more stories from the Bible along with sayings from the text so that both may be retained more firmly. I hope that this may mark a beginning and set an example for others to follow and to improve upon as their talents allow.[66]

I do not think it wrong to paint such stories along with the verses on the walls of rooms and chambers so that one might have God's words and deeds constantly in view and thus encourage fear and faith toward God.[67] And what harm would there be if someone were to illustrate the important stories of the entire Bible in their proper order for a small book which might become known as a layman's Bible? Indeed, one cannot bring God's words and deeds too often to the attention of the common people. Even if concerning God's word, one sings and speaks, lets resound and preaches, writes and reads, and paints and draws it, Satan with his angels and cohorts is always strong and alert to hinder and suppress God's word. Hence our project and concern are not only useful, but necessary—in fact, very badly needed.

I don't care if the iconoclasts condemn and reject this.[68] They do not need our teaching and we don't want theirs, so it is easy for us to part company. I have always condemned and criticized the misuse of [religious] pictures and the false confidence placed in them and all the rest. But whatever is no misuse of pictures I

---

t   Mark 4:11.

u   For a study of attempts to convey Reformation theology on a popular level, see Robert Scribner, *For the Sake of Simple Folk: Popular Propaganda for the German Reformation* (Cambridge: Cambridge University Press, 1981).

The crucifixion of Jesus for 1550 printing
of *Hortulus animae*. In the background,
two scenes are depicted as foreshadowing
this event. On the right, Israelites in the wilderness
gaze upon the bronze serpent lifted on a cross.
On the left, an angel prevents Abraham
from sacrificing his son Isaac.
The monogrammist A.W. has left his mark
at the lower left corner.

Ages. Much art and various forms of literature were devoted to it. See, for example, Richard Kieckhefer, "Major Currents in Late Medieval Devotion," in Jill Raitt, ed., in collaboration with Bernard McGinn and John Meyendorff, *Christian Spirituality: High Middle Ages and Reformation* (New York: Crossroad, 1987), 83–89.

66. Luther encourages here solely the use of Bible stories—not the legends of the saints or the Virgin Mary, which were popular motifs of various forms of medieval art. More generally on Luther, art, and the Reformation, see Carl C. Christensen, *Art and the Reformation in Germany* (Athens: Ohio University Press, 1979).

67. Robert Scribner notes, "Protestant supporters of images, such as Luther, recognized the cognitive value of pictures for the education of pious Christians and strove to create a link between images and word. Iconophobes such as Zwingli denied this possibility: the pious Christian should know God with his or her heart only." Robert Scribner, "Perceptions of the Sacred in Germany," in Roper, ed., *Religion and Culture*, 97.

68. In this paragraph, Luther rejects iconoclastic views. Iconoclasts (destroyers of images) had claimed that images should not be used by Christians because they led to idolatry. Luther had returned from the Wartburg in early 1522 to stop reform moves that included the destruction of images. Luther saw clearly that, though images could be misused, they could also be used for the building up of faith. See also pp. 10–11 in this volume.

69. Just four examples of the forty-nine woodcuts in the 1529 Wittenberg printing of *Little Prayer Book* are included below.

have always permitted and encouraged their retention for beneficial and edifying results. This is the way we teach our common people; those clever fellows shall be neither our pupils nor our masters. May Christ be with all who believe in him and love him. Amen.

[Here followed the woodcuts with Luther's captions].[69]

God creates the world (Gen. 1:1, 31; 2:2)

God created the world. Gen. 1:1, 31; 2:2.

God blows breath into Adam and creates Eve. Gen. 1:27; 2:22-23.

Eve offers an apple to Adam. Gen. 2:10-17; 3:4-5.

Expulsion from the Garden of Eden. Gen. 3:15.

Noah's ark. Gen. 6:5-6; 7:17, 23.

Destruction of Sodom. Gen. 18:20; 19:24-25.

Eating the first Passover meal. Exod. 12:3, 5-6.

Pharaoh drowns in the Red Sea. Exod. 14:27-29.

Moses receives the tables of the law. Exod. 20:1-2; Deut. 4:13.

Rain of manna. Exod. 16:14-15; Deut. 8:3.

The bronze serpent. Num. 21:8; John 3:14-15.

The annunciation of Mary. Isa. 7:14; Luke 1:30-31.

Mary and Elizabeth. Luke 1:39-56.

The birth of Christ. Luke 2:6-7.

Circumcision [of the Infant Jesus]. Luke 2:21.

Adoration of the Magi. Matt. 2:1-3, 11.

Slaughter of the infants [in Bethlehem]. Matt. 2:10-18.

Twelve-year-old Jesus in the Temple. Luke 2:43, 46, 49.

John [the Baptist] preaching. John 1:6-7; Luke 3:3.

Baptism of Christ. Matt. 3:13, 16-17.

Temptation [of Jesus]. Matt. 4:1, 4, 7, 10.

Marriage feast at Cana. John 2:2-3, 10.

Death of John [the Baptist]. Matt. 14:6-11.

Healing of the blind man and raising of Lazarus.
    Luke 18:35, 38; John 11:25-26, 43-44.

Entry on Palm Sunday. Matt. 21:5, 8-9.

Jesus washes the disciples' feet. John 13:4-5.

Lord's Supper. Luke 22:15, 19-20.

Gethsemane. Matt. 26:36ff.; Luke 22:43-44.

Arrest of Jesus. Matt. 26:47-56.

Jesus before Caiaphas. Mark 14:46, 53, 55.

Jesus before Pontius Pilate. Luke 22:66; 23:1, 3.

Scourging [of Jesus]. Luke 23:13, 16; John 19:1.

Soldiers crown Jesus. Matt. 27:27-31.

Pilate shows Jesus to the crowd. John 19:4-5.

Pilate washes his hands. Matt. 27:34-35.

Jesus carries his cross. Matt. 27:31; John 19:17.

Jesus is nailed to the cross. John 19:18-19.

Crucifixion. Luke 23:34, 46.

Jesus taken from the cross. Luke 23:50-53.

Jesus laid in the tomb. John 19:40-42.

Resurrection. Matt. 28:1-4.

The women at the grave. Matt. 28:5-7.

Jesus appears to Mary Magdalene. John 20:11-17.

Rain of manna
(Exod. 16:14 15; Deut. 8:3)

Gethsemane
(Matt. 26:36ff.; Luke 22:43-44)

70. Rather than ending with the last judgment, Luther ends with a picture of messengers, sent two by two, armed with the story portrayed in the preceding forty-nine woodcuts. That story is not just for information; rather, it is "for you." Timothy J. Wengert, "Lutheran Missions," *Lutheran Quarterly* 29 (2015): 77–78. See the accompanying image.

Jesus shows himself to Thomas. John 20:26-27.

Ascension. Mark 16:14-19.

Outpouring of the Holy Spirit. Acts 2:1-4.

Baptism, preaching, and Lord's Supper in a church. Mark 16:20; Acts 2:38, 41.

Christ as judge of the world. Matt. 26:64; 16:27.

Jesus commissions the disciples. Mark 16:15-16; Ps. 19:5.[70]

Jesus commissions the disciples
(Mark 16:15–16; Ps. 19:5)

The Small Catechism

1529

TIMOTHY J. WENGERT

INTRODUCTION

The word *catechism* derives from the Greek verb *katēcheō*, "to sound over," and, hence, to teach by word of mouth.[a] In early Christianity, it simply stood for instructing, as in Gal. 6:6. From there it passed, transliterated, into ancient church Latin. By the fifth century, Augustine (354–430) was employing a Latin noun, *catechismus*, for basic instruction in church teaching. (The equivalent Greek noun also first appears around this time.) By the high or late Middle Ages, these basics came regularly to include especially the Ten Commandments, the Apostles' Creed, and the Lord's Prayer, to which sometimes the *Ave Maria* (Hail Mary) was added. Preachers were to give instruction in the catechism four times a year around the "Ember Weeks" (the third or fourth week in Advent; first week of Lent; Pentecost week; and around Holy

---

a   For the following history, see Robert Kolb, *Teaching God's Children His Teaching: A Guide for the Study of Luther's Catechism*, 2d ed. (St. Louis: Concordia Seminary Press, 2012); Charles P. Arand, *That I May Be His Own: An Overview of Luther's Catechisms* (St. Louis: Concordia, 2000); Timothy J. Wengert, *Martin Luther's Catechisms: Forming the Faith* (Minneapolis: Fortress Press, 2009); Albrecht Peters, *Commentary on Luther's Catechisms*, trans. Thomas H. Trapp, 5 vols. (St. Louis: Concordia, 2009–2013).

Cross Day [14 September], and penitents were to be quizzed in the confessional about their knowledge of the basics.

The Development of Luther's Small Catechism

This tradition is reflected in Luther's early preaching on the Ten Commandments, the Lord's Prayer, and the Creed,[b] and it continued into the 1520s and beyond. In 1520, Luther's sermons on these three parts were gathered into a single tract and in 1522 Luther expanded that into his prayer booklet.[c] Here, for the first time, Luther explains why he orders the parts of catechetical instruction the way he does.

A popular catechism by Dietrich Kolde (c. 1435–1515)[d] had used the Sacrament of Penance as its model for organizing these various parts—beginning with the Creed (which all in a state of sin could confess), moving to the Commandments and other lists of sins (as preparation for contrition and confession to a priest), before introducing the Lord's Prayer (as one prayer to be said to make satisfaction for the punishment for sin remaining after confession had removed one's guilt and reduced one's punishment from eternal to temporal). By contrast, already in 1522 Luther viewed the Commandments as the diagnosis of sin and need for grace, and thus placed them first in his catechetical writings. He then pointed to the Creed as grace, the medicine for sin, and finally he defined the Lord's Prayer as the plea to God to deliver the cure. His *Large Catechism* and *Small Catechism* would retain this same order for these same reasons.

In 1525, the first true forerunner to the *Small Catechism* appeared in Wittenberg from the presses of Nicholas Schirlentz and was quickly translated into *Niederdeutsch* (the dialect of the German lowlands from Magdeburg northward).[e] It contained

---

b   See, for example, *An Exposition of the Lord's Prayer for Simple Laymen* (1519), in LW 42:15–81.

c   See pp. 159–99 in this volume.

d   See Dietrich Kolde, *A Fruitful Mirror, or Small Handbook for Christians*, in Denis Janz, ed., *Three Reformation Catechisms: Catholic, Anabaptist, Lutheran* (Lewiston, NY: Edwin Mellen Press, 1982), 29–130.

e   Timothy J. Wengert, "Wittenberg's Earliest Catechism," *Lutheran Quarterly* 7 (1993): 247–60. For a translation into English, see the

the texts not only of the Ten Commandments, Creed, and Lord's Prayer, but also, for the first time, biblical texts for baptism and the Lord's Supper and instructions on prayers for morning, evening, and mealtimes. At nearly the same time, in his preface to the *German Mass* published in early 1526, Luther himself called on others to write catechisms, giving his *Little Prayer Book* as a guide and also suggesting another form for catechetical instruction.[f] This call resulted in a flood of catechisms produced in many areas by a variety of pastors and theologians.[g] In all, at least ten different booklets were produced in Wittenberg and elsewhere between 1525 and 1529.

Among the people who took up his charge was his former student Johann Agricola (1494–1566),[h] rector of the Latin School in Eisleben, who published three separate catechisms between 1527 and 1529. During the same period, Agricola and Philip Melanchthon (1497–1560) were locked in a struggle over the origin of true repentance, in which the former argued that it arose from the promise of the gospel and the latter from the preaching of the law. This diminution of the law was reflected in Agricola's catechisms, which placed the law as more or less an appendix and introduced it as equivalent to Cicero's rules for rhetoric.[i]

Johann Agricola's Lutheran catechetical instruction for young Christian children was published by Georg Rau in 1527, two years before the publication of Luther's *Small Catechism*. This first edition includes sections on the Ten Commandments, the Lord's Prayer, the Apostles' Creed, the Lord's Supper, and the Trinity.

Booklet for Laity and Children, trans. Timothy J. Wengert, in Robert Kolb and James A. Nestingen, eds., *Sources and Contexts of the Book of Concord* (Minneapolis: Fortress Press, 2001), 1–12.

f   LW 53:64–67; TAL 3:142–46.

g   See Ferdinand Cohrs, ed., *Die evangelischen Katechismusversuche vor Luthers Enchiridion*, 4 vols. (Berlin: Hofmann, 1900–1902; reprint: Hildesheim: Ohms, 1978). For further discussion of the catechisms produced prior to 1529, see Timothy J. Wengert, *Law and Gospel: Philip Melanchthon's Debate with John Agricola of Eisleben over "Poenitentia"* (Grand Rapids: Baker, 1997), 47–75.

h   See also n. *m*, p. 206.

i   Wengert, *Law and Gospel*, 143.

Two other events triggered Luther's decision to write his own catechisms. First, in 1527, under pressure from Wittenberg and from parish pastors like Nicholas Hausmann (d. 1538) in Zwickau (who had also begged Luther to write a catechism), the elector of Saxony, John the Steadfast (1468-1532), decided to take the unprecedented step of authorizing an official visitation of the churches in his territories—something normally carried out by the local bishop. A team of four visitors, consisting of two representatives from the Saxon court and two from the university (one law professor [Jerome Schurff (1481-1554)] and one theologian [Melanchthon, elected by the theology faculty at Luther's insistence]), was sent out, beginning in the summer of 1527, with the tasks of evaluating the administrative, financial, practical, and theological conditions of the parishes, chapels, and monasteries. Luther himself participated in official visitation to parts of Saxony and Meissen from 22 October 1528 through 9 January 1529. As his preface to *the Small Catechism* made clear, these visits outside the confines of the university town of Wittenberg made him realize the abysmal level of Christian instruction, especially in the villages.

Second, in 1528 Johannes Bugenhagen (1485-1558), Wittenberg's chief pastor, was called away to help the cities of Braunschweig and Hamburg reform their churches. Luther was left with all the preaching duties and thus gave three sets of sermons on the catechism at the Vespers services in May, September, and December—still reflecting the medieval practice of expounding the catechism on the Embers.[j] These sermons, along with sermons on confession and the Lord's Supper from Holy Week, 1529, became the basis for the *Large Catechism*, first published in 1529.[k] At the same time, based in part upon summary sentences of the various parts of the Commandments, Creed, Lord's Prayer, and sacraments scattered throughout those sermons, Luther began writing very brief explanations designed to appear on individual broadsheets for each main part of the catechism

A portrait of Johannes Bugenhagen painted in 1532 by Lucas Cranach the Elder (1472-1553)

<hr>

j   For an English translation of transcriptions of the third set of sermons, see LW 51:133–93.

k   See the *Large Catechism*, trans. James L. Schaaf, in BC, 377–480; TAL 2:278–415. For the Holy Week sermons, see *Martin Luther's Sermons from Holy Week and Easter, 1529*, trans. Irving Sandberg (St. Louis: Concordia, 1999).

and daily prayers and addressed to the *Hausvater* (the head of the household).

Although only one of these original Wittenberg printings has survived (a *Niederdeutsch* version of morning and evening prayer, reprints from other cities in both German dialects were gathered into booklet form and preserved. Luther completed work on the Ten Commandments, Creed, and Lord's Prayer in January 1529, when illness intervened, so that he did not complete work on the sacraments until the spring. Almost immediately, Nicholas Schirlentz published these broadsheets in booklet form, now with Luther's preface addressed to parish pastors and preachers, the household chart of Bible passages (later called the Table of Duties), and German liturgies for marriage and baptism (with Luther's prefaces), as well as biblical illustrations for each commandment, article of the Creed, petition of the Lord's Prayer, and sacrament. A second printing from 1531 included a new section on confession and an explanation of the words "Our Father in heaven."[1] The 1529 version was immediately translated into Latin (twice), and the 1531 version saw translations into many other European languages, including a paraphrastic version by Thomas Cranmer (1489–1556) into English.[1] For students learning biblical languages, several midcentury editions featured parallel texts in German, Latin, Greek, and Hebrew. All told, the six-

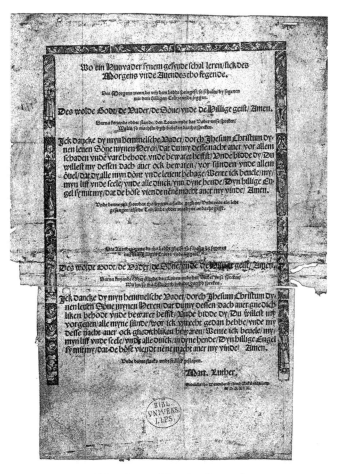

"Morning and Evening Prayers"
from the 1529 Wittenberg edition
of the *Small Catechsim* in the
Low German dialect

1. Later editions published during Luther's lifetime in Wittenberg also occasionally included other additions. In 1536 Schirlentz added Scripture references under each picture along with texts of the *Te Deum* and *Magnificat* (LW 53:171–79). In 1543 he included the "Prayer against the Turks." The version from 1529 also included the *German Litany* (LW 53:153–70).

---

l   The list in WA 30/1:782–804 includes Arabic, Czech, Danish, English, Estonian, Finnish, French, Icelandic, Italian, Slavonic, Latvian, Lithuanian, Dutch, Polish, Prussian (dialect), Swedish, Spanish, and Sorbian. For those printed in German-speaking lands, see also VD 16:L 5035–L 5177.

teenth century produced well over two hundred printings in various languages and dialects.

In contrast to one of Johann Agricola's catechisms, which boasted in its title to contain 130 questions,[m] Luther's *Small Catechism* used a single question throughout, *"Was ist das?"* ("What is this?"). This question invited simple paraphrase of the text in question rather than complicated explanation, thus implying that the catechism's texts were not obscure and needed simply to be put in other words for proper understanding. He added a second question for parts of the Lord's Prayer (for the first three petitions, "How does this come about?" and for the fourth, "What does [the word] daily bread mean?"). For the sacraments, four questions were used in addition to "What is this?"—questions asked about gifts and benefits and the role of faith and, for baptism, what using water signifies, and, for the Supper, the proper preparation.[2] The simple order for private confession contains a series of questions related to preparation for private confession to a pastor or priest.

Content

In contrast to Luther's reputation for verbosity, the *Small Catechism* was uniquely succinct. Using standard texts of medieval catechesis, Luther managed to explain these basics in terms consonant with major themes in his theology. Justification by faith alone had insisted that faith, demanded by the First Commandment, was the center of the Christian life. Thus, Luther took his explanation of that commandment ("fear, love, and trust in God") and applied it to the other nine commandments, where "fear and love" hearken back to the meaning of the First Commandment.[3] Justification also implied for Luther the proper distinction between law and gospel. His consistent use of *wir sollen* ("we are to"), found in both the commandments and his explanations, underscored what human beings *ought* to do but were not able to accomplish.[n]

2. Luther deemed only two texts obscure (the fourth petition and the water of baptism) and thus asked about the meaning of a word (daily bread) and about what an action (baptizing with water) signified.

3. He stated this explicitly in the *Large Catechism*, Ten Commandments, par. 326–29, in BC, 430.

---

m   Johann Agricola, *130 Common Questions for the Girl's School in Eisleben*, trans. Timothy J. Wengert, in Kolb and Nestingen, *Sources and Contexts*, 13–82.

n   See the *Large Catechism*, Ten Commandments, par. 316; Creed, par. 2; Lord's Prayer, par. 2, in BC, 428, 431, and 440–41, respectively.

First in explanations to the Creed, which Luther took as a description of God's triune actions of creating, redeeming, and making holy, Luther expounded the gospel of God's unmerited grace. God created "out of pure, fatherly, and divine goodness and mercy, without any merit or worthiness of mine at all"; God the Son ransomed humanity from the evil "kidnappers" of sin, death, and the devil by his suffering, death, and resurrection; God the Holy Spirit bestows faith and makes holy through forgiveness proclaimed in the Christian assembly.

The Lord's Prayer then pleads for God, now described as a loving Father, to fulfill the very promises made in the Creed by asking first for the word, faith in the word through the Holy Spirit (cf. the third article of the Creed), defeat of enemies of the word and faith (echoing the language of the second article), and then asking in thanksgiving for the gifts of creation (first article). Luther's explanations of petitions for forgiveness of sin, rescue from attacks on faith, and final deliverance from all evil underscore the centrality of God's mercy in the Christian's life. The "amen," which refers directly to commands and promises, also centers on the certainty of faith. Thus, the words "it is going to come about just like this" reflect the threefold paraphrase of the Creed's amen ("This is most certainly true"), which also appears in Luther's translation of Titus 3:5-8, used in question three of baptism, explaining the role of faith.

Luther's explanations of the sacraments move from what they are (question one, related to Christ's institution), to what effect and benefit they provide (forgiveness, life, and salvation), to the role of faith. The fourth question to each sacrament deals with the way they function in the believer's life: involving a daily drowning of the old creature and rising of the new in baptism (and, thus, in 1531 followed by an appended description of private confession, which moved from law to gospel) and the proper inward preparation of faith (as opposed to the outward, medieval practice of fasting) in the Supper.

This practical application continues in the prayers for morning, evening, and mealtimes and in "The Household Chart of Some Bible Passages." While affirming the common practice of regular prayers (based upon medieval models), Luther also directly criticized the late-medieval view of the monastic and mendicant life as being a higher form of Christianity.[4] Instead, in line with his view of Christian vocation in the world, he wrote

4. Such a chart echoed catechetical material prepared by the medieval theologian Jean Gerson (1363–1429).

this chart "for all kinds of holy orders and walks of life." He clearly rejected any division into more and less spiritual walks of life by including the responsibilities of ecclesiastical offices and governmental authority but primarily focusing on the "offices" of the German household of his day. This was also underscored by the inclusion of the liturgies of baptism and marriage, which constituted Christian households before God and in the world, and by the presence of woodcuts, which allowed even the unlettered in the household to visualize the catechism and its relation to Scripture.

The Purpose of the Small Catechism

With the *Small Catechism* in particular and other catechisms in the sixteenth century,[o] Lutheran catechists attempted to achieve several important goals. As a result of the visitations, Luther and others viewed many baptized members of congregations as woefully ignorant and in need of basic catechesis; their pastors were often ignorant themselves and inept teachers. A catechism provided a basic summary of the Christian faith. Moreover, catechisms continued to function as during the Middle Ages in the context of private confession while also providing basic liturgical texts to local pastors and congregants for marriage and baptism. In addition, catechisms provided, as it was often called, a "lay Bible," providing a summary of and introduction to the biblical message.[5] Thus, the combination of law (Commandments) and gospel (Creed and Lord's Prayer) and of word and sacraments gave people the tools by which to hear, understand, and even judge the preacher's sermon[6] and the basic sacramental actions in the congregation (baptism, confession, and the Lord's Supper), while also providing liturgies and biblical guidance for the home.

Even the booklet edition, despite its preface addressed to pastors and preachers, retained the *Small Catechism*'s focus on the household, adding woodcuts (as has been done in this transla-

5. This term was used already in the *Booklet for Laity and Children* of 1525, in the *Large Catechism*, and as a description of Luther's catechisms in the Epitome of the *Formula of Concord* (1576), in BC, 487, par. 5.

6. Mary Jane Haemig, "Laypeople as Overseers of the Faith: A Reformation Proposal," *Trinity Seminary Review* 27 (2006): 21–27.

o　See Johann Michael Reu, ed., *Quellen zur Geschichte des kirchlichen Unterrichts in der evangelischen Kirche Deutschlands zwischen 1530 und 1600*, 4 vols. in 9 (Gütersloh: Bertelsmann, 1904–1935; reprint: Hildesheim: Olms, 1976).

tion) and a chart of Bible passages for the household's various callings, while retaining the captions from each broadsheet addressed to householders. Indeed, in announcing his catechetical sermons to his Wittenberg congregation in November 1528, Luther encouraged the householders to send their children and servants to attend such preaching by stating, "You have been appointed their bishop and pastor; take heed that you do not neglect your office over them." In the first sermon given the next day he reiterated, "Every father of a family is a bishop in his house and the wife a bishopess. Therefore remember that you in your homes are to help us carry on the ministry as we do in the church."[p] With the publication of the *Small Catechism* in a booklet form that included Luther's preface to pastors and preachers, the *Catechism* took on a role in the Evangelical (Lutheran) congregations, thus carrying on the medieval practice of regular instruction in the basics of the Christian faith. Moreover, the *Catechism* quickly found its place in schools, especially with the translation into Latin already in 1529. Thus, households, congregations, and schools all played their part in catechesis.

Luther demonstrated in his explanations what he viewed as the proper way to interpret Scripture by recognizing the commands and promises. The woodcuts tied individual commandments to examples of their being broken in the Old Testament, articles of the Creed to God's biblical actions of creating, redeeming, and making holy, and the petitions of the Lord's Prayer to examples in the New Testament (with the exception of the first petition, which depicts preaching on the Sabbath from Exodus 20). The sacraments show contemporary celebrations in Wittenberg. Only in explaining the Sacrament of Baptism did Luther include several biblical texts (four in all), while in every other portion he simply concentrated on the specific catechetical text. However, in several instances, especially with the Creed, his paraphrases alluded to other biblical texts.

The explosion of catechetical writings in the sixteenth century demonstrates the deep commitment the reformers and their opponents had toward the education of the common people. Luther's *Small Catechism*, however, played an even more important part in catechesis as other preachers and teachers

---

p   See *Ten Sermons on the Catechism* (1528) in LW 51:136–37. These were
    delivered beginning on 29 November 1528.

7. Andreas Osiander (1498–1552).

began, almost immediately, to produce sermons and commentaries on Luther's work, beginning with the Nuremberg preacher Andreas Osiander's[7] *Children's Sermons* of the 1530s, itself a very popular publication throughout the sixteenth century.[q] To help students of theology learn their languages, there were even publications that provided, in four parallel columns, the text of the *Catechism* in German, Latin, Greek, and Hebrew. Moreover, it was not long before theologians were expanding Luther's small work with commentaries and biblically enriched outlines to theology, many of which were based upon or at least provided the text of Luther's *Catechism* as well.[r] Other catechisms, designed for students already proficient in the *Small Catechism*, were also published.[s] In some cases, this approach to instruction obscured the originality of Luther's own work, but it also preserved Luther's *Catechism* for later generations of Lutherans.

This translation uses WA 30/1:239–474, 537–819, and the *Bekenntnisschriften der evangelischen lutherischen Kirche*, 11th ed. (Göttingen: Vandenhoeck & Ruprecht, 1986), 499–542. It is based upon the translator's earlier work in *The Book of Concord*, ed. Robert Kolb and Timothy J. Wengert (Minneapolis: Fortress Press, 2000), 345–75, in which the *Marriage Booklet* and the *Baptismal Booklet* are revisions of Paul Zeller Strodach and Ulrich S. Leupold's translations in LW 53:106–115. The woodcut illustrations are from a facsimile edition of the Wittenberg printing of the *Catechism* from 1536. In that year, the printer Nicholas Schirlentz published a new edition of Luther's *Small Catechism*, in which, as in 1529, he again included woodcuts for each commandment, article of the Creed, petition of the Lord's

q   Mary Jane Haemig, "The Living Voice of the Catechism: German Lutheran Catechetical Preaching 1530–1580" (Harvard University: PhD dissertation, 1996).

r   For two examples among hundreds, see Heinrich Homel, *Catechismus D. Martini Lutheri Minor: Una cum perspicuis et dilucidis scholiis, ex Sacris Bibliis* (Wittenberg: Lehmann, 1584), with a preface by David Chytraeus; and Johann Tettelbach, *Das güldene Kleinodt: D. Martini Lutheri Catechismus, mit mehr christlichen Fragen erkleret* (n.p., 1571), with a preface by Tilemann Heshus.

s   For some of the earliest, see Reu, *Quellen*. Two of the most influential were Johannes Brenz, *Catechismus . . . Deutsch*, trans. Hartmann Beyer (Leipzig: Berwalt, 1553), and David Chytraeus, *Catechesis in Academia Rostochiana ex praelectionibus Davidis Chytraei collecta* (Wittenberg: Johann Krafft, 1554).

Prayer, sacrament, and the marriage and baptismal services, this time adding Bible references for the stories depicted. Such illustrations were included in almost all versions of Luther's catechisms published during his lifetime and beyond, and even in the 1584 official Latin translation of the *Book of Concord*.

Cover of the 1536 printing of the *Small Catechism*.
Otto Albrecht, ed., *Der kleine Katechismus D. Martin
Luthers nach der Ausgabe v. J. 1536* (Halle:
Buchhandlung des Waisenhauses, 1905)

8. German (from the Latin and Greek): *Enchiridion*. In 1501, Erasmus of Rotterdam (1466–1536) had titled his instruction for the Christian life *Enchiridion militis Christiani* ("Handbook [or: Dagger] for the Christian Soldier").

9. This reflects both types of German clergy in Luther's day: pastors (*Pfarrherr*), who bore the major responsibility for pastoral care and worship in congregations, and preachers (*Prediger*).

10. The oldest surviving copy published in Wittenberg is from 1531.

11. See 1 Tim. 1:2 and 2 Tim. 1:2. Luther began using Pauline greetings for his letters exclusively, starting in 1522. When addressing specifically clergy, he sometimes used the greeting found in the Pastoral Epistles, as here.

12. In the medieval church, bishops were charged with regular visitation of their parishes, a formal examination of all aspects of parish life, often overseen by church officials sent by the diocese. In 1527, Elector John of Saxony (1468–1532) ordered an official visitation of churches in his lands, in the absence of cooperation from the local bishops, who normally provided such oversight. The teams consisted of two officials from the court, a professor of law (often Jerome Schurff) and a theologian (usually Philip Melanchthon, who was elected by the theology faculty). As something of an exception, Luther made official visitations of congregations in electoral Saxony and Meissen from October 22, 1528, through January 9, 1529, describing his experiences in a letter to Nicholas von Amsdorf (1483–1565) dated November

HANDBOOK[8]
THE SMALL CATECHISM
FOR ORDINARY PASTORS
AND PREACHERS[9]
MARTIN LUTHER
[1529][10]

[The Preface of Dr. Martin Luther]

MARTIN Luther,[t]

To all faithful and upright pastors and preachers.
Grace, mercy, and peace in Jesus Christ our Lord.[11]

The deplorable, wretched deprivation that I recently encountered while I was a visitor[12] has constrained and compelled[u] me to prepare this catechism, or Christian instruction,[v] in such a brief, plain, and simple version. Dear God have mercy, what misery I beheld! The ordinary person, especially in the villages, knows absolutely nothing about the Christian teaching, and unfortunately many pastors are completely unskilled and incompetent teachers. Yet supposedly they all bear the name Christian, are baptized, and receive the holy sacrament, even though they do not know the Lord's Prayer, the Creed, or the Ten Commandments![13] As a result they live like simple cattle or irrational pigs and, despite the fact that the gospel has returned, have masterfully learned how to misuse all their freedom. O you bishops! How are you ever going to answer to Christ, now that

---

[t] This preface was printed in almost all booklet editions of the *Small Catechism*. In the 1531 edition, Luther's name begins with a large initial "M." Such decorative letters are also found at the beginning of the *Marriage Booklet*, the *Baptismal Booklet*, and, within the latter, for the first word of the exorcism and for the Gospel reading.

[u] A German rhyme: *gezwungen und gedrungen*.

[v] Similar to the introduction to the LC, Short Preface, par. 1-2 (BC, 383).

you have so shamefully neglected the people and have not exercised your office[14] for even a single second? May you escape punishment for this! You forbid the cup [to the laity in the Lord's Supper] and insist on observance of your human laws, while never even bothering to ask whether the people know the Lord's Prayer, the Creed, the Ten Commandments, or a single passage from God's Word. Woe to you forever![w]

Therefore, my dear sirs and brothers, whether pastors or preachers, for God's sake I beg that all of you would fervently take up your office, have pity on your people who are entrusted to you, and help us to bring the catechism to the people, especially to the young. In addition, I ask that those unable to do any better take up these charts and versions[15,x] and present them to the people word for word in the following manner:

In the first place, the preacher should above all take care to avoid changes or variations in the text and version of the Ten Commandments, the Lord's Prayer, the Creed, the sacraments, etc., but instead adopt a single version, stick with it, and always use the same one year after year. For the young and the unlettered people must be taught with a single, fixed text and version. Otherwise, if someone teaches one way now and another way next year—even when desiring to make improvements—the people become quite easily confused, and all the time and effort will go to waste.

The dear [church] fathers also understood this well. They used one form for the Lord's Prayer, the Creed, and the Ten Commandments.[16] Therefore, we, too, should teach these parts to the young and to people who cannot read in such a way that we neither change a single syllable nor present or recite it differently from one year to the next.[17] Therefore, choose for yourself whatever version you want and stick with it for good. To be sure, when you preach to educated and intelligent people, then you may demonstrate your erudition and discuss these parts with as much complexity and from as many different angles as you can. But with the young people, stick with a fixed, unchanging version and form. To begin with, teach them these parts: the Ten Commandments, the Creed, the Lord's Prayer, etc., following the

11, 1528 (LW 49:213–14). In 1528, Luther and Melanchthon together published under their coats of arms theological and practical instructions to the pastors. See LW 40:263–320 (where the title, incorrectly translated, should read *Instruction by the Visitors for the Parish Pastors of Electoral Saxony*).

13. In Luther's day the word *catechism* denoted these three parts, cited here in an order often found in late-medieval manuals.

14. For Luther, the "office" of church leaders constituted their duties and authority. He argued that pastors and bishops had primarily duties regarding teaching, preaching, and administration of the sacraments, in addition to their administrative responsibilities.

15. The word *table* (see n. *x* below) may refer especially to the original printing of the individual sections of the *Small Catechism* on separate broadsheets, which, like posters, could be displayed in homes, schools, and churches.

16. Luther is thinking here of the single Latin versions for the parts of the catechism used in the ancient and medieval church.

17. The reformers insisted that Christian catechesis was not just for the literate. Thus, they stressed memorization as a way of bringing "book learning" to all people. All levels of education stressed the importance of memorization—not as rote but as a way of keeping an author's message in the heart. Here, of course, Luther is not talking about his own explanations but the basic texts on which his explanations were based.

---

w   See Luther's criticism of the bishops in the *Instruction by the Visitors*, 1528 (LW 40:269–73).

x   Literally, in German: *tafeln und forme* (tables and forms).

text word for word, so that they can also repeat it back to you and learn it by heart.

Those who do not want to learn these things must be told how they deny Christ and are not Christians. They should also not be admitted to the sacrament, should not be sponsors for children at baptism, and should not exercise any aspect of Christian freedom,[y] but instead should simply be sent back home to the pope and his officials,[18] and, along with them, to the devil himself. Moreover, their parents and employers ought to deny them food and drink and advise them that the prince is disposed to drive such coarse people out of the country.

Although no one can or should force another person to believe,[z] nevertheless one should insist upon and hold the masses to this: that they know what is right and wrong among those with whom they wish to reside, eat and earn a living.[a] For example, if people want to live in a particular city, they ought to know and abide by the laws of the city whose protection they enjoy, no matter whether they believe or are at heart scoundrels and villains.

In the second place, once the people have learned the text well, then teach them to understand it, too, so that they know what it says. Take up again the form offered in these charts or some other short form that you may prefer, and adhere to it without changing a single syllable, just as was stated above regarding the text. Moreover, allow yourself ample time for it, because you need not take up all the parts at once but may instead handle them one at a time. After the people understand the First Commandment well, then take up the Second, and so on. Otherwise they will be so overwhelmed that they will hardly remember a single thing.

In the third place, after you have taught the people a short catechism like this one, then take up the large catechism[19] and impart to them a richer and fuller understanding. In this case, explain each individual commandment, petition, or part with its

18. German: *Officialen*, diocesan judges who decided administrative, disciplinary, and marriage cases.

19. Luther has in mind not only his own *Deutsch Katechismus*, which others came to call the *Large Catechism*, but also other catechetical books.

---

y　　See also LC, Short Preface, par. 1-5 (BC, 383).

z　　See the letter to Nicholas Hausmann dated March 17, 1522 (LW 48:399–402), the preface to *Instruction by the Visitors*, 1528 (LW 40:273), Luther's announcement for catechetical sermons in December 1528 (LW 51:136), and the LC, Lord's Supper, par. 42 (BC, 471).

a　　See the letter to Thomas Löscher dated August 26, 1529 (LW 49:232–34), and LC, Short Preface, par. 2 (BC, 383).

various works, benefits and blessings, harm and danger, as you find treated at length in so many booklets. In particular, put the greatest stress on that commandment or part where your people experience the greatest need. For example, you must strongly emphasize the Seventh Commandment, which deals with stealing, with artisans and shopkeepers and even with farmers and household workers, because rampant among such people are all kinds of dishonesty and thievery.[b] Likewise, you must emphasize the Fourth Commandment to children and the common people, so that they are orderly, faithful, obedient, and peaceful.[c] Always adduce many examples from the Scriptures where God either punished or blessed such people.[20]

In particular, at this point[d] also urge governing authorities and parents to rule well and to send their children to school. Point out how they are obliged to do so and what a damnable sin they commit if they do not, for thereby, as the worst enemies of God and humanity, they overthrow and lay waste both the kingdom of God and the kingdom of the world.[21] Explain very clearly what kind of horrible damage they do when they do not help to train children as pastors, preachers, civil servants,[e] and the like, and tell them that God will punish them dreadfully for this. For in this day it is necessary to preach about these things, given that the extent to which parents and governing authorities are now sinning in these matters defies description. The devil, too, intends to do something horrible in all this.[f]

Finally,[22] because the tyranny of the pope has been abolished,[23] people no longer want to receive the sacrament, and they treat it with contempt. This, too, needs to be emphasized, with this caveat: That we should not compel anyone to believe or to receive the sacrament and should not fix any law or time

20. Luther's catechisms were always illustrated with woodcuts of biblical scenes. For the Fourth Commandment it was the drunkenness of Noah (Gen. 9:20-27); see illustration on p. 219.

21. As in the *Large Catechism* and his tracts on education listed below (nn. *d* and *f*), Luther emphasizes the importance of education for both church and government.

22. This introduces a final example of how to apply a specific topic from the catechism and is not a fourth step in catechesis. See LC, Lord's Supper, par. 39-84 (BC, 470-75).

23. Luther is referring to the strict medieval requirement to receive the Lord's Supper once a year, especially between Easter and Corpus Christi Day (eleven days after Pentecost).

---

b   See LC, Ten Commandments, par. 225-26 (BC, 416).

c   See LC, Ten Commandments, par. 105-66 (BC, 400-409).

d   This paragraph continues Luther's exposition of the Fourth Commandment. See LC, Ten Commandments, par. 167-78 (BC, 409-410); the *Treatise on Good Works*, 1520 (LW 44:85-100; TAL 1:257-367); and *A Sermon on Keeping Children in School*, 1530 (LW 46:207-58).

e   German: *schreiber*, literally, "notaries" or "clerks."

f   See the LC, Ten Commandments, par. 174-77 (BC, 410); *To the Councilmen of All Cities in Germany That They Establish and Maintain Christian Schools*, 1524 (LW 45:339-78; TAL 5, forthcoming); and *A Sermon on Keeping Children in School*, 1530 (LW 46:207-58).

24. In 1215 the Fourth Lateran Council, canon 21, stipulated that every Christian had to receive the Lord's Supper in the Easter season (up to Corpus Christi Day). See Luther's *Receiving Both Kinds in the Sacrament*, 1522 (LW 36:249), and *The Babylonian Captivity of the Church*, 1520 (LW 36:19–28; TAL 3:9–129).

25. For Luther, the Reformation reshaped the pastoral office, shifting it, for preachers, from moral exhortation to the proclamation of the gospel and, for pastors, from dispensing a grace effective "by the mere performance of rites" (*ex opere operato*) to the declaration of God's grace in audible and visible forms.

26. The titles for each section of the *Small Catechism* stem from the broadsheets of 1529 and were retained in subsequent booklet editions. (The Latin translation of 1529 addresses schoolteachers and students.) In 1531, this sentence was placed on a separate title page, which depicted the Lamb of God above and Luther's coat of arms (the "Luther rose") below. In the booklet form, Luther followed his ordering discussed in the *Little Prayer Book*, moving from Commandments (which diagnose human sin), to the Creed (which describes God's grace), to the Lord's Prayer (which begs God for the very grace needed to fulfill the Commandments). This differed from many medieval catechisms that were oriented toward the Sacrament of

or place for it. Instead, we should preach in such a way that the people make themselves come without our law and just plain compel*ᵍ* us pastors to administer the sacrament to them. This can be done by telling them: One has to worry that whoever does not desire or receive the sacrament at the very least once or four times a year despises the sacrament and is no Christian, just as anyone who does not listen to or believe the gospel is no Christian. For Christ did not say, "Omit this," or "Despise this," but instead [1 Cor. 11:25], "Do this, as often as you drink it. . . ." He really wants it to be done and not completely omitted or despised. "DO this," he says.

Those*ʰ* who do not hold the sacrament in high esteem indicate that they have no sin, no flesh, no devil, no world, no death, no dangers, no hell. That is, they believe they have none of these things, although they are up to their neck in them and belong to the devil twice over. On the other hand, they indicate that they need no grace, no life, no paradise, no heaven, no Christ, no God, nor any other good thing. For if they believed that they had so much evil and needed so much good, they would not neglect the sacrament, in which help against such evil is provided and in which so much good is given. It would not be necessary to compel them with any law to receive the sacrament. Instead, they would come on their own, rushing and running to it; they would compel themselves to come and would insist that you give them the sacrament.

For these reasons, you do not have to make any law concerning this, as the pope did.[24] Only emphasize clearly the benefit and the harm, the need and the blessing, the danger and the salvation in this sacrament. Then they will doubtless come on their own without your forcing them. If they do not come, give up on them and tell them that those who pay no attention to nor feel their great need and God's gracious help belong to the devil. However, if you either do not stress this or make it into a law or poison, then it is your fault if they despise the sacrament. How can they help but neglect it, if you sleep and remain silent? Therefore, pastors and preachers, take note! Our office has now become a completely different thing than it was under

g   German: *dringen, und . . . zwingen*, a rhymed couplet. The Lord's Supper was celebrated each Sunday at St. Mary's Church in Wittenberg, although not many received it that often.

h   The German text uses the third person singular.

the pope.[25] It has now become serious and salutary. Thus, it now involves much toil and work, many dangers and attacks[i] and, in addition, little reward or gratitude in the world. But Christ himself will be our reward, so long as we labor faithfully. May the Father of all grace grant it, to whom be praise and thanks in eternity through Christ, our Lord. Amen.

The Ten Commandments: In a Simple Way in Which the Head of a House Is to Present[j] Them to the Household[26]

Worship of the golden calf (Exodus 32)[27]

The First [Commandment][k]

You are to[l] have no other gods.[28]
What is this?[29] Answer:
We are to fear, love, and trust God above all things.

---

i German: *Anfechtung.*

j German: *furhalten,* used for each section of the catechism, except for the prayers, where Luther suggests they be "taught" (i.e., memorized).

k This word, lacking in the editions of 1529–1535, is present in all other editions of the *Small Catechism* and in the *Book of Concord* of 1580.

Penance and thus began with the Creed, which a person in a state of sin could admit was true, moved to the Ten Commandments as one of many lists of sins the penitent was required to confess, and finally to the Lord's Prayer, often without explanation, as one prayer necessary to recite to satisfy one's remaining temporal punishment for sin.

27. In the printings of the *Small Catechism* during Luther's lifetime, each commandment, article of the Creed, petition of the Lord's Prayer, and sacrament was accompanied by a woodcut and (from 1536) references to the Bible story on which each picture was based. Woodcuts similar to those used in the *Small Catechism* were also included in the *Large Catechism* (see WA 30/1:133–210).

28. Luther uses a common form of the Decalogue that does not always correspond to the texts of either Exodus 20 or Deuteronomy 5 in the Luther Bible. As a result, some later editions, including the Nuremberg editions of 1531 and 1558, correct the text here and elsewhere according to the biblical text. The italicized portions throughout the *Small Catechism* were originally printed using larger type.

29. German: *Was ist das?* This question indicates that Luther viewed his responses more as paraphrase than as a disclosure of hidden meaning. The sense is "In other words" or "That is to say."

Blasphemy of Shelomith's son
(Lev. 24:10-16)

The Second [Commandment]

You are not to take the name of your God in vain.[m]
What is this? Answer:
We are to fear and love[30] God, so that[n] we do not curse, swear,[o] practice magic, lie, or deceive using God's name, but instead use that very name in every time of need to call on, pray to, praise, and give thanks to God.

Breaking the Sabbath (Num. 15:32-36)

The Third [Commandment]

You are to hallow the day of rest.[p]
What is this? Answer:
We are to fear and love God, so that we do not despise preaching or God's Word, but instead keep that Word holy and gladly hear and learn it.

30. Luther uses these two verbs to refer back to the First Commandment. See *Instruction by the Visitors*, 1528 (LW 40:276–77) and LC, Ten Commandments, par. 321–27 (BC, 429–30).

l   Throughout the Commandments the German word *sollen* is translated "are to," as a way of avoiding the confusion in English, where "shall" can mean either "ought to" or "will," and to clarify the paraphrastic nature of Luther's explanations.

m   Following the editions of 1529–1535. The Nuremberg editions of 1531 and 1558 add "for the Lord will not hold that one guiltless who takes his name in vain."

n   German: *das*. This may be rendered either modally ("by not doing") or consequentially ("with the result that we do not").

o   German: *schweren*, here used in the sense of false oaths. See the LC, Ten Commandments, par. 65–66 (BC, 394–95).

p   German: *Feiertag*, literally, "day of rest" (like the Hebrew word *sabbath*), but generally for Sunday and other "holy days." This (traditional) rendering differed from Luther's translation of the text in Exodus 20 and Deuteronomy 5, where he used the terms "holy day" and "Sabbath."

The Fourth [Commandment]

You are to honor your father and your mother.

What is this? Answer:

We are to fear and love God, so that we neither despise nor anger our parents and others in authority[q] but instead honor, serve, obey, love, and respect.

The drunkenness of Noah
(Gen. 9:20–27)

The Fifth [Commandment]

You are not to kill.

What is this? Answer:

We are to fear and love God, so that we neither endanger nor harm the lives of our neighbors,[r] but instead help and support them in all of life's needs.

Cain slays Abel (Gen. 4:1–16)

q   German: *Herrn*, literally, "lords," but used here to denote those in authority, e.g., *Landesherrn* (princes), *Hausherr* (head of the house), or *Pfarrherr* (pastors).

r   Here and in the following explanations, the word *neighbor* is singular in the German.

David and Bathsheba (2 Samuel 11)

The Sixth [Commandment]

You are not to commit adultery.

What is this? Answer:

We are to fear and love God, so that we lead pure and decent lives in word and deed and each person loves and honors his [or her] spouse.

The theft by Achan (Joshua 7)

The Seventh [Commandment]

You are not to steal.

What is this? Answer:

We are to fear and love God, so that we neither take our neighbors' money or property nor acquire them by using shoddy merchandise or crooked deals, but instead help them to improve and protect their property and income.

The Eighth [Commandment]

You are not to bear false witness against your neighbor.
What is this? Answer:
We are to fear and love God, so that we do not tell lies about our neighbors, betray or slander them, or destroy their reputations. Instead we are to come to their defense, speak well of them, and interpret everything they do in the best possible light.

In Latin and Greek versions of Daniel, this story of Susanna and her false accusers was added and is part of the Apocrypha.

The Ninth [Commandment]

You are not to covet your neighbor's house.
What is this? Answer:
We are to fear and love God, so that we do not try to trick our neighbors out of their inheritance or property or try to get it for ourselves by claiming to have a legal right to it and the like, but instead be of help and service to them in keeping what is theirs.

Jacob cheating Laban
(Gen. 30:25–43)

Joseph and Potiphar's
wife (Genesis 39)

The Tenth [Commandment]

You are not to covet your neighbor's wife, male or female servant, cattle or whatever is his.

What is this? Answer:

We are to fear and love God, so that we do not entice, force, or steal away from our neighbors their spouses,[s] household workers, or livestock, but instead urge them to stay and fulfill their obligations.

What then does God say about all these commandments? Answer: God says the following: *"I, the* LORD *your God, am a jealous God. Against those who hate me I visit the sin of the fathers on the children up to the third and fourth generation. But I do good to those who love me and keep my commandments to the thousandth generation."*[t]

What is this? Answer:

God threatens to punish all who break these commandments. Therefore we are to fear his wrath and do nothing contrary to these commandments. However, he promises grace and every good thing to all those who keep these commandments. Therefore we also are to love and trust him and gladly act according to his commands.

---

s   German: *sein weib* (his wife). In sixteenth-century German, *Weib* was the common word for *Frau.*

t   This text does not follow Exod. 20:5-6 or Deut. 5:9-10 as translated in the Luther Bible.

The Creed: In the Very Simple Way in Which the Head of a House Is to Present It to the Household[31]

The First Article: On Creation

I believe in God, the Father almighty, CREATOR[u] of heaven and earth.

What is this? Answer:

I believe that God has created me together with all that exists.[v] God has given me and still preserves my body and soul: eyes, ears and all my abilities; reason and all mental faculties.[32] In addition, God daily and abundantly provides shoes and clothing, food and drink, house and farm, spouse[w] and children, fields, livestock and all property—along with all the necessities and nourishment for this body and life.[x] God protects me against all danger and shields and preserves me from all evil. And all this is done out of pure, fatherly, and divine goodness and mercy, without any merit or worthiness of mine at all! For all of this I owe[y] it to God to thank and praise, serve and obey him. This is most certainly true.[33]

God depicted as a bearded man giving a blessing, surrounded by animals and encircled by clouds and the four winds (cf. Gen. 1–2).

u   Capitalized in the original.

v   German: *Creaturen.*

w   German: *weib,* literally, wife.

x   Some modern commentators and translators connect "shoes . . . property" to the preceding sentence. However, the Latin translations of 1529, the capitalization of "In addition" (*Dazu*) in the original text, and the placement of verbs at the end of each sentence throughout this explanation argue for its inclusion with what follows.

y   German: *schüldig* (indebted).

31. Traditionally, the Creed was divided into twelve articles (for the twelve apostles). Luther here, as already in the *Little Prayer Book*, returns to a still older tradition of dividing the Creed into three parts for the Trinity.

32. Luther here explains more fully what he means by body, using *gelieder* (abilities) to sum up the bodily functions and *sinne* (mental faculties) to sum up the soul's functions.

33. Luther's paraphrase of "Amen." See the explanation to "Amen" in the Lord's Prayer, p. 230, and the reference to the third question in Holy Baptism, p. 231, where the phrase is used to translate Titus 3:8.

Christ crucified
(Matthew 26–27)

The Second Article: On Redemption

And [z] [I believe] in Jesus Christ, his only Son, our Lord, *who was conceived by the Holy Spirit, born of the Virgin Mary, suffered under Pontius Pilate, was crucified, died, and was buried. He descended into hell, on the third day he rose, ascended into heaven, is seated at the right hand of God, the almighty Father, from where he will come to judge the living and the dead.*

What is this? Answer:

I believe that Jesus Christ, true God, born of the Father in eternity, and also a true human being, born of the Virgin Mary, is my Lord.[34] He has redeemed me, a lost and condemned human being. He has purchased and freed me from all sins, from death, and from the power of the devil, not with gold or silver but with his holy, precious blood and with his innocent[a] suffering and death. He has done all this in order that I may belong to him, live under him in his kingdom, and serve him in eternal righteousness, innocence,[b] and blessedness, just as he is risen from the dead and lives and rules eternally. This is most certainly true.

34. Throughout this explanation, Luther uses the familiar image of a lord's responsibility to rescue any kidnapped or imprisoned subjects. See also LC, Creed, par. 27–31 (BC, 434–45).

z   The text corresponds to that used in the 1529 version.
a   German: *Unschüldigen*, literally, "not owed" or "not guilty."
b   German: *Unschuld*, literally, "something not owed."

The Third Article: On Being Made Holy[35]

I believe in the Holy Spirit, one holy Christian church,[36] *the community of the saints,*[c] *forgiveness of sins, resurrection of the flesh and an eternal life. AMEN.*

What is this? Answer:

I believe that by my own reason or powers[37] I cannot believe in Jesus Christ my Lord or come to him. But instead the Holy Spirit has called me through the gospel, enlightened me with his gifts, made me holy and kept me in the true faith, just as he calls, gathers, enlightens, and makes holy the whole Christian church[d] on earth and keeps it with Jesus Christ in the one common, true faith. Daily in this Christian church the Holy Spirit abundantly forgives all sins—mine and those of all believers. On the last day the Holy Spirit will raise me and all the dead and will give to me and all believers in Christ eternal life. This is most certainly true.

The first Pentecost with tongues of fire coming from the disciples' mouths (cf. Acts 2 and Rev. 11:5)

The Lord's Prayer: In the Very Simple Way in Which the Head of a House Is to Present It to the Household

Our Father, you who are in heaven.[e]

[38][What is this? Answer:

With these words God wants to attract us, so that we come to believe he is truly our Father and we are truly his children, in order that we may ask[f] him boldly and with complete confidence, just as loving children ask their loving father.][39]

---

c   German: *heiligen*, literally, holy ones.

d   German: *die gantze Christenheit*. German versions of the Creed predating Luther use this phrase to translate the Latin *ecclesia catholica*.

e   The text of the Lord's Prayer follows a common form used in Wittenberg and not the version in the Luther Bible.

f   German: *bitten*, which means both "ask" and "pray" in early New High German.

---

35. The English word *sanctification* does not preserve the linguistic connection between the Holy Spirit and the Holy Spirit's activity. See LC, Creed, par. 35–36 (BC, 435–36). The sharp distinction between "justification" and "sanctification" first arises later in the sixteenth century.

36. German translations of the Creed before and after the Reformation translate *ecclesia catholica* as Christian church.

37. German: *vernunfft noch krafft*. Luther here is attacking the late-medieval notion that a person could come to faith through his or her own capacities of will (power [Latin: *virtus*]) or intellect (reason [Latin: *ratio*]).

38. Luther first added this explanation to the introduction in the edition of 1531.

39. This explanation, although added later, epitomized Luther's approach to prayer: *not* as a mere recitation of

Preaching the Word of God
(Exod. 20:8-11, 19)

The First Request[g]

May your name be hallowed.[h]

What is this? Answer:

To be sure, God's name is holy in itself, but we ask in this prayer that it may also become holy in and among[i] us.

How does this come about?[j] Answer:

Whenever the Word of God is taught clearly and purely and we live according to it in a holy manner, as God's children. To this end help us, dear Father in heaven![40] However, whoever teaches and lives otherwise than the Word of God teaches profanes the name of God among us. Preserve us from this, heavenly Father!

words but as an earnest begging God for help. In Luther's German the word "prayer" (*beten*) was always associated with asking, so that praise and thanksgiving, as in the explanation to the Second Commandment, were viewed separately.

40. Here Luther combines the "Our Father" with the first petition in an actual paraphrase. Throughout his explanations, he refers to God as Father.

41. See above, the explanation to the third article of the Apostles' Creed.

42. Here Luther connects the third petition's fulfillment to the first two petitions, first quoting the text of those requests and then the meaning (Word and faith).

g   German: *Bitte*, traditionally translated "petition."
h   German: *Geheiliget*, literally, "made holy" or "sanctified."
i   German: *bey*.
j   German: *geschicht*, the same verb as in the third petition.

The Second Request

May your kingdom come.

What is this? Answer:

In fact, God's kingdom comes on its own without our prayer, but we ask in this prayer that it may also come to us.

How does this come about? Answer:

Whenever our heavenly Father gives us his Holy Spirit, so that through his grace we believe his Holy Word and live godly lives here in time and hereafter in eternity.[41]

Because Luther interpreted the Second Petition as a plea for the Holy Spirit, the picture is the same as for the Third Article. See above, p. 225.

The Third Request

May your will come about on earth as in heaven.

What is this? Answer:

In fact, God's good and gracious will comes about without our prayer, but we ask in this prayer, that it may also come about in and among[k] us.

How does this come about? Answer:

Whenever God breaks and hinders every evil scheme and will—as are present in the will of the devil, the world, and our flesh[l]—that would not allow us to hallow God's name and would prevent the coming of his kingdom, and instead whenever God strengthens us and keeps us firm in his Word and in faith until the end of our lives.[42] This is his gracious and good will.

Christ bearing the cross
(Matt. 27:31-32)

---

k   German: *bey.*

l   The syntax of this sentence is rather awkward in the German. Note similarities to the second article of the Creed.

Jesus feeding the five thousand
(John 6:1-15)

The Fourth Request

Give us today our daily bread.

What is this? Answer:

In fact, God gives daily bread without our prayer even to all evil people, but we ask in this prayer that God cause us to recognize what our daily bread is and to receive it with thanksgiving.

What then does [the phrase] "daily bread" mean? Answer:

Everything included in the necessities and nourishment for our bodies,[43] such as food, drink, clothing, shoes, house, farm,[m] fields, livestock, money, property, an upright[44] spouse, upright children, upright members of the household,[45] upright and faithful rulers, good government, good weather, peace, health, decency, honor, good friends, faithful neighbors, and the like.

---

43. See the explanation to the first article of the Apostles' Creed above.

44. German: *frum.* In the sixteenth century this word meant "upright, honest, competent, capable, well-behaved, sensible," but not so much, as in modern usage, "pious or godly."

45. German: *Gesinde,* the house servants and workers. In Luther's day the household was the center of economic activity and thus included both family members and laborers.

46. German: *angefochten,* the verbal form of *Anfechtung,* an important descriptor for Luther of the Christian life. See the Preface to the *Small Catechism,* above, p. 212, and his *Preface to the Wittenberg Edition of Luther's German Writings,* 1539 (LW 34:286–87; this volume, pp. 475–87).

---

m   German: *hoff* (farm buildings or farmstead).

The Fifth Request

And remit our debts," as we remit what our debtors owe.

What is this? Answer:

We ask in this prayer that our heavenly Father would not regard our sins nor deny these requests on their account, for we are worthy of nothing for which we ask, nor have we earned it. Instead we ask that God would give us all things by grace, for we daily sin much and indeed deserve only punishment. So, on the other hand, we, too, truly want heartily to forgive and gladly to do good to those who sin against us.

Parable of the Unforgiving Servant (Matt. 18:23-35)

The Sixth Request

And lead us not in temptation.

What is this? Answer:

It is true that God tempts no one, but we ask in this prayer that God would preserve and keep us, so that the devil, the world, and our flesh may not deceive us or mislead us into false belief, despair, and other great shame and vice, and that, although we may be attacked[46] by them, we may finally prevail and gain the victory.

The temptation of Christ (Matt. 4:1-11). Note Jesus with sheep and the devil with a wolf.

n German: *Schulde*.

Jesus and the Syrophoenician
woman (Matt. 15:21–28)

47. Some later editions of the *Catechism*, printed after Luther's death, add the doxology ("For the kingdom, the power and the glory are yours, now and forever"). Although found in Erasmus's editions of the Greek New Testament and in Luther's translation into German, Luther himself consistently followed the medieval usage in catechesis and omitted it.

48. For the command to pray and the promise to hear prayers, see LC, Lord's Prayer, par. 4–21 (BC, 441–43).

The Seventh Request

But deliver us from evil.

What is this? Answer:

We ask in this prayer, as in the summation, that our Father in heaven may deliver us from all kinds of evil—affecting body or soul, property or reputation—and at last, when our final hour comes, may grant us a blessed end and take us by grace from this valley of tears to himself in heaven.

Amen.[47]

What is this? Answer:

That I should be certain that such petitions are acceptable to and heard by our Father in heaven, for he himself commanded us to pray like this and has promised to hear us.[48] "Amen, amen" means "Yes, yes, it should come about just like this."

Holy Baptism (Matt. 28:16-20)
as practiced in Wittenberg

The Sacrament of Holy Baptism:
In a Simple Way in Which the Head of a House Is to Present It to the Household[49]

First

What is Baptism? Answer:

Baptism is not simply plain water. Instead it is water enclosed in God's command[50] and connected with God's Word.

What then is this Word of God? Answer:

Where our Lord *Christ says in Matt. 28[:19], "Go into all the world, teach all nations,° and baptize them in the name of the Father and of the Son and of the Holy Spirit."*

Second

What gifts or benefits does Baptism grant?[51] Answer:

It brings about forgiveness of sins, redeems from death and the devil, and gives eternal salvation to all who believe it, as the words and promise of God declare.

What are these words and promise of God? Answer:

Where our Lord *Christ says in Mark 16[:16], "Whoever believes and is baptized will be saved, but whoever does not believe will be damned."*

Third

How can water do such great things? Answer:

Clearly the water does not do it, but the Word of God, which is with and alongside[p] the water, and faith, which trusts this Word of God in the water. For without the Word of God the water is plain water and not a baptism, but with the Word of God it is a baptism, that is, a grace-filled water of life and a "bath of the new birth in the Holy Spirit," as St. Paul says to Titus in chapter 3[:5-8], *"through the bath of rebirth and renewal of the Holy Spirit, which he*

49. Baptism, often missing from medieval catechesis (because adults were thought to have sinned away the grace associated with that sacrament), was central to Luther's understanding of the Christian life of faith, as the answer to the fourth question made clear.

50. Luther here moves from the command to baptize to the promises contained in baptism and to faith in such promises.

51. Luther moves from the definition of baptism to its effects.

---

o   German: *Heiden* (heathen).

p   German: *mit und bey.*

52. In Luther's day, baptisms were often performed by immersing the infant in the water and drawing it out again. Luther preferred this method. See *The Babylonian Captivity of the Church*, 1520 (LW 36:67–68; TAL 3:9–129).

53. Literally, the Old Adam.

54. In 1531 paragraphs 15–29 replaced the earlier *A Short Order of Confession*, 1529 (LW 53:116–18), which was found in one Latin version of the *Small Catechism* from 1529 in this place and in one German version of the *Small Catechism* from 1529 following the *Baptismal Booklet*. In 1532 Luther defended this addition and the use of private confession among evangelicals in a letter to the town council and congregation in Frankfurt on the Main, "An Open Letter to Those in Frankfurt on the Main, 1533," trans. John D. Vieker, *Concordia Journal* 16 (1990): 333–51 (= WA 30/3:565–71). In 1531, this title was placed in the same illustrations used for the title page of the *Small Catechism*. Luther, in contrast to medieval theology, viewed confession and forgiveness as the regular living out of baptism's significance, as discussed in question four on baptism.

55. See LC, "A Brief Exhortation to Confession" (BC, 476–80), especially par. 15 (BC, 478). Already in some of his earliest writings from 1517 and later, Luther distinguished two parts of penitence—sorrow for sin (confession) and absolution (forgiveness). This he contrasted to the medieval, Scholastic definition of the Sacrament of Penance as consisting of contrition, confession,

richly poured out over us through Jesus Christ our Savior, so that through that very grace we may be justified[q] heirs in hope of eternal life. This is[r] most certainly true."

Fourth

What then does such baptism with water signify?[52] Answer:

It signifies that the old creature[53] in us with all sins and evil desires is to be drowned and die through daily contrition and repentance and, on the other hand, that daily a new person is to come forth and rise up to live before God in righteousness and purity forever.

Where is this written? Answer:

St. Paul says in Rom. 6[:4] "We were buried with Christ through baptism in death, so that, just as Christ was raised from the dead through the glory of the Father, we, too, are to walk in a new life."

How Simple People Are to Be Taught to Confess[54]

What is confession? Answer:

Confession consists of two parts.[55] One is that we confess our sins. The other is that we receive the absolution, that is, forgiveness, from the confessor as from God himself and by no means doubt but firmly believe that our sins are thereby forgiven before God in heaven.

Which sins is a person to confess?

Before God one is to acknowledge the guilt for all sins, even those of which we are not aware, as we do in the Lord's Prayer.[56]

However, before the confessor we are to confess only those sins of which we have knowledge and which trouble us.[57]

Which sins are these?

---

q   Versions from 1536 and thereafter read instead "righteous and," which is parallel to Luther's Bible.

r   Versions from 1536 and thereafter insert "Surely."

Here, in light of the Ten Commandments, reflect on your place in life:[s] whether you are father, mother, son, daughter, master, mistress, servant;[58] whether you have been disobedient, unfaithful, lazy, ill-tempered, unruly, or quarrelsome;[t] whether you have harmed anyone by word or deed; whether you have stolen, neglected, wasted, or injured anything.

Please provide me with a brief form of confession! Answer:[59] You are to say to the confessor:[60]

"Honorable, dear sir, I ask you[u] to listen to my confession and declare to me forgiveness for God's sake."

Then say this:

"I, a poor sinner, confess before God that I am guilty of all [my] sins.[61] In particular, I confess in your presence that I am a manservant, maidservant, etc., but I unfortunately serve my master[v] unfaithfully, for in this and that instance I did not do what they told me; I made them angry and caused them to curse; I neglected to do my duty and allowed harm to occur.

"I have also spoken and acted impudently. I have quarreled with my equals; I have grumbled about and sworn at my mistresses, etc. I am sorry for all this and ask for grace. I want to do better."

A master or mistress may say the following:

"In particular I confess to you that I have not faithfully cared for my child, the members of my household or my spouse[w] to the glory of God. I have cursed, set a bad example with indecent words and deeds, done harm to my neighbors,[x] spoken evil of them, overcharged them, and sold them inferior goods and short-changed them," and whatever else he [or she] has done against the commands of God and their walk of life, etc.

---

s   German: *Stand* (station or walk of life).
t   The Wittenberg editions of 1535 and following omit: "ill-tempered, unruly, or quarrelsome."
u   Here and throughout Luther uses the formal form of address.
v   Luther shifts from the singular (master) to the plural (they).
w   German: *weib* (wife).
x   German: singular.

---

and satisfaction, where "satisfaction" meant doing good works that satisfied the remaining *temporal* punishment for sin, the eternal punishment having been removed in the priest's absolution.

56. See the fifth petition.

57. This contrasts to the medieval practice, which required that the penitent confess all mortal sins committed since the last confession. See below.

58. The basic positions in a sixteenth-century German household.

59. Much of this form builds upon the medieval practice of private confession.

60. The Wittenberg church still practiced private confession to a pastor, as is depicted on the altarpiece from 1547 painted by Lukas Cranach (1472–1553), which showed the chief pastor in Wittenberg, Johannes Bugenhagen, holding the "keys," forgiving one confessant and binding the sins of another. In an emergency, Luther taught that anyone could function in this way for a Christian whose conscience was especially oppressed by sin.

61. This is the general confession referred to below in par. 25. It prefaces the particular confession here and is the implied beginning of the confessions in paragraphs 23 and 24. In other cases the "general confession" refers to public confession, that is, words spoken at the conclusion of the sermon in worship. Cf. SA, pt. III, art. iii, par. 13 (BC, 314).

62. See *A Discussion on How Confession Should Be Made*, 1520 (LW 39:27–47) and CA XXV.7–12 (BC, 72–75). Medieval practice insisted that the penitent confess *all* sins to the priest with the threat that any omissions placed the entire confession in jeopardy. As a result, long lists of possible sins were often a part of medieval prayer books and catechisms. Contrary to this, the Wittenberg reformers insisted that no such rule should be enforced but, rather, that the individual conscience should be respected and encouraged to seek absolution for particularly those sins that oppressed them.

63. See above, n. 61, p. 233. Luther could have in mind expanding this with the words of the fuller version of general public confession spoken after the sermon by the preacher.

64. German: *angefochten*. See above, n. 46, p. 228.

If, however, some individuals[y] do not find themselves burdened by these or greater sins, they are not to worry or search for and invent further sins and thereby turn confession into torture.[62] Instead mention one or two that you are aware of, as follows: "In particular I confess that I cursed once, likewise that one time I was inconsiderate in my speech, one time I neglected this or that, etc." Let that suffice.

If you are aware of no sins at all (which is really quite unlikely), then do not mention any in particular, but instead receive forgiveness on the basis of the general confession,[63] which you make to God in the presence of the confessor.

Thereupon the confessor is to say:
"God be gracious to you and strengthen your faith. AMEN."

Then let [the confessor] say:
"Do you also believe that my forgiveness is God's forgiveness?"
[Answer:] "Yes, dear sir."

Thereupon he may say:
"'Let it be done for you according to your faith.'[z] And I by the command of our LORD Jesus Christ[a] forgive you your sin in the name of the Father and of the Son and of the Holy Spirit. Amen. Go in peace."[b]

A confessor, by using additional passages of Scripture, can in fact comfort and encourage to faith those whose consciences are heavily burdened or who are distressed and under attack.[64] This is only to be an ordinary form of confession for simple people.

---

y　German: singular.
z　Matt. 8:13.
a　Matt. 16:19; 18:18; John 20:23.
b　Mark 5:34; Luke 7:50; 8:48.

The Sacrament of the Altar:
In a Simple Way in Which the Head of a House
Is to Present It to the Household[65]

The distribution of the Lord's Supper (Matt. 26:26-28).
Above the altar is a depiction of the Last Supper
with Christ communing with Judas.[66] A pastor wearing
a chasuble offers the bread to a kneeling man and
an assistant the cup to a kneeling woman. On either side
of the altar others are waiting to receive the elements.

65. Medieval catechesis was often viewed as preparing persons for the Sacrament of Penance and, hence, did not emphasize the Lord's Supper. Here Luther insisted on the twin gifts of Christ's presence and forgiveness in the Supper, which are received by faith. He thus spelled out a view of the Sacrament of the Altar that differed from those of Ulrich Zwingli (1484–1531), who denied Christ's real presence in the meal, and of Wittenberg's Roman opponents, who argued that the Supper was an unbloodied sacrifice to God offered by the priests on behalf of the sins of the congregation or those for whom the celebration had been purchased, in which faith was unnecessary for the sacrament's effectiveness.

66. This underscored the Lutheran insistence, over against Ulrich Zwingli and others, that unbelievers also received Christ's body and blood in the Supper.

What is the Sacrament of the Altar?[67] Answer:

It is the true body and blood of our Lord Jesus Christ under the bread and wine, instituted by Christ himself for us Christians to eat and to drink.

Where is this written? Answer:

The holy evangelists, Matthew, Mark, and Luke, and St. Paul write thus:

"Our Lord *Jesus Christ, on the night in which he was betrayed, took the bread, gave thanks and broke it and gave it to his disciples and said, 'Take; eat; this is my body which is given for you. Do this in remembrance of me.'*

67. The first three questions here match those in the section on baptism: what is it; what are its benefits; and who receives it properly (namely, through faith)?

"In the same way he also took the cup after the supper, gave thanks and gave it to them and said, 'Take, and drink from it, all of you. This cup is the New Testament in my blood, which is shed for you for the forgiveness of sins. Do this, as often as you drink it, in remembrance of me.'" [c]

What is the benefit of such eating and drinking? Answer:

The words, *"given for you"* and *"shed for you* [d] *for the forgiveness of sins,"* show us that forgiveness of sin, [e] life, and salvation are given to us in the sacrament through these words, [68] because where there is forgiveness of sin, there is also life and salvation.

How can bodily eating and drinking do such a great thing? [f] Answer:

Eating and drinking certainly do not do it, but rather the words that are recorded: *"given for you"* and *"shed for you for the forgiveness of sins."* These words, when accompanied by [g] the physical eating and drinking, are the essential thing in the sacrament, and whoever believes these very words has what they declare and state, namely, *"forgiveness of sins."*

Who, then, receives this sacrament worthily? Answer:

Fasting and bodily preparation are in fact a fine external discipline, [69] but a person who has faith in these words, *"given for you"* and *"shed for you for the forgiveness of sins,"* is really worthy and well prepared. However, a person who does not believe these words or doubts them is unworthy and unprepared, because the words, *"for you,"* require truly believing hearts.

---

68. Beginning with Wittenberg's reform of liturgy in 1523 and included in the *German Mass* of 1526, the words of institution, understood as containing Jesus' testamentary promise, were chanted aloud (as opposed to the medieval practice of the priest whispering them at the altar). This practice, combined with the fact that from 1525 Wittenberg's catechisms included the words of institution as part of the "Lay Bible" to be memorized, meant that the Lord's Supper was no longer a sacrifice to be observed but a meal of God's mercy to be consumed.

69. Medieval practice required fasting before receiving the Lord's Supper. Luther distinguishes here between external preparation and the faith of the heart, which for him is not a human "work" but an action of the Holy Spirit using the gospel (see his explanation to the third article, above, p. 225).

---

c   A conflation of texts from 1 Cor. 11:23-25; Matt. 26:26-28; Mark 14:22-24; Luke 22:19f. Cf. LC, Sacrament of the Altar, par. 3 (BC, 467), and LC, Short Preface, par. 23 (BC, 385–86). This text conforms neither to the words of institution found in *The German Mass and Order of Service*, 1526 (LW 53:80–81), nor in the LC.

d   In this and the succeeding questions the words "for you," stated only once in the German, apply to both phrases.

e   Beginning with the 1536 edition of the *Small Catechism*, "sins."

f   Beginning with the 1540 edition of the *Small Catechism*, "great things."

g   German: *neben* (near, in proximity to).

How the head of the house is to teach the members of the household to say morning and evening blessings[70]

In the morning, as soon as you get out of bed, you are to make the sign of the holy cross and say:

"*God the Father, Son, and Holy Spirit watch over me. Amen.*"

Then, kneeling or standing, say the Apostles' Creed and the Lord's Prayer. If you wish, you may in addition recite this little prayer as well:

"*I give thanks to you, my heavenly Father, through Jesus Christ your dear Son, that you have protected me this night from all harm and danger, and I ask you that you would also protect me today from sin and all evil, so that my life and actions may please you completely. For into your hands I commend myself: my body, my soul, and everything else. Let your holy angel*[71] *be with me, so that the wicked foe may have no power over me. Amen.*"

After singing a hymn perhaps (for example, one on the Ten Commandments[h]) or whatever else may serve your devotion, you are to go to your work joyfully.

In the evening, when you go to bed, you are to make the sign of the holy cross and say:

"*God the Father, Son, and Holy Spirit watch over me. Amen.*"

Then, kneeling or standing, say the Apostles' Creed and the Lord's Prayer. If you wish, you may in addition recite this little prayer as well:

"*I give thanks to you, my heavenly Father, through Jesus Christ your dear Son, that you have graciously protected me today, and I ask you to forgive me all my sins, where I have done wrong, and graciously to protect me tonight. For into your hands I commend myself: my body, my soul, and everything else. Let your holy angel be with me, so that the wicked foe may have no power over me. Amen.*"

Then you are to go to sleep quickly and cheerfully.

70. Luther adapted this material from the Roman Breviary. The expression "say blessings" (*sich segenen*) meant in Luther's day "make the sign of the cross."

71. Luther reflects the common belief of a guardian angel for each person. See Matt. 18:10.

---

h   See LC, Short Preface, par. 24–25 (BC, 386), and Luther's own hymns on the Decalog (LW 53:277–81).

How the head of the house is to teach members of the household to offer blessing and thanksgiving[72] at meals[73]

[The Table Blessing][i]

The children and the members of the household are to come devoutly to the table, fold their hands and recite:

"The eyes of all wait upon you, O Lord, and you give them their food at the proper time. You open your hand and satisfy all living things with delight."[74]

Comment: "Delight" means that all animals receive enough to eat to make them joyful and of good cheer, because worry and greed prevent such delight.

Then they are to recite the Lord's Prayer and the following prayer:

"Lord God, heavenly Father, bless us and these your gifts, which we receive from your bountiful goodness through Jesus Christ our Lord. Amen."

Thanksgiving[j]

Similarly, after eating they should in the same manner fold their hands and recite devoutly:

"O give thanks to the Lord, for he is gracious and his goodness endures forever. He gives food to all flesh. He gives food to the cattle and to the young ravens that cry to him. He takes no pleasure in the power of the horse, nor is he pleased with human strength.[k] *The Lord takes pleasure in those who fear him and wait for his goodness."*[l]

Then recite the Lord's Prayer and the following prayer:

"We give thanks to you, Lord God our Father, through Jesus Christ our Lord for all your benefits, you who live and reign forever. Amen."

---

72. Here Luther uses the well-known Latin terms *benedicite* (blessing) and *gratias* (thanksgiving).

73. The material in this section was adapted from the Roman Breviary already in the 1525 Wittenberg catechism, *Das Buchlin für die leyen und kinder* (*Booklet for the Laity and Children*), in Robert Kolb and James Nestingen, eds., *Sources and Contexts of the* Book of Concord (Minneapolis: Fortress Press, 2001), 7–8. Luther adds here instructions regarding the children's demeanor and a gloss on the word *delight*.

74. Ps. 145:15-16. The gloss that follows matches Luther's comments in his translation of the Bible about the word "pleasure" (*wohlgefallen*) connected with this text and Luke 2:14.

---

i   This title occurs only in the Latin versions: *Benedictio mensae.*

j   Luther, following the 1525 *Buchlin* (*Booklet*), uses the Latin term *gratias.*

k   German: *beinen* (legs).

l   Pss. 106:1; 136:1, 26; 147:9-11. The text follows the translations in the Luther Bible.

The Household Chart[75] of Some Bible Passages

for all kinds of holy orders[76] and walks of life,[m]
through which they may be admonished,
as through lessons particularly pertinent
to their office and duty[77]

For Bishops, Pastors, and Preachers

"A bishop is to be above reproach, the husband of one wife, temperate, virtuous, moderate, hospitable, an apt teacher, not a drunkard, not vicious, not greedy for shameless profit,[78] but gentle, not quarrelsome, not stingy, one who manages his own household well, who has obedient and honest children, not a recent convert, etc."[n] From 1 Tim. 3[:2-4, 6a].[o]

Concerning Governing Authorities

"Let everyone be subject to the governing authority. For wherever the governing authority is, it is ordered by God. But whoever resists the governing authority, resists God's order, but whoever resists will incur judgment, for that authority does not bear the sword in vain. It is God's handmaid, who executes punishment against those who do evil." From Rom. 13[:1-2, 4b].[p]

75. German: *Die Haustafel.* Sometimes translated "table of duties" (a meaning of the term derived from its use here), this section may have been suggested to Luther by Jean Gerson's *Tractatus de modo vivendi omnium fidelium.* Translation of the Bible passages here is based upon Luther's own rendering of the texts.

76. Luther is both criticizing the common use of this term for the monastic life and referring to the three estates: *ordo ecclesiasticus, politicus,* and *oeconomicus* (church, government, and household, respectively). See SA, Preface, par. 14, 1538 (BC, 300; TAL 2:427), and the *Confession Concerning Christ's Supper,* 1528 (LW 37:363–65). This section outlines Luther's understanding of Christian vocations in the world.

77. In his explanation of the Fourth Commandment in the *Large Catechism,* Luther detailed many of the duties outlined here. See LC, Ten Commandments, par. 103–78 (BC, 400–410; TAL 2:314-27). He also mentioned responsibilities in explanations of the Fifth through Eighth Commandments as well.

78. Influenced by a later edition of Luther's German Bible, the 1536 edition replaced "greedy for shameless profit" with "involved in dishonorable work."

---

m German: *Stende* (stations or walks of life).

n In the 1540 edition, using a passage from Titus 1:9 inserted for "etc.": "who holds to the Word that is certain and can teach, so that he may be strong enough to admonish with saving teaching and to refute those who contradict it."

o The 1540 edition adds a section entitled "What Christians ought to do for their teachers and pastors [German: *Seelsorger*]" and includes texts from Luke 10:7; 1 Cor. 9:14; Gal. 6:6-7; 1 Tim. 5:17-18; 1 Thess. 5:12-13; and Heb. 13:17. An abbreviated form, omitting passages from Luke and 1 Thessalonians, is found in Latin translations from 1529.

p The 1542 edition adds a section entitled "What subjects ought to do for the governing authority" and includes texts from Matt. 22:21; Rom. 13:1, 5-7; 1 Tim. 2:1-2; Titus 3:1; and 1 Peter 2:13-14. An expanded form, which includes a reference to, but no text of Matt. 17:24-27, is found in Latin translations from 1529.

79. Here Luther focuses on the household and those stations in life generally found there in the sixteenth century: husband and wife; parents and children; masters, mistresses, and workers; widows; young people.

For Husbands[79]

"You husbands, live reasonably with your wives and give honor, as coheirs of the grace of life, to wives as to the weak[q] instrument, so that your prayers may not be hindered." From 1 Peter 3[:7]. "And do not be harsh with them." From Col. 3[:19].

For Wives

"Let wives be subjected to their husbands as to the LORD, as Sarah obeyed Abraham and called him lord. And you have become her daughters, when you do right and are not afraid of any terrifying thing."[r] From 1 Peter 3[:1, 6].[80]

80. The words "as to the LORD" come from Eph. 5:22.

For Parents

"You fathers, do not provoke your children to anger, lest they become fearful. Instead, bring them up in the discipline and admonition of the LORD." From Eph. 6[:4].

For Children

"You children, be obedient to your parents in the LORD, for this is right. 'Honor your father and mother.' This is the first commandment that has a promise, namely: 'that it may go well for you and that you may live long on earth.'" From Eph. 6[:1-3].

For Male and Female Servants, Day Laborers, Workers, and the Like

81. German: *Knechte* (the male servant in the German household).

"You servants,[81] be obedient to your bodily lords with fear and trembling, with singleness of heart, as to Christ himself; not with service meant only for the eyes, done to please people, but rather as servants of Christ, so that you do the will of God from the heart with compliance.[s] Imagine to yourselves that you are

q   Beginning in the 1536 version: "weakest."

r   The 1536 edition replaced "afraid of any terrifying thing" with "so fearful." See LW 30:87–91 for Luther's sermon on this text from 1522.

s   The 1536 version, following later editions of the Wittenberg translation of the Bible, reads "with a good will."

serving the LORD and not people, and know that whatever good anyone does, the same will that person receive, whether a servant or free."[t]

For Masters and Mistresses[82]

"You masters, do the same to them, and refrain from making threats, and know that you also have a Lord in heaven, and there is no partiality with him."[u]

For Young People in General

"You young people, be subject to your elders and in this way show humility. For 'God opposes the proud but gives grace to the humble.' Therefore humble yourselves under the mighty hand of God, so that he may exalt you in his time." From 1 Peter 5[:5-6].

For Widows

"She who is a real widow and is left all alone sets her hope on God and remains in prayer day and night; whereas she who lives self-indulgently is dead while alive." From 1 Tim. 5[:5-6].

For All in the Community[83]

"Love your neighbor as yourself. In this all the commandments are summarized." From Rom. 13[:9]. "And continually entreat [God] with prayers for all people." From 1 Tim. 2[:1].[v]

Let all their lessons learn with care,
So that the household well may fare.[84]

82. German: *Hausherrn und Hausfrauen*: literally, "the lords and ladies of the house," that is, the heads of households.

83. German: *der Gemeine*. This word may be translated the congregation, the community, or all in common. See *Confession Concerning Christ's Supper*, 1528 (LW 37:367–68).

84. This is most likely Luther's own rhyme. See WA 35:580.

---

t   From Eph. 6:5-8.
u   The 1536 version adds: "Eph. 6[:9]."
v   A loose paraphrase.

1536 section title: "Marriage
Booklet for Simple Pastors"

A Marriage Booklet for Simple Pastors[85]

Martin Luther

"So many lands, so many customs," says the common adage. For this reason, because weddings and the married estate are worldly affairs, it behooves those of us who are "spirituals"[86] or ministers of the church in no way to order or direct anything regarding marriage, but instead to allow every city and land to continue their own customs and practices that are now in use. Some bring the bride to the church twice, in both the evening and the morning; some only once. Some announce it publicly and publish the banns from the pulpit two or three weeks in advance. All these and similar things I leave to the prince and town council to create and arrange as they want. It is no concern of mine.[87]

However, when people request of us to bless them in front of the church or in the church, to pray over them, or even to marry them, we are obligated to do this. Therefore I wanted to offer these words of advice and this order for those who do not know anything better, in case they are inclined to use this common order with us. Others, who can do better (that is, who can do nothing at all and who nevertheless think they know it all), do

85. This text, also printed as a separate pamphlet in 1529, was included in most editions of the *Small Catechism* printed during Luther's lifetime, starting in 1529, and later in several versions of the *Book of Concord* printed in 1580 and 1581. A translation into English, on which this translation is based, is found in LW 53:110–15.

86. German: *Geistlichen*; Luther uses the common term for clergy, monks, friars, and nuns.

87. Here Luther's distancing himself contrasts to the late-medieval church, which used a complicated set of laws to regulate marriage, divorce, and other family matters. Instead, although courts included representatives from the church and the government, marriage and family were understood as legal matters for this world and not related directly to the Christian gospel of forgiveness.

not need this service of mine, unless they might greatly improve on it and masterfully correct it. They certainly ought to take great care not to follow the same practice as others. A person might think that they had learned something from someone else! That would be a real shame!

Because up to now people have made such an impressive, great display at the consecrations of monks and nuns (even though their station in life[w] and existence is an ungodly, human invention without any basis in the Bible), how much more should we honor this godly station of marriage and bless it, pray for it, and adorn it in an even more glorious manner. For, although it is a worldly station, nevertheless it has God's Word on its side and is not a human invention or institution, like the station of monks and nuns.[88] Therefore it should easily be reckoned a hundred times more spiritual than the monastic station, which certainly ought to be considered the most worldly and fleshly of all, because it was invented and instituted by flesh and blood and completely out of a worldly understanding and reason.

We must also do this in order that the young people may learn to take this station in life seriously, to hold it in high esteem as a divine work and command, and not to ridicule it in such outrageous ways with laughing, jeering, and similar levity. This has been common until now, as if it were a joke or child's play to get married or to hold a wedding. Those who first instituted the custom of bringing a bride and bridegroom to church surely did not view it as a joke but as a very serious matter.[x] For there is no doubt that they wanted thereby to receive God's blessing and the community's[89] prayers and not put on a comedy or a pagan farce.

The ceremony itself makes this clear. For all[y] who desire prayer and blessing from the pastor or bishop[90] indicate thereby—whether or not they say so expressly—to what danger and need they are exposing themselves and how much they need God's blessing and the community's prayers for the station of life into which they are entering. For they experience every day how much

88. For a similar criticism see also *The Estate of Marriage*, 1522 (LW 45:17–49), and *The Judgment of Martin Luther on Monastic Vows*, 1521 (LW 44:245–400).

89. Luther is thinking of the general prayers for the couple made by the community in worship.

90. Luther understood that the chief pastor in a town was its bishop. For example, see *Lectures on 1 Timothy*, 1528 (LW 28:281–84); *Answer to the Hyperchristian . . . Book*, 1521 (LW 39:154–56); and *Instruction by the Visitors*, 1528 (LW 40:269–71); as well as the SC, Preface, and Household Chart, above, pp. 212 and 239.

---

w   Here and throughout this tract, the German word *Stand* is translated "station of life" or "walk of life." In older translations it was rendered "estate."

x   See Luther's *Sermon at Marriage of Sigismund von Lindenau*, 1545 (LW 51:363–64).

y   Singular in the original.

unhappiness the devil causes in the marital station through adultery, unfaithfulness, discord, and all kinds of misery.

Therefore we want to deal with the bride and bridegroom (when they desire and demand it) in the following way.

First, publish the banns[91] from the pulpit with the following words:

"John N. and Mary N.[92] wish to enter the holy station of matrimony according to God's ordinance and desire the common Christian prayers[93] on their behalf so that they may begin it in God's name and have it turn out well.

Now should anyone have anything to say against this, let him or her speak at this time or hereafter remain silent. God grant them his blessing. AMEN."

Exchange vows[94] in front of the church with the following words:

"John, do you desire to have Mary as your wedded wife?"
Let him answer[z]: "Yes."
"Mary, do you desire to have John as your wedded husband?"
Let her answer: "Yes."

At this point let them exchange wedding rings and join their right hands together, and say to them:
What God joins together, no human being ought to separate.[a]

Then let the pastor declare to all who are present:

"Therefore, because John N. and Mary N. desire each other in marriage and confess the same here publicly in the presence of God and the world, in testimony of which they have given each other their hands and wedding rings, I pronounce them joined in marriage, in the name of the Father, and of the Son, and of the Holy Spirit. Amen."

In front of the altar[95] let the pastor read God's word from Gen. 2[:18, 21-24] over the bride and groom.

---

91. The "banns" were a legal declaration, usually made by the pastor, announcing the impending marriage of a couple and asking the community to express grounds why the marriage should not take place (usually because of a previous marriage or betrothal). For Luther's opinion of betrothals, a source of much debate in the sixteenth century, see *On Marriage Matters*, 1530 (LW 46:290–91).

92. German: *Hans und Greta*, common names for a couple, but also the names of Luther's own parents.

93. That is, the general prayers made in worship.

94. Luther believed that marriage should follow soon after betrothal. Because the exchange of vows was considered a matter of civil law, it took place at the door of the church.

95. This marks the beginning of the worship service.

z Here and below Luther employs the standard Latin term *dicat*.
a Matt. 19:6.

"Then the Lord *God said, 'It is not good that the human being should be alone; I will make him a helper who will be his companion.'[b] So the* Lord *God caused a deep sleep to fall upon the human being, and he slept; and he took one of his ribs and closed up its place with flesh. And the* Lord *God built a woman out of the rib that he had taken from the human being, and he brought her to him. Then the human being said: 'This is truly bone of my bone and flesh of my flesh. This one will be called woman, because she is taken out of man.' Therefore a man will leave his father and mother and cling to his wife, and the two will be one flesh."*

Then let the pastor turn to both and address them thus:

"Because you both have entered into the married estate in God's name, hear first of all God's commandment concerning this estate. Thus says St. Paul:[c]

"'Husbands, love your wives, just as Christ loved the congregation[d] and gave himself up for it, in order to make it holy, and has cleansed it through the washing of water in the Word, in order to present for himself a glorious congregation,[e] that has neither spot nor wrinkle nor anything of the kind, but instead so that it may be holy and blameless. So also husbands ought to love their wives like their own bodies. He who loves his wife loves himself. For no one ever hated his own flesh, but instead he nourishes it and takes care of it, just as the Lord *does for the congregation.*

"'Wives, be subject to your husbands as to the Lord*. For the husband is the head of the wife, just as Christ is also the head of the congregation, and he is the savior of his body. But as now the congregation is subject to Christ, so also the women are subject to their husbands in all things.'*

"Second, hear also the cross that God has placed upon this station.[f]

---

b   The 1536 version corresponds to the complete edition of the Luther Bible from 1534: "who will stand by his side."

c   Eph. 5:25-29, 22-24.

d   German: *Gemeine* (congregation or community), following the translation of Luther's German translation, the *September Testament* of 1522.

e   The 1536 version corresponds to the complete edition of Luther's 1534 translation of the Bible: "prepare for himself a community that will be glorious."

f   Gen. 3:16-19.

96. The following prayer is an adaptation of a traditional prayer used at nuptial Masses in Luther's day.

97. German: *Kirchen.* Luther did not view marriage as a sacrament but uses the word here as found in the traditional prayer to refer to Eph. 5:32, where the Vulgate translates the Greek *mystērion* with *sacramentum.* See LW 36:92–95. In the gloss on this text in the 1522 translation of the New Testament (WA Bi 7:206), Luther states, "'*geheymnis: sacramentum* or *mysterion* means secret [*geheymnis*] or a hidden thing, which nevertheless has its own signification. Thus, Christ and his congregation is a secret, that is, a great, holy, hidden thing, that one must believe and cannot see. It is signified by a man and wife, as by an external sign; that just as a man and wife are one body and hold all property in common, so also the congregation has everything that Christ is and has."

98. The *Baptismal Booklet,* based upon medieval baptismal rites, was originally published in 1523 (LW 53:95–103). In 1526 a second edition was prepared (LW 53:106–9 with 101–3), which is the basis of the translation here. It was included in the second edition of the *Small Catechism* published in 1529, in all subsequent editions published in Wittenberg during Luther's lifetime, and in some editions of the *Book of Concord.* The rite shows Luther's deep respect for the liturgical tradition, his connection between baptism and the defeat of evil, and his insistence that the promises bestowed in baptism were a lifelong gift from God. Moreover, as his introduction made clear, Luther refocused the liturgical action on the actual baptizing with water, as opposed to the other practices that surrounded it.

"'To the woman God said:

"''*I will create much distress for you in childbirth. You shall bear your children in distress, and you shall cringe before your husband, and he shall be your lord.*'

"'And to the man God said:

"''*Because you have listened to the voice of your wife and have eaten from the tree, about which I commanded you and said, 'You shall not eat from it,' cursed is the ground because of you. In distress you shall nourish yourself your whole life long. The ground shall bring forth thorns and thistles for you, and you shall eat the plants of the field. By the sweat of your face shall you eat your bread, until you return again to the earth from which you were taken. For you are earth and shall return to earth.*'"

"Third, this is your comfort, that you know and believe how your estate is pleasing and blessed in God's eyes. For it is written:[g]

"'*God created human beings in his image, in the image of God he created them. He created them a male and a female, and God blessed them and said to them: "Be fruitful and multiply, and fill the earth and bring it under your control; and have dominion over the fish in the sea and over the birds in the air and over all animals that crawl on the earth." And God saw all that he had made, and look, it was all very good.*'

"Therefore Solomon also says,[h]

"'*Whoever gets a wife, gets a good thing and will obtain delight from the LORD.*'"

At this point let the pastor spread his hands over them and pray:[96]

"*LORD God, who have created man and woman and have ordained them for the station of marriage, have blessed them also with the fruit of the womb, and have therein signified the sacrament of your dear Son, Jesus Christ, and the church,*[97] *his bride: We beseech your never-ending goodness that you would not permit this your creation, ordinance, and blessing to be removed or destroyed, but graciously preserve it among us through Jesus Christ our LORD. AMEN.*"

---

g   Gen. 1:27-28, 31.

h   A paraphrase of Prov. 18:22. The 1536 version reads, "Whoever finds a wife, finds a good thing and obtains a blessing from the LORD."

1536 section title: *The Baptismal
Booklet: Translated into German
and Newly Revised*

99. In the Roman rite only the questions to the sponsors and their responses were not in Latin.

100. German: *ernstlich*. Throughout this preface, Luther repeatedly uses this adverb and other forms of the word, which is translated here either "earnestly" or "seriously."

101. German: *Kinder heben*, literally, "to draw children out of the font." See the order of service below. The sponsors are to hold the child over the font while the priest puts on the christening robe.

The Baptismal Booklet:
Translated into German and Newly Revised[98]

Martin Luther

To all Christian readers: Grace and peace in Christ our Lord. Because daily I see and hear with what carelessness and lack of solemnity—to say nothing of out and out levity—people[i] treat the high, holy, and comforting Sacrament of Baptism for infants, in part caused, I believe, by the fact that those present understand nothing of what is being said and done, I have decided that it is not only helpful but also necessary to conduct the service in the German language. For this reason I have attempted to translate these things[99] in order to begin baptizing in German, so that the sponsors and others present may all the more be aroused to faith and earnest[100] devotion and so that the priests who baptize have to show more diligence for the sake of the listeners.

Out of a sense of Christian commitment, I appeal to all those who baptize, sponsor infants,[101] or witness a baptism to take to

1536 caption: "The figure:
Matthew 28:16-20." See also
the caption for this
image on p. 230.

---

i   Singular in the original.

heart the tremendous work and great earnestness present here. For here in the words of these prayers you hear how plaintively and earnestly the Christian church brings the infant here, confesses before God with such steadfast, undoubting words that the infant is possessed by the devil and a child of sin and perniciousness, and through baptism so diligently asks for help and grace, so that the infant may become a child of God.

Therefore, you have to realize that it is no joke at all to take action against the devil and not only drive him away from the little child but also hang around the child's neck such a mighty, lifelong enemy. For this reason, it is absolutely necessary to stand by the poor child with all one's heart and with a strong faith and to plead with great devotion that God, in accordance with these prayers, would not only free the child from the devil's power but also strengthen the child, so that the child might resist him valiantly[j] in life and in death. I fear that people turn out so badly after baptism because we have dealt with them in such a cold and casual way and have not prayed at all earnestly for them at their baptism.

Bear in mind, too, that in baptism the external ceremonies are least important, such as blowing under the eyes, making the sign of the cross, putting salt in the mouth or spit and clay in the ears and nose, anointing the breast and shoulders with oil, smearing the head with chrism, putting on the christening robe, placing a burning candle in the person's hand, and whatever else has been added by humans to embellish baptism.[102] For certainly a baptism can occur without any of these things, and they are not the actual devices from which the devil shrinks or flees. He sneers at even greater things than these! Here things must get really serious.

Instead, see to it that you are present there in true faith, that you listen to God's word, and that you pray along earnestly.[103] For wherever the priest says, "Let us pray," he is exhorting you to pray with him. Moreover, all sponsors and the others present ought to speak along with him the words of his prayer in their hearts to God. For this reason, the priest should speak these prayers very clearly and slowly, so that the sponsors can hear and understand them and can also pray with the priest with one mind in their hearts, carrying before God the need of the little child with all

102. Many of these practices go back to the rites for baptismal preparation and baptism used in the ancient church, which in turn reflected the actions of Christ in healing the blind and deaf, or the anointing of priests and kings from the Old Testament, or imagery from Paul's letters. See, for example, Mark 7:33; Mark 8:23; Exod. 29:7; 1 Sam. 10:1; and Gal. 3:27. Others reflect the sayings of Christ about Christians as the salt of the earth and light of the world (Matt. 5:13-16).

103. For Luther, prayer was no longer simply holy words that were effective merely by their being spoken (*ex opere operato*), but truly begging God to act, in this case, on behalf of the baptizand. For more on his condemnation of "useless howling and growling" see the LC, Lord's Prayer, par. 4-34 (BC, 441-45, here 444, par. 33).

---

j   German: *ritterlich*, literally, "chivalrously," "like a knight."

earnestness, on the child's behalf setting themselves against the devil with all their strength, and demonstrating that they take seriously what is no joke to the devil.

For this reason it is absolutely right and proper not to allow drunken and boorish clerics[k] to baptize nor to select good-for-nothings as godparents. Instead fine, moral, serious, upright priests and godparents ought to be chosen, who can be expected to treat the matter with seriousness and true faith, lest this high sacrament be abandoned to the devil's mockery and dishonor God, who in this sacrament showers upon us the vast and boundless riches of his grace. He himself calls it a "new birth,"[l] through which we, being freed from the devil's tyranny and loosed from sin, death, and hell, become children of life, heirs of all God's possessions, God's own children, and Christ's brothers and sisters.[m]

Ah, dear Christians, let us not value or treat this unspeakable gift so half-heartedly. For baptism is our only comfort, the entrance into all of God's possessions, and communion with all the saints. To this end may God help us! AMEN.

The Baptizer shall say:
"Depart, you unclean spirit, and make room for the Holy Spirit."

Then he shall make the sign of the cross on both the forehead and the breast and say:
"Receive the sign of the holy cross upon the forehead and the breast.

"Let us pray.
"O almighty and eternal God, Father of our Lord Jesus Christ, I call to you on behalf of this, your servant, N., who asks for the gift of your baptism and desires your eternal grace through spiritual rebirth.

"Receive him," Lord, *and as you have said, 'Ask and you shall receive, seek and you shall find, knock and it shall be open for you,'[o] so give now the blessing to him who asks and open the door to him who knocks on it, so*

---

k   German: *Pfaffen*, often used by Luther in a negative sense.

l   John 3:3, 5.

m   Literally: "brethren."

n   Throughout Luther uses the masculine pronoun for the one being baptized.

o   Matt. 7:7.

that he may obtain the eternal blessing of this heavenly bath[p] *and receive the promised kingdom you give through Christ our Lord. Amen.*

"Let us pray:

"*Almighty, eternal God, who according to your strict judgment condemned the unbelieving world through the flood and according to your great mercy preserved believing Noah and the seven members of his family, and who drowned hardhearted Pharaoh with his army in the Red Sea and led your people Israel through the same sea on dry ground, thereby prefiguring this bath of your Holy Baptism, and who through the baptism of your dear child, our Lord Jesus Christ, hallowed and set apart the Jordan and all water to be a blessed flood and a rich washing away of sins: we ask that through this very same boundless mercy of yours you would look graciously upon N. and in the [Holy] Spirit bless him with true faith*[q] *so that through this saving flood all that has been born in him from Adam and whatever he has added thereto may be drowned in him and perish, and that he, separated from the number of the unbelieving, may be preserved dry and secure in the holy ark of the Christian Church and may at all times, fervent in spirit and joyful in hope, serve your name, so that with all believers in your promise he may become worthy to attain eternal life through Jesus Christ our Lord. Amen.*

"*I adjure you, you unclean spirit, in the name of the Father (+) and of the Son (+) and of the Holy Spirit (+), that you come out of and depart from this servant of Jesus Christ, N. AMEN.*

"Let us hear the holy Gospel of St. Mark:[104, 105]

"'*At that time, they brought little children to Jesus that he might touch them. But the disciples threatened*[r] *those who brought them. But when Jesus saw this, he became annoyed with them and said to them, "Let the little children come to me and do not prevent them. For of such is the kingdom of God. Truly, I say to you, whoever does not receive the kingdom of God like a little child will not enter into it." And he hugged them and laid his hands on them and blessed them.*'"

Then the priest shall lay his hands upon the child's head and pray the Lord's Prayer along with the kneeling sponsors:

104. Mark 10:13-16. First with the 1536 edition does the text match the Luther Bible. Until then the text in the *Small Catechism* represented a free rendering of the text, perhaps based upon the Latin Vulgate.

105. This story came to be depicted in paintings often hung near the font, many of which were executed by Lucas Cranach the Elder. Such images served as an important visual reminder of Lutheran baptismal practices over against those who denied the efficacy of infant baptism.

p   See Titus 3:5.

q   Or: "bless him with true faith in the spirit."

r   The 1536 edition reads: "led away."

"Our Father, you who are in heaven, hallowed be your name, may your kingdom come, may your will come about as in heaven, so, too, on earth. Give us today our daily bread. And forgive us our debts as we forgive our debtors. And lead us not into temptation, but deliver us from evil. Amen."

After this the little child shall be brought to the baptismal font[106] and the priest shall say:

"The LORD preserve your coming in and your going out from now and for evermore."[s]

Then the priest shall let the child through his sponsors renounce the devil and say:

"N., do you renounce the devil?"
Answer: "Yes."
"And all his works?"
Answer: "Yes."
"And all his ways?"
Answer: "Yes."
Then he shall ask:
"Do you believe in God the Father almighty, creator of heaven and earth?"
Answer: "Yes."
"Do you believe in Jesus Christ, his only Son our Lord, who was born and suffered?"
Answer: "Yes."

Jesus blesses the children (Mark 10:13-16), by Lucas Cranach the Elder. The importance of this text for baptisms led the artist and his son to produce many oil paintings of this scene to hang near baptismal fonts in Lutheran churches.

106. According to the medieval rite, the exorcisms took place at the door of the church and the rest of the service at the baptismal font.

s   Ps. 121:8.

"Do you believe in the Holy Spirit, one holy Christian church, the communion of saints,[t] forgiveness of sins, resurrection of the body, and after death an eternal life?"

Answer: "Yes."

"Do you want to be baptized?"

Answer: "Yes."

At this point he shall take the child and immerse[u] it in the baptismal font and say:

"And I baptize you in the name of the Father and of the Son and of the Holy Spirit."

Then the sponsors shall hold the little child over the font, and the priest, while putting the christening robe on the child, shall say:

"The almighty God and Father of our LORD *Jesus Christ, who has given birth to you for a second time through water and the Holy Spirit and has forgiven you all your sins, strengthen you with his grace to eternal life. Amen.*

"Peace be with you."

Answer: "AMEN."

Printed in Wittenberg by Nicholas Schirlentz 1531[107]

---

107. Various editions of the *Small Catechism* also add other material. Editions published in Wittenberg during Luther's lifetime included in 1529: *The German Litany* (LW 53:163–69); in 1536, 1537, and 1539: the German *Te Deum* and *Magnificat* (LW 53:171–79); in 1543: "A Prayer against the Turks" (LW 43:232–33).

---

t   German: *Gemeine der heiligen*, literally, "community of the holy ones."

u   German: *tauchen* (immerse or dip).

A Simple Way to Pray

How One Should Pray, For Peter, the Master Barber

1535

ERIC LUND

INTRODUCTION

During the Lenten season of 1517, only a few months before the posting of the *95 Theses*, Martin Luther preached a series of sermons in Wittenberg on the Lord's Prayer. These were published in April 1519 as *An Exposition of the Lord's Prayer for Simple Laymen.*[a] Sixteen years later, Luther returned to the same topic after being asked by his barber for advice about how to pray. Peter Beskendorf, also known as Peter Balbierer (the Barber), was a close friend of Luther. Luther already knew him in 1517, the year of the Lord's Prayer sermons, because he is mentioned then in a letter written to Christoph Scheurl, a jurist in Nuremberg.[1] Luther greeted him in several other letters and also made a reference to him in a sermon for the eighth Sunday after Trinity, which was published in the House Postil.[b] Peter had a reputation for being "a pious, God-fearing man who gladly listened to and discussed the word

1. Christoph Scheurl (1481–1542) taught canon law and human letters at the University of Wittenberg from 1507 to 1512. He then moved to Nuremberg where he served as legal advisor for the city until his death. He facilitated the publication of Luther's *95 Theses* in Nuremberg. A friend of both Luther and Luther's opponent Johann Eck (1486–1543) of Ingolstadt, he forwarded Luther's writings to the Catholic theologian, which stimulated their later debates.

---

a   *Auflegung deutsch des Vater unnser fuer dye einfeltigen leyen*; WA 2:74–130.

b   Eugene F. A. Klug, ed., *Sermons of Martin Luther: The House Postils*, trans. Erwin W. Koehlinger, James Lanning, and Everette W. Meier (Grand Rapids: Baker, 1996), 2:345; J. G. Walch, *Dr. Martin Luthers sämmtliche Schriften* (Jena, 1740–1753; reprint: St. Louis: Concordia, 1893), 21a:74; WA Br 1:108; WA Br 7:347; WA Br 8:200; WA 37:125.

of God."[c] In response to his barber's request, Luther described how he himself prayed in *A Simple Way to Pray*.[d] As he had done in his sermons of 1517, Luther organized his comments around the seven petitions of the prayer Jesus taught to his disciples (Matt. 6:5-14; Luke 11:1-4).

Luther acknowledges at the start that it is not easy to sustain prayer meaningfully as a daily practice. People become lazy or listless and often get distracted by other mundane tasks that seem more urgent than prayer. Luther notes how Christ commanded prayer and taught both how and what to pray. In *A Simple Way to Pray*, Luther recommends his personal practice of beginning and ending the day with prayer and explicates a method of prayer based on the Lord's Prayer that is both elaborate and flexible. He humbly invites Peter and the readers of the pamphlet to adapt his approach to their own needs or even to improve on it if they can.

Several times in the years between 1517 and 1535, Luther also offered a commentary on the Lord's Prayer in conjunction with an analysis of the Ten Commandments and the Apostles' Creed. All three are treated as devotional texts in his *Little Prayer Book* published in 1522.[e] In that work and in the *Small Catechism* and *Large Catechism*[f] of 1529, Luther focuses first on the law (as summarized in the Ten Commandments), then on the gospel (as revealed in the Creed), and speaks of the Lord's Prayer as medi-

Jesus teaches his disciples about prayer (Matthew 6).

c   Walch, *Dr. Martin Luthers sämmtliche Schriften*, 9:1822.

d   LW 43:193–211; WA 38:358–75.

e   See pages 159–99 in this volume.

f   *Small Catechism*, see pp. 201–51 in this volume; *Large Catechism*, see TAL 2:279–416.

cine one might turn to after learning of the human predicament and the way to salvation. In *A Simple Way to Pray*, Luther also uses the Ten Commandments and the Creed as resources for prayer, but this time adds them as supplements to his initial focus on the Lord's Prayer. Luther's own practice is to combine prayer and meditation.[2] By focusing his mind, in succession, on each of the commandments and the three sections of the Creed, he sets out to "kindle a fire in the heart" and increase his eagerness for prayer. Considering what the Ten Commandments and the Creed reveal about God's will prompts him to offer thanks to God, confess his shortcomings, and finally ask for strength to incorporate what they teach into his life.

Within months of the writing of this piece, the life of Peter Beskendorf took a tragic turn. On the day before Easter, the barber was eating at the home of his daughter, Anna. His son-in-law, Dietrich, who had been a soldier, was apparently reporting on battles he had survived and boasting of his invulnerability to death. Peter, perhaps inebriated, put this to the test and stabbed Dietrich with his own sword at the dinner table. In the *Table Talk*, Luther once mentioned this shocking death and commented that the work of the devil must be behind it.[g] Luther intervened on behalf of his friend and managed to persuade the elector to banish him from Wittenberg instead of executing him. Peter relocated to Dessau, twenty-one miles away, where he had served earlier as barber/surgeon for Prince Joachim I of Anhalt-Dessau (1509–1561). He died in 1538.

A Simple Way to Pray was immediately popular and was printed four times during 1535, in Wittenberg, Nuremberg, and Augsburg. Altogether there were thirteen editions published during Luther's lifetime, including one in Low German and one in Latin.[h]

2. Luther's method bears traces of the *lectio divina* method that was used for the study of Scripture in a monastic setting. In the twelfth century a four-part practice became standardized as: reading, meditation, prayer, and contemplation. Luther later modified this practice and described the proper sequence for the study of theology, in the *Preface to the Wittenberg Edition of Luther's German Writings*, as: prayer, meditation, and testing (*oratio, meditatio, tentatio*); see pp. 477–78 and 482–88 in this volume; WA 50:657–61; LW 34:283–88. See John Kleinig, "The Kindled Heart: Luther on Meditation," *Lutheran Theological Journal* 20, nos. 2–3 (1986): 142–54; Martin Nicol, *Meditation bei Luther*, Forschungen zur Kirchen und Dogmengeschichte (Göttingen: Vandenhoeck & Ruprecht, 1984).

---

g   WA TR 3:70 (#4004)

h   See *Verzeichnis der im deutschen Sprachbereich erschienenen Drucke des 16. Jahrhunderts* (VD 16), at www.gateway-bayern.de/index_vd16.html.

3. The translation offered here is based on the German text in WA 38:358–75 (*Eine einfältige Weise zu beten für einen guten Freund*) and the English translation by Carl J. Schindler found in LW 43:193–211.

4. Peter the Barber is addressed as "Master" because of his senior guild status. A guild member started as an apprentice, became a journeyman, and then a "master."

5. Luther also refers to this state of mind in his *Large Catechism* (1529) when commenting on the Third Commandment. There he associates laziness or weariness with one of the traditional seven deadly sins, namely *acidia* (or *acedia*). He calls this "a malignant plague with which the devil bewitches and deceives many hearts so that he may take us by surprise and stealthily take the Word of God away again" (BC, 400; TAL 2:314). A long tradition of monastic reflection on the danger of this condition goes back to Evagrius Ponticus in the late fourth century.

6. A psalter is a book containing the Psalms and sometimes additional devotional material. Psalters were used in the Latin West from the early eighth century onward, especially by monastic communities, who chanted the Psalms daily. Luther first published a German edition of the book of Psalms in 1524. Over a hundred separate German psalter editions were printed in the sixteenth century. In his 1534 preface to the psalter Luther said the book "might well be called a Little Bible in which the whole Bible is beautifully and briefly collected, and compacted into an enchiridion or Manual" (LW 35:254, WA DB 10/1:100).

The Barber by Lucas van Leyden (1494–1533)

A SIMPLE WAY TO PRAY [3]

HOW ONE SHOULD PRAY, FOR PETER, THE MASTER BARBER [4]

DEAR MASTER PETER: I will tell you as best I can what I do personally when I pray. May our dear Lord grant to you and to everybody to do it better than I! Amen.

First, when I feel that I have become cold and listless[5] in prayer because of other tasks or thoughts (for the flesh and the devil always impede and obstruct prayer), I take my little psalter,[6] hurry to my room, or, if it be the day and hour for it, to the church where a congregation is assembled and, as time permits, I say the Ten Commandments, the Creed, and, if I have time, some words of Christ or of Paul, or some psalms, out loud to myself just as a child might do.

It is a good thing to let prayer be the first business of the morning and the last at night.[7] Diligently guard against those false, deluding ideas, which tell you, "Wait a little while. I will pray in an hour; first I must attend to this or that." Such thoughts get you away from prayer into other affairs that so hold your attention and involve you that nothing comes of prayer for that day. This is especially so in emergencies when you have some tasks that seem as good or better than prayer. There is a saying ascribed to St. Jerome:[8] "Everything a believer does is prayer," and a proverb, "He who works faithfully prays twice." This can be said because a believer fears and honors God in his work[9] and remembers the commandment not to wrong anyone, or to try to steal, overcharge, or embezzle. Such thoughts and such faith undoubtedly transform his work into prayer and a sacrifice of praise.

Then again, the contrary must also be true that the work of an unbeliever is outright cursing and so he who works faithlessly

St. Jerome reading in the countryside,
by Giovanni Bellini (c. 1430–1516)

7. Luther included morning and evening prayers in his *Small Catechism* (1529) and recommended that the head of each family teach all members of the household to say them daily. In his *German Mass*, 1526 (TAL 3:130–61; LW 53:68–69; WA 19:79–80), Luther called for morning (Matins) and evening or afternoon (Vespers) services on Sunday. Luther also said that in towns where there are schools for boys, each day should begin and end with the singing of some psalms in Latin. This practice appears to be inspired by the recitation of canonical hours in monasteries.

8. St. Jerome (c. 347–420) was one of the foremost theologians of the early Western church. Between 382 and 405 he translated the Old and New Testaments from Hebrew and Greek into Latin, producing the *Vulgata*, which became the standard version of the Bible used in the Roman Catholic Church for centuries. The German critical edition (WA) speculated that Luther had in mind Jerome's commentary on Matt. 25:11, but no passage exactly matches the quote. English translation: St. Jerome, *Commentary on Matthew*, trans. Thomas Scheck, *The Fathers of the Church*, vol. 117 (Washington, DC: Catholic University of America Press, 2008). See also MPL 26:186.

9. For Luther, it is not only the clergy who have a religious vocation. Secular forms of work should also be seen as callings ordained by God. In his *To the Christian Nobility* (1520) Luther says: "A cobbler, a smith, a peasant—each has the work and office of his trade. . . . Further, everyone must benefit and serve every other by means of his own work or office so that in this way

10. For Luther, thoughts and feelings were closely connected and interdependent. For him, "heart" (*Herz*) included both reason and emotions, in contrast to modern parlance, which more commonly associates "heart" solely with emotions. Compare Matt. 24:19: "Out of the heart come evil thoughts." See Birgit Stolt, *Martin Luthers Rhetorik des Herzens* (Tübingen: J. C. B. Mohr/Paul Siebeck, 2000); and idem, "Luther's Faith of 'The Heart': Experience, Emotion, and Reason," in Christine Helmer, ed., *The Global Luther: A Theologian for Modern Times* (Minneapolis: Fortress Press, 2009), 131–50.

11. Luke 11 records the Lord's Prayer and a parable pointing to the importance of persistence in prayer. The quoted verse, however, comes from 1 Thess. 5:17.

curses twice. By the thoughts of his heart[10] as well as his work he scorns God. He thinks about violating the commandment and about how to take advantage of his neighbor, to steal and to embezzle. For, what else can such thoughts be but vain curses against God and man, which makes one's work and effort a double curse by which a man also curses himself. In the end such people are beggars and bunglers.

Christ openly speaks of continual prayer in Luke 11,[11] "Pray without ceasing." One must unceasingly guard against sin and wrongdoing, something one cannot do unless one fears God and keeps his commandment in mind, as Ps. 1[:1, 2] says, "Blessed is he who meditates upon God's law day and night, etc."[i]

Yet we must be careful not to break the habit of true prayer and imagine other works to be necessary which, after all, are nothing of the kind. Thus at the end we become lazy and lax, cold and listless toward prayer. The devil who besets us is not lax nor lazy, and our flesh is all too ready and eager to sin and is averse to the spirit of prayer. Now, when your heart has been warmed by such recitation to yourself [of the Ten Commandments, the words of Christ, etc.] and is intent upon the matter, kneel or stand with your hands folded and your eyes are directed toward heaven and speak out loud or think as briefly as you can:

"O Heavenly Father, dear God, I am a poor unworthy sinner. I do not deserve to raise my eyes or hands toward you or to pray. But because you have commanded us all to pray and have promised to hear us and because you have taught us through your dear Son, Jesus Christ, both how and what to pray, I come to you in obedience to your word, trusting in your gracious promise. I pray in the name of my Lord Jesus Christ together with all your saints and Christians on earth as he has taught me: 'Our Father in heaven . . .'"

---

i   Luther paraphrases the text, making one sentence from parts of two verses.

The Lord's Prayer

The First Petition[12]

Pray through the whole prayer, word for word, then repeat one part or as much as you wish, perhaps the first petition: "Hallowed be your name," and say: "Yes, Lord God, dear Father, hallowed be your name, both in us and throughout the whole world. Destroy and root out the abominations, idolatry, and heresy of the Turk, the pope, and all false teachers and factious spirits[13] who falsely bear your name and thus shamefully abuse it and horribly blaspheme it. They insistently boast that they teach your word and the laws of the church, though they really use the devil's lies and trickery in your name to wretchedly seduce so many poor souls throughout the world, even killing and shedding much innocent blood, and in such persecution they believe that they render you a divine service.

"Dear Lord God, convert and restrain [them]. Convert those who are still to be converted that they with us and we with them may hallow and praise your name, both with true and pure

Praying Hands
by Albrecht Dürer
(1471–1528)

12. Although Luther states in the *Small Catechism* that God's will comes about whether we pray or not, he thought every person should form the habit of commending herself or himself to God each day for protection and help in every need. He taught that all true prayers are answered, though not necessarily at the time or in the manner that the faithful request. They should pray boldly, but God may improve on their petitions. If what they ask for glorifies God's name and honors his kingdom, God hears their prayers (WA TR 1:603 n.1212; LW 54:3–114).

13. The Turks were Muslims and denied the divinity and crucifixion of Christ. During the sixteenth century the Ottoman Turks were also seen as a serious political threat because they repeatedly attempted to conquer central Europe. In 1541, Luther wrote a more specific "Appeal for Prayer against the Turks" (LW 43:213–41; WA 51:585–625). In his later polemics, Luther often expressed his belief that the devil was using the Turks, his Catholic opponents, and the more radical Protestant reformers (the *Rottengeister* or factious spirits) to undermine his reform efforts. See Mark U. Edwards Jr., *Luther's Last Battles: Politics and Polemics 1531–1546* (Minneapolis: Fortress Press, 1983).

doctrine and with a good and holy life. Restrain those who are unwilling to be converted so that they are forced to cease from misusing, defiling, and dishonoring your holy name and from misleading the poor people. Amen."

The Second Petition

"Your kingdom come." Say: "O dear Lord, God and Father, you see how worldly wisdom and reason[14] not only profane your name and ascribe the honor due to you to lies and to the devil, but how they also take the power, might, wealth, and glory which you have given them on earth for ruling the world and thereby serving you, and use it in their own ambition to oppose your kingdom.[15] They are many and mighty, thick, fat, and full; they plague and hinder the tiny flock of your kingdom who are weak, despised, and few. They will not tolerate your flock on earth and think that by plaguing them they render a great and godly service to you. Dear Lord, God and Father, convert [them] and defend [us]. Convert those who are still to become children and members of your kingdom so that they with us and we with them may serve you in your kingdom in right faith and true love and that from your kingdom, which has begun, we may enter into your eternal kingdom. Defend us against those who will not turn away their might and power from the destruction of your kingdom so that when they are cast down from their thrones and humbled, they will have to cease from their efforts. Amen."

The Third Petition

"Your will be done on earth as it is in heaven." Say: "O dear Lord, God and Father, you know that the world, if it cannot destroy your name or exterminate your kingdom, is busy day and night with wicked tricks, carrying out many intrigues and strange attacks, whispering together in secret counsel, giving mutual encouragement and support, threatening and spouting off, going about with every evil intention to destroy your name, word, kingdom, and children.

"Therefore, dear Lord, God and Father, convert [them] and defend [us]. Convert those who have yet to acknowledge your good will that they with us and we with them may obey your will and for your sake readily, patiently, and joyously bear every evil,

---

14. Luther was not opposed to the use of reason in its appropriate domain, i.e., worldly affairs and human relations, but said that regarding divine things and matters of faith "reason is like a blind horse" (WA 10/1:530f.). See B. A. Gerrish, *Grace and Reason: A Study in the Theology of Luther* (Oxford: Clarendon Press, 1962), 25–27.

15. Although Luther thought that secular government was ordained by God, he also noted in *On Temporal Authority* (1523) that "the secular lords, who should rule countries and peoples outwardly, do not do so; instead, the only thing they know how to do is to poll and fleece, heap one tax on another, let loose a bear here, a wolf there. There is no good faith or honesty to be found amongst them." (LW 45:109; WA 11:265).

cross, and adversity, and thereby acknowledge, test, and experience your kind, gracious, and perfect will. But defend us against those who in their rage, fury, hate, threats, and evil desires do not cease to do us harm. Make their wicked schemes, tricks, and devices come to nothing so that these may be turned against them, as we sing in Ps. 7[:15, 16].[16] Amen."

The Fourth Petition

"Give us this day our daily bread." Say: "Dear Lord, God and Father, grant us your blessing also in this temporal and physical life. Graciously grant us blessed peace. Protect us against war and discord.[17] Grant to our dear emperor fortune and success against his enemies. Grant him wisdom and understanding to rule unhindered and prosperously over his earthly kingdom. Grant to all kings, princes, and rulers good counsel and the will to preserve their domains and their subjects in tranquility and justice. Especially aid and guide our dear prince N.,[18] under

16. Ps. 7:15-16: "They make a pit, digging it out, and fall into the hole that they have made. Their mischief returns upon their own heads and on their own heads their violence descends."

17. Germany had experienced a significant amount of discord in the decade before this treatise was written. The German Peasants' Revolt, which took over 100,000 lives, ended in 1525. In 1529, a Turkish army under Suleiman the Magnificent (c. 1494–1566) invaded Hungary once again and besieged Vienna.

18. At the time Luther wrote this piece, his prince was John Frederick the Magnanimous (1503–1554), the elector of Saxony, a strong supporter of his Evangelical reforms. Although Emperor Charles V (1500–1558), at the Diet of Worms, declared Luther an outlaw whom anyone could kill without punishment, Luther continued to pray for his well-being. This fits with what he goes on to say about the fifth petition, concerning forgiveness.

Martin Luther and John Frederick I, elector of Saxony (also known as John the Magnanimous), kneel at the cross of Jesus. John Frederick commissioned the Jena edition of Luther's works, in which this woodcut appears.

19. Luther sometimes spoke of three divinely ordained estates (*Stände*): the priestly office, the family, and the civil government (*Kirche, Haus, Staat,* or *ecclesia, oeconomia, politia*). Here, however, he is referring to the traditional medieval division of society into the nobility, the clergy, and the common people. In the sixteenth century, further distinctions were developing within the last category, between the burgher class, made up of citizens of towns who were members of guilds or worked as merchants, and the peasants, who continued to work the land.

20. Revelation 12:9 says that the devil, "the deceiver of the whole world, was thrown down to the earth, and his angels were thrown down with him." Luther did not speculate often about angels but believed that "the evil angels or devils, who are invisible, are enemies more bitter than our visible foes" (LW 4:256; WA 43:319) and that the good angels are busy with the task of keeping these enemies from doing harm (LW 3:270; WA 43:68f.). For Luther's persistent sense of the devil's influence in the world, see Heiko Oberman, *Luther: Man between God and the Devil,* trans. Eileen Walliser-Schwarzbart (New York: Doubleday/Image Books, 1982).

21. During the Middle Ages, it was deemed important to confess all sins specifically to a priest in order to receive absolution. The church distinguished between mortal sins, which condemned one to hell if not confessed, and venial sins or lesser sins, which incurred a penalty that must be removed through the doing of penance or through a process of purgation after death.

whose protection and shelter you maintain us, so that he may be protected against all harm and reign blessedly, secure from evil tongues and disloyal people. Grant to all his subjects grace to serve him loyally and obediently. Grant to every estate[19]—townsmen or farmers—to be devout and to display charity and loyalty toward each other. Give us favorable weather and good harvest. I commend to you my house and property, wife and child. Grant that I may manage them well, supporting and educating them as a Christian should. Defend us and put a stop to the Destroyer and all his wicked angels[20] who would do us harm and mischief in this life. Amen."

The Fifth Petition[21]

"Forgive us our sin as we forgive those who sin against us."[j] Say: "O dear Lord, God and Father, enter not into judgment against us because no man living is righteous before you. Do not count it against us as a sin that we are so unthankful for your ineffable goodness, spiritual and physical, or that we stumble and sin many times every day, more often than we can know or recognize, Ps. 19[:12].[k] Do not look upon how good or how wicked we are but only upon the infinite compassion that you have bestowed upon us in Christ, your dear Son. Grant forgiveness also to those who have harmed or wronged us, as we forgive them from our hearts. They inflict the greatest injury upon themselves by arousing your anger in their actions toward us. We are not helped by their ruin; we would much rather that they be saved with us. Amen." (Anyone who feels unable to forgive, let him ask for grace so that he can forgive; but that belongs in a sermon.)

The Sixth Petition

"And lead us not into temptation." Say: "O dear Lord, Father and God, keep us bold and alert, passionate and eager in your word and service, so that we do not become complacent, lazy, and sluggish as though we had already achieved everything. In that way

---

j   Luther uses the German word *Schuld* in the singular. It can be translated as "sin," "debt," "trespass," or "guilt."

k   Ps. 19:12: "Who can detect their errors? Clear me from hidden faults." (German Bibles list this as v. 13.)

the fierce devil cannot beguile us, surprise us, and deprive us of your precious word or stir up strife and factions among us and lead us into other sin and disgrace, both spiritually and physically. Rather grant us wisdom and strength through your spirit that we may valiantly resist him and gain the victory. Amen."

The Seventh Petition

"But deliver us from evil." Say: "O dear Lord, God and Father, this wretched life is so full of misery, misfortune, and uncertainty, so full of faithlessness and malice (as St. Paul says, "The days are evil" [Eph. 5:16])[*] that we might easily grow weary of life and long for death. But you, dear Father, know our frailty; therefore help us to pass in safety through so much wickedness and villainy; and, when our time comes, in your mercy grant us a gracious final hour and a blessed departure from this vale of sorrows so that in the face of death we do not become fearful or despondent but in firm faith commit our souls into your hands. Amen."

Finally, mark this, that you must always speak the "Amen" firmly. Never doubt that God in his mercy will surely hear you and say "yes" to your prayers. Never think that you are kneeling or standing alone, rather think that the whole of Christendom, all devout Christians, are standing there beside you and you are standing among them in a common, united petition which God cannot disdain. Do not leave your prayer without having said or thought, "Very well, God has heard my prayer; this I know as a certainty and a truth." That is what Amen means.

You should also know that I do not want you to recite all these words in your prayer. That would make it nothing but mere chatter and idle prattle, read word for word out of a book as were the rosaries by the laity and the prayers of the clerics and monks.[22] Rather do I want your heart to be stirred and guided concerning the thoughts that ought to be comprehended in the Lord's Prayer. These thoughts may be expressed, if your heart is rightly warmed and inclined toward prayer, in many different ways and with more words or fewer. I do not bind myself to such words or syllables, but say my prayers in one fashion today,

Luther, however, did not think of sin as specific sinful acts. Instead, he viewed sin more as a general condition of being turned away from God toward one's self (*incurvatus in se*). Citing Rom. 14:23, Luther held that all human acts are sinful until faith restores the relationship with God. See Matt Jenson, *Gravity of Sin: Augustine, Luther, and Barth on homo incurvatus in se* (New York: T&T Clark, 2006).

22. A rosary (from Latin for "garland of roses") is a string of prayer beads. The Dominican Order encouraged people to repeat sets of ten Hail Mary prayers preceded by one recitation of the Lord's Prayer. During the fifteenth century, a German monk introduced the practice of pausing to meditate on a theme after each decade of prayers, but the common people used rosaries more simply to keep track of how many prayers they had said. The German word *Pfaffen*, translated here as "clerics," refers to any individual who has received the clerical tonsure, including bishops, priests, deacons, and subdeacons. Each day, clerics were supposed to recite a set of prayers known as the Divine Office.

I   Eph. 5:16: "Be careful how you live . . . making the most of the time because the days are evil."

23. Luther quotes twice in this text from one of the books of the Apocrypha, the Wisdom of Jesus ben Sirach, also known as Ecclesiasticus. Although Luther did not consider the Apocrypha to be as inspired as the Old and New Testament, he translated it into German and continued to include its books in the complete Bible he published in 1534. Luther's version of Sirach 18:23 is close to the Latin Vulgate, but most modern translations, working from different manuscripts, render the verse quite differently: "Before making a vow, prepare yourself."

24. Luther imagines the priest fulfilling the daily requirement of reciting prayers from a breviary while simultaneously attending to other mundane tasks. The first two Latin phrases are from Psalm 69, which was repeated several times a day at the start of the liturgy of the hours: "Be pleased O God to deliver me" and "Make haste to help me." The third sentence completes the opening lines of the liturgy: "Glory be to the Father, and to the Son, and to the Holy Spirit."

25. In a lecture on Gen. 17:19-22, Luther said: "To pray is not to recite a number of psalms or to roar in churches, as monks usually do, but to have serious thoughts by which the soul establishes a fellowship between him who prays and Him who hears the prayer" (WA 42:662; LW 3:160).

26. The term "canonical hours" is a synonym for the Divine Office, which consisted of psalms, prayers, and lessons publicly chanted in churches or oratories at various times throughout the day. From as early as the fifth century, priests and clerics were expected to recite the hours in private

in another tomorrow, depending upon my mood and feeling. I stay however, as nearly as I can, with the same general thoughts and ideas. It may happen occasionally that I may wander among so many ideas in one petition that I forgo the other six. If such an abundance of good thoughts comes to us we ought to disregard the other petitions, make room for such thoughts, listen in silence, and under no circumstances obstruct them. The Holy Spirit himself preaches here, and one word of his sermon is far better than a thousand of our prayers. Many times I have learned more from one prayer than I might have learned from much reading and speculation.

It is of great importance that the heart be made ready and eager for prayer. As the Preacher says, "Prepare your heart for prayer, and do not tempt God" [Ecclus. 18:23].[23] What else is it but tempting God when your mouth babbles and the heart is distracted? Like the priest who prayed, *"Deus in adjutorium meum intende.* Farmhand, did you unhitch the horses? *Domine ad adjuvandum me festina.* Maid, go out and milk the cow. *Gloria patri et filio et spiritui sancto.*[24] Run, boy. I wish the fever would take you!"[m] I have heard many such prayers in my experience under the papacy; almost all of their prayers are of this sort.[25] This is making a mockery of God and it would be better to admit they are making a game of it if they cannot or do not care to do better. In my day I have prayed many such canonical hours[26] myself, regrettably, and in such a manner that the psalm or the allotted time came to an end before I even realized whether I was at the beginning or in the middle.

Though not all of them blurt out the words as did the above-mentioned cleric and mix business and prayer, they do it by the thoughts in their hearts. They jump from one thing to another[27] in their thoughts and when it is all over they do not know what

---

m   The word translated here as "fever" is *Ritt* in German. It refers to a malaria-like illness characterized by regular intervals of fever and chills.

Das Schlaraffenland (*The Fool's Paradise*)
by Pieter Bruegel the Elder, 1567

they have done or what they talked about. They start with *Laudate*[n] and right away they are in a fool's paradise.[28] It seems to me that if someone could see what arises as prayer from a cold and inattentive heart he would conclude that he had never seen a more ridiculous juggling game.[o] But, praise God, it is now clear to me that a person who forgets what he has said has not prayed well. In a good prayer one fully remembers every word and thought from the beginning to the end of the prayer.

It is just like a good and attentive barber who keeps his thoughts, attention, and eyes on the razor and the hair and does not forget how far he has gotten with his shaving or cutting.[29]

[n] Here *Laudate* ("Praise the Lord") refers to Psalms 148, 149, and 150, which were sung together as one psalm in the canonical hours, especially for Lauds, or Morning Prayer.

[o] In German, a *Gaukler* is a juggler, so *Gaukelspiel* could be translated as "juggling game."

when they could not assist at the public Office. It was considered a serious sin to neglect the hours. When Luther was a monk, he was sometimes so busy with his various daily duties that he fell weeks behind in the required recitation of the Divine Office. Since he took this duty seriously, he would sometimes shut himself up in his cell on weekends without any food or drink and repeatedly read the required texts until he was caught up. See Martin Brecht, *Martin Luther: His Road to Reformation 1483–1521*, trans. James L. Schaaf (Philadelphia: Fortress Press, 1985), 64–65.

27. Luther uses the unusual phrase *"werfen das Hunderste in's Tausendste"* ("throw the hundredth into the thousandth"). This phrase is a reference to calculations being made for currency exchanges. If a moneychanger did not pay close attention, he could record hundreds as thousands. The phrase came to be a way of talking about "getting carried away."

28. Luther uses the term *Schlaraffenland* in reference to a mythical land of plenty. In Middle High German, *schluraff* is a term for a lazy oaf. Sebastian Brant (1457-1521), the humanist social critic from Strassburg, wrote about this mythical land in chapter 108 of *The Ship of Fools* (1494), and Hans Sach wrote a poem, *Schlaweraffen Landt*, in 1530. See Scott Horton's translation, "Hans Sach's Schlaraffenland" in *Harper's Magazine*, July 20, 2008. Compare the medieval French myth of the *pays de cocaigne*, carried over into English literature as "the land of Cockaigne."

29. Sixteenth-century barbers cut hair, gave shaves with a straight razor, and also performed minor medical and dental procedures. On barber-surgeons, see Robert Jütte, "A Seventeenth-Century German Barber-Surgeon and His Patients," in *Medical History* 33 (1989): 184–98.

Etching of a barber,
Frankfurt on Main, 1568

30. This hexameter appears frequently in texts from several regions of Europe. The rhyme between *intentus* and *sensus* suggests that it is medieval in origin.

31. Usually Luther calls the prayer *Der Vater Unser* ("The Our Father"), but in this section he uses the Latin equivalent, *Pater Noster.*

If he engages in lots of conversation at the same time or lets his mind wander or look somewhere else he is likely to cut his customer's mouth, nose, or even his throat. Thus if anything is to be done well, it requires the full attention of all one's senses and members, as the proverb says, *"Pluribus intentus, minor est ad singula sensus"*—"A person engaged in multiple pursuits, minds none of them well."[30] How much more does prayer call for concentration and singleness of heart if it is to be a good prayer!

This in short is the way I use the Lord's Prayer when I pray it. To this day I suckle at the Lord's Prayer[31] like a child, and as an old man eat and drink from it and never get my fill. It is the very best prayer, even better than the psalter, which is so very dear to me. It is surely evident that a real master composed and taught it.

What a great shame[p] that the prayer of such a master is prattled and chattered so irreverently all over the world! How many pray the Lord's Prayer several thousand times in the course of a year, and if they were to keep on doing so for a thousand years they would not have tasted nor prayed one letter or one stroke of a letter of it![32] In a word, the Lord's Prayer is the greatest martyr on earth (along with the name and word of God). Everybody tortures and abuses it; few take comfort and joy in its proper use.

The Ten Commandments[33]

If I have time and opportunity to go through the Lord's Prayer, I do the same with the Ten Commandments. I take one part after another and free myself as much as possible from distractions in order to pray. I divide each commandment into four parts, thereby fashioning a garland of four entwined strands. That is, I think of each commandment as, first, instruction, which is really what it is intended to be, and consider what the Lord God so earnestly demands of me. Second, I turn it into a thanksgiving; third, a confession; and fourth, a prayer. I do so in thoughts or words such as these:

The First Commandment

"I am the Lord your God, etc. You are to have no other gods besides me, etc." Here I first consider that God expects and teaches me to trust him sincerely in all things. It is his most earnest intention to be my God, so I must think of him in this way at the risk of losing eternal salvation. My heart must not build upon anything else or trust in any other thing, be it wealth, prestige, wisdom, might, holiness, or any other creature. Second, I give thanks for God's infinite compassion by which he has come to me, a lost mortal, in such a fatherly way and, without my asking, seeking, or deserving him, has offered to be my God, to care for me, and to be my comfort, protection, help, and strength in every time of need. We poor blind mortals have sought so many gods and would have to seek them still if he did not enable us to hear him

32. Luther may have in mind the many recitations of the Lord's Prayer that were done in his day to complete the penance assigned by priests in the Sacrament of Confession. Although the rosary could be a sophisticated aid to devotion, combining prayer and meditation, many who used it simply counted their beads and rushed through the numerous repetitions of the Lord's Prayer and the Hail Mary prayer.

33. In this treatise, as in his other writings on prayer, Luther looks to a text for instruction and that, in turn, inspires his prayers. He combines catechesis and prayer. For Luther, distinguishing between law and gospel was an essential starting point for the study of Scripture. He always looks first to the law and then to the gospel. The law (as seen in the Ten Commandments) teaches people that they are sick and cannot measure up to what they should do. The gospel (as described in the Creed) shows the sick person where to get the medicine—grace—that restores health. See the preface to his *Little Prayer Book*, pp. 165–67 in this volume.

---

p   Luther uses the phrase "*Jammer über Jammer*" ("sorrow above [all] sorrow[s]"). *Es ist ein Jammer* means "It is such a shame."

openly tell us in our own language that he wants to be our God. How could we ever—in all eternity—thank God enough! Third, I confess and acknowledge my great sin and ingratitude for having so shamefully despised such a sublime teaching and precious gift throughout my whole life, and for having horridly provoked his wrath by countless acts of idolatry. I repent of these and ask for his grace. Fourth, I pray and say: "O my God and Lord, help me by your grace to learn and understand your commandments more fully every day and to live by them in sincere confidence. Preserve my heart so that I shall never again become forgetful and ungrateful, that I may never seek after other gods or other consolation on earth or in any creature, but cling truly and solely to you, my only God. Amen, dear Lord God and Father. Amen."

The Second Commandment

Afterward, if time and inclination permit, the Second Commandment likewise in four strands, in this way: "You are not to take the name of the Lord your God in vain," etc. First, I learn that I should regard God's name as honorable, holy, and beautiful. I should not swear, curse, lie, be boastful, nor seek honor and repute for myself, but instead I should humbly invoke his name, pray, adore, praise, and extol it. I should let it be all my honor and glory that he is my God and that I am his lowly creature and unworthy servant.

Second, I give thanks to him for these precious gifts, that he has revealed and imparted his name to me, that I can glory in his name and be called God's servant and creature, etc., that his name is my refuge like a mighty fortress to which the righteous man can flee and find protection, as Solomon says [Prov. 18:10].[q]

Third, I confess and acknowledge that I have grievously and shamefully sinned against this commandment all my life. I have not only failed to invoke, extol, and honor his holy name, but have also been ungrateful for such gifts and have, by swearing, lying, and betraying, misused them in the pursuit of shame and sin. This I regret and ask grace and forgiveness, etc.

Fourth, I ask for help and strength henceforth to learn [to obey] this commandment and to be preserved from such evil

q   Prov. 18:10: "The name of the Lord is a strong tower [*eine feste Burg*]; the righteous run into it and are safe."

ingratitude, abuse, and sin against his holy name, and that I may be found grateful in revering and honoring his name. I repeat here what I previously said in reference to the Lord's Prayer: if in the midst of such thoughts the Holy Spirit begins to preach in your heart with rich, enlightening thoughts, honor him by letting go of these prepared thoughts; be still and listen to him who can do better than you can. Remember what he says and note it well and you will behold wondrous things in the law of God, as David says [Ps. 119:18].[r]

The Third Commandment

"You are to sanctify the day of rest."[34] I learn from this, first of all, that the day of rest has not been instituted for the sake of being idle or indulging in worldly pleasures, but in order that we may observe it respectfully. However, it is not sanctified by our works and actions—since our works are not holy—but by the word of God, which alone is wholly pure and sacred and which sanctifies everything that comes in contact with it, be it time, place, person, labor, rest, etc. For through the word our works are also sanctified. As St. Paul says in 1 Tim. 4[:5], "Every creature is sanctified by the word and prayer." I realize therefore that on the day of rest I must, above all, hear and contemplate God's word. Thereafter I should give thanks in my own words, praise God for all his benefits, and pray for myself and for the whole world. He who so conducts himself on the day of rest sanctifies it. He who fails to do so is worse than the person who works on the day of rest.

Second, I thank God in this commandment for the great and beautiful goodness and grace which he has given us through his word and preaching. And he has instructed us to make use of it, especially on the day of rest, for meditation by the human heart can never exhaust such a treasure. His word is the only light in the darkness of this life, a word of life, consolation, and supreme blessedness. Where this precious and saving word is absent, nothing remains but empty and terrifying darkness, error and factions, death and every calamity, and the devil's own tyranny, as we can see with our own eyes every day.

34. The Third Commandment concerns the Sabbath, celebrated as a day of rest by Jews from Friday sundown to Saturday sundown. Very early on, the Christian movement switched to observing Sunday as a special day for worship, in commemoration of the resurrection of Christ on the first day of the week. Luther uses a broader word, *Feiertag*, in this section, meaning a holy day or a day of religious celebration. In recent times, the word in German has come to refer more commonly to any kind of holiday.

---

r   Ps. 119:18: "Open my eyes, so that I may behold wondrous things out of your law."

35. Luther was concerned throughout his career with the danger of divisions or schisms within the Christian community. He made clear in his own reform efforts that he was not seeking to create a new church. In 1521 he came out of hiding at the Wartburg to address the confusion created by his university colleague Andreas Karlstadt (c. 1480–1541) and the "prophets" from Zwickau who attempted to introduce radical reforms in worship practices. In his *Invocavit Sermons* of 1522, Luther suggested that reform efforts should be carefully paced and that persuasion rather than force should be used to bring about change. In the same year he wrote a treatise against insurrection and another about the extent to which temporal authorities should be obeyed (see LW 45:51–129; TAL 5, forthcoming). Around the time Luther was writing this work, a new group of "factious spirits" had arisen in Germany. In 1534 Anabaptist radicals took over the city of Münster in Westphalia and renamed it "The New Jerusalem." They exiled many opponents and forcibly baptized others.

36. The barber who prompted Luther to write this piece once proposed himself to write a book warning people about the power of the devil. In response, Luther wrote a humorous poem about this which included the lines:

> So brash and bold the devil is—
> Full of knavery, trick, and guile,
> That Master Peter had better look
>> sharp
> Lest he try to trick the devil
> And it backfires on himself . . .

(LW 52:357–59; Walch, *Dr. Martin Luthers sämmtliche Schriften*, 9:1821–24).

Third, I confess and acknowledge great sin and wicked ingratitude on my part because all my life I have made disgraceful use of the day of rest and have thereby despised his precious and dear word so miserably. I have been too lazy, listless, and tired of the word to listen to it, let alone to have desired it sincerely or to have been grateful for it. I have let my dear God proclaim his word to me in vain, have abandoned the noble treasure, and have trampled it underfoot. He has tolerated this in his great and divine mercy and has not ceased in his fatherly, divine love and faithfulness to keep on preaching to me and calling me to the salvation of my soul. For this I repent and ask for grace and forgiveness.

Fourth, I pray for myself and for the whole world that the gracious Father may preserve us in his holy word and not withdraw it from us because of our sin, ingratitude, and laziness. May he preserve us from factious spirits and false teachers,[35] and may he send faithful and honest laborers into his harvest,[s] that is, devout pastors and preachers. May he grant us grace humbly to hear, accept, and honor their words as his own words and to offer our sincere thanks and praise.

The Fourth Commandment

"You are to honor your father and your mother." First, I learn here to acknowledge God, my Creator; how wondrously he has created me, body and soul; and how he has given me life through my parents and has instilled in them the desire to care for me, the fruit of their bodies, with all their power. He has brought me into this world, has sustained and cared for me, nurtured and educated me with great diligence, carefulness, and concern, through danger, trouble, and work. Up to this very hour he has protected me, his creature, and helped me in countless dangers and troubles. It is as though he were creating me anew every moment. But the devil does not willingly concede us one single moment of life.[36]

Second, I thank the rich and gracious Creator on behalf of myself and all the world that he has established and assured in this commandment the increase and preservation of the human

---

s   Matt. 9:38: "Ask the Lord of the harvest to send out laborers into his harvest."

race, that is, of households and of states.[t] Without these two institutions or governments the world could not stand a single year, because without government there can be no peace, and where there is no peace there can be no family;[u] without family, children cannot be begotten or raised, and fatherhood and motherhood would cease to be. It is the purpose of this commandment to guard and preserve both family and state, to admonish children and subjects to be obedient. This must happen and, if it does not, he will let no violation go unpunished—otherwise children would have torn the household apart long ago by their disobedience, and subjects would have laid waste to the state through rebellion, because they outnumber parents and rulers.

Third, I confess and acknowledge my wicked disobedience and sin; in defiance of God's commandment I have not honored or obeyed my parents; I have often provoked and offended them, have been impatient with their parental discipline, have grumbled about and scorned their

Knight, Death, and the Devil
by Albrecht Dürer, 1513

loving admonition and have preferred to go along with loose company and evil companions. God afflicts such disobedient children and withholds from them a long life; many of them succumb and perish in disgrace before they reach adulthood. Whoever does not obey father and mother must obey the executioner

---

t   Luther uses the German terms *Haus- und Stadtwesen* and then repeats the terms in Latin: *oeconomiam und politiam*.

u   The German term is *Hauswesen*, which can also be translated as "household" or "home."

37. Luther attributes weighty responsibilities to parents. They should not only prepare their children for a successful life in secular society but should also attend to their spiritual training. In his comments on the Fourth Commandment in the *Large Catechism*, Luther states that if they neglect this duty they are at risk of losing divine grace. In turn, since children owe so much to their parents they should view them as God's representatives and accord to them both love and honor. Other superiors such as the schoolmaster and those in positions of civil authority are also owed obedience because their roles are, in a sense, an extension of "fatherhood"; BC, 400–410.

38. Luther may be thinking of 1 Tim. 2:1-4: "First of all, then, I urge that supplications, prayers, intercessions, and thanksgivings be made for everyone, for kings and all who are in high positions, so that we may lead a quiet and peaceable life in all godliness and dignity."

or otherwise come, through God's wrath, to an evil end, etc. Of all this I repent and ask for grace and forgiveness.

Fourth, I pray for myself and for all the world that God would bestow his grace and pour his blessing richly upon the family and the state, so that from this time on we may be devout, honor our parents, obey our superiors, and resist the devil when he entices us to be disobedient and rebellious. Grant that we may help improve home and nation by our actions and thus preserve the peace, all to the praise and glory of God for our own benefit and for the prosperity of all. Grant that we may acknowledge these his gifts and be thankful for them.

At this point we should add a prayer for our parents and superiors, that God may grant them understanding and wisdom to govern and rule us in peace and happiness.[37] May he preserve them from tyranny, from riot and fury, and turn them from such things so that they honor God's word and do not persecute or do injustice to anyone. Such excellent gifts must be sought by prayer, as St. Paul teaches;[38] otherwise the devil will reign in the palace and everything will fall into chaos and confusion.

If you are a father or mother, you should at this point remember your children and the other members of your household.[v]

Scene from a book on prayers before meals
by Johann Hoffer (1534–1583)

---

v   The German term is *Gesinde*, which can also be translated as "servants."

Pray earnestly to the dear Father, who has set you in an office of honor in his name and intends that you also be honored by the name "father." Ask that he grant you grace and blessing to look after and support your wife, children, and workers in a godly and Christian manner. May he give you wisdom and strength to train them well and give them a heart and will to follow your instruction and be obedient. Both your children and the way they develop are God's gifts, both that they turn out well and that they remain so. Otherwise the home is nothing but a pigsty and school for rascals, as one can see among the uncouth and godless people.

The Fifth Commandment

"You are not to kill." Here I learn, first of all, that God desires me to love my neighbor, so that I do him no bodily harm, either by word or action, neither injure nor take revenge upon him in anger, vexation, envy, hatred, or for any evil reason. I should realize that I am obliged to assist and counsel him in every bodily need. In this commandment God commands me to protect my neighbor's body and in turn commands my neighbor to protect my own. As Sirach says, "He has committed to each of us his neighbor."[w]

Second, I give thanks for such ineffable love, care, and faithfulness toward me by which he has placed such a strong protection and wall around my body. All are obliged to look after what is mine and protect me, and I, in turn, must behave likewise toward all others. He upholds this command and, where it is not observed, he has established the sword as punishment for those who do not live up to it. Were it not for this excellent commandment and ordinance, the devil would instigate such a massacre among men that no one could live in safety for a single hour—as happens when God becomes angry and inflicts punishment upon a disobedient and ungrateful world.

---

w   The German critical edition connects this phrase to Ecclus. 9:21. In Luther's 1534 Bible that verse reads, "*Erlerne mit allen vleis deinen nehesten*" ("Learn from [learn to know] your neighbor"). The American edition of Luther's Works (LW) suggests that Luther is referring to Ecclus. 9:14. In Luther's Bible this verse says, "*Übergibt einen alten Freund nicht auf*" ("Do not forsake an old friend"). See also Ecclus. 29:20: "Help your neighbor as much as you can"; and Ecclus. 22:23: "Stand by [your neighbor] when he is in trouble."

Third, I confess and lament my own wickedness and that of the world, not only that we are so terribly ungrateful for such fatherly love and care toward us—but what is especially scandalous, that we do not acknowledge this commandment and teaching, are unwilling to learn it, and neglect it as though it did not concern us or we had no part in it. We amble along complacently, feeling no remorse that, in defiance of this commandment, we despise our neighbors,[x] desert them, persecute, injure, or even kill them in our thoughts.[39] We indulge in anger, rage, and villainy as though we were doing a fine and noble thing. Really, it is high time that we started to deplore and bewail[y] how much we have acted like rogues and like blind, wild, and unfeeling people who tread on, kick, scratch, tear, bite, and devour one another like furious beasts and pay no heed to this serious command of God, etc.

Fourth, I pray the dear Father to lead us to an understanding of this his sacred commandment and to help us keep it and live in accordance with it. May God preserve us from the murderer who is the master of every form of murder and violence. May God grant us his rich grace that we and all others may treat each other in kindly, gentle, and generous ways, forgiving one another from the heart, bearing each other's faults and shortcomings in a Christian and brotherly manner, and thus living together in true peace and unity, as the commandment teaches and requires us to do.

The Sixth Commandment

"You shall not commit adultery." Here I learn once more what God intends and expects me to do, namely, to live chastely, decently, and temperately, both in thoughts and in words and actions, and not to disgrace any man's wife, daughter, or maidservant. More than this, I ought to assist, save, protect, and do everything that serves to uphold their honor and discipline; I should also help to silence the idle loudmouths who want to steal or strip them of their honor. All this I am obliged to do, and God expects me not only to leave my neighbor's wife and family

---

x   This term and the pronouns following are singular in the original.

y   Most literally, "It is bewailing and crying time" (*Hie ist's Klagens und Schreiens Zeit*).

unmolested, but also to uphold and protect his good character and honor, just as I would want my neighbor to do for me and mine in keeping with this commandment.

Second, I thank my faithful and dear Father for his grace and benevolence by which he takes my husband, son, servant, wife, daughter, maidservant into his care and protection and forbids so sternly and firmly anything that would bring them into disrepute. God gives me a safe escort by this commandment and does not let violations go unpunished, even if he himself has to act where someone disregards and violates the commandment and precept. No one escapes; he must either pay the penalty here and now or eventually atone for such lust in the fires of hell. God desires chastity and will not tolerate adultery. That can be seen every day when the impenitent and profligate are finally overtaken by the wrath of God and perish miserably. Otherwise it would be impossible to guard one's wife, child, and servants against the filthy devil for a single hour or preserve them in honor and decency. There would be unbridled immorality[z] and beastliness all over, as happens when God in his wrath withdraws his hand and permits everything to go to wrack and ruin.

Third, I confess and acknowledge my sin, my own and that of all the world, how I have sinned against this commandment my whole life in thought, word, and action. Not only have I been ungrateful for this excellent teaching and gift, but I have murmured against God for commanding such decency and chastity and not permitting all sorts of fornication and rascality to go unchecked and unpunished. God will not allow marriage to be despised, ridiculed, or condemned, etc. Sins against this commandment are, above all others, the grossest and most conspicuous and cannot be covered up or disguised. For this I am sorry, etc.

Fourth, I pray for myself and all the world that God may grant us grace to keep this commandment gladly and cheerfully in order that we might ourselves live in chastity and also help and support others to do likewise.

Then I continue with the other commandments as I have time or opportunity or am in the mood for it. As I have said before, I do not want anyone to feel bound by my words or thoughts.

---

z   Luther uses the colorful term *Hundehochzeiten* ("dog's wedding"), having in mind the unrestrained sexual instincts of animals.

I only want to offer an example for those who may wish to follow it; let anyone improve it who is able to do so and let him meditate either upon all commandments at one time or on as many as he may desire. For the soul, once it is seriously occupied with a matter, be it good or evil, can ponder more in one moment than the tongue can recite in ten hours or the pen write in ten days. There is something quick, subtle, and mighty about the soul or spirit. It is able to review the Ten Commandments in their four-fold aspect[40] very rapidly if it wants to do so and is in earnest.

The Seventh Commandment

"You shall not steal." First, I can learn here that I must not take my neighbor's property from him or possess it against his will, either in secret or openly. I must not be false or dishonest in any transactions, service, or work, nor profit by fraud, but must support myself by the sweat of my brow[a] and eat my bread in honor. Furthermore, I must see to it that in any of the above-named ways my neighbor is not defrauded, just as I wish for myself. I also learn in this commandment that God, in his fatherly solicitude, protects my possessions and solemnly prohibits anyone to steal from me. Where that is ignored, he has imposed a penalty and has placed the gallows and the rope in the hands of Master Jack the hangman.[b] Where that cannot be done, God metes out punishment and they become beggars in the end, as the proverb says, "Who steals in his youth, goes begging in old age." Likewise, "There is no profit in deceit," or "Unjust gain will not remain."[41]

Second, I give thanks for his steadfast goodness in that he has given such excellent teachings, as well as assurance, and protection to me and to all the world. If it were not for his protection, not a penny or a crumb of bread would be left in the house.

Third, I confess my sins and ingratitude in such instances where I have wronged, cheated, or been false to anyone in my life.

Fourth, I ask that God grant to me and all the world grace to learn from this commandment, to ponder it, and to become better people, so that there may be less theft, robbery, mistreatment, cheating, and injustice and that the Judgment Day, for which all

---

40. "These are the Ten Commandments in their fourfold aspect, namely, as a little book of instruction, a book of thanksgiving, a penitential book, and a prayer book" (see p. 277 below).

41. The last proverb is a rhyme: "*Übel gewonnen, böslich zerronnen*" (literally, "What has been gained wrongly melts away"). Today, there is a similar German saying, "*Wie gewonnen, so zerronnen,*" which is comparable to the English proverb "Easy come, easy go." A proverb of this sort exists in all of the major European languages. A Latin equivalent, "*Mala parta male dilabuntur,*" is mentioned in the writings of the Roman orator Cicero (*Orationes Philippicae II*, 27, 65). The Latin version also appears in Erasmus's *Adages* (*Adagiorum chiliades quatuor*) 1, 7, 82.

---

a   Luther's phrase "*Schweiß meiner Nase*" would more literally be translated as "the sweat of my nose."

b   The proverbial "Jack the hangman" is *Meister Hans* in German.

saints and the whole creation pray, Romans 8[:20-23], shall soon bring this to an end. Amen.

The Eighth Commandment

"You are not to bear false witness." This teaches us, first of all, to be truthful to each other, to shun lies and calumnies, to be glad to speak well of each other, and to delight in hearing what is good about others. Thus a wall has been built around our good reputation and integrity to protect it against malicious loud-mouths and false tongues; God will not let that go unpunished, as was said in the other commandments. We owe God thanks both for the teachings and the protection which he has graciously provided for us.

Third, we confess and ask forgiveness for having spent our lives in ingratitude and sin and having maligned our neighbors^c with false and wicked talk, though we owe them the same preservation of honor and integrity which we desire for ourselves.

Fourth, we ask for help to keep the commandment from now on and to have a wholesome tongue, etc.

The Ninth and Tenth Commandments

"You are not to covet your neighbor's house." Similarly, "his wife," etc. This teaches us first that we shall not dispossess our neighbor of his goods under pretense of legal claims, or reduce, divert, or extort what is his, but help him to keep what is his, just as we wish to be done for ourselves. It is also a protection against the subtleties and chicaneries of shrewd manipulators who will receive their punishment in the end.

Second, we should render thanks to him.

Third, we should repentantly and sorrowfully confess our sins.

Fourth, we should ask for help and strength to become devout and to keep this commandment of God.

These are the Ten Commandments in their fourfold aspect, namely, as a little book of instruction, a book of thanksgiving, a penitential book, and a prayer book. They are intended to help the heart come to itself and to be warmed up to pray. Take

---

c   Singular in the German.

care, however, not to undertake all of this or so much that one becomes weary in spirit. Likewise, a good prayer should not be lengthy or drawn out, but frequent and ardent. It is enough to consider one section or half a section which kindles a fire in the heart. This the Spirit will grant us and continually instruct us in when, by God's word, our hearts have been cleared and freed of outside thoughts and concerns.

Nothing can be said here about the part of faith and Holy Scriptures [in prayer] because there would be no end to what could be said.[42] With practice one can take the Ten Commandments on one day, a psalm or chapter of Holy Scripture the next day, and use them to kindle a flame in the heart.[d]

A Simple Exercise for Contemplating the Creed

If you have more time, or the inclination, you may treat the Creed in the same manner and make it, too, into a garland of four strands. The Creed, however, consists of three main parts or articles, corresponding to the three Persons of the Divine Majesty, as it has also been previously divided in the Catechism.[43]

The First Article of Creation

"I believe in God the Father almighty, Creator of heaven and earth." Here, first of all, a great light shines into your heart if you permit it to and teaches you in a few words what all the languages of the world and a multitude of books cannot encompass or grasp in words, namely, who you are, whence you came, whence came heaven and earth. You are God's creation, his handiwork, his workmanship. That is, of yourself and in yourself you are nothing, can do nothing, know nothing, are capable of nothing. What were you a thousand years ago? What were heaven and earth six thousand years ago?[44] Nothing, just as that which will never be created is nothing. But what you are, know, can do, and can achieve is God's creation, as you confess [in the

42. Luther does not refer specifically to the psalms in this treatise, but he recommends eight of them in his *Little Prayer Book* (pp. 159–99 in this volume). He used the psalter for his own prayers throughout his life and said that one can find words for any situation in the psalms (LW 35:256).

In his commentaries and sermons as well as in his treatises on prayer, Luther also drew attention to many examples of prayer that are found in the Bible. For more on that, see Mary Jane Haemig, "Praying amidst Life's Perils: How Luther Used Biblical Examples to Teach Prayer," *Seminary Ridge Review* 13, no. 2 (Spring 2011): 25–40.

43. Luther placed the Apostles' Creed second, after the Ten Commandments and before the Lord's Prayer, in his *Small Catechism* and *Large Catechism*. Medieval catechisms usually divided the Creed into twelve parts. In contrast, Luther understands the Creed as having three parts corresponding to the three persons of the Trinity.

44. In his lectures on Genesis, Luther also stated: "We know from Moses that the world was not in existence before 6,000 years ago" (LW 1:3; WA 42:3).

---

d   The first edition of this writing ends here. Later editions went on to use the three articles of the Creed as the starting point for further prayers.

Creed] by your own mouth. Therefore you have nothing to boast of before God except that you are nothing and he is your Creator who can annihilate you at any moment. Reason knows nothing of such a light. Many great people have sought to know what heaven and earth, humans and creatures are and have found no answer. But here it is declared and faith affirms that God has created everything out of nothing. Here is the soul's garden of pleasure,[45] in which we can stroll, enjoying the works of God—but it would take too long to describe all that.

Second, we should here give thanks to God that in his kindness he has created us out of nothing and provides for our daily needs out of nothing—has made us to be creatures with body and soul, intelligence, and five senses, who are ordained to be masters of earth, of fish, bird, and beast, etc. On this, hear Genesis, chapters one to three.

Third, we should confess and lament our lack of faith and gratitude in failing to take this to heart, or to believe, ponder, and acknowledge it. We are worse than unthinking beasts.

Fourth, we pray for a true and confident faith that sincerely esteems and trusts God to be our Creator, as this article declares.

Page from a copy
of *Hortulus animae*,
first published in 1498

45. The phrase Luther uses here, *Seelen Lustgarten*, would have been familiar to many readers as the title of a popular Catholic prayer book first printed in Strassburg in 1498. *The Pleasure Garden of the Soul*, or *Hortulus animae* in Latin, was the German counterpart to the devotional book known in France and England as the *Book of Hours*. It contained a variety of prayers but at its center was a liturgical devotion known as the Hours of Our Lady. Luther's advice on prayer, however, is notable for the absence of any prayers addressed to Mary or the saints. He thought the *Hortulus animae* needed a thorough reform because "it gave rise to countless false beliefs" (LW 43:11f.). The image of a pleasure garden also reinforces Luther's advice that one should set aside time to pray in a relaxed but focused manner, strolling through the thoughts inspired by the words of the Creed about creation and redemption, rather than rushing through prayers out of habit or repeating them superficially just because one is expected to perform such acts of piety.

The Second Article of Redemption

"And in Jesus Christ, his only Son, our Lord," etc. Again a great light shines forth and teaches us how Christ, God's Son, has redeemed us from death which, after the creation, had become our lot through Adam's fall and in which we would have perished eternally. Now think: just as in the first article you were to consider yourself one of God's creatures and not doubt it, now you must think of yourself as one of the redeemed and never doubt that. Emphasize one word above all others, the first word "our," as in Jesus Christ, "our" Lord. Likewise, suffered for "us," died for "us," arose for "us."[46] All this is ours and pertains to us; that "us" includes yourself, as the word of God declares.

Second, you must be sincerely grateful for such grace and rejoice in your salvation.

46. Luther repeatedly stressed that God is "for us," not "against us." The full significance of Christ becomes apparent only when a person realizes that Christ was given "for me" or "for us."

Man of Sorrows
by Albrecht Dürer, 1509

Third, you must sorrowfully lament and confess your shameful unbelief and mistrust of such grace. Oh, what thoughts will come to mind—the idolatry you have practiced repeatedly, how much you have made of praying to the saints and of innumerable works of yours which have opposed such salvation.

Fourth, pray now that God will preserve you from this time forward to the end in true and pure faith in Christ our Lord.

The Third Article of Sanctification[47]

"I believe in the Holy Spirit," etc. This is the third great light that teaches us where such a Creator and Redeemer may be found and outwardly encountered in this world, and what this will all come to in the end. Much could be said about this, but here is a summary: Where the holy Christian church exists, there we can find God the Creator, God the Redeemer, God the Holy Spirit, that is, the one who daily sanctifies us through the forgiveness of sins, etc. The church exists where the word of God concerning such faith is rightly preached. Again you have occasion here to ponder long about everything that the Holy Spirit accomplishes in the church every day, etc. Therefore be thankful that you have been called and have come into such a church. Confess and lament your lack of faith and gratitude, that you have neglected all this, and pray for a true and steadfast faith that will remain and endure until you come to that place where all endures forever, that is, beyond the resurrection from the dead, in life eternal. Amen.

47. Sanctification refers to the process of renewal that takes place in a person's life through the work of the Holy Spirit. Luther always made a careful distinction between justification and sanctification, though he also saw a cause-and-effect relationship between them. A sinner is justified or viewed with favor by God as a result of the imputation of Christ's righteousness. The righteousness that saves is an "alien and external righteousness," not a product of human efforts to live rightly. Faith in Christ alone makes sinners pleasing to God, but true faith also becomes active in love. In gratitude for the gift of forgiveness, a Christian will struggle against the continuing influence of sinful impulses and will perform good works for the sake of others. Luther attributes this reorientation of a person's life to the work of the Holy Spirit. In *The Small Catechism*, he says: "the Holy Spirit has called me through the gospel, enlightened me with his gifts, made me holy and kept me in true faith" (BC, 355). See also Martin Luther, *The Freedom of a Christian* (LW 31:327–77; TAL 1:467–538).

A Sermon on Preparing to Die

1519[1]

ANNA MARIE JOHNSON

INTRODUCTION

When Luther wrote this sermon in 1519, the controversy that had begun in 1517 with his *95 Theses* was escalating. The church began canonical proceedings against Luther in 1518, and in October of that year he met with the papal legate Tommaso (de Vio) Cajetan (1469–1534) at Augsburg. Cajetan had hoped to hear Luther recant his criticisms and submit to the pope, but, instead, the two theologians quickly found themselves at odds. Soon afterward, Cajetan wrote to Luther's prince, Elector Frederick III of Saxony (1463–1525), demanding that he either extradite Luther to Rome or exile him from his lands. Meanwhile, a theologian from Ingolstadt, Johann Eck (1486–1543), had published an attack on Luther in the spring of 1518. This led to a debate in Leipzig in July 1519 in which Luther further questioned the authority of the papacy (see n. 54 and the image on p. 85).

Luther was preparing for this debate in May of 1519 when he received a request from Mark Schart, a counselor in Elector Frederick's court, to write something on preparing for death. Luther initially responded by saying that he did not have time to do this, and he recommended instead another sermon on death already in print.[a] Within weeks, however, Luther said he would write something on the topic, but he asked Schart to be patient,

1. "Sermon" can mean either a preached sermon or a written essay on a particular topic. In this case, the text originated purely for printed distribution.

saying that the controversy surrounding him was taking all his time.[b] Almost six months later, on 1 November 1519, Luther's *Sermon on Preparing to Die* had been printed.[c]

A short life expectancy and especially the bubonic plague, which raged throughout Europe beginning in the mid-fourteenth century, made death a topic of keen interest in sixteenth-century Germany.[2] By the late Middle Ages, handbooks on how to "die well" became popular. They are often called by their Latin name, *Ars moriendi*, or "The Art of Dying."[d] These handbooks aimed to help dying Christians confess all past sins and fight the temptations that the devil was thought to bring to the deathbed. They were intended either for the dying person or the caregivers, and they typically included questions to ask dying loved ones, such as if they have sinned, if they have contrition for their sins, and if they intend to reject sin. The handbooks also included a formula for confession, prayers, a description of temptations often faced by the dying, and advice for meditating on Christ's passion while on the deathbed. When a priest was available, the dying person also received "the Sacrament of the Altar" (the Lord's Supper) and was administered unction, an anointing with oil that the late-medieval church counted among the seven sacraments.

a   WA Br 1:381.

b   WA Br 1:394; WA Br 1:407.

c   WA Br 1:548; LW 48:130.

d   For more on practices surrounding death in this era, see Mary Catherine O'Connor, *The Art of Dying Well: The Development of the Ars moriendi* (New York: Columbia University Press, 1942); Austra Reinis, *Reforming the Art of Dying: The* Ars moriendi *in the German Reformation, 1519–1528* (Burlington, VT: Ashgate, 2007); Craig Koslofsky, *The Reformation of the Dead: Death and Ritual in Early Modern Germany, 1450–1700* (New York: St. Martin's, 2000); Peter Marshall, *Beliefs and the Dead in Reformation England* (Oxford: Oxford University Press, 2002); Robert Kolb, "'Life Is King and Lord over Death': Martin Luther's View of Death and Dying," in Marion Kobelt-Groch und Cornelia Niekus Moore, eds., *Tod und Jenseits in der Schriftkultur der Frühen Neuzeit* (Wolfenbüttel: Herzog August Bibliothek, 2008), 23–44; Carlos Eire, *From Madrid to Purgatory: The Art and Craft of Dying in Sixteenth-Century Spain* (Cambridge: Cambridge University Press, 1995).

Late-medieval handbooks on death were based on the idea that one's salvation was not decided until the moment of death (see Bosch painting). The emphasis on receiving forgiveness for all past sins and avoiding sin while on the deathbed was meant to ensure that dying Christians received enough grace to enter paradise directly or to have their time in purgatory reduced. The handbooks named five temptations thought to be especially strong on the deathbed: lack of faith, despair over one's sins, impatience in suffering, spiritual pride, and greed or attachment to earthly matters. An illustrated version of the handbooks printed in the early fifteenth century vividly demonstrates the temptations and how to overcome them (see the *Ars moriendi* images below).

The temptations of despair and spiritual pride played an important role in Luther's reinterpretation of practices surrounding death. In late-medieval Western theology, to claim to be certain of one's salvation was considered presumptuous. God

Detail from *Death and the Miser* by Hieronymus Bosch, c. 1485/1490. This painting depicts a man being tempted in his dying moment. While the figure of death enters through the door, an angel bids him to look to the crucifix and to the beam of light coming through the window. Meanwhile, a demon appears at the man's bedside urging him to accept a bag of money, and another demon lurks above his bed.

Woodcut from an illustrated *Ars moriendi* depicting the temptation
to spiritual pride. The demons in this picture tempt the dying man
to pride with banners that proclaim, "Boast," "You are firm in faith,"
"You have earned the crown," "You have persevered in suffering,"
and "Exalt yourself." In the upper left stand God the Father, Jesus,
the Virgin Mary, and several small children in prayer,
ready to help the dying man overcome this temptation.

had made salvation possible through an initial gift of grace, but
Christians had to contribute to their salvation by doing good
works by the power of this initial grace. Theologians taught that
believers could never know if their works were enough to ensure
their salvation. The sin of spiritual pride, then, consisted of a
false sense of assurance in which one felt worthy of salvation.
To counter this sin, the handbooks on death counseled humility
before God and fear of God's judgment.

Such fear must not be overdone, however, lest the dying end
up committing another "deathbed sin," that of despair. Faithful

Christians must not give in to despair over past sins and thereby doubt God's goodness. Instead, they must hold out hope in God's mercy, encouraged by various stories from the New Testament of sinners who were forgiven. On the deathbed and throughout life, Christians were instructed to keep a delicate balance between humility before God's judgment and hope in God's mercy.

Luther, however, was convinced that Christians were saved only by God's grace and not by any good works of their own.[3]

3. Luther's revision to late-medieval theology of grace was focused on grace being unearned. In the predominant late-medieval understanding, God gave an initial gift of grace that enabled good works. Those good works then earned salvific grace. In Luther's understanding, God's grace was freely given out of love and mercy, and it could not be earned in any way. Christians would still do good works out of joy and gratitude for God's grace, but good works did not earn God's favor.

Woodcut from an illustrated *Ars moriendi* depicting the means to overcome the temptation to despair over one's sins. An angel at the foot of the deathbed holds a banner that reads, "You despair for no reason." At the man's head stands St. Peter with the cock that crowed after Peter denied Jesus. Next to him stands Mary Magdalene holding the pot of oil with which she was thought to have anointed Jesus' feet. On the cross is the thief crucified with Jesus to whom Jesus promised salvation. On the floor at the man's feet are Saul of Tarsus and his horse, who were thrown to the ground when a voice spoke to him and he was converted. A demon in the bottom right corner holds a sign that says, "The victory is for me." Another demon flees under the bed, with only its hind legs visible.

They could be certain of God's forgiveness because God had promised to forgive them. In both word and sacrament, that promise becomes concrete and is offered to all Christians. Thus, Luther's instructions for dying removed the threat that one's disposition on the deathbed might put one's salvation in peril. Instead, he focused on laying claim to the promise of salvation and exiting life with a joyful trust in God. The temptations he saw on the deathbed were not the temptations of specific sins but, instead, the temptation to focus on death, sin, and hell instead of life, grace, and salvation. To focus on death, sin, and hell is to rob oneself of the consolation of grace, and to rob God of the honor that is appropriate for such graciousness.

Another important part of sixteenth-century piety surrounding death was the contemplation of Christ's passion. The handbooks on death instructed caregivers to place a crucifix where the dying person could see it and to encourage meditation upon it.[4] The purpose of this meditation was manifold: to encourage compassion for Christ in his suffering, to help ward off temptation, to comfort the dying through its reassurance of God's mercy, to arouse contrition, and to be moved to imitate Christ in his death. One handbook instructed the dying to replicate the five things that Christ did on the cross: to pray, to cry for forgiveness, to weep as a sign of repentance, to commend one's soul to God, and to give up one's soul willingly.[e] Luther discouraged dying Christians from trying to imitate Christ's death. Instead, he saw Christ's passion as another reminder of God's mercy and victory over death. Meditating on Christ's passion from the deathbed, then, should serve to console dying Christians and to assure them of God's grace and the salvation that awaits.

Late-medieval handbooks on death contained little on understanding or approaching the sacraments, although taking the sacraments was encouraged if a priest was available. In Luther's instructions for death, he takes pains to emphasize the importance of the sacraments for the challenges faced by the dying. For Luther, the sacraments were a powerful means of consoling the dying because they are "a sign and promise" of the victory of life, grace, and love over death, sin, and hell. The certainty of God's word declared and made tangible in the sacraments was meant

4. A crucifix, a model of a cross with the crucified Jesus suspended from it, was a common object of public and private devotion in the sixteenth century.

---

e   Reinis, *Reforming the Art of Dying*, 35–40.

to overcome the frightening power of these evils, which threatened to cloud the joy of Christian faith—a joy that was possible even and especially on the deathbed.

Frequent reprints of this sermon spread Luther's message of joy in the face of death. The pamphlet was reprinted in at least eleven editions before the end of 1519.[f] Nine more editions were issued in 1520, including two in Latin.[g] After 1520, reproductions of this text fell sharply, with only eight extant editions from 1521 to 1525,[h] and no known editions after 1525. Throughout the 1520s, however, other Lutheran theologians published pamphlets endorsing their understandings of death and salvation, several of which were modeled on Luther's sermon.[i]

---

[f]   VD 16 L6473–83.

[g]   VD 16 L6484–90; WA 2:683.

[h]   VD 16 L6491–98.

[i]   Reinis, *Reforming the Art of Dying*, esp. 248ff.

A SERMON ON PREPARING TO DIE [5,6]

Martin Luther, Augustinian Monk

FIRST, since death marks a farewell from this world and all its activities, it is necessary that we[j] regulate our temporal goods properly, as we wish to have them ordered, lest after our death there be occasion for squabbles, quarrels, or other misunderstandings among our surviving friends. This pertains to the physical or external departure from this world and to the surrender of our possessions.

Second, we must also take leave spiritually. That is, we must cheerfully and sincerely forgive, for God's sake, all those who have offended us. At the same time we must also, for God's sake, earnestly seek the forgiveness of all those whom we undoubtedly have greatly offended by setting a bad example or by bestowing too few of the kindnesses demanded by the law of Christian brotherly love. This is necessary lest the soul remain burdened by any concerns here on earth.

Third, since everyone must depart this earth, we must turn our eyes to God alone, to whom the path of death leads and directs us. Here we find the beginning of the narrow gate and of the straight path to life [Matt. 7:14].[7] All must joyfully venture forth on this path, for though the gate is quite narrow, the path is not long. Just as an infant is born in peril and pain from the small dwelling of its mother's womb into this immense heaven and earth, that is, into this world, so we depart this life through the narrow gate of death. And although the heavens and the earth in which we dwell at present seem large and wide to us, they are nevertheless much narrower and smaller than the mother's womb in comparison with the future heaven. Therefore, the

---

5. This translation is based on the original German version in the Weimar Edition (WA 2:680–97) and the English translation in the American Edition of *Luther's Works* (LW 42:99–115).

6. See n. 1, p. 283 (sermon).

7. Luther is alluding to Jesus' words in Matt. 7:14: "The gate is narrow and the road is hard that leads to life, and there are few who find it."

---

j Luther alternates between using the universal "one" with generic male pronouns ("he") and using the first-person plural ("we/us") in the first eight of his numbered points. For the sake of readability and conveying the gender-neutral meaning of "one" and "he" in the sixteenth century, all such generic references have been changed to the first-person plural.

death of the dear saints is called a new birth, and their feast day is known in Latin as *natale*, that is, the day of their birth.[8] However, the narrow passage of death makes us think of this life as expansive and the life beyond as confined. Therefore, we must believe this and learn from the physical birth of a child, as Christ declares, "When a woman is in labor she has sorrow; but when she has recovered, she no longer remembers the anguish, since a child is born by her into the world" [John 16:21]. So it is that in dying we must bear this anguish and know that a large mansion and joy will follow [John 14:2].

Fourth, such preparation and readiness for this journey are accomplished first of all by availing ourselves of a sincere confession (of at least the greatest sins and those which by diligent search can be recalled by our memory),[9] the holy Christian Sacrament of the Holy and True Body of Christ, and the Unction.[10] If these can be had, one should devoutly desire them and receive them with great confidence. If they cannot be had, our longing and yearning for them should nevertheless be a comfort and we should not be too dismayed by this circumstance. Christ says, "All things are possible to the one who believes" [Mark 9:23]. The sacraments are nothing other than signs that help incite us to faith, as we shall see. Without this faith they serve no purpose.

Fifth, we must earnestly, diligently, and highly esteem the holy sacraments, hold them in honor, freely and cheerfully rely on them, and weigh them against sin, death, and hell so that they win out by far. We must concern ourselves much more with the sacraments and their powers than with our sins. However, we must know how to give the sacraments due honor and we must know what their powers are. I show them due honor when I believe that I truly receive what the sacraments signify and all that God declares and indicates in them, so that I can say with Mary in firm faith, "Let it be to me according to your words and signs" [Luke 1:38].[11] Since God himself here speaks and acts through the priest, we would do him, in his word and work, no greater dishonor than to doubt whether it is true. And we can do him no greater honor than to believe that his word and work are true and to firmly rely on them.

Sixth, to recognize the power of the sacraments, we must know the evils which they contend with and which we face. There are three such evils: first, the terrifying image of death; second, the awesomely manifold image of sin; third, the unbearable and

8. By 1520, Luther vocally opposed the adoration and invocation of the saints, saying that it encouraged Christians to trust saints instead of God, and that it took time and energy away from the more important work of loving one's neighbor. He instead taught that all Christians were saints through God's gift of grace, and he retained an admiration for Christians who had exhibited strong faith, especially the martyrs. See Robert Kolb, *For All the Saints: Changing Perceptions of Martyrdom and Sainthood in the Lutheran Reformation* (Macon, GA: Mercer University Press, 1987); and Lennart Pinomaa, *Die Heiligen bei Luther* (Helsinki: Luther-Agricola Gesellschaft, 1977).

9. In late-medieval theology, penitents had to confess all their sins to receive forgiveness for them, though some late-medieval theologians reduced that mandate to include only those sins that one remembered, as Luther does here. See Anne Thayer, *Penitence, Preaching, and the Coming of the Reformation* (Burlington, VT: Ashgate, 2002).

10. The Sacrament of Unction, or anointing of the sick, consists of a priest anointing a seriously ill person with oil while reciting a blessing that asks for the forgiveness of sins. It remains one of seven sacraments in the Roman Catholic Church today. Luther ceased to regard it as a sacrament by December 1519 (WA Br 1:594–95).

11. Luther inserts "and signs" into the biblical text here to draw a connection between God's word and the promise contained in the sacrament.

12. Where late-medieval guidebooks for death named five temptations commonly present on the deathbed (doubt, despair, impatience in suffering, spiritual pride, and avarice), Luther instead names three evils, which draw the dying's attention away from God's promise of eternal life through the forgiveness of sin.

unavoidable image of hell and eternal damnation.[12] Every other evil issues from these three and grows large and strong as a result of such mingling.

Death looms so large and is terrifying because our foolish and fainthearted nature has etched its image too deeply within itself and constantly fixes its gaze on it. Moreover, the devil presses us to look closely at the gruesome mien and image of death to add to our worry, timidity, and despair. Indeed, he conjures up before our eyes every kind of sudden and terrible death we have ever seen, heard, or read. And then he also slyly suggests the wrath of God with which he [the devil] in days past sometimes tormented and destroyed sinners. In that way he fills our foolish human nature with the dread of death while cultivating a love and concern for life, so that, burdened with such thoughts, we forget God, flee and abhor death, and thus, in the end, are and remain disobedient to God.

We should familiarize ourselves with death during our lifetime, inviting death into our presence when it is still at a distance and not on the move. At the time of dying, however, this is hazardous and useless, for then death looms large of its own accord. In that hour we must put the thought of death out of mind and refuse to see it, as we shall hear. The power and might of death are rooted in the fearfulness of our nature and in our untimely and undue viewing and contemplating of it.

Seventh, sin also grows large and important when we dwell on it and brood over it too much. This is increased by the fearfulness of our conscience, which

In this 1517 publication by Johann Staupitz, the Trinity is shown above a scene of the Last Judgment, where those destined for heaven and those destined for hell are separated. Hell is depicted as the wide mouth of a devouring animal.

is ashamed before God and accuses itself terribly.[13] That is the water that the devil has been seeking for his mill. He makes our sins seem large and numerous. He reminds us of all who have sinned and of the many who were damned for lesser sins than ours so as to make us despair or die reluctantly, thus forgetting God and being found disobedient in the hour of death.

This is true especially since we feel that we should think of our sins at that time and that it is right and useful for us to engage in such contemplation. But we will find ourselves so unprepared and unfit that now even all our good works are turned into sins.[14] As a result, this naturally leads to an unwillingness to die, disobedience to the will of God, and eternal damnation. This is not the fitting time to meditate on sin. That should be done during one's lifetime. Thus the evil spirit turns everything upside down for us. During our lifetime, when we should constantly have our eyes fixed on the image of death, sin, and hell—as we read in Ps. 51[:3], "My sin is ever before me"—the devil closes our eyes and hides these images. But in the hour of death when our eyes should see only life, grace, and salvation, the devil suddenly opens our eyes and frightens us with these untimely images so that we shall not see the true ones.

Eighth, hell also looms large because of undue scrutiny and stern thought devoted to it at the wrong time. This is increased immeasurably by our ignorance of God's counsel. The evil spirit prods the soul so that it burdens itself with all kinds of useless presumptions, especially with the most dangerous undertaking of delving into the mystery of God's will to ascertain whether one is "chosen" or not.[15]

Here the devil practices his ultimate, greatest, and most cunning art and power. By this he sets us above God, insofar as we seek signs of God's will and become impatient because we are not supposed to know whether we are among the elect. We look with suspicion upon God, so that we soon desire a different God. In brief, the devil is determined to blast God's love from our minds and to arouse thoughts of God's wrath. The more docilely we follow the devil and accept these thoughts, the more imperiled our position is. In the end we cannot save ourselves, and we fall prey to hatred and blasphemy of God. What is my desire to know whether I am chosen other than a presumption to know all that God knows and to be equal with him so that he will know no more than I do? Thus God is no longer God with a knowledge

13. Luther is particularly concerned about those with troubled consciences. His own tortured experience with his conscience during his time in the monastery informed this concern.

14. Good works can become sins for Luther if they are done without faith. In the situation he describes, in which the devil causes the dying Christian to doubt God's grace, the devil has thus brought about a loss of faith.

15. This refers to the doctrine of predestination, the belief that God foreknows who will be given eternal salvation, and that salvation depends only on God's decree and not on human acceptance or action. Luther believed in predestination and emphasized the mystery of God's choices, but he did not advocate a belief called "double predestination," in which God saves some and condemns others. We see here that he had spiritual concerns about the dangers of prying into this mystery.

16. In other words, one should not invite the devil into one's mind by pondering the mysteries of election. This saying is similar to the proverb, "Speak of the devil and he shall appear."

17. That is, in conjunction with images of life, grace, and salvation.

18. Luther might be referring to sudden deaths, which were considered the worst way to die in the sixteenth century because one could not properly prepare for it. A slower, peaceful death was thought to show greater faith in and reconciliation with God. The practice of producing paintings and "death masks" (plaster molds of the deceased's face and hands) was done in part to document the calm, peaceful expression on the face of the deceased.

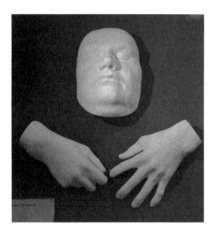

Luther's plaster hands and death mask

surpassing mine. Then the devil reminds us of the many heathen, Jews, and Christians who are lost, agitating such dangerous and pernicious thoughts so violently that we, who would otherwise gladly die, now become loath to depart this life. When we are assailed by thoughts regarding our election, we are being assailed by hell, as the psalms lament so much. Those who surmount this temptation have vanquished sin, hell, and death all in one.

Ninth, in this matter we must exercise all diligence not to open our homes to any of these images and not to paint the devil over the door.[16] These foes will by themselves boldly rush in and seek to occupy the heart completely with their image, their arguments, and their signs. And when that happens we are doomed and God is entirely forgotten. The only thing to do with these pictures at that time is to combat and expel them. Indeed, where they are found alone and not in conjunction with other pictures,[17] they belong nowhere else than in hell among the devils.

But those who want to fight against them and drive them out will find that it is not enough just to wrestle and tussle and scuffle with them. They will prove too strong for them, and matters will go from bad to worse. The one and only approach is to leave them be entirely and have nothing to do with them. But how is that done? It is done in this way: You must see death in the light of life, see sin in the light of grace, and see hell in the light of heaven, permitting nothing to divert you from that view. Adhere to it even if all angels, all creatures, yes, even your own thoughts, depict God in a different light—something these will not do, but it is only the evil spirit who makes it seem that way. What shall we do about that?[k]

Tenth, you must not view or ponder death itself, not in yourself or in your nature, nor in those who were killed by God's wrath and were overcome by death.[18] If you do that you will be lost and defeated with them. But you must resolutely turn your gaze, the thoughts of your heart, and all your senses, away from this picture. Instead, look at death closely and thoroughly only as seen in those who died in God's grace and who have overcome death, particularly in Christ and then also in all his saints.

---

k   Beginning in this paragraph, Luther quite suddenly begins using "you" instead of "we" or "one." This more direct appeal to the reader continues through the end of the sermon.

In such pictures death will not appear terrible and gruesome. No, it will seem contemptible and dead, slain and overcome in life. For Christ is nothing other than sheer life, and his saints are likewise. The more profoundly you impress that image upon your heart and gaze upon it, the more the image of death will fade and vanish by itself, without struggle or battle. Thus your heart will be at peace and you will be able to die calmly in Christ and with Christ, as we read in Rev. [14:13], "Blessed are they who die in the Lord Christ." This was foreshadowed in Exodus 21 [Num. 21:6-9], where we hear that, when the children of Israel were bitten by fiery serpents, they did not struggle with these serpents, but merely had to raise their eyes to the dead bronze serpent and the living ones dropped from them by themselves and perished. Thus you must concern yourself solely with the death of Christ and then you will find life. But if you look at death in any other way, it will kill you with great anxiety and anguish. This is why Christ says, "In the world—that is, in yourselves—you have unrest, but in me you will find peace" [John 16:33].*

Eleventh, you must not look at sin in sinners, or in your conscience, or in those who abide in sin to the end and are damned. If you do, you will surely follow them and also be overwhelmed. You must turn your thoughts away from that and look at sin only within the picture of grace. Engrave that picture in yourself with all your power and keep it before your eyes. The picture of grace is nothing else but that of Christ on the cross and of all his dear saints.[19]

How is that to be understood? Grace and mercy are there where Christ on the cross takes your sin from you, bears it for you, and destroys it. To believe this firmly, to keep it before your eyes and not to doubt it, means to view the picture of Christ and to engrave it in yourself. Likewise, all the saints who suffer and die in Christ also bear your sins and suffer and labor for you, as we find it written, "Bear one another's burdens and thus fulfill the command of Christ" [Gal. 6:2]. Christ himself exclaims in Matt. 11[:28], "Come to me, all who labor and are heavy-laden, and I will help you." In this way you may view your sins in safety without tormenting your conscience. Here sins are never sins, for here they are overcome and swallowed up in Christ.[20] He takes

19. Contemplation of Christ's suffering was an important part of late-medieval piety, especially on the deathbed. In late-medieval practice, it served many functions on the deathbed (see the introduction, pp. 284–85). Luther focuses on only one of these functions, namely, the reassurance of God's mercy and forgiveness of sin.

20. That is, they have lost their power to oppress by threatening damnation.

*The NRSV reads, "In the world you face persecution. But take courage; I have conquered the world!"

your death upon himself and strangles it so that it may not harm you, if you believe that he does it for you and see your death in him and not in yourself. Likewise, he also takes your sins upon himself and overcomes them with his righteousness out of sheer mercy, and if you believe that, your sins will never work you harm. In that way Christ, the picture of life and of grace over against the picture of death and sin, is our consolation. Paul states that in 1 Cor. 15[:57], "Thanks and praise be to God, who through Christ gives us the victory over sin and death."

Twelfth, you must not regard hell and eternal pain in relation to predestination, not in yourself, or in itself, or in those who are damned, nor must you be worried by the many people in the world who are not chosen. If you are not careful, that picture will quickly upset you and be your downfall. You must force yourself to keep your eyes closed tightly to such a view, for it can never help you, even though you were to occupy yourself with it for a thousand years and fret yourself to death. After all, you will have to let God be God and grant that he knows more about you than you do yourself.

So then, gaze at the heavenly picture of Christ, who descended into hell [1 Pet. 3:19] for your sake and was forsaken by God as one eternally damned when he spoke the words on the cross, "Eli, Eli, lama sabachthani!"—"My God, my God, why have you forsaken me?" [Matt. 27:46; Mark 15:34]. In that picture your hell is defeated and your uncertain election is made certain.[21] If you concern yourself solely with that and believe that it was done for you, you will surely be preserved in this same faith. Never, therefore, let this be erased from your vision. Seek yourself only in Christ and not in yourself and you will find yourself in him eternally.

Thus when you look at Christ and all his saints, and delight in the grace of the God who elected them, and continue steadfastly in this joy, then you too are already elected. He says in Genesis 12[:3], "All who bless you shall be blessed." However, if you do not trust in this alone but instead in yourself, you will become adverse to God and all saints, and thus you will find nothing good in yourself. Beware of this, for the evil spirit will strive with much cunning to bring you to such a pass.

Thirteenth, these three pictures or conflicts [of sin, death, and hell] are foreshadowed in Judges 7[:16-22], where we read that Gideon attacked the Midianites at night with three hun-

21. In late-medieval theology, it was considered presumptuous and sinful to claim certainty about one's salvation. Instead, late-medieval Christians were taught to ask for God's mercy and hope that it would be given. Luther, by contrast, tells Christians that they can know and claim their salvation because of God's words and works in Christ.

dred men in three different places, but did no more than have trumpets blown and glass fragments smashed. The foe fled and destroyed himself. Similarly, death, sin, and hell will flee with all their might if in the night we but keep our eyes on the glowing picture of Christ and his saints and abide in the faith, which does not see and does not want to see the false pictures. Furthermore, we must encourage and strengthen ourselves with the word of God as with the sound of trumpets.

Isaiah [9:4] introduces this same figure very aptly against these three images, saying of Christ,[22] "For the yoke of his burden, and the staff for his shoulder, the rod of his oppressor, you have broken as in the days of the Midianites," who were overcome by Gideon. It is as if he said: "The sins of your people (which are a heavy 'yoke of his burden' for his conscience), and death (which is a 'staff' or punishment laid upon his shoulder), and hell (which is a powerful 'rod of the oppressor' with which eternal punishment for sin is exacted)—all these you have broken and defeated. This came to pass in the days of Gideon, that is, when Gideon, by faith and without wielding his sword, put his enemies to flight."

And when did Christ do this? On the cross! There he prepared himself as a threefold picture[23] for us, to be held before the eyes of our faith against the three evil pictures with which the evil spirit and our nature would assail us to rob us of this faith. He is the living and immortal image against death, which he suffered, yet by his resurrection from the dead he vanquished death in his life. He is the image of the grace of God against sin, which he assumed, and yet overcame by his perfect obedience. He is the heavenly image, the

22. Luther and most of his contemporaries read the Old Testament in light of the New Testament, so that Old Testament texts were taken to describe and promise Jesus' coming as the Messiah. See James Samuel Preus, *From Shadow to Promise: Old Testament Interpretation from Augustine to the Young Luther* (Cambridge, MA: Belknap Press, 1969).

23. Many altars in the sixteenth century had a triptych altarpiece, that is, a threefold painting with a center painting and one "wing" painting on each side. (See an example in the image below.) Here Luther tries to paint verbal pictures of life, grace, and salvation to combat the evil pictures of hell, sin, and death. Using images as objects of devotion was a common practice in the late Middle Ages. In the Reformation,

Altarpiece of Calvary by Bernard van Orley, c. 1534, currently in Church of Our Lady in Bruges, Belgium

woodcuts and other images were used by all parties to educate and sway Christians. See Robert Scribner, *For the Sake of Simple Folk: Popular Propaganda for the German Reformation* (Cambridge: Cambridge University Press, 1981).

24. Luther cites words spoken to Jesus by Jewish priests and scribes in the Gospels of Matthew, Mark, and Luke. Many sixteenth-century Christians blamed all Jews for killing Jesus. The unflattering parallel in this text between the devil taunting Christians and Jews taunting Jesus is one example of Luther's antipathy toward Judaism. For more on Luther and Judaism, see Eric Gritsch, *Martin Luther's Anti-Semitism: Against His Better Judgment* (Grand Rapids: Eerdmans, 2012); Brooks Schramm and Kirsi Stjerna, *Martin Luther, the Bible, and the Jewish People* (Minneapolis: Fortress Press, 2012); Heiko Oberman, *Luther: Man between God and the Devil,* trans. Eileen Walliser-Schwarzbart (New York: Doubleday, 1992), 289–97; and Thomas Kaufmann, "Luther and the Jews," in Dean Phillip Bell and Stephen G. Burnett, eds., *Jews, Judaism, and the Reformation in Sixteenth-Century Germany* (Leiden: Brill, 2006), 69–104.

25. Luther sees the images of sin, hell, and death in biblical stories where they are not named as such, here in the destruction of Jerusalem, and above in the fight between Gideon and the Midianites (p. 297).

one who was forsaken by God as damned, yet he conquered hell through his omnipotent love, thereby proving that he is the dearest Son, who gives this to us all if we but believe.

Fourteenth, beyond all this he not only defeated sin, death, and hell in himself and offered his victory to our faith, but for our further comfort he himself suffered and overcame the temptation that these pictures entail for us. He was assailed by the images of death, sin, and hell just as we are. The Jews[24] confronted Christ with death's image when they said, "Let him come down from the cross; he has healed others, let him now help himself" [Matt. 27:40-42], as if to say, "Here you are facing death; now you must die; nothing can save you from that." Likewise, the devil holds the image of death before the eyes of a dying person and frightens his fearful nature with this horrible picture.

The Jews held the image of sin before Christ's eyes when they said to him, "He healed others. If he is the Son of God, let him come down from the cross, etc."—as if to say, "His works were all fraud and deception. He is not the Son of God but the son of the devil, whose own he is with body and soul. He never worked any good, only iniquity." And just as the Jews cast these three pictures at Christ in disarray, so too are we assailed by all three at once in disarray in order to bewilder us, and ultimately, to drive us to despair. The Lord describes the destruction of Jerusalem in Luke 19[:43-44], saying that the city's enemies will surround it with such devastation as to cut off escape—that is death. Furthermore, he says that its enemies will terrify the inhabitants and drive them hither and yon so that they will not know where to turn—that is sin. In the third place, he says that the foe will dash them to the ground and not leave one stone upon another—that is hell and despair.[25]

The Jews pressed the picture of hell before Christ's eyes when they said, "He trusts in God; let us see whether God will deliver him now, for he said he is the Son of God" [Matt. 27:43]—as though they were to say, "His place is in hell; God did not elect him; he is rejected forever. All his confidence and hope will not help him. All is in vain."

And now we note that Christ remained silent in the face of all these words and horrible pictures. He does not argue with his foes; he acts as though he does not hear or see them and makes no reply. Even if he had replied, he would only have given them cause to rave and rant even more horribly. He is so completely devoted to the dearest will of his Father that he forgets about his own death, his sin, and his hell imposed on him, and he intercedes for his enemies, for their sin, death, and hell [Luke 23:34]. We must, similarly, let these images slip away from us to wherever they wish or care to go, and remember only that we cling to God's will, which is that we hold to Christ and firmly believe our sin, death, and hell are overcome in him and no longer able to harm us. Only Christ's image must abide in us. With him alone we must debate and deal.

Fifteenth, we now turn to the holy sacraments[26] and their powers in order to become familiar with their benefits and how to use them. Those who are granted the time and the grace to confess, to be absolved, and to receive the sacrament and unction before death have great cause indeed to love, praise, and thank God and to die cheerfully, if they rely firmly on and believe in the sacraments, as we said earlier. In the sacraments your God, Christ himself, deals, speaks, and works with you through the priest, and these are not the works and words of humans. In the sacraments God himself grants you all the things of Christ that were just mentioned. God wants the sacraments to be a sign and testimony that Christ's life has taken up your death, his obedience your sin, his love your hell, and he has overcome them. Moreover, through the same sacraments you are included and made one with all the saints. You thereby enter into the true communion of saints so that they die with you in Christ, bear sin, and vanquish hell.

It follows from this that the sacraments, that is, the external words of God as spoken by a priest, are a truly great comfort and at the same time a visible sign of divine intent.[27] We must cling to them with a staunch faith as to the good staff which the patriarch Jacob used when crossing the Jordan [Gen. 32:10], or as to a lantern by which we must be guided, and carefully walk with open eyes the dark path of death, sin, and hell, as the prophet says, "Thy word is a light to my feet" [Ps. 119:105]. St. Peter also declares, "And we have a sure word from God. You will do well to pay attention to it" [2 Pet. 1:19]. There is no other help in death's agonies, for everyone who is saved is saved only by that sign. It points to Christ and his image, enabling you to say when faced by the image of death, sin, and hell, "God promised and, in his sacraments, he gave me a sure sign of his grace, that Christ's life overcame my death in his death, that his obedience blotted out

26. The Fourth Lateran Council in 1215 formally declared that there were seven sacraments: baptism, confirmation, penance, Eucharist, ordination, marriage, and extreme unction. When Luther wrote this sermon in 1519, he had rejected the sacramental nature of confirmation, ordination, and marriage. In August of 1520 he wrote a major treatise on the sacraments, *The Babylonian Captivity of the Church*, in which he asserted that only baptism and the Lord's Supper were truly sacraments (see TAL 3:8–129).

27. Luther's definition of the sacraments is based on Augustine. According to this definition, a sacrament is tangible element joined with God's word. Luther's frequent pairing of "sign and promise" in this sermon emphasizes these two aspects of the sacraments, with promise as the word of God and sign as the physical element.

my sin in his suffering, that his love destroyed my hell in his forsakenness. This sign and promise of my salvation will not lie to me or deceive me. It is God who has promised it, and God cannot lie either in words or in deeds." Those who thus insist and rely on the sacraments will find that their election and predestination will turn out well without worry and effort.

Sixteenth, it is of utmost importance that we highly esteem, honor, and rely upon the holy sacraments, which contain nothing but God's words, promises, and signs. This means that we have no doubts about the sacraments or that which they certainly signify, for if we doubt these, we lose everything.[28] Christ says that it will happen to us as we believe. What will it profit you to assume and to believe that sin, death, and hell are overcome in Christ for others, but not to believe that your sin, your death, and your hell are also vanquished and wiped out and that you are thus redeemed? Under those circumstances the sacraments will be completely fruitless, since you do not believe the things that are designated, given, and promised there to you. That is the vilest sin that can be committed, for God himself is looked upon as a liar in his word, signs, and works, as one who speaks, shows, and promises something which he neither means nor intends to keep. Therefore we dare not trifle with the sacraments. Faith must be present for a firm reliance and cheerful venturing on such signs and promises of God. What sort of a God or Savior would he be who could not or would not save us from sin, death, and hell? Whatever the true God promises and effects must be something big.

But then the devil comes along and whispers into your ear, "But suppose you received the sacraments unworthily and through your unworthiness robbed yourself of such grace?" In that event, cross yourself and do not let the question of your worthiness or unworthiness assail you.[29] Just see to it that you believe that these are sure signs, true words of God, and then you will indeed be and remain worthy. Faith makes you worthy; unbelief makes you unworthy. The evil spirit brings up the question of worthiness and unworthiness to stir up doubts within you, thus nullifying the sacraments with their benefits and making God a liar in what he says.

God gives you nothing on account of your worthiness, nor does he build his word and sacraments on your worthiness, but out of sheer grace he establishes you, an unworthy person, on the foundation of his word and signs. Hold fast to that and say, "He

28. In the late-medieval church, Christians were instructed to abstain from the sacrament if they had not confessed their sins, or if they persisted in sin. To take the sacrament in an unholy state risked further divine condemnation, as Paul warned in 1 Cor. 11:27-29: "Whoever, therefore, eats the bread or drinks the cup of the Lord in an unworthy manner will be answerable for the body and blood of the Lord." One sin associated with "unworthy reception" was lack of faith in the promises of the sacrament. Luther was concerned about this sin for two reasons: because it prevented Christians from experiencing the benefits of the sacrament, and because it insulted God by not believing God's words of promise.

29. Crossing oneself, or making the sign of the cross on one's head or torso, was a reminder of the promises of baptism as well as an invocation of Christ against the devil.

who gives and has given me his signs and his word, which assure me that Christ's life, grace, and heaven have kept my sin, death, and hell from harming me, is truly God, who will surely preserve these things for me. When the priest absolves me, I trust in this as in God's word itself. Since it is God's word, it must come true. That is my stand, and on that stand I will die."[30] You must trust in the priest's absolution as firmly as though God had sent a special angel or apostle to you, yes, as though Christ himself were absolving you.

Seventeenth, we must note that those who receive the sacraments have a great advantage, for they have received a sign and a promise from God with which they can exercise and strengthen their belief that they have been called into Christ's image and to his benefits. The others who must do without these signs labor solely in faith and must obtain these benefits with the desires of their hearts. They will, of course, also receive these benefits if they persevere in that same faith. Thus you must also say with regard to the Sacrament of the Altar, "If the priest gave me the holy body of Christ, which is a sign and promise of the communion of all angels and saints that they love me, provide and pray for me, suffer and die with me, bear my sin and overcome hell, it will and must therefore be true that the divine sign does not deceive me.[31] I will not let anyone rob me of it. I would rather deny all the world and myself than doubt my God's trustworthiness and truthfulness in his signs and promises. Whether worthy or unworthy of him, I am, according to the text and the declaration of this sacrament, a member of Christendom. It is better that I be unworthy than that God's truthfulness be questioned. Devil, away with you if you advise me differently."

Just see how many people there are who would like to be certain or to have a sign from heaven to tell them how they stand with God and whether they are elected. But what help would it be to them to receive such a sign if they would still not believe? What good are all the signs without faith? How did Christ's signs and the apostles' signs help the Jews? What help are the venerable signs of the sacraments and the words of God even today? Why do people not hold to the sacraments, which are sure and appointed signs, tested and tried by all saints and found reliable by all who believed and who received all that they indicate?

We should, then, learn what the sacraments are, what purpose they serve, and how they are to be used. We will find that

30. Luther's writings often contain such suggestions for direct dialogue, either with oneself or with the devil.

31. In 1519, Luther still endorsed the practice of praying to the saints and thought that the saints were advocates for the living. This view had changed significantly by 1520. See n. 8, p. 291.

there is no better way on earth to comfort downcast hearts and bad consciences. In the sacraments we find God's Word, which reveals and promises Christ to us, with all the grace that he himself is against sin, death, and hell. Nothing is more pleasing and desirable to the ear than to hear that sin, death, and hell are wiped out. That very thing is effected in us through Christ if we see the sacraments properly.

The right use of the sacraments involves nothing more than trusting that all will be as the sacraments promise and pledge through God's word.[32] Therefore, it is necessary not only to look at the three pictures in Christ, and with these to drive out the counter-pictures, but also to have a definite sign which assures us that this has surely been given to us. That is the function of the sacraments.

Eighteenth, in the hour of their death, Christians should not worry that they are alone. They can be certain, as the sacraments indicate, that a great many eyes are upon them: first, the eyes of God and of Christ himself, for the Christian believes his words and clings to his sacraments; then also, the eyes of the dear angels, of the saints, and of all Christians. As the Sacrament of the Altar indicates, there is no doubt that all of these, as one body, run to Christians as one of their own, help them overcome sin, death, and hell, and bear all things with them. In that hour the work of love and the communion of saints are seriously and mightily active. Christians must see this for themselves and have no doubt regarding it, for then they will be bold in death. Those who doubt this do not believe in the most venerable Sacrament of the Body of Christ, for this sacrament indicates, promises, and pledges the communion, help, love, comfort, and support of all the saints in all times of need. If you believe in the signs and words of God, his eyes rest upon you, as he says in Psalm 32[:8], "*Firmabo*, etc., my eyes will constantly be upon you lest you perish."[m] If God looks upon you, all the angels, saints, and all creatures will fix their eyes upon you. And if you remain in that faith, all of them will uphold you with their hands. And when your soul leaves your body, they will be on hand to receive it, and you cannot perish.

32. Here Luther contradicts the late-medieval teaching that the recipients of the sacrament would not receive the grace conveyed in it if they had an "obstacle to grace" within them. An obstacle to grace was defined as something actively opposed to grace, such as unbelief, unconfessed sin, or malicious intent in taking the sacrament.

m   Psalm 32:8 reads: "I will instruct you and teach you the way you should go; I will counsel you with my eye upon you." Luther adds the Latin "*Firmabo*" to the beginning of this text, meaning "I will strengthen," or "I will support."

Ninth-century depiction of Christ as a heroic warrior—
an illustration of Psalm 91:13 (Stuttgart Psalter, fol. 23)

This is seen in the person of Elisha, who according to 2 Kgs. 6[:16-17] said to his servant, "Fear not, for those who are with us are more than those who are with them." This he said although enemies had surrounded them and they could see nothing but enemies. The Lord opened the eyes of the young man, and they were surrounded by a huge mass of horses and chariots of fire.

The same is true of everyone who trusts God. The words found in Ps. 34[:7] apply here: "The angel of the LORD will encamp around those who fear him, and will deliver them." And in Ps. 125[:1-2], "Those who trust in the LORD are like Mount Zion, which cannot be moved, but abides forever. As the mountains (that is, the angels)" are round about Jerusalem, so the LORD is round about his people, from this time forth and forevermore." And in Ps. 91[:11-16], "For he has charged his angels to bear you on their hands and to guard you wherever you go lest you dash your foot against a stone. You will tread on the lion and the adder, the young lion and the serpent you will trample under

---

n   Luther adds this parenthetical simile.

foot (this means that all the power and the cunning of the devil will be unable to harm you),º because he has trusted in me and I will deliver him; I will protect him because he knows my name. When he calls to me, I will answer him; I will be with him in all his trials, I will rescue him and honor him. With eternal life will I satisfy him, and show him my eternal grace."

Thus the Apostle also declares that the angels, who are countless, are all ministering spirits and are sent out for the sake of those who are to be saved [Heb. 1:14].

These are all such great matters that who can believe them? Therefore, we must know that, even though the works of God surpass human understanding, they happen in such small signs as the sacraments, which teach us what a great thing true faith in God really is.

Nineteenth, we must not presume to perform such things by our own power. Instead, we must humbly ask God to create and preserve such faith in and understanding of his holy sacraments. We must practice awe and humility in all this, lest we ascribe these works to ourselves instead of allowing God the glory. To this end we must call upon the holy angels, particularly our own angel, the Mother of God, and all the apostles and saints, especially since God has granted us exceptional reverence. However, we dare not doubt, but must believe that our prayer will be heard. We have two reasons for this. The first one, which we just heard from the Scriptures, is how God commanded the angels to love and help all who believe, and how the sacrament conveys this. We must hold this before the angels and remind them of it, not that the angels do not know this or would otherwise not do it; but we do it so that our faith and trust in them, and through them in God, becomes stronger and bolder as we face death. The other reason is that God has commanded us to believe firmly in the fulfillment of our prayer [Mark 11:24] and that it is a true Amen.[33] We must also bring this command of God to his attention and say, "My God, you have commanded me to pray and to believe that my prayer will be heard. For this reason I come to you in prayer and trust that you will not forsake me but will grant me a genuine faith."

Moreover, we should implore God and his dear saints our whole life long for true faith in the last hour, as we sing so very

33. "Amen" comes from a Hebrew word that denotes being secure, trustworthy, or sure. It is usually translated into English as "truly," "certainly," or "so be it." See Luther's explanation of the word in his *Exposition of the Lord's Prayer* (LW 42:76–77).

---

o   Again, Luther inserts this commentary into the text in parentheses.

fittingly on the day of Pentecost, "Now let us pray to the Holy Spirit for the true faith of all things the most, that in our last moments he may befriend us, and as home we go, he may tend us."[34] When the hour of death is at hand we must offer this prayer to God and, in addition, remind him of his command and of his promise and not doubt that our prayer will be fulfilled. After all, if God commanded us to pray and to trust in prayer, and, furthermore, has granted us the grace to pray, why should we doubt that his purpose in this was also to hear and to fulfill it?

Twentieth, what more could God do to persuade you to accept death willingly, not to dread it but instead to overcome it? In Christ he offers you the image of life, of grace, and of salvation so that you may not be horrified by the images of sin, death, and hell. Furthermore, he lays your sin, your death, and your hell on his dearest Son, vanquishes them, and renders them harmless for you. In addition, he lets the trials of sin, death, and hell that come to you also assail his Son and teaches you how to preserve yourself in the midst of these and how to make them harmless and bearable. And to relieve you of all doubt, he grants you a sure sign, namely, the holy sacraments. He commands his angels, all saints, all creatures to join him in watching over you, to care for your soul, and to receive it. He commands you to ask him for this and to be assured of fulfillment. What more can or should he do?

From this you can see that he is a true God and that he performs truly great and divine works for you. Why, then, should he not impose something big upon you (such as dying), if he adds to it great benefits, help, and strength, as if he is testing the power of his grace. Thus we read in Ps. 111[:2], "Great are the works of the Lord, selected according to his pleasure."[p]

Therefore, we ought to thank him with a joyful heart for showing us such wonderful, rich, and immeasurable grace and mercy against death, hell, and sin, and to extol and love his grace rather than fearing death so greatly. Love and praise make dying very much easier, as God tells us through Isaiah [48:9], "For the sake of my praise I restrain it [wrath] for you, that I may not cut you off." To that end may God help us. Amen.

34. This quote is the first stanza of a medieval German hymn. In 1524, Luther wrote three new stanzas for the hymn. The hymn is known in English as "Now Let Us Pray to the Holy Spirit" (LW 53:263–64).

---

p   The NRSV translation reads: "Great are the works of the Lord, studied by all who delight in them."

The Magnificat

1521

BETH KREITZER

INTRODUCTION

Luther began his *Commentary on the Magnificat* in late 1520 as a response (and gift) to the young prince John Frederick,[1] nephew of the elector, Frederick of Saxony.[2] This was around the same time that Luther publicly burned the papal bull *Exsurge Domine*,[3] which threatened him with excommunication[4] unless he recanted the teachings criticized in the text. He worked on the commentary and translation of the scriptural text of the Magnificat, Luke 1:46b-55, in earnest in February and March of 1521—the dedicatory preface is dated 10 March—but he was forced to give up working on the text shortly after Easter because he was called to appear at the Imperial Diet in Worms.[5] On 31 March he sent what he had of the text—the first three sections—to the young prince, and hoped to return to the work shortly. However, it was not until he was in hiding in the Wartburg Castle after his condemnation at the diet that he could return to the work. He finished the text and sent it to his friend Georg Spalatin[6] on 10 June to hand over to his printer in Wittenberg. The work was undertaken during one of Luther's most prolific periods of writing seminal texts—the *Address to the Christian Nobility of the German Nation* (August 1520), *The Babylonian Captivity of the Church* (October 1520), and *The Freedom of a Christian* (November

although he was also known as an avid collector of saints' relics.

3. The bull, or official papal declaration, was issued on 10 June 1520, by Pope Leo X (r. 1513–1521). Its official title is "Bull against the Errors of Martin Luther and His Followers," but it is known by its *incipit*, or opening phrase, "Arise, O Lord" (Ps. 74:22). Along with the bull, Luther also burned several copies of canon law books, representing human (that is, the pope's) laws over against God's law.

4. Excommunication is technically a sentence of being barred from the sacraments, but in Luther's day was a far more serious affair. As a publicly declared heretic (once the bull of excommunication, *Decet romanum pontificem*, was issued on 3 January 1521), Luther was in danger of arrest and possibly execution as well; his works could no longer be sold or read, and in some places his publications were gathered and burned. With the support of Frederick, however, Luther managed to stay out of harm's way.

5. The diet was a formal, deliberative assembly of the Holy Roman Empire, presided over by the new emperor, Charles V (1500–1558). Luther was called to the diet to renounce his condemned views, but he refused to recant. Before a sentence was handed down, he escaped the city. Elector Frederick arranged his false "abduction" and escape to the Wartburg Castle.

6. Georg Spalatin (1484–1545), a humanist, close friend, and colleague of Luther, was first tutor to the young Saxon princes, and then chaplain and secretary to Elector Frederick, becoming one of his closest advisors.

Portrait of John Frederick I by Lucas Cranach the Elder (1472–1553). John Frederick, the dedicatee of Luther's commentary and exposition, became elector after the death of his father, John (d. 1532). He reigned from 1532 until his death in 1547.

1520)[a] were published only shortly before this text was begun. Not long after completing his commentary Luther finished his translation of the entire New Testament, published first in September 1522.

Luther was a publishing sensation. In his *Printing, Propaganda, and Martin Luther* (Berkeley: University of California Press,

---

a   *Address to the Christian Nobility* (TAL 1:369–466) and *The Freedom of a Christian* (TAL 1:467–538); *Babylonian Captivity of the Church* (TAL 3:8–130).

1994), Mark U. Edwards Jr. notes the staggering statistics, both of Luther's literary output and the level to which the number of his publications outstripped any other author. The *Commentary on the Magnificat*, too, was popular—at least eight editions were printed in 1521, appearing in Wittenberg, Augsburg, Basel, and Vienna. By 1525, the text was translated into Latin and printed in Strassburg; it was also printed at least twice that same year in a French translation.[b] But despite its contemporary popularity, until recent years Luther scholars have not considered it one of his "serious" theological writings. Wilhelm Maurer dubbed it an *Erbauungsschrift*, or "edifying writing"—the word *edifying* carries a slightly negative connotation in both English and German.[c] At the very least, Luther's commentary, as "edifying" or pious literature, has not been—at least until recently—considered to be serious theology, worthy of extended study and attention.

Luther himself quite consciously wrote this text in German for the *Einfältige*, or simple folk, but the point was not to "water down" or simplify his basic theological ideas for an ignorant crowd. Rather, he intended to reach a wider circle of readers (and listeners, for not everyone could read) and put into practice one of the basic responsibilities of a theologian—increasing piety among Christians. In very practical terms, the text, especially in Luther's new translation, was suited to the "simple" folk, for Mary herself was of low social status, and noted in her song of praise that God would raise up the meek and lowly, while casting down the proud and powerful. In fact, Luther included in his text a long excursus on the meaning of the word *humility*,[7] and suggested that it is not a virtue for which Mary should be praised

The *Bulla contra errores Martini Lutheri*, also known as *Exsurge Domine*, was issued June 15, 1520, by Pope Leo X. It condemned forty-one points from Luther's writings and demanded that he recant these statements within sixty days or face excommunication.

7. Although the Vulgate had translated the Greek ταπείνωσις as *humilitas*, or "humility" (the virtue), Erasmus (1466–1536) clarified in his *Annotations* (1516) on the New Testament that the term does not mean the virtue but, rather, low social status. Luther used both Erasmus's new critical edition of the Greek NT and the Latin Vulgate for his translation.

---

b   See VD 16 L5447–58. See also Christoph Burger's study of the commentary, *Marias Lied in Luthers Deutung: Der Kommentar zum Magnifikat (Lk 1, 46b-55) aus den Jahren 1520/21*, Spätmittelalter und Reformation, neue Reihe, 34 (Tübingen: Mohr Siebeck, 2007), 14–15. The first English translation of the commentary was published in 1538. The text was also included in Luther's collected works, both in German and in Latin.

c   Burger notes that even earlier, by 1929, Von Loewenich had included the Magnificat among Luther's *Erbauungsschriften*. See ibid., 10. For Maurer's comments on Luther's commentary, see his *Von der Freiheit eines Christenmenschen: Zwei Untersuchungen zu Luthers Reformationsschriften 1520/21* (Göttingen: Vandenhoeck & Ruprecht, 1949), 82–158.

8. The *Regina coeli* is a Marian antiphon for Vespers. The first verse reads:

> Queen of heaven, rejoice, alleluia
> The Son whom you merited to bear, alleluia
> Has risen, as He said, alleluia
> Pray for us to God, alleluia.

The Coronation of the Virgin by Fra Angelico (c. 1395–1455). In late-medieval art, Mary was frequently depicted as the Queen of Heaven. Here she is in a traditional scene of receiving her crown.

9. Luther uses the traditional title "Mother of God" (*Mutter Gottes*) for Mary, following the Latin translation of *theotokos*, or God-bearer, as *mater Dei*. The term *theotokos* was affirmed as doctrine at the Council of Ephesus in 431, which stressed that Jesus was both

but, rather, an indication that she was a lowly, poor, and even despised young woman.

There were two important results of this new translation and emphasis: the first is that the high regard and excessive devotion for Mary in the late-medieval church could no longer be maintained, from Luther's perspective. He is very critical, for example, of the words of the hymn *Regina coeli laetare*,[8] which suggest that Mary somehow merited or earned the privilege of bearing God's Son through her great virtue. Any suggestion that Mary deserved this great grace is wrong because we human beings can earn nothing from God—any gift we receive from God comes through pure grace and is undeserved. Ascribing merit or deserving virtue to Mary would, in fact, lessen the value of God's grace, which she herself would not want, Luther notes. Instead, we should take her words seriously, and realize that God deserves *all* the credit here, for he *regarded* her—he looked at and chose someone who was ignored and even despised by everyone else. Luther shifts the focus of this text from Mary (the one who was regarded) to God (the one who deigned to regard her, and likewise all of us).

The second important result of this shift in interpretation is that now, according to Luther, respect for and veneration of Mary can be placed upon the proper footing. She is a simple girl, cleaning house and tending to her chores; she has no high opinions of herself or great expectations or ambitions for the future. She is, in fact, a truly humble person—one who, Luther notes, does not even realize she is humble, because it seems to be such a high virtue (and realizing that one is humble automatically makes one proud, and no longer humble!). Mary should not be praised because of some false notion of "humility," but in fact should be recognized and praised for her great faith and for her willingness, despite the challenges to herself, to be the Mother of God.[9] But as the Mother of God, or even Queen of Heaven (which Luther notes is a true

In the Visitation scene (Luke 1:39–56), Mary comes to help and care for her elderly relative Elizabeth, who is pregnant with John. After Elizabeth greets Mary as the "mother of my Lord," Mary is inspired to sing the Magnificat. Her "haste" in traveling to Elizabeth is usually seen as a sign of her humility and piety.

God and human being, hypostatically joined into one person, thus making Mary quite literally the Mother of God. Luther always maintained this title for Mary, and it is affirmed in the Lutheran tradition in the *Formula of Concord* (SD VIII.24; BC, 510).

name for her), Mary should not be thought of as "a goddess who could grant gifts or render aid" (p. 349). She did nothing to earn these titles, and insists in her own song that all honor be given to God alone. There is no harm (and much good) in regarding her, her actions, her words, even her great blessings and these titles given to her by the church, as long as we remember that all these benefits came, undeserved and unmerited, from God, and that all the glory should be given to God, for "holy is his name."

Although Luther rejected the notion that we somehow need Mary to serve as a mediator for us with God, he closed his commentary with a prayer that Christ would grant us a right understanding of the Magnificat, and asked that it be granted "through the intercession[10] and for the sake of his dear mother Mary." While some have seen in these words a remnant of medieval piety of which Luther would soon rid himself (and that viewpoint is not entirely accurate), it is more helpful to see that, for Luther, Mary is, in fact, helping all of us by providing this beautiful and theologically rich song for us. In the Magnificat she teaches all of us how to pray and models the proper attitude that we should take toward God—and in this aspect, Luther is very influenced by late-medieval mysticism, for he stresses her *gelassenheit*, that is, her "resignation" or "detachment," in her approach both to

10. Invocation, or calling upon the saints for their intercession—that is, that they might pray for the Christian to God—is a practice built upon the communion of the saints. However, in the late medieval period many Christians felt they had to pray to the saints because they were afraid to go directly to Jesus or the Father, or they believed that Mary and the saints had, in themselves, the power to help their petitioners. In this commentary Luther does not reject the idea of asking saints to pray for us. However, the *Augsburg Confession* (1530) (BC, XXI, p. 58) notes that the Bible does not teach the invocation of the saints, while the *Apology* notes (BC XXI, p. 239) that without the testimony of Scripture, it cannot be required, and it can even be dangerous, because people tend to take the practice too far. God has promised to hear our prayers, but we have no guarantee that any human being can hear our prayers or respond to them.

11. *Gelassenheit* is a central concept in the writings of late-medieval mystics such as Meister Eckhart (c. 1260–c. 1328) and John Tauler (c. 1300–1361), both of whom were important influences on Luther. Eckhart especially emphasizes that the human will must conform to the divine will, and that we should accept with equanimity whatever God has planned for us.

12. The "Mirror for Princes" was a common literary genre in the Renaissance and even earlier. These writings offered advice and examples for rulers (especially new rulers) either to emulate or avoid. The most famous example of such works is *The Prince* by Machiavelli, composed around 1513.

her lowly and poor status, and then to her great blessing in being chosen to bear the Christ.[11] She is neither offended nor hopeless in her "low estate," nor is she puffed up with pride in her new status, but equally satisfied by either condition. Instead, she turns all the glory toward God, and praises him alone.

She also intercedes for us in that she serves as a sign—a sign that does not point to itself, saying, "Look at me!," but, rather, says, "Look what God has done for me!" Mary serves as the example of what God will do, and in fact has already done for us. In this sense, "for her sake" does not mean that because she is his mother Jesus should do what she asks but, rather, that she has already received the benefits that God has promised to all of us, and so she stands as the sign and surety that we also will receive blessing and salvation. If Mary and the saints in heaven do pray for us, that is a wonderful thing, but it will never take the place of our own prayer, nor will it help us achieve salvation.

The Magnificat as Mirror[12] for a Prince

Despite the emphasis on Mary's humble status and God's greatness in his regard for the meek and lowly, Luther's stated purpose in writing this commentary is to provide some instruction, or at least reminders, for the young prince John Frederick. It might have seemed more appropriate for Luther to turn to one of the great biblical kings as an exemplar for the future elector—and, in fact, in the epilogue, Luther does provide the story of the young King Solomon asking God for wisdom—but Mary's song is a perfectly appropriate gift for a prince, in Luther's opinion, because it castigates many of the vices and failures that plague those in positions of leadership. That is, it points out very effectively what a good and pious prince should be careful to avoid. The human heart, Luther notes, is prone to presumption—we tend to think that we are pretty special and important. Add to this tendency the wealth, power, and honor that come to those who rule, and the frequent lack of checks and balances, and it is obvious that a ruler will be especially prone to be pleased with himself and to forget about God and the fact that God is the giver of all good gifts (and can take them away again). A ruler, therefore, should fear God and be diligent in piety even more than other people—a ruler has greater temptations, but also greater responsibilities, for "the welfare of many people" rests in his hands. So just as a right understanding of Mary's "humility" can place devotion to her upon the proper footing, so also a right understanding of her song, with its teaching about God and how he regards the proud and the humble, can teach a ruler how to be grateful to God and serve the people with justice.

THE MAGNIFICAT[13]

Translated and Expounded by
Dr. Martin Luther, Augustinian
JESUS

To his serene Highness and Prince, Lord John Frederick, Duke of Saxony, Landgrave of Thuringia, and Margrave of Meissen, my Gracious Lord and Patron.[14]

 Your humble chaplain,
 Dr. Martin Luther.

SERENE AND HIGH-BORN PRINCE, gracious lord! My humble prayers and service are always ready for your Grace.

 Your Grace's kind letters have lately come into my hands, and their cheering contents brought me much joy. By way of reply I send you this little exposition of the Magnificat. I promised it to you long ago, but the troublesome quarrels of many adversaries have repeatedly interrupted it.[15] If I put it off any longer, I shall have to blush for shame. It is not proper for me to make any more excuses; otherwise I may neglect your Grace's youthful heart, which inclines to the love of sacred Scripture and which might be stirred up and strengthened still further by more exercise in it. To this end I wish your Grace God's grace and help.

 And this is really necessary. For the welfare of many people lies in the person of so mighty a prince, once he is taken out of

13. This text is a translation of *Das Magnificat verdeutschet und ausgelegt* (1521), found in WA 7:538–604. It updates the translation of A. T. W. Steinhaeuser, which was originally prepared for the Philadelphia edition (PE) of Luther's Works, *Works of Martin Luther* (vol. III), published in six volumes by Holman/Muhlenberg Press from 1915. Steinhaeuser's translation was included, slightly revised, in LW 21:295–358.

14. The dukes of Saxony, members of the Wettin family, were also rulers of Thuringia and Meissen at this time—it was one of the most powerful families in Europe. Luther showed the expected respect in his address, but he also took on another traditional role for a minister of God's word—that of prophet and teacher—to the young prince.

15. Luther does not specify which opponents he means here, but he may well be referring to the fallout from the debate at Leipzig in June 1519 (see also n. 54, p. 85.). He then entered into some fierce literary debates with Hieronymus Emser (c. 1478–1527) and Augustine von Alfeld (1480–c. 1535), was condemned by the universities of Louvain and Cologne, and continued his literary war with Johann Eck (1486–1543), his opponent at Leipzig. Eck was the leading force behind Luther's condemnation in the papal bull *Exsurge Domine* (see n. 3, p. 308 above).

himself and graciously governed by God; on the other hand, the destruction of many people lies also there if he is left to himself and ruled by God's displeasure. Although the hearts of all people are in God's almighty hand, it is not without reason that only about kings and princes is it said [Prov. 21:1]: "The king's heart is in the hand of God; he turns it wherever he will." Thus God would instill his fear in the mighty lords, that they might learn that they can think nothing at all without his special inspiration. The actions of other people bring gain or loss upon themselves alone, or upon just a few others. But rulers are appointed for the special purpose of being either harmful or helpful to other people; and, the wider their domain, the more people they affect. Therefore Scripture calls pious and God-fearing princes "angels of God" [1 Sam. 29:9] and even "gods" [Ps. 82:6]. But harmful princes it calls "lions" [Zeph. 3:3], "dragons" [Jer. 51:34],[d] and "raging animals" [Ezek. 14:21]. These God includes among his four plagues—pestilence, famine, war, and raging animals [Ezek. 14:13-19; Rev. 6:8].

Since the heart of a human being by nature is flesh and blood, it is prone to presume too much for itself. And when, in addition, power, riches, and honor come to him, these form so strong an incentive to presumption and self-assurance that he forgets God and does not care about his subjects. Being able to do wrong with impunity, he lets himself go and becomes a beast, does whatever he pleases, and is a ruler in name, but a monster in deed. Therefore the sage Bias[16] has well said: "The office of ruler reveals what sort of person a ruler is."[17] As for the subjects, they do not dare to behave however they might want because they are afraid of the government. Since they do not need to fear other people,[18] therefore, all rulers should fear God more than others do, learning to know him and his works and walking diligently, as St. Paul says in Romans 12[:8]: "He who rules, let him rule with diligence."

Now, in all of Scripture I do not know anything that serves such a purpose as well as this sacred hymn of the most blessed Mother of God, which ought indeed to be learned and kept in mind by all who would rule well and be beneficial lords. In it she really sings sweetly about the fear of God, what sort of Lord he is,

---

16. Bias, one of the "seven sages" of ancient Greece, lived in Ionia sometime between 620 and 540 BCE. Many of his sayings were collected by Diogenes Laertius (fl. c. 222–235) in his famous *Lives and Opinions of Eminent Philosophers*, a principal source for the history of Greek philosophy.

17. *Magistratus virum ostendit.* Aristotle cites this saying of Bias in his *Nicomachean Ethics* V, 1.

18. This was hardly the position of the young prince, however; Luther wanted to impress upon him his great responsibility as a ruler. In his *Address to the Christian Nobility of the German Nation*, published in August 1520, Luther had argued for greater responsibility for secular authorities, particularly that they should assume greater oversight in church matters, including the right to call a council to pursue church reform even against the will of the pope and bishops. See TAL 1:369–465.

---

d   Luther has *Trachen*, or "dragons," while the NRSV translates the term in Jeremiah as "a monster."

The Virgin Mary in Prayer by Albrecht
Durër (1471–1528). In her song,
Mary praises God's name and teaches
us all to be led by God's will.

and especially what his dealings are with those of low and high
degree. Let someone else listen to his girlfriend singing a worldly
tune; this pure virgin well deserves to be heard by a prince and
lord, as she sings him her sacred, chaste, and salutary song. It is
not an unreasonable custom, too, that this canticle is sung in all
the churches daily at vespers, and in a special and appropriate
setting that sets it apart from the other hymns.[19]

May the tender Mother of God herself procure for me the
spirit of wisdom profitably and thoroughly to expound this song
of hers, so that your Grace as well as we all may draw from it
wholesome knowledge and a praiseworthy life, and thus come to
chant and sing this Magnificat eternally in heaven. To this may
God help us. Amen.[20]

Herewith I commend myself to your Grace, humbly beseech-
ing your Grace in all kindness to receive my poor effort.

Wittenberg, 10 March 1521

19. For centuries prior to the sixteenth
century, the Magnificat was sung at
Vespers, part of the daily office. Today
it is still used by Roman Catholics,
Lutherans, and Anglicans in their
Vespers services, and many composers
have written beautiful settings of the
text. Luther notes, however, that as
often as this text is sung, it is rarely
properly understood.

20. It is important to note that Luther's
prayer here is directed to God ("may
God help us"), but he is asking Mary for
her intercession, that is, that she should
pray for and help him as well. He notes
elsewhere in the commentary that it is
"right and proper" that we ask others to
pray for us, but it does not replace our
own prayer to God, nor should we think
that we can somehow benefit from their
merits (p. 339).

Preface and Introduction

In order properly to understand this sacred hymn of praise, we need to bear in mind that the Blessed Virgin Mary is speaking on the basis of her own experience, in which she was enlightened and instructed by the Holy Spirit. No one can correctly understand God or his word unless she has received such understanding directly from the Holy Spirit. But no one can receive it from the Holy Spirit without experiencing, testing, and feeling it. In such experience the Holy Spirit instructs us as in his own school, outside of which nothing is learned but empty words and prattle.[21] When the holy virgin experienced what great things God was working in her despite her insignificance, lowliness, poverty, and inferiority, the Holy Spirit taught her this deep insight and

21. Luther soon had to be more cautious in discussing inspiration by the Spirit, for shortly he had to face opponents, the *Schwärmer*, or enthusiasts, who insisted that direct revelation from the Spirit is necessary while the written word (even of the Bible) is not. The Zwickau prophets arrived in Wittenberg at the very end of 1521 and caused great disturbances there, claiming authority as prophets to direct reform. Luther returned from the safety of the Wartburg to reestablish control over reform in Wittenberg on 6 March 1522.

The Annunciation by an unknown artist
(c. 1410–1430). In the Annunciation,
Mary receives a visit
from the angel Gabriel and is
"overshadowed" by the Holy Spirit.

wisdom, that God is the kind of Lord who does nothing but exalt those of low degree and put down the mighty from their thrones, in short, break what is whole and make whole what is broken.

Just as God in the beginning of creation made the world out of nothing, which is why he is called the Creator and the Almighty, so his manner of working continues unchanged. Even now and to the end of the world, all his works are such that out of that which is nothing, worthless, despised, wretched, and dead, he makes that which is something, precious, honorable, blessed, and living. On the other hand, whatever is something, precious, honorable, blessed, and living, he makes to be nothing, worthless, despised, wretched, and dying. No creature can create in this way, able to make something out of nothing.[22] Therefore his eyes look only into the depths, not to the heights; as it is said in Dan. 3[:55][e]: "You sit above the cherubim and look into the depths or abyss."[f] Likewise Ps. 138[:6]: "Though the LORD is the highest, he regards the lowly; but the haughty he perceives from far away," and Ps. 113[:5-6]: "Who is like the LORD, our God, who is seated on high, who looks far down upon the lowly in the heavens and the earth?"[g] For since he is the Most High, and there is nothing above him, he cannot look above him; nor yet to either side, for there is none like him. He must, therefore, look within himself and beneath him; and the farther one is beneath him, the better he sees him.

The eyes of the world and of people, on the contrary, look only above them and are lifted up with pride, as it is said in Prov. 30[:13]: "There is a people whose eyes are lofty, and their eyebrows lifted up on high."[h] This we experience every day. Everyone strives after that which is above him, after honor, power, wealth, knowledge, a life of ease, and whatever is lofty and great. And where such people are, there are many hangers-on—everyone gathers round them, gladly yields them service, and would be at

22. In this passage, Luther combines the traditional belief in the creation *ex nihilo* (God created the world out of nothing, not out of some preexisting matter) with his own emphasis on the hidden God—God tends to work in ways that we least expect, and in ways quite opposite to the values and expectations of "the world," that is, human beings who live in sin, who think that they are in charge, and who do not seek God. In this commentary, the main division is between those who seek God (i.e., the humble or lowly) and those who live fully in the world (i.e., the proud and powerful).

---

e   In Vulgate edition.

f   This portion of Daniel (3:24-90) is in the Septuagint, but not in the Masoretic (Hebrew) text, and thus it does not appear in the NRSV.

g   The Vulgate (Ps. 112:6) has *humilia respicit*—he regards "the lowly" or "low things." The NRSV does not have that phrase, but only reads "who looks far down on the heavens and the earth."

h   Luther's text reads *augprau*, or "eyebrows," while the NRSV reads "eyelids"; likewise the Vulgate reading is *palpabrae*, or "eyelids." It may have been an error on Luther's part, but is still logical in the context.

their side and share in their loftiness. Therefore it is not without reason that the Scriptures describe so few kings and rulers who were godly men. On the other hand, no one is willing to look into the depths, where there is poverty, disgrace, squalor, misery, and anguish. From these all turn away their eyes. Where there are such people, everyone takes to his heels, forsakes and shuns and leaves them to themselves; no one dreams of helping them or of making something out of them. And so they must remain in the depths and in their low and despised condition. There is among human beings no creator who would make something out of nothing, although that is what St. Paul teaches in Rom. 12[:16] when he says, "Dear brethren, set not your mind on high things, but go along with the lowly."

Therefore to God alone belongs that sort of seeing that looks into the depths with its need and misery, and is near to all who are in the depths; as Peter says [1 Pet. 5:5]: "God opposes the proud but gives grace to the humble." And this is the source of the love and praise of God. For no one can praise God without first loving him. No one can love him unless he makes himself known to us in the most lovable and intimate fashion. And he can make himself known only through those works of his which he reveals in us, and which we feel and experience within ourselves. But where there is this experience, namely, that he is a God who looks into the depths and helps only the poor, despised, afflicted, miserable, forsaken, and those who are nothing, there a hearty love for him is born. The heart overflows with gladness and goes leaping and dancing for the great pleasure it has found in God. And there the Holy Spirit is present and has taught us in a moment such exceeding great knowledge and gladness through this experience.[23]

For this reason God has also imposed death on us all and laid the cross of Christ together with countless sufferings and afflictions on his beloved children and Christians. In fact, sometimes he even lets us fall into sin, in order that he may look into the depths even more, bring help to many, perform manifold works, show himself a true creator, and thereby make himself known and worthy of love and praise. Alas, the world with its proud eyes constantly thwarts him in this, hinders his seeing, working, and helping, and our knowledge, love, and praise of him, depriving him of all his glory and itself of its pleasure, joy, and salvation. He also cast his only and well-beloved Son Christ into

23. In Luther's comments on the centrality of experience, God's unexpected actions and works in our lives when we are poor and suffering, and our need to give up our own will and "presumption" in order to live in God's regard, we can see the influence of John Tauler, the German Dominican mystic and preacher whose sermons Luther read and commented upon in 1516.

the depths of all woe and showed in him most plainly to what end his seeing, work, help, method, counsel, and will are directed. Therefore, having most fully experienced all these things, Christ remains through all eternity in the knowledge, love, and praise of God; as it is said in Ps. 21[:6]: "You make him glad with the joy of your presence," namely, in that he sees you and knows you. Thus Psalm 44 also says that all the saints will do nothing in heaven but praise God, because he looked upon them when they were in the depths and there made himself known, beloved, and praiseworthy to them.[i]

The tender mother of Christ does the same here and teaches us, with her words and by the example of her experience, how to know, love, and praise God. For since she boasts, with heart leaping for joy and praising God, that he regarded her despite her low estate and nothingness, we must believe that she came of poor, despised, and lowly parents.[24] Let us make it very plain for the sake of the simple. Doubtless there were in Jerusalem daughters of the chief priests and counselors who were rich, beautiful, young, educated, and held in high renown by all the people, even as it is today with the daughters of kings, princes, and men of wealth. The same was also true in many other cities. Even in her own town of Nazareth she was not the daughter of one of the chief rulers, but a poor and plain citizen's daughter, whom none looked up to or esteemed. To her neighbors and their daughters she was but a simple maiden, tending the cattle and doing the housework, and doubtless esteemed no more than any poor maidservant today, who does as she is told around the house.

For thus Isaiah announced [Isa. 11:1-2]: "There shall come forth a rod out of the stem of Jesse, and a flower shall rise up out of his root, and the Holy Spirit shall rest upon him." The stem

Saints Anna and Joachim. Anna and Joachim were the names traditionally given to Mary's parents, who were considered to be well-to-do. St. Anna (or Anne) became very popular in the late-medieval period. She was the saint to whom Luther cried out during the lightning storm that he would become a monk.

24. The *Protevangelium of James*, a very popular apocryphal Gospel written sometime in the second century, suggests that Mary's parents (named Anne and Joachim) were quite wealthy.

---

i LW 21:301 suggests that Luther is here referring to Ps. 44:7-8, but it is not a clear reference. He may have been thinking of vv. 1-8, in which the people praise God for the blessings given to their ancestors in establishing their land. Verse 3 says that it was through the "light" of God's "countenance" and through God's arm that they were given the victory.

25. The doctrine of the perpetual virginity of Mary—that she remained a virgin before, during, and after the birth of Jesus—has been a common belief in the church since at least the fourth century, when Epiphanius of Salamis (c. 310/315–403) used the term *aeiparthenos* ("ever-virgin") for Mary. Here Luther refers to the belief that Jesus' birth (miraculously) did not break Mary's hymen.

26. See the image on p. 163 of this volume, which depicts a tree growing from the side of Jesse. The tree represents Jesse's progeny. The madonna and child appear in the center of the tree. This image appeared in Luther's *Lustgarten der Seelen* (1548), with woodcuts by the workshop of Lucas Cranach the Elder (1472–1553).

27. The Gospel of Luke notes that Annas and Caiaphas were high priests in Jerusalem when "the word of God came to John son of Zechariah in the wilderness" (3:2). The high priest was the chief religious official in Judaism up until the destruction of the Second Temple in 70 CE.

28. Luther refers here to another concept popular in mysticism: spiritual ecstasy in union with God. The notion of divine sweetness is also common in medieval mysticism, largely drawn from references in the Psalms to the sweetness of God's words, and to the Song of Songs.

29. In his *Lectures on Romans* (1515–1516), Luther notes, again influenced by Tauler, that God does the opposite of what we expect to prepare us to receive his gifts; it is all God's work, and we must suffer passively.

and root is the family of Jesse or David, in particular the Virgin Mary; the rod and flower is Christ. Now, as unlikely, indeed incredible, a thing it is that a fair branch and flower should spring from a dry and withered stem and root, just so unlikely was it that Mary, a virgin, should become the mother of such a child. For I take it that she is called a stem and root not only because she became a mother in a miraculous manner without violation of her virginity[25]—just as it is miraculous to make a branch grow out of a dead tree stump—but also for the following reason. In the days of David and Solomon the royal stem and line of David had been green and flourishing, fortunate in its great glory, might, and riches, and famous in the eyes of the world. But in the latter days, when Christ was to come, the priests had usurped this honor and were the sole rulers, while the royal line of David had become so impoverished and despised that it was like a dead stump, so that there was no hope or likelihood that a king descended from it would ever attain to any great glory. But when all seemed most unlikely—comes Christ, and is born of the despised stump, of the poor and lowly girl![26] The rod and flower spring from her whom the daughter of Lord Annas or Caiaphas[27] would not have deigned to have for her humblest lady's maid. Thus God's work and his eyes are in the depths, but human sight and work are only in the height.

So this is the occasion of Mary's song of praise, which we shall now consider in detail.

46. *My soul magnifies God, the Lord.*

These words express the strong ardor and exuberant joy with which all her heart and life are inwardly exalted in the Spirit. Therefore she does not say, "I exalt the Lord," but, "My soul exalts him." It is as if she said: "My life and all my senses soar in the love and praise of God and in lofty pleasures, so that I can no longer control myself; I am exalted, more than I exalt myself, to praise the Lord." This is the experience of all those who are saturated with the divine sweetness and Spirit: they cannot find words to utter what they feel.[28] For to praise the Lord with gladness is not a human work; it is rather a joyful suffering and the work of God alone.[j,29] It cannot be taught in words but must be learned in

---

j   For the *Lectures on Romans*, see WA 56, esp. 375–77 (LW 25:364–67).

one's own experience. Even as David says in Ps. 34[:8]: "Oh, taste and see that the LORD is sweet; blessed is the one who trusts in him."[k] He puts tasting before seeing, because this sweetness cannot be known unless one has experienced and felt it for herself; and no one can attain to such experience unless he trusts in God with his whole heart when he is in the depths and in sore straits. Therefore David makes haste to add, "Blessed is the one who trusts in God." Such a person will experience the work of God within herself and will thus attain to his sensible sweetness and through it to all knowledge and understanding.

Let us take up the words in their order. The first is "my soul." Scripture divides a human being into three parts, as St. Paul says in 1 Thess. 5[:23]: "May the God of peace himself sanctify you entirely; and may your spirit and soul and body be kept sound and blameless at the coming of our Lord Jesus Christ."[30] There is yet another division of each of these three and the whole of the human being in another way into two parts, which are called "spirit" and "flesh."[31] This is a division, not of the nature of a person but of his qualities. Human nature consists of the three parts—spirit, soul, and body, and all of these may be good or evil, that is, they may be spirit or flesh. But we are not now dealing with this division. The first part, the spirit, is the highest, deepest, and noblest part of a person. By it he is enabled to grasp things that are incomprehensible, invisible, and eternal. It is, in brief, the dwelling place of faith and the word of God. David speaks of it in Ps. 51[:10]: "LORD, create in my inward parts a right spirit," that is, a straight and upright faith. But of the unbelieving he says in Ps. 78[:37]: "Their heart was not right with God, nor was their spirit faithful to God."

The second part, the soul, is this same spirit, so far as its nature is concerned, but viewed as performing a different function, namely, giving life to the body and working through the body. In the Scriptures it is frequently taken for the "life," for the spirit may live without the body, but the body has no life apart from the spirit. We see that even in sleep the soul lives and works without ceasing. It is its nature to comprehend not incomprehensible things but such things as the reason can know

30. This presents the tripartite or trichotomist view of human nature, common in medieval Scholastic theology. Other verses that support this division are Gen. 2:7 and Heb. 4:12. The bipartite view would argue that "soul" and "spirit" are two different terms for the same element.

31. This is the division that Luther emphasized in his treatise *The Freedom of a Christian* (TAL 1:467–538).

---

k The Vulgate has *"gustate et videte quoniam suavis est Dominus,"* instead of *"bonus"* (Ps. 33:9). The NRSV has "O taste and see that the LORD is good" (Ps. 34:8).

EXODI XXVI.

Afleres ex ligno Sitim longitudine cubitorum decem, cum denti-
culis & basibus argenteis, nec non uectibus de lignis Sitim auro ob-
ductis, &c.

Bretter von förn holtz zehen ehlen lang / vnd
anderthalb ehlen breyt / mit jhren zapffen vnd sil
bern füssen. Deßgleichen fünff Rigeln von förn
holtz mit gold vberzogen / etc.

D ij

Virgil Solis (1514–1562) created this woodcut of
the tabernacle interior for a book of images from
the Old and New Testaments. It shows the various
curtains dividing the spaces as well as ritual vessels.

32. The metaphor of the temple was
also applied by others to describe the
human being. For example, Jean Gerson
(1363–1429), theologian and chancellor
of the University of Paris, used this
threefold example in his *Collectorium
super Magnificat* (tract. 7). For
Gerson, the three parts of the temple
corresponded with *mens*, *ratio*, and
anima—which can be roughly translated
as feeling, reason, and soul—three parts
of the human heart.

and understand. Indeed, reason is the light in this dwelling; and unless the spirit, which is lighted with the brighter light of faith, controls this light of reason, it can never be without error. For it is too feeble to deal with divine things. To these two parts the Scriptures ascribe many things, such as wisdom and knowledge—wisdom to the spirit, knowledge to the soul; likewise hatred, love, delight, horror, and the like.

The third part is the body with its members. Its work is only to carry out and apply that which the soul knows and the spirit believes. Let us take an illustration of this from Scripture.[1] In the tabernacle fashioned by Moses there were three separate compartments. The first was called the holy of holies: here was God's dwelling place, and in it there was no light. The second was called the holy place; here stood a candlestick with seven arms and seven lamps. The third was called the "atrium" or court; this lay under the open sky and in the full light of the sun. In this tabernacle we have a figure of the Christian person. His spirit is the holy of holies, where God dwells in the darkness of faith, where no light is; for he believes that which he neither sees nor feels nor comprehends. His soul is the holy place, with its seven lamps, that is, all manner of reason, discrimination, knowledge, and understanding of visible and bodily things. His body is the atrium, open to all, so that all people may see his works and manner of life.[32]

Now Paul prays that God, who is a God of peace, would sanctify us not in one part only, but wholly, through and through, so that spirit, soul, body, and all may be holy. We might mention many reasons why he prays in this manner, but let the following suffice. When the spirit is no longer holy, then nothing is holy. This holiness of the spirit is the scene of the sorest conflict and the source of the greatest danger. It consists in nothing else than

1   Exod. 26:33; 40:1-11.

in faith pure and simple, since the spirit has nothing to do with things comprehensible, as we have seen. But now there come false teachers and they lure the spirit out of doors; one puts forth this work, another that mode of attaining to godliness. And unless the spirit is preserved and is wise, it will come forth and follow these teachers. It will fall upon the external works and rules and imagine it can attain to godliness by means of them. And before we know it, faith is lost, and the spirit is dead in the sight of God.

Then the manifold sects and orders rise up. This one becomes a Carthusian,[33] that one a Franciscan;[34] this one seeks salvation by fasting, that one by praying; one by one work, another by another. Yet these are all self-chosen works and orders, never commanded by God, but invented by human beings. Engrossed in them, they have no eye for faith but only go on teaching people to put their trust in works, until they are so sunk in works that they squabble amongst themselves. Everyone claims to be the greatest and despises the others, as our bragging and blustering Observants do today.[35] Over against such work-saints and seemingly pious teachers Paul prays here, calling God a God of peace and unity. Such a God these divided, discordant saints cannot have or hold on to unless they give up their own things, agree together in the same spirit and faith, and learn that works breed nothing but discrimination, sin, and discord, while faith alone makes people pious, united, and peaceable. As it is said in Ps. 68[:6]: "God makes us dwell in unity in the house"[m]; and in Ps. 133[:1]: "Behold how good and pleasant it is when brothers dwell in unity."

There is no peace except where it is taught that we are made pious, righteous, and blessed not by any work or external thing but solely by faith, that is, a firm confidence in the unseen grace of God that is promised us, as I showed at greater length in the *Treatise on Good Works*.[n] But where there is no faith, there must necessarily be many works; and where these are, discord and disunity follow, and God cannot remain. Therefore St. Paul is not content with saying here simply, "your spirit, your soul," etc.; but

33. The Carthusian order, founded in 1084 by St. Bruno of Cologne (c. 1030–1101), follows its own statutes rather than the Rule of St. Benedict. Its structure is both eremitical (its members are hermits who live in individual cells and spend most of their time alone and in silence) and cenobitical (the members also pray in community several times a day, and the individual cells are part of a larger shared building).

34. The Order of Friars Minor, usually called simply "Franciscans," is one of the orders founded by St. Francis of Assisi (c. 1181–1226). It is a mendicant or "begging" order for men, and they follow the Rule of St. Francis.

35. "Observant" is a general term applied to branches of a number of religious orders beginning in the fifteenth century, a period of reform within religious orders. Observants, as opposed to "conventuals," were stricter in following the founding rules and principles of an order, while conventuals followed the rules that had developed and become more lax over time. These divisions, naturally, caused great disunity within existing orders such as the Dominicans, Augustinians, and Franciscans. The Franciscan order officially split in 1517 into two branches, the Observants and the Conventuals. Luther himself joined a friary of Observant Augustinians.

---

m   The Vulgate (Ps. 67:7) has "*Deus inhabitare facit unius moris in domo*," that is, "God makes those of one way/manner to dwell in a house," while the NRSV reads, "God gives the desolate a home to live in."

n   This treatise, published in 1520, appears in WA 6:196–276, and WA 9:226–301, as well as in LW 44:15–114; and TAL 1:257–367.

he says, "your whole spirit," for on this all depends. He employs a fine Greek expression, ὁλόκληρον ὑμῶν τὸ πνεῦμα—"your spirit that possesses the whole inheritance." It is as if he said: "Let no doctrine of works lead you astray. The believing spirit alone possesses all things. Everything depends on the faith of the spirit. And this same 'spirit that possesses the whole inheritance' I pray God to preserve in you against the false doctrines which would make works the basis of our trust in God and which are but false beliefs, because they do not base such trust upon God's grace alone." When this spirit that possesses the whole inheritance is preserved, both soul and body are able to remain without error and evil works. On the other hand, when the spirit is without faith, the soul together with the whole life cannot but fall into wickedness and error, however good an intention and opinion it may profess, and find in that its own devotion and satisfaction. As a consequence of this error and false opinion of the soul, all the works of the body also become evil and damnable, even though a man killed himself with fasting and performed the works of all the saints. In order, therefore, that our works and our life may not be in vain, but that we may become truly holy, it is necessary that God preserve, first, our spirit, and then our soul and body, not only from overt sins but much more from false and apparent good works.

Let this suffice in explanation of these two words, soul and spirit; they occur very frequently in the Scriptures. We come to the "magnifies," which means to make great, to exalt, to esteem one highly, as having the power, the knowledge, and the desire to perform many great and good things, such as those that follow in this canticle. Just as a book title indicates the contents of the book, so this word "magnifies" is used by Mary to indicate what her hymn of praise is to be about, namely, the great works and deeds of God, to strengthen our faith, to comfort all those of low degree, and to terrify all the mighty ones of earth. We are to let the hymn serve this threefold purpose, for she sang it not for herself alone but for us all, that we might sing it after her. Now, these great works of God will neither terrify nor comfort anyone unless she believes that God has not only the power and the knowledge but also the willingness and hearty desire to do such great things. In fact, it is not even enough to believe that God is willing to do them for others but not for you. This would be to put yourself beyond the pale of these works of God, as is done by those who, because of their strength, do not fear him, and by those of little faith who, because of their tribulations, fall into despair.[36]

That sort of faith is nothing and is dead, like an idea learned from a fairy tale. You must rather, without any wavering or doubt, realize his will toward you and firmly believe that he will do great things also to you, and is willing to do so. Such a faith has life and being; it pervades and changes the whole person; it constrains you to fear if you are mighty, and to take comfort if you are of low degree. And the mightier you are, the more you must fear; the lowlier you are, the more you can take comfort, which no other kind of faith is able to effect. How will it be with you in the hour of death? There you must believe that he has not only the power and the knowledge but also the desire to help you. For it requires indeed an unspeakably great work to deliver you from eternal death, to save you and make you God's heir. To this faith all things are possible, as Christ says [Mark 9:23]; it alone abides; it also comes to experience the works of God and thus attains to the love of God and thence to songs and praise of God, so that a person esteems him highly and truly magnifies him.

For God is not magnified by us so far as his nature is concerned—he is unchangeable[37]—but he is magnified in our knowledge and experience when we greatly esteem him and highly regard him, especially as to his grace and goodness. Therefore the holy mother does not say: "My voice or my mouth, my hand or my thoughts, my reason or my will, magnifies the Lord." For there are many who praise God with a loud voice, preach about him with high-sounding words, speak much of him, dispute and write about him, and paint his image, whose thoughts dwell often upon him and who reach out after him and speculate about him with their reason. There are also many who exalt him with false devotion and a false will. But Mary says, "My soul magnifies him"—that is, my whole life and being, mind and strength, esteem him highly. She is caught up, as it were, into him and feels herself lifted up into his good and gracious will,[38] as the following verse shows. It is the same when anyone does something particularly good for us. Our whole life seems to incline toward that person, and we say: "Ah, I esteem him highly"; that is to say, "My soul magnifies him." How much more will such a lively inclination be awakened in us when we experience the favor of God,

36. Despair (that is, the voluntary act of giving up all hope of salvation) has traditionally been considered a mortal sin, because it denies either that one's sins can be forgiven or that God has the will or power to forgive them. Luther's term, *vorzagen* (*verzagen*), means "to despair" or "give up hope," and he suggests that the despairing person is just as sinful for doubting God's will to forgive as the person who does not care about God at all.

37. The principle of God's unchangeability, or immutability, can be found in a number of Bible passages, such as Mal. 3:6, where God affirms that "I the Lord do not change," and James 1:17, which calls God the "Father of lights, with whom there is no variation or shadow due to change." Luther does not mean, however, that we have no relationship with God, for God hears and responds to us, but, rather, that our understanding of God changes, increases, and deepens when we come to praise and magnify him. God does not become more worthy, but in understanding him better we are moved to praise him more and more.

38. The terms "caught up" and "lifted up" are common terms from mystical theology, but Mary is not in this "ecstasy" unified with God's essence or being. Rather, Luther suggests that she is lifted up into his will.

which is exceedingly great in his works. All words and thoughts fail us, and our whole life and soul must be set in motion, as though all that lived within us wanted to break forth into praise and singing.[39] But here we find two kinds of false spirits that cannot sing the Magnificat properly. First, there are those who will not praise him unless he benefits them; as David says: "He will praise you when you benefit him."[o] These seem indeed to be greatly praising God, but because they are unwilling to suffer oppression and to be in the depths, they can never experience the proper works of God, and therefore can never truly love or praise him.[40] The whole world nowadays is filled with praise and service to God, with singing and preaching, with organs and pipes, and the Magnificat is magnificently sung; but it is regrettable that this precious song should be rendered by us so utterly without strength and flavor. For we sing only when everything is going well with us; as soon as things go badly, we stop our singing and no longer esteem God highly, but suppose that he can or will do nothing for us. Then the Magnificat also is left alone.

The other sort are more dangerous still. They err on the opposite side. They magnify themselves by reason of the good gifts of God and do not ascribe them to his goodness alone. They themselves desire to bear a part in them; they want to be honored and set above others on account of them. When they behold the good things that God has done for them, they fall upon them and appropriate them as their own; they regard themselves as better than others who have no such things. This is really a smooth and slippery position. The good gifts of God will naturally produce proud and self-complacent hearts.[41] Therefore we must here give heed to Mary's last word, which is "God." She does not say, "My soul magnifies itself" or "exalts me." She does not desire herself to be esteemed; she magnifies God alone and gives all glory to him. She leaves herself out and ascribes everything to God alone, from whom she received it. For although she experienced such an exceeding great work of God within herself, yet she was always disposed not to exalt herself above the humblest person on earth. Had she done so, she would have fallen with Lucifer into the abyss of hell.[p]

39. The Psalms frequently indicate that praise of God can and should be sung, even by creatures otherwise unable to speak. For example, Ps. 96:11-13: "Let the sea roar, and all that fills it; let the field exult, and everything in it! Then shall all the trees of the forest sing for joy before the Lord, for he comes. . . ." Luther implies here that the spirit can sing, even when it cannot find the words to speak.

40. In theses 19-24 of the *Heidelberg Disputation* (1518), Luther notes that God has a secret, "foreign" or "alien" work (which breaks us down through the cross and suffering), which then opens the way for his "proper" work of salvation. See LW 31:52-55; WA 1:353-74; TAL 1:83-84.

41. This is the problem that Luther notes in his dedication is a particular issue for rulers, and Mary's rejection of such pride and presumption is why her song (and her example) is so important and helpful as a "mirror" for princes.

o   The Vulgate (Ps. 48:19) has "*confitebitur tibi cum benefeceris ei*," that is, "he will praise you when you benefit him." The NRSV (Ps. 49:18) has "you are praised when you do well for yourself."

p   Cf. Isa. 14:12.

She had no thought but this: if any other young woman had received such good things from God, she would be just as glad and would not grudge them to her; indeed, she regarded herself alone as unworthy of such honor and all others as worthy of it. She would have been well content had God withdrawn these blessings from her and bestowed them upon another before her very eyes. So little did she lay claim to anything, but left all of God's gifts freely in his hands, being herself no more than a cheerful shelter and willing hostess to so great a guest.[42] Therefore she also kept all these things forever. That is to magnify God alone, to count him only as great and lay claim to nothing for ourselves. We see here how strong an incentive she had to fall into sin, so that it is no less a miracle that she refrained from pride and arrogance than that she received the gifts she did. Don't you think that she had a wonderful heart? She finds herself the Mother of God, exalted above all mortals, and still remains so simple and so resigned[q] that she does not think of any poor serving maid as beneath her. Oh, we poor mortals! If we come into a little wealth or might or honor, or even if we are a little prettier than others, we cannot abide being made equal to anyone beneath us, but are puffed up beyond all measure. What would we do if we possessed such great and lofty blessings?

Therefore God lets us remain poor and wretched, because we cannot leave his tender gifts undefiled or keep an even mind, but let our spirits rise or fall according to how he gives or takes away his gifts. But Mary's heart remains strong and the same at all times; she lets God work in her according to his will and draws from it all only a good comfort, joy, and trust in God. Thus we should do also; that would be to sing a right Magnificat.

47. And my spirit rejoices in God, my Savior.

We have seen what is meant by "spirit"; it is that which lays hold by faith onto incomprehensible things. Mary, therefore, calls God her Savior, or her salvation, even though she neither saw nor felt that this was so, but trusted in sure confidence that he was her Savior and her salvation. This faith came to her through the

42. Up until the eighteenth century, the common view of how an embryo came to be formed in the mother's womb was that of "preformation"—that is, the embryo was already contained in tiny form within the father's semen, and simply grew larger in its development. The fact that Luther suggests here that Mary was a "shelter" for or "hostess" to her "guest," Jesus, is not purposefully a diminution of her role as mother. It was, in fact, what people presumed about all mothers.

---

q   Luther here uses the term *gelassen*, which can be variously translated as "resigned," "yielding," "tranquil," even "detached." *Gelassenheit* is a primary concept for medieval mysticism, and was thought to be necessary for the desired union with God.

work God had done within her. And, truly, she sets things in their proper order when she calls God her Lord before calling him her Savior, and when she calls him her Savior before recounting his works. Thereby she teaches us to love and praise God for himself alone, and in the right order, and not selfishly to seek anything at his hands. This is done when one praises God because he is good, regards only his bare goodness, and finds one's joy and pleasure in that alone. That is a lofty, pure, and tender way of loving and praising God and well becomes the high and tender spirit of this virgin.

But the impure and perverted lovers, who are nothing else than parasites and who seek their own advantage in God, neither love nor praise his bare goodness, but have an eye to themselves and consider only how good God is to them, that is, how deeply he makes them feel his goodness and how many good things he does to them. They esteem him highly, are filled with joy and sing his praises, so long as this feeling continues. But just as soon as he hides his face and withdraws the rays of his goodness, leaving them bare and in misery, their love and praise are likewise at an end. They are unable to love and praise the bare, unfelt goodness that is hidden in God. By this they prove that their spirit did not rejoice in God, their Savior, and that they had no true love and praise for his bare goodness. They delighted in their salvation much more than in their Savior, in the gift more than in the Giver, in the creature rather than in the Creator. For they are not able to preserve an even mind in plenty and in want, in wealth and in poverty; as St. Paul says [Phil. 4:12]: "I know how to have plenty and how to have little."

Here apply the words in Ps. 49[:18]: "They will praise you as long as you do well for them." That is to say: "They love themselves and not you; as long as they have good and pleasant things from you, they think nothing of you." As Christ also said to those who sought him [John 6:26]: "Truly, I tell you, you seek me, not because you saw signs, but because you ate your fill [of the loaves]."

Such impure and false spirits defile all of God's gifts and prevent his giving them many gifts, especially the gift of salvation. The following is a good illustration of this: Once a certain godly woman saw in a vision three virgins seated near an altar. During the Mass a beautiful boy leaped from the altar, and approaching the first virgin in a most friendly manner, lavished caresses upon her and smiled lovingly in her face. Then he approached the second virgin, but was not so friendly with her; he did not give her a caress, though he did lift her veil and give her a pleasant smile. But for the third virgin he had not a friendly sign, struck her in the face and tore her hair, thrust her from him and dealt most ungallantly with her. Then he ran swiftly back upon the altar and disappeared.[43]

Afterwards the vision was interpreted for the woman as follows: The first of the three virgins was a figure of the impure and self-seeking spirits, on whom God must lavish many good things and whose will he must do rather than they his; they are unwilling to suffer want but must always find joy and comfort in God and are not content with his goodness. The second virgin was a figure of the spirits that make a beginning of serving God and are willing to do without some things, but not without all or to be free from all self-seeking and enjoyment. God must now and then smile upon them and let them feel his good things, in order that they may learn from this to love and praise his bare goodness. But the third virgin, that poor Cinderella[44]—for her there is nothing but want and misery; she seeks to enjoy nothing and is content to know that God is good, even though she should never once experience it, although that is impossible. She keeps an even mind in both situations and she loves and praises God's goodness just as much when she does not feel it as when she does.[45] She neither falls upon the good things when they are given nor falls away when they are removed. That is the true bride of Christ, who says to him: "I do not seek what is yours, but want to have you yourself; you are no dearer to me when things go well with me, and no less dear when things go badly."

Such spirits fulfill what is written [Isa. 30:21]: "You shall not stray from the even and right way of God, neither to the left side nor to the right." That is to say, they are to love and praise God evenly and rightly and not seek their own advantage or enjoyment. David had such a spirit, for when he was driven from Jerusalem by his son Absalom and was likely to be cast out forever and to lose his kingdom and the favor of God, he said [2 Sam. 15:25-26]: "Go on in. If I find favor in the eyes of the LORD, he will bring me back; but if he says, 'I have no pleasure in you,' then I am ready." Oh, how pure a spirit that was, not to stop loving, praising, and following the goodness of God even in the direst distress![46] Such a spirit is manifested here by Mary,

43. *Exempla*, or "anecdotes," such as this used to illustrate a point, drawn from fables, folktales, legends, or real history, were especially popular in medieval sermons. Jacques de Vitry, a French theologian and bishop (d. 1240), authored one of the most popular collections of these *exempla* around 1200.

44. *Aschenprödel*—the poor stepdaughter forced to work hard and sit and sleep in the ashes of the kitchen hearth— was a popular character in medieval German tales.

45. This resignation and contentment in God's will, whether one experiences good or evil, was the ideal of many medieval mystics, such as Marguerite Porete (c. 1250–1310) and Jan van Ruysbroek (c. 1293–1381), whose work was very influential upon Tauler.

46. The example of David clearly shows that even a king (or a prince, like John Frederick) can have a lowly and resigned attitude and heart. Wealth and power do not necessarily mean one will be proud and presumptuous.

the Mother of God. Standing in the midst of such exceedingly great good things, she does not fall upon them or seek her own enjoyment in them, but keeps her spirit pure in loving and praising the bare goodness of God, ready and willing to have God withdraw them from her and leave her spirit poor and naked and needy.

Now, it is much more difficult to practice moderation in the midst of riches, honor, and power than amid poverty, dishonor, and weakness, since the former are mighty incentives to evildoing. So the wondrous pure spirit of Mary is worthy of even greater praise, because, having such overwhelming honors heaped upon her, she does not let them tempt her, but acts as though she did not see it, remains "even and right in the way," clings only to God's goodness, which she neither sees nor feels, overlooks the good things she does feel, and neither takes pleasure nor seeks her own enjoyment in it. Thus she can truly sing, "My spirit rejoices in God, my Savior." It is indeed a spirit that exults only in faith and rejoices not in the good things of God that she felt, but only in God, whom she did not feel and who is her salvation, known by her in faith alone.[47] Such are the truly lowly, naked, hungry, and God-fearing spirits, as we shall see below.

From all this we may know and judge how full the world is nowadays of false preachers and false saints, who preach so much to the people about good works.[48] There are indeed a few who teach them how to do good works, but the greater part preach human doctrines and works that they themselves have devised and set up. Even the best of them, unfortunately, are so far from this "even and straight road" that they constantly drive the people to the right side by teaching good works and a godly life, not for the sake of the bare goodness of God, but for the sake of one's own enjoyment. For if there were no heaven or hell and if they could not enjoy the good gifts of God, they would let his good things go unloved and unpraised. These people are mere parasites and hirelings; slaves, not children; strangers, not heirs.[49] They turn themselves into idols, whom God is supposed to love and praise and for whom he is to do the very things they ought to do for him. They have no spirit, nor is God their Savior. His good gifts are their savior, and with them God must serve them as their lackey. They are the children of Israel, who were not content in the desert with eating bread from heaven, but wanted meat, onions, and garlic, too [Num. 11:4-6].

47. Here, as elsewhere in the commentary, Luther presents a spiritual experience of God through the *via negativa*, or negative way, where God is found only in total darkness, for the realm of faith is beyond all human comprehension. Negative, or *apophatic*, theology is commonly found in the medieval mystics. For example, in his sermons, Tauler referred to the divinity that is beyond all names and beyond all human capacity for thinking and speaking.

48. Luther echoes here scriptural warnings against false prophets and teachers, e.g., Matt. 24:24: "For false messiahs and false prophets will appear and produce great signs and omens, to lead astray, if possible, even the elect."

49. Jesus notes that the hired hand will not face the wolf to protect the sheep—only the (good) shepherd who owns the sheep and loves them will protect them (John 10:12-15). The people to whom Luther refers are only "hirelings"—they do not love God in himself (his "bare" goodness), but only insofar as it benefits them.

Alas, all the world, all the monasteries, and all the churches are now filled with such people. They all walk in their false, perverted, and wrong spirit, and urge and drive others to do the same. They exalt good works to such a height that they imagine they can merit heaven through them. But the bare goodness of God is what ought rather to be preached and known above all else, and we ought to learn that, just as God saves us out of pure goodness, without any merit of works, so we in our turn should do the works without reward or self-seeking, for the sake of the bare goodness of God.[50] We should desire nothing in them but his good pleasure, and not be anxious about a reward. That will come of itself, without our seeking. For although it is impossible that the reward should not follow, if we do well in a pure and right spirit, without thought of reward or enjoyment, nevertheless God will not have such a self-seeking and impure spirit, nor will it ever obtain a reward. A child serves her father willingly and without reward, as his heir, solely for the father's sake. But a child who serves her father merely for the sake of the inheritance would indeed be a wicked child and deserve to be cast off by her father.

48. For he has regarded the nothingness[r] of his maid. Therefore all generations will call me blessed.

The word *humilitas* has been translated "humility"[s] by some, as though the Virgin Mary referred to her humility and boasted of it; hence certain prelates also call themselves *humiles*.[51] But that is very far from the truth, for no one can boast of any good thing in the sight of God without sin and perdition. In his sight we ought to boast only of his pure grace and goodness, which he bestows upon us unworthy ones; so that not our love and praise

50. Luther argued that he placed good works on their proper footing—that is, a work cannot truly be good if it is done with thought of reward (and in any case heaven is not gained through works or merit), but it can in fact only be good if it flows out of faith and love of God.

51. In other words, Mary would be praising herself rather than God, as if God had chosen her because she was worthy. Likewise Luther saw the use of the word *humble* for wealthy and noble prelates (or bishops) as sheer hypocrisy, for they were simply praising their own virtue. The motto *"exaltavit humiles"* is still used on some bishops' coats of arms.

---

r   Luther here translates the term *humilitas* as *nichtickeyt*, which can be translated as "nothingness" or "emptiness." In the translation of the whole passage that he provides at the beginning of the commentary, he writes instead, *"Denn er hat mich seine geringe magd angesehen,"* or "For he has regarded me, his lowly/small maid." In his translation of the New Testament published in September 1520, he translates the term as *nydrickeyt*, or "lowliness/low estate." In all of these choices he was concerned to present the term *humilitas/tapeinōsis* as low and despised social status (which he felt more accurate to the Greek original), rather than as humility, the virtue.

s   *Demut*, in German.

but his alone may dwell in us and may preserve us. Thus Solomon teaches us in Prov. 25[:6-7]: "Do not put yourself forward in the king's presence or stand [that is, pretend to be something] in the place of the great; for it is better to be told, 'Come up here,' than to be put lower in the presence of the prince." How should such pride and vainglory be attributed to this pure and righteous virgin, as though she boasted of her humility in the presence of God? For humility is the highest of all the virtues, and no one could boast of possessing it except the very proudest person. It is God alone who knows humility, who alone judges it and brings it to light, so that no one knows less about humility than he who is truly humble.

In scriptural usage, "to humble" [*humiliare*] means "to bring down," or "to make into nothing." Hence, in the Scriptures, Christians are frequently called "*pauperes, afflicti, humiliate,*" or poor, afflicted, despised people. Thus, in Ps. 116[:10]: "I am greatly afflicted"—that is, humbled.[t] *Humilitas*, therefore, is nothing else than a disregarded, despised, and lowly way of being or estate, such as that of people who are poor, sick, hungry, thirsty, in prison, suffering, and dying. Such was Job in his afflictions, David when he was thrust out of his kingdom, and Christ, as well as all Christians, in their distresses. Those are the depths of which we said above that God's eyes only look into them, but human eyes look only to the heights, namely, to that way of life or estate that is splendid, glorious, and magnificent. Therefore in the Scriptures Jerusalem is called a city that God's eyes look upon[u]—that is to say, Christendom lies in the depths and is despised by the world; therefore God regards her, and his eyes are always fixed upon her, as he says in Ps. 32[:8]: "I will fix my eyes upon you."

Job's Affliction, a metal engraving by Hans Holbein the Younger (1497/98–1543). Job sits among the ashes with a skin disease, and his wife and friends gather to comfort him. Meanwhile, his possessions are destroyed (background). Despite his suffering and afflictions, Job remained faithful to God's will.

t   *Genidrigt*, or "brought low."
u   Cf. Zech. 12:4.

St. Paul also says in 1 Cor. 1[:27-28]: "God chose what is foolish in the world to shame the worldly wise. God chose what is weak and good for nothing in the world to shame the strong and powerful. God chose what is nothing for the world, that he might make into nothing all things seen as important in the world." In this way he turns the world with all its wisdom and power into foolishness and gives us another wisdom and power. Since, then, it is his manner to regard things that are in the depths and disregarded, I have rendered the word *humilitas* with "nothingness" or "low estate." This, therefore, is what Mary means: "God has regarded me, a poor, despised, and lowly maiden, though he might have found a rich, renowned, noble, and mighty queen, the daughter of princes and great lords. He might have found the daughter of Annas or of Caiaphas, who held the highest position in the land. But he let his pure and gracious eyes light on me and used so poor and despised a maiden, in order that no one might boast of himself before him, as though he were worthy of this, and that I must acknowledge it all to be pure grace and goodness and not at all my merit or worthiness."

Now, we described above at length how lowly was the estate of this tender virgin and how unexpectedly this honor came to her, that God should regard her in such abundant grace. Hence she does not glory in her worthiness nor yet in her unworthiness, but solely in the divine regard, which is so exceedingly good and gracious that he deigned to look upon such a lowly maiden, and to look upon her in so glorious and honorable a fashion. They, therefore, do her an injustice who hold that she gloried, not indeed in her virginity, but in her humility. She gloried neither in the one nor in the other, but only in the gracious regard of God. Hence the stress lies not on the word "low estate [*humilitatem*]," but on the word "regarded [*respexit*]." For not her nothingness but God's regard is to be praised. When a prince takes a poor beggar by the hand, it is not the beggar's lowliness that should be commended but the prince's grace and goodness.

In order to dispel that false opinion and to distinguish true from false humility,[v] we shall have to digress a little and treat the subject of humility, upon which many are quite mistaken. What we call *demut* in German is what St. Paul calls in Greek ταπεινοφροσύνη, and in Latin, *affectus vilitatis* or *sensus humilium*

---

v *Demut*, which is the virtue of humility.

rerum—that is, a spirit and inclination toward lowly and despised things.ʷ Now, we find many here who carry water to the well; that is to say, they affect humble clothing, faces, gestures, status, and words, but with the intention of being regarded by the mighty and rich, by scholars and saints, even by God himself, as people who take pleasure in lowly things. If they knew that no one regarded what they did, they would soon give up. That is an artificial humility. For their villainous eye is fixed only on the reward and result of their humility and not on lowly things apart from a reward. Hence when the reward and result no longer allure, their humility stops. Such people cannot be called *affectos vilitate*, having their heart and will set on things of low degree; for they have only their thoughts, lips, hands, clothes, and outward conduct in them, while their heart looks above to great and lofty things, to which it hopes to attain by that semblance of humility. Yet these people consider themselves to be humble, holy people.[52]

But the truly humble look not to the result of humility but with simple hearts regard things of low degree, and gladly associate with them. It never once enters their minds that they are humble. Here the water flows from the well; here it follows naturally and as a matter of course, that they will cultivate humble conduct, humble words, conditions, faces, and clothing, and shun as far as possible great and lofty things. Thus David says in Ps. 131[:1]: "O Lord, my heart is not lifted up, my eyes are not raised too high." And Job 22[:29] says: "Whoever humbles himself will be lifted up, and he who bows down his eyes will be saved."ˣ Hence honors always come unexpectedly upon them, and their exaltation is a surprise to them; for they have been simply content with their lowly station and never aspired to the heights. But the falsely humble wonder why their glory and honor are so long in coming; their secret false pride is not content with their low estate but aspires in secret ever higher and higher.

True humility, therefore, never knows that it is humble, as I have said; for if it knew this, it would turn proud from con-

---

52. It does not seem that Luther had a specific group of people in mind here, but he may well have been referring to some religious in the observant orders.

---

w   Cf. Acts 20:19; Eph. 4:2; Phil. 2:3; Col. 2:18, 23; 3:12.

x   The Vulgate reads, "*qui enim humiliatus fuerit erit in gloria et qui inclinaverit oculos suos ipse salvabitur*," or "For he who has been humbled shall be in glory; and he who shall bow down his eyes shall be saved." The NRSV has, "When others are humiliated, you say it is pride; for he saves the humble."

templation of so fine a virtue. But it clings with all its heart and mind and senses to lowly things, sets them continually before its eyes, and ponders them in its thoughts. And because it sets them before its eyes, it cannot see itself nor become aware of itself, much less of lofty things. And therefore, when honor and elevation come, they must take it unawares and find it immersed in thoughts of things foreign to honor and elevation. Thus Luke tells us [Luke 1:29] that Mary was perplexed by the angel's greeting and considered in her mind what sort of greeting this might be, since she had never expected anything like it. Had it come to Caiaphas's daughter, she would not have considered in her mind what sort of greeting it was, but would have accepted it immediately, thinking: "Oh, how wonderful! This is just as it should be."

The Annunciation by Johann Christian Schröder (1655–1702)

False humility, on the other hand, never knows that it is proud; for if it knew this, it would soon grow humble from contemplation of that ugly vice. But it clings with heart and mind and senses to lofty things, sets them continually before its eyes, and ponders them in its thoughts. And because it does this, it cannot see itself nor become aware of itself. Hence honors come to it not unawares or unexpectedly, but find it immersed in thoughts of them. But dishonor and humiliation take it unawares and when it is thinking of something far different.

It is useless, therefore, to teach people to be humble by teaching them to set their eyes on lowly things, nor does anyone become proud by setting his eyes on lofty things. Not the things, but our eyes' vision must be changed; for we must spend our life here in the midst of things both lowly and lofty. It is our eye that must be plucked out, as Christ says [Matt. 18:9]. Moses does not tell us in Gen. 3[:7] that Adam and Eve saw different things after the Fall, but he says their eyes were opened and they saw that they were naked, although they had been naked before and were not aware of it. Queen Esther wore a precious crown upon her head,

53. The NRSV, based on the Hebrew canon of the Old Testament, has only ten chapters in the book of Esther. However, the Greek canon, or Septuagint (the basis of Jerome's Latin translation, the Vulgate), has additional material. Jerome inserted this extra material as an additional six chapters (10:4–16:24) beyond the ten in the Hebrew text. Luther's citation of Esther 14:16 is from this material. Esther is speaking to the Lord, and says: "You know my necessity, that I abominate the sign of my pride and glory [i.e. her crown], which is upon my head in the days of my public appearance, and detest it as a menstruous rag, and wear it not in the days of my silence."

54. Augustine (354–430) notes that in our state of sin our loves are disordered. Although we were created to love God above all things, in fact we love ourselves more—hence, love of self is the root of sin. From this perspective, true humility (as Luther paints it here) really is a virtue, because its essence is to turn us away from ourselves and to focus instead upon God and his goodness (whether we receive any of his gifts or not). Luther discusses this aspect of sin in his *Commentary on Romans*, suggesting that we turn in on ourselves because of original sin (*incurvatus in se*). See LW 25 (esp. pp. 245, 291ff., 313, 345, 350).

yet she said it seemed but a filthy rag in her eyes [Esther 14:16].[53] The lofty things were not removed out of her sight, but being a mighty queen, she had them before her in great abundance, and not a lowly thing within sight; yet her eyesight was lowered, her heart and mind did not look at the lofty things, and thus God accomplished wondrous things through her. It is thus not the things but we that must be changed in heart and mind. Then we will teach ourselves how to despise and shun lofty things and how to esteem and seek after lowly things. Then humility is truly good, and steadfast in every way, and yet is never aware that it is humble. All things are done gladly, and the heart is undisturbed, however things may shift and turn, from high to low, from great to small.

Oh, how much pride lurks behind that humble garb, speech, and conduct, of which the world is so full today. People despise themselves, yet so as to be despised by no one else; they fly from honors, yet so as to be pursued by honors; they shun lofty things, but in order to be esteemed and praised, and not to have their lowly things accounted the lowest. But this young woman points to nothing here except her low estate. She was content to spend the remainder of her days in it, never seeking to be honored or exalted or ever becoming aware of her own humility. For humility is so tender and precious a thing that it cannot abide beholding its own face; that belongs to God's eyes alone, as it is said in Ps. 113[:6]: "He looks far down upon the lowly in the heavens and the earth." For if anyone could see his own humility, he could judge himself worthy of salvation and thus anticipate God's judgment; for we know that God certainly saves the humble. Therefore God must reserve to himself the right to know and look at humility, and must hide it from us by setting before our eyes things of low degree and exercising us in them so that we may forget to look at ourselves.[54] That is the purpose of the many sufferings, of death, and all manner of afflictions we have to bear on earth; by means of the trouble and pain they cause us we are to pluck out the false eye.

Thus the word *humilitas* shows us plainly that the Virgin Mary was a poor, despised, and lowly maiden, who served God in her low estate, and did not know it was so highly esteemed by him. This should comfort us and teach us that though we should willingly be humbled and despised, we ought not to despair as though God were angry at us. Rather we should set our hope on his grace, concerned only lest we be not cheerful and contented enough in our low estate and lest our false eye be opened too wide and deceive us by secretly lusting after lofty things and satisfaction with self, which is the death of humility. What profit is it to the damned that they are humbled to the lowest degree, since they are not willing and content to be where they are? Again, what harm is it to all angels that they are exalted to the highest degree, so long as they do not cling to their station with false desire? In short, this verse teaches us to know God aright, because it shows us that he regards the lowly and despised. For she knows God aright who knows that he regards the lowly, as we have said above. From such knowledge flows love and trust in God, by which we yield ourselves to him and gladly obey him.

As Jeremiah says [in chapter] 9[:23-24]: "Let no one glory in his might, riches, or wisdom; but if anyone wants to glory, let him glory in this, that he understands and knows me." And St. Paul teaches in 2 Cor. 10[:17]: "Let the one who boasts, boast in the Lord." Now, after lauding her God and Savior with a bare and pure spirit,^y and after truly singing the praises of his goodness by not boasting of his gifts, the Mother of God addresses herself in the next place to the praise also of his works and gifts. For, as we have seen, we must not fall upon the good gifts of God or boast of them, but make our way through them and reach to him, cling to him alone, and highly esteem his goodness. Thereupon we should praise him also in his works, in which he showed forth his goodness for our love, trust, and praise. Thus his works are simply a great incentive to love and praise his bare goodness that rules over us.

Mary begins with herself and sings what he has done for her. Here she teaches us a twofold lesson. First, every one of us should pay attention to what God does for each one of us rather than to all the works he does for others. For no one will be saved by what God does to another, but only by what he does to you. When in the last chapter of John [21:21-22], St. Peter asked about St. John: "What about this man?" Christ answered him by saying: "What is that to you? Follow me." It is as though he were to say: "John's works will not help you. You yourself must take hold and await what I will do for you." But now the world is captive to

---

y   As Luther discusses God's *blosse guttickeit*, his "bare goodness," later in
     the paragraph, here he notes that Mary praises God "*mit blossem reynen
     geyst*," with a "bare and pure spirit."

55. The medieval church taught that the excess merits of Jesus, Mary, and the saints were kept by the church in a "treasury" of sorts, and could be distributed to the faithful, usually through a (purchased) indulgence in the context of the Sacrament of Penance. Luther had questioned many aspects of this belief system in his *95 Theses on the Power and Efficacy of Indulgences*, and came quickly to reject them (LW 31:17–34; WA 1:233–38; TAL 1:13–46).

56. The cowl, from the Latin *cuculla*, meaning "hood," is the long garment provided to a monk at his solemn profession of vows. There were some who preached (and believed) that simply being buried in monks' garb would help in the process through purgatory, but medieval graves do not seem to show that this was a widespread practice. However, it was not uncommon for rulers (such as Charles V, for example) after an active life to retire to a monastery to pursue in earnest, one would presume, penitential discipline.

a dreadful abuse—the sale and distribution of good works—by which certain audacious spirits would assist others, especially those who live or die without good works of their own, just as if these spirits had a surplus of good works.[55] But Paul plainly says in 1 Cor. 3[:8]: "Each will receive wages according to the labor of each"—certainly not according to that of anyone else.

It would be tolerable if these people prayed for others, or brought their works before God by way of intercession. But since they deal with their works as if they were a gift, it becomes a scandalous piece of business. And, worst of all, they give away works of theirs of whose value in God's sight they themselves are ignorant; for God looks not at the works but at the heart and at the faith by which he himself works with us. To this they pay not the least attention, but trust only in the external works, deceiving themselves and all others besides. They have even gone so far as to persuade people to don the monk's cowl on their deathbeds, pretending that whoever dies in that sacred habit receives indulgence for all his sins and is saved.[56] Thus they have begun to save people not only with the works but even with the clothes of others. Unless we see to it, I fear the evil spirit will drive them on to bring people to heaven by means of monastic diet, cells, and burial. Great God, what great darkness is this, that a monk's cowl makes a man pious and saves him! Where, then, is the need of faith? Let us all become monks or all die in cowls. At this rate,

Renderings of the Benedictine (left) and Carthusian (right) orders. Woodcut by Lucas Cranach the Elder (1472–1553).

all the cloth would go to the making of monks' cowls! Beware, beware of the wolves in such sheep's clothing;[57] they will deceive you and tear you limb from limb. Remember that God also works in you, and base your salvation on no other works than those God works in you alone, as you see the Virgin Mary do here. To let the intercessions of others assist you in this is right and proper; we all should pray and work for one another. But none of us should depend on the works of others, but should only pay attention to how God works within us. Everyone should make an effort to regard himself and God as though God and he were alone in heaven and on earth and as though God were dealing with no one else besides him. Only then might he also glance at the works of others.

In the second place, [Mary] teaches us that each person should strive to be foremost in praising God by showing forth the works he has done to her, and then by praising him for the works he has done to others. Thus we read [Acts 15:12] that Paul and Barnabas declared to the apostles the works God had done by them, and that the apostles in turn told those he had done by them. The same was done by the apostles in Luke 24[:34-35] about the appearances of Christ after his resurrection. Thus there arose a common rejoicing and praising of God, each one praising the grace bestowed on another, yet most of all that bestowed on himself, however much more modest it might have been than that of the other. They were so simple in heart that they did not desire to be first or foremost in possessing the gifts but in praising and loving God; for God himself and his bare goodness were sufficient for them, however small his gifts. But the hirelings and mercenaries grow green with envy when they observe that they are not first and foremost in possessing the good things of God; instead of praising, they murmur because they are made equal to, or lower than, others, like the laborers in the Gospel [Matt. 20:11-12] who murmured against the householder, not because he did them any wrong, but because he made them equal to the other laborers by giving to all the [same] daily wage.

Even so we find many today who do not praise the goodness of God, because they cannot see that they have received the same things as St. Peter or any other of the saints, or as this or that person living on earth. They imagine they also would praise and love God if they possessed as much as these, and they despise the good gifts of God which are showered so abundantly upon them

57. This phrase appears to originate in the Bible, with Jesus' words in Matt. 7:15: "Beware of false prophets, who come to you in sheep's clothing but inwardly are ravenous wolves."

58. This Council (1414–1418), one of the "ecumenical" or general councils of the whole (that is, the Western) church, ended the Great Western Schism (when there were, for a time, three popes) and represents a high point for conciliarism. It was also the council that condemned and executed Jan Hus (1369–1415), the Czech priest and reformer.

and which they altogether overlook—such as life, body, reason, goods, honor, friends, the ministration of the sun and all created things. And even if they had all the good things of Mary, they still would not recognize God in them or praise him because of them. For as Christ says in Luke 16[:10]: "He who is faithful in a very little is faithful also in much; and he who is dishonest in a very little is dishonest also in much." Therefore, because they despise the little and the few things, they are not worthy of the much and the great things. But if they praised God in the little, the much would also be added unto them. They act as they do because they look above them and not beneath them; if they looked beneath them, they would find many that have not half of what they have and yet are content in God and sing his praise. A bird sings and is happy in the gifts it has—it does not murmur because it lacks the gift of speech. A dog jumps happily about and is content, even though he is without the gift of reason. All animals live in contentment and serve God, loving and praising him. Only the selfish, villainous eye of a person is never satisfied, nor can it ever be really satisfied because of its ingratitude and pride. It always wants the best place at the feast as the chief guest [Luke 14:8]; it is not willing to honor God, but would rather be honored by God.

There is a tale, dating back to the days of the Council of Constance,[58] of two cardinals who were riding around when they spied a shepherd standing in a field and weeping.[z] One of the two cardinals, being a good soul and unwilling to pass by without offering the man some comfort, rode up to him and asked him why he wept. The shepherd, who was weeping bitterly, was a long time replying to the cardinal's question. At last, pointing his finger at a toad, he said: "I weep because God has made me so well favored a creature, and not hideous like this reptile, and I have never yet

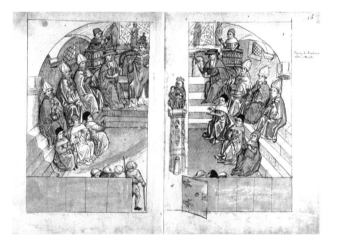

Bishops debating with the pope
at the Council of Constance (1414–1418),
which met to end the Great Western Schism

---

z   Cf. also *The Ten Commandments Preached to the People of Wittenberg* (WA 1:446–47).

acknowledged it or thanked and praised him for it."[a] The cardinal beat his breast and trembled so violently that he fell from his mount. He had to be carried to his lodging, and he cried out: "O St. Augustine, how truly you have said: 'The unlearned start up and take heaven away from us, and we with all our learning, look how we wallow in flesh and blood!'"[b] Now, I am sure that this shepherd was neither rich nor handsome nor powerful; nevertheless he had so clear an insight into God's good gifts and pondered them so deeply that in them he found more than he could comprehend.[59]

Mary confesses that the foremost work God did for her was that he regarded her, which is indeed the greatest of his works, on which all the rest depend and from which they all derive. For when it comes to pass that God turns his face toward a person to regard her, there is nothing but grace and salvation, and all gifts and works must follow. Thus we read in Gen. 4[:4-5] that he had regard for Abel and his offering, but for Cain and his offering he had no regard. Here is the origin of the many prayers in the Psalter—that God would turn his face toward us, and not hide it from us, that he would make his face shine upon us, and the like.[60] And that Mary herself regards this as the chief thing, she indicates by saying: "Behold, since he has regarded me, all generations will call me blessed."

Note that she does not say people will say all sorts of good things about her, praise her virtues, exalt her virginity or her humility, or sing of what she has done. But it is only because God regarded her—that is why people will call her blessed. That is to give all the glory to God as completely as it can be done. Therefore she points to God's regard and says: "For, behold, henceforth all generations will call me blessed. That is, beginning with the time when God regarded my low estate, I shall be called blessed." Not *she* is praised thereby, but God's grace toward her. In fact, she is despised, and she despises herself in that she says her low

59. The theme of the wisdom of the unlearned (and the corresponding ignorance of the learned) is a common one in medieval monastic, especially Franciscan, theology.

60. Such as Ps. 4:6: "Let the light of your face shine on us, O Lord!"; Ps. 27:9: "Do not hide your face from me"; Ps. 31:16: "Let your face shine upon your servant."

---

a A similar story appears in a writing of Jean Gobi the Younger (d. 1350). See the article by Jacques Berlioz, "Le crapaud, animal diabolique: Une exemplaire construction médiévale," in *L'Animal exemplaire au moyen âge (Ve-XVe siècle)*, eds. Jacque Berlioz and Marie Anne Polo (Rennes: Presses universitaires de Rennes, 1999), 267–88.

b Augustine, *Confessions* 8.8. A translation of the *Confessions* into contemporary English is available in the Ignatius Critical Editions, trans. Maria Boulding, O.S.B. (San Francisco: Ignatius, 2012).

61. Luther's exclamation to Mary is a sign of respect, honor, and even of devotion, but it is not intercessory prayer, as he does not ask her to intercede with God on his (or our) behalf.

62. By the late medieval period, Marian devotion was at a height—in one of his prayers, Anselm of Canterbury (c. 1033–1109) said that she should receive the praises of the whole world, for there is "nothing equal to Mary and nothing but God greater than Mary." See his "Prayer to St. Mary" (3:177–78), in *Prayers and Meditations of St. Anselm with the Proslogion*, trans. Benedicta Ward (London: Penguin, 1973).

The "angelic greeting," or *Ave Maria*, was not, in Luther's view, a prayer, but rather a greeting that announced God's regard to Mary.

estate was regarded by God. Therefore she also mentions her blessedness before enumerating the works that God did to her, and ascribes it all to the fact that God regarded her low estate.

From this we may learn how to show her the honor and devotion that are her due. How should one address her? Keep these words in mind, and they will teach you to say: "O Blessed Virgin, Mother of God, you were nothing and all despised; yet God in his grace regarded you and worked such great things in you. You were worthy of none of them, but the rich and abundant grace of God was upon you, far above any merit of yours. Hail to you! Blessed are you, from this hour on and forever, in finding such a God."[61] You do not need to fear that she will take it badly if we call her unworthy of such grace. For undoubtedly she did not lie when she herself acknowledged her unworthiness and nothingness, which God regarded, not because of any merit in her, but solely by reason of his grace.

But she does take it badly that the useless chatterers preach and write so many things about her merits.[62,c] They are set on proving their own skill and fail to see how they spoil the Magnificat, make the Mother of God a liar, and diminish the grace of God. For, in proportion as we ascribe merit and worthiness to her, we lower the grace of God and diminish the truth of the Magnificat. The angel salutes her only as graced by God,[d] and because the Lord is with her [Luke 1:28], which is why she is blessed among women. Hence all those who heap such great praise and honor upon her head are not far from making an idol of her, as though she were concerned that people should honor her and look to her for good things, when in truth she thrusts this from her and would have us honor God in her and would bring us through her to a good confidence in God's grace.

---

c   For a brief review of medieval devotion to Mary in treatises, prayers, and sermons, see Jaroslav Pelikan, *Mary through the Centuries: Her Place in the History of Culture* (New Haven: Yale University Press, 1996), esp. 129–36.

d   Here Luther has *"von gottis gnaden,"* or literally "of God's grace." For a discussion of Luther's translation of the angelic greeting, and later Lutheran interpretation, see Beth Kreitźer, *Reforming Mary: Changing Images of the Virgin Mary in Lutheran Sermons of the Sixteenth Century*, Oxford Studies in Historical Theology (New York: Oxford University Press, 2004), ch. 1.

Whoever, therefore, would show her the proper honor must not regard her alone and by herself, but set her in the presence of God and far beneath him, must there strip her of all honor, and regard her low estate, as she says; he should then marvel at the exceedingly abundant grace of God, who regards, embraces, and blesses so poor and despised a person. Thus regarding her, you will be moved to love and praise God for such grace, and drawn to look for all good things to such a God who does not reject but graciously regards poor and despised and lowly mortals. Thus your heart will be strengthened in faith and love and hope. What do you suppose would please her more than to have you come through her to God this way, and learn from her to put your hope and trust in him, notwithstanding your despised and lowly estate, in life as well as in death? She does not want you to come to her, but through her to God.

Again, nothing would please her better than to have you turn in fear from all lofty things on which people set their hearts, seeing that even in his mother God neither found nor desired anything of high degree. But the masters who so depict and portray the blessed Virgin that there is found in her nothing to be despised, but only great and lofty things—what are they doing but contrasting us with her instead of her with God? Thus they make us stupid and afraid and hide the Virgin's comforting, grace-conveying picture, as the images are covered over in Lent.[63] For they deprive us of her example, from which we might take comfort; they make an exception of her and set her above all examples. But she should be, and herself gladly would be, the foremost example of the grace of God, to incite all the world to trust in this grace and to love and praise it, so that through her the hearts of all should be filled with such knowledge of God that they might confidently say: "O Blessed Virgin, Mother of God, what great comfort God has shown us in you, by so graciously regarding your unworthiness and low estate. This encourages us to believe that from now on he will not despise us poor and lowly ones, but graciously regard us also, according to your example."

What do you think? David, St. Peter, St. Paul, St. Mary Magdalene, and the like are examples to strengthen our trust in God and our faith, by reason of the great grace bestowed on them without their worthiness, for the comforting of all people. Will not the blessed Mother of God also gladly be such an example to all the world? But now she cannot be this because of

63. The term Luther uses here is *gnaden bild,* which can be translated as "wonder-working image." A *gnaden bild* is usually a picture of Mary and child (or another saint), and frequently was used as an icon of sorts—an image before which one would pray, and which could convey grace (or even miracles) to the petitioner. These images, especially the miracle-working ones, were often the site of pilgrimages in the late Middle Ages. Images and crosses in general were covered in Lent (and still are in many churches)—either with a cloth or with folding panels, as in triptychs (three-paneled altars with folding doors). The covering represents both our position as penitents and the fact that Jesus' divinity is "hidden" in his suffering and death, and then revealed again at Easter.

64. Legends of Mary (and other saints) were very popular in the late medieval period. Mary was often presented in these stories as a mother figure who would do anything to help those who were devoted to her—even otherwise questionable folks (thieves, immoral women, etc.) who said a daily prayer to Mary or had some other regular devotion would be saved from disaster by her help.

the excessive eulogists and useless chatterers, who do not show the people from this verse how in her the exceeding riches of God joined with her utter poverty, the divine honor with her low estate, the divine glory with her despisedness, the divine greatness with her smallness, the divine goodness with her lack of merit, the divine grace with her unworthiness. On this basis our love and affection toward God would grow and increase with all confidence, which is why her life and works, as well as the lives and works of all the saints, have been recorded. But now we find those who come to her for help and comfort, as though she were a divine being, so that I fear there is now more idolatry in the world than ever before.[64] But enough of this for the present.

The Latin phrase *omnes generationes* I have rendered in German with "children's children," although literally it means "all generations."[e] But that is an obscure expression, and many have been hard put to it by this passage to know how it can be that all generations shall bless her, since the Jews, the heathen, and many wicked Christians blaspheme her or scorn to call her blessed. They understand the word *generations* of the totality of humankind, whereas its meaning here is rather the line of natural descent, as father, son, grandson, and so on, each member being called a generation. The Virgin Mary means to say simply that her praise will be sung from one generation to another so that there will never be a time when she will not be praised. This she indicates by saying, "Behold, from now on all generations"—that is, it begins now and will continue throughout all generations, to children's children.

The word μακαριοῦσι means more than simply "to call blessed"; its meaning is rather "to bless," or to "make blessed." This consists not merely in saying the words, bending the knee, bowing the head, doffing the hat, making images, or building churches, for this even the wicked can do. But it is done with all one's strength and with downright sincerity, when the heart, moved by her low estate and God's gracious regard of her, as we have seen, rejoices in God and says or thinks with all its heart, "O Blessed Virgin Mary!" So to bless her is to accord her the honor that is her due, as we have seen.

e   Luther uses the term *kinds kind*, rather than *Geschlect*. Modern German has the term *Generation*, which would have been useful for Luther in this context.

49. *For he has done great things for me,*
he who is mighty, and holy is his name.

Here she sings in one breath of all the works that God has done to her, and observes the proper order. In the preceding verse she sang of God's regard and gracious good will toward her, which is indeed the greatest and chief part of grace, as we have said. Now she comes to the works and gifts. For God indeed gives to some many good things and richly adorns them, as he did Lucifer in heaven.[65] He scatters his gifts among the multitudes, but he does not therefore regard them. His good things are merely gifts which last for a season, but his grace and regard are the inheritance which lasts forever, as St. Paul says in Rom. 6[:23]: "The grace of God is eternal life." In giving us the gifts he gives only what is his, but in his regard and grace he gives his very self. In the gifts we touch his hand, but in his gracious regard we receive his heart, spirit, mind, and will. Hence the Blessed Virgin puts his regard in the first and highest place, and does not begin by saying: "All generations will call me blessed, because he has done great things for me," as this verse says; but she begins: "He has regarded my low estate," as the preceding verse shows. Where God's gracious will is, there are also his gifts; but, on the other hand, where his gifts are, there is not also his gracious will. This verse therefore logically follows the preceding verse. We read in Gen. 25[:5-6] that Abraham gave gifts to the children of his concubines; but to Isaac, his true son by his true helpmate Sarah, he gave the whole inheritance. Thus God would not have his true children put their trust in his goods and gifts, spiritual or temporal, however great they be, but in his grace and in himself, yet without despising the gifts.

Nor does Mary enumerate any good things in particular, but gathers them all together in one word and says, "He has done great things for me." That is: "Everything he has done for me is great." She teaches us here that the greater devotion there is in the heart, the fewer words are uttered. For she feels that however she may strive and try, she cannot express it in words.[66] Therefore these few words of the Spirit are so great and profound that no one can comprehend them without having, at least in part, the same Spirit. But for the unspiritual, who deal in many words and much loud noise, such words seem utterly inadequate and wholly without strength or flavor. Christ also teaches us in

65. Lucifer, although not appearing as a name for Satan in the Old Testament, was associated with the devil in the intertestamental period, and thus by early Christians. The only scriptural reference to Lucifer as a name is in Isa. 14:12, which speaks of the king of Babylon as the "morning star," or Lucifer that fell from the heavens. Christians have read this text symbolically as speaking of the devil, who was considered to be a great angel who wanted to rule above God (Isa. 14:13-14), and who was then cast out of heaven (cf. Luke 10:18).

66. Tauler suggests that our joy at uniting with God is "unutterable"—the greater the joy, the less we are able

In this image, printed in a 1547 publication of Luther's *Hauspostil* (a postil is a collection of sermons), the Holy Spirit (represented by the dove) inspires both Elizabeth, who greets Mary as the "Mother of my Lord," and Mary, who sings the Magnificat.

to express it in words (W. R. Inge, ed., *Light, Life, and Love: Selections from the German Mystics of the Middle Ages* (1904). See "Our Aim," www.ccel.org/ccel/inge/light.light_tauler_1.html.

Matt. 6[:7] not to speak much when we pray, as the unbelievers do, for they think that they will be heard for their many words. Even so there is today in the churches a great ringing of bells, blowing of trumpets, singing, shouting, and intoning, yet I fear precious little worship of God, who wants to be worshiped in spirit and truth, as he says in John 4[:24].

Solomon says in Prov. 27[:14]: "Whoever blesses a neighbor with a loud voice, rising early in the morning, will be counted as cursing." For such a person arouses the suspicion that he is endeavoring to embellish an evil situation; he gets so hot under the collar that he makes the situation worse. On the other hand, he who curses his neighbor with a loud voice, rising up early in the morning (that is, not indifferently, but with great zeal and urgency), is to be regarded as a praiser of him. For people do not believe him, but suppose that he is motivated by hatred and a wicked heart; he hurts his own cause and helps his neighbor's. In the same way, if a person presumes to worship God with many words and a great noise, he acts as if God is either deaf or ignorant, and that we must waken or instruct him. Such an opinion of God tends to one's shame and dishonor rather than to his worship. But when one ponders well God's divine works in the depths of his heart and regards them with wonder and gratitude so that he breaks out from very ardor into sighs and groaning rather than into speech; when the words, not nicely chosen or prescribed, flow forth in such a way that the Spirit comes bubbling with them, and the words live and have hands and feet, in fact, the whole body and life with all its members strive and strain for utterance—that is indeed a worship of God in spirit and truth, and such words are pure fire, light, and life.[67] As David says in Ps. 119[:140]: "LORD, your statements are completely fiery,"[f] and again [v. 171]: "My lips will pour forth praise,"[g] even as boiling water overflows and bubbles, unable to contain

67. Cf. Rom. 8:26-27: "Likewise the Spirit helps us in our weakness; for we do not know how to pray as we ought, but that very Spirit intercedes with sighs too deep for words. And God, who searches the heart, knows what is the mind of the Spirit, because the Spirit intercedes for the saints according to the will of God."

f   The Vulgate reads, *"ignitum eloquium tuum vehementer,"* while the NRSV reads, "your promise is well-tried."

g   While the NRSV reads "pour forth," Luther's verb is *scheumen,* "to bubble," which connects the verse with the metaphor of the pot boiling over.

itself for the great heat within the pot. Of this sort are all the words of the blessed Virgin in her hymn—few, but profound and mighty. These people St. Paul calls in Rom. 12[:11] "ardent in spirit," spiritually fervent and bubbling, and teaches us to be that way, too.

The "great things" are nothing less than that she became the Mother of God, in which work so many and such great good things are given to her that no one can grasp it. For on this there follow all honor, all blessedness, and her unique place in the whole of humankind, among which she has no equal, namely, that she had a child by the Father in heaven, and such a child! She herself is unable to find a name for this work, it is too exceedingly great; all she can do is break out in the fervent cry: "They are great things," impossible to describe or define. Therefore people have crowded all her glory into a single word, calling her the Mother of God.[68] No one can say anything greater of her or to her, even if he had as many tongues as there are leaves on the trees, or grass in the fields, or stars in the sky, or sand by the sea. It needs to be pondered in the heart what it means to be the Mother of God.[69]

Mary also freely ascribes all to God's grace, not to her merit. For though she was without sin, yet that grace was far too great for her to deserve it in any way.[70] How should a creature deserve to become the Mother of God? Though certain scribblers make much ado about her worthiness for such motherhood, I prefer to believe her rather than them. She says her low estate was regarded by God, not thereby rewarding her for anything she had done, but, "He has done great things for me," he has done this of his own accord without any doing of mine. For never in all her life did she think to become the Mother of God, still less did she prepare or make herself apt for it. The tidings took her all unaware, as Luke reports [1:29]. Merit, however, is not unprepared for its reward, but deliberately seeks and awaits it.[71]

It is no valid argument to cite against this the words of the hymn *Regina coeli laetare*, "For you have merited to bear," and in another place, "Whom you were worthy to bear." For the same things are sung about the holy cross, which was a thing of wood and incapable of merit. The words are to be understood in this sense: in order to become the Mother of God, she had to be a woman, a virgin, of the tribe of Judah, and had to believe the angelic message in order to become worthy, as the Scriptures

68. In Greek, of course, it is a "single word"—*theotokos*. It is literally translated "God-bearer," but the German and English versions follow the term most commonly used in Latin, *mater Dei*.

69. A reference to Luke 2:19, when, after the visit of the shepherds to the newly born Jesus, and their stories of angelic hosts, Mary "treasured all these words and pondered them in her heart."

70. As Augustine suggested that Mary was the "great exception" to the rule of human sinfulness, Luther also follows tradition here in saying that Mary was sinless. But he does so in the same way that he argues that Mary did not deserve to become the Mother of God, but that it was God's pure gift. He likewise argues that Mary's preservation from sin was not from her own will or strength, but also a gift from God. Some of his later sermons suggest that Luther came to believe that the Holy Spirit purified Mary from sin at some point prior to the conception of Jesus, but not necessarily at her own conception. For more on Luther's views about Mary's conception and sinlessness, see Kreitzer, *Reforming Mary*, 36–45, 123–25.

71. Merit, from the Latin *meritum*, means "reward." In that sense, if Mary were to "merit" to become the Mother of God, it would mean (as can be seen from Luther's discussion) that God would be rewarding her for something she had done (that is, that she had the virtue of humility). "To merit" is not the same as "to earn," although in English that distinction is often lost. But, as Luther here argues, Mary could never merit such a reward in any way.

72. Mary is the Queen of Heaven in the same way that she is the Mother of God. The title refers to her relationship to her Son. Because Jesus is the Son of God, Mary is the *theotokos*, or God-bearer/Mother of God (as affirmed at the Council of Ephesus in 431). Because Jesus is the king of Israel and heavenly king of the universe, Mary is the Queen of Heaven, or *regina coeli*. The Roman Catholic tradition from about the fourth century has held that Mary (either after her death or her Dormition, a "falling asleep") was assumed, body and soul, into heaven—this teaching was formalized into a dogma in the apostolic constitution *Munificentissimus Deus* in 1950. Because she is physically present in heaven then, she is honored as the Queen of Heaven. Luther does not reject either one of these assertions, but insists that her queenship does not then mean she has queenly power.

foretold.[h] As the wood had no other merit or worthiness than that it was suited to be made into a cross and was appointed by God for that purpose, so her sole worthiness to become the Mother of God lay in her being fit and appointed for it; so that it might be pure grace and not a reward, that we might not take away from God's grace, worship, and honor by ascribing too great things to her. For it is better to take away too much from her than from the grace of God. Indeed, we cannot take away too much from her, since she was created out of nothing, like all other creatures. But we can easily take away too much from God's grace, which is a perilous thing to do and not well pleasing to her. One should also be measured and not make too much of calling her "Queen of Heaven," which is a true name[72] and yet

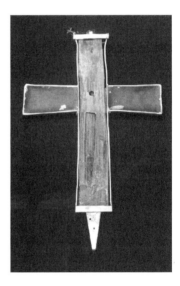

A "Kreuzpartikel"—a fragment of the True Cross—in the Imperial Treasury (Schatzkammer) in Vienna. Mary did not "merit" bearing Christ by her virtues any more than the tree merited becoming his cross. However, after Jesus' death, the cross became a special object of veneration for Christians. According to legend, the True Cross, as it is known, was discovered in 326 by St. Helena, the mother of the emperor Constantine, and pieces of the cross were extremely popular relics even in Luther's day.

---

h   Luther is alluding to Isa. 7:14, and perhaps also to Ezek. 44:2.

does not make her a goddess who could grant gifts or render aid, as some suppose when they pray and flee to her rather than to God.[73] She gives nothing, God gives all, as we see in the words that follow.

"He who is mighty." Truly, in these words she takes away all might and power from every creature and bestows them on God alone. What great boldness and robbery on the part of so young and tender a maiden! She dares, by this one word, to make all the strong feeble, all the mighty weak, all the wise foolish, all the famous despised, and God alone the possessor of all strength, wisdom, and glory. For this is the meaning of the phrase: "He who is mighty." There is no one who does anything, but as St. Paul says in Eph. 1[:11]: "God alone accomplishes all things in all things," and all creatures' works are God's works. Even as we confess in the Creed: "I believe in God the Father, the Almighty." He is almighty because it is his power alone that works in all and through all and over all. Thus St. Hannah, the mother of Samuel, sings in 1 Sam. 2[:9]: "Not by might does one prevail."[74] St. Paul says in 2 Cor. 3[:5]: "Not that we are competent of ourselves to claim anything as coming from us; our competence is from God." This is a most important article of faith, including many things; it completely puts down all pride, arrogance, blasphemy, fame, and false trust, and exalts God alone. It points out the reason why God alone is to be exalted—because he does all things. That is easily said but hard to believe and to translate into life. For those who carry it out in their lives are most peaceable, even-tempered,[i] and simple-hearted folk, who lay no claim to anything, well knowing it is not theirs but God's.

This, then, is the meaning of these words of the Mother of God: "In all those great and good things there is nothing of mine, but he who alone does all things, and whose power works

The Assumption of the Virgin Mary by Titian (1490–1576). Mary's assumption, body and soul, into heaven was not affirmed as dogma until 1950, but it was a common Christian belief from the fourth century.

73. It was common in late-medieval devotion to portray Mary as a merciful mother, while her Son was a strict judge. Fleeing to the mother, then, was a common approach, for Mary could not fail to receive what she asked from her Son.

74. The Song of Hannah, which appears in 1 Sam. 2:1-10, is thematically and organizationally very similar to the Magnificat. The long-barren Hannah sang her song of praise to God after the birth of her promised son, Samuel, and her song has a special status within Judaism as a model of how to pray.

i   Again, *gelassene*.

75. In his commentary on this passage, Augustine notes that God works constantly to sustain all created things, hence the divine title of God the Sustainer.

76. Luther is here suggesting that we can invoke Mary and the saints—that is, ask them to pray to God on our behalf—but they do not accomplish anything for us themselves. All the work is God's alone. In later works such as the *Smalcald Articles* (1537), Luther suggests that as we do not know if the saints in heaven pray for us, we should not invoke their prayer (SA 2; TAL 2:436–37; BC, 305–6).

77. Luther affirms here the notion that he presented in the *Address to the Christian Nobility*, that all Christians have a vocation, andthere is a spiritual value in whatever work they are called to do; he is also offering an implicit critique to those in the church who feel that their spiritual estate exempts them from any work of their hands.

in all, has done such great things for me." For the word *mighty* does not denote a quiescent power, as one says of a temporal king that he is mighty, even though he may be sitting still and doing nothing. But it denotes an energetic power, a continuous activity, that works and operates without ceasing. For God does not rest, but works without ceasing, as Christ says in John 5[:17]: "My Father is still working, and I am also working."[75] In the same sense St. Paul says in Eph. 3[:20]: "He has power to do more than we ask"; that is, he always does more than we ask—that is his way, and that is how his power works. That is why I said Mary does not desire to be an idol; she does nothing, God does all. We ought to call upon her, that for her sake God may grant and do what we request. Thus also all other saints are to be invoked, so that the work may be every way God's alone.[76]

Therefore she adds, "And holy is his name." That is to say: "As I lay no claim to the work, neither do I claim the name and honor. For the name and honor belong alone to the one who does the work. It is not proper that one should do the work and another have the fame and take the glory. I am but the workshop in which he performs his work; I had nothing to do with the work itself. No one should praise me or give me the glory for becoming the Mother of God, but God and his work are to be honored and praised in me. It is enough to be happy along with me and call me blessed, because God used me and did his works in me." Behold, how completely she traces all to God, lays claim to no works, no honor, no fame. She conducts herself as before, when she still had nothing of all this; she demands no higher honors than before. She is not puffed up, does not vaunt herself or proclaim with a loud voice that she is now the Mother of God. She does not seek any glory, but goes about her usual household duties, milking the cows, cooking the meals, washing pots and kettles, sweeping out the rooms, and performing the work of maidservant or housemother in lowly and despised tasks, as though she cared nothing for such great gifts and graces. She was esteemed among other women and her neighbors no more highly than before, nor desired to be, but remained a poor townswoman, one of the great multitude.[77] Oh, how simple and pure a heart was hers, how wonderful a person she was![j] What great things

---

j   According to Grimm's *Deutsches Wörterbuch* (14.II), in Luther's time, "wonderful" (*wunderlich*) had the meaning of "uncommon, remarkable, interesting, astonishing, amazing." See Burger, *Marias Lied*, 104 n.759.

are hidden here under this lowly exterior! How many came in contact with her, talked, ate, and drank with her, who perhaps despised her and counted her but a common, poor, and simple village girl, and who, had they known such a thing, would have fled from her in terror.

That is the meaning of the clause: "Holy is his name." For "holy" means "separated," "dedicated to God," that none should touch or defile it but all should hold it in honor. And "name" means a good report, fame, praise, and honor. Thus everyone should leave God's name alone, not lay hands on it or appropriate it to himself. It is a symbol of this when we read in Exod. 30[:25-32] that Moses made an oil of holy ointment, at God's command, and strictly forbade that it be poured on any person's flesh. That is, no one should ascribe to himself the name of God. For we desecrate God's name when we let ourselves be praised or honored, or when we take pleasure in ourselves and boast of our works or our possessions, as is the way of the world, which constantly dishonors and desecrates the name of God. But as the works are God's alone, so, too, the name should be his alone. And all who thus keep his name holy and deny themselves all honor and glory rightly honor his name, and therefore are made holy by it. Thus we read in Exod. 30[:29] that the precious ointment was so holy that it hallowed whatever it touched. That is, when God's name is kept holy by us, so that we lay claim to no work, fame, or self-satisfaction in it, it is rightly honored, and in turn touches and makes us holy.

Therefore we must be on our guard, because we cannot do without God's good things while we live on earth, and therefore we cannot be without name and honor. When people accord us praise and honor, we ought to profit by the example of the Mother of God and at all times arm ourselves with this verse to make the proper reply and to use such honor and praise correctly. We should openly say, or at least think in our heart: "O Lord God, the work that is being praised and celebrated is yours, so let the name also be yours. Not I but you have done it, for you have the power to do all things, and holy is your name." We ought neither to reject this praise and honor as though they were wrong, nor to despise them as though they were nothing, but refuse to accept them as too precious or noble, and ascribe them to the one in heaven to whom they belong. This is taught by this noble verse, and gives an answer to the question that some might ask, whether one person ought to honor another. St. Paul says in Rom. 12[:10] that we should "outdo one another in showing honor." But no one should accept the honor as accorded to him, nor keep it for himself, but should hallow it and ascribe it to God, to whom it belongs, by performing all manner of good works, from which honor comes. For no one should lead a dishonorable life. But if he is to live honorably, honor will have to be shown him. Yet as an honorable life is the gift and work of God, so, too, the name should be his alone, holy and undefiled by self-complacency. For this we pray in the Lord's Prayer: "Hallowed be your name."

50. *"And his mercy is on those who fear him, from generation to generation."*

We must accustom ourselves to the scriptural usage according to which generations are, as we have said above, the succession of those born in the course of nature, one human being descending from another. Hence the German word *Geschlechter* is not an adequate translation, though I do not know a better one. For by *Geschlechter* we understand families or blood relations. But the word here means the natural succession from parent to child and child's child, where each member of the same succession is called a generation; so that the following would not be a bad translation: "and his mercy endures from children to children of those who fear him." This is a very common expression in Scripture, with its origin in the words of God under the First Commandment, spoken on Mount Sinai to Moses and all the people [Exod. 20:5-6]: "I am your God, strong and jealous, visiting the sins of the fathers upon the children to the third and fourth generation of those who hate me, and showing steadfast love to many thousand generations of those who love me and keep my commandments."

Having finished singing about herself and the good things she had from God, and having sung his praises, Mary now rehearses all the works of God that he works in general in all people, and sings his praises also for them, teaching us to understand the work, method, nature, and will of God. Many philosophers and people of great judgment have also engaged in the endeavor to find out the nature of God; they have written much about him, one in this way, another in that, yet all have gone blind over their task and failed to see the proper perspective. And, indeed, it is the greatest thing in heaven and on earth to know God correctly, if that may be granted to someone. This the Mother of God teaches us here quite well, if we would only understand, just as she taught the same above, in and by her own experience. How can one know God better than in his own works? Whoever understands his works correctly cannot fail to know his nature and will, his heart and mind. Hence to understand his works is an art. And in order that we may learn it, Mary enumerates, in the following four verses, six divine works among six sorts of persons. She divides all the world into two parts and assigns to each side three works and three classes of people, so that either side has its exact counterpart in the other. She describes the works of God in each of these two parts, portraying him so well that it could not be done better.[78]

This division is well conceived and is grounded upon other passages of Scripture. For instance, God says in Jer. 9[:23-24]: "Do not let the wise boast in their wisdom, do not let the mighty boast in their might, do not let the rich boast in their riches; but let those who boast boast in this, that they understand and know me, that I am the LORD who practices mercy,[k] justice, and righteousness in the earth; for in these things I delight, says the LORD." This is a noble text and well agrees with this hymn of the Mother of God. Here we see that he, too, divides all that is in the world into three parts—wisdom, might, and riches—and puts them all down by saying no one should boast in these things, for no one will find him in them, nor does he delight in them. Over against them he sets three others—mercy, justice, and righteousness. "In these things," he says, "I am to be found; indeed, I practice them, so near am I to them; nor do I practice them in heaven, but in the earth, where people may find me. And whoever thus understands me may well boast and trust in that fact. For if she is not wise but poor in spirit, my loving kindness is with her; if he is not mighty but brought low, my justice is by his side to save him; if she is not rich but poor and needy, the more she has of my righteousness."

Under wisdom he includes all spiritual possessions and gifts, by which a person may gain popularity, fame, and a good report,

78. The sixfold division (that is, the threefold division, here of the works of God and earlier of the human person, and then its multiplication by two, so that it splits into two equal threefold sections of good/blessing and evil/punishment) is relatively common in medieval mysticism. For example, in Bonaventure's *Itinerarium mentis in Deum* of 1259, the soul travels through six stages in the ascent to God.

---

k   Luther has here *barmhertzigkeit*, which can also be translated as "lovingkindness." The NRSV has "steadfast love."

as the following verse will show. Such gifts are intellect, reason, wit, knowledge, piety, virtue, a godly life, in short, whatever is in the soul that people call divine and spiritual, all great and high gifts, yet none of them is God himself. Under might he includes all authority, nobility, friends, high station, and honor, whether pertaining to temporal or to spiritual goods or persons—though there is in Scripture no spiritual authority or power, but only servants and subjects—together with all the rights, liberties, and privileges pertaining to them. Under riches are included good health, beauty, pleasure, strength, and every external good that may befall the body. Opposed to these three are the poor in spirit, the oppressed, and those who lack the necessities of life. Let us now consider these six works in order.

The First Work of God, Mercy

Of this the verse says: "His mercy is on those who fear him from generation to generation." She begins with the highest and greatest things, with the spiritual and inward goods, which produce the most vain, proud, and stiff-necked people on earth.[79] There is no rich person or mighty lord who is so puffed up and bold as one such wise guy[I] who feels and knows that he is in the right, understands all about a matter, and is wiser than other people. Especially when he finds he ought to give way or confess himself in the wrong, he becomes so insolent and is so utterly devoid of the fear of God that he dares to boast of being infallible,[80] declares God is on his side and the others on the devil's side, and has the effrontery to appeal to the judgment of God. If such a person possesses the necessary power, he rushes on headlong, persecuting, condemning, slandering, slaying, banishing, and destroying all who differ with him, saying afterward he did it all to the honor and glory of God. He is as certain and sure as hardly any angel in heaven of earning much thanks and merit before God. Oh, how big a bubble we have here! How much Scripture has to say about such people, and how many grievous things it

79. Luther is making a reference to the common complaint about the Israelites, that they were a "stiff-necked" and intractable people (see, e.g., Exod. 32:9; 33:3; Deut. 9:6; Jer. 17:6; and also Acts 7:51).

80. Although this was prior to the official declaration of papal infallibility at the First Vatican Council (1869–1870), the notion was common in medieval theology (as opposed to conciliarism, which argued that councils were the highest authority in the church), and was commonly accepted in the era of the Council of Trent (1545–1563).

I   Luther has here *klugeler*, which can also be translated as "sophist" or "caviller," but those terms seemed a bit highbrow for what he is saying in this passage. Steinhaeuser's original translation had "smart aleck."

threatens them with! But they feel them less than the anvil feels the smith's hammer. This is a great and widespread evil.

Christ says of such people in John 16[:2]: "The hour is coming when whoever kills and drives you out will think that he is offering service to God." And Ps. [10:5-6] says about the same crowd: "He overwhelms all his enemies and says, I shall not meet adversity"; as if he were to say: "I am in the right, I do well, God will richly reward me." Such were the people of Moab, of whom we read in Isa. 16[:6] and Jer. 48[:29-30]: "We have heard of the pride of Moab—he is very proud—of his loftiness, his pride, and his arrogance; his reputation and his wrath are greater than his power." Thus we see that such people would gladly do more in their great arrogance than they are able. The Jews were such a people in their dealings with Christ and the apostles. Such were the friends of St. Job, who argued against him with extraordinary wisdom and praised and preached God in the loftiest terms. Such people will not give you a hearing; it is impossible that they should be in the wrong or give way. They must have their way though all the world perish. Scripture cannot find reproaches enough for such a lost crew. Now it calls them an adder stopping its ears so that it does not hear; now a wild ox that cannot be tamed; again, a raging lion, a mighty, immovable rock, a dragon, etc.[81]

In Goeree's *Voor-bereidselen tot de bybelsche wysheid* (1690), the Behemoth of Job 40 is imagined as a hippopotamus, while the Leviathan of Job 41 is a crocodile.

But nowhere are they more aptly portrayed than in Job 40[:15] and 41[:1] where he calls that same crowd בְּהֵמוֹת.[m] בְּהֵמָה is a single beast, בְּהֵמוֹת a drove of beasts, that is, a people having a bestial mind and unwilling to be ruled by the Spirit of God. In those

81. See Ps. 58:4-5; Ps. 22:21; Ps. 7:2; Jer. 5:3; Ps. 74:13.

m Job 40:15 has "Behemoth," which also is the term here in WA 7:579. Job 41:1 has "Leviathan."

chapters God describes it as having eyes "like the eyelids of the dawn" [41:18], for their prudence is unbounded. His hide is so hard that he laughs at the arrow and the javelin [41:26-28]; that is, when they are preached to, they laugh it to scorn, for their right must not be questioned. Again, his scales "are joined one to another, that no air can come between them" [41:16-17]; that is, they hold so closely together that no Spirit of God can come into them. "His heart," says the Lord, "is as hard as a smith's anvil" [41:24];[n] it is the body of the devil. Therefore he also ascribes the same things to the devil in this passage. Such, above all others, are the pope and his herd today and these many days. They do all of these things, and worse than were ever done; there is no hearing nor giving way, it profits nothing to speak, to counsel, beg, or threaten. It is simply, "We are in the right," and there is an end of it, in spite of everyone else, though it be the whole world.[82]

But someone might say: "How is that? Should we not maintain the right? Should we let the truth go? Are we not commanded to die for the sake of the right and the truth? Did not the holy martyrs suffer for the sake of the gospel? And Christ himself, did not he desire to be in the right? It happens indeed that such people are now and then in the right publicly (and as they whine, before God) and that they do wisely and well." I reply: Here it is high time and most necessary that we open our eyes, for here lies the crux of the whole matter. Everything depends on our proper understanding of "being in the right." It is true, we are to suffer all things for the sake of the truth and the right, and not to deny it, however unimportant the matter be.[83] It may also be that those people are now and then in the right, but they spoil it by not rightly asserting their right, by not going about it in fear or setting God before their eyes. They suppose it is sufficient that it is right, and then they desire to continue and carry it out by their own power. Thus they turn their right into a wrong, even if it was in itself right. But it is much more dangerous when they only think they are in the right, yet are not certain, as they do in the important matters that pertain to God and his right. Let us, however, deal first with the more tangible human right and use a simple illustration that all may grasp.

Is it not true that money, property, body, wife, child, friends, and the like are good things created and given by God himself?

82. During the period in which Luther had to wait for and then deal with the papal bull *Exsurge Domine*, he suggested on several occasions that he was no longer interested in rapprochement with the pope—although he did make an attempt of sorts in the open letter to Pope Leo that introduced his treatise *On the Freedom of a Christian* (published November 1520). When he burned the bull and canon-law books, his decision had been made, as he made clear in his *Why the Books of the Pope and His Disciples Were Burned by Doctor Martin Luther*, published later in December 1520. The critiques of the pope there are similar to those in this section of the commentary.

83. In his *Against the Execrable Bull of the Antichrist* (late October 1520), Luther noted that he could not recant the truth, and no one seemed willing to prove him wrong on the basis of Scripture. If indeed the pope had condemned him (and he suggested in this writing that the bull was probably a fiction invented by Eck), he was willing to condemn the pope as the Antichrist and to suffer any punishment he might have to bear for the sake of the truth. Luther, however, only had the power of his words to use against these enemies, and not the power of force, as those he is here critiquing.

n   The NRSV has "stone."

Since, then, they are God's gifts and not your own, suppose he were to try you, to learn whether you were willing to let them go for his sake and to cleave to him rather than to such gifts. Suppose he raised up an enemy who deprived you of them in whole or in part, or you lost them by death or some other mischance. Do you think you would have just cause to rage and storm and to take them again by force or to be impatient until they were restored to you? And if you said that they were good things and God's creatures, made with his own hands, and that, since all the Scriptures called such things good, you were resolved to fulfill God's word and defend or get back such good at cost of life and limb, not suffering their loss voluntarily or surrendering them patiently—what a farce that would be! To do right in this case, you should not rush in headlong, but fear God and say: "Dear Lord, they are good things and your gifts, as your own word and Scripture says, but I do not know whether you will permit me to keep them. If I knew that I was not to have them, I would not move a finger to get them back. If I knew that you would rather have them remain in my possession than in that of others, I would serve your will by taking them back at risk of life and property. But now, since I know neither and see that for the present you permit them to be taken from me, I commit the case to you. I will await what I am to do, and be ready to have them or to do without them."

That, mark you, is a right soul, and one that fears God. There is God's mercy, as the Mother of God sings. Hence we can see why in times past Abraham, David, and the people of Israel waged war and slew many. They went into battle by the will of God, they stood in fear, and fought not for the sake of the goods but because God commanded them to fight, as the narratives show, in which this command of God is usually set forth at the beginning.[84] In this way the truth is not denied, for the truth declares they are good things and God's creatures. But the same truth declares also and teaches that you should let such good things go, be ready at all times to do without them, if God so wills it, and cleave to God alone. The truth, by saying they are good, does not compel you to take the good things back again, nor to say they are not good; but it does compel you to regard them with equanimity[o] and to confess that they are good and not evil.

84. For example, in Joshua 1, the Lord commands the people to cross over the Jordan and fight to take the land that he was giving to them, and they agree to follow Joshua into battle.

o   Luther has here *"gelassen stehen."* As he notes in the next paragraph, *gelassenheit* is the appropriate response, especially when we are not sure of God's will.

In the same manner we must treat the right and the manifold good things of reason or wisdom. Who can doubt that right is a good thing and a gift of God? God's word itself says right is good, and no one should admit that his good and righteous cause is unrighteous or evil, but should sooner die for it and let go everything that is not God. To do otherwise would be to deny God and his word, for he says right is good and not evil. But if such right is snatched from you or suppressed, would you cry out, storm and rage, and slay the whole world? Some do this; they cry to heaven, work all manner of affliction, ruin land and people, and fill the world with war and bloodshed. How do you know whether or not it is God's will that you keep such a gift and right? It belongs to him, and he can take it from you today or tomorrow, outwardly or inwardly, by friend or enemy, just as he wills. He tries you to see whether you will give up your right for his will's sake, be in the wrong and suffer wrong, endure shame for him, and stick to him alone. If you fear God and think: "Lord, it is yours; I will not hold onto it unless I know that you want me to have it. Let happen what will, just be my God"—then this verse is fulfilled: "His mercy is on those who fear him," who refuse to do anything apart from his will. Then both sides of God's word are observed. In the first place, you confess that the right, your reason, knowledge, wisdom, and all your thoughts are right and good, as God's word teaches. In the second place, you are willing to go without such good things for God's sake, to be wrongfully despoiled and put to shame before the world, as God's word also teaches. To confess the right and good is one thing, to obtain it is another. It is enough for you to confess that you are in the right; if you cannot obtain it, commit that to God. To you is committed the confession, the obtaining God has reserved to himself. If he desires you also to obtain, he will perform it himself or put it in your way, without any thought of yours, so that you must come into possession of it and win the victory, above all that you asked or thought [Eph. 3:20]. If he does not desire you to obtain it, let his mercy be sufficient for you [2 Cor. 12:9]. Though they deprive you of the victory of the right, they cannot deprive you of the confession. Thus we must refrain, not from the good things of God but from wickedly and falsely cleaving to them; so that we may use them or suffer the lack of them with equanimity, and cling, whatever befalls, to God alone. Oh, this is a thing that ought to be known to all princes and rulers who, not content with confessing the right, immediately want to obtain it and win the victory, without the fear of God; they fill the world with bloodshed and misery, and think what they do is right and well done because they have, or think they have, a just cause. What else is that but proud and haughty Moab, which calls and makes itself worthy to possess the right, that fine and noble good and gift of God; while if it regards itself correctly in the sight of God, it is not worthy to live on earth or eat a crust of bread, because of its sins. Oh, blindness, blindness! Who is worthy of the least creature of God? Yet we desire not only to possess the highest creatures, right, wisdom, and honor, but to keep them or regain possession of them with furious shedding of blood and every disaster. Thereupon we go and pray, fast, hear Mass, and found churches, with such bloody, furious, raving hearts, it is a wonder the stones do not burst asunder in our face.

Here a question arises. If a ruler did not defend his land and subjects against injustice, but made no resistance, and let all be taken from him, what would the world come to? I will briefly set down my view of the matter. Temporal power is in duty bound to defend its subjects, as I have frequently said, for it bears the sword in order to keep in fear those who do not heed such divine teaching, and to compel them to leave others in peace. And in this the temporal power seeks not its own but its neighbor's profit and God's honor; it would gladly remain quiet and let its sword rust, if God had not ordained it to be a hindrance to evildoers. Yet this defense of its subjects should not be accompanied by still greater harm; that would be but to leap from the frying pan into the fire.[p] It is a poor defense to expose a whole city to danger for the sake of one person, or to risk the entire country

Referring to 2 Kings 3, this copper engraving by Christoph Weigel (1654–1725) shows Israel destroying Moab by laying siege to the city. The king of Moab is sacrificing his sons in a fire in the background (upper left).

---

p   Luther has "*ein leffel auffgehaben werd, da man ein schussel zutrit.*" That means something along the lines of picking up or protecting a spoon (that is, something small), but breaking the dish (something much bigger). This was a common saying for Luther.

85. Luther's position is similar to that of other just-war theorists in the sixteenth century such as Francisco de Vitoria (1483–1546) and Domingo de Soto (1494–1560), who argued that war is only necessary and just if it prevents a greater evil, and only as much violence as is strictly necessary can be used.

86. While at the Wartburg (1521–22), Luther began to write letters (and this commentary) in which he addressed the issue of the theological basis for political power. He came to a definitive statement, including his two-kingdoms theory, in *On Temporal Authority: To What Extent It Should Be Obeyed* (December 1522, published in 1523). The end of this work was also a "mirror" for princes, in that it explained how one could be a Christian, disliking the use of force, and a ruler, who was required by his office to use force to maintain peace and protect the common good.

87. Luther notes in his treatise *On Temporal [Secular] Authority* (LW 45:75–130; TAL 5, forthcoming) that such rulers do not have the right to legislate the gospel, and any such laws do not need to be obeyed. However, Christians are not allowed to respond with force, so they may in fact have to suffer for the sake of God's word and truth, only able to witness to their faith (possibly even as martyrs, of which there were many in the sixteenth century).

for a single village or castle, unless God enjoined this by a special command, as he did in former times. If a knight robs a citizen of his property and you, my lord, lead your army against him to punish this injustice, and in so doing lay waste the whole land, who will have wrought the greater harm, the knight or the lord? David looked the other way many times when he was unable to punish without bringing harm upon others. All rulers must do the same. On the other hand, a citizen must endure a certain measure of suffering for the sake of the community, and not demand that all others undergo the greater injury for his sake. It will not always be equal—Christ did not want the weeds to be gathered up, lest the wheat also be rooted up with them [Matt. 13:29]. If people went to war on every provocation and overlooked nothing, we should never be at peace and have nothing but destruction. Therefore, right or wrong is never a sufficient cause indiscriminately to punish or make war. It is a sufficient cause to punish within bounds and without destroying another.[85] The lord or ruler must always look to what will profit the whole mass of his subjects rather than any one portion. That householder will never grow rich who, because someone has plucked a feather from his goose, flings the whole goose after him. But there is no time now to go into the subject of war.[86]

We must do the same in things divine, such as faith and the gospel, which are the highest goods and which no one should let go. But the right, favor, honor, and acceptance of them we must cast in the balance and commit them to God. We should be concerned not to obtain but to confess, and willingly endure being reviled before all the world, being persecuted, banished, burned at the stake, or otherwise slain, as unrighteous, deceivers, heretics, apostates, blasphemers, and what not; for then God's mercy is upon us. They cannot take the faith and the truth from us, even though they take our lives.[87] There are not very many, however, who rage and fret to obtain and to win the victory in this matter, as they do in temporal goods and rights. There are also few who confess it aright and on principle. But we should grieve and lament for the others who through the defeat of the gospel are hindered in their souls' salvation. In fact, we should lament and work (yet as in the sight of God) because of the injury to souls inflicted by the Moabites for the sake of their own temporal goods and rights, as we said above. For it is a lamentable thing when God's word does not win the victory, lamentable not so far as the confessor is concerned, but so far as those are concerned who should have been saved by it. Hence we find in the prophets, in Christ, and in the apostles such sorrow and lamentation for the suppression of the word of God, although they were glad to bear any injustice and injury. For far more depends on the obtaining of this good than of any other. Yet no one should employ force or keep or regain such right of the gospel by rage and unreason; he should rather humble himself before God as one who may not be worthy that such a great and good thing be done through him, and commit all to his mercy with prayer and lamentation.

This, then, is the first work of God—that he is merciful to all who are ready to do without their own opinion, right, wisdom, and all spiritual goods, and willing to be poor in spirit.[88] These are the ones who truly fear God, who count themselves not worthy of anything, be it ever so small, and are glad to be naked and bare before God and the world; who ascribe whatever they have to his pure grace, bestowed on the unworthy; who use it with praise and fear and thanksgiving, as though it belonged to another, and who seek not their own will, desire, or honor, but his

Jan Hus, the Czech reformer and theologian, was burned as a heretic at the Council of Constance in 1415. He was recognized as a martyr for his faith by many later Christians, and Luther also recognized him as an important precursor to the Reformation.

alone to whom it belongs. Mary also indicates how much more gladly God shows such mercy, which is his noblest work, than its counterpart, his strength; for she says this work of God endures without ceasing from generation to generation of those that fear him, while his strength endures only to the third and fourth generation, although in the verse that follows it has no time or limit set to it.

88. This explanation, then, connects the work of God's mercy to the Beatitudes, where in Matt. 5:3 Jesus notes that the "poor in spirit" are blessed with the kingdom of heaven (Luke 6:20 refers to the poor, not the poor in spirit).

The Second Work of God, Breaking Spiritual Pride

51. *He has shown strength with his arm and has scattered the proud in the imagination of their hearts.*

I trust no one will be confused by my translation. Above I rendered this verse, "He shows strength," and here, "He has shown strength."*q* I have done this in order that we may the better understand these words, which are not bound to any one time, but are intended to set forth in general the works of God that he always has done, always does, and always will do. Hence the following would be a fair translation: "God is a Lord whose works are of such a nature that he mightily scatters the proud and is merciful to those who fear him." In the Scriptures, the "arm" of God means God's own power, by which he works without the medium of any creature. This work is done quietly and in secret, and no one becomes aware of it until all is accomplished, so that this power, or arm, can be known and understood only by faith. Therefore Isaiah complains [Isa. 53:1] that so few have faith in this arm, saying: "Who has believed the preaching, and to whom has the arm of the LORD been revealed?" These things are so because, as he goes on to say, all is done in secret and without the semblance of power. We also read in Hab. 3[:4] that there are horns coming out of God's hands, to indicate his mighty power; and yet it is said: "There his power was hidden."*r* What is the meaning of this?

It means that when God works by means of his creatures, it is plainly seen where the strength is and where the weakness. Hence the proverb, "God helps those who help themselves."*s* For example, whichever prince wins a battle, it is seen that God defeated the other by him. When someone is devoured by a wolf

---

q   The NRSV has "he has shown strength."

r   The NRSV reads, "The brightness was like the sun; rays came forth from his hand, where his power lay hidden." The Vulgate has "*cornua in manibus eius ibi abscondita est fortitudo eius.*" Like Moses' "horns" in Exod. 34:29-35, this was only one way of translating the Hebrew word, which could mean either "rays" or "horns" depending on the vocalization.

s   Luther has here "*Gott hilfft den sterckisten,*" from the Latin proverb, "*Fortes fortuna adiuvat.*"

or otherwise injured, it is evident that it took place by means of the creature. Thus God makes or breaks one creature by means of another. Whoever falls, falls; whoever stands, stands. But it is different when God himself works, with his own arm. Then a thing is destroyed or raised up before one knows it, and no one sees it done. Such works as these he does only among the two divisions of the world, the godly and the wicked. He lets the godly become powerless and brought low, until everyone supposes their end is near, whereas in these very things he is present to them with all his power, yet so hidden and in secret that even those who suffer the oppression do not feel it but only believe. There is the fullness of God's power and his outstretched arm. For where human strength ends, God's strength begins, provided faith is present and waits on him. And when the oppression comes to an end, it becomes manifest what great strength was hidden underneath the weakness. Even so, Christ was powerless on the cross; and yet there he performed his mightiest work and conquered sin, death, world, hell, devil, and all evil.[89] Thus all the martyrs were strong and overcame. Thus, too, all who suffer and are oppressed overcome. Therefore it is said in Joel 3[:10]: "Let the weak say, 'I am strong'"—yet in faith, and without feeling it until it is accomplished.

On the other hand, God lets the other part become great and exalt themselves mightily. He withdraws his power from them and lets them puff themselves up in their own power alone. For where human strength begins, God's strength ends. When their bubble is full-blown, and everyone supposes them to have won and overcome, and they themselves feel smug in their achievement, then God pricks the bubble, and it is all over. The fools do not know that even while they are puffing themselves up and growing strong they are forsaken by God, and God's arm is not with them. Therefore their prosperity has its day, disappears like a bubble, and is as if it had never been. To this the psalmist refers in Ps. 73[:16-20]. It bothered him when he saw the riches, pride, and prosperity of the wicked in the world. At last he said: "I was not able to understand until I looked into the secrets of God, and then I perceived how it would go with them in the end. I saw that they were exalted only in their self-deception, and were brought to ruin in their exaltation. How they are destroyed in a moment, how quickly it is all over for them! It is as though they had never existed, like a dream when

89. In thesis 20 of the *Heidelberg Disputation* (1518), Luther explains that God is truly revealed in Christ's suffering and weakness, even in his death. God's glory and might are hidden in the humility and shame of the cross. See LW 31:52–53; WA 1:353–74; TAL 1:99. For more on the theology of the cross, see Gerhard Forde, *On Being a Theologian of the Cross: Reflections on Luther's Heidelberg Disputation, 1518* (Grand Rapids: Eerdmans, 1998).

90. Luther explains in the *Heidelberg Disputation* that the "alien" works of God—so named in Isa. 28:21—are when God shows wrath and punishes us, or allows us to suffer (thesis 4), but his "proper" works are "hidden" under these alien works, only visible to those with the eyes of faith. The proper works of God are works of grace and mercy, giving forgiveness, saving, etc. See LW 31:39–70; WA 1:353–74; TAL 1:67–120.

91. This passage resonates with the story of the Tower of Babel in Genesis 11. In that episode, the Lord, seeing the great tower begun by the people united by language, decided to confuse their words and scatter them "over the face of all the earth," so that they would not begin to achieve ever-greater things in their pride and ambition.

The Confusion of Tongues by Gustave Doré (1832–1883). When God destroyed the Tower of Babel (Genesis 11), God scattered the people and confused their languages.

one awakes." And Ps. 37[:35-36]: "I have seen a wicked man overbearing and towering like a cedar from the mountain of Lebanon. Again I passed by, and, lo, he was no more. I asked about him, but he was no longer there."

It is because of our lack of faith that we cannot wait a little, until the time comes when we, too, shall see how the mercy of God together with all his might is with those who fear him, and the arm of God with all severity and power against the proud. We faithless ones grope about with our hands for the mercy and the arm of God, and, unable to feel them, suppose our cause is lost and that of our enemies is won, as though God's grace and mercy had forsaken us and his arm turned against us. We do this because we do not know his proper works and therefore do not know him, neither his mercy nor his arm, for he must and will be known by faith, and so our sense and our reason must close their eyes.[90] This is the eye that offends us; therefore it must be plucked out and cast from us. These, then, are the two contrary works of God, from which we learn that he is minded to be far from the wise and prudent and near to the foolish and those compelled to be in the wrong. This makes God worthy of love and praise and comforts soul and body and all our powers.

We come to the words: "He scatters the proud in the imagination of their hearts." This scattering takes place, as we have said, when their prudence is at its height and when they are filled with their own wisdom; then, truly, God's wisdom is no longer with them. And in what better way could he scatter them than by depriving them of his eternal wisdom and permitting them to be filled with their own temporal, short-lived, and perishing wisdom?[91] For Mary says: "the proud in the imagination of their hearts"; that is, those who delight in their own opinions, thoughts, and reason, which not God but their own hearts inspire, and who suppose that these are right and good and wise above all others. Therefore they exalt themselves above those who fear God, put down and pour shame upon the opinion and right of others, and persecute them to the utmost, so that their own cause may by all means be right and be maintained. When they have accomplished this, they boast and loudly brag, as the Jews did with Christ. Yet the Jews did not see that by this their cause was destroyed and brought down, while Christ was exalted to glory. We observe, then, that our verse treats of spiritual goods and how one can know God's twofold work in them. It shows us that we ought gladly to be poor in spirit and in the wrong and let our adversaries be in the right. They will not long continue; the promise is too strong for them. They cannot escape God's arm but must succumb and be brought as low as they once were high, if we will only believe it. But where there is no faith, God does not perform such works—he withdraws his arm and works openly by means of the creatures, as we said above. But these are not his proper works, by which he may be known; for in them the creatures' strength is mingled with his own. They are not God's own pure works, as they must be when no one works with him and he alone does the work, which he does when we become powerless and oppressed in our right or our opinion and let God's power work in us. Those are noble works![92]

With what mastery Mary here hits the perverse hypocrites! She looks not at their hands or in their eyes, but in their hearts when she says: "the proud in the imagination of their hearts." She refers in particular to the enemies of divine truth, such as the Jews in their opposition to Christ, and even today, the same scholars and saints are not proud of their dress or conduct, [but] pray much, fast much, preach and study much; they also say Mass, go meekly with bowed head, and shun costly clothes. They think there are no greater foes to pride, error, and hypocrisy, nor any better friends of truth and of God than they themselves.[93] How else could they bring such great harm upon the truth if they were not such holy, pious, and learned people? Their doings make a brave outward show and impress the common people. Oh, they have good hearts and mean well, they call upon the good God and pity the poor Jesus, who was so unrighteous and proud, and not so pious as they. He says of them in Matthew 11[:19]: "Divine wisdom is justified by her children," that is: "They are more righteous and wise than I, who am divine wisdom itself; whatever I do is wrong, and I am mastered by them."

92. Here Luther implies that true nobility is unrelated to (high) social status, but in fact the term can (and should more accurately) be applied to those who are in the lowest positions in society, the powerless and oppressed.

93. Luther is drawing a parallel between the Jews of Jesus' day who rejected him (and, in particular, the Pharisees) and the people of his own day (such as the pope and his followers) who make a great show of holiness and wisdom.

These are the most venomous and pernicious people on earth, their hearts abysses of devilish pride. There is no helping them; they will not heed our counsel. It does not concern them; they leave that to poor sinners, for whom such teaching is necessary, but not for them. John calls them "a brood of vipers" in Luke 3[:7], and so does Christ [Matt. 12:34]. These are the right guilty ones, who do not fear God and are fit only that God should scatter them with their pride, because no one persecutes the right and wisdom more than they—yet for the sake of God and of righteousness, as we have said. Hence they must be first and foremost among the three enemies of God on this side, for the rich are the least of his enemies; the mighty are much more hostile; but these learned ones are the worst of all because of their influence on others. The rich destroy the truth among themselves; the mighty drive it away from others; but these wise ones utterly extinguish the truth itself and replace it with other things, the imagination of their own hearts, so that the truth cannot come into its own again. As much as the truth itself is better than the people in whom it dwells, so much worse are the wise than the mighty and the rich. Oh, God is their special enemy, as they well deserve.

Digito compesce labellum.

Multa quidem audienda, pauca vero dicenda.

Dixisse, aliquando poenituit, tacuisse nunquam.

THOMAS VOLFFIVS.

The printer's device, or mark, of Thomas Wolff (fl. 1519–1535) appearing in Luther's *De bonis operibus libellus* shows a scholar coming out of a door with one hand to his mouth and the other lifted in warning. The three mottoes around the picture can be translated as "Much indeed is to be heard, little truly to be learned," "Put your finger to your lip" (or "Be silent"), and "One sometimes regrets having spoken, not staying silent." Scholars are often critiqued for speaking much but saying little of value.

The Third Work, Putting Down the Mighty

52. *He has put down the mighty from their seats.*[t]

This work and those that follow are easily understood from the two foregoing works. God scatters the wise and prudent in their own thoughts and imaginations, on which they depend, venting their pride on those who fear God, who must needs be in the wrong and see their right and their opinion rejected, which happens chiefly for the sake of God's word. Just so he destroys and puts down the mighty and the great with their strength and authority, on which they depend, venting their pride on their inferiors, the godly and weak, who must suffer injury, pain, death, and all manner of evil at their hands. And just as he comforts those who must suffer wrong and shame for the right, truth, and word, so he comforts those who must suffer injury and evil. And as much as he comforts the latter, so much he terrifies the former. But this, too, must all be known and waited for in faith. For he does not destroy the mighty as suddenly as they deserve, but lets them go for a while, until their might has reached its highest point. When it has done this, God does not support it, neither can it support itself; it breaks down of its own weight without any crash or sound, and the oppressed are raised up, also without any sound, for God's strength is in them, and it alone remains when the strength of the mighty has fallen.

Observe, however, that Mary does not say he breaks the seats, but that he casts the mighty out. Nor does she say he leaves those of low degree in their low degree, but he exalts them. For while the world stands, authority, rule, power, and seats must remain.[94] But God will not long permit people to abuse them and turn them against him, inflict injustice and violence on the godly and enjoy it, boast of them, and fail to use them in the fear of God, to his praise and in defense of righteousness. We see in all histories and in experience that he puts down one kingdom and exalts another, lifts up one principality and casts down another, increases one people and destroys another, as he

94. The seat, or throne, is a metaphor for the office or position of a ruler. Mary's point, in Luther's interpretation, is that rulers and offices will still remain in the world, even as God will cast down those who misuse their power. He is definitely not advocating rebellion against authority.

---

t   While the NRSV has "thrones" here, and that is frequently how it is translated in English, Luther uses the term *stuelen* to translate *de sedibus*. *Stuelen* is more accurately translated as "chairs" or "seats," often associated with an office, rather than as "thrones."

95. Assyria ruled a kingdom/empire in south-central Asia, with several periods of rise and decline, from c. 2500 to 605 BCE. The neo-Babylonian Empire, founded by Chaldeans, followed the Assyrian Empire from 608 to 539 BCE. In 550, under Cyrus, the Persians began to assemble their empire, expanding from Mesopotamia in all directions to form the first true world empire. The Persians were defeated by Alexander the Great in 333. The Hellenistic Empire spawned by Alexander split into several "Greek" empires, until its defeat by Rome, which established an empire throughout the entire Mediterranean world. All of these empires experienced rises and falls (sometimes more than once).

did with Assyria, Babylon, Persia, Greece, and Rome, although they thought they would sit in their seats forever.[95] Nor does he destroy reason, wisdom, and right; for if the world is to go on, we must have reason, wisdom, and right. But he does destroy pride and the proud, who use these things for selfish ends, enjoy them, do not fear God, but persecute the godly and the divine right by means of them, and thus abuse the fair gifts of God and turn them against him.

Now, in things divine, the wise guys and proud sages usually make common cause with the mighty and persuade them to take sides against the truth; as it is written in Ps. 2[:2]: "The kings of the earth set themselves, and the rulers take counsel together, against the LORD and his anointed." For truth and right must always be assailed by the wise, the mighty, and the rich, that is, by the world with its greatest and best ability. Hence the Holy Spirit comforts truth and right by the mouth of this mother so that they will not be deceived or afraid. Let them be wise, mighty, rich: it will not be for long. For if the saints and scholars, together with the mighty lords and the rich, were not against but for the right and the truth, what would become of the wrong? Who would there be to suffer evil? No—the learned, saintly, mighty, great and rich, and the best that the world has must fight against God and the right, and be the devil's own. As it is said in Hab. 1[:16]: "His food is rich and choice"; that is to say, the evil spirit has a most delicate palate and is fond of feasting on the very best, daintiest, and choicest morsels, as a bear on honey. Hence the learned and saintly hypocrites, the great lords and the rich, are the devil's own tidbits. On the other hand, as St. Paul says in 1 Cor. 1[:28], those whom the world rejects, the poor, lowly, simplehearted, and despised, God has chosen, causing the best part of the world to bring suffering upon the lowest part, in order that it may be known that our salvation consists not in human power and works but in God's alone, as St. Paul also says [1 Cor. 3:7]. Hence there is much truth in these sayings, "The more men know, the worse they grow";[u] "A prince, a rare bird in

---

u   *Die gelerten die vorkeretenn.* This saying was used frequently by Luther, but was also common among many other writers in the sixteenth and seventeenth centuries. It has its origins in the fifteenth century as a popular phrase to describe theologians and lawyers. See Carlos Gilly, "Das Sprichwort 'Die Gelehrten die Verkehrten' oder der Verrat der

heaven";[96] "Rich here, poor yonder."[97] For the learned will not surrender the pride of their hearts, nor the mighty their oppression, nor the rich their pleasures. And so it goes.

The Fourth Work, Exalting the Lowly

And he has exalted those of low degree.

Those of low degree are here not the humble, but all those who are contemptible and altogether nothing in the eyes of the world. It is the same expression that Mary applied to herself above: "He has regarded the low estate of his handmaiden." Nevertheless, those who are willing to be nothing and lowly of heart, and do not strive to be great, are truly humble. Now, when he exalts them, it does not mean that he will put them in the seats of those he has cast out any more than that when he shows mercy to those who fear him, he puts them in the place of the learned, that is, the proud. Rather he lets them be exalted spiritually and in God, and be judges over seats and power and all might, here and hereafter, for they have more knowledge than all the learned and the mighty.[98] How this is done was said above under the first work and need not be repeated. All this is said for the comfort of those who are suffering and for the terror of the tyrants, if we only had faith enough to believe that it is true.

The Fifth and Sixth Works

53. He has filled the hungry with good things, and the rich he has sent empty away.

We said above that by those of low degree are meant not those who are despised and nothing in appearance, but those who are willing to be in such a state, especially if they have been forced into it for the sake of God's word or the right.[99] Likewise by the hungry are not meant those who have little or nothing to eat,

96. Like the previous proverb, this phrase was popular with Luther. He refers to a prince as a "rare bird" several times in his treatise *On Temporal [Secular] Authority*. The phrase appears to have originated with Juvenal (early second century) in his *Satires* (6.165), where he refers to a perfect wife as a *rara avis*, a "bird as rare upon the earth as a black swan."

97. This phrase brings to mind the parable of Lazarus and the rich man (also known as Dives, which just means "rich man") in Luke 16:19-31, and the comment in Matt. 19:24 that it is easier for a camel to go through the eye of a needle than for a rich person to enter the kingdom of God.

98. At the Last Supper, Jesus told his disciples that they would "eat and drink at my table in my kingdom, and you will sit on thrones judging the twelve tribes of Israel" (Luke 22:30).

99. Here Luther makes clear that "low degree" is not simply a matter of social status, but a matter of attitude and will.

Intellektuellen im Zeitalter der Glaubensspaltung," in A. Rotondò, ed., *Forme e destinazione del messaggio religioso* (Florence: Leo Olschki Editore, 1991), 229–375, esp. 233–37.

100. While Luke mentions that "blessed are those who hunger now, for they will be satisfied" (Luke 6:21), Matthew's version of the Beatitudes makes clear that "blessed are those who hunger and thirst for righteousness, for they will be filled" (Matt. 5:6).

101. When choosing the new king of Israel, the Lord remarked to Samuel, "the Lord does not see as mortals see; they look on the outward appearance, but the Lord looks on the heart" (1 Sam. 16:7).

102. Likewise, the rich man in the parable of Lazarus did not appear to know prior to his death that he would be suffering in hell—at the least, he wanted to return from the grave to warn his five brothers of their impending doom, since they did not seem to take Moses and the prophets seriously.

but those who gladly suffer want, especially if they are forcibly compelled by others to do so for the sake of God or the truth. Who is lowlier, more despised, and needier than the devil and the damned, or than those who are tortured, starved, or slain on account of their evil deeds, or all who are lowly and in want against their will? Yet that does not help them but only adds to their misery. Of them the Mother of God does not speak, but of those who are one with God and God with them, and who believe and trust in him.[100]

On the other hand, what hindrance was their riches to the holy fathers Abraham, Isaac, and Jacob? What hindrance was his royal throne to David, or his authority in Babylon to Daniel? Or their high station or great riches to those who had them or who have them today, provided they do not set their hearts on them or seek their own advantage in them? Solomon says in Prov. 16[:2]: "The Lord weighs the spirit"; that is, he judges not according to the outward appearance, whether one is rich or poor, high or low, but according to the spirit and how it behaves itself within.[101] There must be such differences and distinctions of persons and stations in our life here on earth; yet the heart should neither cling to them nor fly from them—neither cling to the high and rich nor fly from the poor and lowly. Thus it is also said in Ps. 7[:9, 11]: "God tries the hearts and minds, therefore he is a righteous judge." But people judge according to the outward appearance; therefore they often err.

These works are done in secret, like those mentioned above, so that no one is aware of them until they have come to an end. A rich man is not aware how really empty and wretched he is until he comes to die or otherwise suffers loss.[102] Then only does he see how all his goods were altogether nothing, as it is said in Ps. 76[:5]: "They sank into sleep [that is, they died]; all the rich men discovered that they had nothing in their hands."[v] On the other hand, the hungry and thirsty know not how filled they are until they come to the end. Then they find the words of Christ true, in Luke 6:21: "Blessed are those who hunger and thirst, for they shall be filled"; and the comforting promise of the Mother of God here: "He has filled the hungry with good things." It is

---

v   The Vulgate (Ps. 75:6) has "*nihil invenerunt omnes viri divitiarum manibus suis,*" or "all the men of wealth have found nothing in their hands." However, the NRSV reads, "none of the troops was able to lift a hand."

utterly impossible for God to let anyone who trusts in him die of starvation; all angels would have to come and feed him. Elijah was fed by ravens and he and the widow of Zarephath lived for many days on a handful of meal [1 Kgs. 17:6, 15]. God cannot forsake those who trust in him. Hence David says in Ps. 37[:25]: "I have been young, and now am old; yet I have not seen the righteous forsaken, or their children begging bread." Whoever trusts in God is righteous. Again, in Ps. 34[:10]: "The rich*w* suffer want and hunger; but those who seek the LORD lack no good thing." And St. Hannah, the mother of Samuel, says in 1 Sam. 2[:5]: "Those who were full have hired themselves out for bread, and the hungry are filled."

But our wretched unbelief always hinders God from working such works in us, and ourselves from experiencing and knowing them. We desire to be filled and have plenty of everything before hunger and want arrive. We lay up provision against future hunger and need, so that we no longer have need of God and his works. What sort of faith is that which trusts in God, when all the while you feel and know that you have goods laid up to help yourself?[103] It is because of our unbelief that we see God's word, the truth, and the right defeated and wrong triumph and yet remain silent, do not rebuke, speak out, or prevent it, but let things go as they will. Why? We are afraid that we, too, might be attacked and made poor and might then perish of hunger and be forever laid low. That is to esteem temporal goods more than God and to put them in God's place as an idol. If we do this, we do not deserve to hear or to understand this comfortable promise of God: that he exalts the lowly, puts down the mighty, fills the poor, and empties the rich. We do not deserve ever to come to the knowledge of his works, without which there is no salvation. We must therefore be damned forever, as Ps. 28[:5] says: "Because they do not regard the works of the LORD or the work of his hand, he will break them down and build them up no more."

And this is only fair, because they do not believe his promises but count him a fickle, lying God. They dare not venture or begin anything on the strength of his words, so little do they esteem his truth. It is indeed necessary that we give it a go and venture out on his words; for Mary does not say that he has filled

103. Luther may be referring to the parable of the rich fool (Luke 12:16-21), which addresses this point. The man decided to tear down his barns and build bigger ones to store his great harvest, and then told himself, "Soul, you have ample goods laid up for many years; relax, eat, drink, be merry." But God revealed his foolishness, because that very night he was going to die, and would not be able to enjoy any of those earthly treasures.

---

w The NRSV has here "young lions," while the Vulgate (Ps. 33:11) has *divites*.

the full and exalted those of high degree, but "he has filled the hungry and exalted those of low degree." You must feel the pinch of poverty in the midst of your hunger and learn by experience what hunger and poverty are, with no provision on hand and no help in yourself or any other person, but in God only; so that the work may be God's alone and impossible to be done by any other. You must not only think and speak of a low estate but actually come to be in a low estate and caught in it, without any human aid, so that God alone may do the work. Or if it should not come to such a pass, you must at least desire it and not shrink from it. We are Christians and have the gospel, which neither the devil nor people can abide, in order that we may come into poverty and lowliness and God may thereby have his work in us. Think for yourself, and you will see that if God were to fill you before you were hungry or to exalt you before you were brought low, he would have to sink to the level of a conjurer;[104] he would

104. A conjurer has no real power, but is an illusionist or charlatan, someone who deceives his audience with tricks, as in the painting *The Conjurer* by Hieronymus Bosch (c. 1502), whose audience is focused on the tricks while having their pockets picked (see image).

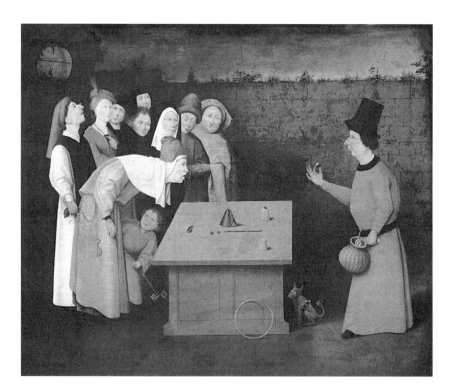

The Conjurer by Hieronymus Bosch, c. 1502.

be unable to do what he promises, and all his works would be a mere jest, whereas it is written in Ps. 111[:7]: "His works are truth and trustworthiness." And even if he were to perform his works as soon as you felt the first pinch of want or lowliness, or to help you in some slight need, such works would be altogether unworthy of his divine power and majesty; for Ps. 111[:2] says of them: "Great are the works of the LORD, sought out according to all his desires."

Let us assume the reverse case. If he were to put down the rich and those of high degree before they became either rich or high, how would he go about it? They must first have risen to so high a place and come into such great riches that they themselves and everyone else supposed—in fact, that it was actually the case—none could put them down, none could stop them, and that they were sure of themselves and said what Isaiah writes of them and of Babylon [Isa. 47:8-9]: "Now hear this, you tender one, who sit securely, who say in your heart, 'I am, and there is no one besides me; I shall not sit as a widow or know the loss of children' [that is, of power and help]: both these things shall come to you in one day." Then God can perform his deeds in them. Thus he let Pharaoh exalt himself against the children of Israel and oppress them, as God himself says about him in Exod. 9[:16]: "For this purpose have I raised you up, to show my power through you, so that my praise may be declared throughout all the earth." The Bible is full of these examples, teaching nothing but the work and the word of God and rejecting human work and word.

Behold, how strong a comfort this is, that not any person but God gives to the hungry, and that he not only gives them this or that but fills and fully satisfies them. Mary says, moreover, "with good things." That is to say, this fullness is to be harmless, wholesome, and saving, benefiting both body and soul, and all their powers. But it also shows that, before being filled, the hungry are lacking in all good things and filled with all want. For, as we said above, riches here include all manner of temporal goods for the supply of bodily needs, to make the soul glad. Even so, hunger here signifies the lack not only of food, but of all temporal goods. For a person can do without everything else but food, so that almost all goods exist for the sake of furnishing him with food, without which no one can live, even though he might be able to live without clothing, house, money, property, and [other] people. Scripture, therefore, here designates temporal goods according to that part of them whose need and use are most essential and which we can least of all do without. Thus it also calls misers and those who covet temporal goods "servants of their own belly" [Rom. 16:18], and Paul calls their belly their god [Phil. 3:19]. How could one be more strongly and comfortably moved to willing endurance of hunger and poverty than by these fine words of the Mother of God—that God will fill all the hungry with good things? Whoever is not moved by these words and such glory and praise of poverty is certainly without faith and trust, a genuine heathen.

On the other hand, how could one bring a more damning accusation against riches, or more grievously terrify the rich, than by saying that God sends them empty away? Oh, how great and overflowing are both God's filling and God's sending away! How utterly vain here is the help or counsel of any creature! A person is frightened when he hears that his father has disowned him or that he has fallen into disfavor with his lord. Yet we who are rich and of high degree are not frightened when we hear that God disowns us—indeed, not only disowns us, but threatens to break, humble, and send us empty away! It is a joy, on the other hand, when one's father is good and one's lord gracious, and many a one sets such great store by these things as to give up life and property for them. We have here such a promise of God and such strong comfort—yet we can neither use nor enjoy them, neither thank him for them nor rejoice in them! Oh, wretched unbelief, hard and firm as stock and stone, not to feel such great things! Let this suffice concerning the six works of God.

54. *He has helped his servant Israel*
in remembrance of his mercy.

After enumerating the works of God in her and in all people, Mary returns to the beginning and to the chief thing. She concludes the Magnificat by mentioning the very greatest of all God's works—the incarnation of the Son of God. She freely acknowledges herself as the handmaiden and servant of all the world, confessing that this work which was performed in her was not done for her sake alone, but for the sake of all Israel. But she divides Israel into two parts and refers only to that part that is God's servant. Now, no one is God's servant unless he lets him be his God and perform his works in him, of which we spoke above. Alas, the phrase "service of God" has nowadays taken on so strange a meaning and usage that whoever hears it thinks not of these works of God, but rather of the ringing of bells, the wood and stone of churches, the incense pot, the flicker of candles, the mumbling in the churches, the gold, silver, and precious stones in the vestments of choirboys and celebrants, of chalices and monstrances,[105] of organs and images, processions and churchgoing, and, most of all, the babbling of lips and the rattling of rosaries.[106] This, alas, is what the service

In this representation of a eucharistic procession, the consecrated host is displayed in a monstrance.

105. A monstrance is a vessel used for displaying the consecrated eucharistic host, usually for a procession or for adoration.

106. The rosary is a string of beads associated with a series of prayers (Hail Mary, Our Father, and Glory Be), with each bead representing a different prayer, and a focus upon different events in the lives of Christ and Mary. The origins of the rosary are associated with the Dominican order, and the devotion began around the fourteenth century.

of God means now. Of such service God knows nothing at all, while we know nothing but this. We chant the Magnificat daily, to a special tone and with gorgeous pomp; and yet the oftener we sing it, the more we silence its true music and meaning. Yet the text stands firm. Unless we learn and experience these works of God, there will be no service of God, no Israel, no grace, no mercy, no God, though we kill ourselves with singing and ringing in the churches and drag into them all the goods in all the world. God has not commanded any of these things, undoubtedly, therefore, he takes no pleasure in them.[107]

Now, the Israel that is God's servant is the one whom the incarnation of Christ benefits. That is his own beloved people, for whose sake he also became incarnate, to redeem them from

107. Luther's scriptural principle—that the Bible is *the* authority in the church—led him to recognize that many demands of churchly law and practice were *adiaphora*, that is, matters indifferent, but other demands were downright dangerous and evil because they were forbidden by God. One example is that of monastic vows, against which he wrote while at the Wartburg in 1521 (see LW 44:243–400; WA 8:573–669). Such vows, considered sacred and binding in the church, were actually against God's command to marry and "be fruitful." Marriage instead was the preferred estate, since few, if any, were actually given the "gift" of chastity.

the power of the devil, of sin, death, and hell, and to lead them to righteousness, eternal life, and salvation. That is the help of which Mary sings. As Paul says in Titus 2:14: "Christ gave himself for us, to purify for himself a people of his own"; and St. Peter in 1 Pet. 2:9: "You are a holy nation, God's chosen people, a royal priesthood." These are the riches of the boundless mercy of God, which we have received by no merit but by pure grace. Therefore she sings: "He has remembered his mercy." She does not say: "He has remembered our merit and worthiness." We were in need, to be sure, but completely unworthy. That is the basis of his praise and glory, while our boasting and presumption must keep quiet. There was nothing for him to regard that could move him except that he was merciful, and that he desired to make that same name [Israel] known. But why does she say, "he remembered" rather than "he regarded" his mercy? Because he had promised it, as the following verse shows. Now, he had waited a long time before showing it, until it seemed as though he had forgotten—even as all his works seem as though he were forgetting us—but when he came, it was seen that he had not forgotten but had continually had in mind to fulfill his promise.

It is true that the word "Israel" means the Jews alone and not us Gentiles. But because they would not have him, he chose certain out of their number and thus satisfied the name Israel and made of it henceforth a spiritual Israel. This was shown in Gen. 32[:24-28], when the holy patriarch Jacob wrestled with the angel, who strained the hollow of his thigh out of joint, to show that his children should henceforth not boast of their fleshly birth, as the Jews do. Therefore he also received a new name, that he should henceforth be called Israel, as a patriarch who was not only Jacob, the father of fleshly children, but Israel, the father of spiritual children. With this the word "Israel" agrees, for it means "a prince with God." That is a most high and holy name and contains in itself the great miracle that, by the grace of God, a person prevailed, as it were, with God, so that God does what that person desires. We see the same thing in the case of Christendom. Through Christ she is joined to God as a bride to her bridegroom, so that the bride has a right to, and power over, her bridegroom's body and all his possessions; all of this happens through faith.[108] By faith the person does what God wills; God in turn does what the person wills.[109] Thus Israel means a god-

108. Jesus refers to himself as the Bridegroom (cf. Mark 2:19; Matt. 9:15; Luke 5:34; John 3:29), and in Eph. 5:22-33, Paul compares the union of a husband and wife to that of Christ and the church. The image of the church as the bride of Christ had a long and colorful history prior to Luther, and the connection was well established.

109. Luther sounds a very similar theme in his *Freedom of a Christian*, completed only a short time before this commentary and published in November 1520. See LW 31:327-78; WA 7:20-38, 42-49; TAL 1:466-538.

like, God-conquering person, who is a lord in God, with God, and through God, able to do all things.

That is the meaning of Israel. For שַׂר means a lord, a prince; אֵל means God. Put them together, and they become יִשְׂרָאֵל according to the Hebrew fashion. Such an Israel God would have. Therefore, when Jacob had wrestled with the angel and prevailed, the angel said to him [Gen. 32:28]: "You shall be called Israel; for since you have power with God, you shall also have power with people." There would be much more to say on this subject, for Israel is a strange and profound mystery.

55. As he spoke to our fathers, to Abraham, and to his seed forever.

Here all merit and presumption are brought low, and God's grace and mercy alone are exalted. For God has not helped Israel on account of its merits, but on account of his own promise. In pure grace he made the promise, in pure grace he also fulfilled it. Wherefore St. Paul says in Galatians 3[:17] that God gave the promise to Abraham four hundred years before he gave the law to Moses, that no one might glory, saying he had merited and obtained such grace and promise through the law or the works of the law. This same promise the Mother of God here lauds and exalts above all else, ascribing this work of the incarnation of God solely to the undeserved promise of divine grace, made to Abraham.

The promise of God to Abraham is recorded especially in Gen. 12[:3] and Gen. 22[:18], and is referred to in many other places besides. It runs thus: "By myself I have sworn: in your Seed shall all families or nations of the earth be blessed." These words of God are highly esteemed by St. Paul [Gal. 3:16] and by all the prophets, as is right. For in these words Abraham and all his descendants were preserved and saved, and in them we, too, must all be saved; for here Christ is contained and promised as the Savior of the whole world. This is Abraham's bosom [Luke 16:22], in which were kept all who were saved before Christ's birth;[110] without these words no one was saved, even if he had performed all good works. Let us examine them more fully.

In the first place, it follows from these words of God that without Christ all the world is in sin and under condemnation, and is accursed with all its doing and knowing. For if he says that

110. The "bosom of Abraham" refers to a place of comfort in Sheol (or, in Greek, Hades) where the righteous dead were believed by the Jews to await judgment day. The idea first appears in texts from the Second Temple period (c. 500 BCE to 70 CE), such as in 4 Macc. 13:17, in which the martyrs expected to be received after their deaths by Abraham, Isaac, and Jacob. In the parable of the rich man and Lazarus (Luke 16:19-31), Abraham's bosom is quite literally the place where Lazarus rests after his death, while the rich man suffers in Hades. It is similar to the early Christian concept of "limbo," a place where the righteous dead go who must await Christ's redemption to pass on to Paradise.

not some but all nations shall be blessed in Abraham's Seed, then without Abraham's Seed no nation shall be blessed. What need was there for God to promise so solemnly and with so mighty an oath, that he would bless them, if they were already blessed and not rather cursed? From this saying the prophets drew many inferences; namely, that all human beings are evil, liars all, false and blind, in short, without God, so that in the scriptural usage to be called a human being is no great honor, since in God's sight that name is no better than the name "liar" or "faithless" in the eyes of the world. So completely is a person corrupted through Adam's fall that the curse[x] is innate with him and becomes, as it were, his nature and being.[111] It follows, in the second place, that

111. Luther spoke of original sin and human nature in many places, but he made clear in his *Against Latomus*, written in June 1521 at the Wartburg, that law reveals to us the corruption of our nature and our sin. The gospel reveals God's grace to us, and through this grace God covers over our sin and forgives us. The sin is not completely removed, however, and we deal with it daily throughout our lives. See LW 32:137–260; WA 8:48–128.

The original sin of Adam and Eve in the garden is the basis for all other human sins, such as gambling, murder, and even suicide, depicted in this sixteenth-century illustration.

---

x   Although most versions have *gebenedeyung*, or "blessing," here, the editor of WA suggests the more logical choice of *vormaledeyung*.

this Seed of Abraham could not be born in the common course of nature, of a man and a woman; for such a birth is cursed and results in nothing but accursed seed, as we have just said.[112] Now, if all the world was to be redeemed from the curse by this Seed of Abraham and thereby blessed, as the word and oath of God declare, the Seed itself had to be blessed first, neither touched nor tainted by that curse, but pure blessing, full of grace and truth [John 1:14]. Again, if God, who cannot lie, declared with an oath that it should be Abraham's natural seed, that is, a natural and genuine child, born of his flesh and blood, then this Seed had to be a true, natural human being, of the flesh and blood of Abraham. Here, then, we have a contradiction—the natural flesh and blood of Abraham, and yet not born in the course of nature, of man and woman.[113] Therefore he uses the word "your seed," not "your child," to make it very clear and certain that it should be his natural flesh and blood, such as seed is. For a child need not be one's natural child, as everyone knows. Now, who will find the means to establish God's word and oath, where such contradictory things lie side by side?

God himself has done this thing. He is able to keep what he has promised, even though no one may understand it before it comes to pass, for his word and work do not demand the proof of reason, but a free and pure faith. See how he combined the two. He raises up seed for Abraham, the natural son of one of his daughters, a pure virgin, Mary, through the Holy Spirit, and without her knowing a man. Here there was no natural conception and birth with its curse, nor could it touch this seed; and yet it is the natural seed of Abraham, as truly as any of the other children of Abraham. That is the blessed Seed of Abraham, in whom all the world is set free from its curse. For whoever believes in this Seed, calls upon him, confesses him, and abides in him, to that one all the curse is forgiven and all blessing given, as the word and oath of God declare—"In your Seed shall all the nations of the earth be blessed." That is to say: "Whatever is to be blessed must and shall be blessed through this Seed, and in no other way." This is Abraham's Seed, begotten by none of his sons, as the Jews always confidently expected, but born of this one daughter of his, Mary, alone.

That is what the tender mother of this Seed means here by saying: "He has helped his servant Israel, as he promised to Abraham and to all his seed." She found the promise fulfilled in

112. In Psalm 51, David makes clear that he was a sinner from his very conception, and Paul notes in Eph. 2:3 that we are "by nature children of wrath." In his comment on Psalm 51, Luther remarks that everyone (except Christ) was conceived in sin, and that is because our "flesh" still remains sinful, even as baptized Christians. Apart from those who were "sanctified in the womb," every human person (again, apart from Christ) was and is born a sinner. See LW 10:236–37; WA 3:293–96.

113. In the Augustinian tradition (that is, the whole Western church), the sexual act itself was generally seen as the conveyor of sin, even within marriage. However, Luther insisted (for example, in his *The Estate of Marriage* of 1522) that the sexual act (leading to the procreation of children) is in fact commanded by God and instituted within human nature—it is only sinful, and conveys sin to a child, because our flesh is already sinful. Here he accepts the idea that, in order for Christ to be sinless in his humanity, he must be conceived outside of the normal manner.

114. Here he is referring not to the blessed waiting area of Hades, but to the covenant made with Abraham mentioned earlier.

115. Luther was still hopeful at this time that if the truth of the gospel were explained to the Jews, they would come to believe in Jesus as the Messiah. It was especially important, he felt, that they be treated kindly and be able to see good examples of pious Christians, not like many of the Christians he saw around him at the time. These thoughts are very similar to what he articulates in *That Jesus Christ Was Born a Jew*, published in 1523 (see LW 45:199–220; WA 11:314–36; TAL, vol. 5, forthcoming). However, over time Luther came to be frustrated and upset that Jews did not convert en masse to Christianity, and he approved their expulsion from the Saxon lands under John Frederick in 1535, and wrote his own very hostile and disturbing tract against them in 1543, *On the Jews and Their Lies* (TAL, vol. 5, forthcoming). And although Luther was hardly out of the ordinary for his time in his feelings toward Jews, in this way he contributed to a long history of anti-Jewish sentiment among Christians. See also Mark U. Edwards Jr., "Against the Jews," ch. 6 in *Luther's Last Battles: Politics and Polemics 1531–46* (Ithaca: Cornell University Press, 1983), 115–42.

116. Of course, these prophets were Jews as well, but Luther is using the term *Jew* to refer to the people within that community who rejected God and God's truth.

herself; hence she says: "It is now fulfilled; he has brought help and kept his word, solely in remembrance of his mercy." Here we have the foundation of the gospel and see why all its teaching and preaching drive us to faith in Christ and into Abraham's bosom.[114] For where this faith does not exist, no advice or help can be given to lay hold of this blessed Seed. And indeed, the whole Bible depends on this oath of God, for in the Bible everything has to do with Christ. Furthermore, we see that all the fathers in the Old Testament, together with all the holy prophets, had the same faith and gospel as we have, as St. Paul says in 1 Cor. 10[:1-4], for they all remained with a strong faith in this oath of God and in Abraham's bosom and were preserved in it. The sole difference is, they believed in the coming and promised Seed; we believe in the Seed that has come and has been given. But it is all the one truth of the promise, and hence also one faith, one Spirit, one Christ, one Lord [Eph. 4:5], now as then, and forever, as Paul says in Hebrews 13[:8].

But the subsequent giving of the law to the Jews is not on a par with this promise. The law was given in order that by its light they might better come to know their cursed nature[y] and more fervently and heartily desire the promised Seed; in this they had an advantage over all the heathen world. But they turned this advantage into a disadvantage; they undertook to keep the law by their own strength, and failed to learn from it their needy and cursed state. Thus they shut the door upon themselves, so that the Seed was compelled to pass them by. They still continue in this state, but God grant not for long, Amen.[115] This was the cause of the quarrel all the prophets had with them. For the prophets well understood the purpose of the law, namely, that people should thereby know their accursed nature and learn to call upon Christ. Hence they condemned all the good works and everything in the life of the Jews that did not agree with this purpose. Therefore the Jews became angry with them and put them to death as ones who condemned the service of God, good works, and godly living, just as the hypocrites and graceless saints ever do, of which we might say a great deal.[116]

When Mary says, "his seed forever," we are to understand "forever" to mean that such grace is to continue to Abraham's

---

y   Luther's term is *vormaledeyet natur*, and he is referring to their human nature, which was cursed in the fall, as it was for everyone.

lineage (that is, the Jews) from that time forth, throughout all time, down to the Last Day. Although the vast majority of them are hardened, yet there are always some, however few, who are converted to Christ and believe in him. For this promise of God does not lie: the promise was made to Abraham and to his seed, not for one year or for a thousand years, but "for the ages," that is, from one generation to another, without end. We ought, therefore, not to treat the Jews in such an unfriendly way, for there are future Christians among them, and they are turning every day. Moreover, they alone, and not we Gentiles, have this promise, that there shall always be Christians among Abraham's seed, who acknowledge the blessed Seed. As for our cause, it rests upon pure grace, without a promise of God. If we lived Christian lives, and brought them with kindness to Christ, it would be the proper measure.[117] Who would desire to become a Christian when he sees Christians dealing with people in so unchristian a spirit? Not so, my dear Christians. Tell them the truth in all kindness; if they will not receive it, let them go. How many Christians are there who despise Christ, do not hear his word, and are worse than Jews or heathen! Yet we leave them in peace and even fall down at their feet and basically adore them as gods. Let this suffice for the present. We pray God to give us a right understanding of this Magnificat, an understanding that consists not merely in brilliant words but in glowing life in body and soul. May Christ grant us this through the intercession and for the sake of his dear mother Mary![118] Amen.

[Epilogue]

In conclusion I come once more to your Grace, craving pardon for my temerity. I know full well that your Grace's youth is amply supplied, each day, with wholesome instruction and admonition. Yet I cannot neglect my duty as a loyal subject, nor keep my conscience from dwelling on and being concerned for your Grace. It is the hope of us all that God may by his salutary grace so direct the future that the rule of Saxony shall come into your Grace's hands, which will be a great and precious thing if it turns out well, but a perilous and wretched one if it turns out ill. We must in all things hope and pray for the best, but nonetheless fear and be prepared for the worst.

117. Luther is insisting that it is the responsibility of Christians to bring the Jews to know and believe in Christ, not through force and certainly not through poor treatment, but instead through kindness and good example. He is here suggesting that if Christians did these things, the number of Jews who converted might not be just the bare minimum to fulfill God's promise, but in fact might instead be a significant and "proper" number.

118. Although Luther's prayer is to God, he is noting here that Mary may well pray (that is, intercede) for us, as do the angels and (possibly) saints in heaven. He later came to reject decisively the practice of asking Mary and the saints to pray for us to God, as there is no scriptural evidence for such a practice and it can be misleading (see introduction, n. 9, p. 310).

Your Grace should reflect that in all the Scriptures God did not permit any heathen king or prince throughout the length and breadth of the world to be praised, but always more to be punished; this is a mighty and terrible example to all rulers. Moreover, even in Israel, his chosen people, he never found a king worthy of praise and not rather of punishment. Above all, in the kingdom of Judah, the chief portion of the whole race of humankind that was exalted by God and beloved of him above all others, there were few, not above six, kings found worthy of praise. And the very best of kings, his own beloved David, who had no peer among temporal rulers before, beside, or after him, filled as he was with the fear and the wisdom of God, and directing his whole rule not after his own reason but according to God's command alone, nevertheless stumbled more than once. Therefore the Scripture, unable to blame his reign and yet finding it necessary to narrate the calamity that befell the people on his account, put the blame not on David but on the people. It says that God's anger was kindled against them so that he let the saintly David be moved by the devil to number the people; on account of this, seventy thousand of them were destroyed by pestilence [2 Sam. 24:1-15].[119]

All these things were foreordained by God in order to terrify those in authority, to keep them in fear, and to admonish them of their peril. For great possessions, glory, power, and favor, as well as the flatterers no lord may be without, surround and lay siege to the heart of a prince, moving it to pride, to forgetfulness of God, and neglect of the people and the common good, to sensuality, blasphemy, arrogance, and idleness, in short, to every sort of vice and evil. Indeed, there is no caste or city that is so heavily besieged and assaulted. Unless, therefore, one fortifies himself by means of such examples, and takes the fear of God for his defense and rampart, how can he endure? For unless a lord and ruler loves his subjects and has for his chief concern not how to live at ease but how to uplift and improve his people, his case is hopeless; he rules only for his soul's perdition. Nor will it avail him to make amends by the foundation of great festivals, monasteries, altars, and what not.[120] God will require of him an account of his office and station and will not be satisfied with anything else.

Therefore, my gracious Lord and Prince, I commend the Magnificat to your Grace, particularly the fifth and sixth verses, in which its chief content is gathered up. I beseech and exhort

119. Along with this somewhat obscure punishment of David (and the people, on his account), there is his "stumble" with Bathsheba (2 Samuel 11–12).

120. Along with chantries (endowments for priests to celebrate Masses for one's soul), wealthy late-medieval people often spent their money—whether officially as penitential works of satisfaction or not—in building churches, endowing altars, funding pilgrimages, etc.

your Grace in all your life to fear nothing on earth, not even hell itself, so much as that which the Mother of God there calls "the imagination of their hearts" [Luke 1:51]. That is the greatest, closest, mightiest, and most destructive enemy of all human-kind, and especially of rulers. Its name is reason, good sense, or opinion; and from it all counsels and all rule must be derived. Your Grace will never be secure from it unless you continually keep it under suspicion and follow it only in the fear of God. I do not mean your Grace's counsels only, but those of all your counselors as well. None should be despised, none trusted. How is this to be done?

Well, your Grace should not leave prayer to the cowls or to the chalices,[121] as it is now the wretched custom to put one's trust in other people's prayers, without praying oneself; but your Grace should pluck up courage and be of good cheer, put away your timidity, and yourself converse with God in your heart or in a secret place, boldly casting down the keys[122] at his feet, and pleading his own system with him, like so: "Behold, O God, my Father, it is your doing and appointment that I was born and created in this estate, to be a ruler.[123] This none can deny, and you yourself also know it. Whether worthy or unworthy, I yet am what you and everyone sees. Grant, therefore, my Lord and Father, that I may rule over your people to your praise and their profit. Let me not follow my own reason, but let you be my reason," and so on.

In this spirit, then, let things go as they will, in God's command. How well such a prayer and such a spirit please God he himself shows in the case of Solomon, who also prayed such a prayer, which I have translated and appended here. May it serve your Grace as a pattern at the close of this proclamation, and awaken in you a consoling trust in God's grace, so that both the fear and the mercy of God may be together, as the fifth verse sings. Herewith I commend myself to your Grace, and your Grace to God. May he grant you a blessed reign. Amen.

How King Solomon made a princely prayer to God,
as a good example to all princes and lords,
found in 1 Kings 3[:5-14]

At the city of Gibeon God appeared to Solomon in a dream by night and said: "Ask what I shall give you." And Solomon said:

121. That is, to monks (cowls are the hoods on a monk's habit) and priests (a chalice is the goblet used during the Eucharist, a sacrament that in Catholic doctrine can only be confected by a priest).

122. In a religious context, the "keys" refers to the bishop's/pastor's authority to remit or to retain a person's sins. It is based upon Jesus' reply to Peter in Matt. 16:19 that he was giving to him "the keys to the kingdom of heaven." In this context, Luther is likely referring simply to the prince's political authority, although Burger suggests that he means the keys to the prince's heart (*Marias Lied*, 175).

123. Although there were limited elections in this era, many offices (such as that of prince) were hereditary.

In this woodcut, Solomon kneels in prayer before a menorah to ask God for wisdom.

"My God, you have shown great grace to my father David, your servant, who walked before you in truth and righteousness and whose heart was right with you; and therefore you have kept for him this great grace, that you have given him a son to sit on his throne this day.

"And now, O LORD, my God, you have made me, your servant, king in place of David, my father, although I am but a little child, who does not know when to go out or come in. And your servant is in the midst of your chosen people, a great people, that cannot be numbered or counted for multitude.

"Give to me, your servant, therefore, a listening heart[z] [one that hears and obeys] to govern your people and discern between good and evil; for who is able to govern your people, so great and brave?"

God was pleased with these words and with the fact that Solomon had asked for these things. And God said to him: "Because you have asked this, and have not asked for yourself long life or riches or the death of your enemies, but have asked for yourself understanding to hear how you should govern, behold, I now do as you have asked. Behold, I give you a wise and discerning mind, so that none like you has been before you and none like you shall arise after you.

"I give you also what you have not asked, both riches and glory, so that no other king shall compare with you, all your days. And if you walk in my ways, keeping my statutes and my commandments, as your father David walked, then I will lengthen your days."

---

z   The NRSV has "understanding mind."

Whether One May Flee from a Deadly Plague

1527

ANNA MARIE JOHNSON

INTRODUCTION

The bubonic plague began in western Europe in the mid-four-teenth century and recurred in cycles through the end of the sev-enteenth century. Its spread was swift and its toll devastating. The plague entered through Italian and French shipping ports in 1347. By 1349 it had reached Germany, and by 1351 it had spread to nearly all of Europe. The initial outbreak abated in 1353, but the disease reappeared in five- to twelve-year cycles throughout the fourteenth century, and in longer intervals thereafter.

There is some question about the biological cause of the dis-ease, but most historians and epidemiologists think that the early modern plague was caused by the bacillus *Yersinia pestis*, a pathogen first identified in 1918.[a] This bacillus is transmit-ted via fleas who feed on infected rats, then bite humans. The increase in trade in the fourteenth century meant that infected rats and fleas were able to spread the disease quickly. The Black Death, as this mid-fourteenth-century epidemic is known, came on the heels of several famines during the late thirteenth and

Allegory of Demon of the Plague, engraved illustration from *Feldtbuch der Wundarzney (Fieldbook of Wound Surgery)* by Hans von Gersdorff (Strasburg, 1540)

---

a   The most thorough argument against this thesis is Samuel K. Cohen Jr.'s *The Black Death Transformed: Disease and Culture in Early Renaissance Europe* (London: Arnold Publishers, 2002).

early fourteenth centuries, which had already taken their toll on society. In the words of historian Edward Peters, the plague "struck a population weakened by hunger and lack of resistance, crowded into cities, more mobile than in any period of Europe's history since the fifth and sixth centuries, and thus extremely vulnerable to contagion—a principle it did not understand."[b]

By the end of the initial 1347–1351 epidemic, approximately one-third of Europe's population had died.[c] Repeated bouts of plague continued to take their toll, and the population did not begin to recover until the late fifteenth century as the epidemic slowed. Even those who survived an infection of the plague were weakened, and thus vulnerable to other diseases. In addition, the plague disrupted the goods and services that sustained health, making life more difficult for survivors. The regional nature of the epidemic meant that some towns and areas were spared entirely, while others were hit hard and even deserted. Estimates on overall fatality rates for the plague have ranged widely, from 30 percent to 60 percent. The German title for this work illustrates the virulence associated with the disease: the English translations have typically called this work "Whether One May Flee from a Deadly Plague," but the original title given to it, probably by the printer, was simply, "Whether One May Flee Death."[d]

The plague could take three forms in humans. In its bubonic form, the lymph nodes near the flea bite would become extremely large, forming the "bubo" that gave this form of plague one of its names. (The other name, "Black Death," comes from the necrotic black plaques that often formed on the skin.) From the lymph nodes, the infection might then travel to the central nervous system, causing high fever, headache, disorientation, and finally death. Sometimes, however, the infection would enter the bloodstream directly, causing the septicemic (blood-borne)

---

b　Edward Peters, *Europe and the Middle Ages*, 3d ed. (Upper Saddle River, NJ: Prentice-Hall, 1997), 332.

c　Jan de Vries, "Population," in Thomas A. Brady Jr., Heiko A. Oberman, and James D. Tracy, eds., *Handbook of European History, 1400–1600: Late Middle Ages, Renaissance and Reformation*, vol. 1: *Structures and Assertions* (Leiden: Brill, 1994).

d　Luther's handwritten manuscript of this work has "OB MAN FVR DEM STERBEN FLIEHEN SOLL" written across the top, although not in Luther's hand (WA 23:338).

form of the disease, a highly fatal form. Another highly fatal form of the plague was pneumonic plague, in which the disease entered the lungs. The pneumonic form was particularly dangerous because it could be spread to others by cough, bypassing the lymphatic system and entering directly into the lungs. When this happened, the fatality rate was nearly 100 percent.[e] The sudden onset and high mortality of the disease fostered an acute concern with the issue of salvation among both theologians and laypeople. One outgrowth of this piqued interest was the appearance of books that advised people what they should do on the deathbed to die a good, Christian death, a genre to which Luther also contributed.[f]

Luther's treatise on whether one may flee when plague strikes was prompted by a request from the clergy of Breslau, a city in Silesia. They wondered whether a Christian could flee home and labors on account of the plague, and they asked the Silesian reformer Johann Hess (1490–1547) to solicit Luther's opinion. Luther did not respond at first, possibly because a health scare on 6 July 1527 had left him with headaches that impeded his reading and writing. Hess repeated the request for counsel at least once, and Luther began his response in late July.[1]

It is very possible that Luther was motivated to write on the topic by rumors that the plague was raging near Wittenberg. Indeed, it reached Wittenberg on 2 August 1527. Within weeks part of the university was moved to Jena. Luther's prince wanted Luther to go to Jena as well, but he refused because he felt he was needed in Wittenberg to minister to the sick and dying. He was also inclined to stay in Wittenberg because he had been experiencing health problems and spiritual trials since April of that year, and he found that the intercessions of his friends in Wittenberg gave him some relief from those trials.[g] The arrival of the plague, as well as Luther's ill health, seems to have interrupted his writing at least twice; Luther's handwritten manuscript shows two distinct shifts in the type of paper he used and in

1. It is not known when Hess first wrote to Luther, nor when he repeated his request. The plague first hit Breslau in August 1525, yet an extant letter from Luther to Hess on 22 April 1526 makes no mention of the request (WA Br 4:60–61).

e   Ann Carmichael, "Bubonic Plague," in Kenneth F. Kiple, ed., *The Cambridge World History of Human Disease* (Cambridge: Cambridge University Press, 1993), 629–30.

f   See his *Sermon on Preparing for Death* in this volume, pp. 283–305.

g   Martin Brecht, *Martin Luther: Shaping and Defining the Reformation 1521–1532*, trans. James L. Schaaf (Minneapolis: Fortress Press, 1990), 207, 209 (hereafter Brecht 2).

his handwriting. The work was finally completed in either October or November, and the plague in Wittenberg ended in the last part of November.

Luther's response was thoroughly pragmatic. It focused on Christians' responsibility to care for the sick and to use the means that God gives to limit the plague's destruction. He lauded those who can face the plague without fear of death, but he emphasized that those with "weak faith" can flee in good conscience as long as they are not needed to care for someone or to maintain a public service. To be sure, the question of whether to flee was a question entertained only by a certain class: those who had somewhere to go and who could afford to suspend their livelihoods. The plague hit the poor harder than the affluent because of their limited ability to flee, their crowded and often rat-infested housing, and their inferior nutrition.[h] Luther's response to the question of fleeing called on those who were able to flee to suspend that privilege if their vocations (either professional or within the household) meant that they were responsible for the well-being of others.

Luther used the opportunity of this open letter to address other plague-related circumstances as well. He encouraged municipalities to create hospitals so that care of the sick was dependable. He urged cities to move graveyards outside of the city so that they would be peaceful places of respect and contemplation. He also addressed extreme pieties that had sprung up in response to the plague. Some argued that Christians should ignore plague precautions because the plague is God's will, and God could heal people through supernatural means. Luther responded that God has given doctors and medicines that ought to be used to ensure that one does not sacrifice one's own life or, much worse, the lives of many others. In all matters related to the plague, love of neighbor was the guiding principle, and that love was manifested best in the faithful and often grueling care for the sick.

---

h   For more on the plague and poverty, see Ann G. Carmichael, *Plague and the Poor in Renaissance Florence* (Cambridge: Cambridge University Press, 1986); Paul Stark, *The Impact of the Plague in Tudor and Stuart England* (London: Routledge, 1985); and A. Lloyd Moote and Dorothy C. Moote, *The Great Plague: The Story of London's Most Deadly Year* (Baltimore: Johns Hopkins University Press, 2004), esp. 75–94.

It is worth noting that Luther lived up to the advice he gave. Far from fleeing, the Luther household took in several people who were infected with the plague. His son and only child at that point, Hans, also became infected but survived. Luther's wife was pregnant with their second child, and Luther worried about both mother and child. The baby, Elizabeth, was born sickly on 10 December, and died just shy of eight months old, quite possibly because of her mother's exposure to the plague during pregnancy.[i] During this time, he spoke often of his spiritual trials and physical ailments, which he attributed to the devil. Ironically, his endurance of those trials seemed to strengthen his fortitude during the plague because he considered the attacks of the devil to be much more fearsome than the plague.

Luther's advice apparently struck a chord with a plague-weary public. This letter was reprinted at least ten times within 1527,[j] and seventeen additional times later in the sixteenth century.[k] Its popularity ebbed and flowed in the second half of the sixteenth century as the plague came and went. It was printed at least five times in the seventeenth century, as the plague continued to preoccupy western Europe.[l]

St. Sebastian was one of the main saints thought to protect and aid those affected by the plague. Sebastian was martyred around 300 C.E. with arrows. In this painting, St. Sebastian pleads before God on behalf of the plague victims seen below while a demon and an angel prepare to fight. The scene on the ground shows several deceased plague victims wrapped in shrouds and a still-living plague victim lying on the ground. Note the swollen lymph gland, or bubo, on the living victim's neck. Painting by Josse Lieferinxe (c. 1497).

---

i   Brecht 2:204.

j   VD 16 L 5513–23.

k   VD 16 L 5524–37; ZV 10175; ZV 18113; ZV 22088.

l   VD 17 1:680482L; 1:680496X; 3:315927D; 14:018701R; 14:668013D.

Title page of *Whether
One May Flee from a
Deadly Plague* (1527)

2. This translation is based on the
original German edition in WA
23:339–79 and the English translation
in LW 43:113–38.

WHETHER ONE MAY FLEE FROM A DEADLY PLAGUE[2]

*To the Reverend Doctor Johann Hess,
pastor at Breslau, and to his fellow-servants of the gospel of Jesus Christ*

Martinus Luther

[Luther's Introduction][m]

GRACE AND PEACE from God our Father and our Lord Jesus Christ. Your letter, sent to us at Wittenberg, was received some time ago. You wish to know whether it is proper for a Christian to run away from

---

m Headings in brackets have been added to the original text to aid
in reading.

a deadly plague. I should have answered long ago, but God has for some time disciplined and scourged me so severely that I have been unable to do much reading or writing.[3] Furthermore, it occurred to me that God, our merciful Father, has endowed you so richly with wisdom and truth in Christ that you yourself should be well qualified to decide this matter or even weightier problems in his Spirit and grace without our assistance.

But now you keep on writing to me and have, so to speak, humbled yourself in requesting our view on this matter so that, as St. Paul repeatedly teaches, we may always agree with one another and be of one mind [1 Cor. 1:10; 2 Cor. 13:11; Phil. 2:2]. Therefore we here give you our opinion as far as God grants us to understand and perceive. This we would humbly submit to your judgment and to that of all devout Christians for them to come to their own decision and conclusion, as is proper. Since the rumor of death is to be heard in these and many other parts also,[4] we have permitted these instructions of ours to be printed because others might also want to make use of them.

To begin with, some people are of the firm opinion that one need not and should not run away from a deadly plague. Rather, since death is God's punishment, which he sends upon us for our sins, we must submit to God and with a true and firm faith patiently await our punishment.[5] They look upon running away as an outright wrong and as lack of belief in God. Others take the position that one may properly flee, particularly if one holds no public office.

I cannot censure the former for their excellent decision. They uphold a good cause, namely, a strong faith in God, and deserve commendation because they desire every Christian to hold to a

Two wings of a plague altarpiece from the Augustinian Monastery zu den Wengen in Ulm by artist Martin Schaffner (1478–1546). In the scene an angry God the Father punishes the sinful with plague arrows. The sufferers send their prayers to God through the mediation of two plague saints, Roch and Sebastian, who pass their pleas to Mary (lower left). Mary, in turn, presents the prayers to her son Jesus, who, showing his wounds, presents the prayers to his father, God.

3. Luther is referring to his many ongoing health problems. By this time, he had experienced kidney stones, angina, fainting spells, and buzzing in his ear. On 6 July 1527, Luther had severe circulatory problems and thought he was dying. After that incident, he suffered from headaches that left him unable to read or write for a time. He interpreted all of these ailments as God's disciplining of him, though he does not name specific sins.

4. When Luther began writing this response, the plague was rumored to be near Wittenberg. It arrived there on 2 August 1527, which suggests that Luther began writing this open letter shortly before then.

5. Nearly all Christians during the late-medieval and Reformation periods

interpreted plagues and other disasters as God's just punishment for sin. See Ronald Rittgers, "Protestants and Plague: The Case of the 1562/63 Pest in Nuremberg," in Franco Mormando and Thomas Worcester, *Piety and Plague: From Byzantium to the Baroque*, Sixteenth Century Essays and Studies 78 (Kirksville, MO: Truman State University Press, 2007).

6. That is, faith in its infancy, and thus only able to drink milk.

7. In other words, those who are strong in faith and willing to accept death cannot expect all Christians to do the same.

8. This is an example of someone who flees death in an unfaithful way.

strong, firm faith. It takes more than a milk faith[6] to await a death before which most of the saints themselves have been and still are in dread. Who would not acclaim these earnest people to whom death is a little thing? They willingly accept God's chastisement, doing so without tempting God, as we shall hear later on.

Since it is generally true of Christians that few are strong and many are weak, one simply cannot place the same burden upon everyone.[7] A person who has a strong faith can drink poison and suffer no harm, Mark 16[:18], while one who has a weak faith would thereby suffer death. Peter could walk upon the water because he was strong in faith. When he began to doubt and his faith weakened, he sank and almost drowned. When those who are strong travel with those who are weak, the strong must try not to walk at a pace based on their strength lest they walk their weak companions nearly to death.*n* Christ does not want his weak ones to be abandoned, as St. Paul teaches in Rom. 15[:1] and 1 Cor. 12[:22ff.].

To put it briefly and concisely, running away from death may happen in one of two ways. First, it may happen in disobedience to God's word and command, for instance, in the case of those who are imprisoned for the sake of God's word and who, to escape death, deny and repudiate God's word.[8] In such a situation everyone has Christ's plain mandate and command not to flee but rather to suffer death, as he says, "Whoever denies me before men, I will also deny before my Father who is in heaven" and "Do not fear those who kill the body but cannot kill the soul," Matt. 10[:28, 33].

[Who must normally stay, and under what conditions they might leave]

Those who are engaged in a spiritual ministry such as preachers and pastors must likewise remain steadfast before the peril of death. We have a plain command from Christ, "A good shepherd lays down his life for the sheep but the hireling sees the

---

n   Here and at some other points in the text, Luther's singular pronouns have been replaced with plural pronouns to avoid the use of generic masculine pronouns.

wolf coming and flees" [John 10:11].[9] For when people are dying, they most need a spiritual ministry which strengthens and comforts their consciences by word and sacrament and in faith overcomes death.[10] However, where enough preachers are available in one locality and they agree to encourage the other clergy to leave in order not to expose themselves needlessly to danger, I do not consider such conduct sinful because spiritual services are provided and because they would have been ready and willing to stay if it had been necessary. We read that St. Athanasius fled from his church that his life might be spared because many others were there to administer his office.[11] Similarly, the brethren in Damascus lowered Paul in a basket over the wall to make it possible for him to escape, Acts 9[:25].[12] And also in Acts 19[:30] Paul allowed himself to be kept from risking danger in the marketplace because it was not essential for him to do so.[13]

Accordingly, all those in public office such as mayors, judges, and the like are under the obligation to remain. This, too, is God's word, which institutes secular authority and commands that town and country be ruled, protected, and preserved, as St. Paul teaches in Rom. 13[:4], "The governing authorities are God's ministers for your own good." To abandon an entire community that one has been called to govern, to leave it without officials or government, exposed to all kinds of danger such as fires, murder, riots, and every imaginable disaster, is a great sin. It is the kind of disaster the devil would like to instigate wherever there is no law and order. St. Paul says, "Anyone who does not provide for family members denies the faith and is worse than an unbeliever" [1 Tim. 5:8]. On the other hand, if in great weakness they flee but provide capable substitutes to make sure that the community is well governed and protected, as we previously indicated, and if they continually and carefully supervise them [i.e., the substitutes], all that would be proper.

What applies to these two offices [church and state] should also apply to persons who stand in a relationship of service or duty toward one another. A servant should not leave his master nor a maid her mistress except with the knowledge and permission of master or mistress. Again, a master should not desert his servant nor a lady her maid unless suitable provision for their care has been made somewhere. In all these matters it is a divine command that servants and maids should render obedience and by the same token masters and ladies should take care of their

9. Priests were often criticized for fleeing when the plague arrived, and it seems they regularly fled. Cf. Robert S. Gottfried, *The Black Death: Natural and Human Disaster in Medieval Europe* (New York: Free Press, 1983). The plague hit clergy particularly hard, likely because the Sacrament of Unction, or last rites, forced clergy to be in close proximity to those who were dying of the disease. The close quarters of monastic communities also made them very susceptible to plague. Cf. Joseph P. Byrne, *Daily Life During the Black Death* (Westport, CT: Greenwood, 2006), 115–30; and William Chester Jordan, *Europe in the High Middle Ages* (London: Penguin Books, 2001), 297.

10. Luther's emphasis on comforting the consciences of the dying diverges from standard late-medieval practice, which urged dying Christians to avoid sin on the deathbed in order to aid in their salvation. See Luther's *Sermon on Preparing for Death* in this volume (pp. 283–305), and Austra Reinis, *Reforming the Art of Dying* (Aldershot, UK: Ashgate, 2007).

11. St. Athanasius (c. 296–373) was a fourth-century bishop of Alexandria best known for his role in formulating the doctrine of Christ as both fully human and fully divine. He was exiled or fled Alexandria numerous times during his tenure there because of opposition to him.

12. Paul was being pursued by Jews who were upset by his recent conversion to Christianity.

13. According to the book of Acts, a riot broke out in the marketplace in Ephesus because of Paul's preaching against a local goddess. Local officials and Paul's companions both urged Paul not to enter the marketplace.

servants.*o* Likewise, fathers and mothers are bound by God's law to serve and help their children, and children their fathers and mothers. Likewise, paid public servants such as city physicians, city clerks, and constables, or whatever their titles, should not flee unless they furnish capable substitutes who are acceptable to their employer.[14]

In the case of children who are orphaned, guardians or close friends are under obligation either to stay with them or to arrange diligently for other nursing care for their sick friends. Yes, no one should dare leave a neighbor unless there are others who will take care of the sick in their stead and nurse them. In such cases we must respect the word of Christ, "I was sick and you did not visit me . . . [Matt. 25:41-46]. According to this passage we are bound to each other in such a way that we not forsake others in distress. Instead, we are obliged to assist and help them, as we ourselves would like to be helped.

[Who may flee]

Where no such emergency exists and enough people are available for the care of the sick—whether voluntarily, by duty, or arranged by those who are weak in faith—so that there is no need for additional helpers, or where the sick do not want them and have refused their services, I judge that they are free either to flee or to remain. If they are sufficiently bold and strong in their faith, let them stay in God's name; that is certainly no sin. If they are weak and fearful, let them flee in God's name as long as they do not neglect their duty toward their neighbors but have made adequate provision for others to provide care. To flee from death and to save one's life is a natural tendency, implanted by God and not forbidden unless it be against God and neighbor,[15] as St. Paul says in Eph. 4 [5:29], "No one ever hates his own flesh, but nourishes and cherishes it." It is even commanded that everyone should as much as possible preserve body and life and not neglect them, as St. Paul says in 1 Cor. 12[:21-26] that God has so ordered the members of the body that each one cares and works for the other.

It is not forbidden but rather commanded that by the sweat of our brow we should seek our daily food, clothing, and all we

14. Luther's advice follows the paradigm he set out most famously in *On the Freedom of a Christian:* "A Christian is a perfectly free lord of all, subject to none. A Christian is a perfectly dutiful servant of all, subject to all" (LW 31:344; TAL 1:488). Here Luther explicates what this means for the plague: the only law a Christian must follow is the law of love—in this case, caring for the sick, maintaining public services, and tending to spiritual needs.

15. Luther argues against a hierarchy of spirit over flesh. Instead, he sees the instinct toward self-preservation as something given by God and not forbidden unless it interferes with the love of God and neighbor.

o   See Eph. 6:6-9 and Col. 3:33—4:1.

need, and that we should avoid destruction and disaster whenever we can, as long as we do so without detracting from our love and duty toward our neighbor. How much more appropriate it is therefore to seek to preserve life and avoid death if this can be done without harm to our neighbor, inasmuch as life is more than food and clothing, as Christ himself says in Matt. 5 [6:25].[16] If you are so strong in faith, however, that you can willingly suffer nakedness, hunger, and want without tempting God and without trying to escape, although you could do so, you may continue that way; but do not condemn those who will not or cannot do the same.

Examples in Holy Scripture abundantly prove that to flee from death is not wrong in itself. Abraham was a great saint but he feared death and escaped it by pretending that his wife, Sarah, was his sister.[p] Because he did so without neglecting or adversely affecting his neighbor, it was not counted as a sin against him. His son Isaac did likewise.[q] Jacob also fled from his brother Esau to avoid death at his hands.[r] Likewise, David fled from Saul, and from Absalom.[s] The prophet Uriah escaped from King Jehoiakim and fled into Egypt.[t] The valiant prophet Elijah, 1 Kgs. 19[:3], had destroyed all the prophets of Baal by his great faith, but afterward, when Queen Jezebel threatened him, he became afraid and fled into the desert. Before that, Moses fled into the land of Midian when the king searched for him in Egypt.[u] Many others have done likewise. All of them fled from death when it was possible and saved their lives, yet without depriving their neighbors of anything, but first meeting their obligations toward them.

Yes, you may reply, but these examples do not refer to dying by pestilence but to death

16. Matt. 6:25: "Therefore I tell you, do not worry about your life, what you will eat or what you will drink, or about your body, what you will wear. Is not life more than food, and the body more than clothing?" (NRSV).

Moses flees Egypt (Exod. 2:15)

---

p   Gen. 12:10-20; Genesis 20.

q   Gen. 26:6-11.

r   Gen. 27:43-45.

s   1 Sam. 19:10-17; 2 Sam. 15:14.

t   Jer. 26:21.

u   Exod. 2:15.

under persecution. Answer: Death is death, no matter how it occurs. According to Holy Scripture God sent his four scourges: pestilence, famine, sword, and wild beasts.ᵛ If it is permissible to flee from one or the other in clear conscience, why not from all four? Our examples demonstrate how the holy fathers escaped from the sword; it is quite evident that Abraham, Isaac, and Jacob fled from the other scourge, namely, hunger and death, when they went to Egypt to escape famine, as we are told in Genesis [40–47]. Likewise, why should one not run away from wild beasts? I hear people say, "If war or the Turks come, we should not flee from our village or town but stay and await God's punishment by the sword." That is quite true; let those who have a strong faith wait for their death, but they should not condemn those who take flight.

By such reasoning, when a house is on fire, no one should run outside or rush to help because such a fire is also a punishment from God.[17] Those who fall into deep water dare not save themselves by swimming but instead must surrender to the water as to a divine punishment. Very well, do so if you can but do not tempt God, and allow others to do as much as they are capable of doing. Likewise, if someone breaks a leg, is wounded or bitten, he should not seek medical aid but say, "It is God's punishment. I shall bear it until it heals by itself." Freezing weather and winter are also God's punishment and can cause death. Why run to get inside or near a fire? Be strong and stay outside until it becomes warm again. We should then need no apothecaries or drugs or physicians because all illnesses are punishment from God. Hunger and thirst are also great punishments and torture. Why do you eat and drink instead of letting yourself be punished until hunger and thirst stop of themselves? Ultimately such talk will lead to the point where we abbreviate the Lord's Prayer and no longer pray, "deliver us from evil, Amen," since we would have to stop praying to be saved from hell and stop seeking to escape it. It, too, is God's punishment as is every kind of evil. Where would all this end?

From what has been said we derive this guidance: We must pray against every form of evil and guard against it to the best of our ability in order not to act contrary to God, as was previously explained. If it be God's will that evil come upon us and

17. In this paragraph Luther shows the foolishness of pseudo-heroism in the name of faith by sarcastically imagining the extreme practices that this line of reasoning might engender.

ᵛ   Ezek. 14:21; Rev. 6:1-11.

destroy us, none of our precautions will help us. We must all take this to heart: first of all, if we feel bound to remain where death rages in order to serve our neighbor, let us commend ourselves to God and say, "Lord, I am in your hands; you have kept me here; your will be done. I am your lowly creature. You can kill me or preserve me in this pestilence in the same way as if I were in fire, water, drought, or any other danger." If we are free, however, and can escape, let us commend ourselves and say, "Lord God, I am weak and fearful. Therefore I am running away from evil and am doing what I can to protect myself against it. I am nevertheless in your hands in this danger as in any other which might overtake me. Your will be done. My flight alone will not succeed of itself because calamity and harm are everywhere. Moreover, the devil never sleeps. He is a murderer from the beginning [John 8:44] and tries everywhere to instigate murder and misfortune."[18]

[Love of neighbor in all circumstances[19]]

In the same way we must accord our neighbors[20] the same treatment in other troubles and perils also, and we owe it to our neighbors to do so. If our neighbors' house is on fire, love compels me to run to help them extinguish the flames. If there are enough other people around to put the fire out, I may either go home or remain to help. If someone falls into the water or into a pit I dare not turn away but must hurry to help the person as best I can. If there are others to do it, I am released from this responsibility. If I see that someone is hungry or thirsty, I cannot ignore that person but must offer food and drink, not considering whether I would risk impoverishing myself by doing so. Those who will not help or support others unless they can do so without affecting their safety or property will never help their neighbor. They will always reckon with the possibility that doing so will bring some disadvantage and damage, danger and loss. No neighbor can live alongside another without risk to one's own safety, property, wife, or child. We must run the risk that fire or some other accident will start in our neighbor's house and destroy us bodily or deprive us of our goods, spouse, children, and all we have.

Those who do not do that for their neighbors, but instead forsake them and leave them to their misfortune, become murderers in the sight of God, as St. John states in his epistles, "All who hate a brother or sister are murderers," and again, "How does

18. Those with weak faith are not condemned here but, rather, encouraged to follow their consciences and to submit themselves to God's will amid all dangers.

19. Luther began this section in mid-September after taking a break in his writing. From this point onward, we see Luther responding not only to the question posed by the Breslau clergy, but also the presence of the plague in Wittenberg at this time (LW 43:125).

20. The German term Luther uses for "neighbor" here is *Nächste*, literally, "whoever is near you."

God's love abide in anyone who has the world's goods and sees a brother or sister in need and yet refuses to help?" [1 John 3:15, 17, NRSV]. That is also one of the sins which God attributed to the city of Sodom when he speaks through the prophet Ezekiel [16:49], "Behold, this was the guilt of your sister Sodom: she and her daughters had pride, excess of food, and prosperous ease, but did not aid the poor and needy." Christ, therefore, will condemn them as murderers on the Last Day when he will say, "I was sick and you did not visit me" [Matt. 25:43]. If that shall be the judgment upon those who have failed to visit the sick and needy or to offer them relief, what will become of those who abandoned them and let them lie there like dogs and pigs? Yes, how will they fare who rob the poor of the little they have and plague them in all kinds of ways?[21] That is what the tyrants do to the poor who accept the gospel. But let that be; they have their condemnation.

[Recommendations for communities]

It would be well, where there is an efficient government in cities and states, to maintain municipal homes and hospitals staffed with people to take care of the sick so that patients from private homes can be sent there—as was the intent and purpose of our forefathers with so many pious bequests, hospices, hospitals, and infirmaries—so that it should not be necessary for every citizen to maintain a hospital in each home.[22] That would indeed be a fine, commendable, and Christian arrangement to which everyone should offer generous help and contributions, particularly the government. Where there are no such institutions—and they exist in only a few places—we must give hospital care and be nurses for one another in any extremity or risk the loss of salvation and the grace of God. Thus it is written in God's word and command, "Love your neighbor as yourself," and in Matt. 7[:12], "So whatever you wish that [others] would do to you, do so to them."

Now if a deadly epidemic strikes, we should stay where we are, make our preparations, and take courage in the fact that we are mutually bound together (as previously indicated) so that we cannot desert one another or flee from one another. First, we can be sure that God's punishment has come upon us, not only to chastise us for our sins but also to test our faith and love—our faith in that we may see and experience how we should act

---

21. In Luther's catechisms and other explications of the Ten Commandments, he emphasizes that the commandments both prohibit and prescribe. Thus, the commandment not to kill means for him that Christians must offer aid for others' physical needs or they are guilty of murder.

22. In sixteenth-century Europe, hospitals existed only in larger towns, and then only where a private citizen or group endowed and sustained them. Those hospitals that existed were usually staffed by convents or monasteries, so the abolition of monasticism in the Reformation threatened the survival of such hospitals. Later in the sixteenth century, specialized plague hospitals were often established to isolate plague patients and to provide them medical and spiritual care. See Otto Ulbricht, *Die leidige Seuche* (Cologne: Böhlau Verlag, 2004).

toward God; our love in that we may recognize how we should act toward our neighbor. I am of the opinion that all the epidemics, like any plague, are spread among the people by evil spirits who poison the air or exhale a pestilential breath, which puts a deadly poison into the flesh.[23] Nevertheless, this is God's decree and punishment to which we must patiently submit and serve our neighbor, risking our lives in this manner as St. John teaches, "If Christ laid down his life for us, we ought to lay down our lives for our brothers and sisters" [1 John 3:16, NRSV].

[Fighting the devil by loving the neighbor]

When anyone is overcome by horror and repugnance in the presence of a sick person we should take courage and strength in the firm assurance that it is the devil who stirs up such abhorrence, fear, and loathing in our hearts. He is such a bitter, knavish devil that he not only unceasingly tries to slay and kill us, but also takes delight in making us deathly afraid, worried, and apprehensive so that we should regard dying as horrible and have no rest or peace all through our life. And so the devil would excrete us out of this life[24] as he tries to make us despair of God and become unwilling and unprepared to die. Then, under the stormy and dark sky of fear and anxiety, he makes us forget and lose Christ, our light and life, and desert our neighbors in their troubles. We would sin thereby against God and humanity; that would be the devil's glory and delight. Because we know that the devil's game is to induce such fear and dread, we should instead minimize it, take courage just to spite and annoy him, and send those terrors right back to him. And we should arm ourselves with this answer to the devil:[25]

"Get away, you devil, with your terrors! Just because you hate it, I'll spite you by going the more quickly to help my sick neighbor. I'll pay no attention to you. I've got two heavy blows to use against you: the first one is that I know that helping my neighbor is a deed well-pleasing to God and all the angels; by this deed I do God's will and render true service and obedience to him. Especially if you hate it so and are so strongly opposed to it, it must be particularly acceptable to God. I'd do this readily and gladly if I could please only one angel who might look with delight on it. But now that it pleases my Lord Jesus Christ and the whole heavenly host because it is the will and command of God, my

23. This theory of how pestilence is communicated reflects the early modern belief, received via Hippocrates and Galen, that infection is spread by foul air. Medieval towns often limited the locations and hours of butchers and leather tanners so that they would not foul the air and thereby spread illness.

24. In sixteenth-century thought, the devil and excretion were closely linked. It was thought that the devil preyed on humans while they were using the toilet because that was where they were most degraded, and thus most vulnerable. Luther once said that he discovered the gospel while on the toilet (WAT 2:177, 8ff.). Whether literally true or not, it illustrates Luther's belief that Christ's redemption reaches the entire range of human experience. See Heiko A. Oberman, *Luther: Man between God and the Devil*, trans. Eileen Walliser-Schwarzbart (New Haven: Yale University Press, 1989), 154–56.

25. Luther often suggests exact wording to use when fighting the devil and reassuring oneself of God's grace.

Father, then how could any fear of you cause me to spoil such joy in heaven or such delight for my Lord? Or how could I, by flattering you, give you and your devils in hell reason to mock and laugh at me? No, you'll not have the last word! If Christ shed his blood for me and died for me, why should I not expose myself to some small dangers for his sake and disregard this feeble plague? If you can terrorize, Christ can strengthen me. If you can kill, Christ can give life. If you have poison in your fangs, Christ has far greater medicine. Should not my dear Christ, with his precepts, his kindness, and all his encouragement, be more important in my spirit than you, roguish devil, with your false terrors in my weak flesh? God forbid! Get away, devil. Here is Christ and here am I, his servant in this work. Let Christ prevail! Amen."

The second blow against the devil is God's mighty promise by which he encourages those who minister to the needy. He says in Ps. 41[:1-3], "Blessed are those who consider the poor. The LORD will deliver them in the day of trouble. The LORD will protect them and keep them alive; the LORD will bless them on earth and not give them up to the will of their enemies. The LORD will sustain them on their sickbed. In their illness he will heal all their infirmities." Are not these glorious and mighty promises of God heaped up upon those who minister to the needy? What should terrorize us or frighten us away from such great and divine comfort? The service we can render to the needy is indeed such a small thing in comparison with God's promises and rewards that St. Paul says to Timothy, "Godliness is of value in every way, and it holds promise both for the present life and for the life to come" [1 Tim. 4:8]. Godliness is nothing else but service to God. Service to God is indeed service to our neighbor. It is proved by experience that those who nurse the sick with love, devotion, and sincerity are generally protected. Though they are poisoned, they are not harmed. As the psalm says, "in his illness you heal all his infirmities" [Ps. 41:3], that is, you change his bed of sickness into a bed of health. A person who attends a patient because of greed, or with the expectation of an inheritance or some personal advantage in such services, should not be surprised if eventually he is infected, disfigured, or even dies before he comes into possession of that estate or inheritance.[26]

But those who serve the sick for the sake of God's gracious promise (though they may accept a suitable payment, to which they are entitled inasmuch as every laborer deserves a wage)

26. Here we see that the plague was sometimes interpreted as a punishment of particular people for particular deeds. Likewise, those who did not become ill when they faithfully nursed the sick are understood as receiving immunity because of their faithfulness.

will have the great assurance that they shall also be cared for. God himself shall be their attendant and their physician, too. What an attendant he is! What a physician! Friend, what are all the physicians, apothecaries, and attendants in comparison to God? Should that not encourage us to go and serve the sick, even though they might have as many contagious boils on them as they have hairs on their bodies, and though we might be bent double carrying a hundred plague-ridden bodies! What do all kinds of pestilence or devils mean over against God, who binds and obliges himself to be our attendant and physician? Shame and more shame on you, you out-and-out unbeliever, for despising such great comfort and letting yourself become more frightened by some small boil or some uncertain danger than emboldened by such sure and faithful promises of God! What would it avail you if all physicians and the entire world were at your service, but God were not present? Again, what harm could overtake you if the whole world were to desert you and no physician would remain with you, but God would abide with you with his assurance?[27] Do you not know that you are surrounded as by thousands of angels who watch over you so that you can indeed trample upon the plague, as it is written in Ps. 91[:11-13], "He has given his angels charge of you to guard you in all your ways. On their hands they will bear you up lest you dash your foot against a stone. You will tread upon the lion and the adder, and trample the young lion and the serpent under foot."

Therefore, dear friends, let us not become so desperate as to desert our own whom we are duty-bound to help, and to flee in such a cowardly way in terror of the devil, or to allow him the joy of mocking us and vexing and distressing God and all his angels. For it is certainly true that those who despise such great promises and commands of God and leave their own people destitute violate all of God's laws and are guilty of the murder of the neighbors whom they abandon. I fear that in such a case God's promise will be reversed and changed into horrible threats and the psalm [41]

356   B E S C H O U W I N G
De P E S T.
Zonden is Peſt.

[Doch] ik zal ze van 't geweld der helle verloſſen, ik zal ze vry maaken van den dood : ô Dood , waar zyn uwe peſtilentien ? Helle , waar is u verderf ? berouw zal van myne oogen verborgen zyn. Hozea XIII: vers 14.

Zo

In this etching by Jan Luiken (1649–1712) or his son Casper Luiken (1672–1708), two men lie dying in the foreground of a town square. One of them is given something to drink by a third man, who holds a hand in front of his mouth. Farther away, a dead person is dragged away, people are dying, and bodies are heaped up against a building.

27. Such chastisement was meant for Luther himself as well as the reader. During Luther's spiritual struggles in 1527 and 1528, he often rebuked himself for succumbing to despair, and he charged himself with blasphemy. Cf. WA Br 4:226,8–227,23.

will then read this way against them: "Accursed are those who do not provide for the needy but escape and forsake them. The LORD in turn will not spare them in evil days but will flee from them and desert them. The LORD will not preserve them and keep them alive and will not prosper them on earth but will deliver them into the hands of their enemies. The LORD will not refresh them on their sickbed nor take them from the bed of their illness." For "the measure you give will be the measure you get" [Matt. 7:2]. Nothing else can come of it. It is terrible to hear this, more terrible to be waiting for this to happen, most terrible to experience it. What else can happen if God withdraws his hand and forsakes us except sheer devilment and every kind of evil? It cannot be otherwise if, against God's command, we abandon our neighbor. This fate will surely overtake everyone of this sort, unless they sincerely repent.

This I well know, that if it were Christ or his mother who was laid low by illness, everybody would be so solicitous and would gladly become a servant or helper. Everyone would want to be bold and fearless; nobody would flee but everyone would come running. And yet they don't hear what Christ himself says, "As you did it to one of the least, you did it to me" [Matt. 25:40]. When he speaks of the greatest commandment he says, "The second commandment is like [the first commandment], you shall love your neighbor as yourself" [Matt. 22:39]. There you hear that the command to love your neighbor is equal to the greatest commandment to love God, and that what you do or fail to do for your neighbor means doing the same to God. If you wish to serve Christ and to wait on him, very well, you have your sick neighbor close at hand. Go to them and serve them, and you will surely find Christ in them, not outwardly but in his word. If you do not wish or care to serve your neighbor, you can be sure that, if Christ lay there instead, you would not serve him either. You would let him just lie there. It is nothing but an illusion on your part that puffs you up with vain pride, namely, that you would really serve Christ if he were there in person. That is nothing but lies. Those who want to serve Christ in person would surely serve their neighbor as well. This is said as an admonition and encouragement against fear and a disgraceful flight, to which the devil would tempt us, so that we would disregard God's command in our dealings with our neighbor and thus fall into sin on the left hand.[28]

28. Those who did not care for the poor are portrayed as being at Christ's left hand in Matthew 25. To sin "on the left hand" means to perpetrate a sin of omission, or not doing something that Christians are commanded to do. To sin "on the right hand" is to do something that is forbidden.

[Those who tempt God]

Others sin on the right hand. They are much too rash and reckless, tempting God and disregarding everything which might counteract death and the plague. They disdain the use of medicines; they do not avoid places and persons infected by the plague, but instead lightheartedly make sport of it and wish to prove how independent they are. They say that it is God's punishment; if he wants to protect them he can do so without medicines or our carefulness. This is not trusting God, but rather tempting him. God has created medicines and provided us with intelligence to guard and take good care of the body so that we can live in good health.

If they make no use of intelligence or medicine when they could do so without detriment to their neighbors, such people injure their bodies and must beware lest they become a suicide in God's eyes.[29] By the same reasoning they might forgo eating and drinking, clothing and shelter, and boldly proclaim their faith that if God wanted to preserve them from starvation and cold, he could do so without food and clothing. Actually that would be suicide. It is even more shameful for them to pay no heed to their own bodies and to fail to protect them against the plague the best they are able, and then to infect and poison others who might have remained alive if they had taken care of their bodies as they should have. They are thus responsible before God for their neighbor's death and are a murderer many times over.[30] Indeed, such people behave as though a house were burning in the city and nobody was trying to put the fire out. Instead they give leeway to the flames so that the whole city is consumed, saying that if God so willed, he could save the city without water to quench the fire.

No, my dear friends, that is no good. Use medicine; take potions which can help you; fumigate house, yard, and street;[31] shun persons and places wherever your neighbor does not need your presence or has recovered, and act like someone who wants to help put out the burning city. What else is the

29. Suicide was considered an unforgivable sin at this time, and one that merited certain damnation.

30. Instead of seeing intentional exposure to the plague as a sign of great faith, Luther sees it as a great sin because it can kill not only the person inviting the exposure, but also many others.

31. Because sixteenth-century Europeans thought that the plague was caused by foul air, one remedy was to cleanse the air through fumigation.

An apothecary prepares medicinal potions with mortar and pestle.

epidemic but a fire which instead of consuming wood and straw devours life and body? You ought to think this way: "Very well, by God's decree the enemy has sent us poison and deadly refuse. Therefore I shall ask God mercifully to protect us. Then I shall fumigate, help purify the air, administer medicine, and take it. I shall avoid places and persons where my presence is not needed in order not to become contaminated and thus perchance infect and pollute others, and so cause their death as a result of my negligence. If God should wish to take me, he will surely find me, and I have done what he has expected of me and so I am not responsible for either my own death or the death of others. If my neighbor needs me, however, I shall not avoid place or person but will go freely, as stated above. See, this is such a God-fearing faith because it is neither brash nor foolhardy and does not tempt God.

Moreover, those who have contracted the disease and recovered should keep away from others and not admit others into their presence unless it is necessary.[32] Though they should receive aid in their time of need, as previously pointed out, after their recovery, they should act toward others so that no one becomes unnecessarily endangered on their account and thus they cause another's death. "Whoever loves danger," says the wise man, "will perish by it" [Ecclus. 3:26]. If the people in a city were to show themselves bold in their faith when a neighbor's need so demands, and cautious when no emergency exists, and if everyone would help ward off contagion as best they can, then the death toll would indeed be moderate. But if some are too panicky and desert their neighbors in their plight, and if some are so foolish as not to take precautions but aggravate the contagion, then the devil has a heyday and many will die. On both counts this is a grievous offense to God and to humanity—here it is tempting God; there it is bringing humanity into despair. Then the one who flees, the devil will pursue; the one who stays behind, the devil will hold captive so that no one escapes.

Some are even worse than that. They keep it secret that they have the disease and go among others in the belief that by contaminating and poisoning others they can rid themselves of the plague and so recover. With this idea they enter streets and homes, trying to saddle children or servants with the disease and thus save themselves. I certainly believe that this is the devil's doing, who helps turn the wheel of fate to make this happen.

32. Luther and others assumed that someone who had been infected could transmit the plague even after recovering from it.

I have been told that some are so incredibly vicious that they circulate among people and enter homes because they are sorry that the plague has not reached that far and wish to carry it in, as though it were a prank, like putting lice into fur garments or flies into someone's living room.[33] I do not know whether I should believe this; if it is true, I do not know whether we Germans are not really devils instead of human beings. It must be admitted that there are some extremely coarse and wicked people. The devil is never idle.

My advice is that if any such persons are discovered, the judge should take them by the ear and turn them over to Master Jack, the hangman, as outright and deliberate murderers.[34] What else are such people but assassins in our town? Here and there an assassin will jab a knife through someone and no one can find the culprit. So these folk infect a child here, a woman there, and can never be caught. They go on laughing as though they had accomplished something. Where this is the case, it would be better to live among wild beasts than with such murderers. I do not know how to preach to such killers. They pay no heed. I appeal to the authorities to take charge and turn them over to the help and advice not of physicians, but of Master Jack, the hangman.

If in the Old Testament God himself ordered lepers to be banished from the community and compelled to live outside the city to prevent contamination [Leviticus 13-14],[35] we must do the same with this dangerous pestilence so that those who become infected will stay away from other people, or allow themselves to be taken away and given speedy help with medicine. Under such circumstances it is our duty to assist those who are infected and not forsake them in their plight, as I have repeatedly pointed out before. Then the poison is stopped in time, which benefits not only the individual infected but also the whole community, which might be contaminated if one person is permitted to infect others. Our plague here in Wittenberg has been caused by nothing but filth. The air, thank God, is still clean and pure, but some few have been contaminated because of the laziness or recklessness of some. So the devil enjoys himself at the terror and flight which he causes among us. May God thwart him! Amen.

This is what we think and conclude on this subject of fleeing from death by the plague. If you are of a different opinion, may God enlighten you. Amen.

33. Numerous rumors of conspiracy circulated in plague-infested areas. In Geneva, authorities condemned some doctors, apothecaries, and plague workers for spreading the plague in order to increase their business. In the later sixteenth century, plagues in some Catholic areas were blamed on Lutherans. Witches and Jews were also frequently accused of spreading plague. See William Naphy, *Plagues, Poisons and Potions: Plague-Spreading Conspiracies in the Western Alps c. 1530–1640* (Manchester: Manchester University Press, 2002).

34. Hangmen learned their trade through an apprenticeship. Those who had completed the apprenticeship and trained others were called "masters" because they had mastered their trade.

35. In the Old Testament, lepers and others with chronic skin diseases were thought to be ritually impure. Leviticus 13:45-46 requires lepers to live alone outside of the community and to identify themselves as unclean. The practice of maintaining lepers' houses, or leprosaria, at the edge of town was revived in Europe in the High Middle Ages.

This section was written after another lull in Luther's writing.

37. Communion was normally administered to the dying as part of a Christian death. See Luther's *Sermon on Preparing to Die* (pp. 283–305) in this volume for more on practices surrounding death.

A priest and two assistants carry a pyx containing the elements of Holy Communion to one who is sick. They are standing below a canopy as in a procession. From a 1523 publication of Luther's *Sermon or Instruction on How a Christian Shall Prepare for Death with Joy*.

38. Confession was the central ritual in preparing for death, both in the late-medieval church and in Luther's revision of the practice. In the late-medieval church, confession and absolution obtained forgiveness for sin, and thus improved the individual's chance for salvation. In Luther's reinterpretation, confession and absolution assured the

[Preparing for death³⁶]

Because this letter will go out in print for people to read, I regard it useful to add some brief instructions on how one should care and provide for the soul in the time of death. We have done this orally from the pulpit, and still do so every day in fulfillment of the ministry to which we have been called as pastors.

First, one must admonish the people to attend church and listen to the sermon so that they learn through God's word how to live and how to die. It must be noted that those who are so uncouth and wicked as to despise God's word while they are in good health should be left unattended when they are sick unless they demonstrate their remorse and repentance with great earnestness, tears, and lamentation. Those who want to live like a heathen or a dog and do not publicly repent should not expect us to administer the sacrament to them³⁷ or have us count them a Christian. Let them die as they have lived because we shall not throw pearls before swine nor give to dogs what is holy [Matt. 7:6]. Sad to say, there are many churlish, hardened ruffians who do not care for their souls when they live or when they die. They simply lie down and die like unthinking hulks.

Second, everyone should prepare in time and get ready for death by going to confession and taking the sacrament once every week or fortnight. They should become reconciled with their neighbor and make their will so that, if the Lord knocks and they depart before a pastor or chaplain can arrive, they have provided for their souls,³⁸ have left nothing undone, and have committed themselves to God. When many are dying and only two or three pastors are on duty, it is impossible to visit everyone, to give instruction, and to teach each one what a Christian ought to know in the anguish of death. Those who have been careless and negligent in these matters must account for themselves. That is their own fault. After all, we cannot set up a private pulpit and altar daily at their bedsides simply because they have despised the public pulpit and altar to which God has summoned and called them.

Third, if someone wants the chaplain or pastor to come, let the sick send word in time to call him and do so early on, before the illness overwhelms the patient and neither senses nor reason remain. The reason I say this is that some are so negligent that they make no request and send no message until the soul is perched for flight on the tip of the tongue[39] and they are no longer rational or able to speak. Then we are told, "Dear Sir, say the very best you can to him," etc. But earlier, when the illness first began, they wanted no visit from the pastor, but instead would say, "Oh, there's no need. I hope he'll get better." What should a diligent pastor do with such people who neglect both body and soul? They live and die like beasts in the field. They want us to teach them the gospel at the last minute and administer the sacrament to them as they were accustomed to it under the papacy when nobody asked whether they believed or understood the gospel but just stuffed the sacrament down their throats as if into a bread bag.

This won't do. If they cannot talk or indicate by a sign that they believe, understand, and desire the sacrament—particularly if they have willfully neglected it—we will not give it to them just anytime they ask for it. We have been commanded not to offer the holy sacrament to unbelievers but rather to believers who can state and confess their faith. Let the others alone in their unbelief; we are guiltless because we have not been slothful in preaching, teaching, exhortation, consolation, visitation, or in anything else that pertains to our ministry and office.[40] This, in brief, is our instruction and what we practice here. We do not write this for you in Breslau, because Christ is with you and without our aid he will amply instruct you and supply your needs with his own ointment. To him be praise and honor together with God the Father and the Holy Spirit, world without end. Amen.

[On cemeteries]

Because we have come upon the subject of death, I cannot refrain from saying something about burials. First of all, I leave it to the doctors of medicine and others with greater experience than mine in such matters to decide whether it is dangerous to maintain cemeteries within the city limits. I do not know and do not claim to understand whether vapors and mists arise out of graves to pollute the air. If this were so my previously stated warnings constitute ample reason to locate cemeteries outside the city. As we have learned, all of us have the responsibility of warding off this poison to the best of our ability because God has commanded us to care for the body, to protect and nurse it so that we are not exposed needlessly. In an emergency, however,

Christian of God's mercy, and thereby offered consolation and assurance of salvation on the deathbed.

39. At this time the soul was thought to exit the body via the mouth.

40. In other words, pastors can refuse to administer the sacrament to someone if they have faithfully carried out their office, and thereby exhorted and encouraged their parishioners to receive the sacrament regularly.

we must be bold enough to risk our health if that is necessary. Thus we should be ready for both—to live and to die according to God's will. For "none of us lives to himself and none of us dies to himself," as St. Paul says, Rom. 15 [14:7].

It is very well known that the custom in antiquity, both among Jews and pagans, among saints and sinners, was to bury the dead outside the city. Those people were just as prudent as we claim to be ourselves. This is also evident in St. Luke's Gospel, when Christ raised from the dead the widow's son at the gates of Nain (for the text [Luke 7:12] states, "He was being carried out of the city to the grave and a large crowd from the city was with her"). In that country it was the practice to bury the dead outside the town.

Christ's tomb, also, was prepared outside the city. Abraham, too, bought a burial plot in the field of Ephron near the double cave where all the patriarchs wished to be buried. The Latin therefore employs the term *efferi*, that is, "to carry out," by which we mean "carry to the grave." They not only carried the dead out but also burned their bodies to powder to keep the air as pure as possible.

My advice, therefore, is to follow these examples and to bury the dead outside the town.[41] Not only necessity but piety and decency should induce us to provide a public burial ground outside the town, that is, our town of Wittenberg.

A cemetery rightfully ought to be a fine quiet place, removed from all other localities, to which one can go and reverently meditate upon death, the Last Judgment, the resurrection, and say one's prayers. Such a place should properly be a decent, hallowed place, to be entered with trepidation and reverence because doubtlessly some saints rest there. It might even be arranged to have religious pictures and portraits painted on the walls.

But our cemetery, what is it like? Four or five alleys, two or three marketplaces, with the result that no place in the whole town is busier or noisier than the cemetery. People and cattle roam over it at any time, night and day. Each house has a door or pathway to it and all sorts of things take place there, probably even some that are not fit to be mentioned. This totally destroys respect and reverence for the graves, and people think no more about walking across it than if it were a burial ground for executed criminals. Not even the Turk[42] would dishonor the place the way we do. And yet a cemetery should inspire us to devout

---

41. In the Middle Ages, Christians began to bury the dead in churches and churchyards in order to be near the holy things contained in a church. Beginning in the late fifteenth century, many cities closed their churchyard cemeteries because of overcrowding and the smell exuded by the corpses. Luther alludes to a debate at the time over whether the smell polluted the air and thereby spread disease, but his main concern is that the graveyard be removed so that it may be a peaceful place. See Craig Koslofsky, *The Reformation of the Dead: Death and Ritual in Early Modern Germany, 1450–1700* (New York: St. Martin's, 2000), esp. 40–77.

42. "The Turk" refers to the people of the Ottoman Empire, which had grown enormously over the fifteenth century and had advanced to the gates of Vienna by the time Luther wrote this work. They were considered a menacing threat to Europe, not least because they were Muslim.

thoughts, to the contemplation of death and the resurrection, and to respect for the saints who rest there. How can that be done at such a common place through which everyone must walk and into which everyone's door opens? If a cemetery is to have some dignity, I would rather be put to rest in the Elbe[43] or in the forest. If a graveyard were located at a quiet, remote spot where no one could make a path through it, it would be a spiritual, proper, and holy sight and could be so arranged that it would inspire devotion in those who go there. That would be my advice. Follow it, who so wishes. If anyone knows better, let him go ahead. I am no man's master.

[Conclusion]

In closing, we admonish and plead with you in Christ's name to help us with your prayers to God so that we may do battle with word and precept against the real and spiritual pestilence of Satan in his wickedness with which he now poisons and defiles the world—that is, particularly against those who blaspheme the sacrament,[44] though there are other sectarians also. Satan is infuriated and perhaps he feels that the day of Christ is at hand. That is why he raves so fiercely and tries to rob us of the Savior, Jesus Christ. Under the papacy Satan was simply "flesh" so that even a monk's cap had to be regarded as sacred. Now he is nothing more than sheer "spirit," and Christ's flesh and word are no longer supposed to mean anything. They made an answer to my treatise long ago, but I am surprised that it has not yet reached me at Wittenberg.[45] [When it does] I shall, God willing, answer them once again and let the matter drop. I can see that they will only become worse. They are like a bedbug which itself has a foul smell, but the harder you rub to crush it, the more it stinks. I hope that I've written enough in this pamphlet for those who can be saved so that—God be praised—many may thereby be snatched from their jaws and many more may be strengthened and confirmed in the truth. May Christ our Lord and Savior preserve us all in pure faith and fervent love, unspotted and pure until his day. Amen. Pray for me, a poor sinner.

43. The Elbe is the river that flows near Wittenberg.

44. This is a reference to Luther's conflict with fellow reformers Andreas Karlstadt (c. 1480–1541) and Ulrich Zwingli (1484–1531), both of whom emphasized the spiritual presence of Christ in the Lord's Supper and rejected Luther's view that Christ's body and blood were physically present in the elements. Their debate was carried on via a pamphlet war from 1524 to 1529 and escalated to include several more theologians. At the Marburg Colloquy in 1529, Luther and Zwingli met in an effort to agree on Protestant doctrine. Their failure to reach agreement on the issue of Christ's presence in the sacrament split the Protestant movement into two distinct factions.

45. From January to March 1527 Luther wrote *That These Words of Christ, "This Is My Body," etc., Still Stand Firm against the Fanatics* (LW 37:13–150; TAL 3:163–274). Zwingli's response, *That These Words . . . Will Always Retain Their Ancient, Single Meaning, and Martin Luther with His Latest Book Has by No Means Proved or Established His Own and the Pope's View*, arrived in Wittenberg on 11 November 1527.

That Christians Should Bear Their Cross with Patience

1530

KEN SUNDET JONES AND MARK C. MATTES

INTRODUCTION

Luther preached a Holy Saturday sermon on the cross and suffering[1] (LW 51:197–208; see also pp. 66–78 in this volume) while he and the Wittenberg party sojourned at the Coburg Castle[2] awaiting the Imperial Diet[3] that was to be assembled at Augsburg and at which Melanchthon would present the Evangelical confession of faith, that is, the *Augsburg Confession*, on 25 June 1530. As an outlaw, following the Edict of Worms[4] (1521), Luther could not leave his prince's territories and the protection that they provided. If he had followed the party to Augsburg he would have been arrested and possibly executed. Luther was not the only person in the entourage in danger, for the edict also proscribed anyone publicly supporting his views. It was a distinct possibility that any and all of them could have faced Luther's same end.

The following translation, *That Christians Should Bear Their Cross with Patience*, is likely sermon notes that Luther drafted in preparation for the sermon. It is not known whether it was composed at Coburg or before, but it bears a clear relationship to the sermon that he preached there. What is not as readily apparent is its connection to Luther's earlier theology of the cross (*theologia crucis*) in his 1518 *Heidelberg Disputation*.[5] In that disputation, the theology of the cross is contrasted with the theology of glory.

1. Along with the Holy Saturday sermon, Luther delivered five others during this time, but did not speak explicitly about the political situation in any of them (LW 51:195–208).

2. The Coburg (see image on p. 67) was part of the holdings of Luther's elector, John of Saxony (1468–1532). Luther was safe from prosecution within the elector's territories. The fortress lies about 130 miles from Augsburg. The elector's first choice for Luther was to stay in Nuremberg, but the city's council declined his request. At the Coburg, Luther was both annoyed and amused by the ravens soaring above the fortress. He complained about their early-morning crowing (WA Br 5, no. 1553) but also wrote George Spalatin (1484–1545) a clever note likening the birds to kings and princes at war with the barley fields (WA Br 5:290–91).

3. The diet was an assembly of the various leaders of the Holy Roman Empire. Its emperor, Charles V (1500–1558), called this assembly specifically to quell religious divisions within the empire and present a united front against the threat of advancing Ottoman troops.

4. Following the Diet of Worms (1521), Charles V issued an edict that outlawed Luther, his publications, and any who supported him. It was because of this edict that Luther was forced to go into hiding at the Wartburg Castle.

5. LW 31:39–70; WA 1:353–74; TAL 1:67–120.

6. The entourage consisted of Luther, Justus Jonas (1493–1555), and Philip Melanchthon (1497–1560), who left Wittenberg and joined Elector John of Saxony, Georg Spalatin, and Johann Agricola (1494–1566) at Torgau. Melanchthon, Jonas, and Agricola would serve as theological consultants and preachers for the Evangelical party at the diet.

There God works the cross in believers' lives so that they are divested of spiritual pride and brought to a dependence upon God's mercy in Christ. By 1530 Luther had expanded his view of the cross to see God at work in upholding people as they confess their faith in the face of persecution and opposition to the faith.

Luther's words here speak to the immediate situation of the Wittenberg entourage.[6] In the face of the uncertainty of the outcome of the diet, and the potential of real suffering and pain before them, Luther, based on these notes, later proclaimed that Christ's "suffering accomplishes everything, while ours does nothing except that we become formed to Christ." Luther's aim is to comfort and give confidence to his fellow reformers that they have been made holy by being "touched with Christ's suffering" (LW 51:208; this volume, p. 77).

These notes, *Feine Christliche gedancken der alten heiligen Veter und Lerer der Kirchen, von D.M.L. angezogen und gebessert, Das ein Christ das Creutz, so jm von Gott auffgelegtist, mit Gedult tragen sol*, were probably never printed separately but were first published in the Jena edition of Luther's collected works (1557) and appeared thereafter in the Wittenberg edition (1557/58), as well as in the later Walch and Erlangen editions.[a] This translation is based on the text of WA 32:547–48.

a   Luthers sämtliche Werke, ed J. G. Walch, 24 volumes (1740–1753), 10:2084–87; D. Martin Luthers sämtliche Werke, ed. J. G. Plachmann and J. K. Irmischer, 67 volumes (Erlangen, 1826–1857), 64:298–300.

Christ Carrying the Cross (1437) by Hans Multscher (1400–1467)

THAT CHRISTIANS SHOULD BEAR THEIR CROSS WITH PATIENCE[b]

Some Excellent and Christian Thoughts of the Ancient and Saintly Fathers and Teachers of the Church, That Christians Should Bear with Patience the Cross Which God Places upon Them, Applied and Elaborated by Luther[c]

THE ANCIENT AND SAINTLY fathers and theologians[7] have contrasted green and dry wood and have allegorized that contrast this way: sin and death came from the green wood;[8] righteousness and life from the dry wood.[9] They conclude: do not eat from the green tree, or you will die, but eat of this dry tree; otherwise, you will stay dead.

7. Although Luther does not specify which theologians he is alluding to, Cyril of Jerusalem (c. 313–386) in the *Catechetical Lectures* 13.31, and John of Damascus (c. 675–749) in *The Orthodox Faith* IV, XI, make this contrast.

8. The Tree of Knowledge of Good and Evil in the Garden of Eden (Gen. 2:17).

9. The Tree of the Cross on Golgotha.

b The original German text uses masculine language. Contemporary usage is reflected throughout this translation.

c The subtitle was most likely added later by an editor.

Adam and Eve eat fruit from the Tree
of Knowledge of Good and Evil (Genesis 3).

You do indeed desire to eat and nibble from a tree. I will direct you to a tree so full that you can never consume all its fruit. But as difficult as it was to stay away from that green tree, so it is just as difficult to enjoy or eat from the dry tree. The first was the figure of life, delight, and goodness, while the other is the figure of death, suffering, and sorrow because one tree is living, the other barren. There is a deeply rooted desire in a person's heart to seek life where there is certain death and to flee from death where there is certain life.

But the cross works in such a way that it causes pain.[d] It must not be self-imposed (as the Anabaptists and all the works-righteous teach), but is instead imposed upon a person.[e]

---

d "Such a cross and pain is necessary; it must be known as such and really bear down painfully, as does some great peril to one's goods and honor . . ." *Sermon vom Leiden und Kreuz* (WA 32:29; see also LW 51:198).

e "It should be the kind of suffering which we have not chosen for ourselves, as the fanatics do in choosing some suffering for themselves to bear . . ." (WA 32:29; LW 51:198).

The Need [for the Cross]*f*

"We must be conformed to the image of the Son of God," Rom. 8[:29].[10]

"All who desire to live a godly life in Christ Jesus must suffer persecution," 2 Tim. 3[:12].*g*

"In the world you have tribulation" [John 16:33]. Likewise, "You will be sorrowful; you will weep and lament, but the world will rejoice," John 16[:20].

"If we share in [Christ's] sufferings we shall also be glorified with him," Rom. 8[:17].

"If you are left without discipline, in which all have participated, then you are bastards and not children," Heb. 12[:8]. Otherwise, what purpose do so many comforting passages of Scripture serve?

The Source [of the Cross]*h*

Because the devil, a mighty, evil, deceitful spirit, hates the children of God.*i* For them the holy cross serves for exercising faith and the power of the word, as well as for subduing whatever sin and pride remain. Indeed, a Christian can no more do without the cross than without food or drink.

The Entreaty*j*

With his touch, Christ sanctifies all the sufferings and sorrows of those who believe in him.*k* Those who do not suffer show that they do not believe that Christ has given them the gift of his own passion. But if they do not wish to bear the cross which

10. In Luther's writings, Scripture quotes are not always verbatim and appear as if Luther is quoting from memory. All but the second quote are slightly paraphrased in this section. In order to retain the flavor of the original quotes in German and retain fidelity to Luther's idiom, we translate Luther literally and so do not follow the NRSV.

---

f *Necessitas.*

g "We must suffer so that we may be conformed to Christ . . . it cannot be otherwise but that each one must have his own cross and suffering" (WA 32:29; LW 51:199).

h *Causa.*

i "The devil . . . is hurt and chagrined that you have one healthy finger . . . but nothing is more hateful to him than the good word [of God]" (WA 32:36; LW 51:206).

j *Precium.*

k "Since they brought Christ into suffering, Christ has hallowed all the sufferings of his Christians . . ." (WA 32:32; LW 51:207).

God places upon them, they will not be compelled to do so by anyone—they are always free to deny Christ.[l] But in so doing they must know that they cannot have fellowship with Christ or share in any of his gifts.

For example, a merchant,[11] a hunter, a soldier[m,n] risk so much pain for the sake of an uncertain gain and victory, while here, where it is certain that glory and blessedness will be the result, it is a disagreeable thing to suffer even for a bit, as Isa. 54[:7], Christ in John 16[:20-22], Peter in 1 Pet. 1[:6], and Paul in 2 Cor. 4[:17] usually put it, "for a little while," and momentarily.[o]

Notice how our adversaries, those torturers from the devil, are torn and divided in their teachings in so many ways that they fail to realize their hopes, since they must be concerned with so much peril and misfortune that they can never act for a moment with certainty or confidence.[12] And these penalties and punishments are only temporal! How can I comprehend their guilt, namely, that without God and through the devil's craftiness they, beset by an evil conscience, are eternally lost? Even though they are uncertain as to the outcome of their endeavor, they keep on rejoicing in a hope that is completely and absolutely lost. Yet we, on the other hand, have God's unfailing promises for our comfort.[13]

In short, since it is the same God and the same matter, in which he has upheld the faith of all the saints so that he might be vindicated, God will not now, just for our own sake, be found a liar. Nor are we to make a liar of him. God grant, whether we do or do not believe, that he will yet defend his word and surely

11. The "Household Chart" in the *Small Catechism* shows that Luther considered these occupations among many vocations in which Christians can serve and bear their cross. See p. 239 in this volume.

12. Luther alludes here to the intrigue and cross-purposes at the Diet of Augsburg and preceding it that hindered the Roman parties from taking decisive action to root out the Lutheran heresy as they had hoped to do.

13. Luther's pastoral practice of providing comfort through God's word comes alive in letters he wrote to the grieving, the sick, and the despairing. Luther not only found comfort in the cross, he also had with him at the Coburg a portrait of his young daughter, Magdalena, that his wife had sent him (WA Br 5:277-78).

---

l "... nor is anybody forced or compelled to it ... you can let it lie and so deny Christ" (WA 32:30; LW 51:199).

m See *Whether Soldiers, Too, Can Be Saved* (1526), in LW 46:87-137; TAL, vol. 5, forthcoming.

n "A merchant ... risks body and life for base gain ... without any assurance" (WA 32:34–35; LW 51:204). "A horseman does the same. He goes to war where so many spears, halberds, and muskets are pointed at him, and has no assurance ..." (WA 32:35; LW 51:204).

o "So suffering becomes sweet and easy and is not eternal but only a tiny bit, which lasts a short time as St. Paul, St. Peter, and Christ also say in the gospel ..." (WA 32:35; LW 51:200).

help [us]. This demands great effort and care so that, in the first place, we turn our eyes from the might [of this world] and second, hold fast to the word. Eve[14] disregarded the word and relied on what was visible, but Christians, in contrast, disregard what they can see and hold to the word. The godless do not do so but rely upon the emperor to uphold them in this world, but because they neglect the word, they will be ruined and lost to eternity. In the year 1530.

14. "Then it will go with us as with Eve in paradise. . . . She let the word go and occupied herself with thoughts of what a fine apple it was." (WA 32:36; LW 51:205).

The visitation of Mary by Master M.S., 1506

Consolation for Women Whose Pregnancies Have Not Gone Well

1542

KRISTEN E. KVAM

INTRODUCTION

Luther's purpose in this text is clear: he wanted to instruct Christians on how they might console parents—particularly mothers—whose expectations for children had been dashed by prenatal and postnatal loss. His text shows his attentiveness to ways these parents would experience anguish—by guilt for how their actions could have contributed to the loss, but especially by fears that the hoped-for child's death prior to baptism would result in the damnation of the expected one. Luther told his audience what they ought not say—not to blame or frighten the mourners. He also told them to offer consolation by reminding the grievers of biblical and theological teachings. Indeed, he offered a treasure trove of examples from Scripture and church history to provide alternatives to thinking either that the mother caused the loss or that the hoped-for child would be condemned to a life separated from God.

The origin of this text is a story in itself. In 1541 Johannes Bugenhagen[1] wrote an interpretation of Psalm 29 and showed it to his friend and colleague Martin Luther. Bugenhagen's commentary prompted Luther to recommend that Bugenhagen add a discussion directed to parents who knew the anguish of encountering death in child bearing.[2] Bugenhagen resisted but

1. Johannes Bugenhagen (1485–1558) was pastor at the Town Church in Wittenberg and professor at the University of Wittenberg where he lectured on and translated the Psalms.

2. According to James Raun, Bugenhagen's use of the phrase "little children" prompted Luther to make this suggestion. Interestingly, such a phrase is not in the wording of the psalm itself; nor is Psalm 29 a lament psalm, making it probable that the phrase was in the now-lost commentary. See Raun's discussion in his introduction at LW 43:245.

was willing to include such an appendix if Luther would write it. Luther thought the project so important that he took up the task, writing this short "afterword" in German to be put at the back of Bugenhagen's text. In an ironic turn of events, Luther's Afterword[a] has outlived the book to which it originally was attached.

The Afterword's first English translation rendered its title *Comfort for Women Who Have Had a Miscarriage.*[b] A recent translation titled it *Consolation for Women Whose Pregnancies Have Not Gone Well.*[c] Each title indicates Luther's pastoral and spiritual concern for women who "have suffered such agony and heartbreak in child-bearing." Yet these translations also signal the difficulty of naming the experiences of agony and heartbreak that Luther would have had in mind. In contemporary English, "miscarriage" tends to refer to the demise of pregnancy far earlier than a pregnancy would have been known or experienced in the sixteenth century. Modern scientific developments in reproductive theory and technology have shaped beliefs and practices in radically different configurations than they had in Luther's time.[d]

---

[a] The German term *Zuletzt* as the heading for this text indicates the text's original status as an afterword or addendum to Bugenhagen's treatise.

[b] The German title is *Ein Trost den Weibern, welchen es ungerade gegangen ist mit Kindergebären.* James Raun translated the Afterword into English in LW 43:243–50, which appeared in 1968.

[c] William R. Russell, "Consolation for Women Whose Pregnancies Have Not Gone Well (1542)," in Timothy F. Lull and William R. Russell, eds., *Martin Luther's Basic Theological Writings,* 3d ed. (Minneapolis: Fortress Press, 2012), 283.

[d] Important discussions concerning medieval and early modern understandings of pregnancy and child bearing include: David Cressy, "Entering the World," in Peter Matheson, ed., *Reformation Christianity,* A People's History of Christianity 5 (Minneapolis: Fortress Press, 2007), 95–119; John M. Riddle, *Eve's Herbs: A History of Contraception and Abortion in the West* (Cambridge: Harvard University Press, 1997); Jane E. Strohl, "The Child in Luther's Theology: 'For What Purpose Do We Older Folks Exist Other Than to Care for . . . the Young?'" in Marcia J. Bunge, ed., *The Child in Christian Thought* (Grand Rapids: Eerdmans, 2001), 134–59; Merry E. Wiesner-Hanks, *Women and Gender in Early Modern Europe,* 3d ed. (New York: Cambridge University Press, 2008). For information on the neglect of children, see John Boswell's *The Kindness of Strangers: The Abandonment of Children in Western Europe from Late Antiquity to the Renaissance* (New York: Pantheon, 1988).

This text demonstrates that parents who knew grief because of stillbirth and other forms of prenatal and postnatal loss were important to Luther. The center of his focus, however, was on those who were in anguish because their awaited child was not baptized. What would be their hoped-for infant's eternal destiny? Anxiety about the fate of an expected infant who died before, during, or shortly after birth was intense in Luther's day. Early modern Christians in western Europe had infants baptized as soon as possible after birth. The dominant understanding of original sin with the attendant teaching that the unbaptized never would experience the full love of God undergirded the practice of requiring the sacrament to follow quickly after a child was born, often within a few days—or even minutes—of birth.[e]

When Luther wrote the Afterword, he recently had experienced the heartbreak of losing an expected child. Katherine von Bora,[3] Luther's wife, suffered at least one miscarriage during her life. In January 1540, the year before Luther asked Bugenhagen to address this type of grief, Katherine had a miscarriage that made her gravely ill. She was so sick, in fact, that she did not walk again until the beginning of March of that year.[f]

The Afterword is a remarkable text in Luther's corpus. It is also a remarkable text in the history of Christian thought. Before Luther, which Christian theologian had offered written advice concerning the particular pastoral needs of parents—especially women—who had hoped for a child and then suffered the anguish of the death of this hope? By pointing to examples of parents and friends praying on behalf of others, he stressed the significance of intercession. By noting examples of praying even when one has no words, he called attention to ways that grief can strip mourners of language. By underscoring the consolation established by the promises of God, he offered his characteristic depiction of the source and font for consoling the grieving, the guilty, and the fearful.

3. Katherine Von Bora (1499–1552) entered a cloister at age five or six, and spent nearly the next twenty years in convent life. She fled from the Nimschen convent near Grimma in April 1523 and later married Luther in 1526. She gave birth to six living children; two daughters died at early ages—Elisabeth (1527–1528) and Magdalena (1529–1542). See Kirsi Stjerna's "Herr Doktor: Katharina von Bora, 1499–1552: The Lutheran Matriarch," in her *Women and the Reformation* (Oxford: Blackwell, 2009), 51–70.

Katherine von Bora. Portrait by Lucas Cranach the Elder, 1528.

---

e   In addition to texts suggested above in n. *d* above, also see Susan Karant-Nunn's *The Reformation of Ritual: An Interpretation of Early Modern Germany*, Christianity and Society in the Modern World (London: Routledge, 1997).

f   Martin Brecht tells of this miscarriage in *Martin Luther: The Preservation of the Church 1532–1546*, ed. James L. Schaaf (Minneapolis: Fortress Press, 1993), 235.

Woodcut depicting midwives
attending a woman in childbirth.
Jacob Reuff. (Zurich, 1554)

This text, *Der XXIX.* || *Psalm ausge=* || *legt/ durch* || *Doctor Johan Bugenhagen/ Pomern.* || *Darinnen auch* || *von der Kinder Tauffe.* || *Jtem von den vn=* || *geborn Kindern/ vnd* || *von den Kindern die man* || *nicht Teuffen kan.* || *Ein trost D.* || *Martini Luthers den* || *Weibern/ welchen es vngerade* || *gegangen ist mit Kinder* || *geberen.* || was printed at least three times in Wittenberg in 1542[g] and appeared in the Wittenberg and Jena collections of Luther's works as well as other subsequent collections.

AFTERWORD[h]

Too often, devout parents—particularly women—have sought consolation from us because they have suffered such agony and heartbreak in child-bearing when, despite their best intentions and against their will, there was a premature birth or miscarriage and their fruit[i] died at birth or was born dead.

We ought not to frighten or sadden such mothers with unkind words. It is not their fault. It is not their carelessness or neglect that caused the birth of their child to go wrong.[4] One must distinguish between them and a woman who resents being pregnant, deliberately neglects her baby, and even goes so far as to strangle or destroy it.[5]

Generally speaking, let us talk with grieving mothers like this:

4. Theories of the prenatal influence of mothers on fetal development were prevalent in Luther's day. See his account in LW 5:380 where, after mentioning "the teaching of physicians," he continues: "in the conception of all living beings . . . special forms or marks are imprinted on the young, both as a result of a mental image and as a result of various objects that appear to the heart or the eyes, not only in the very heat of conception but also after impregnation has taken place."

5. Luther listed parental attitudes toward pregnancy and childbearing in LW 4:304–5, including young women who prevent conception and spouses who do not want to have children.

---

g   VD 16 L6795–97. See also ZV 2694.

h   This translation is based primarily on the recent translation by William R. Russell in Lull and Russell, eds., *Martin Luther's Basic Theological Writings*, 3rd ed., 283–85 (see introduction, n. *c*). The first paragraph uses much of the translation of James Raun in LW 43:247–50. The original is found in WA 53:(202) 205–8.

i   Luther's term here is "*Frucht*," a German word for "fruit."

First, we may not and cannot know the hidden counsel[j] of God in such a case—why, after every possible care had been taken, God did not allow the child to be born alive and baptized. Still, these mothers may find comfort and have faith. God's will is at all times better than our will, even though in the midst of our darkness it looks much different. They need not doubt. God is not angry with them or with others who are involved. This is a trial of one's ability to endure. Also, we know that this kind of case has occurred since the beginning of time. Indeed, Scripture also cites examples of it, as in Ps. 58[:8].[6] St. Paul even calls himself an *abortivum*,[k] "a miscarriage" or "one untimely born" [1 Cor. 15:8].

Second, because the mother is a Christian and a believer, she may hope that God will accept her deep desire to have her child baptized as an effective prayer.[l] True, a Christian in deepest despair does not dare to name, wish, or hope for the help (as it would seem to her) that she would absolutely and gladly purchase with her own life. And, were that possible, find comfort in such help. However, the words of St. Paul in Romans 8[:26] properly apply here: "Likewise the Spirit helps us in our weakness; for we do not know how to pray as we ought," that is, as was said above, we dare not express our wishes, "but that very

6. In the NRSV, Psalm 58:8b is "like the untimely birth that never sees the sun." Robert Alter translates the passage as "a woman's stillbirth that sees not the sun," in *The Book of Psalms* (New York: Norton, 2007), 203.

j   William Russell connects Luther's use here of "*Heimlich Gericht*" to Luther's notion of "the Hidden God," saying, "the Reformer's use here relates to his understanding of the 'Hidden God,' '*deus Absconditus*,'" in "Consolation for Women," 283 n.3.

k   Luther used the Latin *abortivum*, found in the Vulgate's rendering of 1 Cor. 15:8. In his German translation of the passage, he used "*unzeitigen Geburt*."

l   For information about late-medieval and early-modern understandings of infant baptism in the West, see Susan Karant-Nunn's "To Beat the Devil: Baptism and the Conquest of Sin," in her *The Reformation of Ritual*, 44–71; Jaroslav Pelikan's "Luther's Defense of Infant Baptism," in Carl S. Meyer, ed., *Luther for an Ecumenical Age: Essays in Commemoration of the 450th Anniversary of the* Reformation (St. Louis: Concordia, 1967), 200–218. For a different perspective, see Jane Baun, "The Fate of Babies Dying before Baptism in Byzantium," in Diana Wood, ed., *Church and Childhood: Papers Read at the 1993 Summer Meeting and the 1994 Winter Meeting of the Ecclesiastical History Society* (Oxford: Blackwell, 1997), 115–25.

Spirit intercedes for us with sighs too deep for words." And further, "God, who searches the heart, knows . . . the mind of the Spirit . . . ," etc. [Rom. 8:27]. Also Eph. 3[:20], "Now to God who by the power at work within us is able to accomplish abundantly far more than all we can ask or imagine."

One should not despise Christians as if they were Turks, heathens, and God-less persons.[7,m] God regards Christians as precious and their prayer is powerful and great. They have been sanctified by Christ's blood and anointed with God's Spirit. Whatever Christians sincerely pray, especially in the unexpressed yearning of their hearts, becomes a great, unbearable cry in God's ears.[8] God must listen. As God said to Moses in Exod. 14[:15], "Why do you cry out to me?" And Moses had not even whispered a word, because his great need made him so anxious and shaky.[9] His groans and the deep cry of his heart divided the Red Sea and dried it up, led the children of Israel across, and drowned the Pharaoh with all his army, etc. This and even more can be accomplished by a true, faithful longing. Even Moses did not know how or for what he should pray—not knowing how the deliverance would be accomplished—but his cry came from his heart.

---

7. "Turks," for Luther, signified both the political entity of the Ottoman Empire and the adherents of the religion of Islam.

8. Exodus 2:23-35 and 3:7-9 portray God as telling of hearing the suffering cries and groans of the Israelite slaves.

9. The biblical text has Moses being anxious about his speaking abilities at other parts of his story, including Exod. 3:11 and 4:10f.

m   Recent studies on Luther's understanding of Islam include: Matthew Dimmock and Andrew Hadfield, eds., *The Religions of the Book: Christian Perceptions, 1400–1660*, Early Modern Literature in History (Basingstoke, UK: Palgrave Macmillan, 2008); Adam S. Francisco, *Martin Luther and Islam: A Study in Sixteenth-Century Polemics and Apologetics*, History of Christian-Muslim Relations. 8 (Leiden: Koninklijke Brill, 2007); Sarah S. Henrich and James L. Boyce, "Martin Luther—Translations of Two Prefaces on Islam: Preface to the *Libellus de ritu moribus Turcorum* (1530), and Preface to Bibliander's Edition of the Qur'an (1543)," *Word & World* 16, no. 2 (Spring 1996): 250–66; Gregory J. Miller, "Luther on the Turks and Islam," in Timothy J. Wengert, ed., *Harvesting Martin Luther's Reflections on Theology, Ethics, and the Church* (Grand Rapids: Eerdmans, 2004), 185–205; J. Paul Rajashekar and Timothy J. Wengert, "Martin Luther, Philip Melanchthon, and the Publication of the Qur'an," *Lutheran Quarterly* 16 (2002): 221–28; Robert O. Smith, "Luther, the Turks, and Islam," *Currents in Theology and Mission* 34, no. 5 (October 2007):

Isaiah did the same against King Sennacherib." Other kings and prophets likewise accomplished inconceivable and impossible things by prayer, even to their amazement afterward. Before that, however, they would not have dared to expect or wish so much of God. This means we can receive things far higher and greater than we understand or pray for, as St. Paul says in Eph. 3[:20], etc.

Also, St. Augustine declared that his mother prayed, sighed, and wept for him.[10] She did not desire anything more than that he might be converted from the errors of the Manicheans and become a Christian.[11] As St. Augustine puts it, God granted her

St. Monica,
mother of
Augustine
(c. 1464),
painted by
Benozzo Gozzoli
(1420–1497)

10. Monica (c. 331–387) prayed earnestly and repeatedly for the conversion of her son Augustine (354–430). Monica herself had been raised Christian, but Augustine as a young man followed Manicheanism, which was based on the teachings of the Persian teacher Manes (c. 215–275). Monica's upbringing is described in book 9, chapter 8 of Augustine's *Confessions*.

11. Augustine was attracted by the intellectual rigor of Manicheanism, which taught a strict dualism between light and dark, good and evil. Augustine describes the prayers of his mother in his writings. For examples, see *St. Augustine: Confessions*, trans. R. S. Pine-Coffin (New York: Penguin, 1961), 3:11–12; 5:8–9; 6:1–2, 13. In book 8:12, he tells of her joy when he became Christian.

351–64.

cardinem desiderii eius—her chief desire—what she longed for with unutterable sighs: that he would become a Christian. And St. Augustine became a teacher above all others in Christendom. Next to the apostles, Christendom has none that is his equal.

Who can doubt that those Israelite children who died before they could be circumcised on the eighth day were yet saved by the prayers of their parents, in view of the promise that God willed to be their God?[12] God has not limited God's power to sacraments, but has made a covenant with us through God's own word.[o]

Therefore, we ought to speak differently and in a more consoling way with Christians than with pagans or wicked people (the two are often the same), even in such cases where we do not know God's hidden counsel. As Jesus says in Mark 9[:23], and he does not lie, "All things can be done for those who believe," even if they have not prayed, or expected, or hoped for what they would want to see happen.[13] Enough has been said about this. Therefore we must leave such situations to God and take comfort in the thought that God surely has heard our unspoken yearning and done all things better than we could have asked.

12. Luther offered a sustained discussion of circumcision, including its parallels and contrasts with baptism, when he lectured on Genesis 17. The passage that tells of God instituting the circumcision of eight-day-old boys as a sign of faithfulness to the covenant that God made with Abraham; see LW 3:75–146. Luther's consideration of the status of boys who died before the eighth day, as well as of "our own infants, either those who are stillborn or those who die shortly after birth, before they are baptized," begins on page 103 and returns on pages 110, 133, and 137. Concerning what God did with boys who died before circumcision, Luther stated both "I know that I do not know" and "I know that God is merciful."

13. This passage follows Jesus healing a child on the basis of the request of the boy's father.

n   Cf. Isa. 37:4.

o   See LW 43:249 n.8, which states: "At this point the edition of Luther's works by Enders (vol. 15, pp. 55–56) includes some additional material cited in WA 53:207, n. 1:

> that God could without them (word and sacrament) and in ways unknown to us save the unbaptized infants as he did for many in the time of the law of Moses (even kings) apart from the law, such as Job, Naaman, the king of Nineveh, Babylon, Egypt, etc. However, he did not want the law to be openly despised, but upheld under threat of the punishment of eternal curse.
>
> So I consider and hope that the good and merciful God is well-intentioned toward those infants who do not receive baptism through no fault of their own or in disregard of his manifest command of baptism.
>
> Yet [I consider] that God does not and did not wish this to be publicly preached or believed because of the iniquity of the world, so that what God had ordained and commanded would not be despised. For we see that he has commanded much because of the iniquity of the world, but does not constrain the godly in the same way.
>
> In summary, the Spirit turns everything for those who fear him to the best, but to the obstinate he is obstinate (Ps. 18:27).

In summary, see to it that above all else you are a true Christian and that you teach a heartfelt yearning and praying to God in true faith, be it in this or any other trouble.[14] Then do not be dismayed or grieved about your child or yourself. Know that your prayer is pleasing to God and that God will do everything much better than you can comprehend or desire. "Call upon me," God says in Ps. 50[:15], "In the day of trouble; I will deliver you, and you shall glorify me." For this reason, we ought not to condemn such infants. Believers and Christians have devoted their longing and yearning and praying for them. Nor ought we consider them as the same as others for whom no faith, prayer, or yearning are expressed on the part of Christians and believers. God intends that the divine promise, and our prayer or yearning that is grounded in that promise, should not be disdained or rejected, but be highly valued and esteemed.[15]

I have said it before and preached it often enough: God accomplishes much through the faith and longing of another, even a stranger who has no personal faith. And this is given through the channel of another's prayer. In the gospel, Christ raised the widow's son at Nain because of the prayers of his mother apart from the faith of the son [Luke 7:11-17]. And he freed the little daughter of the Canaanite woman from the demon through the faith of the mother apart from the daughter's faith [Matt. 15:22-28]. The same was true of the king's son[16] in John 4[:46-53] and of the paralytic [Mark 2:1-2; Luke 5:17-26][17] and many others of whom we need not say anything here.

14. Luther's admonition coheres with his theology and personal practice concerning prayer with its stress on petitions—even unspoken ones—as keeping the Second Commandment precisely by understanding that the person praying has nothing to offer God. Instead, turning to God in every trouble is a sign of trusting in God's promise to hear the cries of God's people. For examples, see Luther's commentary on the Lord's Prayer in his *Large Catechism* (TAL 2:366–87), as well as other writings in this volume.

15. When lecturing on the death of Abraham and Gen. 25:7-10, Luther stated: "The whereabouts of the souls is the Word of God or the promises in which we fall asleep" (LW 4:314). He went on to criticize those who devised five different places for the dead, including the so-called limbo for infants who died before baptism (see LW 4:314–16).

16. While Luther referred to the father of this child as a king, the NRSV describes him as a "royal official."

17. When telling the story of the healing of a person who was paralyzed, the accounts of Mark and Luke have Jesus perform the healing after he sees the faith of the person's friends; Matthew's account says that Jesus saw the faith of the paralyzed person (Matt. 9:1-8).

Letter from Luther to Thomas Cromwell, secretary to King Henry VIII,
Palm Sunday, 9 April 1536. Luther excuses himself for not responding
to a letter brought by Dr. Barnes and expresses his joy at Cromwell's
zeal for the cause of Christ and his power to advance it.

Selected Letters
of Pastoral
and Spiritual Counsel

JOHN A. MAXFIELD

INTRODUCTION

A very rewarding exercise indeed is a careful reading through
Luther's letters in the excellent volumes prepared by Gottfried
Krodel for the American Edition of *Luther's Works* (vols. 48–50).
Not only does the reader gain insight into the life and character
of the man Martin Luther, but many of the religious, political,
and cultural issues of Reformation Europe also come into view
through Luther's vast correspondence. Arguably the central figure of the sixteenth century, Luther was personally involved in
many of the great issues of his day, and both his reflections on
these events and his involvement in so many of them are put on
display in his letters. Perhaps even more fascinating is the way
Luther's letters reveal his many close relationships with friends,
family members, and colleagues, as well as the way he approached
those in positions of power and authority in his day: temporal
and ecclesiastical rulers, both friend and foe of the Reformation. The texts themselves, as well as the detailed notes prepared
by Dr. Krodel (many of which serve as a guide into the Weimar
edition and other historic editions of Luther's correspondence),
answer many questions about Luther and his times.

In keeping with the theme of this volume in The Annotated Luther, I have combed through the American Edition and

selected letters that display the reformer as a pastor and care-taker of souls (*Seelsorger*). Seeking to provide a window into Luther's development as a theologian and pastor, and to illustrate the many different types of problems he addressed in his letters, some have been selected from earlier in his career (one even "pre-Reformation") as well as others reflecting his concerns as the Evangelical movement he led matured into new church structures and, indeed, a distinct confession existing in conflict (both in his time and largely since) with the Catholic Church led by the papacy in Rome. The letters selected were written to a variety of addressees: colleagues (both close and more distant), close family members, and one to a man he had never met but whom Luther sought to comfort in the face of the death of this man's son, a beloved young student at the University of Wittenberg.

Previous translations[1] have been adapted to capture more literally Luther's German expressions (less frequently his Latin). Bracketed text remains only where it is necessary to convey meaning. Marginal notes and footnotes make use of information supplied in Krodel's very detailed notes and introductions; we are indebted to his excellent scholarship. But for this edition both the number and length of notes are significantly reduced in favor of fewer distractions from Luther's words. Readers should move from these selections to the more detailed notes and introductions in the American Edition (and from there to the critical and historic editions of Luther's correspondence) when conducting more extensive research into the many issues Luther addresses in his letters.

For sixteenth-century humanists (including Luther), letter writing was an important art form as well as a means both of personal communication and for publicizing of ideas and events. Probably most humanist letters were meant to be shared (see, for example, Luther's letter dated 7 February 1546 to his wife, Katie [below], where he instructs her to share even its most intimate details with Philip Melanchthon [1497–1560]), and even many personal letters (not to mention public or "open" letters) were published almost immediately. Erasmus of Rotterdam (1466–1536), who saw to the early publication of his own correspondence, complains in a letter to Luther's supporter Justus Jonas (1493–1555) in May 1521, "I had sent Luther warning in a private letter under seal; it was soon printed in Leipzig."[a] Publication of Luther's personal letters began during his lifetime, in particular

1. In the American Edition, Krodel utilized and adapted translations in the excellent collection edited and translated by Theodore G. Tappert, *Luther: Letters of Spiritual Counsel*, Library of Christian Classics 18 (Philadelphia: Westminster Press, 1955). For other collections of Luther's correspondence in English, see LW 48: xiv. German and Latin texts appear in the sixteen volumes (twelve volumes of texts plus four supplemental volumes) of WA Br. Also important is the Enders edition: *Dr. Martin Luthers Briefwechsel*, ed. E. L. Enders and G. Kawerau, 19 vols. (Frankfurt/Leipzig: Schriften-Niederlage des Evangel, 1884–1932).

within a collection of his writings of comfort (*Trostschriften*) that appeared in 1545, but letters found their place in all sixteenth-century editions of Luther's collected writings.[b]

Although Luther was many things, he was most importantly a pastor, a proclaimer of the word of God and especially of the gospel. The letters presented here (and many more) reveal Luther the pastor at work, comforting, correcting and rebuking, guiding, and caring for others in the body of Christ.

LETTER TO FRIAR GEORGE SPENLEIN[c]

WITTENBERG, 8 APRIL 1516

Luther was formed spiritually through his experience as a friar in the German Reformed Congregation of Augustinian Hermits, first in Erfurt and then in Wittenberg. Both these Augustinian houses were part of the reform (Observant) movement within the Augustinian order, which had become independent of the four provinces of Augustinians in Germany in the fifteenth century

---

a Erasmus goes on to complain of other similar incidents. See Ep. 1202, in Erika Rummel, ed., *The Erasmus Reader* (Toronto: University of Toronto Press, 1990), 212.

b On the editions of Luther's letters, see WA Br 14, as well as Johannes Schilling, "Luthers Briefe und die Abteilung 'Briefwechsel' in der Weimarer Lutherausgabe," in WA, *Sonderedition der kritischen Weimarer Ausgabe. Begleitheft zum Briefwechsel* (Weimar: Hermann Bohlaus Nachfolger, 2002), 25–49. An interesting though flawed analysis (mostly on account of antipathy to Luther and a rather extreme hermeneutic of suspicion) is Lyndal Roper, "'To His Most Learned and Dearest Friend': Reading Luther's Letters," *German History* 28, no. 3 (2010): 283–95.

c LW 48:11–14.

2. Several letters in the American Edition reveal Luther at work pastorally as district vicar, a position he held from 1515 to April 1518. See especially LW 48, nos. 5, 8, 10, and 13.

3. The term *eremite* ("hermit"; Latin: *eremita*) comes from the Greek word for desert, and reflects the tradition of solitary monastic life passed down from the desert fathers of the early church. The Augustinians were first formed in 1256 when several groups of hermits in Italy "in the interests of ecclesiastical efficiency were banded together under the Rule of St. Augustine by Pope Alexander IV" (ODCC, s.v. Augustinian Hermits or Friars).

4. "Jesus Christ" or "Jesus" frequently appears in the salutations of Luther's letters; here and throughout these selections I have retained the punctuation of the salutations as given in WA Br.

5. The so-called Rhenish gulden was a gold coin used as currency in Wittenberg and Electoral Saxony.

6. A major work on logic by Jodokus Trutfetter (c. 1460–1519), one of Luther's teachers at the University of Erfurt, titled *Summulae totius logicae . . . compilatae* (Erfurt, 1501). On Luther's studies in philosophy and Scholastic theology at Erfurt, see LW 48:5, and 59 n.19.

after a bitter struggle to restore the original purity of the order. Over time Luther gained significant respect among his brothers and superiors in Erfurt and later in Wittenberg. In the winter of 1510–11 he was sent to Rome to represent the Observant houses as they attempted to oppose the plan of their elected vicar general, Johann von Staupitz (c. 1460–1524), to unite the Observants with the Conventuals in the Saxon province of Augustinians.[d] In 1515, now at Wittenberg, Luther was elected district vicar.[2]

Friar George Spenlein (c. 1486–1563) had joined the Augustinians in Wittenberg in 1512 and came to know Luther, who that October received his doctorate in theology. Shortly before Luther wrote this letter in April 1516, Spenlein had transferred to the Augustinian cloister in Memmingen. The letter is especially significant because it reveals Luther applying his developing concept of the righteousness of Christ as a gift to the sinner in a letter of spiritual counsel to a brother in the Augustinian order.

Latin text in WA Br 1:35–36.

To the godly and sincere Friar George Spenlein, Augustinian Eremite[3] in the monastery at Memmingen, himself esteemed in the Lord.

Jesus Christ.[4]

GRACE AND PEACE TO YOU from God the Father and from the Lord Jesus Christ. My dearest Friar[e] George: I wish you to know that I sold some of your things for two-and-a-half gulden,[5] namely, the coat of Brussels for one gulden, the larger work of the Eisenach theologian[6] for half a gulden, and the cowl and some other things for one gulden. Some things are left, such as the Eclogues of Baptista Mantuanus[f] and your collections [of other literary materials]. These you must consider a loss, for we have not been able to

d   See Heiko A. Oberman, *Luther: Man between God and the Devil*, trans. Eileen Walliser-Schwarzbart (New Haven: Yale University Press, 1989), 129–50.

e   Or "brother."

f   See *The Eclogues of Baptista Mantuanus,* edited, with introduction and notes, by W. P. Mustard (Baltimore: Johns Hopkins University Press, 1911).

dispose of them. The two-and-a-half gulden which you owe to the Most Reverend Father Vicar[7] we gave him in your name. The other half gulden which you still owe him you must either try to pay or get him to cancel. I felt that the Most Reverend Father was so well disposed toward you that he would not object to doing so.[g]

7. Johann von Staupitz, the vicar general of the German Reformed Congregation of Augustinian Hermits, and Luther's mentor and father confessor at Wittenberg. For a summary description of Staupitz, see LW 48:64 n.1.

Johann von Staupitz

Now I should like to know whether your soul, tired of its own righteousness, is learning to be revived by and to trust in the righteousness of Christ. For in our age the temptation to presumption besets many, especially those who try with all their might to be just and good without knowing the righteousness of God, which is most bountifully and freely given us in Christ. They try to do good of themselves in order that they might stand before God clothed in their own virtues and merits. But this

g   For Staupitz as a theologian and his influence on Luther, see especially the essays in Berndt Hamm, *The Early Luther: Stages in a Reformation Reorientation*, trans. Martin J. Lohrmann (Grand Rapids: Eerdmans, 2014); and David C. Steinmetz, *Luther and Staupitz: An Essay in the Intellectual Origins of the Protestant Reformation* (Durham: Duke University Press, 1980).

8. Luther cradles his description of Christ's righteousness given to the Christian in a theology of the cross.

9. Luther's language here anticipates his vivid descriptions of a "happy exchange" between the believer and Christ in *The Freedom of a Christian* (1520) and other texts. See TAL 1:499–507.

10. In his first lectures on the Psalms (the *Dictata super Psalterium*), given at the University of Wittenberg from August 1513 to late in 1515, Luther on occasion spoke of Christ's righteousness as a gift bestowed upon the Christian, who is cautioned not to be filled with pride when considering this adornment; see, e.g., LW 11:279–84. For Luther's more developed, classic descriptions of justification by faith and the righteousness of faith, see especially his 1520 treatise *The Freedom of a Christian* (LW 31:327–77; TAL 1:466–538); his preface to St. Paul's epistle to the Romans (LW 35:365–80, esp. 370–71); and his reflections in the 1545 *Preface to His Latin Writings* (pp. 489–503 in this volume).

11. In a letter to his younger colleague Philip Melanchthon in August 1521 Luther wrote, "If you are a preacher of grace, then preach a true and not a fictitious grace; if grace is true, you must bear a true and not a fictitious sin. God does not save people who are fictitious sinners. Be a sinner and sin boldly, but believe and rejoice in Christ even more boldly, for he is victorious over sin, death, and the world." Several lines later Luther ended that letter exhorting Melanchthon, "Pray boldly— you too are a mighty sinner" (LW 48:281–82).

is impossible. While you were here, you were one who held this opinion, or rather, error. So was I, and I am still fighting against the error without having conquered it as yet.

Therefore, my dear Friar, learn Christ and him crucified.[8] Learn to praise him and, despairing of yourself, say, "Lord Jesus, you are my righteousness, just as I am your sin. You have taken upon yourself what is mine and have given to me what is yours.[9] You have taken upon yourself what you were not and have given to me what I was not."[10] Beware of aspiring to such purity that you will not wish to be looked upon as a sinner, or to be one.[11] For Christ dwells only in sinners. On this account he descended from heaven, where he dwelt among the righteous, to dwell among sinners. Meditate on this love of his and you will see his sweet consolation. For why was it necessary for him to die if we can obtain a good conscience by our works and afflictions? Accordingly you will find peace only in him and only when you despair of yourself and your own works. Besides, you will learn from him that just as he has received you, so he has made your sins his own and has made his righteousness yours.

If you firmly believe this as you ought (and he is damned who does not believe it), receive your untaught and hitherto erring brothers, patiently help them, make their sins yours, and, if you have any goodness, let it be theirs. Thus the Apostle teaches, "Receive one another as Christ also received you to the glory of God."[h] And again, "Have this mind among yourselves, which you have in Christ Jesus, who, though he was in the form of God, [. . .] but emptied himself" etc. Even so, if you seem to yourself to be better than they are, do not count it as booty, as if it were yours alone, but humble yourself, forget what you are and be as one of them in order that you may help them.

For cursed is the righteousness of the man who is unwilling to assist others on the ground that they are worse than he is, and who thinks of fleeing from and forsaking those whom he ought now to be helping with patience, prayer, and example. This would be burying the Lord's talent and not paying what is due. If you are a lily and a rose of Christ, therefore, know that you will live among thorns. Only see to it that you will not become a thorn as a result of impatience, rash judgment, or secret pride.

---

h Rom. 15:7, with Luther quoting the Vulgate text, as also the following (inexact) quote from Phil. 2:5-7.

The rule of Christ is in the midst of his enemies, as the psalm puts it.[i] Why, then, do you imagine that you are among friends? Pray, therefore, for whatever you lack, kneeling before the face of the Lord Jesus. He will teach you all things. Only keep your eyes fixed on what he has done for you and for all people in order that you may learn what you should do for others. If he had desired to live only among good people and to die only for his friends, for whom, I ask you, would he have died or with whom would he ever have lived? Act accordingly, my dear Friar, and pray for me. The Lord be with you.

Farewell in the Lord.

From Wittenberg, on the Tuesday after *Misericordia Domini* 1516.[12]

> Yours,
> Friar Martin Luther
> Augustinian

12. Luther typically, as here, provides a date according to the church's liturgical calendar. *Misericordia Domini* was in Luther's time the second Sunday after Easter; it takes its name from the antiphon of the Introit from Psalm 33 (Vg. Ps. 32:5): "*Misericordia Domini plena est terra. . . .*"

LETTER TO GEORGE SPALATIN[j]

WARTBURG, 9 SEPTEMBER 1521

George Spalatin (1484–1545) was the chaplain, personal secretary, and private councillor of Elector Frederick the Wise (1463–1525), who protected Luther during his "trial" in the controversy over indulgences and arranged for the protective exile of the reformer after he was declared an outlaw by the emperor in the Edict of Worms (May 1521). As Luther never met the elector personally (apparently they only saw each other when Luther appeared before the Imperial Diet at Worms), Spalatin played a crucial role in the Reformation as the personal mediator between the reformer and the elector, and Luther frequently wrote to him regarding matters of reform in Saxony. In the case of this letter, Luther addressed from his exile the important issue of preaching

---

i   Ps. 110:2 (Ps. 109:2 in the Vulgate).

j   LW 48:305–10.

13. Wolfgang Capito was a humanist who had studied law, medicine, and theology at the University of Freiburg im Breisgau, and from 1515 to 1520 was a preacher in Basel. A close friend of Erasmus, in 1520 he became chancellor to Archbishop Albrecht of Mainz (1490–1545), and like Erasmus he both sympathized with Luther early on in his dispute with Rome and grew critical of Luther's divisiveness. Later he became a leader of the Reformation in Strasbourg; on his role, see James M. Kittelson, *Wolfgang Capito: From Humanist to Reformer* (Leiden: Brill, 1975).

14. Desiderius Erasmus was a humanist scholar of international fame, known by the time of Luther's conflict with Rome for his own satirical criticism of the papal church. By 1521 he had expressed disapproval of Luther's vitriolic language and radical critique of the Roman sacramental system, and later he publicly attacked Luther's theology with his *Diatribe on Free Will* (1524).

Desiderius Erasmus. Engraving by Albrecht Dürer, 1526.

in Wittenberg during his absence. Significantly, he advocates that Philip Melanchthon, the young genius who was called to teach Greek in the Faculty of Arts at the University of Wittenberg in 1518 but who was never ordained to the priesthood, be appointed a preacher in the city of Wittenberg. The letter is thus an important indicator of Luther's understanding of the gospel ministry and the call to that ministry, at least as it had developed early in the Reformation. Luther opens the letter with comments dismissing the negative opinion of him recently expressed by the humanists Wolfgang Capito (1478–1541) and Erasmus of Rotterdam.

    Latin text in WA Br 2:387–89.

Jesus.[k]

GREETINGS. The opinion of neither Capito[13] nor Erasmus[14] moves me in the least.[l] They are only doing what I have suspected. Indeed I have been afraid that someday I should have some trouble with one or the other of them. For I saw that Erasmus was far from the knowledge of grace, since in all his writings he is not concerned for the cross but for peace. He thinks that everything should be discussed and handled in a civil manner and with a certain benevolent kindliness. But Behemoth pays no attention and nothing improves by this.[15] I remember when Erasmus said in his preface to the New Testament, [and he must have been thinking] of himself, "The Christian easily despises glory."[m] I thought in my heart: Erasmus, I am afraid you deceive yourself. It is a great thing to despise glory. But his way of despising glory was to think lightly

---

k   See n. 4, p. 432. The addressee is missing in the autograph, but the contents of the letter, in particular the statement explained in n. 16 below, make clear that Luther is writing to Spalatin.

l   For a reconstruction of the events and correspondence that Luther is responding to here, see LW 48:305 n.4.

m   According to WA Br 2:389 n.4, this statement can be found neither in Erasmus's preface (the *Paraclesis*) to his Greek edition of the New Testament (*Novum Instrumentum*, 1516) nor in the other front matter of that edition. Krodel notes (LW 48:306 n.8), however, that in the letter "To the Reader" that prefaced Erasmus's annotations in this edition of the New Testament "there are certain phrases from which such a statement could be deduced."

of it, not to bear the contempt that others put upon him. Despising glory, however, is nothing if it is only in words; it is even less than nothing if only in thought. The kingdom of God consists in power, says Paul.[n] Therefore up to now I have not dared to boast about anything and am unable to do so, except about the word of truth that the Lord has given to me. Their[o] writings accomplish nothing because they refrain from chiding, biting, and giving offense. For

Young George Spalatin (also known as George Burkhardt from Spalt near Nuremberg). Portrait by Lucas Cranach the Elder, 1509.

when the popes [and bishops] are admonished in a civil manner they think it is flattering and keep on as if they possessed the right to remain uncorrected and incorrigible, content that they are feared and that no one dares to reproach them. These are the kind of people pictured in your Plutarch's little book on flattery.[16] But Jeremiah speaks more gravely and dreadfully of them: "Cursed is he who does the work of the Lord deceitfully."[p] Here the Prophet speaks of the work of the sword against God's enemies. And I am very afraid and my conscience troubles me because, yielding in Worms to your advice and that of our friends, I held my spirit in check and did not show myself as an Elijah to those idols.[17] They would hear other things, if I would come before them again.[18] But enough of this.

Duke John the Elder[19] at last knows where I am; so far he has not known. My host has revealed it to him confidentially. But the Duke should keep it quiet. I am fine here, but I am growing sluggish and languid and cold in spirit, and am miserable. Today,

15. Long before their public dispute in 1524-25, Luther recognized the chasm between his concerns for salvation by grace alone through faith in Christ, and Erasmus's program, which focused on the cultivation of virtue and piety through education, promotion of good literature, and an emphasis on moral improvement. Luther follows Jerome in understanding *Behemoth* (Job 40:15-24) as the devil; see LW 48:306 n.7.

16. Spalatin had published in 1520 a German translation of the book *How to Distinguish between a Flatterer and a Friend* by the Greek biographer Plutarch (c. 46-c. 120).

17. Luther here expresses some regret that he had not spoken more brazenly at the Diet of Worms when he had been denied the opportunity to defend his books but was faced with the demand that he recant them.

18. Now in protective exile at the Wartburg, Luther did indeed "show [himself] an Elijah" through a flood of letters and pamphlets, including a private epistolary rebuke of 1 December 1521 to Archbishop Albrecht of Mainz after Luther had heard in September or October about a sale of indulgences at Halle (see LW 48:339-43), as well as a public blast in a vituperative treatise, *Against the "Idol" at Halle*, begun at this time but held up from publication by Spalatin. See LW 48:344-50.

19. Duke John (1468-1532), brother of Frederick the Wise and elector of Saxony after Frederick's death in 1525.

---

n   1 Cor. 4:20.

o   Capito's and Erasmus's.

p   Jer. 48:10 (Vulgate).

20. Apparently this was the sixth day that Luther was suffering from severe constipation.

21. Luther while at the Wartburg suffered with extreme constipation and rectal sores.

22. Luther wrote this letter just before the time of the Festival of the Exaltation of the Holy Cross, which focused on the relic of the true cross. A year hence Luther would deliver in Wittenberg and later publish *A Sermon on Relics, Decorated with Excess/On the Holy Cross in the Churches*, in which he developed the theme that the Christian is called not to venerate the crucifix but to take up the cross of suffering and of obedience to the will of Christ. On this sermon see John A. Maxfield, "Martin Luther and Idolatry," in Anna Marie Johnson and John A. Maxfield, eds., *The Reformation as Christianization: Essays on Scott Hendrix's Christianization Thesis* (Tübingen: Mohr Siebeck, 2012), 150–58.

23. Philip Melanchthon, Luther's younger colleague, was in the reformer's absence one of the main leaders of the Evangelical movement in Wittenberg, as he would continue to be even after Luther's return the following March.

24. Melanchthon was never ordained and would later decline Luther's urging to complete doctoral studies in theology, instead committing himself fully to the Faculty of Arts and his own program of complementing Evangelical reform with the development of a philosophy and humanism conforming to the Lutheran understanding of law and gospel. However, it is misconstruing Luther's understanding to term Melanchthon a "lay theologian" or "lay preacher," and Luther's urging here to be one of promoting "freedom for the laity to preach" (LW 48:308 n.27).

on the sixth day,[20] I had elimination with such difficulty that I almost passed out.[21] Now I sit aching as if in labor confinement, wounded and sore, and shall have no—or little—rest this night. Thanks be to Christ who has not left me without any relic of the holy cross.[22] I would have been healed from all soreness if the elimination had moved more easily. But whatever heals in four days is wounded again by elimination. I write this not for sympathy but that you may congratulate me, praying that I may be worthy to become fervent in the Spirit.

Now is the time to pray against Satan with all our strength; he is threatening Germany with some fatal tragedy. And in spite of my fear that the Lord will allow him to bring it about, until now I have been sleepy and lazy, both in praying and resisting Satan, so that I am angry at myself, and am a burden to myself. Perhaps it is because I am alone and you are not helping me. I beg you, let us pray and watch that we do not enter into temptation.[q] I have nothing else to write just now. You people in Wittenberg know everything about everyone.

I rejoice that Wittenberg's prestige is increasing, especially that it grows while I am absent, so that the wicked man sees it and grumbles, and his desire perishes.[r] May Christ complete that which he has begun!

I really wish Philip[23] would also preach to the people somewhere in the city on festival days after dinner to provide a substitute for the drinking and gambling. This could become a custom that would introduce freedom and restore the form and manners of the early church.[24] For if we have broken all laws of men and cast off their yokes, what difference would it make to us that Philip is not anointed or tonsured but married?[25] Nevertheless he is truly a priest and actually does the work of a priest, unless it is not the office of a priest to teach the word of God.[26] In that case Christ himself would not be a priest, for he taught now in synagogues, then in ships, now at the shoreline, then in the mountains. In a word, he was always and everywhere all things

q   Matt. 26:41.

r   Ps. 112:10.

to all people at all times. Since, therefore, Philip is called by God and performs the ministry of the word, as no one can deny, what difference does it make that he is not called by those tyrants— who are bishops not of churches but of horses and courtiers.[27] But I know that man's[28] mind. He will not yield to my persuasions. Therefore he has to be called and driven [to preaching] by the order and pressure of the whole congregation.[29] For if the congregation demands and requests it, he ought not and cannot say no. Were I present, I would by all means work on the city council and the people so that they would ask Philip to lecture to them privately in German on the Gospels as he has begun to lecture in Latin, so that little by little he would become a German[-speaking] bishop, as he has already become a Latin[-speaking] bishop. I wish you would do what you can to bring this about, because what the people need above all things is the word of God. Since he is incomparably rich in the word, you can see that it is our duty to call him and not let the word be cheated of its fruit; in addition the conscience urges this and God requires it. You will be able to have this passed by the city council quite easily with the help of Lucas[30] and Christian.[31] May Christ compensate for my absence and silence with Melanchthon's preaching and voice, to the confusion of Satan and his apostles. Origen[32] taught women privately. Why should Melanchthon not undertake something similar, when he can and ought to do it? And this especially since the people are thirsty and in need of such a thing. Please don't be moved too easily by his excuses! He will hide behind the most beautiful fig leaves, as is becoming to him. For he ought not to seek such a duty, but he must be urged and called by the congregation, even begged to serve and to do not what is useful only for himself but rather what is profitable for many. I beg you, work on this most diligently, before all other things. Consult with friends who will help you to push this. Farewell, and remember me before the Lord.

From the wilderness,[s] on the day after the Nativity of Mary.

Yours,
Martin Luther

---

s   *Ex eremo*, which also could be translated "from the hermitage" (see more fully LW 48:263 n.36).

Rather, it is clear that Luther viewed Melanchthon as called to the ministry of the word through his call to the university faculty.

25. Melanchthon had married Katharina Krapp (1497–1557), the daughter of the mayor of Wittenberg, on 27 November 1520; Luther recognizes that the papal bishops would thus never approve his ordination to the priesthood.

26. As this letter clearly indicates (see also LW 48:311–12), the reformer regarded Melanchthon as called by God to the ministry of the word, at least in the university, if not in the City Church.

27. Luther often expressed criticism of the worldly power and pretension of the bishops of the papal church.

28. Melanchthon's.

29. Luther viewed the public call of the congregation as the means through which God places someone in the public ministry of the word.

30. Lucas Cranach the Elder (1472–1553), one of the most famous artists of the Northern Renaissance, was Luther's friend (he later served as the best man at the reformer's wedding) and an important entrepreneur and citizen of Wittenberg. On his contributions to the Reformation, see Steven Ozment, *The Serpent and the Lamb: Cranach, Luther, and the Making of the Reformation* (New Haven: Yale University Press, 2011).

31. Christian Düring (d. 1533), another friend of Luther in Wittenberg. Like Cranach he was a respected businessman in the town.

32. Origen (c. 185–c. 254) was a famous biblical scholar and theologian in

Alexandria, Egypt, but he was ordained to the priesthood only after controversy developed over his being invited to preach by the bishops of Caesarea and Aelia, and later was deposed by his bishop, Demetrius (ODCC, s.v. "Origen"). Luther understates Origen's public role here even while drawing on this example in support of his desire that Melanchthon be called to preach in Wittenberg.

33. LW 48:329–36.

PREFACE TO THE JUDGMENT OF MARTIN LUTHER ON MONASTIC VOWS, ADDRESSED TO HANS LUTHER [33]

WARTBURG, 21 NOVEMBER 1521

As was customary in the time Luther prefaced many of his writings with a dedicatory letter, often addressed to a public person or other figure in some way related to the contents of the book or pamphlet. In this case the letter prefaced The Judgment of Martin

Title page of *De votis monasticis* (Wittenberg, 1522). This title page border is attributed to the workshop of Lucas Cranach the Elder and shows a woodsman and, in a bit of anti-Catholic polemic, a beast in a monastic habit with a rosary.

Luther on Monastic Vows, *dated 21 November 1521 but not published until early in 1522. Luther's letter to his father, Hans, is unique among such prefaces in several ways: (1) his father was no public figure (though he had become by Martin's later youth a successful owner of a copper mine in Mansfeld); (2) he could not be expected to read the letter or the treatise itself (Hans probably could not read and certainly could not read Latin), though he could well have been made aware of the contents of the letter and treatise through others; and (3) the letter exhibits openly yet in a very personal way the relationship Martin had with his father, both their conflict in the past over Martin's disobedience in entering the monastery sixteen years previously, and the restoration that had occurred and, indeed, that Luther was now publicizing through this preface. These characteristics justify selecting the letter for this volume, for even though Luther did not write to his father as a pastor but, rather, as a son and is more self-reflective than directed to the counsel of his father, the letter functioned pastorally and spiritually for the reading public at a time when the subject of monastic vows and clerical celibacy had become one of the most central practical issues of the early Reformation. Within the next few years, many monks and friars sympathetic to the Evangelical reform were renouncing their vows and leaving their monasteries. Many priests as well as former monks and nuns were getting married, in which case they could be prosecuted, forced to separate from their marriage, imprisoned, or even sentenced to death.*[34] *During the summer of 1521 Luther had responded critically to various arguments made by his colleague Andreas Karlstadt (1486–1541) in theses the latter had written on celibacy and monastic vows.*[35] *In the present treatise Luther would put forward his own judgment and its basis in Holy Scripture, and the letter-preface informs the reader of Luther's own experience of monastic vows. He interprets that experience in the light of God's commandments and of the new understanding of Christian freedom that Luther had developed during the course of the controversy over indulgences, which early that year had culminated in his condemnation by both papal church and imperial decree.*

Latin text in WA 8:573–76.[t]

[t] In revising Krodel's translation I have compared a translation of the letter in *Early Protestant Spirituality*, ed. and trans. Scott H. Hendrix (Mahwah, NJ: Paulist, 2009), 16–21.

34. See, e.g., Luther's 1 December letter of protest to Archbishop Albrecht regarding his treatment of priests who had married (LW 48:342–43), and Luther's remarks to Wolfgang Capito concerning a priest who had to abjure his wife (LW 48:377–78). Karlstadt was soon to marry Anna von Mochau (b. 1507) on 19 January 1521 in Wittenberg (see Luther's positive comments on Karlstadt's engagement in a letter to Nicholas von Amsdorf (1483–1565), LW 48:363.

35. Luther responded to Karlstadt's theses, and to his published work on celibacy, in several letters to Philip Melanchthon (and one to George Spalatin) in August and early September 1521 (LW 48, nos. 91–95), as well as in two sets of his own theses on vows, which were published together in October 1521 (see LW 48:311 n.5). Though the preface-letter is dated 21 November 1521, it was not published (along with the treatise) until early 1522.

To Hans Luther, his father, Martin Luther his son sends greetings in Christ.[u]

THIS BOOK I have decided to dedicate to you, dearest Father, not that I might make your name famous in the world and to glory in the flesh, which would be contrary to the teaching of St. Paul.[v] Rather my purpose is to recall, in a short preface, what took place between you and me in order to indicate for pious readers the reason for writing this book as well as its argument, together with an example.

Portrait of Hans Luther (1527) by Lucas Cranach the Elder (1472–1553)

36. As can be understood from his estimation of God's commandments here, Luther's frequent statements regarding the law's uselessness in working salvation for sinners—indeed, its relentless judgment of death upon the sinner—are misconstrued if they are understood to advocate silencing the law or to deny its inherent good as the will of God. See also Luther's 1520 *Treatise on Good Works* (LW 44:21–114; TAL 1:257–367).

To begin with, I wish you to know that your son has reached the point where he is altogether persuaded that there is nothing holier, nothing more important, nothing more religiously to be observed than God's commandment.[36] But here you will say, "Have you been so unfortunate as ever to doubt this, and have you only now learned that this is so?" Most unfortunately

---

u   Luther uses the third-person address of the salutation in the Latin text: "*Johanni Luther, Parenti suo, Martinus Luther filius in Christo salutem.*"

v   Gal. 6:13.

indeed I not only doubted it, but I did not at all know that it is so; and if you will permit me, I am ready to show you that this ignorance was common to both of us.

It is now almost sixteen years since I became a monk,[37] taking the vow without your knowledge and against your will. In your paternal love you were fearful about my weakness because I was then a youth, just entering my twenty-second year (that is, to use St. Augustine's words, I was still "clothed in hot youth"),[38] and you had learned from numerous examples that this way of life turned out sadly for many. You were determined, therefore, to tie me down with an honorable and wealthy marriage.[39] This fear of yours, this care, this indignation against me was for a time implacable. Your friends tried in vain to persuade you that if you wished to offer something to God, you ought to give your dearest and your best. The Lord, meanwhile, was dinning in your ears that psalm verse: "God knows the thoughts of men, that they are vain";[w] but you were deaf. At last you desisted and bowed to the will of God, but your fears for me were never laid aside. For I remember very well[40] that after we were reconciled and you were talking with me, I told you that I had been called by terrors from heaven and that I did not become a monk of my own free will and desire, still less to gain any gratification of the flesh, but that I was walled in by the terror and the agony of sudden death and forced by necessity to take the vow. Then you said, "Let us hope that it was not an illusion and a deception." That word penetrated to the depths of my soul and stayed there, as if God had spoken by your lips, though I hardened my heart against you and your word as much as I could. You said something else, too. When in filial confidence I upbraided you for your wrath, you suddenly retorted with a reply so fitting and so much to the point that I have hardly ever in all my life heard any man say anything which struck me so forcibly and stayed with me so long. "Have you not also heard," you said, "that parents are to be obeyed?"[41] But I was so sure of my own righteousness that in you I heard only a man, and boldly ignored you; though in my heart I could not ignore your word.

See, now, whether you, too, were not unaware that the commandments of God are to be put before all things. If you had known that I was then in your power, would you not have used

37. Luther had entered the Augustinian cloister in Erfurt in July 1505, after a visit home near the beginning of his studies in law at the University of Erfurt.

38. Augustine, *Confessions* II.3(6). The choice of citation is interesting— Augustine is commenting on his father's delight in noticing that young Augustine was showing the signs of sexual maturity: "Indeed, when at the bathhouse my father saw that I was showing signs of virility and the stirrings of adolescence [*inquieta indutum adulescentia*], he was overjoyed to suppose that he would now be having grandchildren." Augustine, *Confessions*, trans. with an introduction and notes by Henry Chadwick (New York: Oxford University Press, 1992).

39. Krodel notes that "this seems to be the only reference from which the marriage plans his father had for Luther can be deduced. These plans seem to be quite in agreement with the father's ambition to see young Martin in the important and influential position of a legally-trained administrator" (LW 48:331 n.10).

40. The following recollection was of a conversation between Luther and his father when Luther celebrated his first Mass, a conversation that struck Luther deeply and that he described frequently. See, e.g., LW 48:301; LW 54:109 (WA TR 1, no. 623); WA TR 1, no. 881; WA TR 3, no. 3556.

41. Luther's father, as also now Luther in his response, refers to the Fourth Commandment of the Decalogue.

_w_ Ps. 94:11 (Vulgate).

42. Luther uttered a vow to St. Anne to become a monk when on his way back to Erfurt he was caught in the midst of a thunderstorm, lightning struck, and he was filled with terror.

43. Luther emphasizes that his rejection of monastic vows (and thus of monastic life) developed out of his *experience* of that life, rather than being the judgment of one who had little or no experience.

your paternal authority to pull me out of the cowl? On the other hand, had I known it, I would never have attempted to become a monk without your knowledge and consent, even though I had to die many deaths. For my vow was not worth a fig, since by taking it I withdrew myself from the authority and guidance of the parent [to whom I was subject] by God's commandment; indeed, it was a wicked vow, and proved that it was not of God not only because it was a sin against your authority, but because it was not absolutely free and voluntary. In short it was taken in accordance with the doctrines of men and the superstition of hypocrites, none of which has God commanded.[42] But behold how much good God (whose mercies are without number and whose wisdom is without end)[x] has made to come out of all these errors and sins! Would you now not rather have lost a hundred sons than not have seen this good?

I think that Satan from my childhood must have foreseen something in me [that is the cause] of those things he now suffers. He has therefore raged against me with incredible contrivings to destroy or hinder me, so that I have often wondered whether I was the only man in the whole world whom he was seeking. But it was the Lord's will, as I now see, that the wisdom of the schools and the sanctity of the monasteries should become known to me by my own actual experience, that is, through many sins and impieties, so that wicked men might not have a chance, when I became their adversary, to boast that I condemned something about which I knew nothing.[43] Therefore I lived as a monk, indeed not without sin but without reproach. For in the kingdom of the pope impiety and sacrilege pass for supreme piety; still less are they considered matters for reproach.

What do you think now? Will you still take me out of the monastery? You are still my father and I am still your son and all the vows are worthless. On your side is the authority of God, on my side there is nothing but human presumption. For that continence of which they boast with puffed-up cheeks is valueless without obedience to God's commandments. Continence is not commanded but obedience is, yet the mad and silly papists will not allow any virtue to be equal to continence and virginity. They extol both these virtues with such prodigious lies that their

x   Ps. 147:5.

very craze for lying and the greatness of their ignorance, singly or together, ought to cast suspicion on all they do or think.

What kind of intelligence do they show when they distort the word of the Sage, "No balance can weigh the value of a continent mind,"[y] to mean that virginity and abstinence are to be preferred to everything else and that vows of virginity cannot be commuted or dispensed with? It was a Jew who wrote these words to Jews about a chaste wife; among the Jews virginity and abstinence were condemned. Thus, too, they apply to virgins that praise of a faithful wife: "This is she who has not known a sinful bed."[z] In a word, although the Scriptures do not laud virginity but only approve it, those who are so ready to inflame souls to lives that endanger their salvation[a] dress it up in borrowed plumes, so to speak, by applying to it the praises the Scriptures bestow on a chaste marriage.[44]

But isn't the value of an obedient soul also beyond all measure? For that reason indeed a chaste soul (that is, a faithful wife) defies every measure, not only because it is commanded by God but also because, as the well-known proverb says, there is nothing in the world more desirable than a chaste wife.[45] But these "faithful" interpreters of Scripture take everything which is said about the chastity that is commanded and apply it to that chastity which is not commanded, and thus make a human evaluation the measure of God's judgment. Thus they grant dispensations from everything, even from obedience to God, [but they grant no dispensation from the vow of chastity], even from that forbidden abstinence which is entered upon against the authority of one's parents. O worthy and truly papistical doctors and teachers! Virginity and chastity are to be praised, but in such a way that by their very greatness men are frightened off from them rather than led to them. This was Christ's way. When the disciples praised continence and said, "If such is the case of a man with his wife, it is expedient not to marry," he at once set their minds straight on the matter and said, "Not all men can receive this precept."[b] The precept must be accepted, but it was Christ's will that only a few should understand it.

44. Luther promoted chaste marriage, that is, marriage in which spouses are sexually faithful to each other, in a number of his writings, e.g., his sermon *On the Estate of Marriage*, published later in 1522 (LW 45:17–49).

45. Hendrix notes, "The value of a faithful, chaste, and modest wife was a topos found in classical writings and in Hebrew wisdom literature. Luther could be paraphrasing a saying attributed to Euripides (485–406 BCE): 'A man's best possession is a sympathetic wife.' Or he might still have in mind Sirach [Ecclus.] 26:15, Wisdom 3:13, or a verse from Proverbs 31:10–31." Hendrix, *Early Protestant Spirituality*, 304 n.17.

---

y   Ecclus. 26:15 (26:20 in the Vulgate and Luther's Bible).

z   Wis. 3:13.

a   I.e., the papists in their promotion and requirement of clerical celibacy.

b   Matt. 19:10-11.

46. The cowl was the hooded portion of a monk's garb, or the hooded robe itself. A tonsure refers to the shaving of a portion of one's hair for religious purposes.

47. Just ten days before (11 November 1521), Luther had written to Spalatin to express his displeasure over Spalatin's communication that Elector Frederick would not allow anything to be written against Albrecht, archbishop of Mainz, saying, "If I have resisted the creator, the pope, why should I yield to his creature?" See LW 48:326, and the excursus on Luther's treatise *Against the "Idol" at Halle*, the publication of which Spalatin had prevented (LW 48:344–50).

But to come back to you, my Father; would you still take me out of the monastery? But so that you would not boast of it, the Lord has anticipated you, and taken me out himself. For what difference does it make whether I retain or lay aside the cowl and tonsure?[46] Do they make the monk? "All things are yours, and you are Christ's," says Paul.[c] Shall I belong to the cowl, or shall not the cowl rather belong to me? My conscience has been freed, and that is the most complete liberation. Therefore I am still a monk and yet not a monk. I am a new creature, not of the pope but of Christ. The pope also has his creatures, but he creates puppets and straw men, that is, masks and idols of himself.[47] I myself was formerly one of them, led astray by the various usages of words, by which even the Sage confesses that he was brought into the danger of death but by God's grace was delivered.[d] But am I not robbing you again of your right and authority? Clearly your authority over me still remains intact, so far as the monastic life is concerned; but this is nothing to me anymore, as I have said. Besides, God, who has taken me out of the monastery, has an authority over me that is greater than yours; you see that he has placed me now not in that fiction of monasticism but in the true worship of God. For who can doubt that I am in the ministry of the word? And it is plain that the authority of parents must yield to this cultus, for Christ says, "He who loves father or mother more than me is not worthy of me."[e] Not that this word destroys the authority of parents, for the Apostle often insists that children should obey their parents;[f] but if the authority of parents conflicts with the authority or calling of Christ, then Christ's authority must reign alone. Therefore—so I am now absolutely persuaded—I could not have refused to obey you without endangering my conscience unless he had added the ministry of the word to my monastic profession. This is what I meant when I said that neither you nor I realized that God's commandments must be put before everything else. But almost the whole world is now laboring under this same ignorance, for under the papal abomination error rules, which Paul also predicted when he said that men would become disobedient

---

c   1 Cor. 3:22-23.
d   Ecclus. 34:12-13.
e   Matt. 10:37.
f   Eph. 6:1; Col. 3:20.

to parents.[g] This fits the monks and priests exactly, especially those who under the pretense of piety and the guise of serving God withdraw themselves from the authority of their parents, as though there were any other service of God than to obey his commandments, which includes obedience to parents.

And so I am sending you this book, in which you may see by what signs and wonders Christ has absolved me from the monastic vow and granted me such great liberty. Although he has made me the servant of all, I am, nevertheless, subject to no one except to him alone.[48] He is himself (as they say) my immediate bishop, abbot, prior, lord, father, and teacher; I know no other superior.

48. This paradox of the Christian being a servant to all while being subject to no one except Christ is the theme of Luther's 1520 treatise *The Freedom of a Christian*; see LW 31:333-77; TAL 1:466-538.

The papal bull *Decet romanum pontificum* of 3 January 1521, issued by Pope Leo X, excommunicated Luther

---

g   2 Tim. 3:2.

Thus I hope that he has taken from you one son in order that he may begin to help the sons of many others through me. You ought not only to endure this willingly, but you ought to rejoice with exceeding joy—and this I am sure is what you will do. What if the pope should slay me or condemn me to the depths of hell! Having once slain me, he will not raise me up again to slay me a second and third time, and now that I have been condemned I have no desire ever to be pardoned.[49] For I trust that the day is at hand when that kingdom of abomination and perdition will be destroyed. Would that we were worthy to be burned or slain by him before that time, so that our blood might cry out against him all the more and hasten the day of his judgment! But if we are not worthy to bear testimony with our blood, then let us at least pray and implore mercy that we may testify with deed and word that Jesus Christ alone is the Lord our God, who is blessed into the age of ages. Amen.

Farewell in the Lord, my dearest Father, and greet in Christ my mother, your Margarethe,[50] along with all our relatives.

From the wilderness,[h] 21 November 1521.

LETTER TO NICHOLAS HAUSMANN[i]

WITTENBERG, 17 MARCH 1522

Just over a week before writing this letter Luther had returned from the Wartburg, responding to the call of the congregation at Wittenberg[j] and in order to deal with the disturbances that had developed in the city as Andreas Karlstadt[51] and others pressed for Evangelical reforms and called for the destruction of images in the church.[k] Luther wrote this letter the day after he had fin-

49. Luther had been excommunicated by Pope Leo X on 3 January 1521 in the bull *Decet romanum pontificem* and thus considered himself at risk of being executed as a condemned heretic.

50. Hans Luder's wife and Martin's mother, Margarethe Lindemann (1463–1531).

51. Andreas Bodenstein von Karlstadt (1486–1541) was Luther's colleague at the University of Wittenberg who took up leadership in advocating Evangelical reforms in the city of Wittenberg while Luther was at the Wartburg. See the image of Karlstadt on p. 8 of this volume.

---

h   See n. *s*, p. 439.

i   LW 48:399–402.

j   See Luther's letters to Elector Frederick, LW 48:386–99 (nos. 116–18).

k   On the Wittenberg disturbances that developed late in 1521 and continued until Luther's return from the Wartburg in early March

ished preaching his famous Invocavit Sermons *from 9 to 16 March in the City Church, thereby taking up leadership of the reform movement in Wittenberg.*[52] *This letter of pastoral counsel shows Luther recommending to his friend Nicholas Hausmann (c. 1478–1538),*[53] *an evangelical pastor in Zwickau, Saxony, that he practice the principles of love, freedom of conscience, and patient teaching that Luther had just finished preaching from his pulpit in St. Mary's Church in Wittenberg.*

Latin text in WA Br 2:474–75.

To the faithful evangelist of the congregation in Zwickau, Mr. Nicholas Hausmann, my dearest brother in Christ.

Jesus.

GREETINGS. My Nicholas, [my friend] in Christ: Although I am in the midst of such great commotion[54] and am occupied with various tasks, yet I could not skip writing to you, especially since the occasion demanded it, and this friend, the carrier of the letter,[55] requested it. I hope you are strong in faith and are growing daily in the knowledge of Christ. Your prophets,[56] who came from your town, are striving for peculiar things; they are pregnant with monstrosities I do not like. If these should be borne, they will cause no small damage. Their spirit is extremely deceitful and specious.[57] The Lord be with us. Amen.

Satan attempted to do so much damage here in my fold that it was hard to oppose him without causing offense to both sides.[58] By all means see to it that you don't permit any innovations, either on the basis of a common resolution or by force.[59]

1522, and Luther's response to them, see Martin Brecht, *Martin Luther: Shaping and Defining the Reformation, 1521–1532,* trans. James L. Schaaf (Minneapolis: Fortress Press, 1990), 25–45, 59–66; Carlos Eire, *War against the Idols: The Reformation of Worship from Erasmus to Calvin* (Cambridge: Cambridge University Press, 1986), 55–73; James S. Preus, *Carlstadt's "Ordinaciones" and Luther's Liberty: A Study of the Wittenberg Movement, 1521–22* (Cambridge: Harvard University Press/London: Oxford University Press, 1974); and Ronald J. Sider, *Andreas Bodenstein von Karlstadt: The Development of His Thought, 1517–1525,* Studies in Medieval and Reformation Thought 11 (Leiden: E. J. Brill, 1974), 148–73.

52. See *The Invocavit Sermons* ("Eight Sermons at Wittenberg"), introduced and translated in this volume (pp. 7–45) and in LW 51:69–100.

53. While in Zwickau, Hausmann had to deal with the so-called enthusiasts or Zwickau prophets (see Luther's *Against the Heavenly Prophets* [TAL 2:39–126]). He also had to face the Zwickau city council, which was attempting to meddle in the affairs of the church. The controversy between Hausmann and the Zwickau city council is important in understanding the relationship of the Reformation churches to secular power (LW 48:399–400).

54. The Wittenberg disturbances.

55. The identity of this friend and messenger could not be determined.

56. The "Zwickau prophets"—Nicholas Storch (d. c. 1536), Thomas Drechsel, and Mark Stübner—had come to Wittenberg in late December 1521, claiming direct revelations from God and contributing greatly to the disturbances that were erupting in the city.

57. Luther had written extensively on 13 January 1522 to Philip Melanchthon regarding how to deal with the Zwickau prophets and their claims. See LW 48:364–72.

58. Luther here shows his sensitivity to the division that had occurred in the Evangelical movement in Wittenberg.

59. Luther advises Hausmann to refrain from making religious changes in the congregation at Zwickau until he has carefully instructed them so that any changes are accepted freely. As he had made clear in his *Invocavit Sermons*, Luther was concerned that religious changes be made in love and after careful teaching rather than forced on the congregation, even if by resolution of the city council or other "common resolution."

60. Karlstadt and others (including the Zwickau prophets) had called for the destruction of religious images, applying the prohibitions of the Mosaic law (Exod. 20:4-5), and violent iconoclasm had occurred in Wittenberg.

61. This paragraph reflects the teaching in Luther's third sermon at Wittenberg, 11 March 1522 (LW 51:79–83; pp. 23–29 in this volume).

62. Luther advocates that traditional practices, or what he terms "external works and regulations"—whether oral confession, ceremonies relating to Communion, or instructions concerning prayer and fasting—can be used "for the sake of the weak" as long as consciences are not being bound and the principle of love rules.

63. That is, on days of prescribed fasting.

Only with the word are those things to be fought which our people tried to accomplish by force and violence; with the word they are to be overthrown, with the word they are to be destroyed! It is Satan who has driven them to their actions.

I condemn the idea that Masses are considered sacrifices or good works; but I do not want to lay hands on the unwilling or unbelieving, or curb them by force. I condemn only with the word; he who believes, let him believe and follow—he who does not believe, let him disbelieve and be dismissed. No one should be forced to faith and to what belongs to faith, but he should be drawn by the word so that, willingly believing, he may come of his own accord.

I condemn images, but with the word; they should not be burned,[60] but trust should not be put in them as was done before and is still done today. They would fall by themselves if people were taught and knew that before God they are nothing.[61]

Likewise I condemn the pope's laws on confession,[l] communion,[m] prayer, and fasting—but I condemn with the word, so that I may liberate consciences from these laws. When the consciences have been freed, then of course people can use all these things for the sake of the weak who are still entangled in them; when the weak have become firm, then these things may be discontinued. This way love will rule with regard to these external works and regulations.[62]

Now nothing is more disgusting to me than our mob of people here who have abandoned the word, faith, and love and can only boast that they are Christians because before the very eyes of the weak they can eat meat, eggs, and milk,[63] receive the Lord's Supper in "both kinds," and neither fast nor pray.

I plead that you, too, take up this way of teaching. Everything has to be exposed to the word, but hearts must be driven slowly,[n] like Jacob's flock,[o] so that first they take up the word of God voluntarily, and when they have finally become strong, do

---

l   See the pamphlet *On Confession, Whether the Pope Has the Power to Require It* (Wittenberg, 1521) (WA 8:140–85).

m   On Luther's concerns to reform the celebration of the Mass or Lord's Supper, see LW 48:324–25.

n   As Krodel notes (LW 48:402 n.14), the word given here as "slowly" is illegible in the autograph and this translation is based on the conjecture and interpretation of the editor of the Weimar edition.

o   Gen. 33:13-14.

everything. Perhaps it is unnecessary to tell this to you because you know this already; but it was the solicitude of love that prompted it.

Farewell in Christ, and support the gospel with your prayers. Wittenberg, Monday after *Reminiscere* 1522.

Yours,
Martin Luther

TO HANS LUTHER[p]

WITTENBERG, 15 FEBRUARY 1530

Although Luther's descriptions of conflict with his father, Hans Luder (Luther), over his entrance into the monastery have fueled interpretations that suggest this conflict was never fully healed,[q] Martin's letter to his father when he learned of his father's serious illness in February 1530 reveals a grown son who deeply loves his father and yearns to be with him in his time of suffering. Martin shows true care for his father, as well as the respect and gratitude owed to his father according to the Fourth Commandment. He expresses confidence that his father is confirmed in the true faith, with its marks of suffering with Christ, and commends his father into the care of his Savior. Described by Krodel as "among the finest of Luther's writings," this letter of spiritual counsel already found a place in the earliest collections of Luther's pastoral writings.[r] Hans Luder died on 29 May 1530 while Luther was at the Coburg during the Imperial Diet at Augsburg.[64]

German text in WA Br 5:239–41.

p   LW 49:267–71.

q   In particular see Erik H. Erikson, *Young Man Luther: A Study in Psychoanalysis and History* (New York: Norton, 1958); and Roger A. Johnson, ed., *Psychohistory and Religion: The Case of Young Man Luther* (Philadelphia: Fortress Press, 1977). See also n. *v*, p. 461.

r   LW 49:268. For bibliographical details, see WA Br 5:238–39; and E. L. Enders and G. Kawerau, eds., *Dr. Martin Luthers Briefwechsel*, 19 vols. (Frankfurt/Leipzig: Schriften-Niederlage des Evangel, 1884–1932), vol. 7, no. 1600.

64. Upon learning of his father's death, Luther wrote to Melanchthon, "This death has certainly thrown me into sadness, thinking not only of the bonds of nature, but also of the very kind love [my father had for me]; for through him my Creator has given me all that I am and have. Even though it does comfort me that [Hans Reinecke] writes that [my father], strong in faith in Christ, had gently fallen asleep, yet the pity of heart and the memory of the most loving dealings with him have shaken me in the innermost parts of my being, so that seldom if ever have I despised death as much as I do now" (LW 49:319).

To my dear Father, Hans Luther, a citizen at Mansfeld[s]
in the valley:
Grace and peace in Christ Jesus, our Lord and Savior. Amen.

DEAR FATHER! Jacob, my brother,[65] has written me that you are seriously ill. As the weather is now bad, and as there is danger everywhere, and because of the season, I am worried about you. For even though God has thus far given to and preserved for you a strong, tough body, yet your age gives me anxious thoughts at this time—although regardless of this, none of us is, or should be, sure of his life at any time. Therefore because of these circumstances I would have liked to come to you personally, but my good friends advised me against it, and have talked me out of it. I myself have to agree, for I did not dare to venture into danger at the risk of tempting God, since you know how lords and peasants feel toward me. It would be great joy for me, however, if it were possible for you and Mother to be brought here to us; this my Katie, too, desires with tears, as do we all. I hope we would be able to take care of you in the best way. Therefore I am sending Cyriac[66] to see whether your weakness [will allow you to be moved]. For if according to God's will this illness brings you to this or to that life,[t] it would be a heartfelt joy for me (as would be only right) to be around you in person and to show, with filial faithfulness and service, my gratitude to God and to you, according to the Fourth Commandment.

In the meantime I pray from the bottom of my heart that the Father, who has made you my father and given you to me, will strengthen you according to his immeasurable kindness, and enlighten and preserve you with his Spirit, so that you may perceive with joy and thanksgiving the blessed teaching concerning his Son, our Lord Jesus Christ, to which you too have been called and have come out of the former terrible darkness and error. I hope that his grace, which has given you such knowledge and

---

65. Luther's younger brother Jacob was a city councillor in Mansfeld; he died in 1570.

66. Cyriac Kaufmann, who had matriculated at Wittenberg in November 1529, was the son of Luther's sister, who lived in Mansfeld.

---

s   See portrait of Hans Luther on p. 442 above. For the location of Mansfeld, see the map at the front of this volume.

t   "Denn es geriet mit Euch nach göttlichem Willen zu diesem oder jenem Leben." Krodel translates, "For if according to God's will your illness turns out to be one either to life or to death" (LW 48:269).

begun his work in you, will preserve and complete it up to the arrival of the future life and the joyous return of our Lord Jesus Christ. Amen.

For God has also sealed this teaching and faith in you and has confirmed them with marks; that is, because of me, you, together with all of us, have suffered much slander, disgrace, scorn, mockery, contempt, hatred, hostility, and even danger. These are but the true marks with which we have to become identical to our Lord Christ, as St. Paul says, so that we may also become identified with his future glory.[67]

Therefore let your heart now be bold and confident in your illness, for we have there, in that life with God, a true and faithful helper, Jesus Christ, who for us has strangled death, together with sin, and now sits there for us; together with all the angels he is looking down on us, and awaiting us, so that when we are to depart, we dare not worry or fear that we might sink or fall to the ground. His power over death and sin is too great for them to harm us. He is so wholeheartedly faithful and good[u] that he cannot forsake us, nor would he wish to do so; only that we desire his help without doubting his promise.

For he has said it—has promised and pledged that he will not and cannot lie to us, nor trick us; there is no doubt about that. "Ask," (he says,) "and it will be given you; seek, and you will find, knock, and it will be opened to you."[v] And elsewhere: "All who call on the name of the Lord shall be saved."[w] The whole Psalter is full of such comforting promises, especially Psalm 91, which is particularly good to be read by all who are sick.

I wished to talk this over with you in writing, because I am anxious about your illness (for we know not the hour),[x] so that I might participate in your faith, struggle,[y] consolation, and gratitude to God for his holy word, which in these days he has given to us so richly, powerfully, and graciously.

67. See Rom. 8:17; Gal. 6:17. Luther regarded various sufferings and persecution as marks by which "the holy Christian people are externally recognized" and through which they "become like their head." *On the Councils and the Church*, 1539 (LW 41:164; TAL 3:430).

---

u   "So ist er so herzlich treu und frumb."

v   Matt. 7:7.

w   Acts 2:21.

x   *Stündlin*, the "little hour." On this concept in Luther's thought, see Gustav Wingren, *Luther on Vocation*, trans. Carl C. Rasmussen (Philadelphia: Muhlenberg, 1957), 213–34.

y   *Kampfs*, literally "fight," "contest," or "combat."

Should it be his divine will, however, for you to wait still longer for that better life, to continue to suffer with us in this troubled and sorrowful vale of tears, to see and hear sadness, or together with all Christians to assist in enduring and overcoming, then he will also give grace to accept all this willingly and obediently. This cursed life is nothing but a real vale of tears, in which the longer a man lives, the more sin, wickedness, torment, and sadness he sees and feels. Nor is there respite or cessation of all of this until one flattens us with the shovel;[z] then, of course, [this sadness] has to stop and let us sleep contentedly in Christ's peace, until he comes again to wake us with joy. Amen.

Herewith I commend you to him who loves you more than you love yourself. He has proved his love by taking your sins upon himself and by paying with his blood, and he has let you know this through the gospel, and has given it to you freely to believe this by his Spirit. Consequently, he has prepared and sealed everything in the most certain way, so that you are not permitted to worry about or be concerned for anything except keeping your heart strong and reliant on his word and faith. If you do this then let him care for the rest. He will see to it that everything turns out well. Indeed, he has already accomplished this in the best way, better than we can understand. May he, our dear Lord and Savior, be with you and at your side, so that (may God grant it to happen either here or there)[68] we may joyfully see each other again. For our faith is certain, and we don't doubt that we shall shortly see each other again in the presence of Christ. For the departure from this life is a smaller thing to God than if I moved from you in Mansfeld to here, or if you moved from me in Wittenberg to Mansfeld. This is certainly true; it is only a matter of an hour's sleep, and all will be different.

I hope that in these matters your pastor and preacher[a] will abundantly demonstrate their faithful service to you, so that you will not need my words. Yet I could not refrain from excusing my physical absence, which (God knows) causes me heartfelt sorrow. My Katie, Hänschen, Lenchen, Aunt Lena, and all my

68. Whether here in this life or in the next, Luther expresses confidence that he will see his father again.

---

z   As Krodel translates literally in the footnote (LW 49:270, n.21); Luther wrote, "bis man uns mit der Schaufel nachschlägt" (WA Br 5:240,67–68).

a   For possible identification, see WA Br 5:214 n.10.

household send you greetings and pray for you faithfully.[69] Greet my dear mother and all my relatives. God's grace and strength be and abide with you forever. Amen.

[Written] at Wittenberg, on the 15th of February in the year 1530.

Your loving son,
Martin Luther

TO PHILIP MELANCHTHON[b]

COBURG, 29 JUNE 1530

In the midst of the flood of correspondence between Luther at the Coburg and the Wittenbergers at the Diet of Augsburg in the spring and summer of 1530,[70] apparently Luther did not receive any mail from Augsburg in the latter weeks of May through early June. Having finally received letters from Philip Melanchthon and Justus Jonas, Luther wrote this extensive letter to Melanchthon that provides a window into his perception of how his colleagues were holding up in the midst of the critical deliberations at the diet regarding the Reformation and the emperor's determination to restore ecclesiastical unity under the papal hierarchy. Luther reacts to the anxiety they had expressed in their letters after the Augsburg Confession *had been publicly read at the diet on 25 June. In words that have been interpreted in various ways since their frequent publication already in the sixteenth century, Luther reacts to the* Augsburg Confession, *which he had recently received (in its final form) along with Melanchthon's letter of 26 June, and to Melanchthon's inquiry about what might be conceded to the papists as negotiations proceeded at Augsburg. Then he turns again, as he had done in a letter two days previously, to console Melanchthon, seeking to relieve his anxiety this time with an exhortation to faith in the midst of the uncertainties and dangers that were confronting the Evangelicals as they confessed their faith*

69. Luther conveys personal greetings from his wife, Katie, his son Hans, his daughter Magdalena (1529–1542), and from Katie's aunt Magdalene von Bora, "a former nun who sometime after 1523 left the nunnery and lived with the Luther household until she died" (LW 49:271 n.28). See also WA Br 5:241 n.11; WA Br 8:19.

70. For the correspondence between Luther at the Coburg and the Lutherans at Augsburg see the many letters of Luther, and Krodel's extensive notes, in LW 48:280–425. Luther's letter of 27 June to Melanchthon, not included in LW, is translated in Tappert, *Luther: Letters of Spiritual Counsel*, 145–47.

b LW 49:324–33.

and defended both the catholicity and the legality of their reforms at the Imperial Diet.

> *Text in Latin, WA Br 5:405–7.*

To my dearest brother, Philip Melanchthon, at Augsburg.*ᶜ*

GRACE AND PEACE IN CHRIST. I have read your*ᵈ* oration, my Philip, with which you people justify yourselves because of your silence.*ᵉ* In the meantime, however, I have twice written a letter to you people in which I have sufficiently explained the reason for my silence (at least in the latter letter, the one which the messenger brings who has been sent by our tax collector to the Sovereign).[71] Today your most recent letters have arrived simultaneously, the one delivered by the messenger, and the other by Februarius.*ᶠ* In these letters you remind me of your work, danger, and tears in such a way that it appears that I, in an unfair way, add insult to injury[72] by my silence, as if I did not know of these things, or sat here among roses and cared nothing. I wish my cause were such as to permit the flow of tears![73] Indeed, had not your first letters, dealing with the arrival of the emperor, come here that evening, I, too, had decided to send a messenger to you the next day at my own expense to find out whether you were alive or dead. Master Veit[74] will testify to this. Still, I believe that all your letters have been delivered to us. For those dealing with the arrival and with the entrance of the emperor into Augsburg came finally, though

---

71. Elector John of Saxony (1468–1532), known as "the Steadfast."

72. Literally, "add pain upon pain by my silence." Krodel describes Melanchthon's and Jonas's letters of this time as lamentations (LW 48:327 n.12), and fear and anxiety characterized their feelings and communications as the *Augsburg Confession* was delivered at the Imperial Diet. In this letter Luther is responding to Melanchthon's fears with a magnificent exhortation to faith.

73. "Here Luther is obviously needling Melanchthon, who on several occasions mentions his tears and the tears of others in connection with the situation in Augsburg" (LW 49:327 n.15). For a careful analysis that puts this correspondence into its broader context, see Heinz Scheible, "Melanchthon und Luther während des Augsburger Reichstags 1530," in Peter Manns, ed., *Martin Luther "Reformator und Vater im Glauben." Referate aus der Vortragsreihe des Instituts für Europäische Geschichte Mainz* (Stuttgart: Franz Steiner, 1985), 38–60.

74. Veit Dietrich (1506–1549), Master of Arts, who lived in Luther's home much of the time between 1527 and 1534, and who stayed with Luther at the Coburg during the Diet of Augsburg. See further LW 49:282 n.13.

c   The address is found only in the manuscript copy deposited in the Landesbibliothek in Stuttgart; see WA Br 13:147, to WA Br 5:405–8 (no. 1609).

d   "Your" is plural. See n. *e* immediately below.

e   This sentence is translated literally, "I have read your oration justifying yourselves concerning your silence, my Philip." Luther is referring to letters of Melanchthon and Justus Jonas wherein they sought to explain why they had not written to him recently. On 7 June Luther had opened his letter to Melanchthon by grumbling, "I see that you have all decided to torment us with silence. Consequently . . . from now on we shall compete with you in the matter of silence" (LW 49:320).

f   Melanchthon's letters of 26 and 27 June, respectively; WA Br 5, nos. 1604 and 1607. "Februarius" is Wolf Hornung (*Hornung* is another name for the month of February).

after some delay, and they arrived almost simultaneously. But some devil or Satan may have been at work here; let him do whatever he has to do.[g]

I have received your *Apologia*,[75] and I wonder what it is you want when you ask what and how much is to be conceded to the papists. In connection with the Sovereign it is another question what he may concede, if danger threatens him.[h] For me personally more than enough has been conceded in this *Apologia*. If the

Portrait of Philip Melanchthon
(c. 1535) by Hans Holbein
the Younger (c. 1497–1543)

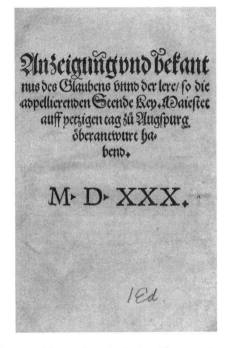

Title page of the *Augsburg Confession*. A late note inserted into the book suggests that this may have been Luther's personal copy. It is very likely a first edition. The first edition of the *Augsburg Confession* and the *Apology* (in German) appeared in the fall of 1531, delayed by the task of translating the *Apology* from the Latin. All subsequent editions have borne on their title page the motto: "I spoke of your testimonies before kings, and was not put to shame."

75. The *Augsburg Confession*. Melanchthon had sent Luther a copy of the *Confession* on 26 June, and inquired of Luther in his letter of that date, "Now it seems to me one has to decide, before our opponents may answer, what we are willing to concede to them in matters of both kinds, the marriage of priests, private mass. . . . Reply on these matters" (LW 49:328 n.25, quoting WA Br 5:397).

g   The last phrase of this sentence is written in German.
h   This sentence is missing in some witnesses (LW 49:328 n.26).

76. For "certainty," Luther uses the Greek word πληροφορία.

77. Duke John Frederick (1503–1554), who succeeded his father as elector of Saxony in 1532.

papists reject it, then I see nothing that I could still concede, unless I saw their reasoning, or clearer Scripture passages than I have seen till now. Day and night I am occupied with this matter, considering it, turning it around, debating it, and searching the whole Scripture; certainty[76] grows continuously in me about this, our teaching, and I am more and more sure that[i] now (God willing) I shall not permit anything further to be taken away from me, come what may.

I had written to the younger Sovereign[77] as you requested, but I afterwards tore up the letter, since I was afraid to give ideas to this genius, and then to hear excuses which I wouldn't like.[j] Here I am sufficiently well off, for it seems that that demon, which till now has beaten me with fists,[k] has given up (as if broken by your prayers and those of the brethren), though I suspect that instead of this demon another one has followed, which will wear down my body. Yet I would rather tolerate this torturer of the flesh than that executioner of the spirit. And I hope that he who defeated in me the father of lies will also overcome that murderer.[l] He has sworn death to me, this I certainly know, and he will have no peace until he has devoured me. All right, if he devours me, he shall devour a laxative (God willing) that will make his bowels and ass too tight for him. Do you want to bet? One has to suffer if he wants to possess Christ.[m] It would be easy indeed for us to triumph if we were willing to deny and calumniate Christ. [Yet] it is written: "Through many tribulations," etc. This is no longer just a word; it has become a reality,[n] and we should act accordingly. Yet he is here who along with the tribulation brings about the escape for the faithful.

I don't like that you write in your letter that you have followed my authority in this cause. I don't wish to be, or be called, the originator in this cause for you people; even though this might be properly interpreted, yet I don't want to hear this term

---

i   The following part of the sentence is written in German.

j   On this sentence, which is missing in two witnesses, see LW 49:329 n.30.

k   See 2 Cor. 12:7 (Luther Bible).

l   John 8:44. The next sentences, with the exception of the one beginning "It would be easy indeed," are all written in German.

m   See n. 67, p. 453.

n   Literally, "but it has come into the work."

["originator"]. If this is not simultaneously and in the same way your cause, then I don't want it to be called mine and imposed upon you. If it is my cause alone then I will handle it by myself.

I believe that all your letters which you have sent by Dr. Jonas's messenger have been delivered to me. Afterwards none were delivered, except the ones dealing with the emperor's arrival and his entrance into Augsburg, and the ones sent thereafter up to this day. Therefore you may also know now that I do have the picture of Vienna.[78] Between the messenger of Jonas and the emperor's entrance, however, you thoroughly crucified us by your silence.[79]

In my last letter I comforted you with thoughts that I hope do not lead to death but to life. What else can I do? The end and the outcome of this cause torture you because you cannot comprehend them. But if you could comprehend them, then I would not wish to be a partner in this cause, much less its originator. God has placed this cause into a certain commonplace,[80] which you don't have in your rhetoric, nor in your philosophy. This locus is entitled "Faith"; in this locus are contained all the things that cannot be seen and do not appear.[81] Should someone attempt to make these things visible, touchable, and comprehendable, as you do, he will bring back, as the reward of his labor, worries and tears such as those you are bringing back to all of us who are vainly protesting. The Lord has promised that he would live in a cloud,[o] and he has made the darkness his hiding place.[p] If someone wants to, let him try to change it.[q] Had Moses attempted to comprehend the outcome by which he might escape the pharaoh's army, then Israel would perhaps to this day be in Egypt. May the Lord increase faith for you and for all of us. If one has faith what may Satan and the whole world do? But if we don't have this faith, why don't we then console ourselves at least with the faith of others? For by necessity there are others who believe in our stead, unless there is no more a church in the world, and Christ has ceased to be with us prior to the consummation of the age. For if Christ is not with us, where, I earnestly wish to know, is he then in the whole world? If we are not the church, or a part of the church, where is the church? Are the dukes of

78. Melanchthon had sent a series of woodcuts by Hans Sebald Beham (1500–1550) on the siege of Vienna along with his letter of 22 May. See WA Br 5:338 n.24; LW 49:330 n.46.

79. Luther had not received letters from Melanchthon (or others at Augsburg) between those of 22 May and 12 June.

80. ". . . *in locum quondam communem,*" an obvious allusion to Melanchthon's method of doing theology (and philosophy) by treating common topics (*loci communes*), and to his 1521 book of that title. For a new translation see Philip Melanchthon, *Commonplaces: Loci Communes 1521*, trans. with introduction and notes by Christian Preus (St. Louis: Concordia, 2014).

81. Luther writes this last phrase ("that cannot be seen and do not appear") in Greek; cf. Heb. 11:1, 3. In his explanation to the first twenty-five psalms that he was writing at this time, Luther on 1 July 1530 continued this very argument in comments on Ps. 20:3. See WA Br 5:408 n.24; text in WA 31/1:347.

---

o   1 Kgs. 8:12.

p   Ps. 18:12.

q   This sentence is written in German.

82. The dukes of Bavaria were strong opponents of Luther and the Reformation, as was Ferdinand (1503–1564), the brother and eventual successor of Emperor Charles V (1500–1558).

83. Johann Brenz (1499–1570) was an important Lutheran reformer in Schwäbisch Hall, a free imperial city in the Duchy of Württemberg.

84. Dr. Casper Lindemann (d. 1536), a physician who was related to Luther through Luther's mother (LW 49:291 n.30).

Bavaria, Ferdinand,[82] the pope, the Turk, and those like them, the church? If we don't have God's Word, who are the people who have it? If God is with us, who is against us?[r] We are sinners and are ungrateful, but God will not therefore be a liar. And yet in this sacred and divine cause we cannot be sinners, even though in our ways we are evil. But you do not even hear this, so distressed and weak does Satan make you. May Christ heal you; for this I pray fervently and without interruption. Amen.

I wish an opportunity would present itself to me to come to you; I am eager to come even without having been asked or invited. These letters to Brenz[83] and Dr. Caspar[84] should have gone with the last letter, but the messenger had already left while the letters were being brought down. Greet all, for I cannot again write to them all.

God's grace be with you and with all of you. Amen.

The Day of SS. Peter and Paul 1530.

    Martin Luther

When[s] I had finished the letter the thought occurred to me that it might perhaps seem to you that I have replied too little to your question as to how much and how far one should make concessions to the opponents. But on the other hand, you have asked in insufficient detail; you have not informed me what demands you think will be made of us. As I have always written, I am ready to concede all things if only the gospel alone is permitted to remain free with us. What fights against the gospel, however, I cannot concede. What else should I answer?

---

r   Rom. 8:31.

s   This postscript is missing in several witnesses (LW 49:333 n.66).

TO MARGARETHE LUTHER[t]

WITTENBERG, 20 MAY 1531

Portrait of Margarethe Luther
by Lucas Cranach the Elder, 1527

*Not a great deal is known from the sources about Luther's mother,
Margarethe, or the relationship between mother and son,[u] but this
has not prevented detailed speculations about how Luther's strict
upbringing by his parents influenced his development[v]—some of
these speculations fueled by the reformer's own cryptic remarks.
For example, in a Table Talk from 1537 Luther is recorded to*

t   LW 50:17–21.

u   But see Ian Siggins, *Luther and His Mother* (Minneapolis: Fortress Press,
    1981), which is a detailed study of the influence of Margarethe and her
    (Lindemann) family circle upon the young Martin.

v   See n. *v*, p. 451 above. Careful and less speculative (if also less
    extensive) interpretations of Luther's home and upbringing in the
    context of his time include treatments by Roland H. Bainton, *Here
    I Stand: A Life of Martin Luther* (New York: Abingdon, 1950), 22–30;
    Martin Brecht, *Martin Luther: His Road to Reformation 1483–1521*,
    trans. James L. Schaaf (Minneapolis: Fortress Press, 1985), 6–21;
    and Oberman, *Luther*, 82–106.

have said, "My parents kept me under very strict discipline, even to the point of making me timid. For the sake of a mere nut my mother beat me until the blood flowed. By such strict discipline they finally forced me into the monastery; though they meant it heartily well, I was only made timid by it."[w] *Certainly, Luther did describe the discipline of both home and school in his childhood and youth as severe, though probably not unusually so for the time, and at times Luther does express some resentment of this severity.*

For this reason Luther's letters to his parents later in his life are crucial witnesses for the way he matured and related to his parents as a grown man. As in the case of his father, so with his mother Luther communicated with tenderness and sensitivity when he wrote to his mother upon hearing from his brother Jacob of her serious illness. Luther wrote the following letter just over a month before his mother died.[85] *It is a profound statement of his love for her and his grief over her illness at a time when he could not be with her, and beautifully displays his personal and spiritual care for her as she suffered from grave illness.*

German text in WA Br 6:103–6.

85. Luther's mother died on 30 June 1531.

Grace and peace in Christ Jesus,
our Lord and Savior, Amen.

MY HEARTILY BELOVED MOTHER! I have received my brother Jacob's[x] letter concerning your illness. Of course this grieves me deeply, especially because I cannot be with you in person, as I certainly would like to be. Yet I am coming to you personally through this letter, and I, together with all the members of my family, shall certainly not be absent from you in spirit.

I trust that you have long since been abundantly instructed, without any help from me, that (God be praised) you have taken his comforting word into your heart, and that you are adequately provided with preachers and comforters.[86] Nevertheless I shall do my part, too, and, according to my duty, acknowledge myself to be your child, and you to be my mother, as our com-

86. Luther expresses his confidence that in the midst of her illness his mother is receiving pastoral care in conformity with the gospel.

w   LW 54:235; WA TR 3, no. 3566A.

x   On Luther's brother Jacob, see n. 65, p. 452.

mon God and Creator has made us and bound us to each other with mutual ties, so that I shall in this way increase the number of your comforters.

First, dear Mother, by God's grace you well know by now that this sickness of yours is his fatherly, gracious chastisement.[y] It is but a slight chastisement in comparison with that which he inflicts upon the godless, and sometimes even his own dear children, when one person is beheaded, another burned, a third drowned, and so on.[87] And so all of us must sing: "For Thy sake we are being daily killed and regarded as sheep to be slaughtered." This sickness therefore should not distress or depress you. On the contrary, you should accept it with thankfulness as being sent by God's grace; recognize how slight a suffering it is—even if it be a sickness unto death—compared with the sufferings of his own dear Son, our Lord Jesus Christ, who did not have to suffer on behalf of himself, as we have to do, but who suffered for us and for our sins.

Second, dear Mother, you also know the true center and foundation of your salvation from whom you are to seek comfort in this and all troubles, namely, Jesus Christ, the cornerstone.[z] He will not waver or fail us, nor allow us to sink or perish, for he is the Savior and is called the Savior of all poor sinners, and of all who are caught in tribulation and death, and rely on him, and call on his name.

He says: "Be of good cheer; I have overcome the world."[a] If he has overcome the world, surely he has also overcome the prince of this world[b] with all his power. But what else is his power but death, by which he has made us subject to himself, held us captives on account of our sin? But now that death and sin are overcome, we may joyfully and cheerfully listen to the sweet words: "Be of good cheer; I have overcome the world." We certainly are not to doubt that these words are indeed true. More than that, we are commanded to accept this comfort with joy and thanksgiving. Whoever would be unwilling to be comforted by these words would do the greatest injustice and dishonor to the dear Comforter, as if it were not true that he bids us to be of good

87. Perhaps Luther is referring to persecutions suffered by Evangelicals in his day, as suggested by the passages he now cites (Ps. 44:22; Rom. 8:36).

---

y   Luther wrote *Rute* ("rod"); cf. Heb. 12:6, 11; Rev. 3:19.

z   Isa. 28:16; 1 Pet. 2:6.

a   John 16:33.

b   See John 12:31.

cheer, or as if it were not true that he has overcome the world. [If we acted thus,] we would only restore within ourselves the tyranny of the vanquished devil, sin, and death, and oppose the dear Savior. From this may God preserve us.

Let us therefore now rejoice with all assurance and gladness, and should any thought of sin or death frighten us, let us in opposition to this lift up our hearts and say: "Behold, dear soul, what are you doing? Dear death, dear sin, how is it that you are alive and terrify me? Do you not know that you have been overcome? Do you, death, not know that you are quite dead? Do you not know the One who says of you: 'I have overcome the world'? It does not behoove me either to listen to your terrifying suggestions, or heed them. Rather I should listen to the comforting words of my Savior: 'Be of good cheer, be of good cheer; I have overcome the world.' He is the victor, the true hero, who gives and appropriates to me his victory with this word: 'Be of good cheer!' I shall cling to him, and to his words and comfort I shall hold fast; regardless whether I remain here or go yonder, he does not lie to me. You would like to deceive me with your terrors, and with your lying thoughts you would like to tear me away from such a victor and savior. But they are lies, as surely as it is true that he has overcome you and commanded us to be comforted.

"Saint Paul also boasts likewise and defies the terrors of death: 'Death is swallowed up in victory. O death, where is thy victory? O hell, where is thy sting?'[88] Like a wooden image of death, you can terrify and challenge, but you have no power to strangle. For your victory, sting, and power have been swallowed up in Christ's victory. You can show your teeth, but you cannot devour, for God has given us the victory over you through Christ Jesus our Lord, to whom be praise and thanks. Amen."

By such words and thoughts, and by none other, let your heart be moved, dear Mother. Above all be thankful that God has brought you to such knowledge and not allowed you to remain caught in the papistic error, by which we were taught to rely on our own works and the holiness of the monks, and to consider this only comfort of ours, our Savior, not as a comforter but as a severe judge and tyrant, so that we had to flee from him to Mary and the saints, and not expect of him any grace or comfort.

But now we know it otherwise of the unfathomable goodness and mercy of our heavenly Father: that Jesus Christ is our mediator[c] and throne of grace,[d] and our bishop[e] before God in heaven,

88. 1 Cor. 15:54-55. The order of the predicates here is reversed from Luther's German Bible: "O death, where is thy sting? O hell, where is thy victory?"

who daily intercedes for us and reconciles all who believe in him alone, and who call upon him;[f] that he is not a judge, nor cruel, except for those who do not believe in him, or who reject his comfort and grace. He is not the man who accuses and threatens us, but rather the one who reconciles us and intercedes for us with his own death and blood, shed for us so that we should not fear him, but approach him with all assurance and call him dear Savior, sweet Comforter, faithful bishop of our souls, etc.

To such knowledge (I say) God has graciously called you. You possess his seal and letter, namely, the gospel, baptism, and the sacrament [of the altar], which you hear being preached, so that you should have no trouble or danger. Only be of good cheer and thank God joyfully for such great grace! For he who has begun [his work] in you will also graciously complete it,[g] since we are unable to help ourselves in such matters. We are unable to accomplish anything against sin, death, and the devil by our own works. Therefore, another appears for us and in our stead who definitely can do better; he gives us his victory, and commands us to accept it and not to doubt it. He says: "Be of good cheer; I have overcome the world"; and again: "I live, and you will live also, and no one will take your joy from you."[h]

The Father and God of all consolation[i] grant you, through his holy word and Spirit, a steadfast, joyful, and grateful faith blessedly to overcome this and all other trouble, and finally to taste and experience that what he himself says is true: "Be of good cheer; I have overcome the world." And with this I commend your body and soul to his mercy. Amen.

All your children and my Katie pray for you; some weep, others say at dinner: "Grandmother is very sick." God's grace be with us all. Amen. On the Saturday after the Ascension of the Lord, 1531.

Your loving son,
Martin Luther

---

c   1 Tim. 2:5.

d   Rom. 3:25 (Luther Bible); Heb. 4:16.

e   1 Pet. 2:25 (Luther Bible).

f   Rom. 8:34; 1 Tim. 4:10; Heb. 7:25.

g   Phil. 1:6.

h   John 14:19; 16:22.

i   Rom. 15:5 (Luther Bible).

89. LW 50:50–53.

TO THOMAS ZINK[89]

WITTENBERG, 22 APRIL 1532

Pastoral care often finds its greatest expression in the face of death, both for the dying and for those who mourn. In this letter of consolation to the father of a young student at Wittenberg who had died, the spiritual care of the reformer is exhibited both in the way he expresses his personal affection for the boy and in the consolation he offers the deceased boy's parents, whom Luther presumably had never met. Luther expresses his own grief and that of others in Wittenberg, expresses his understanding for how the boy's parents will also deeply grieve,[90] and then turns to encourage them to give thanks to God for their son, testifying to the boy's piety and steadfast faith, and comforting them with the assurance that he is now with his true Father in heaven.

Johannes Zink was a very young student who had matriculated in the University of Wittenberg in October 1530, although he and his brother Albrecht had already been tutored under Philip Melanchthon before that time.[j] We learn from Luther's letter that he often sang at the reformer's home, apparently as a boy soprano,[k] and that he was especially dear to Luther. On Palm Sunday (24 March 1532) Johannes became seriously ill and he died on 20 April. Two days later, in the evening, Luther addressed this touching letter of spiritual care to the boy's father, Thomas.

German text in WA Br 6:301–2.

90. Ten years later Luther himself would experience this devastating, parental grief at the death of an older child when his daughter Magdalene, whom he affectionately called *"Lenchen,"* died at the age of thirteen. For a touching description of the reformer's grief over his own child's death, see Steven Ozment, *Protestants: The Birth of a Revolution* (New York: Doubleday, 1992), 167–68; cf. LW 50:238.

91. A small town in lower Franconia.

To Thomas Zink at Hofheim[91]

BEFORE ALL ELSE—grace and peace in Christ, our Lord! My dear Friend! I think that by this time you will have learned that your dear son, Johannes Zink, whom you sent here to study with us, was overtaken by a severe illness and, although nothing was spared in the way of care, attention, and medicine, the disease became too powerful and

j   See n. 92, p. 467.
k   See WA Br 6:300.

took your son away, carrying him off to heaven, to our Lord Jesus Christ. We were all very fond of the boy; he was especially dear to me—so that I made use of him many an evening for singing in my house—because he was quiet, well-behaved, and especially diligent in his studies. Accordingly we all are deeply grieved by his death. We would have been very happy to have him saved, and to keep him with us, had this been at all possible. But he was even dearer to God, who desired to have him.

As is natural, your son's death, and the report of it, will distress and grieve your heart and that of your wife, since you are his parents. I do not blame you for this, for his death grieves us all, and me especially. Yet I exhort you now rather to thank God for having given you such a good, devout child, and for having considered you worthy of investing your money and efforts so well. Let this be your best comfort (as it is ours), that he fell asleep (rather than departed) so peacefully*l* and softly, and with such a fine testimony of faith on his lips and in full possession of his rational faculties*m* that we all marveled. There can be as little doubt that he is with God, his true Father, in eternal blessedness, as there can be doubt that the Christian faith is true. For such a beautiful Christian end cannot miss the kingdom of heaven.

In addition, you should also consider how grateful you ought to be, and how much comfort you ought to derive from this, that he (unlike many others) did not perish in a dangerous and pitiful way. Even if he had lived a long time, you could not, with your efforts, have helped him to anything higher than some sort of office or service. Now, however, he is in that place which he would not wish to exchange for all the world, not even for a moment. Grieve in such a way, therefore, as to console yourselves even more. For you have not lost him, but have sent him on ahead of you to be kept in everlasting blessedness. For so says St. Paul:*n* "You should not mourn over the departed, or those who have fallen asleep, as the heathen do," etc.

I am confident that Master Veit,[92] your son's tutor, will write down for you some of the beautiful words that your son uttered

92. Veit Dietrich (see n. 74, p. 456) was also tutor for Johannes's brother Albrecht Zink, at least since the summer of 1530, when Dietrich (at the time with Luther at the Coburg) had copied out Luther's glosses on the Decalogue and sent them to the brothers so that they might learn by heart the Ten Commandments in Luther's Latin translation (WA Br 6:300).

l Literally, "cleanly."
m Literally, "with such fine faith, clarity of mind, confession."
n Cf. 1 Thess. 4:13.

93. Although it has not been documented that Dietrich sent these statements to the parents, he did include a record of Johannes Zink's final days and last words in his collection of Luther's *Table Talks*. See WA TR 1, no. 249.

94. LW 50:301–6.

before his death, and they will please and comfort you.[93] I, however, have not wished to omit writing these lines to you, out of love for the pious boy, so that you may have a reliable witness of what happened to him.

Christ, our Lord and Comforter, allow me to commend you to his grace. Amen.

In the evening of 22 April 1532.

> Doctor Martin Luther,
> written with my own hand,
> although I too am weak.

LETTERS TO KATHERINE LUTHER[94]

EISLEBEN, 7 AND 10 FEBRUARY 1546

To come to know Luther as a pastor and spiritual counselor one must come to know Luther the man—indeed, a man with a deep and complex personality. That personality comes to the fore in a rich way in Martin's letters to his wife, Katie (Katherine von Bora, 29 January 1499–20 December 1552), whom he married on 13 June 1525. Although apparently Luther wrote many more letters to his wife than are extant, those that have been preserved display a caring husband with a sense of humor even when he was troubled by severe illness and pain, placed under significant stress by the challenges and problems with which he was confronted in both the church and the society in his day, and even in his very last days as he wrote to her from Eisleben, where he had been pressed into a service of reconciliation among the disputing counts of Mansfeld. Tragically, none of Katie's letters to her husband survive. But, thankfully, all extant letters of Luther to his wife appear in volumes 49 and 50 of the American Edition of Luther's Works.

In the salutations of his letters Luther often addresses his wife with a variety of descriptive phrases and titles, many humorous and some with a touch of satire. Katie is "my heartily beloved mistress of the house," "my dear lord," "the lady at the new pig *market," and "Gracious Lady of Zölsdorf (and whatever other names Your Grace has)."* She was also *"my kind and dear Käthen Luther, Brewer and Judge at the pig market at Wittenberg";* *"the highly-learned woman" and "my dear housewife Katherine Ludher, Doctor."* In the second of the letters given here, a central theme of the letter is foreshadowed in the salutation: "To the holy lady, full of worries."*

Both letters selected here are from Luther's last days, and they reveal a great deal about Luther's health and his frustrations with the negotiations with which he was involved in Eisleben during these last weeks of his life. They also reveal a husband giving gentle but somewhat chiding counsel to his wife. With her husband away from her side and apparently having learned of his report to others that a chimney fire had broken out in his room, Katie had grown worried about him. Martin counsels his Katie to let God worry about him, even while informing her of the great trials he was enduring in seeking to reconcile the feuding counts. In the second letter given here, written just over a week before he died, his spiritual counsel takes the form of gentle satire, illustrating how Luther even as a tired, sick old man, overpressed with the problems of others, retained a rich sense of humor and could use it effectively in spiritual counsel.

German texts in WA Br 11:286–87 and 291.

---

o LW 49:312, 401; 50:208. In 1540 Luther had purchased from Katie's brother Hans a small estate, the last of the von Bora family property, at Zölsdorf, which was south of Leipzig. See LW 50:208 n.13; WA Br 8:214–15.

p LW 50:286. The last name and titles are given in the feminine: *Lutherin, Breuerin, und Richterin* (WA Br 11:269).

q LW 50:300–301. It is not known why Luther used the spelling "Ludher" of his last name, but here again the forms are in the feminine: *Katherine Ludherin, Doctorin* (WA Br 11:286).

95. It is no small compliment that the reformer bestows the title of "Doctor" (i.e., of theology) upon his wife. See also n. *q*, p. 469.

96. Either the Gospel or perhaps a volume of Luther's (1537) sermons on John 14–16 (or 14–17), which had been published by Caspar Cruciger (1504–1548) in several printings and which Luther had described in a Table Talk of 1540 as "the best book I have written. Of course, I did not write it; Cruciger did. *The Sermon on the Mount* [LW 21] is also good, but this one is the best." Quoted in LW 24:x. See also WA Br 11:287–88 n.2; WA 28:33–34, 39 (see section no. 2); WA 45:xi, xxxix–xlii; 46:iii–iv, vii–viii).

97. On 25 January 1546 Luther had written to Katie from Halle after a sudden thaw broke the ice on the Saale River and caused the river to overflow its banks. He takes the opportunity to make a joke on Anabaptists as he mentions this flood: "Today . . . we drove away from Halle, yet did not get to Eisleben, but returned to Halle. . . . For a huge female Anabaptist [!] met us with waves of water and great floating pieces of ice; she threatened to baptize us again, and has covered the whole countryside" (LW 50:286).

98. A reference to Wolfgang Seberger, a poor student who was attached to the Luther household for a time as a servant and was trapping birds in the backyard of the Luther house in Wittenberg. See LW 49:158 n.7.

Letter of 7 February 1546 to Katherine Luther

To my dear housewife Katherine Ludher, Doctor,[95] lady of the pig market at Wittenberg— placed into the hands and at the feet[r] of my gracious wife:

GRACE AND PEACE IN THE LORD! You, dear Katie, read John[96] and the Small Catechism, about which you once said: "Everything in this book has been said about me." For you prefer to worry about me instead of letting God worry, as if he were not almighty and could not create ten Doctor Martins, should the old one drown in the Saale,[97] or burn in the oven,[s] or perish in Wolfgang's bird trap.[98]

A drawing of Katherine von Bora Luther
in 1546, the year Luther died

r   Translating literally the technical phrase (the German equivalent of "into the hands") that is normally translated simply with "Personal" (LW 50:301 n.4).

s   See the introduction to this letter.

Free me from your worries. I have a caretaker who is better than you and all the angels; he lies in the cradle and rests on a virgin's bosom, and yet, nevertheless, he sits at the right hand of God, the almighty Father. Therefore be at peace. Amen.

I think that hell and the whole world must now be empty of all devils, who, perhaps for my sake, have congregated here at Eisleben, so hard has this affair[99] run aground. There are also Jews here, about fifty in one house, as I have written to you previously.[t] Now it is said that in Rissdorf—close to Eisleben, where I became ill during my journey[100]—there are supposedly about four hundred Jews living and working. Count Albrecht, who owns all the area around Eisleben, has declared that the Jews who are caught on his property are outlaws. But as yet no one wants to do them any harm. The Countess of Mansfeld,[101] the widow of Solms, is considered to be the protector of the Jews. I do not know whether this is true. Today I made my opinion known in a sufficiently blunt way if anyone wishes to pay attention to it.[u] Otherwise it might not do any good at all. You people pray, pray, pray, and help us that we do all things properly, for today in my anger I had made up my mind to grease the carriage. But the misery of my fatherland, which came to my mind, has stopped me.[102]

I have also now become a jurist, but this will not be to their[v] advantage. It would have been better had they let me remain a theologian, for if I meddle with them, should I live, I will turn out to be a poltergeist who by God's grace will attack vigorously their haughtiness. They behave as if they were God; certainly they had better abandon this attitude soon, before their divinity turns demonic, as happened to Lucifer, who because of his haughtiness simply was unable to remain in heaven. Well, God's will be done.

Please let Master Philip[w] read this letter, for I have no time to write to him. [Instead I wrote to you, however,] so that you could comfort yourself with the knowledge that I would love you if I

99. Luther was at the time involved in (thus far fruitless) negotiations to settle a dispute between the counts of Mansfeld. See the introduction and, more fully, LW 50:281–86.

100. Luther was suffering from heart disease, and probably had a severe attack of angina. See LW 50:290–91, 294.

101. Countess Dorothea of Solms (1493–1578), the widow of Count Ernest II (1479–1531), the father of Counts Philip and John George of Mansfeld.

102. Luther was frustrated and ready to abandon the negotiations between the feuding counts in his "fatherland," but his sense of duty over the conflict kept him in Eisleben.

---

t   See LW 50:291.

u   On this statement see LW 50:303 n.19.

v   I.e., jurists in general and in particular those involved in the negotiations in Eisleben.

w   Philip Melanchthon, Master of Arts.

103. The rest of this sentence suggests that Luther is writing quite frankly about his desire to make love to his wife, were he able (which he wasn't, not only because of physical distance but also because of impotence). A week earlier he had written to Katie, after describing dizziness experienced in his carriage, "But thank God now I am well, except for the fact that beautiful women do not bother me, so that I neither care for nor am afraid of any kind of unchastity" (LW 50:291, adopting the translation suggested in n.10; cf. WA Br 11:276 n.5).

104. Luther wrote *pech,* perhaps a wordplay, since the word can mean "bad luck."

105. Luther wrote *"Fraw Doctorin"* (cf. *q,* p. 469). Krodel translates "Mrs. Doctor" but this connotes in English that she is the wife of a doctor, while *Frau* in German is frequently used to address a woman with her title without reference to her being married. In keeping with Luther's use of the title *Doctorin* in this and other letters at this time it seems best to preserve the German form of polite address.

106. Katie must have mentioned her inability to sleep in a letter Luther had received after his letter of 7 February. For a credible reconstruction of the relationship among extant and nonextant letters between Luther and both Katie and Philip Melanchthon while Luther was in Eisleben, see the excursus in LW 50:307–8.

could,[103] as you know, and as Melanchthon perhaps also knows as far as his wife is concerned, and as he well understands.

We are living well here; for each meal the city council gives me one half *Stübig*[x] of Italian wine,[y] which is very good. Sometimes I drink it with my companions. The native wine is also good, and the beer of Naumburg is very good, except I think that because of its pitch[104] it congests my chest. In all the world the devil has spoiled the beer for us with pitch, and among you people he has spoiled the wine with sulphur. But here the wine is pure, if one disregards the particular quality of the native wine.

So that you do not get confused, you should know that all the letters you had written have arrived here; today those have arrived which you wrote last Friday and sent along with Master Philip's letters.[z]

On the Sunday after St. Dorothy Day 1546.

Your dearest,
Martin Luther, Doctor

Letter of 10 February 1546 to Katherine Luther

To the holy lady, full of worries, Mrs. Katherine Luther, Doctor, the lady of Zölsdorf[a] at Wittenberg, my gracious, dear housewife:

GRACE AND PEACE IN CHRIST! Most holy Frau Doctor![105] I thank you very kindly for your great worry that robs you of sleep.[106] For since the time that you have worried about us, the fire in my quarters, right outside the door of my room, tried to devour me; and yesterday, no doubt because of the strength of your worries, a stone almost

---

x   *"ein halfstubigen,"* either one-half liter or 1–2 liters.

y   *"Reinfal,"* a wine from the South that was highly prized in the Middle Ages; see WA Br 11:288 n.22; and LW 50:304 n.28, where Krodel uses the term *Vinum Rifolium.*

z   As Krodel notes, "There is extant a letter from Melanchthon which c an be dated February 5 with some certainty; WA Br 11, No. 4198. This letter, too, speaks of Katie's worries and fears about her husband's health and general well-being" (LW 50:304 n.34).

a   On these titles see the introduction and nn. *p* and *q,* p. 469.

fell on my head and nearly squashed me as in a mouse trap. For in our secret chamber[107] mortar has been falling down for about two days;[b] we called in some people who merely touched the stone with two fingers and it fell down. The stone was as big as a long pillow and as wide as a large hand; it intended to repay you for your holy worries, had the dear angels not protected me. I worry that if you do not stop worrying the earth will finally swallow us up and all the elements[108] will chase us. Is this the way you learned the Catechism and the faith? Pray, and let God worry. You have certainly not been commanded to worry about me or about yourself. "Cast your burden on the Lord, and he will sustain you," as is written in Psalm 55 and many more passages.

We are chipper and healthy, praise be to God, except that the affair[c] is disgusting to us and that Jonas would also like to have a bad calf, and so he accidentally bumped into a chest. So great is human envy that he did not want me to have a bad calf all by myself.[109]

With this I commend you to God. We would gladly be free now and drive home, if God would will it. Amen.

On the Day of St. Scholastica 1546.

Your Holiness's willing servant,
M. L.

107. I.e., the privy or toilet.

108. I.e., earth, air, fire, and water. The previous July Luther had written to Katie from Zeitz, where he was helping to reconcile some disputing pastors, telling her to sell the property in Wittenberg and plan to move to their little estate in Zölsdorf, for his "heart has become cold" toward Wittenberg and he did not want to return. He wanted her to be settled in Zölsdorf before his death, for "after my death the four elements at Wittenberg certainly will not tolerate you." See LW 50:273–80.

109. From at least the summer of 1543, on the advice of the physician Matthias Ratzeberger (1501–1559) Luther had used an acid, abrasive stone to make and keep a cut (a *fontanella*) in his left calf, which by the release of fluids was supposed to give relief from various ailments, especially headaches and high blood pressure (LW 50:306 n.14). Justus Jonas had apparently injured his calf fairly seriously when he bumped into the chest, or the collision had caused a small wound that had become infected.

b Literally, "for in our secret chamber lime and mortar drizzled from above our head for about two days."

c See n. 99, p. 471.

The first page of Luther's *Preface to the Wittenberg Edition of Luther's German Writings*. This appears in volume 1 of the collected works published in 1539.

Preface

to the Wittenberg Edition of

Luther's German Writings

1539

ERIK H. HERRMANN

INTRODUCTION

Luther's prolific writing was a phenomenon in its own right. Exploiting the print medium, Luther produced a tremendous amount of material, from disputations and treatises to devotional writings, commentaries, and sermons. The German humanists were instrumental in the early demand for and distribution of Luther's writings, whether in Latin or German.[a] But his German writings were particularly popular and influential due to his exceptional ability to communicate in the vernacular. He was easily one of the most widely read authors in print.[b]

It would not be too long before his readers and printers would want some kind of organization and collection of his works.[1]

[1] This was not the first collection of Luther's writings. Already in 1518, the Basel printer Johann Froben (c. 1460–1527) printed an edition of Luther's Latin writings. He published a second edition the next year. For a helpful resumé of the efforts to publish a collection of Luther's writings, see Martin Brecht, *Martin Luther: The Preservation of the Church 1532–1546*, trans. James L. Schaaf (Minneapolis: Fortress Press, 1993), 141–45.

[a] See Bernd Moeller, "The German Humanists and the Beginnings of the Reformation," in *Imperial Cities and the Reformation: Three Essays*, trans. and ed. H. C. Erik Midelfort and Mark U. Edwards Jr. (Philadelphia: Fortress Press, 1972), 19–38.

[b] See Bernd Moeller, "Das Berühmtwerden Luthers," in Leif Grane and Kai Hørby, eds., *Die dänische Reformation vor ihrem internationalen Hintergrund* (Göttingen: Vandenhoeck & Ruprecht, 1990), 187–210; Mark U. Edwards Jr., *Printing, Propaganda, and Martin Luther* (Minneapolis: Fortress Press, 2004).

2. Wolfgang Captio (1478–1541) was a humanist and reformer in Strassburg who worked closely with Martin Bucer (1491–1551). Many of his efforts focused on reconciliation and crafting religious unity. See James Kittleson, *Wolfgang Capito: From Humanist to Reformer* (Leiden: Brill, 1997).

3. Caspar Cruciger (1504–1548) was part of the Wittenberg circle of reformers and taught as a professor of theology at the university from 1528. A humanist specializing in Hebrew, Cruciger was one of the main collaborators in Luther's translation of the Old Testament.

4. Georg Rörer (1492–1557) studied at Wittenberg in 1522 and became deacon in 1525. He also functioned as a personal secretary to Luther and was one of the most important collectors and editors of Luther's writings and sayings, including his *Table Talks*.

In 1528 Stephen Roth (b. 1492), former rector of the schools at Zwickau, tried to initiate the project but failed. After the signing of the Wittenberg Concord in 1536, Wolfgang Capito[2] pursued the idea of a collection to be printed in Strassburg in order to strengthen ties to Wittenberg, but this, too, did not materialize. In 1537 the Wittenbergers undertook the project, with Caspar Cruciger[3] and Georg Rörer[4] as the chief editors. Rörer was even allowed (and paid) by the elector to resign his diaconate and work full time on the project. The first volume was published in 1539. But through it all Luther resisted the idea. He did not view his writings as a corpus of Christian writings, a canon of reformatory works. Rather, he saw all of his writings as occasional pieces shaped by his desire to promote the Scriptures as the sole source for Christian edification and learning. Promoting his own writings for posterity would be, from his perspective, a tragic irony. Nevertheless, having been urged to do so and recognizing that such a collection was inevitable even without his approval, Luther took the opportunity to write a preface that directed his readers back to the sacred Scriptures.

The instruction that Luther offers here is consistent with his earlier efforts at reforming the devotional practices and religious life of Christians. Traditionally, the religious life was measured by the standard of monasticism. Lay piety often modeled itself after this monastic ideal, eschewing various aspects of secular life and taking up monastic patterns of prayer, reading, and contemplation.[c] But Luther rejected such a privileging of monastic life over the life of the common Christian. Through God's commandments and his calling of his people into the daily responsibilities to care for one another, Luther believed that God had sacralized the secular. From this conviction, Luther would gradually reform the common spiritual practices of the lay Christian.

---

c On lay piety on the eve of the Reformation as well as the lay movement of the *devotio moderna*, see Steven Ozment, *The Age of Reform, 1250–1550* (New Haven: Yale University Press, 1981), 73–134; and Bernard McGinn, *The Varieties of Vernacular Mysticism: 1350–1550* (New York: Crossroad, 2013), 96–124.

Here we have an example of the same kind of redirection of traditional lay piety. Luther draws from the familiar monastic *lectio divina* ("divine reading") and modifies it, aligning it more directly with the contours of the Scriptures and the common experiences of daily Christian living.[5] Whereas the *lectio divina* was embodied in various monastic "rules," for instance, the Rule of St. Benedict, the Rule of St. Augustine, the Carthusian Statutes, and others, Luther offers the "rules" of King David in the Psalms. The traditional *lectio divina* followed the pattern of *lectio, meditatio, oratio, contemplatio,* that is, reading, meditation, prayer, and contemplation. In contrast, Luther describes the rules of Psalm 119 as *oratio, meditatio, tentatio,* that is, prayer, meditation, and spiritual trial (*Anfechtung*). While the former practice ran the path of spiritual ascent—from reading, to inward meditation, to contemplation of the divine, it seems that Luther wants to stress that the reading of Scripture directs one toward the ambiguities and trials of one's external earthly life. By the divine descent and pedagogy of God through his Spirit, the Christian learns the promises of the Scripture even while facing temptation and persecution.

Luther's preface first appeared with the initial volume of Luther's collected German writings in the fall of 1539, published in Wittenberg by Hans Lufft (1495-1584).[d] Very quickly, Luther's preface was deemed worth publishing in its own right as an independent pamphlet. In the same year it was published in Nürmberg and then in Augsburg in 1540 under the title *A Christian judgment by D. Martin Luther on his own books. Complete with an instruction on what is necessary if one wants to rightly study the Holy Scriptures and thereby write good books.*[e] The reception of the

5. The *lectio divina* was a regular and disciplined reading of the Scriptures going back to St. Benedict of Nursa (c. 480–543). The description of the practice as a four-stage process was articulated first in the writings of the twelfth-century monk, Guido II the Carthusian (c. 1114–c. 1194), "The Ladder of Monks." On the monastic *lectio divina,* see Jean Leclercq, *The Love of Learning and the Desire for God: A Study of Monastic Culture* (New York: Fordham University Press, 1961). For Luther's continued connection to the monastic reading practices, see Kenneth Hagen, *Luther's Approach to Scripture as Seen in His "Commentaries" on Galatians, 1519–1538* (Tübingen: Mohr, 1993), cf. n.32, below.

---

d   *Der Erste* || *Teil der Bü-||cher D. Mart. Luth.* || *vber etliche Epistel der* || *Aposteln.* || Wittemberg. || M. D. XXXIX. . . . Gedruckt zu Wittemberg || durch Hans Lufft. || M. D. XXXIX.

e   *Ein Christlich Vrteyl* || *D. Mart. Luthers von* || *seinen eigen Buchern.* || *Sampt einer Vnterricht, was darzu* || *gehoere, wen man jnn der heilig Schrifft* || *recht studirn, vnnd darnach gutte* || *Bücher schreiben will.* || M. D. XXXIX. . . . Gedruckt zu Nürmberg, bey || Leonhart Milchtaler. ||; *Ain Christlich Vr-* || *tayl D. Mart. Luthers* || *von seinen aigen Buechern.* || *Sampt ainer Vnterricht, was darz gehoere,* || *wenn man in der hailigen Schrifft recht* || *studieren, vnd darnach gutte* || *Buecher schreiben* || *will.* || M · D · XL · . . . Getruckt z Augspurg, durch || Philipp Vlhart. ||.

preface as Luther's principal instruction for theology and devotion to the Scriptures was widely used and cited by theologians well into the eighteenth century. Both Orthodox Lutheran and Pietist theologians would reproduce and favorably comment on Luther's three "rules" of *oratio, meditatio, tentatio*. One finds examples of Luther's formula in such Orthodox Lutherans as Matthias Hafenreffer (*Loci theologici*, 1600), Johann Valentin Andrea (*Christianopolis*, 1619), Johann Albrecht Bengel (*Cursus theologicus*, 1742), as well as the Pietists Phillip Jacob Spener (*Die allgemeine Gottesgelehrtheit*, 1680) and August Hermann Francke (*Zeugnis vom Werk/Wort und Dienst Gottes*, 1702).[f]

PREFACE TO THE WITTENBERG EDITION OF LUTHER'S GERMAN WRITINGS[6]

Dr. Martin Luther's Preface

I would have been quite content to see my books, one and all, remain in obscurity and go by the board.[g] Among other reasons, I shudder to think of the example I am giving, for I am well aware how little the church has been profited since they have begun to collect many books and large libraries,[7] in addition to and

---

6. The following translation is based on WA 50:(654–56) 657–60 and LW 34:(281–82) 283–88. Likewise, these editions were among the sources consulted for annotations and introductory material.

7. Before the printing press, book collections were normally housed in monastery and university libraries, being the primary places of literacy and book production, though some private collections existed among the upper class. The printing press expanded availability of books and greatly reduced their cost, allowing educated individuals to begin collections, especially in the urban context where circles of intellectuals shared texts and ideas. Scholars as well as wealthy patrons and nobility began significant collections that could be passed down or maintained.

---

f   Cited from Oswald Bayer, *Theology the Lutheran Way*, ed. and trans. Jeffrey G. Silcock and Mark C. Mattes (Grand Rapids: Eerdmans, 2007), 222–23. For a helpful and detailed analysis of the significance of Luther's triadic formula in the *German Preface*, see op cit., 33–66.

g   This was not the first time Luther had expressed the desire to see his writings fall away into obscurity. In 1522 he said, "May all my books besides the Holy Scriptures, and especially since they have stored up, without discrimination, all sorts of writings by the church fathers, the councils, and teachers.[8] Through this practice not only is precious time lost, which could be used for studying the Scriptures, but in the end the pure knowledge of the divine Word is also lost, so that the Bible lies forgotten in the dust under the bench (as happened to the book of Deuteronomy,[h] in the time of the kings of Judah).[i]

Although it has been profitable and necessary that the writings of some church fathers and councils have remained,[9] as witnesses and histories, nevertheless I think, *"Est modus in rebus,"*[j] and we need not regret that the books of many fathers and councils have, by God's grace, disappeared. If they had all remained in existence, no room would be left for anything but books; and yet all of them together would not have improved on what one finds in the Holy Scriptures.

perish; indeed that's what I ask the booksellers to do, if they would just listen to me!" (WA 10/2:329). Likewise, in a preface to a catalogue of his writings, he wrote in 1533, "I wouldn't half mind to suffer the loss of all my works, since by them I have sought nothing else than that the Holy Scriptures and divine truth come to the light of day" (WA 38:133–34). As the collection of his complete German works was just about to be started, he wrote to the Strassburg humanist Wolfgang Capito (9 July 1537) saying, "Regarding my volumes being arranged into books, I am cooler [to the idea] and slower [to give permission]; for instead I desire with a Saturnian hunger to devour them all!" (WA Br 8:99–100). Again, after the Strassburgers asked for permission to publish his works with his preface, Luther said, "I wish all my books were extinct, so that only the sacred books in the Bible would be diligently read. . . . I would prefer to see them preserved for the sake of history, so that people see the condition and the struggle with the pope who was once formidable but is now wavering" (WA TR 3:622–23).

h   That is, "the fifth book of Moses."

i   See 2 Kgs. 22:8f.

j   "Everything in moderation" (literally, "there is measure in all things"); Horace, *Satires* I, 1, 106.

8. In the beginning of the sixteenth century, humanist printers produced complete editions of such revered church fathers as Augustine (354–430) and Jerome (c. 342–420). Previously, the writings of the fathers were often read as collections of excerpted material, or *florilegia*. The authority of the fathers and decrees of church councils vis-à-vis the Scriptures was debated among theologians even before Luther began advocating for the sole authority of the Scriptures (*sola scriptura*). For more on the role that Augustine and Jerome played for Luther, see Heiko Oberman, "Headwaters of the Reformation: *Initia Lutheri—Initia Reformationis*," in Oberman, ed., *Luther and the Dawn of the Modern Era: Papers for the Fourth International Congress for Luther Research* (Leiden: Brill, 1974), 40–88; David Steinmetz, "Luther and the Late Medieval Augustinians: Another Look," *Concordia Theological Monthly* 44 (1973): 245–60; Josef Lössl, "Martin Luther's Jerome: New Evidence for a Changing Attitude," in Andrew Cain and Josef Lössl, eds., *Jerome of Stridon: His Life, Writings, and Legacy* (Aldershot, UK: Ashgate, 2009), 237–45; Erik Herrmann, "Luther's Absorption of Medieval Biblical Interpretation and His Use of the Church Fathers," in Robert Kolb, Irena Dingel, and Lubomir Batka, eds., *The Oxford Handbook to the Theology of Martin Luther* (New York: Oxford University Press, 2014), 71–90.

9. Luther was grateful for the renewed study of the church fathers that the printing press now made available. He studied Augustine and Jerome intensively and also John Chrysostom (d. 407), Ambrose (or Ambrosiaster, d. 397), and Gregory (d. 604). The early ecumenical councils also remained formative for his theology. Nevertheless, his reception and assessment of these writings were always valued relative to Scripture. See Manfred Schulze, "Martin Luther and the Church Fathers," in Irena Backus, ed., *The Reception of the Church Fathers in the West*, vol. 2 (Leiden: Brill, 1997), 573–626.

10. Luther completed his first translation of the New Testament in September 1522 while in exile at the Wartburg. The complete German Bible was published in 1534.

11. In *On the Councils and the Church*, written in the same year as this preface (1539), Luther gives more detailed expression to this image: "[Saint Bernard] regards the holy fathers highly, but does not heed all their sayings, explaining why in the following parable: He would rather drink from the spring itself than from the brook, as do all who once they have a chance to drink from the spring forget about the brook, unless they use the brook to lead them to the spring" (WA 50:519,33—520,10; LW 41:20; cf. WA Br 1:602,44–46 [December 1519]). Bernard of Clairvaux (1090–1153) was a Cistercian abbot revered by many, including Luther, for his devotional writings and sermons. On Luther's relationship to St. Bernard, see Theo Bell, *Divus Bernhardus: Bernhard von Clairvaux in Martin Luthers Schriften* (Mainz: Zabern, 1993); Bernhard Lohse, "Luther und Bernhard von Clairvaux," in Kaspar Elm, ed., *Bernhard von Clairvaux: Rezeption und Wirkung im Mittelalter und in der Neuzeit* (Wiesbaden: Harrassowitz, 1994), 271–301.

12. Luther's caveat here is that mere possession of the Scriptures does not guarantee salvation as if it were the new Protestant relic. Neither ought one to regard the studying and reading of the Bible as an act that in and

It was also our intention and hope, when we ourselves began to translate the Bible into German,[10] that there should be less writing, and instead more studying and reading of the Scriptures. For all other writing is to lead the way into and point toward the Scriptures, as John the Baptist did toward Christ, saying, "He must increase, but I must decrease" [John 3:30], in order that each person may drink of the fresh spring himself,[11] as all those fathers who wanted to accomplish something good had to do.

Neither councils, fathers, nor we, in spite of the greatest and best success possible, will do as well as the Holy Scriptures, that is, as well as God himself has done. (We must, of course, also have the Holy Spirit, faith, godly speech, and works, if we are to be saved.)[12] Therefore it behooves us to let the prophets and apostles stand at the professor's lectern, while we, down below at their feet, listen to what they say. It is not they who must hear what we say.

I cannot, however, prevent them from wanting to collect and publish my works[k] through the press (small honor to me), although it is not my will. I have no choice but to let them risk the labor and the expense of this project. My consolation is that, in time, my books will lie forgotten in the dust anyhow, especially if I (by God's grace) have written anything good. *Non ero melior patribus meis.*[13] He who comes second should indeed be the first

---

k   Luther's Latin works would also be collected a few years later (1545), for which Luther would likewise write a preface. See *Preface to the Complete Edition of Luther's Latin Writings*, pp. 489–503 in this volume.

one forgotten. Inasmuch as they have been capable of leaving the Bible itself lying under the bench, and have also forgotten the fathers and the councils—the better ones[l] all the faster—accordingly there is a good hope, once the overzealousness of this time has abated, that my books also will not last long. There is especially good hope of this, since it has begun to rain and snow books and teachers,[14] many of which already lie there forgotten and moldering. Even their names are not remembered any more, despite their confident hope that they would eternally be on sale in the market and rule churches.

Very well, so let the undertaking proceed in the name of God, except that I make the friendly request of anyone who wishes to have my books at this time, not to let them on any account hinder him from studying the Scriptures themselves. Let him put them to use as I put the "excretes" and "excretals"[m] of the pope to use, and the books of the sophists.[15] That is, if I occasionally wish to see what they have done, or if I wish to ponder the historical facts of the time, I use them. But I do not study in them or act in perfect accord with what they deemed good. I do not treat the books of the fathers and the councils much differently.

Herein I follow the example of St. Augustine, who was, among other things, the first and almost the only one who determined to be subject to the Holy Scriptures alone, and independent of the books of all the fathers and saints.[16] On account of that he

of itself merits grace and salvation. As he details below with the three "rules" for reading the Scriptures, any religious practice—even one as sacred as studying the Bible—is vanity without the Holy Spirit who produces in the heart the disposition to truly hear God's word, believe in it, and live in accordance with it.

13. 1 Kgs. 19:4, "I am no better than my fathers."

14. Protestant books and pamphlets far outnumbered those by Roman Catholics, but the Reformation spurred a flood of literature and propaganda, making the printing press one of the most dynamic and expanding businesses in early modern times. However, Luther is easily the most-influential and most-read author of this time with an estimated 2,200 writings in print by 1530. For more on the Reformation's impact on printing, see Edwards, *Printing, Propaganda, and Martin Luther.*

15. Luther often called the Scholastic theologians "sophists," connecting their methods to the ancient Greek rationalists who often argued merely for the sake of being clever or procuring fees without regard for truth.

16. Cf. *Ep.* 82:1, 3; MPL 33:277; CSEL 34:354: "I have learned to yield this respect and honor only to the books of Scripture which are now called 'canonical': of these alone do I most firmly believe that the authors were completely free from error. . . . As to all other writings, in reading them, however great the superiority of the authors to myself in sanctity and learning, I do not accept their teaching as true on the mere ground of the opinion being held by them; but only because they have succeeded in convincing my judgment

---

l For Luther's view on the authority of the councils and fathers, see *On the Councils and the Church* (1539), TAL 3:317–443.

m Read "decrees and decretals." The translation attempts to replicate in English Luther's scatological pun, "*Drecket und Drecketal.*"

of its truth either by means of these canonical writings themselves, or by arguments addressed to my reason."

17. Augustine and Jerome carried on a debate for over a decade (394–405) through an exchange of eleven letters on Jerome's translation of the Bible and the proper interpretation of Paul in Galatians. See Robert B. Eno, "Epistulae," in Allen D. Fitzgerald, ed., *Augustine through the Ages: An Encyclopedia* (Grand Rapids: Eerdmans, 1999), 298–308.

18. Luther first began to consider the possibility of the pope being the true Antichrist after his meeting with the papal legate, Cardinal Cajetan (1469–1534), in 1518. It was Cajetan's reliance on Scholastic authorities rather than Scripture that troubled him the most. Cf. *Acta Augustana* (1518), WA 2:17,5–12; LW 31:275–76; cf. Luther's letter to Wenceslaus Linck, 18 December 1518, WA Br 1:270,11–14. See also Leif Grane, *Martinus Noster: Luther in the German Reform Movement, 1518–1521* (Mainz: Verlag Philipp von Zabern, 1994), 23–29, 38–44.

19. "Prayer, Meditation, Spiritual Assaults [*Anfechtung*]." By retaining the Latin names, Luther appears to be making a connection to the traditional monastic practice of the *lectio divina*, i.e., *lectio, meditatio, oratio, contemplatio*, i.e., reading, meditation, prayer, and contemplation. Cf. introduction, n. 5.

20. The original printing as a preface to Luther's German writings did not have these headings demarcating the three rules, *oratio, meditatio, tentatio*, but they were included when the text was printed as a separate pamphlet. Published in the same year, these pamphlets were

got into a fierce fight with St. Jerome,[17] who reproached him by pointing to the books of his forefathers; but he did not turn to them. And if the example of St. Augustine had been followed, the pope would not have become Antichrist,[18] and that countless mass of books, which is like a crawling swarm of vermin, would not have found its way into the church, and the Bible would have remained on the pulpit.

Moreover, I want to point out to you a correct way of studying theology, for I have had practice in that. If you keep to it, you will become so learned that you yourself could (if it were necessary) write books just as good as those of the fathers and councils, even as I (in God) dare to presume and boast, without arrogance and lying, that in the matter of writing books I do not stand much behind some of the fathers. Of my life I can by no means make the same boast. This is the way taught by holy King David (and doubtlessly used also by all the patriarchs and prophets) in the one hundred nineteenth psalm. There you will find three rules, amply presented throughout the whole psalm. They are *oratio, meditatio, tentatio.*[19]

Oratio[20]

Firstly, you should know that the Holy Scriptures constitute a book that turns the wisdom of all other books into foolishness, because not one teaches about eternal life except this one alone.*[n]* Therefore you should straightway despair of your reason and understanding.[21] With them you will not attain eternal life, but, on the contrary, your presumptuousness will plunge you and others with you out of heaven (as happened to Lucifer) into the abyss of hell. But kneel down in your little room [Matt. 6:6] and pray to God with real humility and earnestness, that he through his dear Son may give you his Holy Spirit, who will enlighten you, lead you, and give you understanding.

Thus you see how David keeps praying in the above-mentioned psalm, "Teach me, Lord, instruct me, lead me, show me,"

---

n   Cf. LW 52:176: "There is no book that teaches the faith except Scripture."

ORATIO

St. Dominic Praying by El Greco (1541–1614)

entitled *A Christian judgment by D. Martin Luther on his own books. Complete with an instruction on what is necessary if one wants to rightly study the Holy Scriptures and thereby write good books.*

21. Luther's negative assessment of reason is twofold. First, because reason is arguably the highest natural gift to human beings, it is easily a source of pride and self-sufficiency—an unfit disposition for one who wishes to be a student of the Scriptures. Second, because reason is such a noble faculty, human beings are prone to consider its naturally derived conclusions as compatible or even normative for divine matters rather than subject them to the conclusions of the Scriptures (sometimes called the distinction between the magisterial and ministerial use of reason). For Luther, the problem is not with reason per se, but with the sinful abuse of it—the higher the gift, the greater the fall. See, for example, the *Heidelberg Disputation* (1518), thesis 24: "Yet that wisdom is not of itself evil, nor is the law to be evaded; but without the theology of the cross man misuses the best in the worst manner" (LW 31:41, 55; TAL 1:84, 101).

and many more words like these.[o] Although he well knew and daily heard and read the text of Moses and other books besides, still he wants to lay hold of the real teacher of the Scriptures himself, so that he may not seize upon them pell-mell with his reason and become his own teacher. For such practice gives rise to factious spirits who allow themselves to nurture the delusion

---

o E.g., Ps. 119:12, 26, 33, 35, 64, 68, 108, 124, 135.

22. A series of medieval tales and dialogues between King Solomon and Markolf, a coarse trickster who, through his impudence and disregard for convention, often outwits the wise king. Both German and Latin editions were printed near the end of the fifteenth century and were popular especially among humanists in Germany as a subversive text of the "wise fool" type. See Jan M. Ziolkowski, *Solomon and Marcolf*, Harvard Studies in Medieval Latin 1 (Cambridge: Harvard University Press, 2008).

23. Luther had a high regard for *Aesop's Fables* and even began editing a version of them while in Coburg Castle in 1530. Yet precisely because Aesop is such a fine example of morality derived from natural reason, Luther cites it here as a foil for that which the Scriptures teach. For more on Luther's relationship to *Aesop's Fables* see Carl Springer, *Luther's Aesop*, Early Modern Studies 8 (Kirksville, MO: Truman State University Press, 2011).

24. Luther's emphasis on the external (*eusserlich*) connects the study of the Scriptures to God's promise to give the Spirit through the external means, i.e., the word. This stands in contrast to the interiority of the monastic *lectio divina*, which moves from the external reading of the text to the inward rumination and introspection of meditation and prayer, and culminates in union with the divine through contemplation. For Luther the reading of Scripture is not a springboard for spiritual ascent, but the context of divine descent, presence, and promise.

that the Scriptures are subject to them and can be easily grasped with their reason, as if they were *Markolf*[22] or *Aesop's Fables*,[23] for which no Holy Spirit and no prayers are needed.

Meditatio[p]

Secondly, you should meditate,[q] that is, not only in your heart, but also externally,[r] by actually repeating and comparing[s] oral speech and literal words of the book, reading and rereading them with diligent attention and reflection, so that you may see what the Holy Spirit means by them. And take care that you do not grow weary or think that you have done enough when you have read, heard, and spoken them once or twice, and that you then have complete understanding. You will never be a particularly good theologian if you do that, for you will be like untimely fruit which falls to the ground before it is half ripe.

Thus you see in this same psalm how David constantly boasts that he will talk, meditate, speak, sing, hear, read, by day and night and always, about nothing except God's word and commandments. For God will not give you his Spirit without the external[t] word; so take your cue from that. His command to write, preach, read, hear, sing, speak, etc., outwardly[u] was not given in vain.[24]

---

p   See n. 19, above.

q   *Meditirn.*

r   *Eusserlich.*

s   *Treiben und reiben.*

t   *Eusserlich.*

u   *Eusserlich.*

MEDITATIO

St. Jerome in His Study (1514)
by Albrecht Dürer (1471–1528)

Tentatio[v]

TENTATIO (Anfechtung)

Head of a Shouting Man (c. 1520) by
Matthias Grünewald (c. 1470–1528)

Thirdly, there is *tentatio, Anfechtung.* This is the touchstone that teaches you not only to know and understand, but also to experience how right, how true, how sweet, how lovely, how mighty, how comforting God's word is, wisdom beyond all wisdom.

Thus you see how David, in the psalm mentioned, complains so often about all kinds of enemies, arrogant princes or tyrants, false spirits and factions, whom he must tolerate because he meditates, that is, because he is occupied with God's word (as has been said) in all manner of ways.[w] For as soon as God's word takes root and grows in you, the devil will harry you, and will make a real doctor of you, and by his assaults[x] will teach you to seek and love

---

v   See n. 19, above.

w   E.g., Ps. 119:22-23, 51, 61, 69-71, 78, 84-87, 95, 110, 115, 134, 141, 143, 150, 153, 157, 161.

x   *Anfechtungen.*

Preface to the Wittenberg Edition
of Luther's German Writings
487

God's word.[25] I myself (if you will permit me, mere mouse-shit, to be mingled with pepper)[26] am deeply indebted to my papists that through the devil's raging they have beaten, oppressed, and distressed me so much. That is to say, they have made a fairly good theologian of me, which I would not have become otherwise.[27] And I heartily grant them what they have won in return for making this of me, honor, victory, and triumph, for that's the way they wanted it.

There now, with that you have David's rules. If you study hard in accord with his example, then you will also sing and boast with him in the psalm, "The law of thy mouth is better to me than thousands of gold and silver pieces" [Ps. 119:72]. Also, "Thy commandment makes me wiser than my enemies, for it is ever with me. I have more understanding than all my teachers, for thy testimonies are my meditation. I understand more than the aged, for I keep thy precepts," etc. [Ps. 119:98-100]. And it will be your experience that the books of the fathers will taste stale and putrid to you in comparison.*y* You will not only despise the books written by adversaries, but the longer you write and teach the less you will be pleased with yourself. When you have reached this point, then do not be afraid to hope that you have begun to become a real theologian, who can teach not only the young and imperfect Christians, but also the maturing and perfect ones. For indeed, Christ's church has all kinds of Christians in it who are young, old, weak, sick, healthy, strong, energetic, lazy, simple, wise, etc.

If, however, you feel and are inclined to think you have made it, flattering yourself with your own little books, teaching, or writing, because you have done it beautifully and preached excellently; if you are highly pleased when someone praises you in the presence of others; if you perhaps look for praise, and would sulk or quit what you are doing if you did not get it—if you are of that stripe, dear friend, then take yourself by the ears, and if you do this in the right way you will find a beautiful pair of big, long, shaggy donkey ears.[28] Then do not spare any expense! Decorate them with golden bells, so that people will be able to hear you wherever you go, point their fingers at you, and say, "See, See! There goes that clever beast, who can write such exquisite books

---

25. Cf. Ps. 119:71, "It is good for me that I was humbled, so that I might learn your statutes."

26. A common saying, indicating the dilution of a precious commodity with something common. Luther self-deprecatingly applies the saying to himself. See Karl Friedrich Wilhelm Wander, ed., *Deutsches Sprichwörter-Lexikon*, Band 3 (Leipzig, 1873), 548.

27. Luther often talked about the role and importance of *Anfechtung* for his theological and spiritual formation, e.g., LW 54:50-51, no. 352: "I didn't learn my theology all at once. I had to ponder over it ever more deeply, and my spiritual trials were of help to me in this for one does not learn anything without practice"; WA TR 4:489-92, no. 4777: "If I live longer, I would like to write a book about *Anfechtungen*, for without them no person is able to know Holy Scripture, nor faith, the fear and love of God; indeed he is not able to know what the Spirit is, having never been in temptations."

28. Luther regularly used the image of the donkey against his opponents, especially the papacy (see, for example, the "pope-ass," already depicted by Lucas Cranach [1472–1553] in 1520). The reference to having the ears of the ass is probably an allusion to the story of King Midas who preferred the reedy, earthy music of Pan to the divine music of Apollo. As punishment, Midas received the ears of an ass, which he tried to hide from the public, but ultimately to no avail (cf. Ovid, *Metamorphosis* II, 172–93). Luther is making a similar point about the absurdity of preferring human writings to the divine Scriptures. He makes the same point in an earlier writing against Jerome Emser (1477–1527), stating

---

y See n. 16, above.

that the pope's reliance on his own teachings rather than the word of God is impossible to conceal, just as if he had the ears of an ass sticking out from under his hat (see LW 39:195). For more on Luther and the papacy, see Scott Hendrix, *Luther and the Papacy: Stages in a Reformation Conflict* (Minneapolis: Fortress Press, 1981); Lawrence P. Buck, *The Roman Monster: An Icon of the Papal Antichrist in Reformation Polemics*, Early Modern Studies 13 (Kirksville, MO: Truman State University Press, 2014).

29. That is, the Bible.

and preach so remarkably well." That very moment you will be blessed and blessed beyond measure in the kingdom of heaven. Yes, in that heaven where hellfire is ready for the devil and his angels. To sum up: Let us be proud and seek honor in the places where we can. But in this book[29] the honor is God's alone, as it is said, "God opposes the proud, but gives grace to the humble" [1 Pet. 5:5]; to whom be glory, world without end, Amen.[z]

z   The Scripture citation and the final sentence are in Latin in the original text.

Preface
to the Latin Works

1545

ROBERT KOLB

INTRODUCTION

In the early years of movable type no living personality had commanded sufficient interest to warrant publication of a "complete works" until Martin Luther came on the scene. In the printing center of Basel, Johannes Froben (c. 1460–1527) recognized that Luther's writings commanded a market already in 1518 and set the cathedral preacher and professor of theology Wolfgang Capito (1478–1541) to work on editing what Luther had published to that point, the first "complete" oeuvre of a living author to appear in print, in five hundred pages. The collection contained only his Latin publications.[a] Froben's close friend Desiderius Erasmus (1466–1536) objected, certain that his own works deserved similar treatment, but other printers assumed the project.[b] By early 1520, editions of Luther's German works could be purchased.[c] The prohibition of the publication of Luther's writings

Portrait of Johannes Froben
(c. 1522/23) by Hans Holbein
the Younger (1497/98–1543)

a   *Ad Leonem X. pontificem maximvm, Resolutiones . . .* (Basel: Froben, 1518).

b   *Ad Leonem X. . . . Resolutiones* (Strassburg: Schürer, 1519); *Prima [Secvnda . . .] pars opervm Reverendi patris, ac sacrae theologiae Doctoris Martini Lvtheri . . .* (Basel: Cratander, 1520); *R. P. Doct. Martini Lvtherii . . . lvcvbrationvm pars vna . . .* (Basel: Petri, 1520).

c   *Martini Luthers der waren go[e]ttlichen schrifft Doctors/Augustiner zu Wittenbergk mancherley bu[e]chlin vnd tractetlin . . .* (Basel: Cratander,

1. Holy Roman Emperor Charles V (1500–1558) issued this edict banning Luther's writings and labeling him a heretic and enemy of the state.

2. See, for example, Martin J. Lohrmann, "A Newly Discovered Report of Luther's Reformation Breakthrough from Johannes Bugenhagen's 1550 Jonah Commentary," *Lutheran Quarterly* ns 22, no. 3 (2008): 324–30.

3. Core essays in this debate may be found in *Durchbruch der reformatorischen Erkenntnis bei Luther* (Darmstadt: Wissenschaftliche Buchgesellschaft, 1968), and *Durchbruch der reformatorischen Erkenntnis bei Luther: neuere Untersuchungen* (Stuttgart: Steiner, 1988).

by the Edict of Worms (1521)[1] dampened printers' enthusiasm for so extensive a project, although publication of individual works, both those previously published and new works from Luther's pen, proceeded apace. It was not until the late 1530s that a "complete works" was again envisioned, this time arising within the Wittenberg circle. The first volume of the German works appeared in 1539.[d] By the early 1540s Luther's official amanuensis, salaried by the electoral Saxon court, Georg Rörer (1492–1557),[e] with help from Georg Spalatin (1484–1545), pastor in Altenburg and former secretary to Elector Frederick, were gathering the materials to be published in the first volume of Latin works in the early 1540s.

The preface that Luther was asked to prepare for the first of seven Latin volumes in this "Wittenberg edition" took the form of an autobiographical reflection because, although the Wittenberg edition is thematically organized, its first volume presented the earliest publications from Luther's pen. His preface therefore focused on these years in order to aid the reader in distinguishing positions expressed in some of these writings from later, more mature positions. The preface is important because it provides a significant summary of Luther's own recollections of the earliest days of the Wittenberg movement for reform. His recollections are in large part confirmed by other reports[2] from the period; his memory seems to have been quite accurate. This preface has also assumed a key role in the twentieth-century debate over Luther's "tower experience"[f] or "evangelical breakthrough," the attempt to identify the time of Luther's "reformational discovery."[3] This search produced a variety of answers to the question of "when"

1520); *Martini Luthers . . . mancherley bu[e]chlin vnnd tractetlin . . .* (Strassburg: Matthias Schürer, 1520). On these first *"opera omnia,"* see Robert Kolb, *Martin Luther as Prophet, Teacher, and Hero: Images of the Reformer, 1520–1620* (Grand Rapids: Baker, 1999), 139–41; Eike Wolgast, "Geschichte der Luther-Ausgaben vom 16. bis zum 19. Jahrhundert," in WA 60:431–60. For fuller details, see Eike Wolgast, "Die Wittenberger Luther-Ausgabe, Zur Überlieferungsgeschichte der Werke Luthers im 16. Jahrhundert," *Archiv für Geschichte des Buchwesens* XI, 1-2, 1–336.

d   See pp. 475–87 above.

e   See the introductory discussion of the preface in WA 54:174–79; Stefan Michel and Christian Speer, eds., *Georg Rörer (1492–1557), der Chronist der Wittenberger Reformation* (Leipzig: Evangelische Verlagsanstalt, 2012).

f   See pp. 501–2 below.

Luther "discovered" the "gospel." Some scholars answered the question by identifying when Luther first used what they considered to be his most important insight. Others dated the "discovery" to the time when he consistently used their own key idea in his thinking. In fact, documentary evidence suggests that Luther, like most thinkers, experienced a gradual maturation of his theology, in which he experimented (as he would continue to do his entire life) with concepts and expressions, refined or rejected them, and synthesized them in ways that sometimes became permanent features of his thinking and sometimes did not. The accuracy of his memories of what constituted his turning point to his understanding of the gospel need not be questioned, even if he himself posed alternative explanations of his coming to the gospel at other times.[g]

PREFACE TO LUTHER'S LATIN WORKS[4]

4. The translation is based on WA 54:179–87, the edited version of the 1545 printing of the first Latin volume of the "Wittenberg edition" of his works.

MARTIN LUTHER sends greetings to the pious reader.

For a long time I have strenuously resisted those who wanted my books, or more accurately the confused ideas in my notations, to be edited. I did not want my novelties to bury the labors of the ancients and to impede readers from reading them. Furthermore, by God's grace there now exist a great many books that present theology according

---

g   E.g., his dedication of the *Resolutiones disputationem de indulgentiarum virtute* to Johann von Staupitz (c. 1460–1524), which pointed to his coming to a recognition of the biblical meaning of *poenitentia* (WA 1:525,4–526,23; LW 48:65–68).

5. In Luther's usage both "theologian" and "bishop" can refer to the pastor of a parish.

6. John Frederick the Elder (1503–1554) was the son of Elector John (1468–1532), nephew of Frederick the Wise (1463–1525), and an ardent supporter of Luther's reform efforts. The "etc." refers to his other titles as duke, margrave, etc.

Engraving of Erasmus Sarcerius

to an organized method. Among them Philip's *Loci communes*[h] is the best. With these a theologian and bishop[5] can be exquisitely and fully formed to preach proper doctrine effectively, especially since the Holy Bible itself can be had in nearly every language. Besides, one thing led to another; simply because the course of events permitted nothing else, my books are not in any order, and are something of a chaotic, crude mess.[i] By this time even I find it difficult to arrange them properly.

These reasons have led me to wish that all my books would be buried in perpetual oblivion to make room for better ones.[j] But other people were audacious—impertinently persistent—filling my ears every day with the argument that in the future, if I did not permit them to be issued while I was still alive, most certainly people would edit them after my death, and they would not know precisely the reasons why things took place or the times in which they took place. The result would be that one confusion would simply create many. Their impertinence, if I may say it that way, prevailed, with the result that I am permitting these writings to be published. At the same time our most illustrious prince, Elector John Frederick, etc.[6] added his wish and command to these arguments, and he directed that the printer not only print the edition but actually expedite it.

Above all else, I implore the sincere reader (and I implore this for the sake of our Lord Jesus Christ himself) to read these things judiciously, and with a great deal of sympathy. May the reader remember that I was at the time a monk and a most madly

---

h Philip Melanchthon (1497–1560) wrote his handbook to reading the book of Romans in 1521, under the title *Loci communes rerum theologicorum* (MLStA 2/1:15–185). He expanded it in 1535 and re-edited this version in 1543 (MLStA 2/1:164–352; 2/2:353–780). Another of Luther's followers, Erasmus Sarcerius (1501–1559), had also published his *Locorum communivm ex consensu divinae scripturae, & sanctorum patrum . . . confirmatio* (Basel, 1540) at this point.

i Ovid, *Metamorphoses*, I, 7, Loeb Classical Library (Cambridge: Harvard University Press, 1999), 212/213: *Chaos-rudis indigestaque moles.*

j Cf. similar expressions by Luther in his preface to the "Fragments" of Johannes Goch (1522) (WA 10/2:329,6–2); preface to the *Catalog or Register of All the Books and Writings of Luther* (1533) (WA 38:133, 1–134,25); preface to the first volume of the Wittenberg edition of Luther's German Works (1539) (WA 50:657,31–658,28; also see pp. 475–87 in this volume).

devoted papist, when I began this whole affair. I was so inebriated, so really immersed, in the dogmas of the pope, that I was completely prepared to kill, if I could, or cooperate with and support anyone who was killing those who would redirect obedience away from the pope with a single syllable. So great a Saul was I,[7] as are many to this day. I was not such a lump of frozen ice in defending the papacy as Eck[8] and those like him,[9] who appeared to me to be defending the pope for the sake of their own bellies rather than taking the matter seriously. I took the matter very seriously as a person who was tremendously afraid of the Last Day and nevertheless desired from the bottom of my heart to be saved.

Thus, in my earlier writings you will find how many things (and such important things) I most humbly conceded to the pope, which I later came to regard and condemn as the height of blasphemy and abomination—and I still do. Therefore, you should attribute this error or contradiction (as those who slander me call it), sincere reader, to the times or my own lack of experience. At first I was alone, and certainly very inept and very unskilled in conducting matters of such great importance when I fell into this turmoil by accident, without wanting to do so or intending to do so. I call upon God himself as my witness.

Therefore, when in 1517 indulgences were being sold (I wanted to say "palmed off") in these regions for most shameful gain—I was at the time a preacher,[10] just a fresh-baked (as they say) doctor of theology,[k] and I began to discourage the people, urging them not to lend an ear to the clamor being made by the indulgence preachers: they had better things to do.[l] I was certain in this case that I would have a strong supporter in the pope, on whose trustworthiness I depended since in his decrees he had very clearly condemned the lack of propriety among the plaintiffs, as he called the preachers of indulgences.[11]

7. A comparison of himself with Saul at the stoning of Stephen, Acts 7; on Luther's early practice of drawing parallels between his own ministry and that of biblical figures, cf. Timothy J. Wengert, "Martin Luther's Movement toward an Apostolic Awareness as Reflected in His Early Letters," *Lutherjahrbuch* 61 (1994): 71–92.

8. Johann Eck (1486–1543) was Luther's foremost opponent; he had initially greeted Luther's ideas but feared a breakdown of the papal system and became not only a critic in his publications but also active in the pursuit of the legal case against Luther. See the reports from the Leipzig Debate between Eck and Luther (WA 2:254–83, LW 31:307–325).

9. Luther could have had in mind a number of early critics of his reform, including Johannes Cochlaeus (1479–1552), Johann Faber (1478–1541), Hieronymus Dungersheim (1465–1540), and Hieronymus Emser (1477–1527); see David Bagchi, *Luther's Earliest Opponents: Catholic Controversialists, 1518–1525* (Minneapolis: Fortress Press, 1991).

10. As a monk, Luther had preaching duties for the monastic community but also in Wittenberg and became quite a popular preacher soon after his arrival in the town.

11. The doctrine of indulgences had not been developed in detail and clarity at this point, nor had rules for the practice of their distribution been established. That came in part in the reaction of Thomas de Vio (Cardinal Cajetan) [1469–1534] against Luther; see Bernhard Alfred R. Felmberg, *Die Ablasstheologie Kardinal Cajetans (1469–1534)* (Leiden: Brill, 1998).

---

k Cf. *Wider Hans Worst*, WA 51:539,1–3; LW 41:231: "at that time I was preacher in the monastery, a young Doctor just out of the oven."

l Cf. Luther's sermons of 27 July 1516, 31 October 1516, and 24 February 1517 (WA 1:63–65, 94–99, and 138–41), and his recollections in *Wider Hans Worst* (1541) (WA 51:538,21–546,32; LW 41:231–37).

12. The bishop within the episcopal system of governing the church, who was the superior of all ordained clergy in the geographical area of his bishopric.

13. Archbishop Albrecht did not act himself in reaction to Luther's letter and the *95 Theses* but instead sent the matter to Rome for action on 13 December 1517. In Rome the matter was placed in the hands of the Dominican order, traditionally charged with the prosecution of heresy. Charges were issued in late January and late May 1518. Luther received the citation on 7 August.

Portrait of Albrecht
von Brandenburg, archbishop
of Mainz, by Lucas Cranach
the Elder, 1526

14. Emperor Maximilian I (1459–1519).

Soon afterward I wrote two letters, one to Archbishop Albrecht of Mainz (1490–1545),*ᵐ* who was receiving half of the money from the indulgences, (and the other half went to the pope, which I did not know at the time) and the second to my Ordinary,**¹²** as they called him, the bishop of Brandenburg, Jerome, asking that they restrain the impudence and blasphemy of these plaintiffs. But this poor little brother got only contempt: they despised me. I published the theses for a disputation and at the same time a German sermon on indulgences,*ⁿ* and a little later the *Explanations*,*ᵒ* in which with respect for the pope I argued that indulgences certainly not be condemned, but that good works of love should be preferred over the indulgences.

This was tearing down heaven and consuming earth with fire. The pope brought formal charges against me. I was cited to the Holy See, and the whole papacy rose up against just me.**¹³** These events took place in 1518 when Maximilian**¹⁴** held the diet in Augsburg, for which Cardinal Cajetan**¹⁵** served as legate for the pontifical party. The most illustrious duke of Saxony, Frederick,**¹⁶** Prince Elector, approached him [Cajetan] regarding my case and implored him not to force me to go to Rome, saying that he himself [Frederick] would summon me, examine me, and resolve the matter. Soon the diet adjourned.**¹⁷**

Meanwhile, because the Germans were tired of all the suffering caused by the pillaging, trafficking, and endless impositions of the idle rascals from Rome, they were waiting with bated

m   WA Br 1:110–12, no. 48; see Martin Luther, "Letter to Cardinal Albrecht, Archbishop of Mainz," ed. Timothy J. Wengert (TAL 1:47–55); and Robert Kolb, "Luthers Appell an Albrecht von Mainz—Sein Brief vom 31. Oktober 1517," in Irene Dingel and Henning P. Jürgens, eds., *Meilensteine der Reformation: Schlüsseldokumente der frühen Wirksamkeit Martin Luthers* (Gütersloh: Gütersloher Verlagshaus, 2014), 80–88. The letter which accompanied Luther's *95 Theses* to his own bishop, Hieronymus (Jerome) Scultetus (1460–1522), bishop of Brandenburg, is lost; his letter to the bishop sending his *Resolutiones* on the theses is found in WA Br 1:138–40, no. 58.

n   *The Sermon on Indulgences and Grace*, published in March 1518 (WA 1:243–46; see TAL 1:56–65).

o   *The Explanations of the Ninety-Five Theses*, August 1518 (WA 1:525–628; LW 31:77–252).

breath to see how such an important matter would be resolved since no one before, neither bishop nor theologian, had dared to touch the subject.[18] In any case the mood among the people was on my side because they were disgusted with all the maneuverings and Romanations[19] with which they [the papal supporters] had filled the world and worn it out.

Thus, I came to Augsburg on foot, without resources, supplied with food and letters of commendation from Prince Frederick to the municipal senate and certain well-disposed men. I was there three days before I went to the cardinal since those highly placed men dissuaded me, using all their powers of persuasion, arguing that I should not approach the cardinal without the emperor's safe conduct. The cardinal had me summoned each day through a certain spokesman. He [the spokesman] was rather annoying to me and kept pestering me to recant—then all would be well. But as great as the wrong, so long is the labyrinth that leads out of it.[p]

Finally, on the third day, he came, demanding to know why I did not come to the cardinal: he supposedly expected me and had the kindest of intentions. I answered that I had to respect the advice of those very fine men to whom I had been commended by Prince Frederick, and it was their advice that in no way should I go to the cardinal without the emperor's safe conduct and protection. Once I had it, I would come immediately (and they were taking action through the imperial council to obtain it). At this point he blew up. "What?" he said. "Do you think that Prince Frederick will take up arms in your behalf?" I said, "I do not want that to happen under any condition." "And where will you find refuge?" I replied, "Under the heavens." Then he said, "If you had the pope and the cardinals in your power, what would you do?" I said, "I would show them all respect and honor." He wagged his finger in response with an Italian gesture, and said "hmm!" And at that he went away and did not return.

15. Thomas de Vio, Cardinal Cajetan, the General Master of the Dominican order and bishop of his native Gaeta, was a leader in the revival of the theology of Thomas Aquinas (c. 1225–1274) and of humanistically influenced biblical studies within the Roman Catholic Church. Luther reported on their interaction in letters to Spalatin, 14 October 1518 (WA Br 1:214–15, no. 99), to Cajetan, 14 October 1518 (WA 2:9–16), and 17 October 1518 (WA Br 1:220–21, no. 103), and in his report, *The Proceedings at Augsburg* (1518) (WA 2:6–26; LW 31:253–92).

16. Frederick III of Saxony (1463–1525), one of the seven princes who elected the German emperor, and marshal of the empire, never met Luther personally, in part because he seldom resided at his castle in Wittenberg but spent most of each year at his castle in Torgau. Although he never publicly supported Luther, he defended him by refusing to hand him over to imperial or papal authorities.

17. Formal meetings of the diet began in July; it adjourned on 22 September, but representatives remained in Augsburg for a time to conduct further business. Luther arrived on 7 October and appeared before Cajetan on 12 and 14 October. See *The Proceedings at Augsburg* (TAL 1:121–65).

18. In fact, Erasmus in *The Praise of Folly* and a number of other theologians had criticized the practice and/or raised questions about its practice.

19. Luther invented the term *Romanationes* to emphasize that the papal court applied diplomatic pressure through what he regarded as trickery.

p   Virgil, *Aeneid*, 1:335–42, in *Virgil: Eclogues, Georgics, Aeneid I-VI*, Loeb Classical Library (Cambridge: Harvard University Press, 1999), 284/285.

20. *Acta Augustana* (1518) (WA 2:6–26); *The Proceedings at Augsburg* (1518) (LW 31:253–92; TAL 1:121–65). Luther's reports on his debate with Johann Eck in Leipzig (1519) and his report on his appearance at Worms did appear in later volumes of the Wittenberg edition (WA 2:158–61; WA 7:815–87), at least in part: Wittenberg edition, Latin, I:CCXLa–CCXLIb (Leipzig), and II: 171a–75b (Worms).

21. Melanchthon arrived in Wittenberg on 29 August 1518, and gave his inaugural lecture on 2 September (StA 3:30–42).

22. That was certainly the result, but at the time the motivation of the Wittenberg faculty was primarily to fill a position in the arts faculty with a professor of Greek.

23. *Squamae*, literally "scales," here a negative designation for "adherents" or "followers."

24. Something of an intrusion into his account of his conflict with the papal party, this estimate of his colleague Philip Melanchthon indicates that at the end of his life Luther did not find reason to express disapproval of Melanchthon's teaching, thus challenging later scholars who assert significant differences between the two by the 1540s.

25. The papal legate Marinus Caraccioli (1469–1538) accompanied Jerome Aleander (1480–1542) to Germany in this period. They confronted Frederick at Mass on 4 November 1519, in Cologne, after his attendance at the coronation of Charles V in Aachen on 23 October, demanding action against Luther. Frederick rejected their overture.

On the same day the imperial council informed the cardinal that the emperor's protection or safe conduct had been granted to me, admonishing him that he should not have any harsher designs against me. He is said to have replied, "All right, but nevertheless, I will do what my duty demands." These events were the beginning of the turmoil. The rest can be learned from the accounts included later.[20]

In that same year Master Philip Melanchthon was called here by Prince Frederick to teach Greek literature,[21] without doubt so that I might have a colleague for the work in theology.[22] For his achievements demonstrate most adequately what the Lord has accomplished through this tool of his, not only in the humanities but in theology, despite Satan and all his reptiles[23] fuming with rage.[24]

In the following year, 1519, Maximilian died in February, and Duke Frederick became the vicar for the empire according to imperial law. Thereupon the storm let up a bit, and gradually contempt for the excommunication or the thunderbolts of the papacy increased. For when Eck and Caraccioli[25] brought a bull from Rome condemning Luther, and Eck promulgated it here, Caraccioli delivered it to Duke Frederick. He was at Cologne at the time together with the other princes in order to receive Charles, who had recently been elected [emperor]. Frederick was most indignant, and with great courage and steadfastness he reproved the pontifical rascal because he and Eck had fomented unrest in his and his brother John's lands while he, the elector, was away. The prince upset them so superbly that they left him in great embarrassment and disgrace. He, endowed with incredible insight, caught on to the devices of the Roman Curia[26] and knew how to deal with them in a fitting manner, for he had a very acute nose[q] and got more and more of a deep whiff of what was going on than the Romanist could hope or fear.

---

q   Cf. Horace, *Satires*, I,4,8, in *Horace: Satires, Epistles and Ars poetica*, Loeb Classical Library (Cambridge: Harvard University Press, 1930), 48/49: *emunctae naris*.

Thus, they refrained from pushing him too far after that. He did not regard the "Rose" which they call "golden,"[27] which Leo X bestowed upon him the same year, as worth anything. He actually ridiculed it. Therefore, the Romanists were forced to despair of their efforts to deceive a prince of this character. The gospel advanced with great success under the shadow of this prince and was spread over a wide area. His authority persuaded many. Only those who hated him could have suspected him of wanting to nourish and protect heresy or heretics. This did the papacy great harm.

The same year the Leipzig debate[28] was held, to which Eck summoned us two, Karlstadt[29] and me. But could I, in spite of all the letters I sent, get a guarantee of safety from Duke George?[30] Thus, I came to Leipzig not as one who could debate but as a spectator under the safe conduct granted to Karlstadt. Who stood in my way I do not know, for up to that point Duke George had not been hostile to me. That I know for certain.

A golden rose commissioned by Pope John XXII (1316–1334) and given to Rudolph III of Nidau

26. The papal court and its legion of functionaries, which saw to the disposition of the church's legal cases.

27. The Golden Rose was an annually awarded medallion of the popes; it was intended to bestow on outstanding rulers special blessings. Papal nuncio Karl von Miltitz (see n. 32, p. 499) was to present it to Frederick, who instead sent three advisors to receive it in his stead, Fabian von Feilitysch, Haubold von Einsiedel, and Günther von Bünau, on 25 September 1519.

28. Held June and July 1519 at Pleissenburg Castle (see the image on p. 85 of this volume).

29. Andreas Bodenstein von Karlstadt (1480–1541), Luther's older colleague, erstwhile ardent supporter, was the senior member of the Wittenberg theology faculty at the time and thus the one designated to debate with Eck. He later abandoned Luther's reform, opting for the medieval model of a biblicistic, moralistic, anticlerical, antisacramental primitivist reform; see Amy Nelson Burnett, *Karlstadt and the Origins of the Eucharistic Controversy: A Study in the Circulation of Ideas* (New York: Oxford University Press, 2011).

30. George, duke of Saxony (1471–1539), represented the Albertine line of the Wettin house, a cousin of Frederick the Wise, and ruler of ducal Saxony, an unremitting opponent of Luther and Wittenberg reform. Leipzig was in his territory.

In Leipzig Eck came to me in my lodging and said that he had heard that I declined to debate. I replied, "How can take I part in the debate without a guarantee of safety from Duke George?" He said, "If I cannot debate with you, I do not want to debate with Karlstadt either. I came here because of you. What if I obtain the guarantee for you? Would you debate with me then?" "Get it," I said, "and it will take place." He went away and soon the safe conduct was given me, too, and the opportunity to debate was arranged.

Eck did this because he perceived that he would reap certain fame because of my proposition, in which I denied that the pope was by divine right the head of the church. This opened a wide field for him, the best opportunity for attracting flattery and for earning favor among the papal party while burying me with hatred and envy. He devoted all his strength to that through the entire disputation, but nevertheless, he did not prove his own position or confute mine, with the result that Duke George himself said to Eck and me at breakfast, "Whether the pope is pope by human right or divine right, he is the pope." If he had not been moved by my arguments, he would never have said that. But only Eck earned his approval.

Here, in my case, you may also see how hard it is to fight your way out of errors and escape them when they have been confirmed by the example of the entire world and have been transformed by extended practice into something that seems natural. How true is the proverb: "It is hard to give up that to which one has become accustomed,"r and "the customary is second nature."s How correctly Augustine said, "if the customary is not resisted, it becomes necessity."t I had most diligently read the Scriptures privately and publicly and taught them for seven years,[31] so that I had memorized them almost completely. I had begun to have some sense of the knowledge of Christ and faith in him, that is, that we become righteous and are saved not by

31. Luther here dates his teaching career from the reception of the degree Doctor in Biblia, 19 October 1512.

r   Scholion on Juvenal, *Satires* 6, 87: *difficile est desespere consuetudinem*. Cf. *Juvenal and Perseus*, Loeb Classical Library (Cambridge: Harvard University Press, 2004). On the *scholion*, see WA 54:183 n.6.

s   Cicero, *De finibus*, 5, 25, 74, in *Cicero. De finibus bonorum et malorum*, Loeb Classical Library (London: Heinemann, 1931), 476/477: *Deinde consuetudine quasi alteram quandam naturam effici*.

t   Augustine, *Confessions*, book 8, chapter 5, section 10.

works but by faith in Christ. Indeed, I had even defended the proposition about which I am speaking, that the pope is not by divine right head of the church. Nevertheless, I had not seen that the consequence was that the pope must be of the devil. For what is not from God is by necessity from the devil."

Thus, as I have said, the example of the church's conduct, and the fact that it claimed the name "holy church," along with my own way of thinking, had such a grip on me that I conceded to the pope a human right, that nevertheless, if it were not founded on divine authority, is a lie and diabolical. For we obey parents and rulers not because they command it but because it is God's will, 1 Pet. 3 [2:13]. That is why I can tolerate those who tenaciously adhere to the papacy without getting terribly upset, especially if they have not read the sacred or even the profane writings, since I most ardently persisted in this belief while reading the sacred writings all those years.

In 1519, Leo X (1475–1521) sent the Rose, as I have said, with Karl von Miltitz[32] [to Frederick]. Miltitz had many arguments why I should be reconciled with the pope. He had seventy apostolic documents stating that, if Prince Frederick would hand me over to him, as the pope sought to have done by means of the Rose, he could tack one up in each city and thus safely transport me to Rome.ᵛ But he betrayed what he had really been imagining in his heart to me when he said, "O Martin, I thought that you were some old theologian, who was sitting behind the stove disputing with himself. Now I see that you are young and strong. If I had twenty-five thousand armed men, I would not be confident that I could get you to Rome, for I have sounded out the people's minds all along the way to learn what they thought of you.ʷ Look! Where I found one who stood by the pope, three were standing on your side against the pope." That was ridiculous. He had sounded out simple little women and girls in inns, asking what they thought of the Roman see.[33] Not knowing this

32. Karl von Miltitz (1490–1529), a Saxon nobleman in the diplomatic service of the papal court, strove to find a peaceful solution to the Luther problem. In doing so, he seems to have exceeded what he was actually authorized to do. He did not attain his goals.

33. Luther is making a word play on the Latin *sedes*, the word for "chair," which was also used to designate the papal throne.

---

u   On the gradual intensification of Luther's rejection of the papacy, see Scott H. Hendrix, *Luther and the Papacy: Stages in a Reformation Conflict* (Philadelphia: Fortress Press, 1981).

v   Cf. Luther's reports in letters to Johann Sylvius Egrantus (1480–1535), 2 February 1519 (WA Br 1:313, no. 140), and to Johannes von Staupitz, 20 February 1519 (WA Br 1:344–45, no. 152).

w   WA TR 3:308, no. 3413.

expression and thinking of a regular place to sit, they said, "How should we know what kind of chairs you have in Rome, wood or stone?"

Therefore, he pled with me to give consideration to whatever would make for peace, and he would make every effort that the pope would do the same. I vigorously assured him that I would do everything I could in good conscience with respect for the truth as quickly as I could. I, too, desired peace and was eager to attain it. I had been drawn into this turmoil by force and driven by necessity, and I had done all that I could do. I was not the guilty one.[34]

He summoned Johann Tetzel, the Dominican, who was the chief author of this tragedy, and with rebukes and threats from the pope he broke this man, who had up to that point seemed so threatening to all, an undaunted loudmouth. The result was that Tetzel began wasting away and was finally consumed with mental illness. When I learned of this, I consoled him with a kindly letter, urging him to be of good cheer and not to fear my memory. But he must have succumbed to his conscience and the anger of the pope.[35]

Karl [von Miltitz] was regarded as not worth much and his advice was not worth much, but in my opinion, the matter would not have developed into such turmoil if they had immediately quenched Tetzel's raging right at the beginning and had taken my advice when the man in Mainz[36] received my admonition, and before the pope had condemned me without a hearing and raged with his bulls. Karl did take my advice at this point, but too late. The entire guilt rests on [the archbishop of] Mainz, whose wisdom and cleverness fooled him [Albrecht] since he thought his threats would serve to suppress my teaching and to secure his money which he was acquiring from the indulgences. Now approaches [to solving the problem] are being sought in vain, and all efforts are in vain. The Lord has awakened, and he is standing in judgment on the people. Even if they could kill us, they would not accomplish what they want.[37] They would have less than if we remain alive and well. Some of them who have not totally lost their sense of smell have gotten enough of a whiff of this.

Meanwhile, that same year, I returned to interpreting the Psalms, building on the fact that I was more skillful after I had lectured on Saint Paul's epistles to the Romans, Galatians, and

34. At Altenburg in January 1519 Luther agreed to refrain from attacking opponents, and Miltitz promised that the Roman party would also abandon their criticism, which, of course, proved a vain gesture. Cf. Luther's letter to Elector Frederick on the agreement, 5 or 6 January 1519 (WA Br 1:289–91, no. 128).

35. Johann Tetzel (c. 1460–1519) entered the Dominican order in 1489 and in 1504 began service as a preacher of indulgences for the Teutonic Knights in Saxony. Elector Frederick the Wise obtained a pardon for him at a time when he was scheduled to be executed for adultery. He became sub-commissioner for indulgences in the bishopric of Meissen in 1516 and the following year was appointed general sub-commissioner for the preaching of the indulgences for Saint Peter's cathedral in Rome by Archbishop Albrecht of Mainz. Cf. Luther's mention of his letter of consolation to him in his last days, *Ad aegocerotem Emserianum M. Lutheri additio* (1519) (WA 2:667,13–21).

36. Archbishop Albrecht.

37. In 1545 Luther continued to stand under condemnation to death by both the papacy and the emperor.

the epistle addressed to the Hebrews.ˣ Indeed, an extraordinary passion for learning Paul had seized me in his epistle to the Romans. Up to that point it was not the cold blood around the heartʸ that had blocked my path, but a single word in chapter 1 [v. 17], "the righteousness of God is revealed in it." I hated that word "righteousness of God" because according to the usage and idiom of all the teachers I had been taught to understand it in terms of philosophy,[38] that righteousness is a formal or active righteousness by which God is righteous and punishes sinners and the unrighteous.

Although I was living an irreproachable life as a monk, I felt that I was a sinner before God with an extremely distressed conscience. I could not have confidence that it could find peace through my performance of satisfactions.[39] I did not love—I hated!—the righteous God who punishes sinners. Secretly, I expressed my anger with God, if not in the form of blasphemy, at least with intense grumbling. I said, "As if, indeed, it is not enough that miserable sinners, who are eternally ruined through original sin, are crushed by every kind of calamity by the law of the Decalogue, without having God add affliction to our affliction by the gospel and also by the gospel threatening us with his righteousness and wrath!" I raged with a savage conscience that was in turmoil. Nevertheless, I impertinently hammered on Paul over this passage, passionately wanting to know what Paul was after.

At last, by the mercy of God, as I was meditating day and night on what was holding this passage together—"the righteousness of God is revealed in it, as it is written: the righteous lives by faith"—there I began to understand that the righteousness of God is that by which the righteous person lives by the gift of God, namely, by faith. And this is the meaning: the righteousness of

38. As is often the case when he speaks of "philosophy," Luther here referred specifically to the anthropology of Aristotle, in which human performance defined the ultimate essence of the "animal rationalis," the human creature.

39. Third part of penance, the performance of satisfactions by the penitent.

---

x   Luther's lectures on Romans, 1515–16 (WA 56; LW 25); on Galatians, 1516–17 (published 1519) (WA 2:443–618; cf. WA 57/2:5–108; LW 27:153–410), and on Hebrews, 1517–18 (WA 58/3:5–238, LW 29:109–241).

y   Cf. Virgil, *Georgics*, 2, 484, in *Virgil: Eclogues, Georgics, Aeneid I-VI*, 284/285. According to David O. Ross Jr., *Virgil's Elements: Physics and Poetry in the Georgics* (Princeton: Princeton University Press, 1987), 228, this expression can be traced back at least to Empedocles, who held that thinking takes place in the blood around the heart. The failure of intellect was defined as "cold blood around the heart."

God is revealed by the gospel, namely, the passive righteousness with which the merciful God justifies us through faith, just as it is written: the righteous lives by faith. At this point I felt that I had been completely born again and had entered paradise itself through wide open doors. There a completely different face of the entire Scripture appeared to me. At that, I ran through the Scriptures as I had them in my memory, and I gathered together in other words parallel expressions, such as "work of God," that is what God effects in us, "power of God," by which he makes us powerful, "wisdom of God," by which he makes us wise, "strength of God," "salvation of God," "glory of God."

Then, just as much as I had hated the word "righteousness of God," I now loved it and praised it as the sweetest of all words, and this passage of Paul became truly the gate of paradise. Afterward, in reading Augustine's *De spiritu et littera*[z] I found that, contrary to what I had hoped, he, too, interpreted the righteousness of God in a similar way, as the righteousness with which God clothes us when he justifies us. Although he expressed these things imperfectly and did not explain everything having to do with imputation clearly, it was nevertheless reassuring that this idea—that God's righteousness is that by which we become righteous—had been taught earlier.[a]

More fully armed by these thoughts, I began to interpret the Psalter a second time, and the work would have grown into a large commentary if I had not again been compelled to leave the task I had begun because Charles V convened the diet at Worms in the following year.[40]

40. Luther received the imperial summons to appear at the Diet of Worms in late March 1521 and interrupted his lectures at Psalm 21. At this point in the preface he seems to end abruptly, but he is introducing his writings up to 1520, which appeared in this volume for which he was preparing this preface.

z   Augustine, *De spiritu et littera*, 1, ix, x, 15–16. Luther does not state that this was his first reading of *De spiritu et littera*. He had probably read only excerpts from the work in the florilegia as he cited it in 1509/1510 in his lectures; see Jun Matsuura, ed., *Martin Luther: Erfurter Annotationen 1509–1510/11*, AWA 9 (Cologne/Weimar/Vienna: Böhlau Verlag, 2009), civ. This account reflects his return to this work of Augustine which he had read earlier in excerpts or in whole; at this point in time with his new insight in mind he found there confirmation for it.

a   On Luther's critical but appreciative use of Augustine, see Wolfgang Bienert, "'Im Zweifel näher bei Augustin?' Zum patristischen Hintergrund der Theologie Luthers," in Damaskinos Papandreou, et al., eds., *Oecumenica et patristica* (Stuttgart: Kohlhammer, 1989), 281-94.

I am telling these things, good reader, so that, if you read these puny works of mine, you keep in mind that, as I said above, I was all alone and one of those who, as Augustine wrote about himself, gained proficiency by writing and teaching. I did not spring to the top out of nowhere, suddenly, though such people do not amount to anything, not having worked at their thinking nor having struggled with temptation and acquired experience. They take one look at Scripture and have exhausted their entire mind.[41]

Up to this point, to the year 1520 and 1521, the indulgence matter was running its course. After that the sacramentarian and Anabaptist matters arose. Regarding these a preface shall be written to other tomes if I live.[42]

Farewell in the Lord, reader, and pray for the spread of the Word against Satan. Strong and evil, and now really enraged and violent as well, he knows that his time is short and that the reign of his pope is threatened. But may God confirm in us what he has accomplished and complete his work which he has begun in us [Phil. 1:6], Amen. 5 March 1545.

41. This passage suggests that Luther saw the development of his own theology not as a sudden or abrupt "discovery" or "breakthrough" but, rather, as a maturation.

42. The second volume of the Wittenberg edition of Luther's Latin works appeared in late 1546; the preface was written by Philip Melanchthon.

Image Credits

xii, xiii (maps): © 2006 Lucidity Information Design, LLC. Used by permission.

3, 9, 13, 16, 22, 25, 27, 39, 43, 46, 49, 59, 69, 97, 124, 146, 163, 168, 182, 183, 197, 254, 261, 272, 292, 311, 322, 332, 338, 342, 345, 366, 375, 384, 406, 414, 440: Courtesy of the Richard C. Kessler Reformation Collection, Pitts Theological Library, Candler School of Theology, Emory University.

5, 7, 8, 12, 31, 35, 52, 55, 67 (Veit Dietrich), 72, 86, 138, 141, 166, 204, 266, 279, 286, 303, 309, 310, 319, 340, 348, 364, 391, 433, 437, 442, 447, 461, 470, 494: Wikimedia Commons.

11: photograph by K. H. Jurgens, Cologne.

15: Universitäts- und Landesbibliothek Sachsen-Anhalt.

18: public domain / from Paul Drews, Der evangelische Geistliche in der deutschen Vergangenheit" (Jena: Diederichs, 1905).

60: Wikimedia Commons / Digitalisat der UB Düsseldorf (173612).

67: Thinkstock Photos; Cleary.

85: Superstock / Interfoto.

107, 390, 428, 457: (Augsburg Confession) The Lutheran School of Theology at Chicago (Gruber Rare Books Collection). Used by permission.

113, 120, 143: Wikimedia Commons / scan vom Reprint Spyer, 2008.

129: Wikimedia Commons / National Gallery.

149, 418: Album / Art Resource, NY.

158, 198–200: public domain / scanned from facsimile of 1529 printing of *Ein bet buclin / mit eym Calender und Passional/ hubsch zu gericht Martin. Luther*. Wittenberg.

161: Courtesy Houghton Library, Harvard University.

162, 297, 315, 413, 425, 483, 486: Wikimedia Commons / Web Gallery of Art.

175: Wikimedia Commons / Rijksmuseum Amsterdam online catalogue.

179, 265, 308, 349, 372: Wikimedia Commons / The Yorck Project.

193: Wikimedia Commons / www.culture.pl.

Index of Scriptural References

Index of Names

Abel, biblical figure, 125, 219, 341
Abraham, patriarch, 9, 28, 95–96,
  197, 240, 345, 357, 370, 377–81,
  395–96, 408, 426–27
Achan, biblical figure, 200
Adam, biblical figure, 3, 53–54, 198, 250,
  280, 335, 378, 414
Aesop, 484
Agricola, Johann, 58–59, 66, 203, 206,
  291, 412
Albertine family, 497
Albrecht, Otto, 211
Albrecht of Mansfield, Count, 66, 471
Albrecht von Brandenburg, Cardinal,
  Elector, and Archbishop, 30–31,
  436–37, 441, 446, 494–95, 500
Aleander, Jerome, 496
Alexander IV, Pope, 432
Alexander the Great, 368
Alfeld, Augustine von, 313
Alfonso X of Castile, the Wise, 149
Alfrich, 55
Alter, Robert, 423
Ambrose (Ambrosiaster), 196, 479
Amsdorf, Nicholas von, 7–8, 22,
  212–13, 441
Andrea, Johann Valentin, 478
Anna/Anne, Saint, mother of Mary, 319,
  444
Annas, 320, 333
Anselm of Canterbury, 342
Anthony, Saint, 100–101
Apollo, 487
Aristotle, 55–56, 101, 314, 501
Athanasius, Saint, bishop of Alexandria,
  393

Attila the Hun, 55
Augustine, Saint, 23, 39, 175, 201, 263,
  297, 299, 336, 341, 347, 350,
  425–26, 432, 443, 477, 479,
  481–82, 498, 502–3

Balbierer, Peter, Master (the Barber),
  253–56, 270
Barnabas, 339
Barnes, Dr., 428
Bathsheba, 220, 382
Bede, Venerable, 196
Beham, Hans Sebald, 459
Bellini, Giovanni, 257
Benedict of Nursa, Saint, 323, 477
Bengel, Johann Albrecht, 478
Bernard of Clairvaux, Saint, 480
Bertram, Martin H., 151, 164
Beskendorf, Peter, 253–56, 270
Beyer, Christian, 10
Birgitta of Sweden (Saint Bridget), 166
Bonaventure, Saint, 196, 353
Bora, Hans von, brother-in-law, 469
Bora, Katharine von. See Luther,
  Katharine/Katherina (Katie), wife
Bora, Magdalene (Lena) von, aunt,
  454–55
Bosch, Hieronymus, 285, 372
Brant, Sebastian, 265
Brecht, Martin, xi, 13, 18, 41, 49, 51, 66,
  85, 150, 159–60, 265, 387, 389,
  421, 449, 461, 475
Brenz, Johannes, 210, 460
Bridget, Saint (Birgitta of Sweden), 166
Bruegel, Pieter, the Elder, 265
Bruno of Cologne, Saint, 323

Index of Works
by Martin Luther and Others

Index of Subjects

abbots, 63

absolution, 44–45, 88–89, 232–34, 262, 301, 406–7. *See also* forgiveness

adiaphora, 19, 375

adultery, 70, 156, 169, 173, 220, 243–44, 274–75, 500

Advent, 13, 50, 97, 201

allegories, 103, 385, 413

All Saints Church, 8, 24

altars and altarpieces, 297–98

Amen, 223, 304

Anabaptists, 82–83, 163, 202, 270, 414, 470, 503

Anfechtung, 217, 228, 477, 482, 486–87

angels, 97, 304, 381

Anglicans, 315

anthropology, 501

Antichrist, 194
    pope as, 25, 356, 482, 488

anticlericalism, 9
    antiphon: of Introit, 435
    Latin, 119
    Marian, 310

Apocrypha, 154, 221, 264, 319

Apostles' Creed, 115–16, 349
    in catechism, 201–10, 212–13, 216–17, 223–28, 237
    and prayer, 254–56, 267, 278–81
    in prayer book, 162–64, 167, 171, 178–83, 192

apothecaries, 403

Ars moriendi, 4, 162, 284–87

Ascension, 147–48, 154, 164–65, 200, 465

ascension
    of soul, 353
    spiritual, 477, 484

Asia, 80, 368

Assyria, 154, 368

Augustinians, 7–8, 24, 26, 36, 41, 51, 57–58, 62, 105, 109–10, 123–24, 151, 290, 313, 323, 379, 391, 431–33, 435, 443, 479

authority, temporal. *See* temporal authority

avarice, 285, 292

Ave Maria. See Hail Mary

Babylon, 345, 367–68, 370, 373

baptism, 3, 5, 9, 37, 44, 49, 59, 62–63, 65, 88–90, 116, 270, 299–300, 379, 419, 421, 426–27, 465, 470
    in catechism, 203, 205–12, 214, 223, 230, 231–34, 235, 246, 247–52
    of infants, 3, 248, 250, 423
    in prayer book, 159, 182, 191, 199–200

barbers, 265–66

bare goodness, 337

Beatitudes, 361, 370

Behemoth, 355, 436–37

Benedictines, 59, 338

Bible, as authority in church, 375. *See also* New Testament; Old Testament; Scriptures

bipartitism, 321

bishops, 213, 439, 494

Black Death. *See* plague

blasphemy, 62, 69, 184, 194, 218, 259, 293, 344, 349, 360, 382, 401, 409, 493–94, 501

blessings and thanksgiving
    in catechism, 226, 237–41